THE IMMENSE MAJESTY

A History of
Rome and the
Roman Empire

G CORPORATION

llinois 60004

THOMAS W. AFRICA
STATE UNIVERSITY OF NEW YORK
AT BINGHAMTON

THE IMMENSE MAJESTY

A History of Rome and the Roman Empire

FOR OUR CHILDREN
DEBBIE AND TOM

Preface

*A*ccording to Thomas Mann, *"only the exhaustive can be truly in-*
teresting." Yet, "a big book," Callimachus said, "is a big bore." The
present work tries to observe the spirit of both dicta and to summarize
a millennium of human experience without sacrificing scope or the
insights provided by factual details. Though there is little mention of
art, there is much on literature, religion, and social history. The reader
will get his or her fill of politics and family ties, for such things loomed
large in the Roman world, but administrative and technical terms
have been kept to a minimum. While collective nouns, such as class,
Senate, or church, are used out of necessity, the author realizes that
such words are mere labels for galaxies of divergent individuals.
Wherever feasible, anecdotes and personal data have been included to
illuminate a man, a movement, or an era. Since there is no "verdict of
history" but only the considered opinions of historians, historiographi-
cal comments are frequent in this book. Scholars will recognize the
author's indebtedness to many predecessors, ancient and modern.

A special note of acknowledgment is due my wife Ursula, who
despite ill health edited the manuscript with her usual acumen and
sensitivity. Whatever merit this book may possess reflects her devoted
efforts.

Vestal, New York   T.W.A.
August, 1972

Acknowledgments

The author wishes to thank the following publishers for permission to reprint copyright material:

BOBBS-MERRILL COMPANY:

    F. C. Grant, *Ancient Roman Religion,* 1957.

COLUMBIA UNIVERSITY PRESS:

    Macrobius, *Saturnalia,* trans. P. V. Davies, 1969.

FABER & FABER, LTD.:

    Plotinus, *Enneads,* trans. S. MacKenna, 1962.

FARRAR, STRAUS, AND GIROUX, INC.:

    Apuleius, *The Golden Ass,* trans. R. Graves, 1969.

HARPER & ROW, INC.:

    A. H. M. Jones, *A History of Rome through the Fifth Century,* 1968.

HARVARD UNIVERSITY PRESS AND THE LOEB CLASSICAL LIBRARY:

    Ammianus Marcellinus, trans. J. C. Rolfe, 1952.
    Cassius Dio, trans. E. Cary, 1925.
    Cato, *On Agriculture,* trans. W. D. Hooper, 1953.
    Dionysius of Halicarnassus, *Roman Antiquities,* trans. E. Cary, 1937.
    Livy, trans. E. T. Sage and A. C. Schlesinger, 1938.

ix

A. S. Hunt and C. C. Edgar, *Select Papyri*, 1934.
E. H. Warmington, *Remains of Old Latin*, 1940.

HOUGHTON MIFFLIN COMPANY:

L. R. Lind, ed., *Latin Poetry in Verse Translation*, 1957.

LUTTERWORTH PRESS:

H. Leitzmann, *A History of the Early Church*, 1961.

OXFORD UNIVERSITY PRESS:

A. J. Toynbee, *A Study of History*, 1939.

POCKET BOOKS INC.:

Polybius, trans. M. Chambers, ed. E. Badian 1966.

PRINCETON UNIVERSITY PRESS:

The Theodosian Code, trans. C. Pharr, 1952.

RANDOM HOUSE, INC.:

C. J. Kramer Jr., ed., *The Complete Works of Horace*, 1936.

ROUTLEDGE & KEGAN PAUL, LTD.:

F. A. Wright, *The Poets of the Greek Anthology*, 1924.

ST. MARTIN'S PRESS:

Peter Arnott, *The Romans and Their World*, 1970.

UNIVERSITY OF CHICAGO PRESS:

Pindar, *Odes*, trans. R. Lattimore, 1947.

UNIVERSITY OF TEXAS PRESS:

C. Pharr, ed., *Ancient Roman Statutes*, 1961.

Contents

INTRODUCTION   1

1 THE PEOPLES OF EARLY ITALY   3

    The Land   3
    The Italians   5
    The Etruscans   14
    The Greeks in Italy and Sicily   25

2 THE EMERGENCE OF ROME   37

    Through a Glass Darkly   37
    The Beginnings of Rome   45
    The Expansion of Roman Power   54

3 THE WAYS OF ROME   67

    Roman Virtues   67
    Roman Society: *Fides*   69
    Roman Religion: *Pietas*   81
    The Nobles: *Dignitas*   91

4 THE PATH OF EMPIRE   100

    The World Beyond Italy   100
    The Roman Conquest from Pyrrhus to Hannibal   115
    The Roman Conquest from Philip V to Numantia   129
    A Digression on Roman Imperialism   139

5 THE BURDEN OF SUCCESS   142

    The Best of Times, the Worst of Times   142
    The Gracchi and Marius   154
    A Wilderness of Tigers   163

6 *THE OLD ORDER PASSES*   172

    The Gravediggers of the Republic   173
    The Caesareans   187
    The Golden Age of Roman Literature   208

7 *THE IMMENSE MAJESTY*   218

    The Heritage of Augustus   220
    The "Golden Age" of Rome   235
    Bodies and Souls   262

8 *A KINGDOM OF IRON AND RUST*   284

    The Army and the Throne   286
    The Totalitarian State   298
    The Dark Night of the Soul   314

9 *THE CHRISTIAN REVOLUTION*   325

    A Shoot from Jesse, a Star out of Jacob   327
    The Beginnings of Christianity   334
    The Trials and Triumph of Christianity   346

10 *THE END OF THE ROMAN WORLD*   358

    The Christian Roman Empire   360
    The End of a World   370
    After the Deluge   388

EPILOGUE   401

RECOMMENDED READING   403

GENEALOGICAL CHARTS   411
    1 *The Aemilii, the Cornelii Scipiones, and the Gracchi*   413
    2 *The Gracchan Alliance*   414
    3 *The Marital Connections of Sulla, Marius, Caesar, and Pompey*   414
    4 *The Marital Connections of Cato and Brutus*   415
    5 *The Julio-Claudian Dynasty*   416
    6 *The Hasmonean and Herodian Dynasties*   417
    7 *The Flavian Dynasty*   417
    8 *The Antonine Dynasty*   418

Contents

9 *The Severan Dynasty*   418
10 *The Constantinian Dynasty*   419
11 *The Valentinian-Theodosian Dynasty*   419

INDEX   421

Maps

1. Ancient Italy   8
2. Expansion of the Roman Empire to 133 B.C.   138
3. The Empire in 40 B.C.   199
4. The Empire to the Death of Trajan, A.D. 117   242
5. The Empire and the Germanic Kingdoms in A.D. 527   377

Illustrations

A Villanovan Hut Urn   6
Lid for a Bronze Cist from Praeneste   11
Etruscan Ploughman from the Fourth Century from Arretium   19
A Roman of the Early Republic   65
Negro Boy   75
Patrician with busts of his ancestors   95
Antiochus III on a silver tetradrachm   111
Pompey   180
Cicero   182
Caesar   189
Cleopatra   193
Obverse: Brutus. Reverse: Liberty Cap and Daggers (the Ides of March)   196
Octavian   197
A panel from the *Ara Pacis* showing members of the imperial family   205

A panel from the *Ara Pacis* showing the Earth Mother sur-
rounded by symbols of fertility and plenty   205
Nero   232
Interior of the house of the Vettii, a wealthy family of Pompeii 237
Trajan   239
Scene from Trajan's Column of soldiers helping wounded
comrades   241
Hadrian   243
Marcus Aurelius sacrificing on the Capitol   246
Scene of gladiators in the Circus   265
The Pont-du-Gard   274
Interior of a factory   274
The tomb of the Haterii showing construction machinery   276
Asclepius   281
Caracalla   289
Tetrarchs (Diocletian, Maximian, Galerius, Constantius
Chlorus)   302
Constantine   312
Isis, holding an Egyptian ritual rattle and a jar of water from
the Nile   318
Relief depicting Phanes and the Zodiac   320
Jesus as the Good Shepherd   352
A Christian sarcophagus of the third century   355
Theodosius I flanked by Valentinian II and Arcadius   364
Stilicho with his wife and son   374
Justinian flanked by clergymen and courtiers   395

Introduction

*O*nce an obscure people in ancient Italy, the Romans embarked on an imperial career that changed the course of world history. In the Mediterranean basin and Western Europe, they established an international order that lasted for centuries. The name "Roman" conjures up images of empire and power, war and brutality, but also the rule of law and civic rights, a republic that flourished before it foundered, and an attempt at responsible despotism. The heritage of Rome is still felt in law, architecture, and politics. The Catholic church operates on a Roman imperial model, and the United States was designed as a "Roman" republic. To a great extent, the linguistic and religious map of Europe is drawn on Roman boundaries. The spectacular success of the Roman empire prompted imitations by Charlemagne, medieval kaisers, and Napoleon, and the baser side of Rome served as a model for fascism. Better men revered the Roman Republic and tried to emulate it, vainly in Rienzo's Rome and revolutionary Paris, more successfully in the republics of the Americas. While posterity has aped them for good and ill, the Romans warrant attention on their own merits for what they were and what they did. Moralists find homilies in Roman history, and scholars seek paradigms of human behavior in the Roman experience. Their insights must be tempered with factual details that emphasize differences as well as similarities between the past and the present. The past may be a storehouse of lessons and warnings, or merely a fascinating spectacle worthy of study for its own sake. In either case, as Cicero said: "To be ignorant of what happened before you were born, is to remain forever a child." [1]

[1] Cicero *Orator* 34.120.

1

The peoples of early Italy

THE LAND

*I*n the beginning was the land, a long mountainous peninsula jutting out from the underbelly of Europe. Across this land that we call Italy came the men: first nameless tribes, then Etruscan and Greek settlers, Celtic invaders and Roman garrisons, later Hannibal's Africans and Germanic barbarians. Some of the intruders settled and built cities; others simply pillaged and destroyed. Today, its forests have been ravaged, and towns pockmark its surface, but the land remains, beautiful under the Mediterranean sun.

To Thomas Hardy, Italy was one of the claws of a dragonlike Europe, but most men visualize the peninsula as a great boot. Though the Po Valley is often cold and damp, most of Italy enjoys a mild Mediterranean climate. In the summer, hot sirocco winds from North Africa scorch Sicily and southern Italy, but usually there is sufficient rainfall during the rest of the year to compensate for the summer drought. In antiquity, Italy was a fertile and prosperous land, and its harvests awed Greek tourists. Much of Italy is mountainous, and the Apennines form a backbone running north and south. Throughout history, earthquakes have plagued the Italians, and many of the mountains were volcanoes; (Etna and Vesuvius are still active). Yet volcanic ash has enriched the Italian soil, and volcanic dust was used in the concrete that made possible the massive architecture of the Romans. There were also mineral deposits in Etruria and iron on Elba; near Tivoli was the limestone that Romans used for building. Originally, many parts of Italy were covered with dense forests, and settlers had to struggle for years to clear the land for agriculture. In the hills were verdant meadows, and pastoral tribes moved their herds from pasture to pasture with the seasons.

In the North, Italy is cut off from Europe by the great wall of the Alps, but the Celts, Hannibal, and various Germans proved that this

3

was not an insurmountable barrier. Traversed by the only river of great size in Italy, the Po Valley was once a region of swamps and forests, but over the centuries pioneers drained the swamps and cleared the trees until it became a major cereal-producing region. On the northern coast of the Tyrrhenian Sea, the mountains of Liguria held great tracts of timber and deposits of Carrara marble. Etruria was a region of fertile hills and good farmland, but the dense Ciminian Forest was almost impassable. Despite coastal swamps, Latium was an area of rich farms and vineyards, thanks to the volcanic soil. Commanding a ford on the Tiber River, Rome had a convenient central location for travelers going north or south, but its seaport at Ostia was not a major port until the first century A.D.

South of Latium, the Plain of Campania was covered with volcanic soil from Vesuvius, and the region produced grain, olives, and fine wines. Falernian wine was the best of the Campanian vintages. Puteoli was the most important port in western Italy, and the lovely Bay of Naples has been a popular resort area throughout history. Settled by both Etruscans and Greeks, Campania was the most advanced economic area in early Italy, a center of metalwork and later of glass manufacturing. In the hills of the South was good grazing land, and there were rich farmlands on the instep of the Italian boot. The major port of the area, Tarentum, profited from fishing and farming. From the sea, the Tarentines also harvested the murex, a shellfish from which they produced a purplish dye used in coloring textiles. Despite the summer drought, Sicily was a rich agricultural region, coveted by Greeks, Carthaginians, and Romans. Its soil enriched by volcanic ash, the island was a major producer of wheat, olives, and wine, and it had large stands of timber and fine grazing lands. Sicily was also a resort area; tourists climbed the heights of Etna to view the smoking crater. The timber of Corsica was exploited by Etruscans, and Sardinia held mineral deposits. Because of its many swamps, Sardinia was considered unhealthy by the Italians, and the Romans established penal colonies on the island. Later, when the swamps were drained, Sardinia became a center of cereal production.

The natural resources of Italy and Sicily made possible large populations, and Rome drew upon this reservoir of manpower for its armies. The central location of Italy was favorable for control of the Mediterranean basin, but there is nothing inherent in geography to explain Roman imperialism. Empires are the work of men, and the Romans were driven neither by poverty nor overpopulation to seize the lands of others.

THE ITALIANS

The well of the past is deep, dark, and fathomless, and history shows only what lies immediately below the surface. Like a lamp lowered into the depths, archeology casts a feeble and distorted glow on some of what lies below. Although the methods of archeologists are scientific and their triumphs are impressive, there is danger in conclusions which rely solely on archeology for proof. By its very nature, prehistory is the domain of the archeologist, and its importance as the seedbed of historical cultures is undeniable. Yet what passes for prehistory is at best a groping in the dark, an approximation of what happened in the remote past. The "facts" of prehistory are based on chance finds, and the interpretations of these facts are sometimes fanciful. From a few finds, an entire culture can be created and an unknown people provided with a history of sorts. Too often, a migration or cultural development inferred solely from archeological evidence becomes a historical fact for some historians, and later finds may seriously undermine the original theory. This is not to deny the cumulative effect of massive archeological evidence, but only to sound a note of caution. The constant activity of archeologists requires that each generation write its own prehistory.

Because the prehistory of Italy (before c. 800 B.C.) is a topic of great uncertainty, any account of prehistoric peoples and cultures can only be a sketch based on some concrete evidence and a great deal of theorizing. We know neither the faces nor the tongues of the prehistoric inhabitants of Italy, but a great deal can be inferred from their artifacts and burial customs. In the second millennium B.C., Italy was in the Bronze Age, and the Terramara culture of a people who lived in pile dwellings flourished in the Po Valley. The term *terramara* refers to the "black earth" compost heaps that first attracted the attention of archeologists. The Terramara folk burned their dead and buried the ashes in urns. In the hills of central and southern Italy dwelt pastoral peoples of the so-called Apennine culture, who buried their dead. About 1000 B.C. the use of iron appears in Italy, perhaps as a result of the migration of new peoples. The most famous of the iron-using cultures is called Villanovan after a site near Bologna. The Villanovans occupied the Po Valley, Etruria, Latium, and Umbria, and cremated their dead, placing the ashes in biconical urns that were then buried. In Latium, the urns were shaped as huts, which provide striking evidence of the actual living quarters of the prehistoric inhabitants of central Italy. In Villanovan graves are also found weapons and other items for the use of the dead, indicating a belief in an afterlife. After 750 B.C. the Villanovans in central Italy practiced both inhumation and cremation.

In the eighth century B.C., Italy was divided between peoples who

Villanovan Hut Urn. Rome, Villa Giula. *Editorial Photocolor Archives.*

buried and those who burned their dead. If a line were drawn across a map of Italy, beginning in the West somewhat south of Rome and ending at Rimini on the east coast, cremation was generally the custom north of the line; south of the line and in Sicily inhumation was almost universal. The same line can also serve as a linguistic boundary for prehistoric Italy. South of the line were Indo-European speaking peoples; north of the line, the Etruscans and (probably) the Ligurians spoke non-Indo-European tongues. The linguistic affiliation of the Villanovans is not known. The Ligurians seem to have been a surviving group of the aborigines who were occupying Italy when the Indo-Europeans arrived. Perhaps the Etruscans were another enclave of the aboriginal population, though an Asian origin for the Etruscan ruling class seems more likely. Were the Villanovans Indo-European invaders whose culture resembles in part that of the peoples who left great urn fields in Hungary? Or were the Villanovans a non-Indo-European group ancestral to the Etruscans? The inhumating Indo-Europeans of the South seem to be descendants of the Apennine peoples. Did they enter Italy from the North or across the Adriatic from the Balkans? At present, all these questions are unanswerable. Paradoxically, the Latin tribes near Rome spoke an Indo-European language but generally burned their dead in the earliest period. Perhaps there is no paradox here, for ethnic distinctions based on burial custom and language are modern scholarly devices. Like moderns, primitive peoples adopted the cultural ways of neighbors.

In historical times, most of the Italian tribes spoke Indo-European languages. The major divisions of the Italic languages were Latin, Osco-Umbrian, and the eastern tongues, such as Veneti and others related to Balkan languages. The Osco-Umbrian peoples lived in central and southern Italy, and most spoke Oscan (Sabellian) or Oscan-type (Sabellic) languages. A characteristic of Oscan was a "p" sound where Latin has a "q," thus Latin *quis* is *pis* in Oscan. Though the Italic languages were related, there were numerous regional and tribal variations. Later, when Rome dominated the peninsula, Latin was the language of the ruling classes and was gradually adopted by the common people as well. Eventually the local tongues were submerged in a tide of Latin, although regional variations were frequent.

A number of cultural traits were common to most Italians, but there were regional and tribal characteristics. The evidence, however, is uneven and fragmentary. Though slight in build, the Ligurians in Northwest Italy were hardened by hard work, their lives conditioned by poverty. The women of Liguria labored beside their men, and the Greek philosopher, Posidonius, knew an entrepreneur from Massilia who was familiar with the hardiness of Ligurian women. The Massiliote had employed a gang of Ligurians as ditchdiggers, not knowing that one of the

Map 1. Ancient Italy.

women was about to bear a child. Unobserved by the employer, she briefly left the work site, gave birth, and hid the baby in bushes, returning to her labor in order not to lose her wages. Though he noticed that she was working painfully, the Massiliote did not learn the cause until late in the day, whereupon he paid the woman and dismissed her. Grasping the coins, she rescued her infant, bathed and swaddled it, and returned home.[1] The stark poverty which prompted such heroism was, of course, not confined to Ligurians. As a result of their hard lives, the Ligurians were fierce fighters and foolhardy sailors. In battle, Ligurians would challenge Gauls to single combat, and though short and slim, a Ligurian would often vanquish a Celtic giant. The Romans later had difficulty subduing the hardy hillmen of the Northwest. In the Northeast, the Veneti wore black clothing and auctioned their marriageable young women. Naturally, large sums were paid for attractive women, and the money was then used as dowries for less favored ladies. In the fifth century B.C., Celtic tribes invaded the Po Valley, and the influx of new peoples soon resulted in a blend of Italic, Etruscan, and Celtic cultures. Under Roman control, the Po Valley would become the home of two giants of Latin literature—Vergil came from Mantua and Livy from Patavium.

On the eastern coast of Italy, the Picentes and Iapygians were related to Balkan peoples across the Adriatic. According to Aristotle, the Messapii in the heel of the Italian boot and the Bruttii in the toe maintained common messes for the men, as did the Spartans and Dorians of Crete. In Etruria, the rural population was Italic, but the cities were held by Etruscans who likely were Asian immigrants. Both the Latins and the tribes of Campania were greatly influenced by the urban culture of the Etruscans. Similarly, the Sabine tribes northeast of Rome and Volscian hillmen south of Latium were influenced by Etruscan and Latin culture. In the late Roman Republic, Cicero and Marius came from what was once Volscian territory, while the former Sabine region produced the writers Varro and Sallust. Generally, the Sabellian hill tribes held aloof from the Greeks who settled the coasts of southern Italy. Subdued by the Romans and later Latinized, the Sabellian region was the home of the poet Horace in the time of Augustus. Early in the Iron Age, Sicels from Italy had overwhelmed the native Sicans of Sicily, but the Sicels in turn were exposed to Greek and Punic expansion on the much coveted island. Whatever their local peculiarities, the Italians had a common culture and economy. Almost all were farmers or herdsmen, and according to Greek observers, they were a sturdy peasant stock.

---

[1] Strabo 3.4.17. Cf. Diodorus Siculus 4.20.1–3; 5.39.1–8.

The most important Sabellian group were the Samnites, who bitterly contested the Roman conquest of southern Italy. Though their armies were not as tightly organized as those of the Romans, the Samnites were fierce fighters and masters of guerrilla warfare. A hardy mountain folk, they were peasants and herdsmen. The Oscan-speaking Samnites buried their dead and practiced divination by observing the flights and calls of birds. Like other Italians, the Samnites occasionally proclaimed a Sacred Spring, promising to sacrifice to the god Mamers every child and beast born the following spring. In practice, the rite was a device to relieve population pressures, for the newborn were not slain but were raised until maturity when they and their herds were sent away to found another settlement. The migration of the "sacrificed" generation was led by a sacred animal or bird which presumably guided them to their new home. Like hillmen throughout the world, the Samnites often raided the richer communities of nearby plains. Sometimes their aggression was prompted by overpopulation, not booty. In the fifth century, the Samnites pushed into Campania, seizing Capua from the Etruscans in 423 and Cumae from the Greeks in 421. Though Samnium contained villages and towns, most Samnites lived a pre-urban existence and were scattered in quarreling tribes. Disdaining kings, the highlanders created tribal republics with councils, assemblies, and elected magistrates. According to the Roman historian Livy, the Samnite republics were "democratic," and the masses frequently forced policy on their leaders. However, the bulk of the evidence shows that a landowning aristocracy monopolized magistracies and dominated the tribes. Despite the separatist tendencies of tribal life, the Samnite groups formed a confederation by the middle of the fourth century; the principal function of the Samnite League was military. Though never a nation, the Samnites were a proud people with a deep sense of ethnic unity. Disdaining the attractions of nearby Greek culture, the mountaineers did not adopt writing until they conquered the Etruscans of Campania. Samnite humor was rough and pithy, and Oscan comedies with stock characters and rude satire were later popular at Rome, particularly among young people. Perhaps the comic forms were borrowed from the Etruscans, but the wit was rural and earthy. Although Roman tradition attributed the origin of gladiatorial combats to the Etruscans, the bloody games were probably a Samnite "contribution" to Roman culture, and Campania was a center for training gladiators. Originally, the combats were held as funeral sacrifices to the dead, but in time the spectacles degenerated into a sadistic sport. Whatever their faults, the Samnites were fiercely independent and the most formidable rivals the Romans met in Italy. By 354, the Samnite League controlled about 6000 square miles and was the largest po-

Lid for a bronze cist from Praeneste showing two Latin warriors carrying a dead comrade. Rome, Villa Giulia. *Alinari—Scala.*

litical "unit" in Italy; it may have controlled the largest population as well. When the Romans conquered Samnium early in the third century, the Roman victory meant the triumph of municipal life over Italian tribalism. The Samnites were restive under the Roman yoke and led more than one uprising against the imperial republic.

In its wars with the Italian tribes, Rome represented the cause of urban civilization, but the early Romans shared a common culture with the other Italians. Though the extant Latin and Italic evidence offers little more than a collage, it is possible to reconstruct the general culture of the early Italians. Throughout Italy, the tribe was the major unit in society,[2] but upper-class families also belonged to a clan (*gens*) which with its retainers wielded considerable influence. Gentilician loyalties were strong, and the rivalry of the clans was sometimes divisive to a tribe or community. All Italians had a personal name (*praenomen*), and many had a clan name (*nomen*), for retainers often assumed the names of their patron's clan. In warfare, the tribesmen wore similar armor and adorned their helmets with horns or feathers. The Italians fought with swords and javelins and often carried rectangular shields. Because they

---

[2] In early societies, a tribe is an aggregate of kin groups (clans) and their dependents. Later, tribal membership may be determined by residence in a particular territory, a principle which undercuts kinship ties.

practiced human sacrifice, it was not uncommon for warriors to choose a voluntary death in battle to win divine favor and victory. Essentially, Italian religion was agrarian and conservative with great emphasis upon venerable rites and exact formulas. The custom of the Sacred Spring was widespread, and the most common form of divination was observing the flight and calls of birds. Since all Italians believed in magic and feared witchcraft, numerous taboos enmeshed their lives and required frequent acts of purification. Though many animistic concepts survived, the gods of historical times were generally anthropomorphic, probably due to Etruscan and Greek influence. Heading each Italian pantheon was the sky god, Jupiter, but the god of war and agriculture, Mamers (Mars), was closer to the hearts of the people. Mamers's female counterpart was the goddess Diana, whose shrine at Aricia in Latium was tended by a strange priest. A runaway slave, who had slain his predecessor, prowled the sacred grove, sword in hand, waiting to fight any challenger.[3] Various forms of the Earth Mother were cherished by the farmers of Italy, and hordes of minor deities presided over prosaic activities. Though religious practices were complex and precise, the early Italians had no need of formal mythologies. Later, they borrowed Apollo from the Greeks as well as the divine twins, Castor and Pollux. In southern Italy, the Bacchic cult of Dionysus was taken up by some natives. In general, the simple rural cults of the prehistoric Italians were cherished by their descendants throughout antiquity, despite the novel deities who flourished at Rome and other urban centers.

A valuable insight into the religious mentality of the early Italians is preserved on bronze tablets from the Umbrian town of Iguvium, later known as Gubbio, where Saint Francis had a famous encounter with a wolf. The Iguvine tablets deal with rites of expiation but also include curses upon the Etruscans and other hostile neighbors. In part, the tablets read:

> When the voices of the birds are heard, the one sitting in the enclosure shall announce it, calling the priest by name, "[I announce] favorable owls, favorable crows, a male woodpecker on the right hand, a female woodpecker on the right hand, birds on the right, voices of birds on the right hand for thee, for the community of Iguvium, at this particular time." For all these sacred acts, for the procession about the people, for the expiation of the city, he must carry the sacred staff. The sacrificial

---

[3] Whoever challenged the "king" of the grove had first to pluck a bough from a sacred tree. Accounts of the bizarre customs at Aricia stimulated a great classic of anthropology, Sir James Frazer's monumental and often fanciful *The Golden Bough*.

hearth at the Treblanian gate, which is to be laid for the expiation of the city, thou shalt so arrange that fire may be kindled from fire. So likewise at the two other gates. . . . Before the Treblanian gate, three oxen shall be sacrificed to Jupiter Grabovius. At the offering shall be said: . . . "If in the town of Iguvium the due rites are neglected, [look upon it] as if it had been unintentional. O Jupiter Grabovius, if in thine offering [anything] is amiss or neglected or omitted or [fraudulently] held back or at fault, or if in thine offering there be any blemish, whether seen or unseen, O Jupiter Grabovius, let it be expiated by these fat oxen for an expiation, as is right. . . . O Jupiter Grabovius, preserve the Fisian city, preserve the town of Iguvium; full citizens, sacred rites, slaves, cattle, fruits of the field, preserve. Be kind, be gracious with thy favor to the Fisian city, to the town of Iguvium, the name of the city, the name of the town.[4] O Jupiter Grabovius, with these fat oxen as an expiation . . . , I call upon thee." . . . The whole prayer shall be said silently. Then lay [the parts of the sacrifice] upon the altar and announce what has been laid on, add the measured-out round cakes of meal and the morsels of the sacrifice, and offer fruits of the field. This sacrifice is to be accompanied by wine or water. . . . Thus the city is expiated. If anything interrupts the sacrifice, it is invalid, the birds must be consulted; go back to the Treblanian gate and begin again as before and offer the sacrifice there.[5]

In the mental world of the Iguvine tablets, man was totally dependent upon the gods and had to expiate all affronts to them. Even unintentional errors might offend the gods. Through ritual sacrifices, the anger of the deities could be averted, but the rites had to be performed strictly according to time-honored prescriptions. If an error or omission occurred, the ritual was repeated. The willingness of the gods to accept the rite was indicated by the cries of birds which were considered emissaries of Heaven. Since the gods were rustics like their worshipers, the animals and foodstuffs for the sacrifice were simple fare. This rural religion with its "fear of the Lord" and rigid conservatism was typical of all Italian cults. Though subject to Etruscan influence, the early Romans were Italians and shared the common religion and culture of Italy. The *ius gentium* of later Roman jurisprudence was simply the "international law" of early Italy—the generally accepted values of the Italian tribes.

[4] The "name" may mean "race" or more likely the sacred name of the city. To primitives, the name of anything is an entity as real as the physical substance of a thing and must be protected from calamity or witchcraft.

[5] Iguvine Tablets VI.A 16, 22, 27–29, 31–34, 56–57, VI.B 47, trans. Frederick C. Grant, *Ancient Roman Religion* (New York: Liberal Arts Press, 1957), pp. 5–7. For the text, linguistic analyses and a variant translation, see James W. Poultney, *The Bronze Tablets of Iguvium*, Monographs of the American Philological Association XVIII (1959), 238–40, 244–46, 248, 266.

THE ETRUSCANS

Of the non-Greek peoples of early Italy, the most advanced and urbane were the Etruscans, whose heartland, Etruria, lay west of the Apennines between the Arno and Tiber rivers. The Romans called them Etruscans; to the Greeks, they were Tyrrhenians or Tyrsenians; but they called themselves Rasenna. Unlike that of most Italians, their language is not Indo-European. So much about the Etruscans is unknown or conjectural that an aura of mystery surrounds them, and they are the subjects of considerable scholarly controversy.

Their Greek and Roman rivals described the Etruscans as cruel and corrupt, and some modern writers have echoed the ancient charges. *The Cambridge Ancient History,* for example, took a dim view of the Etruscans:

> We have no record of Etruscan intellectual life and it seems doubtful if there was much to record. From their remains, however, and from literary references, we can imagine the curious mixture of cruelty, superstition, immorality, and luxury which occupied most of their time. Their fundamental cruelty does not really emerge until the end of the fifth century when it permeates all their art, but it is perceptible in the extreme brutality of the games depicted in the sixth and early fifth century. . . . Entirely un-Greek are the immoral scenes in the paintings of the frieze in the "Tomba delle Bighe." [6]

Such indignation is both subjective and self-refuting. At the opposite end of the emotional spectrum, a fevered Etruscomania sometimes seizes romantic souls. D. H. Lawrence wrote enthusiastically of the painted tombs at Tarquinii:

> There is a haunting quality in the Etruscan representations. Those leopards with their long tongues hanging out: those flowing hippocampi; those cringing spotted deer, struck in flank and neck; they get into the imagination and will not go out. And we see the wavy edge of the sea, the dolphins curving over, the diver going down clean, the little man climbing up the rock after him so eagerly. Then the men with beards who recline on the banqueting beds: how they hold up the mysterious egg! And the women with the conical head-dress, how strangely they lean forward, with caresses we no longer know! The naked slaves joyfully stoop to the wine-jars. Their nakedness is its own clothing, more easy than drapery. The curves of their limbs show pure pleasure in life, a pleasure that goes deeper still in the limbs of the dancers, in the big, long hands thrown out

[6] S. Casson, *The Cambridge Ancient History* (Cambridge: Cambridge University Press, 1954), IV, 432. (Henceforth this work is cited as *CAH.*)

and dancing to the very ends of the fingers, a dance that surges from within, like a current in the sea. It is as if the current of some strong different life swept through them, different from our shallow current today: as if they drew their vitality from different depths that we are denied.[7]

Though his *Etruscan Places* may serve to awaken interest in the art and vitality of a lost people, Lawrence was dying of tuberculosis and sucked life from his dreamy visions of the Etruscans. In both of these passages, the key words are "imagine" and "imagination." Where evidence is lacking or obscure, historians must sail on the winds of imagination, but they should never lose sight of the shores of reality. Archeology reveals a great deal about the inhabitants of Etruria, and the literary evidence has value when used with caution, but any discussion of the Etruscans must be tentative and include a number of suppositions.

The most hotly disputed topic in Etruscology is the origin of the Etruscans. In the Periclean age, the Greek historian Herodotus claimed that the Tyrsenians were descendants of Lydians who had fled from Asia during a famine.[8] Though he did not specify a date, Herodotus's other comments on Lydian history would place the migration in the thirteenth century. In antiquity, all writers, save one, accepted the theory of an Asian origin, as do most moderns. It is tempting to identify the Tyrsenians with the Tursha, who assaulted Egypt in the reign of Merneptah. Among the other "Sea Peoples" who plagued the Pharaoh were the Sherden, who eventually sailed on to Sardinia. While the Tursha may have been "Tyrsenians," the Etruscan civilization in Italy did not appear until five centuries later, and there is no archeological evidence for a colony of the "Sea Peoples" in Italy. In the Augustan era, another Greek historian, Dionysius of Halicarnassus, investigated the origins of the Tyrrhenians and challenged the Herodotean thesis. Dionysius noted that the Etruscans and Lydians differed in language, laws, and religion, and he offered a counterproposal, that the Etruscans were in fact aborigines of Italy.[9] The indigenous theory has support among some modern scholars, mostly Italians, who view the Etruscans as a remnant of the original Mediterranean stock who were surrounded and usually absorbed by Indo-European invaders. Similar ethnic islands exist in the modern world—for example, the Basques—and current disciples of Dionysius claim that Etruscan culture evolved from the Villanovan, though they do not explain why the other Villanovans did not produce an Etruscan-type civilization. A third theory was offered by

---

[7] D. H. Lawrence, *Etruscan Places* (New York: Viking Press, 1957), pp. 81–82.
[8] Herodotus 1.94.   [9] Dionysius of Halicarnassus 1.25–30.

Dionysius's contemporary, Livy, who remarked that the Etruscans were related to an Alpine tribe, the Raetians.[10] However, few moderns feel that the "Rasenna" were kin of the Raetians, for Raetian is an Indo-European language, and Etruscoid inscriptions in Alpine valleys are probably the work of refugees who had fled from the Po Valley to escape the Celtic invasions.

The origin of the Etruscans is best explained by combining the Asian and the indigenous theories. The evidence of an Asian element in Etruria is unmistakable and ranges from artistic motifs and shoes with pointed toes to divination through liver analysis. On the Isle of Lemnos off the coast of Asia Minor, inscriptions have been found which date from the seventh century and are written in a language very similar to Etruscan. One or more migrations from Asia would account for the sudden burst of urban civilization with an oriental flavor on the soil of Italy at the end of the eighth century. Because the land was already populated by Villanovans, the resultant culture was a blend of Italian and Asian elements. As the more advanced group, the Asian invaders dominated the aborigines, and the speech of the literate ruling class, Etruscan, became the language of Etruria. How much the Villanovan dialects were submerged is difficult to say, since the peasants left no records, and we have only the inscriptions of the rulers. No doubt debates on Etruscan origins will continue, but the topic is less important than the achievements of the Etruscans and the role which they played in spreading urban culture in Italy.

At best, Etruscan history is only a sketch, like a faded drawing in a tomb. In the early Iron Age, Etruria was occupied by Villanovans who cremated the dead and buried the ashes in urns. About 750, burials by inhumation increased, grave goods became more elaborate, and there is evidence of an orientalization of culture, probably as a result of Asian penetration. By 700, the eminent dead were buried in monumental tombs, and a full-blown urban society was flourishing in Etruria. Among the prominent cities were Caere, Tarquinii, Vulci, Veii, Clusium, Volsinii, Arretium, and Populonia. Each city was independent and ruled by a king (*lucumo*), who was simultaneously magistrate, war chief, and priest. In public, the *lucumo* was preceded by a lictor, an attendant bearing a *fascis,* a bundle of rods bound around a double-bladed axe, which symbolized magisterial authority. Annually, the *lucumones* of twelve leading cities met near Volsinii at the sanctuary of Voltumna and discussed common problems. There, the kings elected one of their number to head the loose amphictyony which we call the Etruscan League; for a year, the *lucumo* so honored was attended by

[10] Livy 5.33.

twelve lictors with *fasces*. Though less a political entity than a religio-cultural organization, the League promoted cooperation among the cities in time of war. Like early Greece, Etruria was a land of hills and thick forests, and the terrain encouraged separatism among the communities. Although doubtless proud of their culture, the Etruscans lacked the strong sense of nationality which their Roman neighbors possessed.

The seventh and sixth centuries were a golden age for the ruling class of Etruria, whose prosperity was based on rich farms, extensive trade, and a flourishing metal industry. The luxury-loving rulers imported gold, silver, and ivory and exported lump iron and fine bronzes. Connoisseurs of Greek art, the *lucumones* and the nobles collected Attic vases in great numbers. An outward-looking maritime people, the Etruscans were also active in piracy, a main facet of ancient sea power. Their Greek rivals complained bitterly of Etruscan pirates, and a Homeric hymn noted a Tyrsenian raid on Ionia. Though legends told of Tyrrhenians raping and looting in Attica, the Greeks too had a bad reputation for piracy. In more legitimate endeavors, Etruscan merchants sailed to Spain, Greece, Carthage, and Egypt. Closer to home, their ships prowled Italian waters, and the ocean between Italy, Sicily, Sardinia, and Corsica is still called the Tyrrhenian Sea. However, Carthaginians settled on Sardinia, and Greeks established a menacing colony at Massilia. Though they welcomed Greek businessmen in the coastal cities of Etruria, the Etruscans challenged Hellenic colonial expansion. Making an expedient alliance with Carthage, the Etruscans attacked a Greek settlement on Corsica in 535. Though Herodotus claims that his countrymen won the battle of Alalia, the Greeks were driven from Corsica.

On land as on sea, the Etruscans were a formidable power. Like the Greeks, they fought as hoplites, well-armored and disciplined infantrymen. In the sixth century, the Etruscans expanded northward into the Po Valley, occupying communities such as Felsina (later Bologna) and the Greek trading center of Spina. Though their political control was probably limited to the southern areas of the valley, Etruscan influence reached throughout the Po basin, and Etruscan goods have been found in many localities in northern Italy. Beyond the Alps, Celtic tribes were eager consumers of Etruscan products. South of Etruria, the Etruscans dominated Latium, and an Etruscan dynasty, the Tarquins, made Rome into a major city. Moving into Campania, the Etruscans occupied Capua and challenged the Greeks for control of the South. Bypassing hostile Cumae and the Bay of Naples, the Etruscans established strongholds on the Gulf of Salerno. The Greeks of Campania did not welcome the Etruscan intrusion, and the city of Cumae repelled an attack by the Etruscans of Capua in 524. At the peak of Etruscan expansion, a series of political upheavals overthrew the monarchies throughout the Etruscan world. Though these developments took place in various cities at different times, the end result was always the same—oligarchy. In most cities, the *lucumones* were replaced by annually elected magistrates with the title of *zilath,* who were comparable to Roman praetors and took over the lictors and *fasces* of the former kings. Since cliques of noble families monopolized the office of *zilath,* there was probably little popular government in the oligarchic republics. The most famous of the revolutions was the ousting of the Tarquin dynasty from Rome, but there the overthrow of the monarchy involved an ethnic revolt of Latin nobles against Etruscan rule. Although the ruler of Clusium, Lars Porsenna, briefly conquered the recently liberated Romans, the Etruscan hold on Latium was soon broken, and the Etruscan cities lost overland access to Campania. In 474, the Etruscans suffered a major naval defeat at the hands of the Syracusan fleet off Cumae. Steadily, Etruscan power continued to contract as Samnite tribes pushed into Campania, and by 423 Capua had fallen to the highlanders of the South.

In central Italy, the Etruscans were exposed to Roman expansion, but most cities of Etruria held aloof during Rome's war with the city of Veii, which the Romans conquered in 396. Apparently the Etruscan republics had no sympathy with Veii, where the institution of monarchy had been restored. In the North, the Po Valley was overrun by waves of Celtic invaders, and by 350 Felsina had fallen to the barbarians. Under Celtic occupation, the Etruscans of the North preserved the remnants of urban life, much like the inhabitants of Roman towns during the Germanic invasions that toppled the Roman empire. Throughout the fourth century, Roman pressure on Etruria continued, and the Etruscans joined the Samnites in a vain resistance in the early third century. By 280 Etruria was firmly under the Roman yoke, but the benefits of the new order were considerable, and the Etruscans fought loyally for Rome during the Hannibalic War. In the late Republic, men of Etruscan origin moved among the Roman aristocracy—the most famous was Maecenas, the confidant of Augustus. In Imperial Rome, Etruscomania was not unknown, and the emperor Claudius was a renowned Etruscologist. Yet, except for antiquarians and devotees of religion, Etruscan civilization had faded away under the dominant culture of Rome, and even the language of the Etruscans disappeared.

Whatever their later fate, the Etruscans had a glorious past and had enjoyed the fruits of success. The wealth of Etruria was proverbial, and archeology has substantiated tales of Etruscan luxury and good living. Originally, the Asian elements in Etruscan society had been drawn to Italy by the mineral deposits of Etruria, and they fully exploited its copper mines to produce superior bronze works. On the offshore Isle of Elba were rich iron deposits that provided ore for the smelting furnaces of Populonia on the Etrurian coast. Truly the "Birmingham of ancient Italy," Populonia was a major center of iron production, and the site of the city is surrounded by ancient slag heaps, from which iron is still being extracted by modern methods. Metal was not the only source of Etruscan prosperity. The dense forests of the Etrurian hills provided lumber for the construction of ships and homes. Etruria was also a rich farming region, and the Etruscans increased their agricultural production through elaborate irrigation networks and drainage systems, particularly in southern Etruria. In many crafts, the Etruscans were justly renowned. Goldsmiths made delicate filigrees with gold strands and created stunning decorations with masses of gold granules, and dentists crowned and bridged teeth with gold. Etruscan cobblers were famed for fine shoes that found a wide market in Italy. Under Roman rule, Etruscan prosperity continued, and Livy describes the contributions of the Etruscan cities to the Roman war effort in 205: Perusia, Volaterrae, Clusium, and Rusellae promised lumber and grain, Caere grain and other supplies, Populonia iron, Tarquinii sailcloth, and Arretium alone offered 120,000 measures of wheat, 3,000 shields, 3,000 helmets, 50,000 pikes, 50,000 javelins, 50,000 spears, and enough axes, shovels,

Etruscan ploughman from the fourth century from Arretium. Rome, Villa Giulia. *Scala New York / Florence.*

sickles, and other gear for forty warships.[11] In the late Empire, Etruria was still a productive region, although there was an economic decline in the coastal regions due to malaria.

During their heyday, the Etruscans had produced impressive works of art. The bronzes of early Etruria were superbly done, and a desire to portray accurately the features of the deceased led to a tradition of realism in funerary art. This concern for realism was soon reflected in sculptures of public figures as well. Though greatly indebted to Greek models, Etruscan artists had their own distinctive styles and a fondness for animals and strange monsters. Unlike the Greeks, Etruscan architects did not use marble, and stone was employed primarily for city walls and the foundations of buildings, the structures of which were wooden and decorated with terracotta. In some tombs and gates, the Etruscans utilized a false arch, which stimulated the Romans to develop the true arch. Typical Etruscan temples were almost as wide as they were long and contained three cellae at the rear to accommodate a triad of gods. Fond of color, the Etruscans painted their wooden structures with bright hues. Like many early peoples, they filled their tombs with treasures and artifacts to be used by the dead in the afterlife. In Lawrence's words, "splendid was the array they went with into death." [12] Etruscan painters used vibrant colors to decorate tombs with scenes of feasting and play, and since the tombs remained sealed for centuries, many paintings have survived to delight and inform us today.

Thanks to the evidence of the tombs and literary accounts from antiquity, much is known of the life of the Etruscan upper classes. The statues in the tombs often display the deceased as well-fed if not portly, so it would seem that Etruscan nobles deserved their reputation as proponents of *la dolce vita*. As with many early Mediterranean peoples, seminudity was common for men, who often wore only loincloths. For decoration and warmth, jackets were used as well as a mantle which later developed into the Roman toga. Though beards were characteristic of the early Etruscans, most men were clean-shaven after 500. Women of the upper classes wore long, sometimes diaphanous, gowns, and some dyed their hair blond. According to the Greeks, Etruscan women were beautiful but lewd. The principal source of this charge of immorality was the freedom that women enjoyed in Etruscan society, dining with the men and enjoying spectacles together. Etruscan funerary statues often portray married couples reclining together in honest affection. Such domestic equality shocked the Greeks who treated women as inferiors. Etruscan ladies were fond of mirrors, cosmetics, and jewelry, but

---

[11] Livy 28.45.   [12] Lawrence, *Etruscan Places*, p. 24.

their sexual reputation was surely exaggerated.[13] All Etruscans loved music and dancing, and games, work, and even punishment were conducted to the music of flutes. Actors were very popular, and the art of the mime was passed from Etruria to Rome. Etruscan men were fond of sports and enthusiastic over horse racing. Less pleasant were gladiatorial games, which the Etruscans may have learned from the Samnites in Campania. An undeniably Etruscan entertainment was a brutal spectacle in which a man, blinded by a hood and armed with a club, had to fight off a vicious hound. Probably the cruel aspects of Etruscan life reflect the decadence of an aristocracy which was overfed and bored for amusement. In Etruria, as elsewhere, the pleasures of the poor were few and simple.

In the Etruscan world, society was kin-based with severe class lines. Family feeling was strong, and like the other Italians, the Etruscans employed a gentilician name system, in which personal names were followed by clan names. Among the aristocracy, it was common to add a patronymic, and some inscriptions include the name of the mother as well. This latter custom has prompted some imaginative scholars to claim a matriarchal element in Etruscan society, but there is no need to revive the outmoded theories of Bachofen.[14] The Etruscans regarded women highly, and some were proud of their mothers, but there was no *Mutterrecht* in Etruria. In the days of the *lucumones,* a small group of noble clans dominated each Etruscan city, and later they competed for the office of *zilath.* In the commercial centers, there was a middle class, but it played no significant role in politics. Apparently, some Etruscans were clients of the noble families, for they were honored by having their ashes interred in the cavernous sepulchers of their patrons. In addition to a large number of slaves owned by the nobility, there was a lower class of artisans and farmers; the latter may have worked the nobles' fields as serfs or perhaps as tenants. In classical Etruscan society, the oppressed classes were subservient, but there are accounts of social unrest in the days of Etruscan decline and of a major slave revolt at Volsinii in the third century.

Except for about one hundred words, the Etruscan language cannot be read by moderns. Scores of philologists have failed to solve the mys-

---

[13] Similar charges were made against the women of Sparta who, by Hellenic standards, were emancipated.

[14] A nineteenth-century Romantic, Johann J. Bachofen was the first scholar to recognize matrilineal descent, but he erroneously equated it with matriarchy and insisted that he had discovered a universal pattern preceding patriarchal societies. Engels found his theory useful, and it has been revived by some feminists today.

tery, for Etruscan is not related to Indo-European or any known linguistic family. However, funerary inscriptions dealing with names, families, and offices held can be read with considerable certainty, and the meanings of some Etruscan words were recorded by scholars in antiquity. The Romans borrowed a number of Etruscan terms, such as *lanista* (a trainer of gladiators), *histrio* (actor), and *persona* (mask). Unfortunately, very few Etruscan texts have survived—the most famous is a religious calendar written on linen and later used to wrap an Egyptian mummy, now in the Zagreb Museum. Recently, three gold tablets were discovered at Pyrgi, the port of Caere; one of the tablets is written in Punic, and the others comprise a longer Etruscan version of the Carthaginian material. The Punic document can be dated about the beginning of the fifth century, and it mentions the dedication of the sanctuary by the ruler of Caere to the Carthaginian goddess, Astarte. Because the Punic tablet is briefer than the two Etruscan tablets, Etruscology still lacks a Rosetta Stone. However, the tablets provide interesting evidence of Carthaginian diplomatic activity on the coast of Etruria at an early period. In their writings, the Etruscans used an alphabetic script which was an adaptation of the Western Greek alphabet. Within the Etruscan sphere of cultural influence, the modified alphabet was passed on to more backward Italic peoples. As for Etruscan literature, its nature can only be surmised. Obviously religion played an important part, but the Etruscans were also interested in secular themes and probably borrowed them from the Greek world, for figures from Hellenic literature are prominently featured in Etruscan art. The Romans credited the Etruscans with originating the popular Fescennine songs, which were satirical and ribald. In the second century, an Etruscan poet, Volnius, wrote Greek-style tragedies in his native tongue. In the first century B.C., the Roman antiquarian Varro wrote at length on Etruscan matters and quoted from "Tuscan Histories." For the benefit of the Roman public, an Etruscan scholar, Tarquitius Priscus, translated the sacred lore of Etruria into Latin. Later, the emperor Claudius, who could read Etruscan, managed to fill twenty books with Etruscology, but unfortunately these are no longer extant. Even if the Etruscan language is never deciphered, the recovery of these lost Latin authorities would greatly enlarge our knowledge of the history and ways of the Etruscans.

In antiquity, all societies were devoted to religion, but Livy claims that the Etruscans were the most religious nation on earth.[15] Not content with worshiping the gods and imploring their aid, the Etruscans were anxious to learn the wishes of Heaven and implement the divine intent. The crowded Etruscan pantheon was headed by the sky god,

---

[15] Livy 5.1 Cf. Herodotus 2.37.

Tinia, who wielded thunderbolts. In the famed Capitoline temple that the Etruscans built at Rome, the statue of Tinia was flanked by the images of two female deities, his consort Uni and the goddess of urban affairs, Menerva. The two goddesses were originally Italian deities, as was the war god Maris. From Greece, the Etruscans borrowed the gods Apollo and Heracles. According to Varro, the national deity of Etruria was a protean god, Voltumna, at whose shrine the Etruscan League held its meetings. Though their gods were anthropomorphic, Etruscan priests devised a theology which included mysterious divinities whom even Tinia had to obey. Unlike the Greeks and Romans, the Etruscans had a revealed religion based on a collection of sacred texts that were cherished and followed to the letter. Some of the texts were attributed to a prophetess, Vegoia or Begoë, but the major scriptures were believed to be the revelations of Tinia's grandson, Tages, who had the face of a child and the white hair of a sage. The holy books of Etruria were divided into three categories: haruspication, lightning lore, and ritual. They also included tracts on such varied subjects as civil affairs, mensuration, life after death, and the mysteries of time. According to the Etruscans, fate had allowed their nation a life span of ten *saecula;* the average length of a *saeculum* was a little over a century, but the later *saecula* seem to have varied. Although the eighth era ended in 88 B.C. with the sound of a celestial trumpet (or so Plutarch tells us),[16] an Etruscan diviner claimed that the comet of 44 B.C. heralded the end of the ninth *saeculum.* Apparently the Etruscans were not sure about the length of a *saeculum,* but they were convinced that the course of history was predetermined. The Etruscans were equally certain that man was immortal. In the era of Etruscan expansion, tomb paintings show scenes of a pleasant afterlife of banqueting and joy, but Etruscan eschatology grew gloomy in the days of national decline. By the fourth century, Etruscan art emphasized a nightmarish underworld peopled with fearful demons. The Greek ferryman of the river Styx, Charon, was transformed into a ghostly blue figure of death, Charun, and the winged monsters of the underworld included the frightful Tuchulcha, who had a vulture's face with donkey's ears and serpents in his hair. Despite a morbid concern with demonology, Etruscan religion also provided rites of salvation which promised the deceased an afterlife of bliss.

The aspect of Etruscan religiosity that most impressed the Romans was their mania for divination. Driven by a compulsion to bridge the gap between the world of man and the supernatural, they needed desperately to know the explicit wishes of the gods. To the Etruscans, nothing happened at random or without an esoteric meaning—every

[16] Plutarch *Sulla,* 7.

phenomenon had a supernatural significance, the key to which could be found in the holy books. In Etruria, divination was regarded as a science, and its practitioners were men of learning and prestige. The *fulgurator* interpreted lightning flashes, and the *haruspex*, the Etruscan diviner *par excellence,* read meanings into the markings on the livers of sacrificed animals. The premise of these practices was an assumption that the cosmos was divided into sixteen areas presided over by various divinities, some benevolent and others hostile. When the diviner faced south, he was oriented to the cosmic pattern, and by their location lightning flashes and thunder claps revealed to him which god was speaking through celestial fireworks. Thunder on his left (east) was a good omen, but thunder on the right (west) boded ill; the types and shapes of lightning were classified, and only a highly skilled *fulgurator* knew all their forms and significances. Similarly, during the rites of divination, a sacrificial liver became a gory map of the cosmos with the future revealed by the formations on the organ. At Piacenza, a bronze model of a liver has been found which is marked with the cosmic divisions and the names of the appropriate gods. The origins of haruspication lay in the Near East where it had been practiced for millennia, and the haruspices of Etruria took their "science" seriously. Wearing pointed hats and fringed robes, the haruspices held the future in their hands as they examined the bloody livers. So the masses believed, and no doubt the rulers and the haruspices as well shared the national delusion. Not only did the Etruscan scriptures contain the arcana of thunder, lightning, and liver analysis, but also rites to avert the wrath of Heaven and prevent calamity.

Though it required accurate observations, divination precluded the rise of a truly scientific spirit. The Roman scholar Seneca dryly observed the difference between Etruscan lore and Greco-Roman science:

> While we believe that lightning is released when clouds collide, they believe that clouds collide in order to release lightning. Since they ascribe everything to the divine, they cannot accept that things have a meaning because they happen, but rather they believe that things happen in order to have a meaning.[17]

Few Romans were as skeptical as Seneca, however, and most stood in awe of Etruscan haruspices. Whenever their own augurs were at a loss, the Romans would call upon the services of Etruscan diviners even down to the end of the Empire. Translated into Latin in the late Republic, the scriptures of Etruria were added to the sacred texts the Roman state consulted in times of stress.

In the Augustan age, the Roman poet Propertius mused on the fallen glory of the Etruscans:

[17] Seneca *Quaestiones Naturales* 2.32.2.

> Veii, thou hadst a royal crown of old,
> And in thy forum stood a throne of gold!
> Thy walls now echo but the shepherd's horn,
> And o'er thine ashes waves the summer corn.[18]

Now, Rome too is only ruins and memories, but the effect that nations have upon history usually lasts longer than their physical remains. In the remote past, the Etruscans urbanized Rome and made an enduring impression on its political and cultural development.

THE GREEKS IN ITALY AND SICILY

The third major group in ancient Italy were the Greeks. So numerous were they and so long established were their cities, that southern Italy, not old Hellas, was called Magna Graecia by the Romans. The Greeks contributed much to the general stream of Italian culture and to the spread of urbanization. In Italy and Sicily, the Hellenes had a history and a cultural life as significant as those of the mainland Greeks.

In the second millennium B.C., Minoans and Mycenaeans had penetrated the western Mediterranean and established trading posts in Italy and Sicily, but these contacts ended and were probably forgotten in the Dark Ages following the fall of the Mycenaean world about 1100 B.C. To the early Greeks who braved unknown seas in search of trade and adventure, the West was a land of wonders filled with witches, cannibals, and rude savages. In Sicily dwelt primitive pastoralists with the eye of the sun tattooed on their foreheads; in legend, they became the Cyclopes. Memories of the strange peoples of the West were incorporated into the *Odyssey,* but later Greeks were not discouraged by the tall tales of Homer.

In the Dark Ages, the Greeks had expanded across the Aegean to the western coast of Asia Minor, but in the eighth and seventh centuries there was a veritable explosion of colonization and exploration. Greek settlements were established around the Black Sea, in Egypt and Libya, and in the West. Traders and merchants were prompted by greed and set up trading posts, but other Greeks sought new lives in the colonies. In old Hellas, expanding populations had caused a scarcity of land, and economic changes had reduced many Greeks to pauperism, but across the seas lay new opportunities and land which would give them status again. Not all immigrants were driven by poverty. Some colonists were refugees from foreign invaders, and others were political malcontents

---

[18] Propertius 4.10, trans. George Dennis, *Cities and Cemetaries of Etruria* (London: John Murray, 1878), I, 16.

whose emigration was encouraged by the ruling oligarchies of their homelands. In the motivations and behavior of the colonists, Greek immigration to the West resembles later European migrations to the Americas. Greek pioneers were not concerned with the rights of natives whose lands they coveted and seized. In particular, the fertile lands of Sicily attracted the avarice of Hellenes, who often treated the native Sicels with treachery and eventually overwhelmed them. The Italian tribes offered greater resistance, and the history of Greek Italy was punctuated with bitter frontier wars. However they got their lands, the Greeks introduced olives and viniculture.

The early history of the western Greeks is based largely on the researches of the Hellenistic Sicilian historian, Timaeus, who relied in part on the writings of Antiochus of Syracuse, published soon after 424 B.C. Obviously many details of this tradition invite suspicion, particularly precise dates for the early period, but archeology has confirmed the general accuracy of the accounts. The first Greek settlement in the West was off the Bay of Naples on the island of Pithekoussai (Ischia) near the southern boundary of the Etruscan sphere of influence—the purpose of the colony was trade. On the coast north of the Bay of Naples, the city of Cumae was founded about 750 B.C. A flourishing community, Cumae later set up a colony of its own, Neapolis, which is now Naples. From Cumae, the Chalcidian form of the Greek alphabet spread to the Etruscans and eventually to the Italians. Some of the settlers in Campania were called Graioi, which the Latins transformed into Graeci and applied the term to all Hellenes. On the western side of the straits between Sicily and Italy, Cumaeans and other Greeks founded the strategic town of Zancle, later called Messana. The oldest Greek settlement in Sicily was Naxos, established traditionally in 735. A year later a more important city, Syracuse, was founded, on the finest harbor on the island. A Corinthian colony, Syracuse soon became the largest and most powerful city in the Greek West. Later, the town of Leontini was founded nearby.

In southern Italy on the Gulf of Taranto, three major Greek cities were established: Sybaris, Croton, and Tarentum. Prospering from both trade and rich farms, Sybaris was a powerful commercial city enclosed by eight miles of walls. Active in overland trade with the Etruscans, the Sybarites set up a colony, Posidonia, on the western coast south of Campania. Flaunting its wealth, Sybaris held international games which rivaled those at Olympia. Because the prosperous Sybarites enjoyed conspicuous consumption, the city became synonymous with ostentatious luxury, but most tales of Sybarite decadence were libels spread by their hostile neighbors at Croton. Life in Hellas was not comfortable, and visitors were awed that the streets of Sybaris were clean and shaded, that food was well-prepared, and that noisy occupations were kept outside the walls. Such Sybarite inventions as the chamber pot were considered decadent, and other Greeks were genuinely shocked when the men of Sybaris dined with their wives, as did the Etruscans. According to the Crotonites, a gentleman of Sybaris was ruptured by the sight of men at work, and another Sybarite was ruptured by just hearing about it. The intense rivalry between the two towns was further inflamed when Croton fell under the control of Pythagorean puritans. Like Sybaris, Croton was a prosperous city, and it supported a major medical school. Crotonite doctors were famed for their skills, and one, Democedes, served as court physician to Darius the Great. Enjoying the reputation of a healthy locale, Croton was a mecca for health faddists. The Crotonites were devoted to athletics, and their champion Milo was a frequent victor in the Olympic games. At Tarentum, Sparta had founded a colony and manned it with unwanted bastards who had been born during the First Messenian War. Whatever their ancestry, the Tarentines had the best harbor in southern Italy and grew rich from both trade and agriculture.

Early in the seventh century, Rhegium was founded on the Italian shore of the Straits of Messana. Nearby on the Ionian Sea was Locri, which feared the aggressions of Rhegium and Croton and often sought alliances with Syracuse. According to a doubtful tradition, Locri produced the earliest law code in the Hellenic world, but its lawgiver Zaleucus is a legendary figure whose legislation suggests later Pythagorean notions, and Timaeus denied that he had ever lived. Nevertheless, stable laws were essential in the Greek cities of the West, for the populations of new communities were usually mixed and sometimes unruly. On the coasts of central Sicily, two famous towns were founded, Gela in the South and Himera in the North. Gela in turn established Acragas which in time would rival the importance of Syracuse. It was also to be the home of the famous philosopher, Empedocles. North of Sicily, freebooters from Rhodes had seized the Lipari Islands and set up a communistic pirate state with common messes and communal ownership of land. Eventually the Lipari pirates abandoned communism, but periodically they redistributed land.

In the lands west of Italy, Greeks from the Ionian city of Phocaea were active in exploration and trade. The Phocaeans had commercial connections with the great city of Tartessus (the Biblical Tarshish) on the Atlantic coast of Spain. Near the mouth of the Rhone, Phocaeans founded the town of Massilia which profited from trade with the tribes of Gaul. Despite occasional forays by the barbarians, Massilia became a rich and prosperous city and was later a center of education. The Massiliotes introduced olives and viniculture to the region that is now southern France. On the coast of Spain, Massilia had numerous trading emporia. By 500, the Carthaginians had closed the Strait of Gibraltar to Greek ships, and Etruscan traders captured the inland markets north of the Alps, once monopolized by Massiliotes. Earlier, when Ionia fell to the Persians, half of the population of Phocaea had fled to the West, but the refugees were ousted from Corsica by Etruscans and Carthaginians. Finally, the Phocaeans settled at Elea (Velia) on the Italian coast near Posidonia. Though not a major city, Elea would become famous as the home of the philosophers, Parmenides and Zeno.

Although the Hellenes often drove natives from their own lands or enslaved them as serfs, there was considerable intermarriage between the Greeks and the Italians and Sicels. Despite frequent acts of aggression and treachery, the coming of the Greeks meant the spread of urban civilization, and even the Sicels, who resented the pushy pioneers, adopted the Chalcidian alphabet. In Etruria, the Greeks behaved better, for they were anxious to trade with the Etruscan cities. As early as the seventh century, Greek trading posts were established in Etruria, where Corinthian and later Attic vases were especially desired. According to legend, a Corinthian nobleman, Demaratus, migrated to Etruria with his family and retainers who were skilled craftsmen. The story becomes implausible when it adds that Demaratus was the father of Tarquin, the first Etruscan king of Rome. However, the basic tale of a Hellenic noble seeking a civilized life in Etruria is probable enough. No doubt, an urban environment seemed more attractive to a nobleman than clearing farmland or battling barbarians in the new colonies.

A proud and emotional people, the Greeks were quick to shed blood and bore grudges for generations. Class conflicts between rich and poor, power struggles between oligarchs and democrats, and bitter rivalries between cities made Greek politics lively and fierce. Originally, the early colonies were controlled by oligarchies, but in time many cities broadened the franchise and some became democracies. Whatever the form of government, each city in the West held dissatisfied elements who wished to seize power and were willing to use violence to gain it. Exhausted by internal strife, many cities succumbed to tyrants or dictators who provided stability at the price of political despotism. Often the tyrants, backed by mercenaries, terrorized and abused their subjects, but many were able autocrats who ruled with moderation and the cooperation of leading citizens. In Italy, raids by Italian tribesmen prompted some cities to raise military leaders to supreme power, while in Sicily the threat of Carthage drove many towns into the arms of tyrants. The Carthaginians considered western Sicily their sphere of influence and had established strongholds there, but Punic policy was not aimed against the Greeks as such. Carthage itself was a great consumer of Hellenic goods, and the African state often allied itself with various Greek cities in Sicily to combat a mutual enemy, Syracuse. In the sixth century, the Carthaginians seized Sardinia and helped the Etruscans drive Greeks from Corsica, but Carthage did not wage an anti-Hellenic crusade in Sicily. More dangerous than Punic pressure were predatory local tyrants, such as Phalaris of Acragas, who reputedly roasted his enemies in a bronze bull. The tales of Phalaris's cruelties were magnified with each retelling, but later at Carthage, Polybius saw a bronze bull equipped with a door for inserting victims. The Carthaginians claimed that they had captured the device at Acragas centuries earlier. Restored to Acragas by the Romans, the bull became a famous tourist attraction.

In southern Italy, some Greek cities had the novel experience of being ruled by intellectual elites. In 530, the philosopher Pythagoras arrived at Croton, which had recently been shaken by a defeat in a war with Locri. A charismatic figure, Pythagoras formed a semireligious community of disciples at Croton. Other Crotonites of the leisure class endorsed his notion of an intellectual elite and formed political clubs which soon seized control of the city. Though Pythagoras himself probably took little part in politics, the Pythagorean clubs turned Croton into a "city of God" not unlike Calvin's Geneva. Puritanical and doctrinaire, the elect at Croton loathed the nearby "Sodom" of Sybaris, which was also their hereditary enemy. In 510, a pretext for a holy war against Sybaris arose, and a Crotonite army led by Milo crushed the Sybarite forces and razed the city. To complete their triumph, the victors diverted a river to flow over the ruins of Sybaris. Under the aegis of Croton, Pythagorean oligarchies were established in many neighboring cities, but democrats were restive under the oppressive rule of the saints. About the middle of the fifth century, the Pythagorean regimes were overthrown by popular uprisings, and many of the elect were burned alive by their former subjects. After this debacle, the Pythagorean brotherhood avoided politics and concerned itself with intellectual activity. However, individual Pythagoreans, such as Archytas of Tarentum, still engaged in politics.

In Campania, a picturesque tyrant arose at Cumae. In 524 a large force of Etruscan and Italian allies marched against Cumae but were repulsed. The hero of the victory, Aristodemus, became a champion of the Cumaean commons against their oligarchic rulers. Late in the century, the Latins were threatened by the Etruscan monarch Lars Porsenna and asked Cumae for aid. Leading a relief force, Aristodemus helped the Latins defeat the Etruscans near Aricia. In the battle, the Cumaean general slew Porsenna's son, who commanded the Etruscan army. Returning to Cumae, Aristodemus turned tyrant, seizing the city and disarming the citizenry. Appealing to the poor, the tyrant abolished debts and redistributed land. To break the aristocracy, Aristodemus closed the gymnasia frequented by the sons of the rich and forced them to labor in the fields. He also played host to the exiled Tarquin of Rome. Supposedly, the tyrant wallowed in luxury and debauchery, for he earned an epithet as "the Effeminate." In nearby Capua, refugees from Cumae plotted his overthrow, and about 490 they infiltrated Cumae and murdered Aristodemus. With the tyrant's death, oligarchy returned to Cumae. It is regrettable that most details of Aristodemus's career come from a late source, the Augustan writer Dionysius of Halicarnassus, who depicts Aristodemus as a typical "stage tyrant" of the Hellenistic era. Perhaps Dionysius relied on some lost "Annals of Cumae," but more likely he used a Hellenistic historian, such as Timaeus or perhaps Hyperochus of Cumae, who knew little about the real Aristodemus. At best, Dionysius's account is highly suspect.

More authentic than Aristodemus are the tyrants of Sicily. Early in the fifth century, Gela was ruled by a Machiavellian tyrant, Hippocrates, who harassed the Sicels and conquered many Greek cities in Sicily. At his death about 485, the tyranny at Gela passed to one of his generals, Gelon, who is a major figure in Sicilian history. When democrats took over the government of Syracuse, the ousted oligarchs appealed to Gelon for aid. The tyrant restored order in Syracuse but seized the city for himself and made it the capital of a military empire. In some Greek towns, Gelon deported the population, transporting the upper classes and skilled workmen to Syracuse and selling the poor as slaves. Allied with Gelon was the powerful tyrant of Acragas, Theron, whose aggressions drove various cities into the arms of Carthage. One of Gelon's enemies was the ruler of Rhegium, Anaxilas, who seized Zancle and renamed it Messana. Anaxilas's son-in-law, the tyrant of Himera, was ousted by Theron and Gelon and appealed to Carthage for aid. Anaxilas also pleaded with the Carthaginians to intervene. In 480, a large Punic army under Hamilcar marched against Himera, but Gelon and his allies defeated the invaders, and Hamilcar immolated himself to appease the gods of Carthage. Many Greek historians believed that the battle of Himera was synchronistic with Xerxes' defeat at Salamis, and the fourth-century writer, Ephorus, claimed that Carthage and Persia had attacked the Greeks in the West and East as part of a concerted plan, but Aristotle had the good sense to reject the notion. During the Persian invasion of Greece, Gelon had envoys waiting at Delphi with instructions to present Xerxes with a great treasure *if he won.* After the victory at Himera, Gelon was lenient with Anaxilas and other pro-Punic tyrants. Now lord of most of Sicily, he had no need for revenge.

Two years after the battle of Himera, Gelon died and was succeeded by his brother Hiero, who was equally able and brutal. Syracuse flourished under the tyrant, and famous poets flocked to his court, for Hiero was a generous patron. In Pindar's words,

> They come their ways
> to the magnificent board of Hieron,
> who handles the scepter of dooms in Sicily, rich in flocks,
> reaping the crested heads of every excellence.
> There his fame is magnified
> in the splendor of music, where
> we delight at the friendly table.[19]

The citizens of Syracuse were less enthusiastic about Hiero the magnificent. Interested in Italy, the tyrant of Syracuse supported Locri against Rhegium and came to the assistance of Cumae, which was again menaced by the Etruscans. In 474, Hiero's fleet won a great victory over the Etruscans off Cumae. Pindar obligingly celebrated the event:

> Kronion [Zeus], I beseech you, bend your head in assent
> that the Phoenician and the war-crying Tyrsenian keep
> quietly at home, beholding the shame of their wreck by
> sea at Kyme,
> the things they endured, beaten at the hands of Syracuse's lord,
> how he hurled their young men out of their fleet-running
> ships on the sea,
> gathering back Hellas from the weight of slavery.[20]

Despite the success at Cumae, Hiero was unable to extend his empire to Italy, but fear of his intentions drove Rhegium into an alliance with Tarentum. In 466, the tyrant died and was succeeded by an inept brother, but a democratic revolution soon overthrew the tyranny at Syracuse. Similarly, the tyrants at Acragas and Rhegium were also replaced by popular governments. Though Syracuse was now a democracy, the age of tyrants in Sicily had only been interrupted.

At mid-century, a native leader, Ducetius, tried to rally the Sicels against Greek domination, but despite some early successes, he eventually failed, and the Sicel cause foundered after his death. In 445 Syracuse won a victory over Acragas and strengthened its hegemony over the Greek cities. During the Peloponnesian War, Athens meddled in Sicily and sent a great armada to attack Syracuse, but the expedition was totally defeated in 413 and Athenian prisoners were forced to labor as slaves in the quarries at Syracuse. Late in the century, Carthage re-

---

[19] Pindar *Olympia* 1, trans. Richmond Lattimore, *The Odes of Pindar* (Chicago: University of Chicago Press, 1947), p. 1.
[20] Pindar *Pythia* 1, ibid., p. 46.

took the offensive in Sicily and sacked Acragas, but the Punic threat brought about a revival of tyranny at Syracuse.

In 405, the citizens of Syracuse elected the wily Dionysius as commander-in-chief to fight the Carthaginians. Backed by a large mercenary force, Dionysius made himself tyrant and built a superb military force, replete with specialists and large mobile siege towers. Though heavily taxed, Syracuse flourished under his regime. Generally successful in his wars against the Carthaginians, Dionysius never tried to expel them completely from Sicily, for he needed the foreign menace to justify his regime. The tyrant subdued the Greek cities and the Sicels. Allied with Locri, Dionysius attacked Rhegium, the government of which had earlier angered him by offering the hangman's daughter as his bride. Taking Rhegium after a long siege, he sold most of the survivors as slaves. Croton too fell to the Sicilian tyrant who extended his sway to Tarentum and established garrisons on the Adriatic coast of Italy and in the Balkans. At the peak of his power, Dionysius had created the greatest military empire in the West. An amateur poet, the tyrant was renowned as a patron of the arts, and Plato and other intellectuals were attracted to his court. Though the philosopher hoped to advise the despot, Dionysius considered Plato naive and sent him back to Athens. In 367 Dionysius died and was succeeded by his son, Dionysius II, whom Plato sought to influence but again without success. In 356 the new tyrant was overthrown by a coalition led by his uncle Dion, a brother-in-law of the older Dionysius. A friend of Plato, Dion favored oligarchic government and soon quarreled with the democratic leaders in Syracuse. Impatient with opposition, Dion became tyrannical and was assassinated by one of Plato's disciples, who in turn tried to establish a tyranny at Syracuse. Eventually, Dionysius II returned to power but was ousted in 344 by the famous idealist, Timoleon, who also beat back the Carthaginians. Resigning from power, Timoleon left Syracuse in the hands of a moderate oligarchy. With the fall of Dionysius II, the hold of Syracuse on southern Italy had been broken.

Pressed by warlike Italian tribes, Tarentum invited the assistance of mercenary captains, all of whom chanced to be royalty. King Archidamus of Sparta brought a force to Tarentum but soon quarreled with his employers. In 338 the Spartan king died in battle against the Italians. Next came Alexander of Epirus, the uncle of a more famous Alexander. In defending Tarentum, the Epirote was more successful than Archidamus, but in 330 he was assassinated by an Italian. Finally, the Tarentines employed a Spartan prince, Cleonymus. An overbearing dynast, he captured various Greek towns and abused their inhabitants. When Cleonymus was defeated by the Italians, the Tarentines sent him away in 303. However, the patriotic Livy claims that the Spartan adventurer had been frightened off by the Romans, which is not very likely. In the future, Tarentum would again seek the aid of a royal adventurer, but then it would be Pyrrhus and against Rome. Late in the fourth century, Syracuse fell into the hands of a colorful and able tyrant, Agathocles, who made himself King of Sicily. A resourceful commander, he fought the Carthaginians in Africa. Though he took Croton about 300, Agathocles failed to establish an empire in Italy.

Like the Etruscans, the Greeks represented urban civilization, and through trade with the Hellenes, the peoples of Italy were exposed to Greek culture. Hellenic deities and religious concepts impressed the Etruscans, the Romans, and many other Italians. The Greeks believed that the gods often spoke through raving women. At Cumae, a holy woman, the Sibyl, tended the shrine of Apollo and delivered frenzied oracles when the god seized possession of her. Venerated by neighboring peoples, the Cumaean Sibyl would later be Aeneas's guide to the underworld in Vergil's *Aeneid*. According to a pious legend, Apollo had fallen in love with the Sibyl and had granted her a thousand years of life. However, when she refused his advances, the deity allowed the Sibyl to retain her miraculous longevity, but he ordained that she should age like any mortal. Wizened and wrinkled, the Sibyl shrank to a tiny size, and in Roman times the once awesome oracle was supposedly kept suspended in a jug. Playing about the shrine at Cumae, children taunted the presumed inhabitant of the jug and asked the Sibyl what she wanted. According to Petronius, the mocking children heard a hoarse whisper, "I wish to die." In her heyday, the Cumaean Sibyl had been one of the great oracles of the Hellenic world.

The early Greeks also stood in awe of shamans, mystic seers who in trances made spirit-journeys to distant lands and even to the world of the dead. The shamans were believed to be able to assume the shape of birds, and many were credited with miraculous reappearances after their death. At the Crotonite town of Metapontum, Herodotus saw a statue of the Scythian shaman Aristeas, who (the local citizens claimed) had once appeared there and told them that he had earlier visited Italy in the shape of a crow and in the company of Apollo. On the orders of the shaman, the people of Metapontum built an altar to the god.[21] Elements of shamanism appear in the lives and teachings of the western sages Pythagoras, Empedocles, and even Parmenides.

To the western regions, the Greeks brought the mystery cults of old Hellas, and votive pictures found at Locri suggest themes of the great Eleusinian Mysteries. To the average Greek, the afterlife was a dismal, blurred existence, but devotees of mystery cults anticipated a paradise

---

[21] Herodotus 4.15. See also the miracle at Metapontum in Athenaeus 13.605 CD.

in the next world. A few Greeks were Orphics, who believed in reincarnation and punishment in this life for the sins of a prior existence. The principle of atonement explained why Zeus neglected to hurl his lightning at notorious sinners. However, through ritual purity and a sinless life, Orphics expected to escape the wheel of rebirth. In some graves in southern Italy, golden tablets have been discovered which express "Orphic" doctrines. These leaves from "a Greek Book of the Dead" instruct the deceased how to find his way in the underworld. In part, the tablets read:

> Thou shalt find to the left of the House of Hades a Well-spring,
> And by the side thereof standing a white cypress.
> To this Well-spring approach not near.
> But thou shalt find another by the Lake of Memory,
> Cold water flowing forth, and there are Guardians before it.
> Say: "I am a child of Earth and of Starry Heaven;
> But my race is of Heaven [alone]. This ye know yourselves.
> And lo, I am parched with thirst and I perish. Give me quickly
> The cold water flowing forth from the Lake of Memory." [22]

By drinking the holy water, the deceased would recall his prior existence in "starry Heaven." The forbidden spring contained the water of forgetfulness which would doom him to rebirth.[23] The golden tablets also exalt the beatification of the deceased:

> Hail, thou who hast suffered the Suffering. This thou hadst never suffered before.
> Thou art become God from Man. A kid thou art fallen into milk. . . .
> Out of the Pure I come, Pure Queen of Them Below. . . .
> For I also avow me that I am of your blessed race.
> And I have paid the penalty for deeds unrighteous. . . .
> I have flown out of the sorrowful weary Wheel;
> I have passed with eager feet to the Circle desired. . . .
> Happy and Blessed one, thou shalt be God instead of Mortal.[24]

Not only did the deceased escape "the sorrowful weary wheel" of rebirth, but he became divine again, returning to the pure race of Heaven. Such eschatological longings appealed even to Romans, and a similar tablet was found in the tomb of Caecilia Secundina at Rome. Orphism

---

[22] Jane Harrison, *Prolegomena to the Study of Greek Religion* (Cambridge: Cambridge University Press, 1922), pp. 659–60. The translation is by Gilbert Murray.

[23] The latter idea appears in Plato's myth of Er and Vergil's *Aeneid,* and both streams are found in the Earthly Paradise at the climax of Dante's *Purgatorio.*

[24] Ibid., pp. 662, 669.

is a muddled and controversial subject, and the southern Italian tablets may be Hellenistic. The doctrines stem from an earlier period, however, for salvation cults are as old as Greece and reincarnation was taught by both Pythagoras and Empedocles. There was a mystic strain in the Greeks of Italy, and in time some Romans would have need of it.

The cultural life of the Greek West was rich and varied. Art was ornate, with a touch of the grand, and the famed temple of Zeus at Acragas was characteristically large. Even in the sixth century, Himera produced a prominent lyric poet, Stesichorus, who wrote disparagingly of Helen of Troy. Aware that the West was not a cultural wasteland, the philosopher Xenophanes moved to Sicily, and Pythagoras assumed that Croton would be compatible to a man of intellectual interests. The poets Simonides, his nephew Bacchylides, Pindar, and Aeschylus enjoyed the patronage of Hiero, and later Plato tried to play a political role at Syracuse. Plato also visited Pythagorean communities in Italy.

At Croton, Pythagoras taught the doctrines of reincarnation in human and animal forms, and he promised salvation through philosophic purification. Also interested in science and mathematics, Pythagoras believed in the sphericity of the earth. Pythagoreanism had overtones of mysticism, and his disciples in Italy devised a strange world of numerology that saw numbers as physical entities. Under Pythagorean control, the medical school of Croton continued to flourish, and there Alcmaeon proclaimed that the brain is the seat of sensation. In the fifth century, another Pythagorean, Philolaus, concocted a cosmology in which the earth and its seven satellites (sun, moon, and five visible planets) daily circled a central fire; a counter-earth across the cosmos brought the total of heavenly bodies to ten, a perfect number by Pythagorean standards. Though numerological nonsense, the system of Philolaus put the earth in motion. Plato's friend, the Tarentine politician Archytas, was also a Pythagorean and interested in mechanical automata and mathematical theories. At Elea, the philosopher Parmenides claimed divine inspiration to justify his doctrines, which denied change and motion. Stretching words to the semantic breaking point, Parmenides' disciple Zeno described a motionless world in which an arrow can never reach a target. The antics of the Eleatics made philosophers wary of loose definitions and more careful in their logic.

In fifth-century Sicily, the philosopher Empedocles played an active role in democratic politics at Acragas. He was also a shaman and claimed, as did Pythagoras, to be a "purified soul" returned to earth. An advocate of cosmic cycles, Empedocles devised an interesting theory of evolution with a kind of "natural selection." Less colorful than Empedocles was the famous sophist, Gorgias of Leontini, who taught that nothing exists and if something did exist, it would be incomprehensible and could not be communicated—at least in theory. Sicily boasted historians, and the works of Antiochus of Syracuse were apparently consulted by Thucydides. A friend of Dionysius I, Philistus, wrote a major history of Sicily, but the greatest of the western historians was Timaeus of Acragas who fled from the tyranny of Agathocles. A bitter émigré in Athens, Timaeus wrote voluminously on the past glories of the western Greeks and the wickedness of tyrants. He also popularized the practice of dating events by Olympiads.

From Tarentum came the "workers' poet," Leonidas, who was a contemporary of Pyrrhus and ended his days wandering in Greece. Unlike most Hellenistic writers, Leonidas celebrated "the short and simple annals of the poor." Unashamed of his own poverty, the vagrant poet described the daily toil and homely joys of fishermen, peasants, and artisans. The works of Leonidas reveal the quiet country life of Italy and Greece, and the shepherds in his poems were real workingmen—tired, dirty, and proud of their labor. A valuable glimpse of a lifetime of toil is preserved in his portrait of a simple spinning woman:

> Her morning rest, her evening sleep,
> Old Platthis oft refused to keep;
> And spindle still and distaff plied
> To ward grim Hunger from her side.
>
> Oft would she see the bright dawn come
> While yet she laboured at her loom
> With wrinkled hand on wrinkled knee,
> Smoothing the threads for weaving free.
>
> Though near she stood to withered eld
> Still something of youth's charm she held
> And while she worked sweet music made
> Calling the Graces to her aid.
>
> So eighty years had passed and flown
> Ere Platthis laid her weaving down
> And closed her eyes to see beneath
> The waters of the lake of death.[25]

Old Platthis and her peers produced the wealth which cities spent on public monuments and despots squandered on war. Inured to poverty and toil, exploited and despised, the rural masses labored quietly throughout antiquity. Without their labor to fill her coffers, Rome could not have built an empire. Without their sons to fill her armies, Rome could not have captured a world.

[25] F. A. Wright, *The Poets of the Greek Anthology* (London: George Routledge & Sons, 1924), pp. 35–36. See also Edwyn Bevan, *The Poems of Leonidas of Tarentum* (Oxford: Clarendon Press, 1931), pp. 70–71.

CHAPTER TWO

The emergence of Rome

THROUGH A GLASS DARKLY

*W*hether *of men or of nations, beginnings are always small,* and the Romans freely admitted that their origins were humble by physical standards. In the time of Augustus, the poet Propertius reminded his fellow Romans how tiny and simple their city had once been:

> All that you see here, stranger, where great Rome now stands,
> Was once, before Phrygian Aeneas came, native hill and turf.
> Where now rises the Palatine, sacred to Phoebus Mariner,
> Evander's cows, refugees, sank down to rest. Where now,
> For gods of clay, these gilded temples have been built,
> A rough and artless shelter, formerly, was no shame. . . .
> Our oxen drank from Tiber, then a foreign stream. . . .
> The Curia, now the lofty seat of a togaed senate,
> Held fathers wearing skins tied with the rustic cord.[1]

Proof of the poet's words were two straw hovels with thatched roofs, each called the "hut of Romulus," that were preserved with religious care, one on the Palatine, the other on the Capitoline hill. Tradition, too, insisted that the Rome of Romulus had been a small community of shepherds and outcasts. In their days of glory with its attendant problems, many Romans looked back wistfully to the squalor of their nation's birth.

Yet an imperial people requires an epic past and usually invents one. If early Rome was physically simple, it nonetheless had to be the home of heroes, and Roman writers readily supplied the details. From a minimum of facts, many dubious traditions, and a great deal of imagination,

---

[1] Propertius 4.1.1–12, trans. Frances Fletcher, in L. R. Lind, ed., *Latin Poetry in Verse Translation* (Boston: Houghton Mifflin, 1957), p. 193.

Roman historians and poets produced an epic historical tradition, studded with unforgettable characters and tuned to a central theme, the manifest destiny of the Roman people. From the flaming ruins of Troy emerged the heroic Aeneas, bearing his father and the household gods, the very epitome of Roman piety. Disdaining the love of Dido and a throne in Africa, he followed his destiny to Italy and sowed the seed from which the Roman stock would spring. Centuries later, a virginal descendant of Aeneas bore twin sons sired by the god Mars, but their wicked granduncle, the local king, set the boys adrift in a basket on the Tiber. Rescued and suckled by a she-wolf, the twins, Romulus and Remus, were raised in wholesome poverty by peasants. About 753 B.C. the adult Romulus founded his own town, a tiny group of villages called Rome. A warlike man, he killed Remus in a fit of anger, adding a fratricidal note to the themes of Roman history. To gain wives, Romulus's followers stole women from the nearby Sabines, but the two groups were soon reconciled, and Romulus's successor as king was a pious Sabine, Numa, who founded the Roman state cult. After two kings of little note, the throne passed to an able Etruscan, Tarquin, who began the urbanization of Rome. Tarquin's son-in-law and successor was the Latin Servius Tullius, who put walls around the city and established many lasting institutions. However, the good king was murdered by his evil daughter and her husband, another Tarquin, who seized the throne. Rome languished under the tyranny of Tarquin the Proud until the monarchy was overthrown in 509 B.C., presumably because a Tarquin prince had raped the chaste Lucretia. The revolution was led by the stolid L. Junius Brutus, who helped to establish a republican government at Rome. The new republic was dominated by aristocratic patricians who only grudgingly relinquished political power to plebeian commoners. Gradually through years of compromise and concession, the classic Republic took form, with popular assemblies electing magistrates and making laws under the watchful eye of a venerable Senate. Under the Republic, the Romans became a great military power, vanquishing Etruscans, Latins, Gauls, and Italic tribes until Rome dominated Italy by the beginning of the third century B.C. Naturally, the heroes who built Roman success were awesome types—Brutus killed his own sons when they conspired against the Republic, and other men slew their sons for disobeying military orders even when the outcome was a victory for Rome. Horatius at the bridge, Scaevola holding his hand in the fire, Decius Mus sacrificing his life to win victory—the roster of valor could be extended at length. Though the Gauls burned the city in 387 B.C., the Roman people rallied behind the great Camillus and drove the barbarians away. Not only the heroic leaders, but the Roman commons themselves had the stuff of greatness in them. Moreover, the Republic was not a hectic Greek democracy, for it had a mixed constitution, delicately balancing powers and rights. Rule by law was part of the Roman achievement. Disciplined, valorous, and just, Republican Rome would be a beacon of liberty and courage for ages to come. These are the stories on which schoolboys were raised not so long ago, and such was the image that dazzled Jefferson and Robespierre.

The epic of early Rome is a great one, but is it true? In modern times, Beaufort, Niebuhr, and other historians launched a frontal assault on the edifice of early Roman history and demolished it stone by stone. Though scholarship gained, mankind lost much in the bargain, as Goethe sadly noted:

> Up to now the world believed in the heroism of a Lucretia and a Mucius Scaevola, and thus let itself be warmed and inspired. But now historical criticism appears and says that those persons have never lived, but must be regarded as fictions and fables, dreamed up by the great mind of the Romans. What are we to do with such a miserable truth? If the Romans were great enough to invent such things, we should at least be great enough to believe in them.[2]

To be sure, the world is poorer when idols topple and heroes are brought low. By their achievements or strength of character, heroes show us what we might be and rarely are. However, the social utility of a parable cannot justify its acceptance as truth. Perhaps critical history is a cruel craft, but it serves a better purpose than furthering what Plato termed "noble lies."

Not all poets shared Goethe's antipathy to historical criticism. In the *Lays of Ancient Rome,* Lord Macaulay, who believed that the epic of Rome was based on ballads, took his stand with the critics:

> That what is called the history of the kings and early consuls of Rome is to a great extent fabulous, few scholars have, since the time of Beaufort, ventured to deny. It is certain that, more than three hundred and sixty years after the date ordinarily assigned for the foundation of the city, the public records were, with scarcely an exception, destroyed by the Gauls. It is certain that the oldest annals of the commonwealth were compiled more than a century and a half after this destruction of the records. It is certain, therefore, that the great Latin writers of the Augustan age did not possess those materials, without which a trustworthy account of the infancy of the republic could not possibly be framed. Those writers own, in-

[2] Johann P. Eckermann, *Gespräche mit Goethe* (Lahr: Moritz Schauenburg, 1948), p. 121.

deed, that the chronicles to which they had access were filled with battles that were never fought, and consuls that were never inaugurated.[3]

Macaulay adds that many plausible episodes have "that peculiar character, more easily understood than defined, which distinguishes the creations of the imagination from the realities of the world in which we live." [4] Livy's account of the downfall of Servius Tullius reads like *Macbeth* and is pure Hellenistic melodrama. Though stranger than fiction, truth rarely reads as well. Even more disturbing than detailed reports of remote events are the glaring contradictions that exist, often side by side, in the writings of Livy, Dionysius, and Plutarch. The ancients freely admitted that Roman sources could not be reconciled.

Obviously, the lack of adequate records and reliable reports were major problems for Roman historians. Moreover, the ancient writers viewed history as a didactic art to be used to instill morals, justify political positions, and glorify men and families. Objectivity or even restraint were not conspicuous qualities among Roman historians. Though admitting that the era of the kings was lost in the mists of antiquity, Livy still drew portraits of Romulus and Numa so vivid that his readers had no difficulty grasping the contemporary moral hidden in his account of the distant past. In Romulus, who was loved by the people and the army and murdered by senators, the figure of Caesar emerges, while the "second founder of the city," Numa, was a man of peace and piety, who tamed his warlike followers with religion and is clearly Augustus (as the emperor saw himself). In utilizing the past for present purposes, Livy was following in the footsteps of earlier writers, who had filled their histories with political fictions. The recurring theme of class conflict—aristocratic patricians versus plebeian commoners—lent itself to anachronism. While partisans of the popular faction painted the early tribunes as gallant defenders of oppressed plebeians, conservative historians glorified patrician government and damned the tribunes as demagogues.[5] Not only was history a vehicle for political propaganda, but moralists grew ecstatic over the rustic virtues of early Rome before wealth and greed tainted men's souls. The bucolic purity of the primitive Romans became axiomatic, and the record of subsequent centuries was a harrowing tale of corruption and lost virtue, worthy of a Hebrew prophet and just as hyperbolic.

[3] Thomas B. Macaulay, *The Works of Lord Macaulay* (London: Longmans-Green, 1898), II, 313.

[4] Ibid., p. 314.

[5] Comparable is the myth of the "Norman yoke" devised by British reformers to convince their countrymen that they had been robbed of their "Saxon liberties" by villainous Normans; thus, reform was really a restoration of lost rights.

In the late Republic, many Romans doubted the details of the epic past. According to some writers, the wolf that suckled Romulus was really a woman of such bestial sexual appetite that she was called "Lupa," and Livy insists that Numa pretended to converse with a goddess in order to persuade the masses to accept his reforms.[6] Every Roman was aware that the great families had concocted imaginary glories and high offices for their early ancestors. Cicero scoffed at false claims in funeral orations that passed for history:

> The panegyrics have packed our history full of errors, for many things are claimed that never took place—imaginary triumphs, multiple consulships, false genealogies, and forged ascents from plebeian to patrician status, whereby lowborn people were eased into another family of the same name. It is as if I would claim descent from Manius Tullius the patrician, who was consul with Servius Sulpicius in the tenth year after the expulsion of the kings.[7]

When these claims were embodied in the historical tradition, the historian's task was made almost impossible. Livy is quite explicit:

> It is difficult to choose one version over another, or one authority over another. In my opinion, the record has been corrupted by funeral panegyrics and forged inscriptions on busts, for each family has deliberately appropriated false exploits and honors. Both individual careers and public records have been confused, and no contemporary writer has survived who could be relied upon as an authority.[8]

In the light of such testimony, the literary tradition for early Roman history must be treated with great skepticism.

If the details of the tradition are suspect, what of the lists of consuls and triumphs that provide a chronological framework? In 18 B.C. such a roster, the *Capitoline Fasti,* was inscribed on the Arch of Augustus in the Roman Forum, and portions have been preserved. Though complementary lists can be pieced together from Livy, Dionysius, and other writers, there are a number of contradictions in these sources. The *Capitoline Fasti* were probably based on the researches of the learned antiquarian Varro. Ultimately, Varro's list was derived from the *Annales Maximi* composed by the Pontifex Maximus, P. Mucius Scaevola, about 125 B.C. Among the duties of the high priest was the recording of important data for each year on a whitewashed wooden tablet—the names of consuls and triumphant generals, the price of grain, solar and lunar eclipses, wars, and extraordinary omens. Lack of space prevented

---

[6] Livy 1.4.7; 19.5.   [7] Cicero *Brutus* 16.62.   [8] Livy 8.40.3–5.

the recording of much else, and the priests were not interested in history as such. Since the tablets became illegible over the years, the scholarly Scaevola compiled them into eighty books, the *Annales Maximi,* filled largely with religious material. The only extant fragment (from Book XI) apparently deals with an episode after 300 B.C.;[9] if so, the first ten books of the *Annales Maximi* covered the entire period from Romulus to c. 300, and the other seventy dealt with the era from c. 300 to Scaevola. Obviously, there was little material for secular history in such a collection. Cato scoffed that the pontifical tablets were skimpy, and Cicero dismissed the *Annales Maximi* as a meager collection.[10] Another list of magistrates, written on linen rolls, was kept in the temple of Juno Moneta, but Roman historians who cite these rolls do not agree on the details. The *Annales Maximi* is the keystone of early Roman history, but its accuracy can be questioned. Presumably, the pontifical tablets could have been carried to safety before the Gauls sacked the city, yet Livy says that almost all public records were destroyed. A strong argument in favor of the *Fasti* is the inclusion in the early years of the Republic of consulships for families which were later unknown. Why would historians interpolate the names of obscure or forgotten families, when they were busily adding names from the great houses of their own time? On the other hand, many early consulships were held by men from plebeian families, including the Junii Bruti; yet the literary tradition insists that plebeians were barred from the consulship until 367 B.C. Either the early *Fasti* are forgeries, or the literary tradition is, as usual, overwrought; the latter is more likely.

Even if the *Fasti* are generally authentic, we still lack a reliable historical tradition that can raise early Roman history above the level of a meager chronicle. So significant a theme as the plebeian struggle to wrest political rights and power from the patricians rests upon questionable literary sources. For events prior to 387 B.C., Livy had little faith in either the *Annales Maximi* or the literary tradition:

> These matters are obscure not only because of their great antiquity, like things so far away that they can hardly be seen, but because in those times there was little use of written records, the only reliable custodians of the memory of past events, and also because even the commentaries of the pontiffs and other public and private records, almost all were destroyed in the burning of the city.[11]

His doubts, however, did not prevent Livy from writing at great length on this period for didactic purposes. A more thorough skeptic might

---

[9] Aulus Gellius 4.5.1–6.   [10] Aulus Gellius 2.28.6. Cicero *de Legibus* 1.1.6.
[11] Livy 6.1.2. Cf. Plutarch *Numa* 1.1, *Romulus* 8.7.

wish to question the entire Roman tradition before the third century B.C. With regard to evidence, there are fads in scholarship, alternate waves of skepticism and credulity. Sometimes the shifts are the result of more evidence or new insights, but in addition each generation of scholars tends to take a different stand in order to supplant their mentors. This dialectic advances knowledge and prevents any view, no matter how reasonable, from becoming orthodox. Because a disreputable source can contain a valuable kernel of fact, even skeptical historians search the Latin writers for such nuggets. On the other hand, there are few events in early Roman history that are factual in the sense that the assassination of Caesar on March 15, 44 B.C. is a fact. When Livy is skeptical, moderns should not be credulous.

Made by men, history is also written by men, who view the past through the prism of bias. Most writers who created the traditional history of Rome were senators or hangers-on of the great houses, and so the tradition has an upper-class, generally conservative tone. For the most part, these historians were narrow-minded toward other nations and interested in them only as foils for Rome. However, an ethnocentric bias did not prevent Roman writers from imitating the more extravagant habits of Hellenistic historians, rhetorical speeches and dramatic embellishment. Yet the Romans did not need Hellenic models to persuade them of the pragmatic use of history for moralistic and partisan aims, for sententiousness was a national trait. As with most peoples, history came late to Rome. Late in the third century B.C., the first Roman historian, Q. Fabius Pictor, wrote in Greek, probably to impress the "lesser breeds" with the intrinsic virtues and consistent rectitude in foreign affairs of his countrymen. A pious and conservative senator, Fabius was a veteran of the Hannibalic War, an apologist for the Senate, and a diligent glorifier of the Fabian clan. Polybius used his work but criticized his ultrapatriotic bias. Although lesser writers followed Fabius's lead in writing Roman history in Greek, Cato the Elder soon established Latin as the proper mode in which to celebrate the national past. A self-made man who loathed hereditary nobles, Cato refused to name the consuls and generals who had won Rome's victories and only identified them by their titles. On the other hand, he praised himself to the skies. Angered by the contemporary fad for Hellenism, Cato emphasized the Italian heritage of Rome and treated the Italic peoples in his work. A fierce moralist, he denounced the decline of piety and patriotism from the rustic virtue of the early Republic. Another senator, Cn. Gellius, viewed history as entertainment and wrote a voluminous account of the Roman past, packed with drama and digressions. Less prolific was the stern L. Calpurnius Piso Frugi, who opposed the Gracchi and worried about moral decay. From Piso's angry

pen came tales of fifth-century demagogues who proposed land programs as did Tiberius Gracchus, or who wanted to distribute cheap
grain as did Gaius Gracchus; needless to say, these "scoundrels" failed
and came to violent ends. Less dyspeptic than Piso was L. Coelius Antipater, a careful historian who compared sources and dealt chiefly
with the Hannibalic War. However, Antipater also enjoyed dramatic
scenes, the supernatural, and literary flourishes.

In the first century B.C., Roman historians were even more active. An
inept hanger-on of the Claudian clan, Q. Claudius Quadrigarius invented documents, inflated statistics, and exalted the Claudii, some of
whom were questionable characters. All the worst features of Hellenistic
and Roman historiography culminated in the many volumes of Valerius
Antias. Though not a member of the noble Valerii, Antias took up
their cause with enthusiasm and filled his annals with Valerian dignitar-
ies. Like Quadrigarius, Antias inserted imaginary documents in his
work, and Livy balked at his incredible statistics. Politically conservative, Antias relied heavily on Fabius and Piso but also wove Sullan
apologies into the tradition. Equally partisan but more respectable was
the senator, C. Licinius Macer, who damned Sulla and glorified the
popular faction. A champion of the tribunate, Macer portrayed the
early tribunes in glowing colors and emphasized class conflict in the
early Republic. So cavalierly did Macer insinuate the names of Licinii
into the tradition that Livy grew suspicious. Another annalist, Aelius
Tubero, perhaps a friend of Cicero, was apparently interested in legal
history but depended on the undependable Antias. In the last days of
the Republic, the learned M. Terentius Varro did extensive antiquarian
research on the Roman past and was especially interested in religion.
Astonishingly, Livy made no use of Varro although he drew heavily on
Valerius Antias, Licinius Macer, Tubero, and Claudius Quadrigarius.
Livy's frequent name-dropping (e.g. Fabius Pictor or Piso) only reveals
his borrowed learning. However, Livy was a literary artist, and his history of Rome in 142 books from Aeneas to Augustus eclipsed all his
predecessors, who survive today only in fragments.[12] Pious and patriotic, Livy yearned for the simple virtues of the early Republic (as he
fancied it) and accepted the Augustan settlement as a necessary antidote
to a corrupt and violence-ridden society (for so he viewed the late Republic). Though he composed a magnificent work of art, Livy had no
experience in politics or warfare; he was at the mercy of his sources,

[12] The long-winded history of the early Republic by Livy's Greek contemporary,
Dionysius of Halicarnassus, pales in comparison, as do Plutarch's cluttered
lives of renowned Romans, though both of these Hellenic writers preserve
much useful material.

and like them he wrote history for a didactic purpose—not truth but moral uplift. Nevertheless, Livy's history embodied for all time the great epic tradition of Rome on its march to greatness. It is a pity that so much of the story is not true.

THE BEGINNINGS OF ROME

A casual reader of the *Aeneid* might be inclined to dismiss the tale of Aeneas as a literary contrivance of Vergil to bolster Roman prestige by connecting the origin of Rome with Homer's prophecy that Aeneas would continue the royal line of Troy. Ironically, the story of Aeneas was part of Roman consciousness in the days of the Etruscan kings. Aeneas was well-known to the Etruscans; a statue of him has been found at Veii, and the fifth-century Greek writer Hellanicus connected the Trojan hero with the foundation of Rome. While not historical, Aeneas was at least venerable. However, Romulus is more difficult to assess, for a galaxy of legends surround the eponymous founder of Rome, who was sired by a god and a virgin. When a hostile father figure tried to kill him, the infant was set adrift on a river; a kindly animal saved the infant hero; though raised in poverty, Romulus was really of royal blood; the hero fulfilled his destiny and founded a kingdom, but he also killed his brother. Some of these themes go back to the propaganda of Sargon of Agade in the third millennium B.C.; others are universal mythic attributes of a hidden hero. The wolf totem was a suitable foster mother for the founder of Rome, but his twin Remus seems to be a late addition. There could well have been a historical Romulus, a chieftain of distinction in the remote past, though not the imposing figure of Roman tradition. At any rate, the dead Romulus was incorporated into the Sabine god Quirinius.

On April 21, the Romans celebrated the anniversary of the city's founding, but there was some doubt about the year. Vergil and Pompeius Trogus favored 848 B.C., but Timaeus had set it in 814, linking the foundation of Rome with that of Carthage. Cato insisted on 752; Polybius, Diodorus, and Cicero preferred the following year. The canonical year, 753, rests on the authority of Varro, whose astrologer friend, Tarutius, was even more explicit—the nativity of Rome was on April 9 between about seven and eight o'clock in the morning.[13] Regrettably, modern scholars cannot be so precise, but archeology is more reliable than astrology, and archeological evidence is employed in the

[13] Plutarch *Romulus* 12.3–6.

following account of Roman origins.[14] As for personalities and events, the literary tradition is utilized as far as it seems plausible.

Unlike Alexandria, St. Petersburg, or Washington, D.C., the city of Rome was not founded at all; rather, like Topsy, it just grew. Fifteen miles from the ocean and precious salt flats, the site was favorable, a group of hills commanding an important ford across the Tiber through which ran primitive trails and trade routes. By the middle of the second millennium B.C. men were living on the hills, but these Bronze Age settlements were not continuous. In the Iron Age, Latin tribes occupied the area, and a community of shepherds dwelt in daub-and-wattle huts on the Palatine hill by the mid-eighth century. The swampy marshes of the future Forum were used as a cemetery. On nearby hills, other villages coalesced, and the blending of burial customs (both cremation and inhumation) suggests the mingling of Sabines and Latins which is part of the Roman tradition. By 670 B.C. the Forum area was inhabited, but floods were frequent until the region was drained about 625. Probably in the early seventh century, the villages on the Palatine, Esquiline, and Caelian hills joined into a single community. This unification was celebrated with a festival, the *Septimontium,* though the "seven hills" at that time excluded the Capitoline, Aventine, Quirinal, and Viminal. Primitive Rome continued to grow, incorporating other hills into an expanded collection of villages inclosed by a ritual farrow (*pomerium*).

The inhabitants of early Rome were pastoralists who tended cattle and sheep. Their huts were squalid, and their cultural level low. A law attributed to Numa prescribed that whoever moved a boundary stone was to be sacrificed to the god Terminus. Though he is a legendary Moses type, Numa and others in the tradition were Sabines, and the Sabine contribution to early Rome was considerable. Organized into three tribes, the Romans were essentially Latins and participated in the annual festivals of Jupiter Latiaris, which the Latin peoples held in the Alban hills. They also revered the shrine of Diana at Aricia. It is not likely, however, that the villagers of Rome would have qualified as members of the Latin League, a loose coalition of communities that recognized the validity of marriages and contracts between members of the component groups. Despite the elaborate tales of Romulus and Numa and early wars of conquest in Latium, Rome was only a cluster of rude villages, where pigs and goats roamed about the scattered huts. No doubt the Romans had chiefs, perhaps even Romulus and Numa, but

---

[14] Einar Gjerstad has issued a monumental archeological study, *Early Rome,* 4 vols. (Lund: GWK Gleerup, 1953–60). See also his *Legends and Facts of Early Roman History* (Lund: GWK Gleerup, 1962) and the criticism by A. R. Momigliano, "An Interim Report on the Origins of Rome," *Journal of Roman Studies* 53 (1963): 95–121.

they were hardly kings. Assembled in 30 kinship groups called *curiae,* the villagers elected the chiefs who were both priests and commanders in war, but like their subjects the "kings" of early Rome were simple folk.

In the sixth century B.C., the Etruscans seized the strategic site of Rome and made it into a city. In 616 according to Varro but about 575 by archeological evidence, Rome was occupied by foreign rulers, the Tarquins of Etruria. In Roman literary accounts the first Tarquin monarch was portrayed as a man of such merit that the Romans elected him king, but a military conquest is more likely in the heyday of Etruscan expansion. Under the superior culture of the Etruscans, Rome was rapidly urbanized, and the Forum, now paved with pebbles, became the center of the city. Economically, there was an industrial boom as Etruscan craftsmen set up shops, and in the countryside the advanced methods of Etruria prompted a shift from pastoralism to agriculture. Though some Etruscan nobles moved to Rome, the Latin aristocrats enjoyed the general prosperity and became wealthy under the kings. A Senate of Etruscan and Latin nobles advised the rulers on policy matters, and probably the formality of election by the Curial Assembly was continued. Nevertheless, the king was an absolute monarch—judge, general, and priest—and like his counterparts in Etruria, he dressed in purple robes and was preceded by lictors bearing *fasces.* Culturally, the Etruscans introduced their elaborate systems of divination, especially hepatoscopy, and a twelve-month lunar calendar with an intercalary month every second year. Later Romans attributed the lunar calendar to Numa, but they never questioned the primacy of Etruscan diviners in the occult arts.

The details of history during the Etruscan occupation are vague, despite a wealth of traditional stories. The first Tarquin began the sewer constructions which became the Cloaca Maxima. His successor, Servius Tullius, ringed the city with earthwork fortifications, though the "Servian" wall of stone is of later construction. He also built a temple for Diana on the Aventine Hill to rival the Latin shrine at Aricia. In Roman tradition, Servius is credited with establishing the Centuriate organization of the Roman citizenry. A military muster, the Centuries were groups of cavalry, hoplite infantry, and supporting troops; membership in a particular Century was determined by a specific amount of wealth, for the Etruscans observed the Greek principle that a citizen supplied his own armor and weapons. Because nobles made up the cavalry and the poor were relegated to a few unimportant Centuries, the core of the new system was the phalanx of hoplite infantrymen who had to be property owners. Formerly, war had been a disorganized melee with an emphasis on individual champions; now, success in battle depended upon phalanx tactics and the armed middle class, who were quick to realize their importance in the new order.[15] Servius is also said to have established new tribes based upon residence to replace the old Latin tribes. Thus the Roman citizenry were organized into four urban and sixteen rural tribes; under the Republic, the number of rural tribes rose to 31. So important was Servius Tullius in the tradition that the Romans insisted that he was a Latin son-in-law of Tarquin, albeit of servile origin. However, the emperor Claudius claimed that Servius was really an Etruscan, Mastarna; frescoes at Etruscan Vulci show a hero, Macstrna, whose allies are slaying a foe labeled Tarchunics Rumach (i.e. Tarquin of Rome), suggesting that good king Servius Tullius ousted his fellow Etruscan, Tarquin, by force. Be this as it may, Servius was succeeded by Tarquin the Proud, who plays the role of a tyrant in Roman tradition. Under him, Rome was apparently a major power in Latium, and the establishment of a Roman settlement at Ostia by the mouth of the Tiber should probably be dated to this era. On a stone foundation on the Capitoline hill, Tarquin the Proud built a large wooden temple, decorated with terra cotta, to house Jupiter, Juno, and Minerva. Dedicated in 509, the Capitoline temple of Jupiter Optimus Maximus became the greatest and most venerated shrine in Rome. The statues of Jupiter and the goddesses were made by the famed sculptor, Vulca of Veii. Despite the splendor of his building operations, Tarquin the Proud was a high-handed ruler, and the Latin gentry resented his tyranny. About 509, Tarquin was driven from Rome, and a republic replaced the Etruscan kingdom. If the account is true, a rural aristocracy ousted a sophisticated urban regime.

The overthrow of the Tarquins is so draped in melodramatic details that even its historical core has been doubted. Some scholars feel that the passing of monarchy from Rome was evolutionary as at Athens. However, memories of kingship left a bad taste at Rome, and the very name of king (*rex*) became a hated term. In many Etruscan cities, the nobility had overthrown the *lucumones* or eased them from power, and Rome was no exception, regardless how Tarquin departed. Still, many Roman nobles were Etruscans, and Etruscan names appear in the traditions of the early Republic. Archeologically, there is no break in Etruscan culture at Rome until c. 475 when there is a noticeable drop in luxury imports. Similarly, many temples were dedicated in the period from 509 to 475, a symptom of prosperity contrasting with the depressed period that followed. Presumably, the economic slump reflected Rome's withdrawal from the Etruscan sphere. According to tradition and the

---

[15] Supposedly, Servian Rome could field an army of 6,000, but this figure may be too large.

Fasti, Rome resisted an attempt by the king of Etruscan Clusium, Lars Porsenna, to reinstate the Tarquins; awed by the heroics of Horatius and Scaevola, Porsenna abandoned the siege of the city. However, Tacitus and Pliny the Elder preserve a more plausible report that Porsenna captured the city and tried to forbid the Romans the use of iron weapons.[16] There is no reason to assume that Porsenna had any interest in restoring the Tarquins; rather, he aimed at dominating Latium until defeated near Aricia about 506 by a coalition of Latins and Cumaeans under Aristodemus. When the Etruscan yoke was finally lifted from Rome is not sure, and some scholars would date it as late as the mid fifth century, when Etruscan power was visibly contracting in central Italy. Perhaps soon after Porsenna's defeat by the Latins is a more realistic date. However and whenever Rome was freed from the Etruscans, the city's debt to Etruria was great, for the Tarquin dynasty had made Rome an urban center and a major force in Latium.

The early days of the Republic are obscure, although the traditional account is filled with glorious military campaigns and momentous constitutional changes. Many of the political developments probably occurred later, and the wars were mostly border raids. Nevertheless, Rome was frequently at war in the fifth century with the result that the Romans became proficient in arms and a power in central Italy. Internally, the citizen soldier who fought for the Republic demanded an increasing share in political life. Rome's first opponents were her Latin kinsmen who resented the Republic's attempts to restore the supremacy in Latium which the Tarquins had probably held. Friction between the Romans and the Latin League, which excluded Rome, culminated in the battle of Lake Regillus about 499 B.C. Though the gods Castor and Pollux fought beside the Romans, the battle was probably a draw, and so was the war. The peace treaty in 493 expressed equality between partners, not a dictated peace:

> Between the Romans and all the cities of the Latins, there shall be peace toward one another, so long as both heaven and earth maintain their present position. And they neither shall wage war against one another nor shall invite enemies from abroad nor shall provide safe passage for those bringing war; they shall aid with all their strength those persons on whom war is waged and each shall obtain an equal portion of spoils and of booty from their common wars. And judgments on private contracts shall be rendered within ten days in the city where the contract was made.[17]

---

[16] Tacitus *Historiae* 3.72. Pliny the Elder *Naturalis Historia* 34.139.

[17] Dionysius of Halicarnassus 6.95.2, trans. Clyde Pharr, ed., *Ancient Roman Statutes* (Austin: University of Texas Press, 1961), p. 8. (Henceforth this work is cited as *ARS*.)

The last clause reflected the Latin League's principle of mutual recognition of commercial contracts. Rome and the Latins needed each other, for Latium was threatened by incursions of the nearby Aequi and Volscian tribes. Between the Volsci and the Aequi lay the Hernici, with whom Rome formed a military alliance in 486, the first in a long line of diplomatic ploys whereby the Republic sought allies flanking or behind its immediate foes. In war, this policy was highly successful, but the ever-widening circle of alliances led Rome into unexpected confrontations with new enemies and more cycles of wars.

The struggle against the Aequi and Volscians continued for a century with endless forays, occasionally brightened by a dramatic episode such as the victories of Coriolanus against the Volsci and the subsequent treachery of the hero against an ungrateful Rome. Leading the enemy against Rome itself, Coriolanus was finally dissuaded by his mother from destroying his fatherland. Unfortunately for history, Coriolanus's name does not appear in the *Capitoline Fasti,* and he may have been a Volscian. More edifying was the noble Cincinnatus, who, wiping the sweat of honest toil from his face, left his plow to lead the armies of Rome against the Aequi. By the turn of the fourth century, the Romans and Latins had subdued the Volsci and Aequi. As in the days of the Etruscans, the Roman infantry were armed with swords, round shields, and long thrusting spears and probably fought in a phalanx formation. A survival of pre-Servian military concepts was evident at the battle of the Cremera in 479 when the Fabii marched out as a clan against the troops of Veii and perished almost to a man. If there is any truth in the tale, the experience must have discredited the outmoded idea of warfare by kin groups and reinforced the value of the hoplite phalanx. Unfortunately for the credibility of the account, the single Fabian boy who survived the debacle turned up as consul only ten years later. Obviously, Fabius Pictor was embellishing with a vengeance.

The Republic served by such heroes evolved slowly over the years. The details of its development are filled with contradictions, anachronisms, and duplicated episodes. In 287 B.C., for example, the decisions of the plebeian assembly were made legally binding on all Romans, an unquestionable historical fact; yet Livy claims that the same law had been passed in 449 and amazingly again in 339! [18] Either Roman legislators were remarkably forgetful, or historians sought to represent the reform of 287 as a restoration of lost privileges. Any reconstruction of Roman constitutional history must be tenuous and arbitrary. In the beginning of the Republic, the old *curiae* elected the magistrates, but its elective function soon passed to the Centuriate Assembly, and the

[18] Aulus Gellius 15.27.4. Livy 3.55.3; 8.12.15.

Curial Assembly became a purely formal body conferring military authority (*imperium*) on men elected by the Centuries. The magistrates were two praetors, later called consuls, who presided over the assemblies, conducted judicial affairs, and led the armies of Rome.[19] In the latter capacity, they held *imperium* with the power of life and death over men under their command outside the city limits of Rome. After serving a year in office, the consuls entered the Senate, which was filled with elder statesmen who could squelch unwanted acts by the assemblies, for the consent of the Senate was necessary to confirm elections and legislation. Republican Rome contained two hereditary social classes: an aristocracy of patricians who monopolized religious and important political offices, and the commons, known as plebeians. In theory, patricians alone were eligible for the consulship, and control of the state was in their hands, yet plebeian names appear in the *Fasti,* and it is reasonable to assume that the ruling circles broadened to accept some wealthy plebeians. The Servian military reform had made the commons aware of their importance, and the embattled Republic could hardly have blocked all plebeian aspirations to high office. Nevertheless, financial limitations excluded most plebeians from aspiring beyond their station, and the role of the patriciate was dominant for a time. Minor officials, quaestors, assisted the consuls by investigating murders and later served as paymasters with the legions. In times of crisis, the consuls turned over the state to a dictator who held *imperium* and almost absolute powers, but this potentially dangerous office lasted only six months, and apparently none of the dictators of early Rome ever sought to exploit their opportunity. Since the dictatorship was exceptional, the consulship was the key office, and election to it was in the hands of the Centuriate Assembly, a timocratic body dominated by property owners. The Centuriate Assembly also legislated, made formal declarations of war and peace, and served as an appellate court on capital charges to which any Roman citizen might appeal.

Though the Roman commons had acquired considerable rights since the days of the kings, many poor plebeians felt that they lacked a stake in the Republic. The patricians were their allies against foreign foes, but at home a great landowner might be an economic enemy. By 475 the prosperity of the Etruscan era was ended and economic distress was common. Roman farms were small, and many plebeians had difficulty making a profit, yet they were often called to leave their fields and serve in war. Still primitive in many respects, Roman law countenanced en-

---

[19] A consular army was called a legion; its strength in the early Republic is a matter of debate. In the second century B.C., the size of a legion was about 4,200 men.

slavement for debt, and the Roman poor lived in dread of sinking into slavery. Agitation for economic relief led to a secession by the plebeians supposedly in 494 or more likely in 471. En masse, the common people simply abandoned the city and returned only after the Senate accepted the existence of a plebeian assembly organized by tribes, the *concilium plebis,* and recognized its elected officials, two (or five) tribunes, who served as defenders of the masses. The persons of the tribunes were sacrosanct, for the plebeians swore to sacrifice to Jupiter anyone who harmed them. Within the city limits of Rome, a tribune could veto any act of the state, and the doors of his house were open day and night to any plebeian in distress. Like the consulship, the tribunate was an annual office and the tribunes were assisted by minor officials, two aediles who supervised the markets and municipal affairs. The decisions (*plebiscita*) of the *concilium plebis* were not binding on patricians unless ratified by the Centuriate Assembly which alone could make laws. In the traditional accounts, early Roman history was filled with class conflict and the tribunes are portrayed as either scheming demagogues or heroic champions of the people against an unfeeling patriciate. Whatever the truth of these tales, the masses had won a great weapon in the tribunician veto. Class conflict cut across social classes, however, for the interests of wealthy plebeians lay with the patricians if the aristocrats allowed them access to the consulship.

By mid-century, the pressure of wealthy plebeians for a legal statement of their right to the consulship was increasing, as was patrician intransigence. Many aristocrats were willing to admit a deserving plebeian to high office as long as there was no concession of his automatic right to hold it. The patricians appear to have tried to maintain their privileged position at all costs. Though it was impossible to quiet popular demands for a codification of laws, it might be possible to manipulate the code to patrician advantage. The events surrounding the publication of the code and a patrician counterattack are melodramatic and implausible, but there may be a core of truth in the theme of patrician overreaction. There is no question, however, about the code, the Twelve Tables, fragments of which survive. In 451, constitutional government was suspended and a board of ten patricians, the *decemviri,* took over the state with authority to formulate a basic legal code. Headed by Appius Claudius, the *decemviri* produced ten tables of laws. The following year, the board was reconstituted with half of its members plebeians but still headed by Appius Claudius. Suddenly, Claudius became an oppressive tyrant and lusted after a plebeian maiden, Verginia, until her father slew her to save her virtue. The new *decemviri* also produced two more tables of what Cicero says were "bad laws," including a prohibition on intermarriage between patricians and plebeians, astonishing if our understanding of the composition of the board is accurate. Outraged by the turn of events, the plebeians seceded again from the city in 449, the *decemviri* were overthrown, and constitutional government was restored with the number of tribunes raised to ten. Shortly afterwards, the *concilium plebis* was expanded into the Tribal Assembly, organized also by tribes but presided over by a consul and including patricians. Unlike the Centuriate Assembly where wealth alone counted, the Tribal Assembly was a truly popular body and became in time the principal legislative assembly at Rome. Since the patricians did not always attend its meetings, the Tribal Assembly was often only the *concilium plebis* and as such was presided over by tribunes; ancient writers confused the two bodies, and the term *comitia tributa* is used to describe either. Though popular control of legislation had increased, the consent of the Senate was still required before the acts of the Tribal Assembly became laws.[20] One of the first legislative acts of the restored tribunate was the *lex Canuleia* in 445, which abolished the recently enacted prohibition of intermarriage between the classes. After a lively debate, the Senate accepted the *plebiscitum* as a law.

The fragments that survive of the Twelve Tables are an invaluable guide to the realities of early Rome, far more reliable than the heroic tales of Livy. In general, the code reveals a crude rural society. A Roman father had the right of life and death over his children and could sell his son three times into slavery. Arsonists were burned alive, and a thief who stole crops by night was sacrificed to Ceres. Creditors could seize defaulting debtors, hold them in bonds for sixty days, and if the debt was still unpaid, either kill or sell them "across the Tiber." Interest was limited to one-twelfth of the principal and was probably computed annually. Extravagant funerals were curtailed, and nocturnal meetings in the city were forbidden. For personal injuries, the *lex talionis* ("an eye for an eye") prevailed unless the injured party accepted other compensation. However, no Roman citizen could be executed without being tried and convicted, and anyone convicted on a capital charge could appeal to the Centuriate Assembly. Amid the stern and sometimes grotesque code of a rude people stood the laws that guaranteed trial and appeal, rights that would make Roman citizenship an object of envy. Though in antiquity no rights were inalienable, rule by law and protection under the law were longstanding Roman concepts. "When we were boys," mused Cicero, "we learned the Twelve Tables

---

[20] Not until 287 B.C. were the *plebiscita* of the *concilium plebis* considered *leges*. In the Late Republic, patricians probably attended the *concilium plebis*. At any rate, the niceties of Roman procedure have been reconstructed by modern scholars from vague, inadequate, and sometimes contradictory evidence.

as a required formula, but now no one learns them." [21] Once, the mere publication of the laws had seemed precious to Romans.

THE EXPANSION OF ROMAN POWER

In the period between the restoration of constitutional government in 449 B.C. and the ultimate hegemony of Rome over Italy in the early third century, the Romans suffered many vicissitudes and a shattering defeat at the hands of the Gauls only to emerge stronger and more expansive. Part of the credit was due to the abilities of the senatorial class, but much was also due to the staying power of the Roman masses who fought the wars that made Rome supreme in Italy. In the process, the commons capitalized on the state's need of their military services to win a greater share in the political life of Rome.

So intense was the military pressure upon Rome that in 445 a new office was created—the military tribune with consular powers. Unlike the consuls, their annual number was not limited to two, and in fifty-one of the years between 445 and 367 consular tribunes headed the state and led the legions. A variant explanation for the consular tribunate was provided by Licinius Macer, who claimed that the office was a sop to plebeians who were agitating for admission to the consulship. Since consular tribunes did not celebrate triumphs or enter the Senate after their year in office, the cunning patricians had pawned off a second-class consulship on the plebeians. However, Macer also claims that the first plebeian to hold the consular tribunate did not serve until 400. Possibly two other plebeians held the office in 444 and 422 respectively. If the purpose of the change was to uplift plebeians, it is extraordinary that only one plebeian, three at the most, held the office for the first forty-five years of its existence. It should also be noted that plebeians had held consulships before 445. Because the Roman executives, whether consuls or consular tribunes, were preoccupied with military affairs, another office, the censorate, was created in 443. The two censors served for eighteen months, held a census of the citizenry, and assigned men to the Centuries. The censors also kept an eye on the expenditure of state funds and became in time watchdogs of public morals. Originally appointed, they were later elected by the Centuriate Assembly, theoretically every five years. In the hands of a strong man, the censorate could be an enormously powerful office though it lacked *imperium*. Conventionally, only distinguished ex-consuls could hope to be censors, for the prestigious office was the high point of a public career.

---

[21] Cicero *de Legibus* 2.23.59.

Early in the fifth century, Rome had fought extensive wars with its traditional rival, the nearby Etruscan town of Veii, ending in a truce about 474. Late in the century, the struggle with Veii revived, and the Romans laid siege to the city, intent on destroying it once and for all. Traditionally, the siege lasted ten years, but this figure suggests the Trojan War, and it is doubtful that Rome could have sustained an operation of such duration. During the war with Veii, Rome began paying its soldiery, thus adding to the hoplite ranks men who otherwise could not afford the expense of military service. However, the Roman army was still limited to property owners. To pay the increased costs of war, the Republic imposed a minimal one tenth of one percent land tax on its citizens. By 396, Veii had fallen, the city was destroyed, and the land of Veii was distributed among the Roman commons. To publicize his victory, the hero of the war, Camillus, sent a golden bowl to Delphi. Rome was now the largest and most powerful city in Latium, and her Latin allies resented the arrogance that the leaders of the Republic sometimes displayed.

While Rome basked in the triumph over Veii, a new enemy, the Gauls, fell upon the Romans and brought them to their knees. So catastrophic was the Roman defeat that ancient writers saw the Gallic fury as divine punishment for Roman *hubris*. Divine agents or not, the Gauls were formidable warriors who fought with barbaric frenzy and iron broadswords. Emerging from central Europe, they had occupied the Po Valley and shattered Etruscan rule in the North. Bypassing the walled cities of Etruria, a Gallic host swept aside a Roman army of 10,000 men and occupied Rome itself in 387. The population had fled before the barbarians arrived, although a garrison held the sacred precincts on the Capitoline hill. Roman pride later insisted that the Capitol was spared the looting and burning which the Gauls perpetrated in the city below, and a pleasant legend told how the sacred geese of Juno alerted the defenders when a Gallic party tried to scale the hill. However, the poet Silius Italicus preserved an almost forgotten tradition that the Capitol also fell to the Gauls.[22] Unable to drive the invaders from Rome, which now lay in ashes, the Senate bribed the barbarians with 1,000 pounds of gold to abandon the city. As the gold was being weighed, the Gallic chief tossed his sword on the scale to increase the ransom and silenced the protesting Romans with the stern dictum of the victor: "Woe to the vanquished!" Laden with booty, the barbarians returned to northern Italy, harassed by Camillus and the remnants of the Roman army, or so patriotic Roman writers assure us. The city of Rome had been

---

[22] O. Skutsch, "The Fall of the Capitol," *Journal of Roman Studies* 43 (1953): 77–78.

gutted, and Roman prestige faltered for a generation as the Latins and the Hernici ignored their old alliances with the fallen city.

Rome's allies acted hastily, for they underestimated Roman capacity for recovery. From the ashes Rome rose stronger than ever, for she had learned to profit from defeat by eliminating its causes. The Roman people also displayed (not for the last time) the doggedness that impressed friends and foes alike and prompted Polybius to observe that the Romans could not accept the notion of defeat in war but would fight on regardless.[23] To preclude another easy seizure of the city, Rome was fortified with five and a half miles of stone walls, the so-called "Servian" Wall, built by imported Greek masons and completed about 378. Since both the tactics and equipment of the past had proven inadequate against the Gallic onslaught, Camillus began a major overhaul of the Roman military apparatus. A long rectangular shield replaced the round hoplite shield, and the thrusting spear was supplanted by a javelin. After throwing his javelin, the legionary closed with the enemy and fought with his sword. Camillus may also have reorganized the legion into 30 maniples, numbering 120 men each, with the battle line ten maniples across and three maniples deep; intervals between the maniples allowed for greater flexibility. Each maniple had two centuries, and each century was commanded by a centurion, chosen by the legion's commander from the ranks. Unlike the tight formations of the phalanx, the new manipular army had greater maneuverability. However, the actual date of the manipular reform is controversial, and it may well have been undertaken during the Samnite wars.

Secure behind her new walls, Rome sent forth the legions to retrieve her lost position in central Italy. In obscure wars, the Romans defeated various Etruscan towns and beat back probing invasions by the Gauls. Ironically, the Gallic threat gave Rome a new role as the symbol of successful resistance to the enemies of all Italians. Within the city, the Roman commons pushed for new concessions. By the Sexto-Licinian laws of 367, interest paid on loans was to be deducted from the principal, and perhaps a limit of 500 *iugera* (about 300 acres) was set on the amount of public land which one man could occupy. As Roman power expanded, considerable land had been seized from defeated foes, and some senators had carved estates from the property of the Republic. If a limit was set at this time, the later Gracchan legislation was a revival of fourth-century policies; if not, the land limit of 367 is an anachronistic forgery. There is no question, however, that the tribunes, C. Licinius and L. Sextius, abolished the consular tribunate and established by law

[23] Polybius 1.37.7.

that at least one consul should be plebeian.[24] The following year, Sextius was elected consul; later, Licinius was supposedly convicted of violating the land limitation law. In 366, a new magistracy, the praetorship, was created to ease the burdens of the consuls. Elected by the Centuries, the praetor held *imperium* and performed the military and judicial duties of a consul, though he was mostly concerned with the civil administration of the city. In effect a junior consul, the praetor entered the Senate after his year in office. The number of aediles was increased to four, two of whom, the curule aediles, also supervised public games. After the right of plebeians to hold the consulship had been confirmed, plebeians soon reached the dictatorship and censorate. Only the priesthoods remained a patrician preserve, for the pontiffs and augurs could only be patricians, and they co-opted their members.

Externally, the power of Rome expanded in Italy. The Hernici were humbled and became allies again though no longer as equals. By 358 the Latins returned to the Roman alliance, but the armies of the Latin League were now subordinate to Roman commanders. The Etruscan cities either accepted truces or alliances with Rome. In 348 the Romans signed a commercial treaty with Carthage that probably renewed a similar treaty enacted in the early days of the Republic. Though the heart of the treaty dealt with Roman promises to avoid the Carthaginian sphere of influence, the clauses pertaining to Punic raids into Latium reveal Rome's callous attitude toward her Latin kinsmen:

> If the Carthaginians capture a city in Latium that is not subject to the Romans, they shall retain the booty and men captured but shall turn the city over to Rome. If any Carthaginians capture any persons who have a treaty of peace with the Romans but are not subjects of Rome, they shall not bring such persons into Roman harbors; but if such a person is brought there and a Roman claims him as free, he shall be freed. The Romans shall observe a similar prohibition.[25]

Always practical, the Romans had no intention of inconveniencing their powerful Punic friends. In southern Italy the Romans acquired more allies. In 354 a common fear of the Gauls had prompted the Samnite League to form an alliance with Rome; the allies then proceeded to carve up the territory of the Volsci. According to Roman tradition, Rome clashed briefly (343–341) with the Samnites over a tiny tribe, the Sidicini, who were menaced by the Samnites, but the details of the war

[24] In practice, this provision was not always fulfilled, but the principle of plebeian consuls had been conceded.

[25] Polybius 3.24.5—7, trans. Mortimer Chambers, ed. E. Badian *Polybius: The Histories* (New York: Washington Square Press, 1966), p. 111.

are highly dubious, and in any case the Romans soon handed the Sidicini over to the Samnites.

In 341 the exasperated Latins rose against the Romans; the Samnites stood by their alliance with Rome, but the great Campanian city of Capua backed the Latins. By 338 the Latin revolt was crushed, and Rome dissolved the Latin League. However, the victorious Republic showed restraint in dealing with its defeated foes. Four or five Latin cities received full Roman citizenship; others were allied to Rome by individual treaties which recognized marriages and commercial contracts as well as stipulating military obligations. Capua and other towns in Campania received Roman citizenship without the right to vote. Though the generosity of the settlement of 338 contrasts favorably with the atrocities inflicted by Athens or Sparta on defeated foes, Roman policy was not altruistic. By slowly spreading a web of Roman or quasi-Roman cities throughout Italy, the Republic bound the Italians to her and made Roman interests Italy's interests. Even in allied cities, the ruling circles were often given Roman citizenship to attach them closer to Rome. In certain coastal areas, Rome established small naval garrisons manned by Roman citizens. More common and larger were the "Latin" colonies made up of former Roman citizens who had given up their citizenship and become nominal Latins. Later, "allies of the Latin name" (a term that included both original Latins and the descendants of former Romans) could acquire Roman citizenship by residing at Rome. In time, the Italians would become restless as Rome niggardly granted the choice status of full citizenship to favored towns, but for the present, the Romans displayed statecraft of the highest order. When dangerous invaders such as Pyrrhus or Hannibal appeared in Italy, Rome reaped the fruits of her intelligent treatment of the Italians.

The stresses of the Latin revolt furthered the growth of popular government at Rome. In 339 under the dictatorship of the plebeian Q. Publilius Philo, the Centuriate Assembly passed a law requiring that the Senate give its consent to the legislative acts of the centuries. A few years later the Senate also surrendered its right to withhold approval of Centuriate elections. In 326 debt slavery was abolished, and "the liberty of the Roman people had, as it were, a new beginning." [26] In the South, however, new problems erupted, for the Samnites were uneasy over Roman penetration of Campania. As long as Alexander of Epirus was active at Tarentum, the Samnites had been preoccupied, but his death about 330 freed them to challenge Rome in a struggle that would decide the mastery of Italy. The Roman ruling circles also contained men anxious to win laurels in a war that would make Rome dominant in the

[26] Livy 8.28.1.

peninsula. In 326 Rome went to war against the Samnite League, but the details of the long struggle are contradictory. Accounts of imaginary victories cannot obscure the humiliation of 321 when the Samnites trapped a Roman army at the Caudine Forks and forced it to surrender; the humbled Romans had to pass beneath a symbolic yoke of spears. Similar fiascoes soon brought the war to an end, and Rome bought time with a peace treaty. Outfought by the hillmen of the South, the Romans may have adopted manipular formations at this time. In 316 Rome attacked the Samnites again but with such little success that Capua briefly bolted from the Roman alliance. The Etruscans, too, tried to aid the Samnites but were quickly cowed by a Roman invasion. By 304, the inglorious Samnite war ended with a stalemate peace. During the struggle Rome had been forced to prolong some military commands beyond the customary annual limit for magistrates, thus creating the offices of proconsuls and propraetors. Another result of the Samnite war was the construction of a paved military highway from Rome to Capua, the Via Appia, which was the first of the great Roman roads.

The Appian Way was the work of the famed censor, Appius Claudius Caecus, who also built Rome's first aqueduct. The need for more water in the city indicates an increased population. During his censorship in 312, Claudius attempted some far-reaching reforms, but the details are confused. Apparently he allowed members of the four urban tribes to register in the rural tribes. As the city contained many proletarians and freedmen, the effect would have been to democratize the Tribal Assembly in which the rural tribes were a majority. A hostile tradition claims that the liberal censor tried to enroll the sons of freedmen in the Senate, but so drastic an innovation is unlikely even for a high-handed Claudian. In 304 the censors revoked Claudius's arrangement of the tribes. To aid plebeian politicians who were unfamiliar with the arcana of government, the aedile Cn. Flavius, a protegé of Claudius, published a handbook on legal procedures and technicalities. He also posted in the Forum the official state calendar listing the days on which court could be held; this roster was useful to all citizens. A freedman's son, Flavius attained the tribunate, and his career demonstrates the social mobility of Roman society; of course, Claudius's backing was essential. In 300 the last stronghold of the patricians was breached when the tribunes Gnaeus and Quintus Ogulnius passed legislation that added four plebeians to the five patrician pontiffs and five plebeians to the four patrician augurs. Though liberal in political matters, Appius Claudius was a haughty patrician and opposed the Ogulnian reform but to no avail.

Early in the third century, the Samnite League made a final attempt to break the Roman hold on Italy. Allied with the Gauls, the Samnites met the Romans in a decisive battle at Sentinum in 295. The consul, P. Decius Mus, sacrificed his life in a ritual death to assure the victory which the military skill of his Fabian colleague won. Shattered at Sentinum, the Gallic-Samnite front collapsed, and after more defeats the Samnites surrendered by 290. The Romans seized the best land in Samnium and forced the Samnites to accept the status of allies. In 284 the Gauls were active again and some Etruscan cities joined them in challenging Rome, but the allies were defeated at Lake Vadimo in 283. The Gauls withdrew, and all of Etruria was allied to Rome by 280. At Sentinum and Vadimo, the last bids for Italian independence had failed. Except for the Greek cities in the far South, all Italy below the Po Valley was under Roman control. The primary benefit to the Roman state was military, for the allied towns and tribes had to supply armed contingents on demand. However, the allies did not have to pay tribute to Rome, although all inhabitants of the Roman sphere, whether citizen or ally, had to pay a minimal customs duty. The major economic advantage of supremacy in Italy was the exploitation of conquered lands by both the Roman commons and the senatorial class. Quite apart from military and economic benefits, the Romans enjoyed the new sense of superiority and power to decide the fates of others. In 302 the masses in Etruscan Arretium had expelled the ruling family, the Cilnii, but Rome intervened and restored the unpopular aristocrats. In 265 the slaves (more likely serfs) of Volsinii rose against their masters, who appealed to Rome for aid. The Romans quickly crushed the revolt and destroyed the city, settling the former masters elsewhere. In both instances, Rome came to the defense of property and conservative government, a role which she would often play in history. Though they resented Roman arrogance, the ruling classes in Italy realized that Rome would back them in any outbreak of class conflict.

At Rome, stress between the classes had been resolved through judicious concessions to the commons. In 287 the strains of the Samnite wars had driven many plebeians into debt, and the Senate provided no relief for them. When the outraged commoners rioted and seceded from the city, a plebeian dictator, Q. Hortensius, somehow resolved the problem of debts, and the plebeians returned to Rome. Hortensius also forced the Senate to grant a major constitutional concession, the automatic approval of all *plebiscita* of the *concilium plebis*. No longer dependent upon the consent of the Senate, the Tribal Assembly (which the *concilium plebis* was in effect) was now an unfettered legislative body. Though the Centuriate Assembly, too, could legislate, the plebeians had won control of the lawmaking process of Rome. The centuries still elected magistrates with *imperium* and the censors, but the *lex Hortensia* made Rome a limited democracy, and the extraordinary powers of the tribunate gave the Roman people protection unequaled elsewhere in history. However, what appears to be a popular government in theory may turn out to be the reverse in practice.

Like its British counterpart, the Roman constitution was an evolutionary product of compromise and accommodation, hence its durability and also its flexibility. Though they prided themselves on conservatism and adherence to convention, the Romans were consummate pragmatists and willing to accept the necessity of change. Cato scoffed at societies that were bound to written constitutions devised by one man, often a doctrinaire idealist: "Our constitution is superior to other states because it was the work not of one genius but many; and . . . it was founded, not in one generation, but over a long period of many centuries and by many men." [27] Slowly over the years, the Romans evolved their complex political system. As Rome acquired an empire, its success awed many observers, and Polybius attributed the "Roman miracle" to the merits of its constitution. [28] According to Polybius, the Romans had devised a mixed constitution which blended the three basic forms of government (monarchy = consuls, aristocracy = Senate, and democracy = assemblies) in a perfect balance, preventing the abuses that normally spring from an excess of each of the three—despotism, oligarchy, and mob rule. As long as the balance was maintained, Polybius alleged, Rome would flourish both internally and externally. Of course, Polybius knew quite well that the balance was an illusion and that Rome was in fact run by an oligarchy, but it would be ungracious for us to insist that political theories correspond to facts. Long after Rome was only a memory, the image of the Republic haunted men's minds, and when popular governments were instituted in France and America at the end of the eighteenth century, Rome was their model. France had a First Republic and an unfortunate First Consul, and the United States still cherishes its Senate and the doctrine of balance of powers. In *Federalist 63*, James Madison noted that "history informs us of no long-lived republic which had not a senate, . . . instructive proofs of the necessity of some institution that will blend stability with liberty." [29] In the same document, Madison also had a good word for the tribunes whose suc-

---

[27] Cicero *de Republica* 2.1.2.

[28] The greatest of Hellenistic historians, Polybius of Megalopolis covered the crucial years of Roman imperial expansion down to 145 B.C. in forty books. A thorough researcher, he is generally reliable on factual matters but highly biased against Spartans, Aetolians, and democrats, and unduly favorable to the family of his patron, Scipio Aemilianus. A believer in historical cycles, Polybius felt that Rome's constitution allowed it to delay the "natural" cycle of rise and decline. As a Greek, he also acknowledged the role of chance in history.

[29] James Madison, *The Federalist* (New York: The Heritage Press, 1945), pp. 424–25.

cess "proves the irresistible force possessed by that branch of a free government which has the people on its side."[30] His contemporaries were more wary of tribunes, and the American constitution was carefully constructed to prevent any outbreak of democracy.[31] The Roman oligarchs would have approved.

Though Rome had no written constitution, the aggregate of laws, procedures, and conventions that is called the Roman constitution displays some basic concepts. A timocratic strain ran through the Roman system, and no official or magistrate received a salary, though the state furnished funds for operating expenses. At Rome, a poor man could not afford to hold office, and it is no surprise that all Roman leaders, including the tribunes, were men of substance. Similarly, the nobility became increasingly exclusive and tried to keep the number of "new men" entering the Senate to a minimum. In the *Fasti,* the same names recur with a consistency that reveals the composition of the Roman Establishment. In all offices, save the dictatorship, more than one man held the same office concurrently and could block the actions of a colleague. Though not always invoked, the notion of collegiate authority kept many an unruly official in line. Social pressure and ambition also cooled the ardor of firebrands. After their year in office, consuls, praetors, and eventually tribunes entered the Senate, and they had no desire to antagonize the august body where they would spend the rest of their lives. Ambitious tribunes had their eyes on the consulship through which they could win glory and booty in war, and it was not wise to anger powerful men who could swing elections. It is the nature of the political animal to seek to improve his lot, and even the aediles in their role as sponsors of public games won popularity by spending their own funds to increase the magnificence of the entertainment; later, the voters would remember them well.

At Rome, the legislative and elective process took place in the assemblies. Eclipsed by the Centuriate and Tribal Assemblies, the *comitia curiata* soon became a constitutional fossil, concerned with religious functions and conferring *imperium* as a formality. In the late Republic, three augurs and thirty lictors, one for each *curia,* made up the once important Curial Assembly. On the Field of Mars (Campus Martius) outside the *pomerium,* the Centuriate Assembly legislated, decided war and peace, served as a court of appeals, and elected consuls, praetors, and censors. All Roman males over seventeen were enrolled in the *comitia centuriata* according to wealth. Its terminology was military, for once the Assembly had been the Roman nation in arms. The patricians

---

[30] Ibid., p. 429.

[31] See Gilbert Chinard, "Polybius and the American Constitution," *Journal of the History of Ideas* 1 (1940): 38–58.

and very wealthy plebeians filled eighteen centuries of *equites* or cavalry; the middle class made up eighty centuries of heavy infantry; ninety centuries of light infantry were composed of the lower middle class and small farmers. Below the infantry were four centuries of "musicians" and artisans, followed by a final century of *proletarii,* propertyless men whose only contribution to the state was offspring (*proles*) and who did not perform military service. Within each of the military centuries, the members were divided into "seniors" (aged forty-six to sixty) and "juniors" (aged seventeen to forty-five). Though the sources are not in agreement and many details about the centuries are controversial, the total number of centuries was probably 193. Whatever their number, the poor were crowded into the lowest century and deprived of real voting power. Since the Romans believed in block voting, each century had but one vote; 97 made a majority in the Assembly, and the *equites* and "heavy infantry" together accounted for 98 votes. The *equites* began the voting, and if they and the "heavy infantry" stuck together, a majority was reached before the lower middle class was ever consulted. Of this system, Cicero says with approval:

> The greatest number of votes belonged, not to the common people, but to the rich, and put into effect the principle which always ought to be followed in the commonwealth, that the greatest number should not have the greatest power. . . . Thus, while no one was deprived of the suffrage, the majority of votes was in the hands of those to whom the highest welfare of the state was most important.[32]

The timocratic nature of the Centuriate Assembly was obvious to all. At some time between the First and Second Punic Wars, the centuries were slightly reformed in favor of the middle classes, but at all times the Centuriate Assembly represented the interests of men of wealth, and the poor were excluded from a major role in electing magistrates or deciding war and peace.

In the modern sense of the word, the only democratic body at Rome was the Tribal Assembly which performed most legislation and met in the Forum. As the *comitia tributa,* it was made up of all adult male citizens and elected quaestors and two curule aediles; the presiding officer was a consul or praetor. As the *concilium plebis,* it was limited to plebeians, elected tribunes and two aediles, and was presided over by a tribune. Since the patricians dwindled to a handful of families and were not likely to participate much in its activities, the Tribal Assembly was usually the *concilium plebis.* Though technically inaccurate, the use of the term *comitia tributa* for both bodies reflected a political reality, for

[32] Cicero *de Republica* 2.22.39–40.

the Tribal Assembly was the stronghold of plebeians. By 241, the number of tribes had reached thirty-five, four urban and thirty-one rural, and each tribe had one block vote. Membership in a tribe was hereditary, and members of rural tribes who moved to the city of Rome still voted in the tribes of their origin. Many of the members of the urban tribes were proletarians, and freedmen were customarily enrolled in the urban tribes, but the "liberal" votes of the urban populace could easily be swamped by the rural majority in the Tribal Assembly. As Roman citizens were spread about central Italy, the only voters to appear for a rural tribe would be farmers who lived near the city, wealthy men who could travel in for the occasion, or former rural residents who now lived in Rome but were likely the dependents of noble families. Unless a particular issue could attract a large attendance by rural residents, the nobles had little difficulty manipulating the rural votes in the Tribal Assembly. A large portion of rural proletarians could sway the vote in another direction, and this was the case in the Gracchan crisis of the second century. If the Tribal Assembly did not always reflect the wishes of the people, neither did the tribunes, few of whom intended to end their political careers in the tribunate. The collegiate nature of the office hampered all but the most aggressive tribunes, for at least one of the ten could be persuaded to block the unwanted activities of a colleague. Though it had originated as a defense for oppressed plebeians, the tribunate was a weapon that cut both directions, and astute nobles often utilized tribunes to obstruct the acts of the commons. The democratic side of Roman politics operated under severe handicaps.

The heart of the Roman Establishment, the stronghold of the nobles, was the Senate. After 287 it could no longer withhold its consent from the actions of the Assemblies and could only advise consuls and tribunes before elections and legislative acts. However, the forms of politics do not always reveal where power lies, and real decision making was in the hands of the Senate. In the famous formula *Senatus Populusque Romanus* the Senate came before the People, and such was the reality of Roman politics. The Assemblies elected officials and passed legislation, but the Senate controlled the disbursement of state funds, directed foreign policy, administered public lands, and gave out patronage to magistrates in the form of military commands.[33] Without money, laws and programs could not be enforced; without knowledge of secret treaties and diplomacy, declarations of war and peace had little meaning. While cooperative magistrates received opportunities to win glory in major wars and later govern rich provinces, difficult magistrates were

---

[33] Sometimes, lots were drawn for military commands, but an elite so pragmatic in their manipulation of omens would hardly have allowed a chance lot to place an incompetent general in an important command.

A Roman of the Early Republic. Rome, Museo Capitolino. *Alinari —Scala.*

given inglorious military commands and poverty-stricken provinces. The Senate's handling of funds and public lands was under the scrutiny of the censors, themselves revered members of the Establishment; few censors caused trouble as did Appius Claudius Caecus and Cato the Elder. Though the membership of the Senate was about three hundred, an inner circle of consular nobles dominated the chamber, speaking first on all matters. Heading the elder statesmen was the *Princeps Senatus,* who began all debates; few of the junior "back-bench" senators would care to antagonize the *Princeps* or his friends. Unless recognized by the presiding officer, a junior senator could not even speak but could only scurry to one side or the other to indicate which group he voted with, hence the scornful term *pedarii* (footmen) for junior senators. The preeminence of the inner clique of the Senate was based on their service to Rome or the prestige of their families. No ruling group is monolithic, and the Senate was often divided into factions, for personal and family rivalries were keen. Yet the Senate as a body was conscious of its power which grew as Roman power expanded, and jealous of its prerogatives when challenged by maverick magistrates or tribunes. Above all, the Senate was a continuing body unlike the magistrates and officials who held power for only a year. In times of crisis when the consuls were preoccupied and the electorate absent in war, the Senate became in effect the Roman government, particularly during the long strain of the Hannibalic War. Because of the background and age of its members, the Senate was conservative in temper and suspicious of impatient politicians, but there is no evidence of enduring opposition between it and the Assemblies or even the tribunate. What it lacked in genius, the Senate made up for in experience, and for the most part it served Rome well.

Despite the empty theorizing of Polybius, Rome did not have a mixed constitution. The Republic was run by an oligarchy of senatorial nobles who were sensible enough to allow the masses to elect officials and pass laws without participating in real decision making. A similar pragmatic wisdom was shown in the recruitment of wealthy plebeians into the nobility through service to the state. If the main concern of a ruling group is to maintain power, preventing revolution by listening to complaints from the commons and making concessions is more practical than severe acts of repression, which only drive the masses to desperation. Whatever their faults, however limited their horizons, the Roman oligarchs knew when to bend with the storm and concede rights without surrendering essential power. Rome survived many confrontations between classes without resort to the bloody revolutions that so often erupted in Hellas. The rights granted to the people were by no means negligible, and the plebeians were no fools. The masses took politics seriously and participated actively in the Assemblies, even at the price of physical discomfort, for Roman voters disdained seats as effeminate Greek devices and stood in the sun and rain. Despite the predominance of the oligarchy, the Roman people had a considerable role in deciding much of what affected their lives. Oligarchic realities and machine politics notwithstanding, the Republic was a viable institution for centuries. If any people had a genius for politics—both good and bad—they were the Romans.

CHAPTER THREE

The ways of Rome

ROMAN VIRTUES

*A*ccording to Ennius, "moribus antiquis res stat Romana virisque"—the Roman state was founded on old customs and real men.[1] Few epigrams express so well how Republican Romans saw themselves. The poet used the term *vir* and not *homo* which simply meant a man; *vir* was a man with courage and virility, foremost in battle and unfailing in bed. The aggregate of these qualities was *virtus,* manliness, and when the Romans talked of virtue, they meant aggressive masculinity and not the pallid "virtue" of Christian cant. Without the "old customs," however, the *viri* would have been no better than the rustic hooligans who flocked to Romulus's camp. Tamed by custom, they became Republican heroes and world conquerors. The ways of the ancients (*mos maiorum*) conditioned the Roman folk, who, even in the Late Republic, paid lip service to the old ways. Conspicuous among Roman virtues were *fides, pietas,* and *gravitas.* Absorbed in their own prestige (*dignitas*), the nobles bore themselves accordingly. Though gravity and aloofness often masked mediocrity, foreign observers admitted that the Roman ruling class was impressive in appearance and decorum. Of course, the studied seriousness (*gravitas*) of the nobles was calculated to impress spectators. All classes were expected to display *pietas,* concern for the long established rites of the gods, a rigid adherence to public and family cults. So long as religious customs were dutifully observed, the Roman state had no interest in personal belief or the lack of it. As piety kept peace between men and gods, so good faith (*fides*) bound men together in society. Loyal to the state, true to his friends and dependents, and faithful to his word, the ideal Roman was a man to be relied upon. Roman virtues were not abstractions of goodness, but essential conditions for the

[1] Cicero *de Republica* 5.1.1.

67

survival of society. If piety was neglected, the wrath of heaven was sure to follow. If nobles lacked dignity, they would cease to be leaders. If men did not observe good faith with one another, the fabric of society would collapse. Without manliness, the armies of Rome would be swept aside by their many enemies.

The degree to which Roman virtue was practiced varied with men and times. The Greek historian Polybius paid the Romans a high compliment:

> Public servants among the Greeks, even if entrusted with no more than a talent, and if provided with ten secretaries, ten seals, and twice as many witnesses, are unable to fulfill their trust; but among the Romans, people in office and in embassies handle large amounts of money and protect what is entrusted to them on account of the force of their oath alone. In other nations it is rare to find a man who keeps his hands off public money and is above reproach in this respect; but in Rome it is rare to find a man who has been detected in such a practice.[2]

Perhaps there is a note of sarcasm in the last phrase, for in discussing Roman conquests of the second century B.C., Polybius admitted that the integrity of magistrates was becoming a thing of the past, and he emphasized that at least Aemilius Paullus and his son, Scipio Aemilianus, who was Polybius' friend, were exceptions to the growing venality in Roman public life.[3] Even Livy's account of the early Republic, when virtue was supposedly unsullied, contains episodes of shady dealings and self-interest. When wealth was not at stake, Romans found it easier to observe their vaunted fidelity.

Pacifism was not a Roman virtue, and threads of violence run through Roman history. Despite the emphasis upon orderliness in the tradition, public disorders were not unknown, and private violence was frequent, for Rome had no police force before Augustus, and citizens had to defend themselves as best they could. The virtue of *fides* increased occurrences of violence, for nobles would summon their dependents to battle for them, and commoners called on friends and neighbors for aid. The aura of senatorial dignity that permeates traditional accounts obscures the highly emotional quality of the Romans, who were not inhibited Puritans but volatile Italians. Family pride was intense, feuds were common, and all Romans freely displayed sorrow and anger. Fond of laughter, they preferred low comedy to high tragedy and enjoyed rowdy festivals. Noble or commoner, the typical Roman bore little resemblance to either of the Catos, who were both considered odd by their contemporaries.

[2] Polybius 6.56.13—15, trans. Chambers, ed. Badian, p. 264.   [3] Polybius 18.35.1—12.

ROMAN SOCIETY: FIDES

The economic base of Roman society was agriculture, and the Romans were essentially a farming people. Farms were small; the basic measure of land was a *iugerum*, two-thirds of an acre. Early in the fourth century, Roman veterans received lots of seven (or four) *iugera* from the territory of Veii, but no one could subsist on such tiny parcels. The *lex Acilia* of 111 B.C. specified thirty *iugera* as a reasonable size for a farm. Nobles, of course, had much larger estates. Most farmland was in cereal production, but olives and viticulture became important through contact with the Greeks of the South. Though oxen were used for plowing, human muscle power was the main source of energy in agriculture and industry as well. By modern tastes, the Roman diet was appalling, for the main dish was a salted mush made of emmer flour or beans, augmented by a few garden vegetables. With the introduction of "naked wheat," bread became the staple food of Rome after 300 B.C. Sweets were limited to fruits and honey. Most Romans did not care for fish and ate little flesh; what meat there was on the table was goat, lamb, or preferably, pork. Like Greek chefs, Roman cooks were liberal with the use of garlic. The principal beverage was originally a mixture of milk and water; later, wine, also diluted with water, was popular. Olive oil was used for cooking and as fuel for lamps. Roman houses were simple one-room constructions of wood; later, brick was common, and tile roofs replaced thatch. Fancier homes had more rooms and an *atrium,* which was probably the old farmyard incorporated as a central court surrounded by a complex of rooms. Few Romans at any time could afford large homes, and all houses were simply furnished. In time, Rome developed small industry and a minority of the population was engaged in crafts or trade, but the typical Roman shop or factory was simply the owner's home facing on the street.

In antiquity, the agrarian output of Italy was considerable, as Varro boasts:

> Is there any useful product that does not grow in Italy and to perfection? What spelt is comparable to Campanian, what wheat to Apulian, what wine to Falernian, what oil to Vanefrian? Italy is so covered with trees that it seems to be an orchard. Is Homer's "vine-clad Phrygia" more covered with vines than this land, or his "grain-filled Argos" more covered with wheat? In what land does one *iugerum* bear ten and fifteen *cullei* [4] of wine as do some parts of Italy? [5]

---

[4] A culleus held 120 gallons. [5] Varro *Rerum Rusticarum* 1.2.6–7.

So productive was Italian agriculture that the peninsula supported a large population, from which Rome could levy armies. In the second century B.C., Cato offered advice on where in Italy goods could best be bought:

> Tunics, togas, blankets, smocks, and shoes should be bought at Rome; caps, iron tools, scythes, spades, mattocks, axes, harness, ornaments, and small chains at Cales and Minturnae; spades at Venafrum, carts and sledges at Suessa and in Lucania; jars and pots at Alba and at Rome; and tiles at Venafrum. Roman ploughs will be good for heavy soil, Campanian for black loam. Roman yokes are the best made. You will find detachable ploughshares the best. The following cities are the best markets for the articles named: oil mills at Pompeii and at Rufrius's yard at Nola; nails and bars at Rome; pails, oil-urns, water-pitchers, wine-urns, other copper vessels at Capua and at Nola; Campanian baskets from Capua will be found useful; pulley ropes and all sorts of cordage at Capua; Roman baskets at Suessa and Casinum.[6]

Since Cato was a canny agrarian capitalist, his advice was surely sound. The list might well have included the fine woolens of Apulia or the excellent pottery of Arretium.

In Cato's time, Rome had a money economy, but originally wealth had been computed in non-monetary terms. The word for money, *pecunia,* was based on *pecus,* a head of cattle, and fines in early Rome were stated as so many sheep or cattle. Soon after 300 B.C., Rome issued a bronze coin, the *as,* and by 269 a silver *sestercius* worth 2½ (later four) *asses.* About 187, the famed silver *denarius* appeared, worth four sesterces. For large sums of money, the Romans used the Greek term, a talent, for 6,000 *denarii.* By modern standards, the Romans were not a heavily taxed people. In Italian ports, a 2½ percent customs duty was levied, and an owner freeing a slave paid the Roman treasury five percent of his value. Roman citizens, but not allies, paid the *tributum simplex,* a one-tenth of one percent property tax. In times of war, the *tributum simplex* was increased because of additional state expenditures, and war loans were floated, but it was expected that the state would repay not only the loans but also the increased war taxes. The Republic also drew revenue from rent on public lands. When Rome acquired an overseas empire, provincial taxes swelled the Roman treasury until the Roman citizenry was spared all direct taxation in the second century B.C. The early Romans, however, paid their own way, and the expenditures of the state had not been great.

---

[6] Cato *de Agri Cultura* 135.1–3, trans. William D. Hooper, *Cato and Varro* (Cambridge, Mass.: Harvard University Press, 1935), p. 117.

Kinship was a cherished concept among the Romans, and familial ties were extremely strong. As with other Italians, the major elements in Roman society were the clan (*gens*) and the family. In historical times, the Roman tribes were primarily territorial units dominated by the leading resident clans. In history the major significance of the clans was the role they played among the nobility. However, every Roman belonged to a family headed by a *paterfamilias,* who was not necessarily the progenitor but was the ranking male. Legally, the *paterfamilias* held the lives and destinies of family members in his hand, but his powers of life and death were rarely invoked even in the early Republic. In religious affairs, the *paterfamilias* conducted rites for the household, and in economic matters, he administered the family's holdings.

While politically the Romans had evolved beyond the tribal concepts of the early Italians, the gentilician structure was still important even though people on the bottom of society belonged to no clan. Thus men like C. Marius or Q. Sertorius, who rose from humble beginnings, had no clan names, or at least none are known. Every Roman had a personal name (*praenomen*) such as Marcus or Gaius; many had a clan name (*nomen*), such as Tullius or Julius; all had a surname (*cognomen*), such as Cicero or Caesar. These family names often originated in some distinction of an ancestor; the *cognomen* Rufus indicated redheads in the family tree, and Q. Fabius Pictor had an ancestor who was a painter despite his patrician lineage. Why Cicero's family was named after a chick-pea is open to speculation. Whatever its prominence, the Roman family was a source of love, respect, and obligation.

In addition to kinship relations, most Romans were bound by the ties of mutual obligation that linked patrons and clients. Clientage is found in many societies, including some modern tribes in East Africa. At Rome, clientage was highly institutionalized and played a key role both socially and politically. Its origins are controversial, but the most likely explanation is that poor men attached themselves to powerful families for aid and protection in the rough days of Roman prehistory. The relationship became hereditary though clients did change patrons in the late Republic. In discussing the "laws of Romulus," Dionysius of Halicarnassus succinctly described patronage and clientage:

> It was the duty of the [patrons] to explain to their clients the laws, of which they were ignorant; to take the same care of them when absent as present, doing everything for them that fathers do for their sons with regard both to money and to the contracts that related to money; to bring suit on behalf of their clients when they were wronged in connection with contracts, and to defend them against any who brought charges against them. . . . It was the duty of the clients to assist their patrons in providing dowries for their daughters upon their marriage if the fathers had not

sufficient means; to pay their ransom to the enemy if any of them or of their children were taken prisoner; to discharge out of their own purses their patrons' losses in private suits and the pecuniary fines which they were condemned to pay to the state, making these contributions to them not as loans but as thank-offerings; and to share with their patrons the costs incurred in their magistracies and dignities and other public expenditures, in the same manner as if they were their relations. For both patrons and clients alike, it was impious and unlawful to accuse each other in lawsuits or to bear witness or to give their votes against each other or to be found in the number of each other's enemies; and whoever was convicted of doing any of these things, . . . might lawfully be put to death by any man who so wished as a victim devoted to the Jupiter of the Infernal Regions.[7]

The Twelve Tables confirm the sanction of ritual death: "If a patron defrauds a client, he shall be sacrificed." In time, such rigid rules relaxed, but the social pressure against breaking the bond was enormous. According to Cato, the patron-client relationship overrode even kinship ties: "One testifies in a client's behalf against one's relatives, and no one testifies against his client. A father is first in honor, but next after him a patron." [8] When both patron and client observed *fides,* the mutual benefits were great. While the client had a powerful protector in high places, the patron could draw on both the financial and political support of his clients, and many a noble rose to office on the block votes of clients. Clients took pride in the prestige of their patrons and often adopted their names to the confusion of prosopographers.[9] In war, clients preferred to serve under patrons, and in civil wars some nobles raised private armies of clients.

In all societies of antiquity, the specter of slavery lurked behind the scene. Though there were few slaves in early Rome, success in war brought increasing numbers of captives to work for Roman masters. Skilled slaves were especially desired and much of the small handicraft of Rome was produced by servile craftsmen. In Italian agriculture, slave labor was not important until the growth of large plantations after the Second Punic War. Most Romans were too poor to afford a slave, but all subscribed to the system. Legally, a slave was not human but was a piece of property totally at the master's disposal, and many labored

[7] Dionysius of Halicarnassus 2.10.1–3, trans. Earnest Cary, (Cambridge, Mass.: Harvard University Press, 1937), I, 341–43.

[8] Aulus Gellius 5.13.4.

[9] The study of elites, prosopography, concentrates on the careers, families, and marital connections of prominent men. Crucial for the study of Roman history, prosopographical techniques have also been employed by the Lewis Namier school in British history and by Charles Beard in his classic study of the Founding Fathers of the United States.

under the lash. Only a fool would whip his horse or slave to death, but in neither case would the law interfere. Although no slave could escape a sadistic master, household slaves and those with skills enjoyed a better lot than rural field hands. All slaves, female and male, were subject to the master's lust if he was so inclined. On large estates, slaves were bred like other stock. All slave-owning societies enforce obedience with brutality, and disobedient slaves dreaded being sent to the mills (the Roman equivalent of being "sold up river"):

> Where naughty slaves grind barley-meal in tears,
> The Whackland Islands, Ironclanky Isles,
> Where dead ox-leather slashes living men.[10]

The author of these lines, Plautus, had once worked as a millhand beside slaves and knew their agony. Though antiquity produced no Frederick Douglas to record the horror of slavery from a bondman's view, Plautus recorded the angry voice of a master raging at his chattel:

> Outside! Come on, keep moving! I was a fool
> To buy you, and a bigger fool to keep you.
> Can't you get it into your stupid heads
> To do just one thing right for a change? (whack)
> That's the only treatment you understand;
> The only way I'll get my money's worth.
> Look at those ribs. They're all over welts,
> More like donkeys than human beings.
> A waste of good rawhide, that's what you are.
> Give you a chance, and you're picking and stealing,
> Guzzling my wine, and running away.
> It's safer to use a wolf as a sheep-dog
> Than leave this lot in charge of the house.
> They don't seem too bad when you look them over.
> Making them work is another matter.
> All right! Pay attention! Your master's speaking!
> Wipe the sleep out of your eyes! Look lively
> Or I'll beat you till you look like patchwork quilts.
> You'll be prettier than a Persian carpet.
> I gave you all your duties yesterday,
> But your skulls are so thick you need a thrashing
> To refresh your memory. That's the way you're made.[11]

To uncounted wretches, this scene of brutality and degradation was an everyday experience. Not every master was a brute, and some Romans,

10 Plautus *Asinaria* 33–35, trans. J. Wight Duff, CAH, VIII, 409.
11 Plautus *Pseudolus* 133–151, trans. Peter D. Arnott, *The Romans and Their World* (New York: St. Martin's Press, 1970), p. 87.

like Varro and Seneca, advocated humane treatment of slaves. Cases of slaves who were loyal to kind masters are not unknown, but slavery as a system requires force, and few men can resist the psychological intoxication of treating other men as chattel.

Even before the horrors of the plantation era, the lot of a Roman slave was not enviable. Skilled slaves in crafts or trade, however, were usually allowed to retain a share of the profits and ultimately bought their freedom. On small farms, aging slaves were often freed to avoid the expense of feeding them in their nonproductive years. Compared to American slaveowners, Romans were generous in granting freedom to slaves, and a considerable portion of Roman society in the Late Republic was made up of freedmen or their descendants. The formalities of manumission varied, and some freedmen owed minor obligations to former masters, but these ties were not burdensome or hereditary. Moreover, the freedman was a Roman citizen, absorbing this privilege from the status of the former master who was now his patron. Freedmen usually adopted the names of former masters and bore them in pride and gratitude. This liberal attitude toward freedmen probably reflected conditions when Romans themselves had been debt slaves. Unlike the American freed slave, the Roman freedman was totally integrated into Roman society and had most rights and privileges of other citizens.[12] As the number of freedmen increased, the worried Senate took care to enroll them in the urban tribes where their votes would always be overwhelmed by the rural tribes. In high society, servile ancestry was a social handicap, but freedmen moved freely in all circles at Rome, and the poet Horace was not ashamed to boast that his father had once been a slave.

In the ancient world, men were enslaved because they had lost a battle and could not run fast enough or were kidnapped by pirates; slavery did not rest on a rationale of race. There was no color line in antiquity. To the Romans, black skin was a curiosity, like the great height of Gauls compared to short Italians, but pigmentation was not a badge of inferiority. In the Roman context, the term "African" referred to inhabitants of North Africa who were usually Semites or Berbers with a slight infusion of Negroid peoples from below the Sahara. Black skins were more common in Egypt because of its proximity to the Sudan, and it was well known that Ethiopia was a black kingdom. The Greeks and Romans were aware that there were varying degrees of civilization and savagery among the black nations, and Ethiopians had a reputation for virtue and nobility of spirit. In the Roman world, there were few Ne-

---

[12] A freedman was ineligible for military service or the higher magistracies, but his son suffered no such disability. Philip V, the astute king of Macedon, advised the Greeks to imitate Roman liberality toward freedmen.

Negro Boy. New York, Metropolitan Museum of Art. *The Metropolitan Museum of Art, Rogers Fund, 1918.*

groes, and most probably arrived as slaves, but once manumitted they circulated as freely as any other freedman. The evidence for black Romans is sparse, but there are unmistakably negroid individuals shown in art; and the great playwright, P. Terentius Afer, who was a slave born at Carthage, had a dusky complexion (*colore fusco*).[13] Given the small number of black people in the Roman Empire, the absence of prominent Negroes is not strange. Like all nations, the Romans had their ethnic biases and made unfavorable comments about "little Greeks," "sneaky Syrians," and above all, "treacherous Carthaginians," but eventually all these peoples were integrated as Roman citizens, and Rome had emperors from Spain, Africa, Syria, and the Balkans.

Traditionally, the role of Roman women was high, and Greeks were scandalized by the outspoken, confident ladies of Rome. Though legally under their husbands' control, women could own property and, when divorced, they retained their dowries. Marriage rites were simple and divorce was easy though infrequent. Women married early, and brides of twelve years of age were common. Though families were large, infant

---

[13] Suetonius *vita Terentii* 5.

mortality was great, and most babies did not survive into adulthood.[14] Among the poor, unwanted children were exposed, a common practice in antiquity. The ideal Roman woman was fecund as a mother and accomplished as the mistress of a household, spinning wool and keeping order among the children and slaves. Though most women were given no *praenomen* (even aristocratic ladies received generic names such as Fabia or Valeria), Roman history is filled with individualistic females, and henpecked husbands were not unknown. According to a doubtful tradition, Numa had forbidden Roman ladies to drink wine, and kinsmen were authorized to kiss them to see if they had been sampling the wine jars. Sumptuary legislation tried vainly to limit female expenditures on cosmetics, jewelry, and other luxuries. During the Hannibalic War, Roman women were forbidden to own more than a half-ounce of gold, wear purple-trimmed garments, or ride in a carriage within the city, but in 195 B.C. the women of Rome agitated for the repeal of these wartime decrees. Though Cato delivered a sarcastic antifeminist diatribe, his colleague in the consulship recommended that the women's demands be granted. When two tribunes threatened to veto the repeal, a crowd of women rioted at their doors until the tribunes meekly gave in. In 43 B.C., a similar tumult broke out when Antony and Octavian tried to levy funds from the wealthy women of Rome. In the Forum, the outraged ladies denounced the dynasts to their faces and raised such a commotion that the government quickly compromised. Though they lacked the franchise, the women of Rome were not afraid to raise their voices on public issues. As in all societies, the private influence of wives and mistresses was far greater than the legal positions afforded women.

Though historians recorded the deeds of prominent ladies, gravestones at Rome preserve the memories of simple women who played no role in history but whose passing was grieved by loving husbands:

> Stranger, my message is short. Stand by and read it through. Here is the unlovely tomb of a lovely woman. Her parents called her Claudia by name. She loved her husband with her whole heart. She bore two sons; of these she leaves one on earth; under the earth has she placed the other. She was charming in converse, yet proper in bearing. She kept house, she made wool. That's my last word. Go your way.[15]

Another epitaph honors the freedwoman, Aurelia, whose husband was a freedman and a butcher:

[14] Of the twelve children of Cornelia and T. Sempronius Gracchus the Elder, only three reached adulthood, and this was in one of the greatest noble houses of Rome with the best available care.

[15] E. H. Warmington, *Remains of Old Latin* (Cambridge, Mass.: Harvard University Press, 1940), IV, 13. (Henceforth this work is cited as *ROL*).

She who went before me in death, my one and only wife, chaste in body, a loving woman of my heart possessed, lived faithful to her faithful man; in fondness equal to her other virtues, never during bitter times did she shrink from loving duties.[16]

Another freedwoman, Publia Horaea, received an eloquent epitaph:

I was a woman respected by the good and hated by no respectable woman. To my old master and mistress I was an obedient servant, but to him yonder my husband I was a dutiful wife; for they gave me freedom, and he arrayed me in a robe. For twenty years since my girlhood I maintained the whole house. My last day delivered its judgment and death took away my breath, but took not the splendor of my life.[17]

Far removed from circles of power and wealth, the lives of many of these humble women were filled with love and satisfaction. How many aristocratic ladies could look back on their deathbeds on "lives of splendor?"

Because writers were attracted to the bizarre or amusing, details for the social history of Rome are often unsatisfactory, for ordinary things lacked interest and were not always recorded. Yet many aspects of Roman life are known. In the morning, the Romans rose early in order to utilize every minute of daylight. Meals were light with the main meal at midday in the early Republic, at evening in the Late Republic; a siesta followed lunch in summer. Both sexes wore loincloths as underwear and simple tunics as outer garments; men's tunics were short, women's much longer. For men, formal dress consisted of a long white cloth, the toga, draped about the body and worn over the tunic. Hot in summer and drafty in winter, it was heavy, difficult to arrange, and easily disarrayed. Yet the toga was the symbol of citizenship and Romans wore it proudly, even though it was quickly shed at home or at work. Children and magistrates wore togas with a purple border, and the assumption of the plain toga of an adult was a major event in a boy's life. In early Rome, all men wore beards, and older men and philosophers continued to do so throughout Roman history. In the second century B.C., Romans aped the Greeks and began to shave; Scipio Aemilianus was supposed to have started the fad of being clean-shaven.

The Romans did not, however, share the Hellenic fondness for athletics. Though hunting was popular with those who could afford the time, Romans did not engage in sports apart from physical exercises in military service. In all societies, a life of leisure is necessary for a sportsman; the Roman masses had no leisure, and the nobles considered ath-

---

[16] *ROL,* IV, 23.   [17] *ROL,* IV, 53.

letics trifling. At Rome, spectator sports alone were popular, and all classes enjoyed chariot races. The Circus Maximus, where races were held, supposedly dated from the days of the kings. In 264 B.C., the first gladiatorial combat was staged at Rome, but the grisly spectacles were infrequent during the Republic. In the fourth century, Rome imported Etruscan entertainers who danced to music and improvised songs, but the Romans soon transformed the shows into a type of burlesque. In the third century, Greek tragedies in translation were introduced, but Roman taste preferred bawdy farces, and comedy—not tragedy—was the typical Roman fare. Given the emphasis of the Roman stage, the social status of actors was low. The Romans preferred music loud and lively, and Polybius indignantly reports that a troupe of accomplished Greek musicians was forced to put on a mock musical combat for an audience at Rome.[18] At heart, the Romans were farmers with earthy tastes, and they loved buffoons, not artists. The Romans were also fond of gambling, especially with dice.

The Latin language evolved slowly over the centuries, borrowing some words from Etruscan and Greek. The earliest known example of Latin is inscribed on a brooch found at Praeneste, probably made in the late seventh or early sixth century B.C.: *Manios med fhe fhaked Numasioi*—in classical Latin, *Manius me fecit Numerio,* "Manius made me for Numasios" (Numerius).[19] The famed *Lapis Niger* in the Roman Forum is a fragmentary sixth or early fifth-century inscription, apparently dealing with religious taboos and containing the word *recei,* "to the king." To Romans of Cicero's time, the Latin of the past was roughhewn and not always easy to understand. In time, Latin became a rich language, though Heinrich Heine dismissed it as fit only "for military commands, governmental reports, usurers' judgments, a lapidary speech for the flinty Roman folk." [20] It would become a means of elegant argument for Cicero and a vehicle of beauty for poets. Though most of the poor could not read, literacy was relatively widespread among the Romans, who read aloud when reading. Augustine marveled that Ambrose perused books in silence. Literary interests came late in Roman history, for the Romans were more concerned with recording public and private documents of all kinds—laws, meetings of the Senate, contracts, dedications, land deeds, and similar material—where accuracy was more important than elegance.

To the Romans, legal relationships were important, and many laws accumulated after the Twelve Tables. The aggregate that we call Roman Law was a composite of the Twelve Tables, statutes of the Assemblies,

---

[18] Polybius 30.22.1–12.   [19] *ROL,* IV, 196.
[20] L. R. Lind, *Latin Poetry,* p. xxvi.

magistrates' edicts, and interpretations by learned jurists.[21] The cumulative result was an unwieldy body of laws, edicts, and decisions which only specialists could master, and not all magistrates were familiar with the rulings of their predecessors. Also many matters were left vague, for the practical Romans believed in rule by men as well as laws. There was no doubt, however, about the precious rights of Roman citizens: franchise, appeal, formal trial, and immunity from torture and degrading execution (such as crucifixion). In antiquity no one had immutable human rights, for all status and privilege stemmed from society, but Rome had given its members a number of rights that were envied by non-citizens.

In upper-class households, some books were available, usually of a practical nature, for the Romans felt that the head of a family should be versed in medicine, agriculture, and things that concern daily life. Originally such knowledge had been passed on by word of mouth, but by the second century B.C. manuals on a variety of subjects were written, and the Roman encyclopedic tradition was in full swing. The most famous of the early handbooks, Cato's monograph on farm management, included timeworn advice on home medicine. Like Pythagoras, Cato had great faith in the medicinal properties of cabbage and urine:

> If you save the urine of a person who eats cabbage habitually, heat it, and bathe the [debilitated] patient in it, he will heal quickly; this remedy has been tested. Also, if babies are bathed in this urine they will never be weakly; those whose eyes are not very clear will see better if they are bathed in this urine; and pain in the head or neck will be relieved if the heated urine is applied.[22]

According to Plutarch, Cato prided himself on his medical skills and fed sick members of his household on diets that gave them nightmares. Under his ministrations, both his wife and a son died.[23] In his role as family physician, Cato not only prescribed diets and urine baths, but voodoo as well:

> Any kind of dislocation may be cured by the following charm: Take a green reed four or five feet long and split it down the middle, and let two men hold it to your hips. Begin to chant: "motas uaeta daries dardares astataries dissunapiter" and continue until they meet. Brandish a knife over

---

[21] Most Republican jurists were senators who studied the law and taught young men of their own class. They also supplied advice to magistrates and thus molded the law itself. According to the Twelve Tables, a father could sell his son three times, but the code did not mention daughters; the jurists decided that a daughter could be sold only once.

[22] Cato *de Agri Cultura* 157.10, trans. Hooper, p. 149.

[23] Plutarch *Cato Maior* 23–24.

them, and when the reeds meet so that one touches the other, grasp with
the hand and cut right and left. If the pieces are applied to the dislocation
or the fracture, it will heal. And none the less chant every day, and, in
the case of a dislocation, in this manner, if you wish: "huat haut haut is-
tasis tarsis ardannabou dannaustra".[24]

Such was native Roman medicine, a blend of Italic magic and quackery
from Magna Graecia. Late in the third century B.C., Hellenistic doctors
began to practice in Rome though the first Greek physician, Archaga-
thus, was too free with the knife, cauterizing iron, and catheter, and was
nicknamed "Butcher." [25] Almost as crippling were the fees that Greek
doctors charged.

Roman attitudes toward time-reckoning were almost as crude as
Roman medicine. In early Rome, the sun was the only "clock," but during the Hannibalic War, a large sundial was brought to Rome as booty
from Syracuse. It took the Romans fifty years, however, to realize that
Syracuse and Rome were on different latitudes. In 159 B.C., the censors
adjusted the sundial and provided against future mishaps by installing a
water-clock to time the meetings of the Senate. The Roman year had
355 days and began in March; hence December is the "tenth" month; in
the second century B.C., the beginning of the year was moved to January for political reasons. March, May, July, and October had 31 days,
February 28, and the other months 29. The first day of each month was
called the Kalends. In the long months, the Nones fell on the seventh
and the Ides on the fifteenth; in the short months, the Nones were the
fifth and the Ides the thirteenth. Until the dictatorship of Caesar, the
Romans clung to the obsolete lunar "calendar of Numa" and reconciled
it with the solar year by inserting an intercalary month every second
February. However, the length of the year affected the duration of contracts and magistracies, and so the pontiffs cavalierly decided when and
if to intercalate, often for political reasons. The Roman week had eight
days; the last was a market day, on which the Assemblies could not
meet. The Assemblies also did not convene during public festivals or
games or on "unlucky" days. A clever magistrate could avoid unwanted
acts by the Assemblies by juggling the calendar adroitly.

Roman mathematics were more precise than Roman calendrics. For
large sums, an abacus was used, but the Romans were highly skilled in
finger-counting:

It was a real art with strict rules which enabled the two hands to indicate
any whole number from 1 to 1,000,000. The last three fingers of the left
hand indicated the numbers 1 to 9, according to the extent that they were

[24] Cato, *de Agri Cultura* 160, trans. Hooper, p. 153.
[25] Pliny the Elder *Naturalis Historia* 29.12–13.

bent towards the palm. Tens were indicated by the relative positions of the thumb and first finger of the same hand. The right hand was used in the same way—first finger and thumb, last three fingers—to indicate hundreds and thousands. Tens and hundreds of thousands were indicated by the position of the left or right hand in relation to the chest, navel, or thigh-bone. A million was indicated by the two hands locked together.[26]

Finger reckoning was used in the markets and courts or wherever a Roman needed to calculate quickly.

Of necessity, historians must deal with a few prominent men and relegate the rest to faceless anonymity under loose labels like "the masses" or "the Romans." Yet millions of men and women lived in the Roman world, and though they did not win a place in history, their lives had meaning. The voters in the Assemblies, the farmers in the fields, the soldiers in the legions, the slaves at the mill—all were individuals although they affected history only en masse. Across the centuries some Romans still cry to be remembered:

> Young man, though you are in a hurry, this little stone asks you to look at it, and then to read the message with which it is inscribed. Here lie the bones of Lucius Maecius Philotimus the hardwareman. I wanted you to know this. Farewell.[27]

More poignant was the epitaph raised by the father of a dead child:

> Here an unhappy parent has laid to rest his one and only daughter, Nymphe, whom he cherished in the joy of sweet love while the shortened hours of the Fates allowed it. Now she is torn away from her home —earth covers her, dear to her own; now her fair face, her form too, praised as fair—all is airy shadow and her bones are a little pinch of ashes.[28]

The role of Philotimus was a humble one, and Nymphe died before her life had really begun, but once they lived, the hardwareman who was proud of his honest profession and the girl who was the darling of her father—they, too, were Romans.

ROMAN RELIGION: PIETAS

As Fustel de Coulanges recognized long ago, the core of Roman life was religious. Like other Italians, the Romans cherished simple agrar-

---

[26] Henri I. Marrou, *A History of Education in Antiquity* (New York: The New American Library, 1964), p. 219.
[27] *ROL,* IV, 25.   [28] *ROL,* IV, 29.

ian cults and were concerned primarily with the proper performance of venerable rites. Originally, the gods were vague sexless spirits, indistinct but powerful forces of nature. From the Etruscans and Greeks the Romans acquired more definite notions of deities and a smattering of myth, but mythology paid little role in Roman religion, and there was no theology to systematize the unknowable. To the early Romans, life after death was not important, for the dead did not congregate in any heaven or hell. Collectively, the dead were *Di Manes,* a host of ghosts still hovering on the earth, and each family propitiated the spirits of its dead ancestors. Extremely formalistic, the rites of Roman religion were similar to those of the Iguvine Tablets. So anxious were the Romans to perform rituals faithfully that any divergence in word or deed negated a ceremony, and rites might be repeated thirty times until they were done properly. Conservative, unimaginative, and meticulous, Roman *pietas* was not concerned with ethics. Though the gods might reward good and punish evil, a Roman was pious if he observed the traditional cults; the state of his soul was not a matter of interest to Rome. *Pietas* was *fides* toward the gods and their time-honored rituals.

In the words of the Psalmist, "the fear of the Lord is the beginning of wisdom." The Romans would have agreed, for fear and dread lay behind much of the animistic base of Roman religion. Living close to nature, the early Romans had an awe of dark, secluded places. Even the sophisticated Seneca felt an ancient shudder in the dim recesses of the forest:

> If you have ever come on a dense wood of ancient trees that have risen to an exceptional height, shutting out all sight of the sky with one thick screen of branches upon another, the loftiness of the forest, the seclusion of the spot, your sense of wonderment at finding so deep and unbroken a gloom out of doors, will persuade you of the presence of a deity. Any cave in which the rocks have been eroded deep into the mountain resting on it, its hollowing out into a cavern of impressive extent not produced by the labors of men but the result of processes of nature, will strike into your soul some kind of inkling of the divine. We venerate the sources of important streams; places where a mighty river bursts suddenly from hiding are provided with altars; hot springs are objects of worship; the darkness or unfathomable depth of pools has made their waters sacred.[29]

Awe of the forces of nature, fear of darkness, an awareness that something or someone is there in the shadows—such were the roots of Roman religion. The concept of sacredness, too, had a grim side, for

[29] Seneca *Epistulae Morales ad Lucilium* 41.3, trans. Robin Campbell, *Letters from a Stoic* (London: Penguin, 1969) , p. 87.

the word *sacer* meant not only sacred but accursed and was applied both to holy places and things (as in the modern sense of sacred) and to individuals who were to be sacrificed to the gods.

According to Varro, the Romans worshiped the gods without images for 170 years.[30] Though so precise a figure was an antiquarian's guess, Varro was aware that the Etruscans introduced idols to Rome. Greek influence increased the anthropomorphic trend to the detriment of true piety, Varro insists, for men ceased to fear the gods when they could see them. Though awe and devotion replaced the more primitive element of dread, Roman religion preserved an undercurrent of anxiety, for the will of heaven was often arbitrary even toward pious men. Heading the Roman pantheon was the Italic sky deity, Jupiter, king of the gods and father of heroes, master of storms and lightning and protector of the Roman folk. Another revered Italic god was Mars (Mamers), who was both an agricultural deity and a war god. The two-faced Janus was the god of beginnings and crossings. In the Late Republic, the closing of the door of his temple symbolized peace. The cult of Vesta originated in one of the oldest concerns of mankind, the need for fire. Vesta personified the flame in the household hearth, and at Rome, six patrician virgins tended the perpetual fire of the hearth of the city, which was never allowed to go out. Since the Vestal Virgins served for thirty years, elevation to the holy sisterhood was often unwanted by the women involved, despite the great honor it brought to their families. By the fifth century, some Greek gods had become popular among the Romans, and the divine twins, Castor and Pollux, shared a temple at Rome in 484. Both tradesmen and farmers cherished the rowdy Hercules, and all classes respected the phallic prowess of Priapus. In 293, the serpentine god of medicine, Asclepius, was brought to Rome to stay a plague. As polytheists, the Romans admitted the existence of all gods, but their devotion was reserved for old familiar deities.

In addition to the high gods of the state cult, the Romans paid homage to a myriad of minor spirits, barely deserving the title of gods, who presided over every aspect of nature and human life, no matter how petty. The curious reader can refer to Augustine's sarcastic recitation of their names and functions.[31] Even sophisticated pagans were embarrassed by what Seneca called "this ignoble crowd of gods whom the superstition of ages has amassed." [32] Besides the motley "gods" mocked by Augustine and Seneca, the Romans honored nameless spirits associated with the home and farm. Guarding the cupboard, the Penates were household gods, while the Lares hovered in the fields; later, the

---

[30] Augustine *de Civitate Dei* 4.31. Plutarch *Numa* 8.
[31] Augustine *de Civitate Dei* 4.8,11; 6.9.   [32] Augustine *de Civitate Dei* 6.10.

Lares were included in ceremonies in the home. Every family worshiped the spiritualized virility (*genius*) of the *paterfamilias*. Genital in origin, the *genius* became in time something like a soul but never lost the aura of potency. Because hostile forces, too, inhabited the world, the Romans tried to defend themselves with spells and amulets against unseen enemies and malign spirits. Witches were especially dreaded, and the Romans lived in fear of the evil eye, a belief which is still common in modern Italy. The phallus was a symbol of potency, and people of all classes wore phallic amulets against the dreaded evil eye. The phallus was also a symbol of good luck, and statues of the Greek god Priapus, often portrayed as a comic figure with an enormous erection, stood in many Roman gardens.

At Rome, official priests presided over the state cult, but in the home and on the farm, the *paterfamilias* conducted the simple rites of everyday religion. In February the Romans set aside six days for a public honoring of the dead, the Parentalia, with visits to graves where the living placed flowers and poured libations; the memorial days ended with a family banquet. In May, however, the Romans celebrated a grimmer ceremony, the Lemuria, in which the dead were viewed as hostile ghosts to be exorcized by the *paterfamilias*. At midnight the head of the house filled his mouth with black beans and walked through the home, nine times spitting out beans and chanting, "With these, I redeem me and mine." He was careful not to look around lest he see the ghosts gathering the beans. The ceremony ended with the clashing of brass and a nine-fold cry for the ghosts to depart. Unlike the pleasant Parentalia, the Lemuria reflected a primitive time when even the ghosts of relatives were feared.

In the countryside, old ways last longest, and the *paterfamilias* performed many rites, learned not from books but from his father. A farm was purified by sacrificing a pig, a ram, and a bull to "Father Mars," after the beasts had been led around the boundaries of the property. When clearing land, the Roman farmer employed a rite and prayers of great antiquity. Cato preserves "the Roman formula to be observed for thinning a grove":

> A pig is to be sacrificed, and the following prayer uttered: "Whether thou be god or goddess to whom this grove is dedicated, as it is thy right to receive a sacrifice of a pig for the thinning of this sacred grove, and to this intent, whether I or one at my bidding do it, may it be rightly done. To this end, in offering this pig to thee I humbly beg that thou wilt be gracious and merciful to me, to my house and household, and to my children. Wilt thou deign to receive this pig which I offer thee to this end." If you wish to till the ground, offer a second sacrifice in the same way, with the addition of the words: "for the sake of doing this work." So long

as the work continues, the ritual must be performed in some part of the land every day; and if you miss a day, or if public or domestic feast days intervene, a new offering must be made.[33]

The god in the woods was animistic, for neither its name nor sex was known, but its fearful presence was real to the farmer, who carefully performed the rite in the ancestral way.

In the city of Rome, frequent festivals enlivened the year with holidays from work and opportunities for spectacle and rowdy exuberance. Most of the festivals included rites of great antiquity. On the Ides of February, the Lupercalia was celebrated at the foot of the Palatine Hill by a cave where the wolf was supposed to have suckled Romulus. After two goats and a dog were sacrificed, the goats were skinned and their blood smeared on the foreheads of two naked youths. Girded with the goat pelts and brandishing strips of hide, the youths ran around the base of the hill striking women with the strips, which were believed to bring fertility. On the Ides of October, a horse was slain with the spear of Mars in the Campus Martius. The horse's tail was rushed to the Regia, the former home of the kings, where the blood was collected for later use in fertility magic. The people then fought over possession of the horse's head, and the winning group carried it off as a sacred trophy. Though Timaeus foolishly connected the ceremony with the Trojan horse, Polybius aptly noted that horse sacrifices were commonplace among barbaric peoples.[34] Since Mars was an agricultural as well as a war god, the slaughtered horse probably represented a "corn-spirit." On April 21 during the Parilia, the coagulated blood of the October Horse was sprinkled on a bonfire, and men and women jumped through it. At the end of April and beginning of May, the Romans celebrated the festival of Flora, in which the ancient Italian fertility goddess was honored with considerable sexual activity. On the seventeenth of December began the most famous of Roman holidays, the Saturnalia, which eventually lasted seven days though the emperors tried to restrict its duration. An old Italic deity, Saturn was viewed as a prehistoric king of Latium who had presided over a classless Golden Age of bliss. During the Saturnalia, the Golden Age briefly returned, for slaves were given great license and were waited on by their masters at a feast. Visits were paid to friends and gifts were exchanged, a custom that carried over into Christian usage when Christmas usurped the winter solstice festivities. According to Seneca, the whole city went mad during the Saturnalia, and it was difficult to get any work done in December because of the growing excitement and preparations.[35]

[33] Cato *de Agri Cultura* 139–40, trans. Hooper, p. 121.
[34] Polybius 12.4b. Cf. Plutarch *Moralia* 287B.
[35] Seneca *Epistulae Morales ad Lucilium* 18.1.

The solemn side of Roman religion was reflected in the great priest-hoods that supervised the state cult. Unlike the clergy of Egypt and the Near East, Roman priests were not a sacerdotal class devoted solely to religious affairs. With few exceptions, the Roman priesthoods were held by men who also served the state as magistrates or officials. In 300 B.C. the Ogulvian law had broken the patrician monopoly on the priesthoods and augurates. Originally a self-perpetuating co-optative body, the nine pontiffs were elected after 104 B.C. by seventeen of the thirty-five tribes chosen by lot. The same special voting assembly elected the nine augurs, who interpreted omens and the results of divination. Heading the religious establishment was the Pontifex Maximus, who chose the Vestal Virgins and minor priests. Heir to the religious functions of the kings, the Pontifex Maximus lived in the Regia, the former royal resi-dence, and the prestige of the office made it highly desired. An elected position since the third century, the supreme pontificate was a political office in a society that did not separate church and state. The Pontifex Maximus was spared the onerous taboos that surrounded the priest of Jupiter (*flamen Dialis*), who could not ride a horse, wear an unperfor-ated ring, touch or even mention raw flesh, ivy, beans, dogs, or goats, eat leavened bread, or enter a burial place. He could have no knots in his clothing, and his cut nails and hair were carefully buried to prevent witchcraft being worked against him. Since he could not view an army, the public career of the *flamen Dialis* was somewhat limited.

In Roman political life, the augurs played a major role. Though mag-istrates took the auspices to read the will of heaven, the augurs inter-preted and verified them. The gods revealed their intent through light-ning flashes, the flight of birds, the eating habits of sacred chickens, and the livers of sacrificed beasts; for the latter, a *haruspex* (usually an Etruscan) was employed, and in all matters of divination, Etruscan ex-perts were consulted on difficult points. However, regardless of what ac-tually occurred in nature, the augurs decided whether or not the omens were favorable, and their decisions were often based not on the pedan-try of experts but on immediate political considerations. Thus elections and legislation could be aborted on religious grounds when other means of obstruction failed. Even the renowned Q. Fabius Maximus, whose piety was beyond doubt, frankly admitted that, when he was an augur, whatever was in the public interest had good omens, and whatever was not for the public good, did not.[36] Such manipulation of the state cult was common among Roman politicians, and the cynical practice reached outrageous lengths in the Late Republic.

Though Roman religion had no revealed book, the state did in times

---

[36] Cicero *de Senectute* 4.11.

of emergency consult a three-volume collection of oracles, the Sibylline Books, which were supposedly peddled to Tarquin the Proud by the Cumaean Sibyl. Kept in the temple of Jupiter on the Capitol, the books were guarded by a board of ten distinguished men. The introduction of Greek gods and religious practices usually had a Sibylline sanction. When the books were accidentally burned in 83 B.C., a new collection was made with substantial borrowings from the Erythraean Sibyl in Asia Minor, but Varro rejected many of the new oracles as spurious. Genuine or not, the Sibylline oracles cited by historians are a farrago of ambiguities that could mean anything and usually did. The Romans had good reason to be suspicious of holy books of reputed antiquity. In 181 B.C., a forger produced the lost books of Numa, but the Senate, after examining them, ordered the volumes burned as subversive.[37]

Despite the sizeable element of fraud in the state cult, Roman religion was permeated by genuine piety and a faithful observation of venerable rites. Among the duties of the censors was a ritual purification (*lustrum*) of the Roman citizenry, whereby a ram, pig, and ox were led around the assembled host and then sacrificed to the gods. The Salian priests of Mars bore ancient shields that "had fallen from heaven" and performed war dances singing lyrics unintelligible to Varro and Horace. The priests of the Arval Brotherhood chanted archaic songs and leapt frantically, crying for Mars to aid the Roman folk. Such survivals from the earliest days of Rome lasted long into the Imperial era. When Hannibal threatened Rome in 217 B.C., the Romans had recourse to the old Italic practice of a Sacred Spring, vowing all the animals born that year to be sacrificed to the gods.

One of the most ancient Roman rites was that of the *fetiales,* twenty priests who conducted ritual declarations of war and peace. As sacred ambassadors, the *fetiales* presented Roman demands to foreign peoples; if the demand was rejected, the priests stood at the border, assured the gods that Rome was guiltless of provoking war, and hurled a bloody spear with a fire-hardened tip into the enemy territory. Thus, all Roman wars were just wars in the eyes of heaven. The fetial priests also sanctified peace treaties by sacrificing a pig with a flint knife:

> From these terms, as they have been publicly recited from beginning to end without fraud, from these tablets or this wax, and as they have been this day clearly understood, the Roman people will not be the first to depart. If they shall be the first to depart from them by general consent with malice aforethought, then on that day do thou, great Diespiter, so smite the Roman people as I today smite this pig, and smite them so much harder as thy power and strength are so much greater.[38]

[37] Livy 40.29.2–14. Plutarch *Numa* 22. Augustine *de civitate Dei* 7.34.
[38] Livy 1.24.7–8.

The primitive magic of the rite and the use of a flint knife testify to the great antiquity of the *fetiales*. In time, the fetial practices became obsolete and hypocritical, and the ritual spear was tossed into a plot of land at Rome symbolizing the enemy territory. During the second century B.C., the *fetiales* were eclipsed until the rites were revived for the Spanish wars in 136. In declaring war on Cleopatra in 32 B.C., Octavian acted as a *fetialis*.

The world of the *fetiales* was one of magic and concern for the gods. A similar view was embodied in the Roman rite of *evocatio,* whereby the deities of the enemy were seduced into abandoning them and joining the side of Rome, thus leaving the Romans free to sack the city without fear of retaliation from the gods of the land. Macrobius preserves the formula used in the Third Punic War:

> To any god, to any goddess, under whose protection are the people and state of Carthage, and chiefly to thee who art charged with the protection of this city and people, I make prayer and do reverence and ask grace of you all, that ye abandon the people and state of Carthage, forsake their places, temples, shrines, and city, and depart therefrom; and that upon that people and state ye bring fear and terror and oblivion; that once put forth ye come to Rome, to me and to mine; and that our places, temples, shrines, and city may be more acceptable and pleasing to you; and that ye take me and the Roman people and my soldiers under your charge; that we may know and understand the same. If ye shall so have done, I vow to you temples and solemn games. With those words victims are to be sacrificed, and the import of the entrails examined to see if they indicate a fulfillment of the above.[39]

With such prayers, Juno had been lured from Veii. Being practical people, the Romans offered the divine defectors a temple, honors, and worship at Rome. The Romans were also anxious to be assured by the entrails of sacrificed beasts that the enemy's gods had indeed departed. When they were confident that the gods were agreeable to the bargain and had deserted their former worshipers, the Romans then "devoted" the city, that is, consigned it to utter destruction. Macrobius also preserves the formula for devoting a city, which reads in part:

> Father Dis, Veiovis, and ye spirits of the world below, or by what other name ye should be called, do all of you fill with panic and fear and terror that city of Carthage and the army whereof it is my purpose now to speak, and those who shall bear arms and weapons against our legions and army; take away and deprive of the light of day that army, those en-

[39] Macrobius *Saturnalia* 3.97–9, trans. Percival V. Davies (New York: Columbia University Press, 1969), p. 218.

emies, those people, their cities and lands, and those who dwell in these places and parts, fields and cities; . . . hold devoted and doomed those cities and fields, the lives, of whatever age, of those people. . . .[40]

With the slaughter of three black sheep, the curse was confirmed, and the city was destroyed; the inhabitants were slain or sold as the Romans saw fit. Since the gods had already abandoned the city, it was safe to indulge in pillage and massacre. With such prayers, the Romans devoted Veii, Carthage, Corinth, and numerous other towns throughout the Mediterranean.

Lest baleful magic be used against Rome, the city had a secret name which was also the name of its tutelary god. Only the pontiffs knew the god's name, and it was death to reveal it. In antiquity, scholars offered many guesses as to the secret name, and some suggested that the god was Eros, whose Latin name, Amor, was Roma spelled backwards. At Pompeii, a curious graffito has been found:

```
ROMA
O     M
M     O
AMOR
```

Apparently, whoever scribbled the graffito felt the quadrangle confirmed the identity of Rome and Amor. After all, Aeneas was the son of Aphrodite.

In all primitive societies the gods have a taste for blood, human as well as animal. To win the favor of heaven, the early Romans were willing to give the gods the most precious gift of all, human life. Valor and skill did not always ensure success in battle, and at times the Romans tried to buy victory with the ritual death of a human victim. Any commander with *imperium* could select a soldier, devote him ritually to the gods, and send him to certain death with the intent that heaven would keep its side of the bargain and furnish victory in return. If by chance the "devoted" man did not die, an effigy of him was made and buried, presumably to fool the gods. On occasion, the commander might devote himself. Livy records the *devotio* of P. Decius Mus during the Latin Revolt in 340 B.C.:

In a loud voice, Decius the consul called out to Marcus Valerius: "We have need of heaven's aid, Marcus Valerius. Come now, supreme pontiff

[40] Macrobius *Saturnalia* 3.9.10, trans. Davies, pp. 218–19.

of the Roman people, dictate the words that I may devote myself to save the legions." At the pontiff's direction, Decius put on the purple-bordered toga, veiled his head, and with one hand touching his chin, stood upon a spear laid under his feet and said: "Janus, Jupiter, Father Mars, Quirinius, Bellona, Lares, . . . ye gods in whose power are both we and our enemies, and you divine Manes, I invoke and worship you, I beseech and beg your favor that you further the might and victory of the Roman people . . . and visit the foes of the Roman people . . . with fear, shuddering, and death. As I have spoken these words on behalf of the republic of the Roman people . . . and of the army, the legions, and the auxiliaries of the Roman people . . . , do I devote the legions and auxiliaries of the enemy, together with myself, to the divine Manes and to the Earth." [41]

After completing his prayer, Decius plunged into the ranks of the enemy and perished. Inspired by his action, the Romans won the battle. In 295 at the battle of Sentium, his son, P. Decius Mus, also devoted himself, and the Romans were again victorious. At Ausculum in 279 B.C., the grandson, P. Decius Mus, tried to devote himself, but Pyrrhus sent word that his soldiers had orders to spare the "devoted" consul. Decius was dissuaded, and the Romans lost. However, a tradition preserved by Cicero claims that Decius succeeded in devoting himself, yet the Romans still lost the battle. In any case, after Ausculum, the Decii lost their taste for *devotio*.

In early Rome, human sacrifices had been conducted in annual ceremonies. Gradually the Romans modified the practice by substituting symbols for men. On the Ides of May, the pontiffs and Vestal Virgins hurled into the Tiber twenty-seven straw puppets shaped like men, surrogates for what had once been human victims. During national crises the Romans reverted to the barbaric ways of the past. About 226 B.C., two Gauls and one or two Greeks were buried alive at Rome, because the Sibylline Books had said that Greeks and Gauls would occupy the city.[42] After the great defeat at Cannae in 216, the Romans again buried alive two Gauls and two Greeks,[43] and the same number were buried in 104 to purify the city because of a scandal among the Vestal Virgins.[44] In 97, human sacrifice was abolished by a decree of the Senate.[45] However, in 46 during the dictatorship of Caesar, the pontiffs sacrificed two soldiers in the Campus Martius and hung their heads on the Regia.[46] In the first century A.D., Pliny the Elder mentions that human sacrifices still took place in Italy, presumably in backward country districts.[47] It is likely that the mock kings elected by the revelers during the Saturnalia were sacrificed as well.

[41] Livy 8.9.4–8.   [42] Orosius 4.13. Zonaras 8.19.   [43] Livy 22.57.6.
[44] Plutarch *Moralia* 284B–C.   [45] Pliny the Elder *Naturalis Historia* 30.12.
[46] Cassius Dio 43.24.4.   [47] Pliny the Elder, *Naturalis Historia* 28.12.

Whatever moderns may think of its darker side, Roman religion added enormously to the cohesion of Roman society. Polybius, who considered religion the opium of the people, praised the Romans for their religiosity:

> What other peoples hold in reproach is precisely what binds together the political institutions of the Romans: I mean superstition. This element is dramatized and brought into action among them, both in their private lives and in their public affairs, to the highest possible degree.[48]

Polybius adds that Roman sophisticates who mocked religion were doing great damage to the state. During the second century B.C., the fad for Greek philosophy and scholarship among Roman intellectuals undermined many traditional beliefs. More important, however, was the fact that the old agrarian cults meant little to an urban population that had lost its ties with rural life. The city populace had not become irreligious; they simply began to look to other cults to satisfy their spiritual needs. The religious reformation of Augustus did much to restore the formal practice of the old religion of Rome. Regardless of urban religious developments, the country people clung to the ways and beliefs of their fathers. In the Imperial Era, travelers in the countryside often came across sacred stones, on which flowers had been freshly laid, proof that *pietas* was still a Roman trait.

THE NOBLES: DIGNITAS

> In all ages, whatever the form and name of government, be it monarchy, republic, or democracy, an oligarchy lurks behind the facade; and Roman history, Republican or Imperial, is the history of the governing class.[49]

There is much truth in these epigrams of Sir Ronald Syme.[50] The realities of Roman politics reveal the rule of an elite and the perversion of popular government in the interests of the oligarchs. Obviously, there was more to Roman history than the machinations of the ruling group, but it was the nobles who made decisions at Rome, contrived, directed, and profited from its wars, administered the empire, and ultimately pulled down the Republic that their ancestors had created.

[48] Polybius 6.56.6—8, trans. Chambers, ed. Badian, p. 264.
[49] Ronald Syme, *The Roman Revolution* (Oxford: Clarendon Press, 1939), p. 7.
[50] In his epoch-making *Roman Revolution* (1939), Syme treated the Late Republic and the Augustan regime with cold realism and a biting wit. His work is much indebted to the German prosopographers, Friedrich Münzer and Matthias Gelzer.

The Romans talked a great deal about liberty, but they did not believe in equality. Holding a monopoly on *dignitas*, the nobles were convinced that they were superior to the commons. The masses, in turn, deferred to the nobility and asked only that worthy commoners be permitted to infiltrate its ranks. For the most part, wealthy commoners were content to marry their daughters to unimportant nobles. Not infrequently, the nobles allowed able and ambitious commoners to attain political office, but few reached the consulship, and back-bench senators were expected to be grateful to the great families who had backed them. Within the prestigious ranks of the Senate, the nobles formed a privileged group, an oligarchy within an oligarchy. This small circle, the *nobiles*, were the real rulers of Rome.[51]

Originally the nobles of Rome were patricians, but plebeians had attained consulships even in the early Republic, and noble status was conferred on all who had served as consuls and on their descendants. The proportion of patricians dwindled slowly until the nobility were actually a blend of patrician and plebeian families, separated from the rest of Roman society by the aura of the consulship. Perhaps the early Romans had included praetors in the ranks of the nobility, but the nobles of the Late Republic were all consuls or descendants of consuls. A patrician name was always a source of pride, and certain religious offices were reserved for patricians, but those whose families had fallen on evil days were in effect *declassé* and outranked by the great plebeian nobles. Whether patrician or plebeian in origin, the nobles were haughty and insisted on their right to monopolize consulships and positions of power in the state. Generally, the status-conscious Roman commons acceded to them. The source of the nobles' wealth was landed estates, and they were forbidden by law to engage in trade or finance, though money-hungry nobles circumvented the prohibition through dummy corporations. As the class that supplied Rome with most of its generals and governors, the nobles found additional sources of income in war booty and provincial extortion. Ideally, the Roman noble was a man of the soil, his mind unsullied by sordid affairs of commerce and finance, but it was considered proper for him to loot the property of Rome's enemies and accumulate a fortune in graft as long as he was not flagrant about it.

Among the great noble families, certain patrician houses had particular luster. In the early Republic, the Fabii wielded great power and continued to do so through the end of the third century B.C. The fortunes of

---

[51] The key work on this important topic is Matthias Gelzer's *Die Nobilität der römischen Republik*, 1912, now available in his *Kleine Schriften* (Wiesbaden: Franz Steiner Verlag, 1962), I, 15–135. It has been translated by Robin Seager (Oxford: Blackwell, 1969). See also Friedrich Münzer, *Römische Adelsparteien und Adelsfamilien* (Stuttgart: J. B. Metzlersche Verlagsbuchhandlung, 1920).

the Valerii were more varied. In the middle of the third century, the Aemilii suffered an eclipse but rallied and drew new strength through an alliance with the Cornelii, of whom the Scipios are most renowned. Originally a Sabine clan, the Claudii were famed for their pride, and "there was no epoch of Rome's history but could show a Claudius intolerably arrogant towards the *nobles* his rivals, or grasping personal power under cover of liberal politics." [52] Perhaps Syme's judgment is too harsh, but the Claudii did supply Roman history with some of its most colorful personalities. Less prestigious but nonetheless powerful were the great plebeian noble houses, such as the Semperonii Gracchi, who produced three consuls, a censor, and two memorable tribunes.

When the nobility opened its ranks to allow another plebeian to enter, the new consul was considered a "new man" (*novus homo*) who had to prove himself. Though their responses differed, Cato the Elder, Marius, and Cicero were all uncomfortable as *novi homines*. Cato resented the superior attitude of the hereditary nobles and openly attacked them, but few "new men" had the nerve or inclination to play such a role; most followed the same path as Cicero and ingratiated themselves as staunch supporters of the Establishment. Their sons, who did not suffer the disability of being *arrivistes*, were quietly absorbed into the hereditary nobility. The number of "new men" to hold the consulship from 367 to the end of the Republic is not certain, but it was not large and only fifteen are specifically called *novi homines*. After the Second Punic War, the nobility was quite restrictive:

> The effective government was in the hands of some ten or twenty families. Of the 108 consuls between 200 and 146 B.C. only eight came from new families, and perhaps only four were strictly *novi homines*, two of whom were helped by aristocratic friends, Cato by Valerius Flaccus, Glabrio by the Scipios. Sallust remarks that the nobility passed on the consulship from one to another. Of the 200 consuls, who held office from 234 to 134 B.C., 159 were members of twenty-six families, 99 of ten families.[53]

Such statistics reveal the essential pattern of Roman politics under the Republic.

In noble families, it was expected that males would serve the Republic in both military and political capacities, hopefully in the highest magistracies. A young man who showed little interest in either role would not only disgrace the family name but also weaken their power in the state, for every family wished to be represented as much as possible

---

[52] Syme, *The Roman Revolution*, p. 19. Cf. Suetonius *Tiberius* 1–2.
[53] Howard H. Scullard, *A History of the Roman World from 753 to 146 B.C.*, 3rd ed. (London: Methuen, 1961), p. 325. Cf. Sallust *Bellum Jugurthinum* 63.6.

in the Senate, the army, and the public offices. Few young nobles lagged in the pursuit of public careers. As children, noble boys were educated for public service by their fathers and family elders. In early Rome, senators brought their adolescent sons to hear debates in the Senate, but the custom was no longer observed in the second century B.C. Oratory was an important weapon in political life, and the scions of noble houses were trained in the art of persuasive pleading. Since future generals needed to know a minimum of astronomy to calculate time at night, a superficial acquaintance with science was also part of the boys' education. By the third century, schools for the rich had appeared in Rome, but most noble families preferred to have Greek tutors, either hired or slave, to teach their children literature and academic matters. Because the Romans read aloud while reading, the family was aware of the content of the books studied. For the most part, the nobility of Rome was reasonably well educated, but the camp and the Forum were considered the greatest schools of all.

To a young noble, the family was paramount, and he was carefully conditioned to consider its *dignitas* and advancement the main interest of his life. From earliest childhood, he was indoctrinated with the glorious deeds of his ancestors and the need for him to add further honors to the family. When one of the prominent men of the family died and was given a public funeral in the Forum, eulogists recounted the greatness of the deceased and the glories of his ancestors. These long-dead heroes were not vague abstractions, for the boys had seen their faces displayed in their homes. In the funeral procession, the ancient dead actually came alive, as Polybius describes in his discussion of a nobleman's funeral at Rome:

> Afterward, when they have buried him and have performed the customary ceremonies, they place the image of the deceased in the most prominent place in the house, enclosed in a small wooden box. This image is a mask, made with extreme fidelity both in its modeling and in its coloring. They bring these images out at public sacrifices and decorate them handsomely; and when some notable man of the family passes away, they bear the images to his funeral and put them on men who seem most like those whose masks they wear, in build and general appearance. These men also put on togas; if the deceased held the office of a consul or praetor, the togas have a purple border; if he was a censor, they are solid purple; if he held a triumph or won other military honors, they are embroidered in gold. The men themselves proceed in chariots; in front of them are carried *fasces,* axes, and the other insignia that customarily accompany the several offices, the ones used in the procession being chosen according to the rank of political office attained by each man in life. When they arrive at the Rostra, they all sit down in a row on ivory chairs. It would not be easy to behold a more inspiring sight to a young man who is ambitious

Patrician with busts of his ancestors. Rome, Palazzo Barberini. *Alinari—Scala.*

for glory and admires the good generally. Indeed, who would not be moved at seeing in one place all the images of men famous for their character, looking as if they were alive and breathing? [54]

If the spectacle was inspiring to young men, its effect on young children must have been tremendous. To the Roman mind, the dead were never really gone. Their ghosts hovered in the house, their masks stared down on the living, and at public funerals, the dead walked again in the Forum. Every Roman noble knew that one day he would join the eternal parade.

[54]Polybius 6.53.1—10, trans. Chambers, ed. Badian, p. 262.

The obsession of the nobles with increasing the power and glory of the family was intensified by such means as masks and eulogies. Their devotion was further sharpened by the fact that self-interest and unbridled ambition could be cloaked under the socially acceptable motive of adding to the family's fame. The epitaph of Cn. Cornelius Scipio Hispanus, who was praetor in 139 B.C., epitomizes the identification with the family which all nobles felt:

> By my good conduct I heaped virtues on the virtues of my clan; I begat a family and sought to equal the exploits of my father. I upheld the praise of my ancestors, so that they are glad that I was created of their line. My honors have ennobled my stock.[55]

To die without adding to the family's capital of prestige was a cause for grief almost equal to the pain of personal loss. When one of the sons of Scipio Africanus died young, his epitaph expressed regret that the deceased had not won his "destined" place in life:

> Death caused all your virtues, your honor, good report and valiance, your glory and your talents to be short-lived. If you had but been allowed long life in which to enjoy them, an easy thing it would have been for you to surpass by great deeds the glory of your ancestors. Wherefore, O Publius Cornelius Scipio, begotten son of Publius, joyfully does Earth take you to her bosom.[56]

His sister, Cornelia, compensated for the glories that Publius failed to attain, for she was the mother of the Gracchi.

Among the Roman nobility, women too served the interests of the family. Mothers impressed family pride on their children, and daughters could anticipate marriages of political convenience, for alliances between the families were tightened with marital bonds. In the interest of politics, it was common for prominent men to put aside wives of many years in order to marry a woman related to a new ally. The effect of such loveless marriages and divorces without cause was considerable on the women involved as well as on their children. Some women resented being pawns and became promiscuous, betraying the unwanted spouse, but most women stoically accepted their lot as necessary for the good of the family. Even a cynical marriage of convenience might develop into a lasting love, as did Pompey's marriage to Caesar's daughter, Julia. When Cicero's daughter, Tullia, died, his friend Servilius Sulpicius Rufus tried to comfort him with words that summarized a Roman noble's view of a woman's life well-lived:

---

[55] *ROL*, IV, 9.   [56] *ROL*, IV, 5.

> She saw you, her father, elected praetor, then consul, then augur; she had been successfully the bride of more than one youth of the highest rank; she enjoyed almost every blessing in life; with the fall of the Republic, she ceased to live. What reason have either you or she for quarreling with fortune on this score? [57]

Rufus tactfully avoided the realities of Tullia's life. Married at thirteen, she lost her first child and was a widow at twenty-one; her second marriage ended in divorce, and her third marriage was extremely unhappy. As a *novus homo,* Cicero had forced his daughter into the first two marriages with noble families; his wife had engineered the third. Many women of the hereditary nobility had lives no happier than Tullia's.

At Rome, much political maneuvering was actually family politics. The great families gloried in their own successes and relished the frustration inflicted on their rivals. Competition for high offices was fierce. When oratory and clientage failed to sway sufficient voters, bribery was freely employed, and the word for canvassing for office (*ambitio*) begat the word for bribery (*ambitus*). To succeed in politics, noble families needed alliances with other great houses, and thus marriage was an important weapon in the struggle. Linked by marital bonds, the families formed powerful coalitions, and the Romans would have appreciated Sir Robert Peel's angry complaint that the Whig leaders were all cousins. Besides his relatives, a Roman politician relied upon his friends for mutual support. This bond of friendship was called *amicitia,* but opponents called it *factio.* In ancient Rome, there were no political parties or organized groups with opposing ideologies, nor was there any lasting conflict between the Senate and the people. The moving force of Roman political life was the struggle of noble factions. In the Late Republic, nobles who openly sought popular support in the Tribal Assembly were labeled *populares,* but they were still nobles, jealous of their *dignitas,* and even the *novi homines* were wealthy men of the minor gentry. The masses might support a particular faction, but the commons did not initiate political movements. For the most part, the Roman electorate gave its loyalty to the families and the factions.

Historical analogies are often misleading, but H. H. Scullard aptly compares Republican Rome with eighteenth-century England:

> A Roman noble of the time of Cato might not have felt much out of his element in England during the period of the Whig oligarchy under the first two Georges when "about seventy great families, in alliance or in rivalry among themselves, exercised the power and patronage of the State." . . . The Roman nobles had their equivalents to "pocket," "rotten," and

---

[57] Cicero *ad Familiares* 4.5.5.

"crown" boroughs, and they resembled the "big landowners who, if united, were the deciding influence in 39 out of 40 English counties." *Mutatis mutandis,* two observations could well be applied to Rome: "About 1750 there were no parties in our sense of the term. . . . Eighteenth-century administrations, not being able to control individual members through a party machine and a party-trained electorate, had to bind their following by posts of honor, places of benefit, contracts, and pensions"; and "the number of men in the Parliament of 1761 who were unsupported by family, party, or local connections, but sat merely because they had money and were prepared to spend it on elections, was exceedingly small." [58]

A major difference between the two systems, similar though the ruling groups were, was the military side of the Roman magistracies.

Though all ruling elites want power, prestige, and profit, the Roman nobility had an additional aim—glory in arms. The frequent wars of Rome provided ample opportunities to win glory, both for the individual and for the family. No doubt booty was a factor in many generals' minds, but everlasting fame was the greatest prize of war. The supreme moment of a Roman noble's life was his public celebration of a triumph, a custom borrowed from the Etruscans. At the head of his troops, the victorious consul led a festive parade through the Forum, displaying prominent captives and booty to the cheering multitude. As *triumphator,* his robe was purple embroidered with gold, his head was wreathed with laurel, and his face was painted red to match the color of the statue of Jupiter, for the conqueror was temporarily a god king. The celebrant rode in a special chariot with his children about him and a slave behind him to whisper, "Remember that you are mortal." At the foot of the Capitoline hill, the triumphal parade ended, and the general climbed the steps of the Temple of Jupiter Optimus Maximus to report his victory to the god; that night, he dined in the temple. So impressive was the total effect that the Senate claimed the prerogative to approve triumphs, and funds for them could be withheld from an uncooperative commander. Every noble boy dreamed of the day when he could celebrate a triumph, and in later years he was not averse to military adventures that might fulfill his dream. Though the origins of any war are complex, the decision-making groups at Rome contained men whose deliberations on war and peace were influenced by the hopes of triumphs.

In 221 B.C., a great public funeral was held for L. Caecilius Metellus, who had been twice consul, once dictator, and was Pontifex Maximus

---

[58] Howard H. Scullard, *Roman Politics 220–150 B.C.* (Oxford: Clarendon Press, 1951), p. 30. The second quotation is from Lewis Namier's classic study of British politics under George III.

when he died. His son, Quintus, delivered a glowing eulogy, listing the splendid career of his father and noting that he had been the first Roman ever to display elephants in his triumph. Warming to the occasion, the orator declared that Metellus had achieved the ten greatest aims for which wise men strive all their lives: He had been able to be a superior warrior, a great orator, and a brave general; to direct matters of great import, to enjoy the highest honors, to be very wise, to be considered the most eminent member of the Senate, to gain wealth in an honorable fashion, to leave many children, and to attain the highest distinction in the state.[59] Such were the ideals of the Roman nobility—to serve one's self and one's family by serving the Republic. Brave and proud, the great families sent forth their men to die for Rome if need be, but enough returned to add their laurels to the immortal glory of the family. Vain and factious, they also warped the course of history with their bitter feuds and boundless ambition.

[59] Pliny the Elder *Naturalis Historia* 7.139–140.

CHAPTER FOUR

The path of empire

There is, I trust, no one so sluggish and dull as not to be curious how, and because of what qualities in Roman government, practically the whole inhabited world in less than fifty-three years [220–167 B.C.] fell completely under the control of Rome—the like of which, it will be found, has never happened before.[1]

Actually it took a little longer for Rome to secure mastery of the Mediterranean world. Though he posed a meaningful question, Polybius's answer that Roman success was due to the virtues of the mixed constitution is simplistic nonsense. There is no single answer, for there was no inexorable march to victory, no master plan of imperial expansion. The cumulative effect of Roman success is so startling that it gives an illusory impression of continuity. In reality, the causes of Rome's many wars were varied, and theorizing on Roman imperialism should be deferred until Rome's rise to supremacy has been described.

THE WORLD BEYOND ITALY

Roman conquests did not take place in a vacuum, and it is advisable to survey briefly the nations that succumbed. Whether rivals or victims, Rome's foes were more than just foils for the imperial Republic. With the submission of the Samnites, Rome was the major power in Italy, though the Gauls in the Po Valley and the Greek cities of the South were still free of the Roman yoke.[2] Across the straits of Messana lay the troubled towns of Sicily, caught between the power plays of Syracuse and Carthage. When King Agathocles died of cancer of the jaw in 289 B.C., the Syracusan domination of Greek Sicily dissolved, and ty-

[1] Polybius 1.1.5, trans. Chambers, ed. Badian, p. 1.
[2] For the cities and culture of Magna Graecia, see above, pp. 25–36. The misadventures of Pyrrhus in Italy are described in the present chapter, pp. 116–17.

rants seized power in many cities. At Messana, a band of Campanian mercenaries, the Mamertines (Sons of Mars), took over the strategic town. Seeking to profit from the chaos, the Carthaginians invaded the eastern part of the island and attacked Syracuse. In desperation, the Greeks appealed for aid to Pyrrhus of Epirus, who was bogged down in a war with Rome and was anxious to leave Italy. In 278, the king and his troops arrived in Sicily and drove the Carthaginians back until only the great naval stronghold of Lilybaeum was in Punic hands. However, Pyrrhus was high-handed with his allies, and the Greeks soon asked their obnoxious savior to leave. In the aftermath of Pyrrhus's fiasco, many Greek cities returned to their alliances with Carthage.

After Pyrrhus departed in 276, the major figure in Sicilian affairs was the Syracusan general Hiero who had risen from humble beginnings. By 269, he had inflicted a major defeat on the Mamertines, though he did not take Messana. Buoyed by success, he assumed a royal title as Hiero II and dominated the Greeks of western Sicily. For half a century, Hiero ruled Syracuse with benevolence and efficiency, and the Sicilians willingly accepted his leadership. Unlike the bloody rulers of the past, Hiero had seized and maintained power without killing, exiling, or injuring anyone, and more than once, the Syracusans refused to let him abdicate his throne.[3] In his domains the king farmed the collection of taxes to municipal leaders, who collected most payments in kind. If the harvest was poor, Hiero took a loss, for his share was ten percent of the crop. Generally the system worked fairly. In 215, the beloved king died at over ninety years of age. Under his regime, Syracuse had prospered as a center of commerce and shipbuilding. The docks of the city were equipped with great cranes, and Hiero's workmen were capable of constructing enormous ships like the 4,000-ton "Lady of Syracuse." Built for ostentation, the mammoth vessel was a white elephant and Hiero soon renamed it "Lady of Alexandria" and sent it off to Ptolemy IV, who also fancied big boats. Syracuse produced a major poet in Theocritus, who got little patronage from Hiero, left Sicily, and graced the Ptolemaic court. In his *Idylls,* Theocritus wrote lovingly of the Sicilian countryside, its green hills mottled by flocks of sheep while the warm summer sun shone down on a shimmering sea. The poet also wrote amusing sketches of urban life in sprawling Alexandria. Though he neglected Theocritus, Hiero appreciated science and technology and supported the research of Archimedes, the greatest scientist of the Hellenistic era. A kinsman of the king, Archimedes excelled in both theoretical mathematics and practical mechanics. The founder of the science of hydrostatics, he devised the "endless screw,"

---

[3] Polybius 7.8.1–8.

which was used to pump water from mines in Spain and is still employed by the fellahin of Egypt. With pulleys and levers, Archimedes was able to move huge weights with the aid of a single boy. After a disastrous brush with Rome during the First Punic War, Hiero utilized Archimedes' talents to fortify Syracuse with an amazing array of weapons that held a Roman army at bay in the Second Punic War.

Opposite Sicily in Tunisia lay the city of Carthage, the greatest power in the Western Mediterranean and the most important Semitic state since Assyria. Late in the ninth century, Phoenicians from Tyre had founded Kart-Hadasht ("New Town") as a trading post near the site of modern Tunis. The traditional date of 814 B.C. was established by Timaeus, who consulted Tyrian sources and recounts the tale of a princess, Elissa, who fled from Tyre with her followers. After visiting Cyprus, Elissa led the immigrants to North Africa, where she founded Carthage and voluntarily perished in a ritual fire.[4] Timaeus adds that the Africans called Elissa Dido, a name later immortalized by Vergil who cast her as the tragic queen loved and deserted by Aeneas. If she was anything like her grandaunt Jezebel, Elissa was probably made of sterner stuff than Vergil's Dido. In any case, archeology confirms Phoenician settlements at Carthage in the eighth century. Though the territory of Carthage never expanded beyond Tunisia, the city gradually built a great commercial empire and a loose hegemony over other Phoenician towns, such as nearby Utica, Motya in Sicily, and Gades in Spain. Subject to Carthage were the Berbers of Numidia and later the tribes of southern Spain. Like their Phoenician forebears, the Carthaginians were accomplished sailors, and their ships ranged far afield in search of trade. Though primarily carriers, they produced cheap imitations of Greek goods to barter to the barbarians of the West. The Carthaginians, despite their image as merchants, were skillful farmers, and Tunisia was filled with rich plantations worked by natives who were restless under Punic taskmasters.

The men who made policy at Carthage were both merchant princes and plantation owners; thus it is difficult to identify a commercial group favoring expansion and a rural block advocating isolation, but there were military families who were interested in imperial adventures. Originally the city had been ruled by kings, who were soon replaced by two executives (suffetes), elected annually by the people. As at Rome, an aristocratic senate was the decision-making body of Carthage. When the suffetes and the senate disagreed, the matter was submitted to a popular assembly. Unlike Roman consuls, the suffetes did not exercise military

---

[4] Felix Jacoby, *Die Fragmente der Griechischen Historiker* (Leiden: Brill, 1950), Vol. IIIB, No.566 F 82. Cf. Josephus *Contra Apionem* 1.18.125.

authority. The Carthaginian senate entrusted its armies to professional generals, who were not limited to one-year commands but often paid for defeat with their lives. Despite the hazards of failure, Punic generals enjoyed great power in the field, and a board of 100 or 104 "judges" was established to keep an eye on them. In time, the 100 judges played an increasing role in defending oligarchic control against both the commons and ambitious generals. Though the ruling class at Carthage had a reputation for venality, Aristotle admired the stability of their government, and Cicero conceded that the Punic system was praiseworthy "for 600 years." [5]

In the seventh century, Carthage established strongholds in Western Sicily, and in the sixth century Punic armies frequently campaigned on the island, often allied with one Greek city against another. Sardinia fell to the Carthaginians, who then joined the Etruscans in driving Greek settlers from Corsica. In Italy, Carthage had friendly relations with Sybaris and treaty rights on the coasts of Etruria and Latium; the first Punic-Roman treaty is dated 509 B.C. As Carthaginian power expanded, an aristocratic general, Mago, began hiring mercenaries on a large scale to avoid wasteful expenditures of Punic manpower in foreign wars. Though mercenaries were sometimes unreliable, the professionalism of Punic generals won the loyalties of the hired soldiery. Carthage also drew troop levies from its subject peoples, and the Berber horsemen of Numidia made Punic cavalry a force to be feared. The Spaniards were superb infantry, and the Balearic Islands furnished slingers who insisted on being paid in women instead of money. Most Punic armies included a number of African elephants with black mahouts. On the seas, the Carthaginians were equally formidable, for their swift warships, quinqueremes with five men to an oar, were designed for ramming. The success of Punic arms increased the prestige of the Magonid family and prompted the establishment of the 100 judges to curtail the power of the generals. The Magonids were responsible for the campaign against Gelon of Syracuse which ended catastrophically at Himera in 480 with the destruction of a Punic army and its accompanying fleet. By the middle of the fifth century, the Magonids were in eclipse.

After Himera, Carthage was limited to the western third of Sicily and turned its attention to Africa and Atlantic exploration. Earlier, the Phoenicians had sailed to Britain for tin, and now a Punic explorer, Himilco, made a voyage to the Tin Islands or at least to Brittany. Under the Magonid Hanno, another expedition explored the coast of West Africa as far as Sierra Leone, possibly to the Cameroons. A

[5] Cicero *de Republica* 1, fragment 3.

Greek version of Hanno's report of his trip has been preserved. Though some of the details are controversial, the account is a vivid tale of savages, volcanoes, prairie fires, and "hairy men called gorillas," possibly chimpanzees. In the open ocean, the Carthaginians did not dare to sail too far, but they reached the Canaries, the Madeiras, and possibly the Azores.

During much of the fifth century, the Carthaginians kept to their own sphere in Sicily and held aloof when an Athenian expedition attacked Syracuse, because the Athenians had talked rashly about conquering Carthage next. Soon after the Athenian defeat, a quarrel among the Sicilian cities resulted in an invitation for Carthage to intervene. A large Punic army landed in Sicily and was joined by many Sicels. In 409, the Carthaginians sacked Himera and three years later plundered Acragas, but these atrocities angered the other Greeks and solidified resistance. In the last phase of the Peloponnesian War, the hard-pressed Athenians negotiated with Carthage for aid against Sparta, which was allied with Syracuse. While Athens got no help from Carthage, the Punic threat panicked Syracuse and allowed Dionysius I to seize power. In 397, the tyrant launched an anti-Carthaginian war and stormed Motya. After years of sporadic warfare, Carthage and Dionysius divided Sicily at the Halycus River in 375. Sometime in the fourth century, Carthage adopted the Hellenic institution of an elite hoplite corps of 3,000 citizens, the Sacred Band. In the chaos that followed the fall of the house of Dionysius, the Sacred Band was sent to fight in Sicily, but Timoleon's troops annihilated them in 341, and Carthage returned to its old reliance on mercenaries. In 339, the Halycus boundary was restored. Late in the fourth century, Carthage clashed with Agathocles and landed a force to besiege Syracuse, but the wily tyrant invaded Africa in 310 and threatened Carthage itself. Although a general called Bomilcar attempted an abortive coup within the city, the Carthaginians survived the strain of the siege and watched impassively as Agathocles' troops ravaged the countryside. The invaders had underestimated Punic tenacity, and in 307 Agathocles abandoned the siege. Though his invasion had been a fiasco, the Syracusan tyrant had grasped the strategy that one day Rome would use against Hannibal.

At the height of its power, the city of Carthage probably had a population of about 400,000, including slaves. Most of the populace was of Semitic descent, but there were also a large number of Berbers and some Greeks and Negroes. Though Punic clothing was Near Eastern in design, Hellenic influence was considerable in art and architecture. The conservative Carthaginians worshiped the gods of Canaan: Melqart of Tyre, Eshmoun the healing god of Sidon, and the ubiquitous Baal. However, the most popular deities were Baal Hammon, who was a blend of Canaanite and African agricultural gods, and his consort, Tanit (the Face of Baal), who was a goddess of the moon and fertility. The prominence of Baal Hammon and Tanit may reflect the African orientation of Carthage in the fifth century and the growing importance of agricultural factors. Since the gods of Canaan were bloodthirsty, the precinct of Tanit contained a *topheth* where pious Carthaginians burned their children to honor Baal. Many mothers refused to sacrifice their babies, however, and animals and birds were sometimes substituted. During the siege by Agathocles, the Punic government discovered that wealthy families had been offering slave children in place of their own, and hence the invaders were seen as instruments of divine wrath. To appease the angry gods, two hundred babies were chosen from the best families and "passed through the fire to Baal." In a burst of piety and patriotism, three hundred more children were offered voluntarily. Apparently, the gods were satisfied, for Agathocles' siege failed. The episode revealed that not all Carthaginians were religious fanatics, but under pressure many were capable of extreme devotion to the public interest. Little is known of the literature of Carthage, which was written in a variant of the Phoenician alphabet. However, there are tantalizing references to Punic histories, and Augustine spoke highly of the books of ancient Carthage, though perhaps the African saint was prejudiced.[6] In 129 B.C., Carneades' successor as head of the Platonic Academy was a Carthaginian, Hasdrubal, who adopted the Greek name of Clitomachus. The advanced agricultural methods of Carthage prompted the Roman Senate to order a translation of Mago's manual on scientific farming. Both Aristotle and Eratosthenes praised the merits of the Carthaginian constitution, and various Greek historians of Sicily wrote pro-Punic accounts of the wars between Carthage and Rome. Roman tradition was hostile, however, and Latin writers portray the Carthaginians as a nation of hucksters—dour, venal, cruel, and crafty. To the Carthaginians, of course, the Romans were bumpkins—stiff-necked, avaricious, brutal, and treacherous.

In the Carthaginians and the Greeks of Sicily, Rome encountered civilized foes, but in Western Europe, Romans battled Celtic barbarians, kinsmen of the Gauls who had sacked Rome in 387. Spain, Gaul, Britain, and the Po Valley were inhabited by Celtic peoples, who had once occupied central Europe as well. Though Celtic prehistory is vague, archeologists have determined that about 700 B.C. the continental Celts had developed a common iron-using culture, labeled Hallstatt. Around 500 B.C., the Hallstatt culture was replaced by the La Tène culture which lasted until the Roman conquest. One distinctive feature of La

---

[6] Augustine *Epistulae* 17.2.

Tène iron work was the nailed horseshoe, which was not commonly employed in antiquity. Apparently, the shift from Hallstatt to La Tène indicated tribal movements, for the trade routes down the Rhone valley were interrupted about 500 to the detriment of Massilia and the profit of the Etruscans, whose commerce with the Celts increased. About 400, Celts from Austria overwhelmed the Etruscan settlements in the Po Valley, which in time became known as Cisalpine Gaul. Other Gauls sacked Rome, and a century later a Gallic horde moved through the Balkans, assaulted Macedon and Greece, and attacked Delphi in 279. Another Celtic host crossed into Asia Minor and eventually settled in the interior, giving their name to the region which became known as Galatia.

To the Romans and Greeks, the Celts seemed fierce blond giants. Tall and well-built, the men wore their hair long and had prominent mustaches. The Celts loved bright clothing, and the males wore trousers and short cloaks in winter. An emotional outgoing people, they were famed for hospitality, boasting, and heavy drinking. Though beer was the national beverage, wine was preferred, and Greek merchants did a lively business shipping liquor to the thirsty Celts, who would trade a slave for a jar of wine. According to Greek visitors, the Celts were lecherous, and homosexuality was common among them. In battle, the barbarians carried great iron swords and huge shields, and some wore helmets with horns. Though armor was not uncommon, many Celts fought naked even in winter, trusting to magic charms to divert the weapons of the enemy. The frenzy of Celtic warriors frightened civilized foes, and their war chants unnerved Roman veterans. The Celts also collected heads, and every warrior's lodge was decorated with grisly trophies. After a victory, they would bury booty as a gift to the gods of war. Chiefs were sometimes slain in ritual deaths, and on the funeral pyres of prominent men, wives and slaves were burned together with heaps of treasure. Human sacrifice was widespread, and Druid priests divined the future in the steaming entrails of men. On high festivals, the priests burned captives in huge wickerwood figures of men. In Gaul and Britain, the Druids were rigidly organized in a hierarchy and served as judges in disputes between both tribes and individuals. Though illiterate, the Druids committed astral lore and tribal traditions to memory. The Druids, whose shamanistic trances awed laymen, were both the Celtic intelligentsia and a dreaded corporation of priests. Probably the foolhardy bravery of Celtic warriors was due in part to confidence in the Druid doctrine of reincarnation, an intellectualization of totemic beliefs in the continuity of life and kinship with animals. In the Po Valley and the region around Massilia, some Celts acquired literacy, and the cultural influence of Greeks and Romans was considerable in border areas. The basic economy in Gaul was agricultural, and towns began to develop. In Caesar's time, aristocratic clans had reduced much of the Gallic peasantry to the status of serfs. Because the Celts never advanced beyond tribalism, and warfare between tribes was widespread, Celtic factionalism would one day be a crucial factor in easing the Roman conquest of Gaul.

In Britain, the tribes of Kent were agrarian, but in the interior, pastoralism was common. The island held rich mineral deposits, particularly tin, though copper had to be imported. Culturally, the Britons were more barbaric than their neighbors in Gaul. Communal marriages were frequent, and British warriors dyed their bodies blue. In Scotland, the tattooed savages were simply called Picts; cannibalism was reportedly practiced in Ireland. Throughout the British Isles, the Druids held sway, and Greek writers report a circular temple of Apollo where great festivities were held on the vernal equinox every nineteen years. Apparently the Druids were aware of the Metonic cycle and celebrated the reconciliation of the solar and lunar years at the great sanctuary of Stonehenge, which they had occupied. The Iberian peninsula was also in Celtic hands though much of the pre-Celtic population was probably related to the Berbers of Africa. Like the modern Spaniards, the Celtiberians were a proud people who preferred to dress in black. Though clean in every other respect, the Iberians bathed and brushed their teeth in urine. The Lusitanians of modern Portugal were fierce hill fighters who preyed on the Celtiberians. All Iberians were noted for their courage, and Spanish women would slit their children's throats to save them from Roman slavers. Despite the warlike nature of the Iberians, both Carthaginians and Romans considered Spain a worthy prize, for the land was rich in gold and silver mines. In Gibbon's words, "Spain, by a very singular fatality, was the Peru and Mexico of the old world," [7] and the ancient Spaniards suffered the same fate that their descendants would impose upon the American Indians.

North of the Alps and across the Rhine stretched the great forests of central Europe, dark, dense, and foreboding, inhabited by warlike Germans who had ousted the Celts. Though most Germans were primitive hunters, some tribes practiced agriculture. Fond of drinking and battle, the fierce Germans were feared by the Celts of Gaul. Unlike the Celts, the Germans had no established priesthood and worshiped their gods in forest clearings. Tiwaz, the war god, and Thor the Thunderer were prominent deities among the Germans, who also cherished fertility gods. Human sacrifice was widespread, and captives were often offered

[7] Edward Gibbon, *The History of the Decline and Fall of the Roman Empire*, ed. J. B. Bury (London: Methuen, 1896), I, 159.

to the gods. Like many primitive peoples, the Germans believed that continence increased a warrior's prowess, and men did not marry until the age of twenty. Rude and violent, the Germans fascinated Roman ethnographers. Tacitus describes the ethos of a German warband:

> The Germans have no taste for peace; renown is easier won among perils, and you cannot maintain a large body of companions except by violence and war. The companions are prodigal in their demands on the generosity of their chiefs. It is always "give me that war-horse" or "give me that bloody and victorious spear." As for meals with their plentiful, if homely, fare, they count simply as pay. Such open-handedness must have war and plunder to feed it. You will find it harder to persuade a German to plough the land and to await its annual produce with patience than to challenge a foe and earn the prize of wounds. He thinks it spiritless and slack to gain by sweat what he can buy with blood. When not engaged in warfare, they spend some little time in hunting, but more in idling, abandoned to sleep and gluttony. All the heroes and grim warriors dawdle their time away, while the care of house, hearth, and fields is left to the women, old men and weaklings of the family. . . . They love indolence, but they hate peace.[8]

Based on the observations of Pliny the Elder who had served on the Rhine frontier, Tacitus's account is reminiscent of the habits of the warlike tribes of North America. Such folkways are common among primitive war-oriented societies throughout the world.

Like the sun, civilization had risen in the East and slowly worked its way westward. The West was the heart of darkness, where civilized towns like Massilia or Gades were outposts on the shores of barbarism. In the central Mediterranean, civilized life flourished in Sicily and Magna Graecia, Roman Italy, and Punic Africa. However, Rome and Carthage were staid in their ways, and much of the primitive still clung to them. The two republics had become great powers without losing the habits of their youth. Despite their nation's wealth and prestige, many Romans were boorish farmers and many Carthaginians had peddlers' minds. In the Hellenistic East, civilization was an old established way of life, and men were comfortable with city living. Like farmers everywhere, the rural populace was superstitious and ignorant, but Egypt, Asia, and Greece were studded with towns where men knew books, loved art, and had broader vision. In the taverns of Alexandria, captains from Gades supped with sailors who had sailed to India, and at the Museum were scholars who could chart the stars and measure the circumference of the earth with amazing accuracy. The Hellenistic

[8] Tacitus *Germania* 14–15, trans. Harold Mattingly, *Tacitus on Britain and Germany* (London: Penguin, 1948), pp. 112–13.

world had paid a high price for sophistication. Democracy was passé, and the city-states had been gobbled up by great nations ruled by kings who were worshiped as living gods. Though trade flourished as never before, immense wealth was squandered on dynastic wars, and class conflict was an ever-present reality. If the West was a New World— rude, awkward, and rowdy—, the East was the Old World—clever, worried, and fitful. In time, the internal dissensions of the Hellenistic world would facilitate its conquest by the Romans.

After the death of Alexander the Great in 323 B.C., his generals had struggled for a generation over the disposition of his unwieldy empire and exterminated the royal family of Macedon in the process. From the fierce power struggle emerged the great kingdoms of the Hellenistic age: Ptolemaic Egypt, Seleucid Syria, and Antigonid Macedon. While Rome and Carthage fought over mastery of the West in the third century, Egypt flourished under the Ptolemies, Macedon sought to dominate Greece, and the Seleucid empire came apart in chunks. The Greek cities floundered along as best they could and sought alliances with the kings to suit the needs of the moment.

By far the richest kingdom was Egypt, which supplied vast amounts of grain for Mediterranean markets. The Ptolemies also had a monopoly on the production of papyrus, the "paper" of antiquity. To wring every possible profit from their "spear-won" land, the Ptolemies combined the canny greed of Greek business techniques with the age-old bureaucracy of Egypt. Organized for maximum production, the economy of Egypt was controlled in every minute detail by governmental decrees. The tax burden of the masses was heavy, and even the upper classes had to perform services for the state. Dominated by a Greco-Macedonian ruling class, the fellahin labored to make the Ptolemies rich, and for almost a century the natives were forbidden to bear arms. In theory, the kings of Egypt were living gods, but the later Ptolemies faced many urban riots, for the turbulent population of Alexandria ceased to fear their Macedonian rulers. A teeming international port, Alexandria was probably a city of half a million. The cultural center of the Hellenistic world was the Alexandrian Museum, a great state-supported institute for research in the humanities and science. The resident scholars included Euclid, Eratosthenes, Herophilus, Erasistratus, Archimedes, and probably Aristarchus of Samos, and they had access to the vast collection of books in the Alexandrian Library. The king also supplied condemned criminals for medical experiments. In state arsenals, skilled engineers improved on war machines, and in the countryside, the king's agronomists tried to increase agricultural production. Under the Ptolemies, Cyrene produced large quantities of silphium, a plant much used in medicine and cooking and also prized as an aphrodisiac. In the third century, Egypt was a great naval power and dominated parts of Greece and Asia Minor, but the Macedonian fleet broke the Ptolemaic attempt to rule the Eastern seas. Once a highly professional mercenary force, the Ptolemaic army became an indolent military caste and failed to protect Egypt against its enemies. Faced with a Seleucid invasion in 217, Ptolemy IV armed the Egyptian peasants and led them successfully at the battle of Raphia against the mercenaries of Antiochus III. As Ptolemaic prestige declined in the second century, peasant risings were common, for inflation was rampant and the pressure of the state was unrelenting. Falling grain prices added to Egypt's ills. The success of an absolute monarchy requires a series of able kings, but unfortunately for Egypt, the later Ptolemies were a sorry lot. Only Roman intervention saved the country from being conquered by Antiochus IV in 168. Once within the Roman sphere of influence, Egypt survived as a national entity by the sufferance of Rome.

Originally, the Seleucid empire had been the largest of the Hellenistic kingdoms, stretching from Asia Minor to the Indus Valley. Like the Ptolemies, the Seleucid kings were worshiped as living gods, but they had great difficulty holding their sprawling realm together. The Indian provinces were lost early, and Iran soon broke away; there the Parthians sought to revive the lost glories of the Persian empire and became troublesome neighbors. In central Asia, a rebel state was set up in Bactria ruled by Greek dynasts, who in the second century occupied the Punjab. The core of the Seleucid kingdom was Syria and Mesopotamia, and both regions were filled with rich farms and bustling cities, such as the twin capitals, Antioch in Syria and Seleuceia on the Tigris. Through Seleucid territory ran the great commercial routes of Asia, bringing goods from China and India; other oriental wares came by sea, and the Ptolemies too sent ships to India. Despite their potential for great wealth, the Seleucids were not always solvent, for they wasted much treasure on vain wars with Egypt, and their Near Eastern subjects had experience in withholding taxes from kings. Late in the third century, Antiochus III restored Seleucid prestige by a showy Eastern campaign and forced Parthia and Bactria to acknowledge his suzerainty. Though his hold on Bactria and Parthia soon slipped, Antiochus "the Great" had acquired a reputation as a conqueror that made Rome uneasy. In time, he came to grief at Roman hands. Under the Seleucids, Hellenic culture was popular among the urban classes of the Near East, but the wily kings took care to please the priests of Mesopotamia as well. In 167, however, Antiochus IV tried to enforce religious Hellenization on the Judaic population of Palestine. Though many Jews favored his policy, the Hasmonean family rallied the orthodox faction and resisted the king, who soon abandoned the brief persecution. After Antiochus's

Antiochus III on a silver tetra-drachm. *American Numismatic Society, New York.*

death in 163, Seleucid power waned rapidly, and the Hasmoneans took advantage of Seleucid civil wars to make Judea independent and themselves its kings. The rapid decline of the Seleucids was accelerated by the Romans, who harassed the regime in Antioch and encouraged Hasmonean separatism. By 129, the Parthians seized Mesopotamia, and the Seleucids were left with only Syria, which soon became an impotent state, torn by civil strife and beset by Arab raiders. Yet, in the palmy days of Antiochus III, the Seleucid kingdom had seemed the greatest power in the Hellenistic world.

At the crossroads of the Eastern Mediterranean lay the island of Rhodes, a major center of commerce and banking. At the entrance to the harbor of Rhodes stood a colossal statue of Apollo. The self-appointed guardians of the sea lanes, the Rhodians maintained an effective war fleet that cleared the seas of pirates. In 226, a great earthquake devastated much of the city and toppled the Colossus, but the major Hellenistic powers sent relief supplies, and Rhodes was soon rebuilt. So vital was Rhodes's role as policeman of the seas that the quarreling kingdoms had temporarily cooperated for the common good. Less savory was the reputation of the Attalid rulers of Pergamum, the dominant power in Asia Minor. Once subject to the Seleucids, Pergamum had become an independent state, and the Attalids imitated the Ptolemies in squeezing profit from their subjects. The Pergamenes exported parchment, perfume, and pitch for shipbuilding, and their brocades were justly famous. In the interior of Anatolia, the Galatians had established a warlike state that threatened both the Seleucids and Pergamum. The Seleucids bought off the barbaric Celts with subsidies, but Attalus I of Pergamum defeated them by 230 and crowned his success by assuming a royal title. An astute politician, Attalus sought Roman aid against

Macedon, and his son, Eumenes II, joined the Romans in humbling Antiochus III. Through a lackey of Rome, Eumenes was generous in donating gifts to the cities of Greece, and he immortalized a victory over the Galatians by erecting the great Altar of Zeus, which became a showpiece at Pergamum; Christians called it the "throne of Satan." [9] Like Alexandria, Pergamum boasted a large library and was later the seat of a major medical school.

Under the Antigonids, Macedon had recovered from the hectic reign of Alexander the Great, who had squandered its manpower in his grandiose wars. Though descended from the erratic Demetrius Poliorcetes, the Antigonids were responsible and popular rulers. Unlike the Ptolemies and Seleucids, they were not worshiped by their own subjects, though the Greek cities paid them divine honors. The capable Antigonus II repelled a major Celtic invasion, saved the Peloponnesus from Pyrrhus, and conquered Athens, which was occupied by a Macedonian garrison until 229 B.C. Both Antigonus and his successors struggled to reduce Greece to satellite status, and many Greek tyrants were puppets of Macedon. In 221, the able young Philip V ascended the Macedonian throne and surprised the Greeks by quickly defeating the warlike Aetolians. At a famous conference, the defeated Aetolian leaders warned Philip against "the clouds rising in the West," referring to the war then raging between Hannibal and Rome. Whoever won, the Aetolians claimed, would turn on Macedon next, and then Philip would need the help of the Greeks. [10]

The Hellenistic age was a time of steady decline for most of the cities of Greece. Outclassed by the great powers, the Hellenic towns tried to survive through alliances with the kings, who treated them as despised puppets. To endure in the new era, some cities joined federal organizations. In the Peloponnesus, the towns of the Achaean League shared federal citizenship, paid some common taxes, and provided troops for the federation. In northwestern Greece, the Aetolian League was similarly organized, but most Greeks belonged to neither confederacy. The belated experiments in federalism did not save the Greeks from being pawns in the power struggles of the day. In many cities, petty tyrants had arisen, for Greece was in a state of chronic depression and political strife was endemic. Inflation was constant, prices were high, and wages were low. Both the urban and rural poor barely subsisted, and slave competition retarded the wages of free labor. The once prosperous Greek economy had contracted as former markets became centers of production and new rivals in international trade. Ptolemaic Egypt placed prohibitive tariffs on Greek wine and olive oil. Unable to support more children,

[9] Apocalypse of John 2.13.   [10] Polybius 5.104.1–11.

the poor in Hellas exposed unwanted babies, and Polybius complained that even the rich were curtailing families in the second century.[11]

As economic stress gave rise to political unrest, class conflict racked the cities of Greece. When the masses raised the perennial cry of Greek reformers, "abolish debts and redivide the land," [12] the terrified rich turned for protection to tyrants or to Macedon, the traditional defender of property and the status quo. Once the symbol of conservatism, Sparta became the spearhead of social revolution under the controversial Cleomenes III, who abolished debts, gave land to the Spartan poor, and enlisted freed serfs in his army. In the guise of reviving the theoretical equality of the Lycurgan system, the opportunistic king had restored Sparta as a major military power in order to conquer the Peloponnesus. In the Achaean cities, his agitators promised the poor social reforms, and a number of towns submitted to Cleomenes, who failed to fulfill the pledges. When the desperate leaders of the Achaean League asked Antigonus III to intervene, the Macedonian king insisted on control of Corinth as the price of stopping the Spartan advance. In 222 at the battle of Sellasia, the Macedonians and Achaeans decisively defeated Cleomenes, who fled to Egypt and later committed suicide. At Sparta, the revolutionary system collapsed, and the Macedonian hegemony was restored in Greece. Though the Spartan Revolution had failed, the cities of Hellas were still beset with class conflict, for the distress of the poor had not been resolved, and the rich were uneasy even under the protection of Macedon. The memory of Cleomenes haunted well-to-do Greeks, who would one day welcome Rome as a bulwark against social revolution.

With its god-kings and hectic politics, the Hellenistic East held little attraction for Romans. Culturally, however, the East was far in advance of Rome. Old cultural boundaries had collapsed, and sophistication had replaced the parochialism of classical Hellas. Koine Greek was the common language of trade and government, and cosmopolitanism was general among the intelligentsia. While Rome was still a scientific backwater, Aristarchus of Samos was toying with the idea that the earth was a satellite of a stationary sun, and that the illusion of solar movement was caused by the diurnal rotation of the earth. The hypothesis created more problems than it solved, however, and Hellenistic astronomers contrived the concept of planetary motion in eccentric epicycles about a

---

[11] Polybius 36.17.7.

[12] The proposals of Hellenistic reformers were not as radical as might appear. From Solon to Agathocles, demands for the abolition of debts were common in Greek politics; redistribution of land made property owners out of paupers, and no one proposed the abolition of slavery. Nevertheless, the Romans took a dim view of Greek "radicals."

static earth and supported their views with accurate sightings and complex mathematics. Using laboratory demonstrations, the great physiolo-
gist Erasistratus refuted the Hippocratic doctrine of the four humors. In
urban centers, education was widespread among the upper and middle
classes who eagerly consumed popularizations of science and history.
Despite scientific advances, the anxiety of the age encouraged the
growth of personal religion and a lust for immortality. Mystery cults
promised a blissful afterlife to their initiates, and the Egyptian goddess
Isis was widely worshiped as the loving mother of mankind. Astronomers succumbed to the growing craze for astrology and lent it spurious
dignity as a "science."

In the Hellenistic age, the Platonic Academy surrendered to skepticism, and the most popular philosophies were escapist. According to
the Epicureans, mankind was in bondage to superstition and fear of
death, but it could be liberated by disdaining conventional religion and
seeing the universe as nothing but atoms in a void. There were no terrors in the tomb or hostile gods in heaven, only pure atomic deities remote and aloof in some faraway corner of the universe, models of philosophic detachment. Insisting that the aim of life is the avoidance of
pain, Epicurus warned his disciples against immoderation in matters of
the flesh and forbade such futile activities as politics. The Stoics, on the
other hand, viewed the universe as directed by Divine Providence, which
set each man his role to play. Since an uncomplaining performance of
duty was the paramount virtue, ambitious Stoics sought to fulfill their
obligation to Providence by serving kings as advisers. The monarchs, in
turn, appreciated the notion that the status quo was divinely ordained.
In theory, court Stoics tried to guide their employers in the paths of Divine Reason, but in reality, most were sanctimonious apologists for conservative regimes. Scientifically, the Stoics were fervent advocates of astral determinism. The liveliest philosophic sect were the Cynics,
militant anarchists who rejected all conventions as fraud and preached a
return to nature. Long-haired, barefooted, and dirty, the Cynics denounced science and society and harangued passers-by on the evils of
property. Delighting in shocking bourgeois audiences, Cynics performed
natural acts in public and begged food from the same persons they insulted. Impudent and surly, the Cynics were caustic critics of an unjust
world, but they offered no solution other than total rejection of civilization. Thus, although many Hellenistic philosophers were impressive,
wise, and even saintly individuals, none tried to remedy the glaring ills
of the world. Epicurean withdrawal was total escapism, Stoic acceptance sanctified existing evils, and Cynic antics were futile acts of despair. Though they appreciated the achievements of Greek science, the
Romans viewed Hellenistic intellectuals with suspicion, and only Stoics

were really welcome at Rome. Welcome or not, Greek cultural influence could not be avoided when the Romans increased their contacts with the Hellenistic states.

THE ROMAN CONQUEST FROM PYRRHUS TO HANNIBAL

According to Roman tradition, the men who established Rome's supremacy in the West and East were men of valor, devotion, and hardihood. No doubt most Roman soldiers were brave and reliable, but no nation has a monopoly on martial virtue. In war, numbers are usually decisive, and Rome was a formidable power both in total population and in men at arms. Few statistics have survived from antiquity, but the Roman data is better than most, and Livy often mentions census figures, which list the number of adult male citizens. Ultimately, the census figures for the third century B.C. derive from Fabius Pictor, and some seem reliable. In 280 on the eve of the war with Pyrrhus, Rome had 287,222 adult male citizens; in 264, when the First Punic War broke out, 292,334. Enormous war casualties reduced the figure to 241,212 in 246, but by 234 the postwar generation was reflected in the figure of 270,212, which agrees with Polybius's figure of 273,000 for 225.[13] These statistics suggest a Roman population of about a million at mid-century; the number of Italians was at least double that of Romans, so the total population of Italy was between three and four million. Nothing is known of the population of the Punic empire, and guesses as to the populations of the Hellenistic states are futile, for there is simply no evidence.[14] In the first century A.D., the population of Egypt was seven and a half million,[15] and it may be safely inferred that Ptolemaic Egypt and the Seleucid kingdom were more populous than Italy in the Hellenistic era, but Macedon surely had less people.

In a famous passage,[16] Polybius surveyed Roman military manpower about 225: Rome had four overstrength legions (20,800) and 1200 cavalry in the field, 20,000 infantry and 1500 cavalry in reserve at Rome, and two legions (8400) and 400 cavalry in Tarentum and Sicily, totaling 52,300 citizens under arms. With the consuls in the field were 30,-000 allied soldiers and 2000 allied cavalry; an equal force of allies were with the Roman reserves, raising the grand total of soldiers at Rome's immediate disposal to over 116,000. The pool of manpower in Roman

---

[13] Livy *Periochae* 13,19,20. Eutropius 2.18. (The census figure in Livy *Periocha* 16 is a scribal error.) Polybius 2.24.16.

[14] Mikhail Rostovtzeff, *The Social and Economic History of the Hellenistic World* (Oxford: Clarendon Press, 1941), II, 1135–42.

[15] Josephus *Bellum Judaicum* 2.385.   [16] Polybius 2.24.

Italy was large, and Polybius claims that about 94,000 more allied troops stood ready to be called. Even without this last group, the Roman and allied force of 116,000 was a formidable army by ancient standards. In a useful comparison, Toynbee observes that "the army mobilized by the Roman commonwealth in 225 B.C. . . . was nearly twice as strong as Antiochus III's army at Raphia, not much less superior than this to Ptolemy IV's army at Raphia, more than four times as strong as Antigonus Doson's army at Sellasia, and more than six times as strong as Cleomenes III's army at Sellasia." [17] At Raphia, the fate of Egypt had been at stake, and Sellasia was an all-out effort by both Macedon and Sparta. Furthermore, the bulk of the royal armies were made up of mercenaries as were the forces of Carthage, while Rome had a solid core of citizen soldiers and generally loyal Italian allies. In her wars with Carthage and the Hellenistic states, Rome enjoyed numerical superiority and the benefit of citizen soldiery. During colonial campaigns in the West, the Romans often faced greater odds, but the discipline of the legions eventually triumphed over the barbarians, whose impetuosity and factionalism negated their numbers.

Rome's first prominent opponent with a reputation beyond Italy was the warlike king of Epirus, Pyrrhus, whom Roman tradition portrays as a gallant and chivalrous foe. Though Hannibal admired him as a tactician, Pyrrhus was vain, erratic, and a bane to both Epirus and Hellas. A kinsman of Alexander the Great and once married to a daughter of Agathocles, the Epirote king was unhinged by dreams of empire and had snatched control of Macedon, only to quickly lose the country through ineptitude. At best a predatory warlord, Pyrrhus was invited to Italy by the Tarentines, who resented Roman interference in their sphere of influence. By subduing the Samnites, the Romans had found themselves on the borders of Magna Graecia and soon began meddling in Italo-Greek affairs. Menaced by hill tribes, Thurii turned to Rome for aid rather than to Tarentum, and the Romans established a garrison in the city in 282 knowing that it would infuriate the Tarentines. Probably, the intervention was prompted by plebeian politicians who sought to win glory in a possible clash with Tarentum; at any rate, many senators lacked enthusiasm for the war when it came. Summoning Pyrrhus to assist them, the Tarentines expelled the Romans from Thurii, attacked Roman ships in Tarentine waters (claiming that Rome had violated an old treaty not to sail there), and insulted Roman envoys with a coarse Greek jest.

In 280, Pyrrhus landed at Tarentum with 25,000 mercenaries and

---

[17] Arnold J. Toynbee, *Hannibal's Legacy* (London: Oxford University Press, 1965), I, 502.

twenty Indian elephants and soon defeated a Roman force near Heraclea, where the legionaries for the first time encountered elephants. Backed by the Samnites and some Greeks, the king marched on Rome, hoping to awe the Italians into joining him, but Capua and Naples closed their gates to the invaders, and at Rome even proletarians were armed to defend the Republic. Only forty miles from Rome, Pyrrhus turned back, aware that he could not storm the city. Instead, he sent an eloquent envoy, Cineas, with sufficient gold to emphasize the advantages of peace. Though Cineas was successful with the peace faction in the Senate, Appius Claudius Caecus, aged, blind, and revered, made an impassioned speech against negotiating with an undefeated enemy, and the Senate rejected Cineas's offer. The scene was dear to the hearts of Roman moralists, but even without Claudius's great speech, Rome was not about to give up Samnium or let the Tarentines go unpunished. Later, Cineas remarked that the Senate was "an assembly of kings," which may not have been a compliment. In 279, Pyrrhus won another victory over the Romans at Ausculum, but his own losses were great. Weary of Pyrrhic victories, the king began talks with Sicilian envoys who asked his aid against Carthage. Hoping to keep Pyrrhus occupied in Italy, Carthage sent Rome a sizeable subsidy in silver, and both republics signed a vaguely worded alliance that did not commit Rome to fight in Sicily. Leaving a force in Tarentum, Pyrrhus moved his operations to Sicily in 278. Two years later, he returned crestfallen to Italy and was defeated by the Romans at Beneventum. In 275, the king withdrew to Hellas, where he died ingloriously. By 272, Tarentum submitted to Rome, and the rest of Magna Graecia soon followed suit. The territory of the Samnites was reduced, and the Samnite League was dissolved. All Italy below the Po Valley was now under Roman control, and in 268 on the Adriatic coast at the southern tip of the Po Valley, a Latin colony was established at Ariminum to keep an eye on the Gauls. The Roman victory over Pyrrhus did not go unnoticed in the Hellenistic East, and ambassadors were soon exchanged between Rome and Ptolemaic Egypt.

According to the Sicilian historian Philinus, Rome had agreed by treaty (probably in 306) not to intrude into Sicily without being invited by Carthage. Though Polybius denied that such an agreement had been made, the treaty is likely enough, and in any case the Roman-Punic alliance of 279 implied that the island was a Punic sphere of influence. However, a squabble at Messana brought the allies into confrontation with each other. Menaced by Hiero II, the Mamertines who controlled Messana asked a passing Punic fleet for aid. When the Carthaginians landed, Hiero withdrew but the Mamertines feared that their rescuers might try to make Messana a Punic naval base. Accordingly, the Mamertines offered to become allies of Rome. Though the city had strategic value at the straits between Sicily and Italy, the Mamertines were an unsavory crew, and Rome had recently suppressed similar freebooters at Rhegium. More importantly, intervention at Messana could mean war with Carthage, and the Senate was divided on what action to take. Following Fabius Pictor, Polybius claims that the Senate equivocated and the consul, Appius Claudius Caudex, persuaded the war-weary voters of the Tribal Assembly to approve the alliance as beneficial for the masses. Perhaps the prospect of booty was appealing, for the Mamertines' contribution to Rome's military pool would not have substantially reduced the obligations of the Roman commons. However, Fabius's account exonerated the Senate from responsibility for a dubious adventure, and Livy says that the Senate, not the people, decided the issue after a spirited debate.[18] As economic exploitation of defeated foes was not yet part of the Roman system, the motives of the war faction would seem to have been the prospect of glory for commanders and booty for the troops. In 264, Appius Claudius Caudex led a Roman force to Messana, but the Carthaginians had already evacuated the town. Furious over the loss of face, the Punic government executed the admiral who had abandoned Messana, and declared war on Rome for violating the treaty of 306 (or 279). Convinced that the Italian power had designs on Sicily, Carthage was reluctantly drawn into a war for which many Romans had little enthusiasm. Meanwhile, Hiero had joined the Carthaginians against the common enemy, and Claudius declared war on Rome's behalf against Syracuse and Carthage. When the Romans marched against Syracuse in 263, Hiero abandoned his Punic allies, made peace with Rome, and became an ally of the invaders. During the First Punic War, Syracuse made a handsome profit selling supplies to the Romans.

For a generation, Rome and Carthage were locked in mortal combat over control of Sicily. The struggle cost the Romans many casualties and much treasure but the prize was worth it. Ironically, Carthage the Mistress of the Seas fared badly in naval engagements, and her most successful endeavors were on land. Caught between the Romans and Carthaginians were the Greeks, who preferred to be left alone but considered Carthage less of a menace than Rome. In 262, the Romans sacked the city of Acragas to impress the Greeks with the folly of supporting the African power. In western Sicily, the Carthaginians had two major naval bases, Lilybaeum and Drepana, and Rome needed a fleet to wrest control of the seas from Carthage. Though her traditions were that of a land power and her naval experience limited, Rome quickly acquired 120 quinqueremes built in record time by the master ship-

---

[18] Livy *Periocha* 16.

builders of Syracuse and Magna Graecia; Greek pilots also served with the fleet.[19] Because the Punic captains were experts at ramming, the Romans equipped their new battleships with boarding bridges, closed with the enemy, and sent marines over the bridges to battle on the decks of the Punic vessels. Within the next few years, the Romans won an impressive series of naval victories, seized Corsica, and increased the size of their fleet. In 256, the consul M. Atilius Regulus invaded Africa and laid siege to Carthage, but the Carthaginians rallied to the threat and hired a Spartan condottiere, Xanthippus, who used a frontal attack by elephants and flanking attacks by cavalry to all but annihilate Regulus's legions in 255. The ill-fated consul died in captivity and became a martyr in Roman folklore. Most of the Roman ships that carried away the survivors were lost in a storm at sea. In 253, another Roman fleet was destroyed in a tempest, but in Sicily the Romans held most of the island and threatened Lilybaeum.

In 249, the consul P. Claudius Pulcher suffered a major naval defeat off Drepana and was recalled to Rome and fined. Pious Romans viewed the disaster as divine punishment for sacrilege. While consulting the omens, Claudius had grown angry when the sacred chickens did not eat, and he had tossed the birds overboard. However, Claudius's pious colleague also suffered a defeat at Punic hands and lost his remaining ships in a storm. Yet Carthage could not take advantage of the Roman disasters, for Hanno "the Great" had persuaded the Punic government to concentrate on Tunisia and suppress rebellious tribes in the interior. The Punic fleet was recalled to Carthage to use the crews as infantry. Nevertheless, the energetic Hamilcar Barca harassed the Romans in Sicily and raided the Italian coasts. Resolving to end the costly war, the Senate floated a major war loan, payable upon victory, and built a new fleet, which blockaded Drepana and in 241 drove off a Punic attempt to relieve the base. At Carthage, Hanno's faction pressed for peace, and Hamilcar was authorized to negotiate an end to the war. Though Hamilcar agreed to the evacuation of Sicily and the payment of 2200 talents in twenty annual instalments, the Senate increased the indemnity to 3300 talents payable in ten instalments and added new stipulations: Carthage could not recruit mercenaries in Italy or sail in Roman waters, and Rome was to receive not only Sicily but the isles between Sicily and Italy (obviously the Lipari Islands). Exhausted by the long war, Carthage accepted the peace terms, for possession of Sicily was not essential for the African city. For Carthage, the First Punic War had been

[19] Polybius repeats the silly tale that the Romans built the ships themselves, using as a model the hulk of a wrecked Punic warship, and trained the crews on benches on dry land. So perverse and unnecessary a procedure would be difficult to imagine.

expensive and humiliating. The Romans had won Sicily and a large indemnity which paid off the war loan, but the census figures for 246 suggest that the Roman war effort had cost the lives of 50,000 citizens and who knows how many allied lives.

In the immediate aftermath of the war, Carthage received two more crippling blows, one self-inflicted, the other dealt by Rome. When Hamilcar's mercenaries returned to Carthage and demanded their back wages, the Punic government (perhaps influenced by Hanno) refused to pay them, for the war was over and Carthage needed money to meet the indemnity to Rome. Outraged, the mercenaries mutinied, and dissatisfied natives in Libya and Numidia joined them in a major revolt. On Sardinia, other mercenaries rebelled. Unable to handle the crisis, Hanno was replaced by Hamilcar who tried to treat captives leniently, but the rebel leaders began systematic atrocities, and the mercenaries' revolt soon became a truceless war with savage cruelties inflicted by both sides. Ignoring the provisions of the treaty of 241, Rome allowed Carthage to recruit reliable mercenaries in Italy, and Hamilcar was able to crush the African rebellion by 237. When Hamilcar was about to move against the rebels on Sardinia, Rome suddenly announced jurisdiction over the island and declared war on Carthage, claiming that Sardinia was one of the "isles between Sicily and Italy." Furthermore, the Romans insisted on an additional indemnity of 1200 talents. Her fleet lost in the First Punic War, her treasury depleted by the mercenaries' revolt, Carthage could only capitulate and accept the Roman *Diktat*. Even the pro-Roman Polybius admits that Rome had committed a shameless act of piracy. Unwittingly, Rome had laid the foundations for the Second Punic War, for every Punic patriot now ached for revenge against the predatory Italians. Apparently Corsica had been in Roman hands since the recent war; though not stipulated in 237, it, too, fell to Rome. On Sardinia, the natives were not pleased with their new masters, but when they rebelled, the Romans hunted them down with fierce hounds.

In acquiring overseas possessions, Rome had become an imperial power, but her institutions were ill-designed for such responsibilities. In Sicily, Syracuse and Messana were allied territories, and Hiero controlled about a quarter of the island. For services rendered to Rome in the First Punic War, a few other Greek cities received favored treatment with regard to taxes, but former Punic holdings became the public property of Rome, and the remaining half of Sicily became a tribute-paying province, owned by the Roman people. Rather than adding new allies as in Italy, the Romans had embarked on a momentous course, the results of which could not be perceived at the time. Rome did not need additional allied troops, and the Sicilians were accustomed to paying taxes to either Hiero or Carthage. Always pragmatic, the Romans simply left existing conditions unchanged with the exception that the revenue now went to Rome. Adopting Hiero's tax system, the Romans imposed a ten percent tithe on the harvest, cash payments on grazing stock, and five percent harbor dues. The collection of taxes was farmed out to local leaders, for Rome had no bureaucracy to handle such problems. A similar system was applied in Sardinia and Corsica. For the time being, the Roman yoke was light on the Sicilians, but later Roman businessmen would bid on the tax contracts, and the provinces would be plundered unmercifully by the publicans. The aftermath of the First Punic War also forced Rome to expand its magistracies. A second praetorship was created to deal with non-citizens at Rome; though his duties were essentially judicial, the praetor peregrinus held *imperium* and entered the Senate after his year in office. In 227, two more praetorships were established to serve as provincial governors, one in Sicily, the other in Sardinia-Corsica. Like all elected officials of Rome, the praetors received no salary, though the Republic paid for their expenses while on duty. Served by a small staff of friends, the praetor wielded great power in his province and could enforce his decrees with troops. In the Mediterranean world, the bribery of officials is a time-honored custom, and Roman governors always welcomed gifts from loyal provincials, but at times the gifts were involuntary, and many Roman nobles viewed a governorship as an opportunity to extort a fortune from defenseless people.

Internally, the Republic felt the strains of the First Punic War. The citizen soldiers, who had fought so long and well, demanded a greater role in the Centuriate Assembly, the stronghold of timocracy. Soon after the war, the centuries were somehow reorganized in favor of the middle classes. The details are vague and confusing, and no modern explanation is wholly satisfactory. Probably the total number of centuries remained the same, but the "light infantry," received ten additional centuries at the expense of the "heavy infantry," and primacy in voting was moved from the *equites* to one of the "heavy infantry" centuries chosen by lot. Thus, if a majority was not reached early, even the lower centuries might participate, but the weight of votes still lay with the property-owning classes. Apparently, the "reform" was in the interests of the farmers who made up the bulk of the legions. According to Mommsen, the flamboyant C. Flaminius sponsored the reform, but a recently discovered inscription suggests that its author was the dour conservative, Q. Fabius Maximus.

Whether or not he was responsible for the changes in the Centuriate Assembly, Gaius Flaminius was a favorite of the farmers. As tribune in 232, he distributed homesteads on public land near Ariminum to proletarians, who were willing to settle on the Gallic frontier. The policy made landowners of former paupers and added to Rome's pool of citizen soldiers, but the Senate resented the tribune's "usurpation" of its prerogatives in disposing of public land, and Polybius echoed conservative sentiments when he damned Flaminius for beginning the "corruption of the masses." [20] The Celts were already alarmed over Rome's intentions in the Po Valley, and a Gallic force had earlier made a feint toward Ariminum. The arrival of new settlers convinced the barbarians that they had to make a final stand against Rome's northward expansion. Reinforced by war bands from beyond the Alps, the Gauls moved southward, but the Romans, remembering past defeats, mobilized their allies and sacrificed two Gauls and two Greeks to guarantee the favor of heaven. In 225, a Gallic army ravaged Etruria but was decisively defeated at the battle of Telamon. As consul in 223, Flaminius campaigned vigorously in the Po Valley, and his successors pacified the region by 220. The same year, Flaminius was censor and completed the military highway which led from Rome to Ariminum, the Via Flaminia. In the Campus Martius at Rome, he built a racecourse, the Circus Flaminius. In 218, Flaminius was the only senator to support a tribune, Q. Claudius, who passed a law forbidding senators to own ocean-going ships (i.e. engage in trade). According to the tradition preserved by Polybius and Livy, Flaminius was a demagogue catering to the masses, and the ancient historians emphasize his impiety and impetuosity. Yet his use of public land in 232 and his support of Claudius in 218 suggest that he was really an imaginative conservative like Tiberius Gracchus. Despite his damnation by historians, Flaminius was consul twice and reached the censorship, an unlikely attainment for a "demagogue," and later his son was consul.

Piracy in the Adriatic prompted Rome's first venture into the Balkans. In 229, a Roman punitive expedition was sent against corsairs in Illyria, and a permanent protectorate was established on a stretch of coast north of Epirus. In 219, the Romans sent another expedition against a troublesome puppet of theirs, Demetrius of Pharos, who fled to Philip V of Macedon and complained bitterly of the "Roman menace." Already alarmed by the Roman presence in the Balkans, Philip did not venture to challenge Rome, but he was clearly irritated and later allied Macedon with Hannibal.

While Rome was concerned with Gauls in the Po Valley and pirates in the Adriatic, Carthage had recovered from the First Punic War, but few Carthaginians were reconciled to the loss of Sicily and Sardinia. Turning westward, the Punic government sent Hamilcar Barca to Spain in 237 to restore Carthaginian prestige and expand its holdings in the

[20] Polybius 2.21.8.

Iberian peninsula. Soon, most of southern and eastern Spain were in Punic hands. Spanish gold and silver filled Hamilcar's coffers, and rugged Iberian tribesmen hired on as mercenaries in his armies. The Massiliotes, who had outposts on the eastern coast of Spain, were irritated by Hamilcar's success, and his death by drowning in 229 did not relieve their apprehensions. Hamilcar was succeeded by his able son-in-law, Hasdrubal, who used diplomacy more than warfare to bind the tribes closer to Carthage. After the death of his Punic wife, Hasdrubal married an Iberian and founded a capital for Punic Spain at New Carthage, modern Cartagena. Nagged by Massilia to contain Hasdrubal and worried that he might support the hostile Celts in the Po Valley, the Romans signed a treaty with Hasdrubal in 226, specifying the Ebro River as the northern boundary of Punic Spain. When Hasdrubal was assassinated by a Spaniard in 221, his successor was the greatest of the Barcids, Hamilcar's twenty-five-year-old son, Hannibal.

A military genius of the highest order, Hannibal was the most formidable foe ever faced by Rome. From his father and from years of campaigning in Spain, he had learned mastery in the arts of war. Like Hasdrubal, Hannibal was a skilled diplomat and had married a Spaniard. In Punic politics, he was "a friend of the people," a stance that proved useful in his anti-Roman crusade. Above all, Hannibal was a charismatic leader, and his troops were fiercely loyal to him, despite the varied ethnic composition of his Punic, Numidian, and Spanish forces. The Romans feared Hannibal and paid him the highest compliment that hate and fear can concoct, posthumous vilification. In Roman tradition, Hannibal was a prince of darkness—crafty, cruel, treacherous, and terrible in battle. To Carthaginians, of course, he was a patriotic hero who almost brought Rome to its knees. In later life, Hannibal told Antiochus III that as a nine-year-old boy, he was brought by his father to the altar of Baal and there swore eternal hatred of Rome. In the postwar era, the theme of Barcid vengeance was eagerly seized upon by both Roman and Punic apologists, for the dramatic vendetta of Hamilcar and his son obscured the responsibility of both Rome and Carthage for the Second Punic War. In 219, Hannibal stormed the town of Saguntum which had expelled its pro-Punic faction and warred against tribes under his protection. Though Saguntum lay south of the Ebro River,[21] Rome had made a treaty with the city and backed it now. The date of the alliance is unknown, but if prior to 226, it was abrogated by the treaty with Hasdrubal, and if later, it violated the treaty with him. In subduing Saguntum, Hannibal was legally correct, but he was also

---

[21] Livy blandly claimed that Saguntum lay north of the Ebro, and even Polybius, who knew better, implies as much.

deliberately provoking Rome in order to start a war of revenge. At Rome, the Senate was divided with the Cornelii anxious for war and the Fabii counseling restraint. In 218, Rome issued an ultimatum demanding the surrender of Hannibal as a war criminal, but he received the full backing of the Punic government. Carthage was willing to challenge Rome again, although Hamilcar's old enemy Hanno had misgivings about the outcome of the new war.

The Second Punic War is reasonably well "documented," for Livy's complete account is extant as are important portions of Polybius. However, the Polybio-Livian account is weakened by patent propaganda in favor of the Aemilii and the Cornelii Scipiones (the real and adopted ancestors of Polybius's patron), and a tendentious emphasis on the merits of aristocrats and the follies of "new men" such as Flaminius and Varro. Of course, the sterling qualities of Fabius Maximus were not slighted in Fabius Pictor's history. Amid the overlays of distortion, two plausible themes appear—the individual genius of Hannibal and the perseverance of the Romans who refused to accept defeat. For interesting *dramatis personae,* the Second Punic War is unsurpassed—the indomitable Fabius Maximus, the scientific wizard Archimedes, the colorful Scipio Africanus, and above all the satanic figure of Hannibal as seen by his Roman foes. For Romans of succeeding generations, the Hannibalic War was what 1812 is to Russians, the great Patriotic War, the heroic defense of the fatherland against the greatest military genius of the age.

A man of vision, Hannibal intended to destroy Rome by carrying the war to Italy, rallying the Celts of the Po Valley, and prying the Italians loose from their alliances to Rome. While his brother Hasdrubal protected Spain, Hannibal marched a sizeable army over the Pyrenees and across southern Gaul, evading a Roman force that waited to intercept him at Massilia. In the snowy wastes of the Alps, he lost many men and most of his elephants, but the Punic forces that descended on northern Italy were about 26,000 strong and included the superb Numidian cavalry. His troops augmented by Gallic volunteers, Hannibal smashed two consular armies at the Trebia River and occupied Bologna for the winter. During the campaign, he contracted a serious eye infection and lost the sight of his right eye, but even half-blind, Hannibal was more than a match for the Romans. Shocked by the Carthaginian's success, the voters of the Centuriate Assembly elected the popular Gaius Flaminius consul for 217. Able but overconfident, Flaminius led his troops into an ambush by Lake Trasimene and suffered a major defeat. Though the consul died bravely in the battle, the hostile Roman tradition portrayed him as an impious fool who deserved the disaster, but Flaminius merits a better epitaph, for he had served Rome well both in war and domestic affairs. To advertise the Roman defeat and his own generosity, Hannibal released the Italian allies who had been taken prisoner at Lake Trasimene.

Despairing of impetuous generals, the Centuriate Assembly elected a cautious patrician, Q. Fabius Maximus, as dictator. Conservative in politics and careful in war, Fabius inaugurated a policy of avoiding pitched battles with the seemingly invincible Carthaginian and harassing him from the hills where Hannibal's cavalry would be less effective. The Fabian strategy also included preying on Italian cities that defected to the invader. To restore popular morale, the dictator proclaimed a Sacred Spring, but the promised slaughter of the animals did not take place until years later. Though eminently practical, Fabius was not a glamorous figure, and his countrymen grew impatient for a spectacular victory. His own Master of Horse (and briefly co-dictator) M. Minucius Rufus dubbed Fabius a delayer, and the consuls for 216, L. Aemilius Paullus and C. Terentius Varro, decided on a clash with Hannibal. The result was the battle of Cannae, Rome's greatest defeat and a classic example of the envelopment of a larger force by a smaller. Despising the Celts and Spaniards who made up Hannibal's center, the Romans pressed against the barbarians who stood firm while the Numidian cavalry and African infantry swept around the Roman flanks and closed up the rear. Over half the Roman army fell in battle, and thousands were captured. Since Paullus died at Cannae, Varro, who escaped, was blamed for the debacle, and the luckless *novus homo* became a scapegoat in the pro-Aemilian tradition. While profiting from the folly of both consuls, Hannibal had trusted in the fighting skills and discipline of Celts and Spaniards and his own sense of timing.

Though still safe behind its walls, Rome was severely shaken by the defeat at Cannae, and two Greeks and two Gauls were promptly sacrificed to appease the angry gods. The property tax was doubled, and slaves were freed to fill two legions. As always, Rome's greatest resource was its manpower—central Italy remained loyal, and Carthage would soon be opposed by twenty-five legions. However, in the aftermath of Cannae, Hannibal's prospects looked bright, though he did not dare to assault Rome itself. In the South, the Samnites rallied to him as did the Campanians. At Capua, the masses overthrew the pro-Roman oligarchs, trusting in the Barcid reputation for supporting popular government. In 215, Hiero of Syracuse died, and his grandson Hieronymus allied his city with Hannibal. Though the royal family was slain in an abortive pro-Roman *Putsch*, the new democracy at Syracuse was soon in the hands of Punic agents. Also impressed by Cannae, Philip V of Macedon allied himself with Carthage and attacked Roman bases in Illyria. Unfortunately for Hannibal, the Macedon-Magna Graecia-Syracuse axis proved to be of little aid to Carthage. To contain Philip in Hellas, the Romans made an alliance with the Aetolians in 211 but did little to aid them against the king. By 206, the Aetolians made peace with Philip, as did Rome the following year on a status quo basis. Though the First Macedonian War had a negligible effect on the Hannibalic War, Rome had entered the Greek world and had a score to settle with Macedon.

In Sicily, the Romans under M. Claudius Marcellus had brutally sacked Leontini but failed to prevent the Carthaginians from taking Acragas. By land and sea, Syracuse was besieged by Marcellus, but the city was well protected by Archimedes' war machines. Catapults and crossbows, set to cover specific ranges, mowed down the Roman infantry, and cranes swung out from the walls to seize luckless soldiers—one or two victims were sufficient to terrorize the rest. In the harbor, similar devices capsized small crafts and dropped great weights on larger vessels.[22] Thus one old man defended Syracuse with ropes and pulleys.[23] Despite his mechanical skills, Archimedes had not anticipated human weakness, and the Syracusans grew overconfident and careless. During a festival in 212, the guards on the walls became drunk, and the Romans stormed into the suburbs. In 211, a Spanish mercenary betrayed a strategic gate to Marcellus, whose forces swept into the inner city. The Roman general allowed his troops to plunder at will and seized some works of art himself; later, the statues were set up at Rome. However, Marcellus failed to capture the greatest prize of war, Archimedes, who was slain in the chaos by a common soldier. A year later, Acragas was stormed and sacked, but it emerged again in history as Agrigentum. All Sicily was in the harsh grasp of Rome. In Italy, Tarentum had defected to Hannibal, but Capua lay under a Roman siege. To relieve his ally, Hannibal made a feint toward Rome in 211 and rode within sight of the Colline Gate, but the stubborn Romans did not abandon the siege of Capua, where the defenders despaired and surrendered. Unlike Syracuse, Capua was not sacked, but its lands were forfeited to Rome and became part of the public lands of the Republic. By 209, Tarentum was betrayed to Fabius Maximus who sacked the town and sold many of its inhabitants. The fire that burned so brightly at Cannae was being reduced to embers.

In Spain, the fortunes of war had varied as Hannibal's brother, Hasdrubal, and other Punic generals struggled with the Roman commanders, Cn. and P. Cornelius Scipio. By 211, both Scipios had fallen

---

[22] Polybius 8.3.1–7.9. Plutarch *Marcellus* 15–17. Livy 24.34.

[23] The legendary burning mirrors are a product of the fertile imagination of late antiquity.

in battle, and Hasdrubal hoped to lead an overland expedition to reinforce his brother in Italy. In 210, the Centuriate Assembly disregarded formalities and bestowed a proconsular command on the son and namesake of the late Roman general, P. Cornelius Scipio, soon to be renowned as Africanus. Despite his youth (twenty-five years), Scipio was an able and energetic leader, skilled in tactics and diplomacy. According to his admirers, he was also inclined to mysticism and claimed revelations from the gods, though the rationalistic Polybius viewed such stories skeptically. In Spain, the young general trained his troops to fight in flexible formations and armed them with a local sword that slashed as well as stabbed. In 209, Scipio took the Punic stronghold of New Carthage, but he was calculatingly lenient with captured Spaniards to win the tribesmen away from their loyalties to the Barcids. Though he could not prevent Hasdrubal from leaving with a relief army for Hannibal, Scipio completed the reduction of Punic Spain by 206. Meanwhile, Hasdrubal had arrived in northern Italy in 207 and was faced by a consular army. He sent a message to Hannibal in Apulia, but the couriers were intercepted by the consul, C. Claudius Nero, who was trying to contain Hannibal in the South. To prevent a juncture of the Barcids, Nero made a rapid march to the North and joined his colleague in crushing Hasdrubal's forces at the Metaurus River. With typical Roman delicacy, Nero had Hasdrubal's head hurled into his brother's camp. In 205, another Barcid, Mago, seized Genoa but failed to rally the Celts, who had been impressed by the Roman victory at the Metaurus. Though Mago's abortive expedition was soon recalled, the Romans still faced Hannibal.

To drive Hannibal from Italy, Scipio advocated attacking Carthage, a sound strategy employed a century earlier by the Syracusan tyrant Agathocles. However, Fabius and others vehemently opposed the proposal as long as the invader was still in Italy. In 205, the Fabian clique could not prevent Scipio's election as consul with authority to invade Africa, but he was given only two legions in Sicily made up of disgraced survivors from Cannae. With an army augmented by volunteers and a surly quaestor called Cato, Scipio invaded Africa in 204 and began negotiations with Carthage to withdraw his troops if Hannibal would evacuate Italy. With more sincerity, Scipio plotted with the Numidian chief, Masinissa, whom he had met in Spain and who was anxious to unseat the pro-Carthaginian ruler of Numidia, Syphax. In 203, Scipio and Masinissa made a surprise attack on Syphax's camp and the Carthaginians who came to his aid. While Scipio accumulated more victories, Masinissa hunted down and slew Syphax. Now, the Romans could use the fine Numidian cavalry. When Scipio laid siege to Carthage, the Punic government succumbed to war-weariness and agreed to evacuate Italy, give up its empire, limit its fleet to twenty ships, and pay an indemnity of 5,000 talents. Bitter at the Punic peace faction and still unbeaten in battle, Hannibal returned to Africa, where his arrival put new heart into Punic patriots although the Roman Senate had accepted the peace treaty. An attack by starving Carthaginians on a Roman supply convoy provided Hannibal with a pretext to revive the war, and the Punic government backed his gamble. In 202, Hannibal and Scipio clashed at the hard-fought battle of Zama. For the first time, the Carthaginian commander used elephants against the Romans but to little effect; the staying power of Scipio's legions and an enveloping sweep by Masinissa's cavalry gave the victory to Scipio, now Africanus. Carthage paid a high price for Zama. The peace treaty of 201 reduced the Punic fleet to ten ships and increased the indemnity to 10,000 talents. Its territory stripped to roughly the limits of modern Tunisia, Carthage was to be a client state with its foreign policy subject to Roman approval. Masinissa was recognized as king of Numidia and ally of Rome with full rights to recover "the lands once held by his ancestors," a vague and dangerous clause that placed Carthage under a permanent threat from Numidia. Accepting the verdict of Zama, Hannibal advised his countrymen to submit to the harsh peace settlement.

The effects of war are in many ways incalculable, for the lives of millions of individuals are changed by it, and who knows what the dead might have done had they not perished. The concrete results of the Second Punic War are more obvious. Most Italians had stayed loyal to Rome, and of the major defectors, Capua had been humbled and its lands were forfeited to the Republic. In the Po Valley, the Celts were still restive, and Roman control was not completely restored until 192. Because of the constant crises of war, military commands had frequently been extended, and the career of Scipio Africanus had been unconventional to say the least. The prestige of the Senate, which had guided Rome to victory, had never been higher, and conservatives would later recall the Punic Wars as the Golden Age of the oligarchy. Since the *novi homines,* Flaminius and Varro, were blamed for ignominious defeats, the great families tightened their monopoly on the consulship, and few new men were allowed to enter the circle of privilege in the ensuing century. In parts of Italy, the devastation of war had been considerable, but ravaged cities were soon repaired, and nature healed the scarred fields. Not counting war booty and the indemnity from Carthage, the profits of victory had been great. Syracuse was under the Roman yoke, and Spain with its mineral wealth had been added to the empire. East of Ptolemaic Egypt, North Africa was now made up of allied or client states. Triumphant in the West, Rome was about to turn its attention eastward.

THE ROMAN CONQUEST FROM PHILIP V TO NUMANTIA

In the postwar years, Carthage—for long an obsession with Romans —receded as a matter of concern for the Senate. To pay off the indemnity, the Punic government increased taxes for the common people, who turned to Hannibal for redress. Elected suffete in 196, the war hero reformed the corrupt treasury office and expelled venal officials, who appealed for protection to the 100 judges, the stronghold of the Punic oligarchy. Undaunted, Hannibal pushed through a drastic constitutional change that required the annual election of judges and forbade them consecutive terms. His reforms brought Carthage closer to democracy, and his insistence on honesty in officials produced adequate funds to pay the indemnity without raising taxes. Appealing to old war hatreds, Hannibal's Punic foes informed the Roman Senate that his reforms were the first step in a planned military revival of Carthage. Though Scipio Africanus defended his former enemy on the floor of the Senate, a Roman commission was sent to Carthage in 195 to deal with Hannibal. Knowing Roman justice, he fled to the East and eventually to the court of Antiochus III, a move that increased Roman fears of the Seleucid monarch. Though few of his adult years were spent at Carthage, Hannibal had performed extraordinary services for his city both as a soldier and statesman, "first in war and first in peace."

Rome's real concern was with Philip V, who had chosen the losing side in the Second Punic War but had soundly trounced Rome's Aetolian allies. Another bone of contention was Rome's holdings in Illyria which, the Senate felt, were threatened by Philip. To the Greeks, Philip was a troublesome aggressor, but legally Hellas was none of Rome's affair. At war with Philip, the government of Rhodes and King Attalus of Pergamum appealed vainly to the Aetolians, then turned to Rome for aid. Before the Senate, their envoys played on Roman resentment of Philip and raised the specter of an alliance between Macedon and Antiochus III to attack Rome. Though there was little likelihood of such a plan by the rival kings, "the phantom of the 'Seleucid peril,'" Holleaux has observed, "was the constant preoccupation of the Romans. . . . Had they been more keen-sighted and less easily alarmed, they would not have come to dominate the Hellenic world." [24] Fear and hatred are powerful emotions, and the Senate resolved on a "preventive" war against Philip.[25] In 200, the consul demanded a declaration of war, but the war-weary voters of the Centuriate Assembly rejected the proposal.

[24] Maurice Holleaux, *CAH*, VIII, 239.
[25] Because of Livy's confused account, the origin of the Second Macedonian War has been the subject of much modern controversy. The chronology of events is obscure, and so are Roman motives—but philhellenism was not a factor.

Undaunted, the Senate sent the king an arrogant ultimatum to make reparations to Attalus and refrain from war against any Greek state— as if Hellas were a Roman protectorate and Macedon not a sovereign power. Happily for Rome, Philip became embroiled in a squabble with Athens, which asked for Roman assistance. An inflammatory speech by the presiding consul that Rome would have to fight Philip in Italy if not in Greece, brought a grudging declaration of war from the Centuriate voters.

As expected, the king of Macedon rejected Roman interference in Greek affairs. In 199 the Aetolians joined Rome, but the war did not take a decisive turn until the consul for 198, T. Quinctius Flamininus, took command. A glib opportunist and crafty diplomat, Flamininus spoke grandly of freeing Greece from the Macedonian yoke. Though not impressed by Roman propaganda, the Achaean League was fearful of the radical king of Sparta, Nabis, who had freed slaves and plundered the rich and whose example was exciting the urban poor in Achaean cities. The Achaeans, too, joined the coalition against Macedon. Hard-pressed by the allies, Philip renounced areas that he had already lost, but he wished to retain his garrisons at Corinth and elsewhere in Greece. When the Greeks demanded the complete evacuation of Hellas, Flamininus advised the king to appeal to the Senate, which might easily betray its Greek allies. The wily Roman, however, was also scheming to prolong the war and his own command. When the Senate rejected the peace proposals, Philip abandoned Argos to Nabis, who promptly unleashed a reign of terror on the rich in the city. However, Nabis was a practical revolutionary and soon joined Rome against Philip. In 197 at Cynoscephalae, Flamininus and his Aetolian allies decisively defeated Philip, who was outflanked by a movement reminiscent of Scipio's tactics. The victory of the legions over the famed Macedonian phalanx added new prestige to the already inflated Roman image. By the terms of the peace settlement, Philip withdrew his garrisons from Greece and paid Rome an indemnity of 1000 talents, but the Aetolians, who received little territory for their troubles, grumbled over Roman ingratitude. To complete the disillusionment of the Aetolians, Rome made an alliance with Philip, who would be useful against the dreaded Antiochus.

To reassure the Greeks, Flamininus staged an impressive show at the Isthmian Games in 196 when his heralds proclaimed that Rome would impose neither tribute nor garrisons on Hellas, and that the Greek cities were to be "free and governed by their own laws." The holiday crowds cheered the announcement, and centuries later Livy mused contentedly on the altruism of his ancestors:

There was one people in the world which would fight for others' liberties at its own cost, to its own peril and with its own toil, not limiting its guarantees of freedom to its neighbors, to men of the immediate vicinity, or to countries that lay close at hand, but ready to cross the sea that there might be no unjust empire anywhere and that everywhere justice, right, and law might prevail.[26]

Such sentiments would have made the cynical Flamininus smile. To Rome, the Greeks were now clients under Roman patronage and were expected to be loyal and obedient. Moreover, Rome distrusted democracy and the restless lower classes, and the rich in Hellas expected Roman intervention against domestic as well as foreign threats. In Thessaly, for example, Flamininus squelched attempts at democracy and put the cities in the hands of property owners, "those whose interest it is to make things safe and quiet." [27] When the Achaeans insisted that Argos be liberated from Nabis, Flamininus easily defeated the revolutionary king and stripped Sparta of its coastline, but despite Achaean clamors, he left Nabis in control of Sparta as a check against the Achaeans. A weakened and dependent Greece was the reality of the slogan Freedom for Hellas. In 194, Flamininus withdrew his troops from Greece, despite the objections of Scipio who wanted Hellas as his consular command. Scipio and other Roman leaders were nervous over Antiochus who was reoccupying former Seleucid holdings in Thrace, but the king had no desire for a clash with Rome.

Roman suspicion of Antiochus was further aggravated by the intrigues of Eumenes II of Pergamum who wished to embroil Rome in an anti-Seleucid war. His grim warnings of the "Eastern peril" seemed confirmed when the refugee Hannibal arrived at Antiochus's court. When the king rejected a Roman demand to withdraw from Thrace, Rome threatened to "liberate" the Greeks of Seleucid Asia. Angered by Roman interference in his affairs, Antiochus decided to assert his authority by "liberating" Greece. Already digruntled with Rome, the Aetolians had invited the king to land in Hellas, and they assured him that the poor in every city would rally to his banners. Though Philip stayed aloof, Nabis joined in the plot, but the Aetolians thought twice about the crafty Spartan and had him assassinated in 192. To the horror of the Aetolians, Antiochus landed in Greece with only a small army and evoked little enthusiasm from the masses. Apparently, the king had planned a show of force rather than a major war, but in 191 the Romans drove him from Greece and soon compelled the Aetolians to sur-

[26] Livy 33.33.5–7.   [27] Livy 34.51.5–6.

render.[28] With bulldog tenacity, Scipio Africanus insisted that Antiochus be beaten decisively in Asia. Unable to hold the consulship for 190, Africanus saw to it that his brother, Lucius, received the office and the Asian command. He also accompanied Lucius as his legate and in reality directed the campaign. With Philip's aid, the Scipios marched overland through Thrace and invaded Asia, while Roman ships with assistance from Rhodes and Pergamum won command of the seas. Perhaps jealous of his famous guest, Antiochus failed to employ the talents of Hannibal and wasted the great tactician on naval duties. Rejecting an offer of peace, the Romans forced Antiochus to make a stand in 189 at Magnesia, where he was decisively defeated by Lucius Scipio and Eumenes. Other Roman generals penetrated into Galatia and seized enormous amounts of booty. At Apamea in 188, Antiochus surrendered all Seleucid territory north and west of the Taurus mountains and paid Rome a staggering indemnity of 15,000 talents. Eumenes received the bulk of the surrendered territory and planned further gains with Roman aid.

After the defeat of Antiochus, Hannibal had fled to Bithynia, but a Roman commission under Flamininus demanded his extradition in 183. Rather than be dragged to an ignominious death at Rome, the great general took poison. The postwar years were also bitter for Scipio Africanus, whose great prestige was shattered by the vindictive attacks of Cato. In 187, Cato had accused Lucius Scipio of embezzling funds received from Antiochus, but Africanus tore the account books to shreds before the Senate. Cato continued the attack in the Tribal Assembly where a tribune threatened to arrest Lucius. Another tribune, Tiberius Sempronius Gracchus, intervened to save Lucius, but the Scipios had lost face. In 184, Africanus was himself accused of treason with Antiochus, and though the wild charge was not pressed, the ingratitude of his countrymen broke his spirit. Withdrawing into seclusion, Africanus died despondent a year later. So, in 183, the two giants of the Hannibalic War died, lonely, embittered men.

Philip's final years were not much happier, for the king, who had aided the Scipios against Antiochus, fell from Roman favor. Moreover, his younger son, Demetrius, who had been a hostage at Rome, was angling for Roman support to supplant his older brother, Perseus, as Philip's successor. Persuaded by Perseus that Demetrius was a traitor, the king executed him but lived to doubt the charge. On Philip's death in 179, Perseus released political prisoners and abolished some debts to

---

[28] The final peace treaty with the Aetolians illustrates the new order in Hellas, for the Aetolians had to promise to always "uphold the empire and majesty of Rome."

relieve the poor. In the Greek cities, his agents promised the masses abolition of debts if they would support the cause of Macedon. Sincere or not, the king seemed a champion to the desperate poor who had been excited by Nabis and disenchanted with Antiochus. His rival for leadership in Hellas, Eumenes of Pergamum, journeyed to Rome in 172 and denounced Perseus for undermining Rome's conservative puppets in Greece in order to restore the Macedonian hegemony. For good measure, the Pergamene monarch added that Perseus was plotting to have the entire Roman Senate poisoned. Though no one took Eumenes' wilder charges seriously, the Romans were concerned over Perseus's appeal to the Greek poor, which was a danger to the established order. Rome, which had earlier engineered a "preventive" war with Philip, now resolved on a preemptive strike against Perseus, and envoys were sent to beguile the king with negotiations while Rome prepared to attack him. This consummate deceit prompted Livy to observe that "those in the Senate to whom the pursuit of advantage was more important than that of honor prevailed." [29] In 171, Rome attacked Perseus, but the war bogged down under incompetent Roman generals until neutral Rhodes offered to negotiate a peace settlement between the warring powers. However, the consul for 168, L. Aemilius Paullus, was a capable and aggressive commander. The son of the "hero" of Cannae, the brother-in-law of Africanus, and the father of Polybius's patron, Paullus has received a good press among ancient and modern historians, but the evidence reveals him as a cold-blooded imperialist. In 168, his legions cut to pieces the obsolete Macedonian phalanx at the battle of Pydna. Expecting to be treated like a king, Perseus surrendered but was dragged in Paullus's triumph at Rome and died in a Roman dungeon. Cultured as well as cruel, Paullus seized the royal library of Macedon as part of his share in the war booty. With the defeat of Perseus, the Antigonid monarchy was extinguished, and Macedon was divided into four republics under oligarchies dependent on Rome. Half of the former royal revenue became tribute for the Romans.

In the immediate aftermath of the Third Macedonian War, Rome abandoned what little tact she had previously shown toward the Greeks. In Aetolia, hundreds of "Macedonian sympathizers" were butchered with Paullus's approval. From Achaea a thousand leading citizens were deported to Italy on vague charges of sympathy with Perseus. Never given formal trials, few of the Achaean exiles lived to return home fifteen years later. Among the deportees was Polybius, an impeccable conservative. The people of Epirus fared even worse, for the Senate had authorized Paullus's army to loot the little nation. After seizing the

[29] Livy 42.47.9.

movable wealth of the citizenry by deception, Paullus ordered his men to enslave the Epirotes themselves, and 150,000 hapless people were sold to slave traders in one day. When the price of slaves dropped immediately, the Roman veterans grumbled. Even Rome's old allies, Pergamum and Rhodes, received shabby treatment. Suspected of secret negotiations with Perseus, Eumenes was not allowed to defend himself, for the Senate forbade the appearance of any king at Rome, though the august fathers had recently welcomed the contemptible Prusias II of Bithynia who appeared before them dressed as a freedman! A rejected lackey, Eumenes kept his resentment to himself, and Pergamum remained an ally of Rome under his successors. For daring to suggest peace during the recent conflict, Rhodes narrowly escaped war with Rome, for only Cato's objection and a tribunician veto prevented a declaration of war. To punish Rhodes, Rome established the Athenian isle of Delos as a free port, diverting so much trade from Rhodes that its harbor dues fell 85 percent. With its revenues shrunken, Rhodes could no longer maintain the war fleet that had policed the Eastern Mediterranean, and pirates soon swarmed over the seas. As a result of the unwarranted injury to the Rhodians, Rome would have to contest control of the sea lanes with corsairs who established strongholds in Cilicia and Crete.

An extraordinary demonstration of Roman power took place in 168 when Antiochus IV invaded Egypt to establish a protectorate over his squabbling nephews, Ptolemy VI and VIII. A three-man Roman commission arrived and presented the Seleucid king with the Senate's ultimatum to withdraw from Egypt. Unbacked by ships or spears, the Senate's arrogant envoy, C. Popillius Laenas, drew a circle in the sand about Antiochus's feet and rudely ordered the king to reply before stepping out of the circle. Humiliated and fearful, Antiochus withdrew his forces from Egypt. After Antiochus's death, the Romans further weakened the Seleucids by insisting on limitations on its armed forces and by extending protection to the rebellious Hasmonean state at Jerusalem. A complex series of dynastic struggles and the rising power of Parthia in the East accelerated the decline of the Seleucid kingdom, which dissolved into chaos under shadow kings by the end of the second century. Unlike the Seleucid realm, Ptolemaic Egypt remained intact though racked by peasant revolts and dynastic squabbles. The Ptolemies constantly appealed for Rome to settle their quarrels. In the process, prominent senators collected handsome bribes from Ptolemaic contenders, and Egypt was kept weak and sometimes divided. Polybius dryly remarked that the Romans profited from other men's errors and posed as the benefactors of those whom they exploited.[30]

[30] Polybius 31.10.7.

Long before the Romans arrived in Greece, the cities of Hellas were in serious economic straits. In desperation, the urban and rural poor had turned to Cleomenes, Nabis, Antiochus III, and Perseus, but the kings had proved to be false messiahs. Popular leaders rose in their places, but they lacked real power and their agitation panicked the rich into the arms of Rome. Under Roman control, the agony of Greece increased and the population dropped drastically. Even the wealthy classes fretted in their humiliating dependence on the western "barbarians." In 149, a pretender, Andriscus, claimed to be the son of Perseus and rallied the Macedonians against Rome. Despite initial successes, he was crushed and Macedon was reduced to provincial status in 148. When the leadership of the once stolid Achaean League passed into the hands of democrats, Rome sought to shatter the League by separating Corinth, Argos, and other towns from its control. Gambling that the Romans were preoccupied with wars in Spain and Africa, the Achaean democrats challenged Rome and won support among the urban masses elsewhere in Greece. In 146, Roman armies easily crushed the Greek rebels, and the Senate made an example of Corinth, a hotbed of anti-Roman democratic nationalism. The ancient city was sacked and leveled to the ground, its inhabitants were sold, and its art treasures were sent to Rome. Elsewhere, ex-rebels were executed, democracies were abolished, and safe oligarchies were set up in their places. Henceforth, the Romans promptly punished attempts at popular government and social reform in Hellas. An inscription, which probably should be dated in 115, deals with the Achaean town of Dyme where democrats had burned public records and abolished debts:

Quintus Fabius Maximus son of Quintus, proconsul of the Romans, to the magistrates, council, and city of Dyme. Whereas the councilors of the year of Cyllanius have notified me of the wrongful acts committed in your city—I mean the burning and destruction of the archives and public records, the leader of the whole commotion being Sosus son of Tauromenes, who also proposed laws contrary to the constitution given by the Romans to the Achaeans—on which matter we discussed the details at Patrae with the present council; since then the perpetrators of this deed seemed to me to be giving the example of the worst disposition and disorder to all the Greeks; for their action not only suited their policy of breach of mutual contracts and cancellation of debts, but also was alien from the freedom granted to all the Greeks in common and from our policy; I, the accusers having submitted true charges, have judged Sosus, the leader of the affair and the proposer of legislation destructive of the constitution granted to you, deserving of death and have executed him.[31]

[31] W. Dittenberger *Sylloge*³, 684, trans. A. H. M. Jones, *A History of Rome Through the Fifth Century* (New York: Harper & Row, 1968), I, 101–2.

With such methods, the Romans defended property and public order in captive Greece.

In the West, the Roman juggernaut crushed other free nations, including its ancient enemy, Carthage. A hapless puppet of Rome, the African city had been subject to constant harassment by Masinissa, who piecemeal seized Punic territory to add to his own domains. Carthaginian complaints to Rome brought little results, and one senatorial investigating commission in 153 was headed by the irascible Cato, who returned to Rome demanding the destruction of Carthage. On the floor of the Senate, Cato insisted on the extermination of the traditional foe, and no doubt his harangues inflamed public opinion, though there were few veterans of the Punic Wars like Cato among the decision makers at Rome. To counter Cato, Africanus's son-in-law, P. Scipio Nasica Corculum, suggested that the continued existence of Carthage was a salutary challenge to Rome. Apparently, an influential group in the Senate paid lip service to Cato's hate-filled rhetoric but was really concerned that Masinissa might conquer Carthage and make it the capital of Greater Numidia. Should this development occur, the aged king might prove difficult to control. In 151, the Punic government was dominated by "democrats" who were heirs to the popular sympathies and ardent patriotism of the Barcids. When the Carthaginians declared war on Numidia, Masinissa complained that they were acting without Roman approval and in violation of the peace settlement of 201. Though Carthage soon purged the rash nationalists, the Senate decided on war, and Roman armies landed in Africa in 149. Laying siege to Carthage, the Romans demanded 300 noble hostages and total disarmament of the city. When the Carthaginians complied, the consuls revealed their secret instructions to destroy Carthage and resettle the population ten miles from the sea, a death warrant for the city and for Punic commerce. Both Carthage and Masinissa had been betrayed. Outraged by Roman duplicity, the Carthaginians closed their gates and resolved to die fighting; the factories of the city quickly supplied new arms. Grumbling that Rome had no need of him, Masinissa withdrew his troops and soon died of old age.

Since loyal tribes in the interior kept Carthage supplied with food, the siege dragged on for three years, and the Roman public grew impatient. During the African war, P. Cornelius Scipio Aemilianus distinguished himself and became a popular hero. The son of Aemilius Paullus, he had been adopted into the Scipionic family on his father's death. Like Paullus, Scipio was a ruthless warlord whose merits have been exaggerated by sympathetic historians. Though technically ineligible, he received the consulship in 147, and the Tribal Assembly duly ratified the illegal election. Scipio soon won the victory he had schemed to attain, and his troops stormed Carthage in 146 amid frightful scenes of carnage.[32] The city burned for seventeen days, the survivors were sold, and the ruins were cursed. The former territory of Carthage became the Roman province of Africa. According to Polybius, Scipio had stared at the burning city and mused that one day the same fate might befall Rome.[33] However, Scipio's awareness of the mutability of human affairs did not prevent him from lusting for more wars and cities to burn.

The subjugation of Spain is one of the most discreditable chapters in the history of Roman imperialism. The grim record resembles the Spanish conquest of the Americas and the treatment of Indian tribes by the United States. Rome had seized the Punic territories in southern and eastern Spain as a prize of the Second Punic War. To protect these new frontiers, the Romans eventually subdued Lusitania and other areas in the Iberian Peninsula, though the hill tribes of northwestern Spain did not submit until the time of Augustus. A fierce and proud people, the Iberian barbarians resisted the Roman conquest in a protracted struggle waged with brutality on both sides. Though they claimed to represent the cause of civilization, the Romans made treacherous attacks on unarmed natives, massacred or enslaved them, and frequently repudiated peace treaties. Rome's incentives in Spain were glory and gold, for war was the occupation of the Roman ruling class, and the mineral wealth of the peninsula was fabulous by ancient standards. In the first decade of Roman rule, Spain yielded in plunder or extortion 4,000 pounds of gold and 130,000 pounds of silver. The silver mines near New Carthage produced 25,000 denarii a day, and 40,000 miners toiled under wretched conditions to keep the river of silver flowing to Rome. Given such treasures, the cupidity of Roman governors is understandable, but their conduct toward natives was a total repudiation of the "ancient virtues" lauded by romantic apologists for Rome.

Not all Romans, of course, were brutes. Tiberius Sempronius Gracchus the Elder tried to promote urbanization and win the loyalties of the tribes. Even the stern Cato had impressed the Spaniards with his iron rectitude, and they later turned to him for help against oppressive governors. In 171, a special commission made up of Cato and other patrons of the Iberians was established to deal with complaints from Spain. By 149, a permanent court was formed to deal with extortion in the provinces,[34] but its effectiveness was limited by the natural reluc-

---

[32] Appian *Punica* 127–132, preserves Polybius's eyewitness account of the horrors of the fall of Carthage.

[33] Polybius 38.21–22.

[34] Another permanent result of the Spanish War was calendric. In 153, the beginning of the Roman year was moved from March to January to facilitate a change of military command.

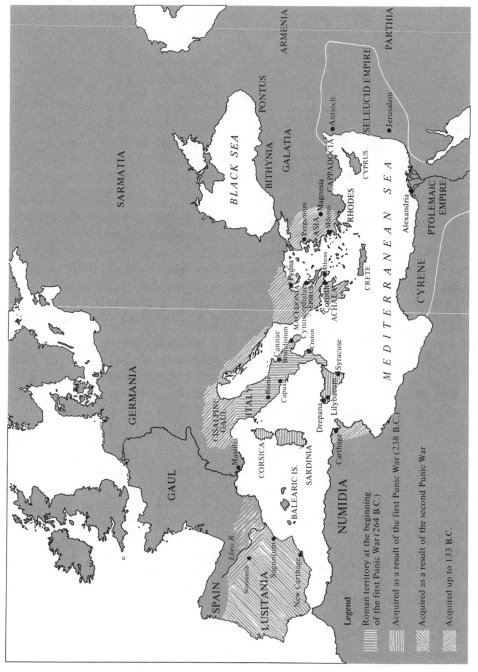

Map 2. Expansion of the Roman Empire to 133 B.C.

Legend

Roman territory at the beginning of the first Punic War (264 B.C.)

Acquired as a result of the first Punic War (238 B.C.)

Acquired as a result of the second Punic War

Acquired up to 133 B.C.

tance of senators to convict their peers. The same year, a tribune indicted Sulpicius Galba, who had tarnished the honor of Rome by persuading the Lusitanians to disarm and then massacring most of them. At an emotional trial before the Tribal Assembly, the dying Cato castigated Galba, who pleaded for mercy with equal eloquence and bribed enough voters to secure an acquittal. Among the survivors of Galba's massacre was an outraged patriot, Viriathus, who led a major resistance among the Lusitanians until the Romans had him assassinated in 139. Two years later, in a pass in Central Spain, 8,000 tribesmen from Numantia trapped the consul, C. Hostilius Mancinus, and 20,000 of his troops. Because the Spaniards trusted the Gracchan name, Tiberius Gracchus the Younger negotiated a treaty with the Numantines, which was promptly repudiated by the Senate at the urging of Scipio Aemilianus. To restore Roman honor, the Senate handed over Mancinus to the Numantines, but the proud Spaniards refused to accept him. With the rejection of the treaty, Tiberius Gracchus lost face with his Numantine clients, and he never forgave his brother-in-law, Scipio Aemilianus, for sabotaging it. The conqueror of Carthage aimed at new glories in Spain and cared little for Tiberius's resentment. As consul in 134, Scipio laid siege to Numantia with a force of 20,000 Romans and 40,000 Spanish allies. Inside the brave town, 4,000 Numantines resisted for eight months until they were reduced by starvation to eating their own dead. In 133, a handful of gaunt survivors surrendered the town to Scipio, who put it to the torch. After the destruction of Numantia, the Iberian Peninsula was pacified for a generation, but the natives waited eagerly for another leader to challenge the might of Rome.

A DIGRESSION ON ROMAN IMPERIALISM

At the beginning of the present chapter, Polybius was quoted to the effect that Rome conquered the Mediterranean world so swiftly because of the merits of its political system. In reality, the Republic owed more to the courage and loyalty of the Roman legionary than to the largely imaginary mixed constitution. Rome also benefited from superior manpower and from the military ability of individual leaders. The awe and envy that is implicit in Polybius's apology was shared by many contemporaries, including the author of *First Book of Maccabees*,[35] for the whole Mediterranean world was dazzled by the momentum of Roman expansion. There was, however, no master strategy, no secret plot handed down by generations of senators to rule the known world. The

[35] First Maccabees 8.1–16.

Senate was often divided on foreign policy. Few men in history have much foresight, and fewer still can anticipate all the results of a given action.

Many Roman conquests were originally expeditions to protect current holdings and importuning clients. "By defending our allies," Cicero dryly remarked, "our people have come to dominate the whole world." [36] His ancestors could have stated the same with a straight face. Rome had fought Carthage to protect Messana and wound up in control of most of Sicily. To this gratuitous gain was added the deliberate imperialism of seizing Sardinia. The Second Punic War was a natural outgrowth of the aftermath of the First Punic War. Other wars were prompted by purely emotional feelings, hatred of Carthage and Philip, fear of Philip and Antiochus, and conservative sympathies with the wealthy classes in Hellas who felt threatened by Perseus. The lure of new commands and martial glory prompted the intrigues of Flamininus and Scipio Aemilianus, and Roman nobles enjoyed the profits of war in the crass form of booty. The Senate had not challenged Carthage to win the tribute of Sicily, but once the taxes rolled in, the decision makers were not averse to adding new regions of potential revenue. However, there was no business lobby active in promoting foreign wars, nor was any farm lobby worried over competition from African grain. The imperialist wars of Rome did not resemble the patterns of nineteenth-century capitalism. Rather, by 167, Rome had developed a national industry, the empire, which produced a huge profit in tribute and required only the export of soldiers. In that year, the Roman people ceased paying direct property taxes, so lucrative had the business of imperialism become.

The very notion of empire is somewhat flexible, for imperialist endeavors are not confined to outright annexations of another people's territory. An imperial power can hold sway over other nations by the mere threat of intervention, by crushing its friends in the iron grip of protection, or by warning its enemies not to penetrate its sphere of control. When Flamininus pulled his legions out of Greece, Rome did not release Hellas from its custody although the Senate had no plans for annexation. As for the Hellenistic world, Rostovtzeff has succinctly stated the case:

> Rome may have honestly thought that her first two wars with a Hellenistic power were necessary for her political safety. The Roman Senate certainly knew little of Eastern affairs and may have been alarmed by the successes of Philip and Antiochus. However this may be, after Cynoscephalae and Magnesia, Rome was very well informed regarding the conditions that prevailed in the Hellenistic states. The Senate could not seri-

[36] Cicero *de Republica* 3.23.35.

ously think that an independent Macedonia or a well-organized Syria was a danger to Rome's Western empire. Their policy of demoralizing the Hellenistic world, of dictating to it, and of chastising any state that disobeyed their orders, was not a policy of self-defense, but of prepotency and imperialism. Imperialism does not always involve the intention of acquiring an increase of territory. The desire for political hegemony, the wish to play the leading role in the political life of the civilized world, cannot but be regarded as a form of imperialism.[37]

In the process of establishing this hegemony, the Romans gobbled up some states and wrecked the rest. Even life as a client king was precarious and filled with demands for troops in war and bribes in peace.

The Romans did not apply the same standards of conduct toward barbarians as were extended to civilized powers, though the double standard was little comfort to the citizens of Syracuse, Corinth, or Carthage. With barbarian foes, the Romans did not even invoke the excuse of the exigencies of war. They hunted down Sardinians with dogs and treated Spaniards with callous brutality. Rome's march to dominion did not begin by design, and much of it was the fortuitous result of bumbling policies, but the Romans acquired a taste for lording it over others and eating the fruits of other men's labors. Centuries later, when the world basked in the Roman Peace, and a common culture had spread throughout the Mediterranean lands, apologists claimed that Roman conquest had ultimately meant the triumph of civilization. However, altruism had not been the intent, much less the practice, of the conniving senators and swaggering generals of the imperial Republic. Butchery, rape, plunder, enslavement, and extortion were the first fruits of the manifest destiny of Rome. With supremacy came an exhilarating sense of superiority, but also a constant fear of rebellion. The theme of Rome's uneasy triumph was expressed by an unknown Roman author, writing sometime after the destruction of the rebellious Latin city of Fregellae in 125 B.C.:

> By the Roman people Numantia was destroyed, Carthage razed, Corinth demolished, Fregellae overthrown. Of no aid to the Numantines was bodily strength; of no assistance to the Carthaginians was military science; of no help to the Corinthians was polished cleverness; of no avail to the Fregellans was fellowship with us in customs and in language.[38]

It was a grim record of old and famous cities destroyed, root and branch, by a nation that preyed on the world but still feared its victims.

[37] Rostovtzeff, *Social and Economic History of Hellenistic World*, I, 70–71.
[38] *Rhetorica ad Herennium* 4.27.37, trans. Harry Caplan (Cambridge, Mass.: Harvard University Press, 1954), p. 323.

CHAPTER FIVE

The burden of success

Success is a burden that few men or nations bear well, but not because some moralistic Providence or jealous deities lay a rose-strewn path for our downfall. Rather, success changes men into something quite different than they were before, something that they may not want to be. Being a superstitious people who worried about luck, the Greeks whined that pride always goes before a fall. The Romans, to whom pride was a virtue, had little patience with such a view. Having been poor so long, they coveted wealth and power and did not anticipate the results. During the second century B.C., the empire caused profound social, economic, and cultural changes in Roman life that ultimately brought on a series of political crises. When the military needs of the empire required the employment of professional soldiers, a factor was introduced that eventually wrecked the Republic. To later Romans, it was obvious that something had gone wrong in the second century. Sallust superficially suggested that the key cause was the removal of the perpetual challenge of Carthage in 146.[1] The moralists were on sounder ground when they deplored the luxuries that came with the loot of the world, for the new style of living among the rich was symptomatic of the sociological changes that were unalterably making a different Rome. Whatever the dangers so obvious to those with hindsight, the Republican leadership had gladly taken up the burden of empire, and the journey was begun that led through tortuous turns to the bloody dictatorship of Sulla.

THE BEST OF TIMES, THE WORST OF TIMES

Perhaps the most famous, surely the most picturesque, of the Romans of the second century was Marcus Porcius Cato, who had fought Hasdrubal at the Metaurus and lived to help precipitate the Third Punic

[1] Sallust *Bellum Jugurthinum* 41.2–3.

142

War. A red-haired rustic from Tusculum, Cato made a splendid career by posing as the defender of ancient virtue against modern corruption. Crafty and aggressive, he was a powerful orator and rose politically with the backing of the Valerian and Fabian houses. As consul in 195, Cato campaigned in Spain and later fought against Antiochus III. Proud of his own abilities, he loathed the haughty patricians, Scipio Africanus and Flamininus, and shook their prestige by indicting their brothers for misconduct. His vendetta against Scipio was particularly vindictive and successful. Despite the opposition of many nobles, Cato won the censorship in 184 by constantly harping on the venality and decadence of the ruling class. As censor, he tried vainly to stem the social currents of the age and restore old-time rectitude. By his puritan posture, Cato wielded an influence out of all proportion to his status as a "new man," but as a reformer, he was a failure, for his contemporaries applauded his rhetoric and ignored his injunctions. No one could really take seriously Cato's wild charge that Greek physicians had conspired to murder the Roman people with their newfangled medicine.[2]

Were it not for his unquestioned honesty, Cato might seem a complete hypocrite, for he was a man of many masks. An outspoken foe of the aristocracy, he married his son to the daughter of Aemilius Paullus. Though he spoke and read Greek well, Cato opposed the intrusion of Hellenic culture into Rome. Seemingly a rural boor, he wrote a number of treatises and a major history of Rome, emphasizing its Italic heritage, omitting the names of nobles, and praising himself whenever possible. For the use of his young son, Cato made a copy of the history written in large letters. Despite his severity, the old veteran opposed Roman penetration of the East and defended the rights of oppressed Spaniards. Though sincere in his obsessive hatred of Carthage, he could hardly have felt that the city was still a threat in 149. Lyric in his praises of farming and rural life, Cato lusted after cash and invested in a variety of business enterprises so successfully that he left a sizeable fortune to his children, who, as descendants of a consul, were nobles.

In his handbook on agriculture, Cato displayed the views of a tight-fisted agrarian capitalist. His maxims resemble *Poor Richard* at his worst:

> Sell worn-out oxen, blemished cattle, blemished sheep, wool, hides, an old wagon, old tools, an old slave, a sickly slave, and whatever else is superfluous. The master should have the selling habit, not the buying habit. . . . In rainy weather try to find something to do indoors. Clean up rather than be idle. Remember that even though work stops, expenses run on none the less.[3]

[2] Pliny the Elder *Naturalis Historia* 29.13–14.
[3] Cato *de Agri Cultura* 2.7,39.2, trans. Hooper, pp. 9, 57.

No doubt avarice is a rustic virtue, but selling old and ill slaves was considered poor form even by Roman standards. After getting many years of labor from him, a gentleman would free a slave and bask in the gratitude of a new client. But Cato, who worked in the fields beside his slaves and drank from the same bucket, preferred the pittance he could get for a decrepit bondsman. To insure their future loyalties, he had his wife suckle slave children who presumably absorbed fondness for Cato with the woman's milk. Never missing a chance for profit, the old patriarch made his male slaves pay a fee for sleeping with female slaves.

Though few were as niggardly as Cato, many Romans were as pious, and all conservatives were concerned about the growing influence of Greek and Asian religions in Italy. In 205 the Sybilline books had declared that Hannibal could be driven from Italy only with the aid of Cybele, the great mother goddess of Phrygia. The Senate invited the deity to move to Rome, and in the following year, a delegation of noble matrons welcomed the arrival of her sacred black stone, which was installed in a temple on the Palatine Hill. The Romans, however, were not prepared for the orgiastic rites of Cybele or the antics of her eunuch priests, and citizens were forbidden to participate. As Rome became more involved in the Greek world, Hellenic influences increased, particularly in religious matters, although the Romans had already been exposed to Greek ideas and customs in Sicily and southern Italy. As a major metropolis, Rome attracted quacks and fortune-tellers from Hellas and the East, much to the dismay of Romans of Cato's persuasion who preferred their superstition home-grown and venerable.

Strong in Magna Graecia and especially in Campania, the exuberant Bacchic cult won converts at Rome and in the Italian countryside. However, the secrecy of Bacchic rites aroused the suspicions of the Roman Establishment, which always frowned on nonpublic religious practices. In 186, the Senate denounced the Bacchic worshipers for conspiring against public order and accused them of nocturnal orgies and murder plots. A relentless persecution was launched with arrests, tortures, and executions; Livy says that seven thousand persons were hounded. Ignoring the local autonomy of its allies, the Senate ordered all cities in Italy to take similar measures to suppress the Bacchic cult.[4] As polytheists, the Romans did not prohibit private devotions to Bacchus, but they crushed the Bacchic priesthood and put the cult under a cloud of opprobrium. The causes of Rome's first religious persecution are not entirely clear. The charges of crime and sexual aberration are highly colored, and similar accusations were later made against Christians. Possibly some Bacchic devotees were involved in a murder plot, for similar scandals

[4] A copy of the Senate's decree is still extant (*ROL,* IV, 255–59); Livy's account (39.8–18) of the affair is highly sensational.

occurred among the Roman aristocracy, but this alone would not warrant an attack on the cult itself. As for private orgies, the Romans were not puritans, and the Bacchic religion was later allowed to flourish. In the first century B.C., Bacchism was quite popular and a "House of the Mysteries" still stands at Pompeii. Probably the Senate suspected that secret cults among the lower classes and especially among slaves could become networks of sedition. As increasing numbers of foreign slaves appeared in Italy, there was concern that their religious practices masked hostile intents toward their masters. Cato specifies that a slave woman "must not engage in religious worship herself or get others to engage in it for her without the orders of the master or the mistress; let her remember that the master attends to the devotions for the whole household." [5] Who knew what dire things slaves asked of their alien gods, what malign witchcraft was practiced at night, or what plots were whispered in their outlandish tongues?

Less sensational than the Bacchic "threat" was the infusion of Hellenic thought among the Roman upper classes. Children of the Roman ruling class were taught by Greek tutors, and adults were expected to display a familiarity with the classics. No matter how inappropriate, a Homeric quotation was a standard ploy in polite repartee and writing. When Polybius wanted the Senate to make restitution to the Achaean exiles who were returning home, Cato—the arch foe of Hellenism—reminded him that Odysseus did not return to the Cyclops' cave to pick up his cap.[6] Greek culture exposed Romans not only to Homer and Sophocles but also to Epicurus, who sneered at traditional religion, and to clever philosophers who could argue either side of a question with equal persuasiveness. Cato and other conservatives fought vainly to halt the spread of sophistication. In 173, two Epicureans were banished from Rome, and in 161, all philosophers and rhetoricians were ordered expelled. When the Academic Carneades visited the city as an ambassador in 155 and stayed to give public lectures,[7] Cato prompted the Senate to hurry the distinguished philosopher back to Greece and "leave the youth of Rome to give their attention to the laws and the magistrates as they did in the past." [8] In 139, the Senate ousted many astrologers from Rome, but only those who were obvious charlatans were expelled, for few men doubted the scientific base of astrology. Ultimately, the Romans encountered a Greek philosophy compatible with their

[5] Cato *de Agri Cultura* 143.1.   [6] Plutarch *Cato Maior* 9.

[7] The conservative historian L. Calpurnius Piso was sure that Rome fell from grace in 154 B.C., and he may have had the visit of Carneades in mind. Another symptom of "corruption" was an attempt to construct Rome's first stone theater in that memorable year, but Scipio Nasica Corculum defeated the project.

[8] Plutarch *Cato Maior* 22.

tastes, the austere tenets of Stoicism, which preached duty and restraint. The Stoic Panaetius, who was one of the few thinkers to reject astrology, became a confidant of Scipio Aemilianus, and a watered-down version of Stoicism was added to the intellectual baggage of the Roman ruling class. Pompey sponsored a prominent Stoic, Posidonius, and Cato the Younger was a practicing Stoic, but Caesar favored the views of Epicurus as did his foe Cassius. While Cicero preferred the skepticism of the New Academy, Brutus venerated Plato and the Old Academy, and Crassus was interested in Aristotle. Despite their intellectual affectations, however, the men who made Roman history were not swayed by philosophic doctrines but conditioned by ambition and family pride—their hearts were in the Forum and the camp, not in books.

To Cato's chagrin, even Latin literature had emerged under a Greek aura. Early in the third century, a captive Greek from Tarentum, Livius Andronicus, translated the Odyssey into Latin and wrote tragedies based on Greek models. The Campanian, Gnaeus Naevius, composed plays and a verse epic on the Punic Wars, which included a digression on the origin of Rome that influenced Vergil. An outspoken critic of the Metelli, Naevius was imprisoned and exiled for libeling the great family. "Mighty in genius, rude in art," [9] Ennius was the first great Latin poet, but even he claimed to have three hearts—Roman, Italian, and Greek. A Calabrian, Ennius praised Pyrrhus in his epic history of the Roman past, the *Annales,* but he also had the good sense to laud Scipio Africanus. Though his works were filled with quotable epigrams, the poet could produce a monstrosity of alliteration: *"O Tite tute Tati tibi tanta tyranne tulisti."* [10] Despite his exhortations to antique virtue, Ennius wrote a prose work popularizing the theory of Euhemerus that the traditional gods were really deified kings and benefactors of the past. Thus, Jupiter was an ancient ruler who had abolished cannibalism and instituted cults in honor of himself, like a Hellenistic monarch. Naturally, Cato, who had once aided Ennius, was horrified. Even the first Roman historians, Q. Fabius Pictor and his immediate successors, wrote in Greek—an intolerable situation that Cato remedied with his own history. The two major writers of Latin comedy, Plautus and Terence, freely adapted Hellenistic plays for Roman tastes. The plays of T. Maccius Plautus, who had once worked as a mill-hand, are filled with burlesque humor and vivid sketches of popular life. More sophisticated were the comedies of P. Terentius Afer, a dark-skinned ex-slave from North Africa, who may have been a friend of Scipio Aemilianus. Like Joseph Conrad, Terence became a master of an acquired language. His most famous line—"I am a man, and nothing human is alien to me" [11]

[9] Ovid *Tristia* 2.424.   [10] Ennius *Annales* fragment 109.
[11] Terence *Heautontimorumenos* 77.

—is close to the spirit of his model, Menander. Whether arriving directly, through Greek visitors, or insinuated in the emerging Latin literature, the tide of Hellenism was irresistible. Less dependent on Hellas was the Latin tradition of satire begun by C. Lucilius, a well-born Campanian friend of Scipio Aemilianus. In vigorous verse, the poet poked fun at his contemporaries and pilloried the foes of Aemilianus. Lucilius's niece was the mother of Pompey, but his intellectual heir was the great satirist Horace.

In addition to obvious intellectual influences, there were psychological currents from Hellas that disturbed Cato and the old guard. Rome had never lacked prominent men or self-seeking opportunists, but ambition was supposed to operate behind a screen of families and the Senate. The Hellenistic world was one of kings and dictators, where the glorification of the successful individual knew little bounds. Now, Roman generals, too, enjoyed the adulation of foreign crowds and wielded enormous power over cities and nations. Flamininus was the first Roman statesman to receive divine honors in Hellas, and he issued coins there bearing his own portrait. Such procedures shattered precedent and betrayed a new egoism that was not limited to Flamininus. According to Polybius, when Scipio Africanus was asked to name the statesmen who best combined wisdom and courage, the conqueror of Hannibal coolly replied, "Agathocles and Dionysius of Syracuse," [12] an odd answer for an old Roman. Perhaps Scipio only admired the tyrants as able opponents of Carthage, but maybe Cato knew Scipio better than Scipio's modern admirers do. Of course, it was the reality of power, not observation of Greek models, that made some Romans giddy.[13]

At a lower level of experience, there was a growing taste for luxury and a growing ability to gratify it. Previously, Romans had frowned on living in the grand style because they were too poor to afford it. Now, the upper classes were used to wealth and comfortable with luxury. Conspicuous consumption became an accepted mode of life for the rich, who built villas in the countryside and filled their homes at Rome with works of art. Once staid matrons now dressed in diaphanous gowns and piled their hair in careful coiffures. The entourage of a prominent Roman included butlers, maids, chefs, tutors, and perhaps a kept intellectual. After the war with Perseus, Polybius maintains, banqueting became a craze, and young men of good families emulated the homosexual tastes of Hellas. The gilded youths would pay a talent for a pretty boy

---

[12] Polybius 15.35.6.

[13] One curb on noble ambitions was the *lex Villia annalis* in 180 that provided minimal ages for magistrates—consuls, for example, had to be at least 42, presumably an age when maturity and experience would make them more restrained.

and three hundred denarii for a jar of pickled fish. Cato snorted that the Republic was toppling when a male whore cost more than a field, and a jar of fish more than a slave ploughman.[14] The extent of homosexuality in Roman society should not be exaggerated, for homosexual soldiers were publicly scourged. The frequent charges of *stuprum cum masculo,* made against rival politicians and unpopular emperors, proves that the practice was looked upon with disfavor by most Romans. Until Scipio Aemilianus made it fashionable, daily shaving was considered an affectation of the effeminate Greeks. Despite a series of sumptuary laws beginning in 161, extensive banquets and luxury consumption continued to infuriate moralists, and the repetition of the laws only indicates their ineffectuality.[15]

In the second century, immense amounts of movable wealth accrued to the Roman state in the form of booty, indemnities, and tribute. From Livy's account of the period from 201 to 157 B.C., Tenney Frank calculated that the Senate received about 161,000,000 denarii from such sources [16]—the actual figures would be much higher. After 167, the Roman citizenry were no longer required to pay direct property taxes. The Republic held vast tracts of public land in Italy, including the lands seized in Campania after the fall of Capua. While a good amount of cash was spent on war in this period, the Roman economy absorbed much of the new wealth, causing a steady inflation. The profits of empire excited the avarice of businessmen who sought contracts as tax farmers (publicans) to collect rents on public lands, custom duties, and tribute in the provinces. Because the Senate failed to create a civil service for the empire, the publicans were a necessary evil whose worst abuses were reserved for defenseless provincials. In the provinces, unpaid Roman officials were easily bribed to ignore complaints of oppressive taxation and to provide troops to assist the publicans. The unfavorable image of publicans in the *New Testament* testifies to the hatred felt by victims of these "caterpillars of the commonwealth." Organized in companies, the publicans became a major force in the economic life of the imperial Republic. Businessmen also reaped additional profits in contracts to supply the armies of Rome. The rise of a wealthy middle class produced a minor gentry, for rich commoners were enrolled in the eighteen top centuries as *equites.* Soon, the name, *equites,*[17] which

[14] Polybius 31.25.4–6.
[15] Aulus Gellius (2.24) gives a good summary of sumptuary legislation.
[16] Tenney Frank, *An Economic Survey of Ancient Rome* (Baltimore: Johns Hopkins Press, 1933), I, 126–38. (Henceforth this work is cited as *ESAR*).
[17] The singular noun, *eques,* is sometimes rendered as knight, but this has a military connotation in English which is inappropriate for Roman financiers. The adjective "equestrian" also has an awkward tone but it is unavoidable.

meant "cavalrymen" and was also applied to nobles in the Centuriate Assembly, came to signify the plutocratic class of Rome. Recognized as gentry, *equites* wore distinctive gold rings and were entitled to specific privileges such as sitting in the first fourteen rows of the theater. Though they often intermarried with noble families, the *equites* as a class did not aspire to high office but were content to make money while the nobles scrambled for honor and glory. Generally, the interests of senators and *equites* coincided, but Gaius Gracchus would raise the *equites* to a position of rivalry with the Senate.

Unlike the *equites,* senators were forbidden to engage in commerce, but many were silent partners in business endeavors. The ideology of the nobility insisted that farming was the only legitimate means of making money. In the second century, many senators became agrarian capitalists on a grand scale by amassing large estates from public lands. Theoretically, individual holdings had been limited to 500 *iugera* (about 300 acres) by the Licinian law in 367. Cato implied in a speech that the Licinian law was still on the books in 167,[18] but its provisions were not observed, for senators were exploiting the public lands, and the Senate was not about to police itself. Besides illegally held public land, estate owners bought up the holdings of indigent small farmers. On their huge estates (*latifundia*), agrarian capitalists adopted a plantation economy, employing slave labor in large numbers and concentrating on a few crops. Cereal and vegetable production were abandoned in favor of olives and vineyards, and elsewhere farms were converted to pastures to produce meat, wool, and hides, commodities easily saleable to army contractors. The economic revolution in agriculture evolved slowly, and most *latifundia* were concentrated in Etruria and Campania, but the effects on Italy were drastic. The number of small farms decreased, and the level of efficiency on the *latifundia* was low. Both Varro and Pliny the Elder testify to the superiority of free laborers over slave workers in agricultural production.[19]

Essential for the plantation system in Italy was the importation of large numbers of slaves. As war captives, hordes of luckless slaves had been dragged from Hellas, the East, Africa, and Spain to labor for Roman taskmasters. Skilled individuals were usually employed at their former trades, and so both education and industry were largely in servile hands. Many small businessmen were slaves whose masters made a handsome profit and allowed them to retain enough cash to eventually buy their freedom. The ubiquity of freedmen in professional life and the lower levels of economic activity was characteristic of Republican

[18] Aulus Gellius 6.3.37.
[19] Varro *Rerum Rusticarum* 1.17.3. Pliny the Elder *Naturalis Historia* 18.21.

Rome. A handful of slaves became domestics in the homes of rich Romans. Less fortunate and far greater in number were unskilled slaves, who labored as field hands and were often brutally treated. At the bottom of the hell of slavery were miserable wretches who toiled in the mines. Quoting Posidonius who had seen the mines in operation, Diodorus Siculus describes the sufferings of miners in Spain:

> The slaves who are engaged in the working of [mines] produce for their masters revenues in sums defying belief, but they themselves wear out their bodies both by day and by night in the diggings under the earth, dying in large numbers because of the exceptional hardships they endure. For no respite or pause is granted them in their labors, but compelled beneath blows of the overseers to endure the severity of their plight, they throw away their lives in this wretched manner, although certain of them who can endure it, by virtue of their bodily strength and their persevering souls, suffer such hardships over a long period; indeed, death in their eyes is more to be desired than life, because of the magnitude of the hardships they must bear.[20]

Everywhere in the slave economy, force or the threat of force was constant. To the trauma of capture and the degradation of being sold like an animal was added the extended agony of life as a slave. Many a master who was kind to his household slaves was justly hated by hundreds of faceless bondsmen who labored in his fields. Unruly slaves were beaten and tortured, and many rural owners chained their chattel at night to prevent their escape. Runaways were common despite the fear of punishment when caught. Especially difficult to control were shepherds and cowboys on large ranches. Having no hope of return to their homelands, runaway slaves became bandits and added to the crime rate in the countryside. As hordes of slaves were scattered about Italy, the danger of slave revolts—always a pressing worry in antiquity—increased, for both negligence and brutality encouraged resentful slaves to strike for freedom. In the economy, the slave was a humanoid machine, on stage a figure of ridicule, but he could become a fearful apparition when he rose in rebellion.

The world of millionaires and slaves was the product of Roman conquests, achieved not only by ambitious generals and cunning senators but also by thousands of anonymous legionaries who fought and died that Rome might be supreme. The Roman army was a conscript force, for every male between 17 and 46 was eligible to be called to serve

[20] Diodorus Siculus 5.38.1, trans. C. H. Oldfather, (Cambridge, Mass.: Harvard University Press, 1939), III, 199–201.

with the legions. In theory, however, proletarians had too little stake in society to be required to serve in the army. Though most Romans considered it an honor, military service became an increasingly heavy burden as the wars of Rome multiplied. In 171, when the consuls were enrolling troops for the war against Perseus, ex-centurions grumbled at not receiving their former rank in the new levy. Livy has preserved an interesting exhortation to patriotism by one veteran who shamed his fellows by recounting his services to Rome:

I, Spurius Ligustinus of the tribe of Crustumina, come of Sabine stock, fellow citizens. My father left me a *iugerum* of land and a little hut, in which I was born and brought up, and to this day I live there. When I first came of age, my father gave me as wife his brother's daughter, who brought with her nothing but her free birth and her chastity, and with these a fertility which would be enough even for a wealthy home. We have six sons and two daughters, both of whom are now married. Four of our sons have assumed the toga of manhood, two wear the boys' stripe. I became a soldier in [200 B.C.]. In the army which was taken over to Macedonia I served two years as a private soldier against King Philip; in the third year, for my bravery, Titus Quinctius Flamininus made me centurion of the tenth maniple of the advance formation. After the defeat of Philip and the Macedonians, when we had been brought back to Italy and discharged, immediately I set out for Spain as a volunteer soldier with Marcus Porcius [Cato] the consul. . . . This general judged me worthy to be assigned as centurion of the forward first century of the advance formation. For the third time I enlisted, again voluntarily, in the army which was sent against the Aetolians and King Antiochus. . . . I was given the rank of centurion of the forward first century of the main formation. When King Antiochus had been driven out and the Aetolians beaten, we were brought back to Italy; and twice after that I was in campaigns where the legions served for a year. Then I campaigned twice in Spain, [181 and 180]. . . . I went back to the province [in 180] because Tiberius Gracchus asked me. Four times within a few years, I held the rank of chief centurion; thirty-four times I was rewarded for bravery by my generals; I have received six civic crowns. I have done twenty-two years of service in the army, and I am over fifty years old. But if all my years of service had not been completed and my age did not yet give me exemption, still, since I could give you four soldiers in my place, . . . it would be fair to discharge me. . . . For my part, as long as anyone who is enrolling armies considers me fit for service, I will never beg off. Of what rank the military tribunes think me worthy is for them to decide; I shall see to it that no one in the army surpasses me in bravery. . . . It is fair for you, too, fellow soldiers, even though you are within your rights in this appeal, since, when you were young you never did anything against the authority of the magistrates and the Senate, now also to submit to the consuls and the Senate, and to consider every place honorable in which you will be defending the Republic.[21]

A poor man, Ligustinus had spent over two decades in the army. After his moving speech, the grateful consuls made him chief centurion again.[22]

Though the case of Ligustinus was exceptional, many Romans were forced to spend long years away from their farms and families. The strain on the fidelity of Roman wives was considerable, and the role of the *paterfamilias* suffered in many homes. Because poor Romans did not own slaves, the absence of the husband could be economically catastrophic, for the farm often went to ruin and the wife was forced to mortgage it. Many veterans came home to find their farms neglected and themselves in debt. Widows, too, found it difficult to maintain a homestead. With the growth of *latifundia,* rich neighbors were ready to buy out impoverished farmers, and few wanted them as tenants. Ousted from their ancestral homes, dispossessed veterans became day laborers working for a pittance or drifted into the slums of Rome to join the growing mass of proletarians who were often unemployed. Bitter and indigent, the urban poor lived from hand to mouth and received little aid from noble patrons. Largely unskilled, they drifted into construction work, but the raising of public buildings was a fitful affair, dependent upon overseas booty. A minor source of income for the poor was bribery of proletarian voters. Should they find a champion, the proletarians could become an important factor in the Tribal Assembly. In the second century, the population of the city of Rome changed its composition and tone as dislocated veterans and alien freedmen joined its ranks. Rootless and insecure, they turned readily to clubs (*collegia*) for a sense of sodality and to novel religions. The state cult was a hollow formality and its agrarian emphasis had little meaning to urban dwellers. Ligustinus's old commander, Tiberius Gracchus the Elder, viewed the changing citizenry with alarm. As censor in 168, he enrolled all freedmen in one tribe to lessen their impact on the Tribal Assembly.

If Rome was indifferent toward proletarians and snobbish toward freedmen, the imperial Republic behaved even worse toward its old allies, the Italians, who made up two-thirds of the available military manpower at Rome's disposal. Despite ties of blood and culture, the Romans were stingy with the precious grant of citizenship, and in 188 Arpinum, Formiae, and Fundi were the last Italian towns to receive the

---

[21] Livy 42.34.2–15, trans. Evan T. Sage and Alfred C. Schlesinger, (Cambridge, Mass.: Harvard University Press, 1938), XII, 389–95.

[22] Though Livy may have invented him, Ligustinus is nonetheless true as a type. The details of the speech have the ring of authenticity.

status of full citizenship. In the distribution of war booty, the Italians were at the mercy of Roman generosity. In 173, when the consuls distributed captured lands in Liguria and the Po Valley, Romans received ten *iugera* and "Latins" three. The growing arrogance of Romans toward Italians was manifested in many ways. As aedile in 182, the elder Gracchus had made both Italians and provincials pay for the lavish games he conducted. In 173, a consul intimidated the local magistrates of Praeneste into meeting him on foot, providing entertainment during his stay, and furnishing transport animals on his departure. Later in the century, Gaius Gracchus revealed that a consul had ordered the officials of an Italian town to clear the public baths in order that his wife might bathe. When the woman complained that the officials had not acted quickly enough and that the baths were dirty, the consul had the chief magistrate scourged. About the same time, a haughty young noble had an Italian peasant beaten to death for joking about the Roman being carried in a litter.[23] To escape such outrageous treatment, Italians needed the protection afforded by Roman citizenship, but Rome ignored their constant agitation for the prized status. Although municipal oligarchs and businessmen often received the honor, the mass of the Italian population was denied Roman citizenship. Good enough to fight and die for Rome, the Italians were not considered fit to share in citizenship.

In the provinces, whole nations fretted under the publican's yoke and the brutalities of the Roman army. Though tribute was an onerous burden and the arrogance of Roman officials intolerable, the provincials were usually left to their own devices, and Rome did not interfere much in the economic life of its subjects. In 167, the Senate closed the silver mines in Macedon to keep them out of the publican's hands, or so Livy claims.[24] At any rate, the mines were operating again by 158. In a much disputed passage, Cicero remarks that (when they had extended their control to Narbonensian Gaul) the Romans forbade the Transalpine Gauls to cultivate the olive or the vine, in order to protect the products of Italy.[25] Since no mention was made of other Western provinces that produced wine and olives, it would seem that Rome was acting not on behalf of Italian producers, but rather for its old ally, Massilia, which would be interested in monopolies in southern Gaul.[26] Later the Romans refined the arts of exploitation, for by 69 B.C. Cicero described Gaul as being in an economic stranglehold: "Gaul is packed with traders, crammed with Roman citizens. No Gaul ever does business independently of a citizen of Rome; not a penny exchanges hands

23 Aulus Gellius 10.3.3–5.   24 Livy 45.18.3–4.
25 Cicero *de Republica* 3.9.16.   26 Frank, *ESAR,* I, 172–74.

in Gaul without the transaction being recorded in the books of Roman citizens." [27] Even allowing for Ciceronian hyperbole, the situation depicted was a classic scene of imperialism after a military conquest has been effected. In the second century, similar conditions prevailed in many provinces as evidenced by the universal hatred of Roman businessmen both in Spain and in Asia. In the words of a modern scholar, "it was plain that many Romans believed that they were born booted and spurred where other men were born saddled and bridled." [28]

THE GRACCHI AND MARIUS

The spectacular dominion that Rome enjoyed by the middle of the second century masked the shaky foundations upon which Roman power rested. In the provinces, the subject nations waited eagerly for messiahs to lead them against their oppressors. Closer to home, the Romans faced hordes of surly enemies in the slaves who plotted revolts. To survive, Rome depended on the might of the legions, but the Italians resented their second-class status, and the reservoirs of Roman manpower were drying up as more and more veterans slipped into the ranks of the proletarians. In the city of Rome, urban poverty increased as the slum population grew, and the antique ways lauded by Cato had long since become an anachronism. The proliferation of *latifundia* in the countryside alarmed perceptive Romans. For the most part, however, the senatorial oligarchy lacked much concern for provincials, Italians, or proletarians. As in all societies, there were few men of vision at Rome. Some problems the Romans were willing to face while others were evaded, but even the solutions brought results unanticipated by their advocates.

The protracted wars in Spain were a constant source of crisis, for the Roman masses had little enthusiasm for colonial adventures in the Far West. In 151, the reluctance of conscripts to serve in Spain caused a clash between the consuls and a tribune who briefly imprisoned the magistrates. To spur volunteers for the unpopular war, young Scipio Aemilianus offered to serve in Spain. In 139, the tribune A. Gabinius passed a law providing for the secret ballot in elections in the assemblies. The following year, resistance to the draft resulted in tribunician action against the consul, P. Cornelius Scipio Nasica Serapio, and his colleague. In 140, the dwindling supply of men available for conscription had prompted Scipio Aemilianus to back a proposal by the consul,

[27] Cicero *pro Fonteio* 11, trans. Frank, *ESAR,* I, 281.
[28] Sir Frank Adcock, *CAH,* X, 604.

C. Laelius, to resettle proletarians on public land. While Aemilianus hoped to increase the supply of cannon fodder, some of his senatorial colleagues illegally held large tracts of public land and opposed the measure, which Laelius then withdrew. A new threat soon aroused many senators to the dangers of the *latifundia*. About 135, a major slave revolt broke out in Sicily, led by a Syrian wonder-worker, Eunus, who set up a rebel state with himself as "King Antiochus." The slaves seized a number of important towns and defeated the Roman forces sent against them. As consul in 133, the historian L. Calpurnius Piso Frugi campaigned in Sicily, and his successor in 132 crushed the slaves with veterans from Numantia. Though Eunus died in a Roman dungeon, his rebellion had far-reaching results, for there were outbursts in Italy as well, and news of the Sicilian revolt prompted slaves to rise in Attica and on Delos. Though the slave rebellions were ruthlessly put down, the Roman ruling class was now fearful of the strangers in their midst.

In 133, the time was ripe for a reform that would replenish Rome's military manpower and reduce the threat of slave revolts. A land program to resettle proletarians on public land was devised by the *Princeps Senatus* Appius Claudius Pulcher, the consul P. Mucius Scaevola,[29] and Scaevola's powerful brother, P. Licinius Crassus. The reformers also had the backing of Scipio Aemilianus and most of the Senate. The spokesman for the land program was an able young tribune, Tiberius Sempronius Gracchus the Younger, who was Pulcher's son-in-law. To later generations, Tiberius Gracchus was either a champion of the masses or a scheming demagogue. In reality, he was a Roman aristocrat of the bluest blood who felt destined for consular glories. His father, the conservative censor Tiberius Gracchus the Elder, had died when the younger Tiberius was a child. The boy had been raised by his mother, Cornelia, who was the daughter of Scipio Africanus.[30] Tiberius's sister, Sempronia, was married to Scipio Aemilianus, although there was ill feeling between the two men over Scipio's repudiation of the treaty that Tiberius had negotiated with Numantia. Both Tiberius and his brother, Gaius, were well educated, and Cornelia maintained a fashionable salon frequented by Greek intellectuals. Though Scipio's friend, the Greek historian Polybius, growled that land reform corrupted the masses, both Aemilianus and Gracchus saw the measure as essential for the military rejuvenation of the Roman body politic. As a politician, Tiberius was not insensitive to the utility of building up a following of grateful voters, and he was alarmed by the *latifundia* and the slave gangs that he had seen in Etruria on his way back from Spain. Above all, Gracchus was a

---

[29] Later, as Pontifex Maximus, Scaevola compiled the *Annales Maximi*.
[30] For defending Lucius Scipio in 187, the elder Gracchus had received Cornelia's hand and her father's support.

Roman noble who, like Laelius, had fought beside Scipio at Carthage, and he hoped one day to lead the augmented armies of citizen soldiers to win glory in foreign wars.

Appealing to the ill-observed precedent of the Licinian law of 367, Tiberius proposed a bill to the Tribal Assembly that would limit holdings of public land to 500 *iugera* (with perhaps 500 more for a man with two children). The state would repossess excess acreage but reimburse former holders for any improvements they had made, an astute sop for senators who stood to lose by the reforms. From the repossessed lands, the state would provide proletarians with small homesteads of probably 30 *iugera* and lend the settlers funds for setting up their farms. The land so given would be inalienable and elevate ex-proletarians into freeholders and potential draftees. Roman squatters, who were holding small parcels of public land, were also protected by the bill. However, the Pontifex Maximus, Scipio Nasica Serapio, and others who had seized large estates at public expense, opposed the measure and prompted another tribune, M. Octavius, to veto the proposal. Angered, Tiberius dropped the provision of reimbursement and reintroduced the measure at the next meeting of the Tribal Assembly, warning Octavius that he would not tolerate further obstruction. The urban poor were enthusiastic for the bill, and rural laborers trooped into the city to add their support. Secure in the Senate's backing, Gracchus was highhanded like his grandfather, Scipio Africanus. When Octavius again threatened a veto, Tiberius unseated his rival by a unanimous vote of the tribes, who then passed the land bill. Though tribunician vetoes had been ignored in the past, no one had dared to remove a tribune even in the name of the people's will. The obstruction of Nasica's small clique had pushed Gracchus into a constitutional innovation of far-reaching consequence, for, if pushed to its logical conclusion, Tiberius's action had converted Rome into a democracy, which was not his intention. In the Senate, his supporters began to have second thoughts about the rash tribune. To implement the land program, a commission—made up of Tiberius, his brother Gaius, and his father-in-law, Pulcher—was established, but Scipio Nasica prevailed upon the Senate to allot only nine sesterces a day for the operating expenses of the land program. In time, more money would have been forthcoming, for the Senate supported the reforms, but it seemed necessary to tame Gracchus. Meanwhile, Attalus III of Pergamum had died and left much of his kingdom to Rome. Because the Gracchi were patrons of Pergamum,[31] the Asian envoys contacted Tiberius and presented him with a large portion of the royal trea-

---

[31] In 165, Tiberius Gracchus the Elder had visited Pergamum and later defended Eumenes' interests at Rome.

sures, which he accepted on behalf of the Roman people and applied to the land program. Since foreign affairs and graft were its cherished prerogatives, the Senate was furious, and Nasica awaited the end of Tiberius's tribunate when the maverick noble might be harassed with impunity.

Again shattering convention, Gracchus announced that he would run for reelection. Sure of the support of ex-proletarians and rural voters, he may also have made overtures to the urban masses, but accounts of his programs were later confused with those of his brother. When it appeared that Tiberius might win the election, hostile tribunes vetoed the proceedings and his supporters rioted. In the Senate, Nasica demanded the declaration of a state of emergency, but the consul Scaevola naturally declined to act, whereupon Nasica turned to lynch law. Though he was Tiberius's cousin, the Pontifex led a mob of nobles and clients who hunted down and killed Gracchus and massacred three hundred of his followers. To legalize the murders, a special tribunal was set up in 132 to try other Gracchan supporters for sedition. The board scrupulously ignored Tiberius's high-born allies and acquitted the radical intellectual, Blossius of Cumae, who defiantly proclaimed his loyalty to the martyred tribune. When he returned from Numantia, Scipio Aemilianus was asked his opinion of the lynching of his brother-in-law; the general coolly replied that Tiberius deserved his fate. However, the murder of the popular tribune backfired on Nasica and his friends as Cornelia worked assiduously to canonize her son as a martyr who had died for the masses. Aemilianus lost popularity, and Nasica soon left Italy and died in Pergamum under suspicious circumstances. In 131, Gaius Gracchus's father-in-law, Crassus, was consul, and the same year, a Gracchan tribune, C. Papirius Carbo, introduced the secret ballot for legislative votes in the assemblies. As the Senate had not opposed the Gracchan land program, the commission, on which Crassus had replaced Tiberius, had continued to operate and may have placed 75,000 proletarians on the land.

In Asia, Rome tried to collect the legacy of Attalus III, who had willed his royal property to the Roman people to prevent the throne from passing into the hands of Aristonicus, a bastard of Eumenes II. Having no children, Attalus had handed his nation to the rapacious Romans out of spite against his half brother. However, Aristonicus proclaimed a war of national resistance and won the backing of many of the Greek cities of Asia, though Pergamum supported Rome. Apparently, the pretender had great popular appeal, for many peasants rallied to him and the city of Pergamum was forced to grant freedom to slaves who did not defect to his banners. When he lost control of the coast, Aristonicus withdrew to the interior and proclaimed his rebel government a City of the Sun, appealing to local beliefs in the sun as a god of justice and equality. Interestingly, Blossius, who bypassed the rebellious slaves of Sicily, fled to Aristonicus and may have been involved in the sudden death of Nasica at Pergamum. Another Gracchan, the proconsul Crassus, was less friendly to the citizens of the sun and died leading Roman armies against them. In 130, a general who had taken Eunus in Sicily captured Aristonicus, and the embers of revolt were stamped out by poisoning the wells used by rebels. When the sun state collapsed, Blossius committed suicide, and Aristonicus was later strangled at Rome. Whatever religio-ideological appeal it had for slaves, the City of the Sun had no place in the Roman world, and the Pergamene kingdom became the Roman province of Asia.

In Italy, the land commission continued its work, and Gaius Gracchus was joined by M. Fulvius Flaccus and Carbo, replacing the deceased Pulcher and Crassus. In their rigor, the commissioners expelled Italians who were holding public lands but whose deeds were lost or invalid. For aid, the Italians turned in 129 to their old commander Scipio Aemilianus, who proposed that the consuls take over the functions of the Gracchan commission. One morning, when Scipio was scheduled to deliver a speech on the Italians and their rights, the famous general was found dead, and foul play was suspected. Though no charges were pressed, the suspects included Gaius Gracchus, Cornelia, Carbo, and even Scipio's wife, Sempronia, who was deformed and had been unhappy married to the famous warlord. Perhaps to quiet the agitation over land or even for more statesmanlike reasons, the Gracchans now took up the cause of the Italians. As consul in 125, Flaccus wished to grant them citizenship, but the Senate opposed the measure and the Roman masses were indifferent. When Massilia asked for assistance against the Gauls, Flaccus gladly departed for the wars.[32] Disillusioned by Flaccus and despairing of Roman justice, the town of Fregellae rebelled and was destroyed by the praetor L. Opimius. Though cowed by the brutal act, the Italians did not cease lobbying and soon found a champion in Gaius Gracchus.

Like his brother, Gaius Sempronius Gracchus was a controversial figure, whose aims and acts are clouded by the propaganda of later writers. A forceful orator, he insisted that the martyred Tiberius had ordered him in a dream to carry on the struggle for the masses. Though any such claim by a politician is suspect, the story is psychologically plausible. More astute politically than Tiberius, Gaius made as broad an appeal as possible and sought to ally the *equites* with the commons

---

[32] Within a few years, the Romans subdued the southern coast of Gaul and annexed it as the province of Gallia Narbonensis. The new province excluded the territory of Rome's old ally, Massilia.

against the more reactionary members of the Senate. It is absurd, however, to view him as a democrat, for no Gracchus intended to end his career as a tribune—Cornelia raised her sons to be consuls and conquerors like her father. A veteran of Numantia, Gaius was a land commissioner and had served as quaestor on Sardinia. As tribune in 123, he pushed through a variety of bills, continuing the land commission, improving roads in rural areas, providing clothing for soldiers, and indicting officials who had persecuted the followers of Tiberius. To relieve the urban poor, Gaius proposed colonies at Tarentum and later at Carthage. The urban masses were at the mercy of grain speculators, and he established a system whereby the state bought up grain and resold it to the people at a fixed low price. While he did not create a dole, Gaius won many votes by this measure. To win over the *equites,* he had the censors auction the tax contracts for Asia at Rome, but only the wealthiest businessmen could afford to cover such large sums. Then (or perhaps the following year), Gracchus made a major bid for the support of the *equites* when one of his allies, the tribune Manius Acilius, passed a law excluding senators from the courts that judged complaints from the provinces.[33] The juries of perhaps 75 members were now drawn from a board of 450 wealthy non-senators. By protecting corrupt governors, senatorial juries had earned a poor reputation, but the *equites* would do no better, for Gaius had given them an opportunity to plunder Asia and other provinces with impunity. Solicitous about the Roman masses and friendly to the Italians, he treated provincials with typical Roman arrogance. Possibly, in setting up the *equites* as a counterweight to the Senate, Gaius was influenced by Polybius's notions of a balance of power in the state, but no experienced politician needed an aged Greek historian to enlighten him on the realities of Roman politics.

In 122, Gaius Gracchus seemed at the height of his power. He was reelected tribune, and Flaccus, though a consular noble, joined him in the tribunate to further their joint programs. Another friend, C. Fannius, was consul. Overconfident, Gaius left Rome to organize the colony at Carthage, which was having difficulties. In his absence, Flaccus was unable to counter the activities of a rival tribune, M. Livius Drusus, who outbid the Gracchans with unrealistic promises of land for the masses and made other gestures to win popular support. An opportunist, Drusus served the interests of Opimius and the extreme anti-Gracchan faction in the Senate. Returning to Rome, Gaius tried to extend citizenship to Latins, but Drusus vetoed the bill, and the voters in the Tribal Assembly then rejected a desperate Gracchan measure to give

---

[33] Portions of the *lex Acilia* are extant. See *ROL,* IV, 316–71 and *ARS,* pp. 38–46.

the franchise to all Italians. The sources are not clear on these matters, and Gaius may have intended only Latin rights for the Italians and been blocked even there by Drusus's veto. Sensing the mood of Rome, Fannius had deserted the Gracchans and expelled all Italians from the city during the voting. The Roman voters had no interest in the Italian cause, and the *equites* had nothing more to gain by supporting Gaius, whose coalition had collapsed due to the intrigues of Drusus. Whatever his motives in championing the Italians, Gaius Gracchus had risen to the heights of statesmanship, but unfortunately he had lost his grasp on the political machinery at Rome. Had his bill been passed, Rome and the Italians would have been spared the fierce rebellion that erupted a generation later.

Defeated for a third term as tribune, Gaius was only a land commissioner in 121, but Opimius was consul. When a riot broke out between Gaius's followers and those of his enemies, Opimius persuaded the Senate to grant him emergency powers (*senatus consultum ultimum*) to restore order. The consul dispatched a posse of his sympathizers against the Gracchans. Gaius was hunted down and committed suicide, and Opimius summarily executed 3,000 of his supporters. Since Opimius had offered to pay its weight in gold for Gaius's head, a canny thug scooped out the brain and filled the skull with lead. The folly of resorting to violence after Drusus had broken the Gracchan hold on the Tribal Assembly revealed the incompetence as well as the vindictiveness of Opimius and his clique. Now, both of the Gracchi were martyrs in the eyes of those Romans who favored measures on behalf of the masses. By twice employing lynch law, the reactionary faction in the Senate had shown its political bankruptcy and set a precedent in atrocity which would be magnified a hundredfold in the next generation. Once masters of cunning and compromise, the Roman ruling class had embraced the politics of violence and set the stage for the assassinations, purges, and civil wars that would destroy the Republic.

In the post-Gracchan era, men who may be labelled Optimates and Populares rose to prominence, though these terms were only used in the Ciceronian period. In no sense are the labels equivalent to modern party designations, for the Roman system did not evolve a party apparatus. Because politics at Rome operated through the Establishment, the Populares and Optimates were nobles or would-be nobles, not party chiefs but leaders of rival factions. In general, the Populares posed as friends of the people and usually supported land programs and measures calculated to benefit the masses, who expressed their gratitude in the Assemblies. The Gracchi were heroes in the eyes of Populares, whose ranks included Marius and Caesar. Their opponents, the self-styled Optimates ("best people"), were generally more conservative and preferred to operate through the Senate, but that body also contained Popular nobles. Sulla, Cicero, and Cato the Younger were famous Optimates. Neither group was particularly doctrinaire in its positions, and expediency prompted opportunists such as Pompey to slide back and forth between the factions. No doubt some senators were sincerely liberal or conservative, but the Romans were a flexible folk when it came to politics. Family alliances or old vendettas explain more about Roman history than do the programs of reform and reaction so dear to orators and historians.

After destroying Gaius Gracchus, Opimius and his friends survived indictments for their illegal assaults on the Gracchans. Even Carbo became a turncoat and was rewarded with the consulship for 120, but he was prosecuted on some charge and driven to suicide a year later. In 119, the land commission was abolished, and by 111 settlers could sell their lots, but the Gracchan program had been a success and there was little public land left in Italy outside of Campania. One of the tribunes in 119 was an ambitious *eques* from Arpinum, Gaius Marius, who had fought at Numantia and was backed by the noble Metelli. Though opposed to an extension of the Gracchan grain program, Marius irritated his patrons by a measure which made it more difficult for nobles to keep an eye on their clients' voting. By 115, he was praetor and soon married into the patrician Caesarean family; his wife was the aunt of Julius Caesar. Politically, Marius was a Popular leader, but he had no firm commitments to anyone and no love for the masses. Because of his military ability, Marius recovered favor with the Metelli, but he would soon betray them. An unabashed opportunist, Marius believed in his own destiny. In childhood, he had come across seven eagles, and in later life, Marius was convinced that fate had reserved seven great honors for him.

Through war and political intrigue, Marius worked to fulfill the omen of the seven eagles. In North Africa, Rome had been drawn into a difficult war against Masinissa's grandson, Jugurtha, who had served with Marius at Numantia. In seizing power in Numidia, Jugurtha had made the error of massacring Roman businessmen when he stormed the capital of a rival prince. Though the outraged *equites* insisted on war in 111, the Optimate consul L. Calpurnius Bestia was bribed by Jugurtha to halt hostilities. When the king received a safe-conduct to testify on the affair before the Tribal Assembly, an Optimate tribune vetoed the proceedings. Leaving Rome, Jugurtha sneered that the venal city was up for sale and might soon find a buyer. The war in Numidia resumed with humiliating defeats for the Romans until the consul for 109, Q. Caecilius Metellus Numidicus, restored some honor to Roman arms. However, Metellus could not defeat Jugurtha, and his own aide, Marius, was plotting to replace him. Appealing to the impatient *equites* and masses at Rome, Marius won the consulship in 107 by maligning his old patron. Though he received the Numidian command, the "new man" was short of troops, for Rome was also concerned with menacing barbarians in Gaul. To fill his legions, Marius ignored property qualifications for soldiers and enlisted proletarians among his volunteers. An emergency measure by an impatient consul, the new policy was to have far-reaching effects as the poor filled the ranks of the Roman army. With great efficiency, Marius put his troops to use in Numidia and crushed Jugurtha by 105 when the king was taken by treachery. A year later, Jugurtha was dragged in Marius's triumph at Rome and strangled. In the Numidian campaign, Marius had been ably served by his quaestor, Sulla, who later claimed credit for much of the victory. From that time on, the two men loathed each other.

In Europe, Optimate bungling of a major war gave Marius a chance for new glories. In 109, Gaul had been invaded by hordes of Celtic and Germanic barbarians, loosely called Cimbri and Teutones. A fierce people whose women egged their men to battle, the invaders asked the Senate for permission to settle in southern Gaul and offered to serve as auxiliaries with the Roman armies. When the Senate rejected the proposal, the barbarians defeated the Roman forces sent against them. In 105 the proconsul, Q. Servilius Caepio, suffered a major defeat at their hands near Arausio.[34] So great were the Roman losses that the voters at Rome quickly elected Marius consul for 104 and kept him in the office for five years to repel the northern menace. No one had ever held so many consulships, and Marius's vanity was inflated accordingly. His predecessor in 105, P. Rutilius Rufus, had begun to reform the Roman armies by introducing severe training and better weapons. Marius continued the process and forced his men to carry their baggage. He also remodeled the legion itself and raised its strength to 6,000 men, organized in ten cohorts of six centuries each. As the army became professionalized, the centurions emerged as a seasoned cadre of company-grade officers, whose expertise could counteract the errors of inexperienced commanders. To build loyalty to the unit, each legion received a silver eagle on a standard, to which the troops offered religious devotions as the embodiment of their collective spirit. In 102, Marius put his new model army to use and defeated the Teutones in Gaul. A year later, he decisively routed the Cimbri who had invaded the Po Valley. Hailed as the "new Camillus," Marius was the savior of his country, and he easily received a sixth consulship in 100.

[34] In 106, Caepio had passed a law that divided the extortion courts between senators and *equites*. After Arausio, the *equites* regained control of the juries in 104.

While Marius was engaged in the northern wars, Rome slightly expanded the democratic process. Since the third century, the Pontifex Maximus had been chosen by a vote of seventeen tribes in the Tribal Assembly selected by lot, but he had to be elected from among the co-optative priesthoods. In 104, a law was passed providing that the seventeen tribes elect all pontiffs and augurs. Less easily solved was the problem of slave unrest. So active were the buccaneers of the Eastern Mediterranean that many plantations in Sicily were filled with individuals who had been kidnapped by corsairs and sold to Roman traders. When asked by Marius for troops for the war against the Cimbri, Nicomedes III of Bithynia complained that pirates had enslaved most of his men and publicans had got the rest. Many of the Sicilian slaves were, in fact, Bithynians. After investigating numerous complaints, the Senate ordered the release of illegally held slaves, but when the owners protested, the governor of Sicily refused to enforce the decree. In 104, the infuriated slaves rose under able leaders and seized parts of the island. Not until 100 was the slave revolt finally crushed by veterans from the Cimbric wars. The Sicilian revolt had awakened the Senate to the problem of piracy, and in 102 part of Cilicia was made a province to facilitate its use as a naval base against the corsairs, whose major lairs were in Cilicia and Crete. In 96, Rome picked up another Eastern property when a Ptolemaic prince willed Cyrene to the Republic, but the Romans only took possession of the crown lands, including the silphium monopoly, and did not annex the region as a province until 74.

A WILDERNESS OF TIGERS

The career of Marius represents a watershed in Roman history, for the great general had unwittingly created the client armies that would soon subvert the Republic. By enlisting proletarians, he made military service a means for the poor to enrich themselves with pay and booty in war and land grants after discharge. Although conscription was not abandoned, the conscript warriors of the past were largely replaced by professional soldiers, who served for sixteen years and developed a sense of loyalty to their units and commanders that outweighed allegiance to the Republic. Able generals, such as Marius, Sulla, Pompey, and Caesar, had little difficulty recruiting volunteers, for soldiers knew that service under a proven commander increased their chances of surviving to enjoy the fruits of victory. Prolonged military commands increased the bonds between the troops and their leaders. Besides ability, a successful general needed a war chest to pay and supply his men, and he also had to have land for his veterans. Money and land were provided by political allies at Rome, who might call upon the general to furnish his men as voters and brawlers. Since the leading men of Rome were both politicians and generals, the implications of the client armies would become obvious when a general who was thwarted politically turned to his troops for assistance. Marius, however, was unaware of the ultimate possibilities of the client army. A "new man," he yearned for acceptance by the nobles, who resented him as an upstart.

In his heyday, Marius's chief political ally was an Optimate opportunist, L. Appuleius Saturninus, who had joined the Populares. As tribune in 103, he provided land grants for Marius's veterans and set up a permanent court of *equites* to try cases of treason, which was redefined as any act that diminished the honor (*maiestas*) of the Roman people. Like *incivisme* in the French Revolution, the charge of *maiestas* was deliberately nebulous and could cover almost anything. When another tribune prosecuted Caepio for the defeat at Arausio, Optimate tribunes tried to veto the proceedings but were driven from the Assembly with violence. In 100, Saturninus was again tribune and restored the Gracchan policy of selling grain at a fixed price; he also secured Gallic land for Marius's veterans and proposed some Latin colonies, which would benefit the Italian allies. The latter measure was not popular with Roman voters, and the *equites* disapproved of Saturninus's demagogery and use of violence. The land bill included a proviso that senators had to swear to uphold it or suffer fines and exile. The consul Marius equivocated; old Metellus Numidicus went into exile. Running for reelection as tribune, Saturninus tried to pack the tribunates and quaestorships with his own supporters, including a freedman who pretended to be a son of Tiberius Gracchus. When riots broke out and an Optimate tribune was slain, the Senate demanded that Marius take action against Saturninus and his followers who took refuge on the Capitoline Hill. Never known for loyalty, Marius sent troops against Saturninus and his men, who surrendered and were placed in the Senate house for safekeeping. While an Optimate mob broke through the roof and stoned the prisoners to death, Marius's guards stood idly by. No doubt Marius expected the Senate's gratitude for his betrayal of Saturninus, but the Optimates were not impressed and the Populares resented his sudden shift. Probably the old general was sincere in his rejection of the rowdy tactics of Saturninus, but he had offended both factions and would never reach the censorship, which he had assumed was the seventh glory promised by the omen of the eagles.

In the first decade of the first century B.C., the Optimates were generally in control, but little was accomplished beyond circumventing the programs of Saturninus. The Italians clamored vainly for citizenship and the provincials cried for an end to extortion, but the Roman Establishment was in no mood for reform. In 92, the *equites* convicted P. Rutilius Rufus of extortion in Asia, though in reality he had tried to protect the provincials from the publicans. A persistent enemy of Marius and the *equites,* Rufus retired from public life and wrote bitter memoirs which lie behind much of the tradition on this era. The same year, the Senate made an ineffective ban on Latin teachers of rhetoric; perhaps the bill was aimed at orators who backed the Populares. In 91, Rufus's nephew, M. Livius Drusus, who was the son of Tiberius Gracchus's opponent, entered on a memorable tribunate. An enlightened Optimate, Drusus proposed a revival of the Gracchan programs of cheap grain, homesteads, and colonies. To reconcile the *equites* and senators, he wished to add 300 *equites* to the Senate and then fill the courts with juries composed of both classes. Most importantly, Drusus was a champion of the exasperated Italians and intended to extend citizenship to all Italy. Regrettably, reactionary Optimates cancelled his bills on a legal technicality, and Roman voters were not likely to approve sharing the franchise. However, the anger of the Italians was mounting, and Drusus himself warned the consuls of Italian plots against their lives. His program a failure and his hopes for Italy dashed, Drusus was assassinated by unknown assailants, perhaps reactionary Romans or even disappointed Italians.

The failure of Drusus was the last straw for the Italians, who abandoned any hope of justice from Rome. Though their arms had helped to win an empire for Rome, they had been treated as inferiors and were often subjected to arrogant behavior from Roman officials. Even Gaius Gracchus had only belatedly urged justice for Italy, and the Gracchan land program had driven many Italians from their homes. At Asculum, the townspeople lynched a haughty Roman praetor and massacred every Roman in sight. At the news from Asculum, the Marsi of Central Italy and the Samnites of the South rose in rebellion. Though the Etruscans, Latins, and Greeks stayed loyal, the Italians had challenged Rome and soon set up a rebel capital, Italia, at Corfinium only seventy-five miles from Rome. The Italian government was probably a confederacy with decision making in the hands of a representative Senate and elected magistrates, such as the able Samnite "praetor" Pontius Telesinus. Appropriately, the coins of Italia featured an Italian bull goring a Roman wolf. Although support came from troops overseas and colonies within Italy, Rome was engaged in a desperate struggle for survival against angry men with a cause. Despite his hope to win new glory in the war, Marius did not receive a command until one of the consuls for 90 had fallen in battle. With Sulla's aid, he broke the Marsic resistance. The consul, L. Julius Caesar, was successful in the South, but even more so in diplomacy, for he acknowledged the justice of Italian grievances. At

Caesar's behest, a law was passed granting citizenship to Italians who remained loyal or surrendered. In 89, more Italians submitted and received the status of citizens, and Latin rights were bestowed on those who lived north of the Po River. Meanwhile, Sulla fiercely harried the Samnites, and by 88 the Italian revolt had ended. Except for a few die-hard Italian nationalists, the rebels had received what they wanted, Roman citizenship, and by granting their demand, Rome admitted its earlier errors. However, thousands of lives had been wasted in the war, and Roman armies had become accustomed to fighting former comrades in arms. In previous conflicts, the enemy had always been strangers, but in the Italian Revolt, men of similar speech and like uniforms fought each other to the death. It was a dress rehearsal for the fratricidal wars of the future. Having granted the Italians' demands under duress, the Senate displayed its real feelings by confining the new citizens to eight tribes in the Assembly. Yet there was no danger of being swamped by the new voters, for only wealthy Italians would have the leisure to travel to Rome to cast votes. The extension of Roman citizenship to all Italians south of the Po greatly enlarged the ranks of the *equites* and somewhat changed their role as a social class. The Italian *equites* were often rural-oriented municipal gentry who were less interested in the empire than were the high financiers at Rome. At any rate, the Italians as a whole had won dignity and equality under Roman law.

News of the Italian Revolt had excited the oppressed nations of the East, who soon rose against Rome under a colorful messiah, Mithridates VI of Pontus, the tarnished shield of Asia. Crafty and courageous, the Pontic king was one of the ablest monarchs of his time. His ancestors had been Persian grandees, and his subjects were Anatolian peasants, but Mithridates and his nobles were thoroughly Hellenized. From his base in Pontus on the southern shore of the Black Sea, he had gradually gained control of the northern shore and seized the Greek cities of the Crimea, posing as their defender against the menacing Scythians. Wealthy and ambitious, Mithridates was a formidable potentate with a flair for the dramatic. According to legend, he built up an immunity to poison by taking tiny daily doses of toxic matter. Anxious to expand westward, Mithridates took advantage of Rome's preoccupation with the Italian Revolt to invade the client kingdoms of Bithynia and Cappadocia, but he withdrew when ordered by Manius Aquilius, the Roman governor at Pergamum. In 88, urged on by Aquilius, Nicomedes IV of Bithynia marched against Mithridates, who accepted the challenge and declared a war of liberation against Rome and its lackeys. Brushing aside the troops of Nicomedes and Aquilius, the Pontic monarch occupied Pergamum and had molten gold poured down the luckless governor's throat. Appealing to social unrest and Hellenistic nationalism, he abolished debts and conducted a pogrom in which 80,000 "Romans" perished—mostly publicans, Italian businessmen, and their families. Twenty thousand more "Romans" died when Mithridates' fleet took Delos, but the island of Rhodes resisted the king. At Athens, democrats seized control of the ancient city and welcomed Mithridates' generals as they occupied central Greece. Like earlier kings, the Pontic monarch posed as a champion of the urban poor and a defender of Hellas against the Italian "barbarians." On his coins, Mithridates posed as Hercules draped in a Roman wolf's pelt instead of the conventional lion skin.

In 88, Sulla was consul and looked eagerly to the Mithridatic war as a chance to win glory and booty restoring Roman power. A threadbare patrician, L. Cornelius Sulla had married into money and spent it freely. Blond, blue-eyed, and red-faced from heavy drinking, the consul was a prominent rake with a sardonic sense of humor. He also had a superstitious confidence in his own good fortune and gloried in the epithet Felix (Lucky). Politically, Sulla was an Optimate, but his only real loyalty was to himself. In the Numidian and Italian wars, he had proven to be an able and ruthless soldier. While Sulla prepared for the Eastern campaign, his old enemy, Marius, made a final bid for glory. A statesmanlike tribune, P. Sulpicius Rufus, wished to enroll freedmen and the new Italian citizens in all the tribes of the Assembly. To gain support for his bill, he proposed the expulsion of debtors from the Senate, the recall of political exiles, and the handing over of Sulla's command to Marius, who was now almost seventy. Despite his eloquence—which Cicero considered the most moving he had ever heard [35]—Rufus could only count on the votes of the four urban tribes that included freedmen and the eight tribes in which the Italians had been enrolled, but Marius's veterans and the *equites* could swing the votes of six more tribes needed to carry the Assembly. When Sulla tried to stop the voting, riots broke out in the Forum, and the consul took refuge in the home of Marius, who helped him to escape after he had promised to cease obstructing Rufus. Once free of Rome, Sulla hurried to the army he had assembled for the Eastern war, and informed them that the expected booty would be snatched from their hands by the troops that Marius would enlist. Rallying the men to his personal cause and deserted by all but one of his officers,[36] Sulla led his legions back to Rome and took the defenseless city after a few hours of fighting. Balked in his ambition, a patrician opportunist had realized the potential of the client army and carried off Rome's first revolution. Cowed by Sulla's troops, the Senate and the Assembly outlawed Marius and Rufus, who had fled. Though

---

[35] Cicero *Brutus* 55.203.
[36] The officer may have been L. Licinius Lucullus, who later edited Sulla's memoirs.

the tribune was quickly hunted down and slain, Marius escaped his pursuers after many close calls and made his way to Africa where some of his veterans had settled. Hiding from Sulla's agents, he sulked in a hut in the ruins of Carthage. "There," says Velleius Paterculus, "Marius, as he gazed upon Carthage, and Carthage, as she beheld Marius, might well have offered consolation to each other." [37]

Before leaving Rome for the East, Sulla made arbitrary constitutional changes to prevent a return to power by the Populares.[38] To circumvent the tribunes, the Centuriate Assembly resumed its long dormant role as the legislative body of Rome, but even it was subjected to prior approval by the Senate. By force of arms, Sulla had turned the clock back two centuries. Even Optimates were shocked by his revolutionary acts and ignored his recommendations for the consuls for 87. Despite Sulla's opposition, an able Popularis, L. Cornelius Cinna, was elected consul together with a safe Optimate, Cn. Octavius. Since his troops were anxious to depart for Greece, Sulla glumly accepted the elections and sailed for the Eastern war. As soon as Sulla was gone, Cinna tried to reinstate the legislation of Rufus, but Octavius drove him and other leading Populares from the city. To replace Cinna, Octavius appointed as consul the *flamen dialis* which meant in effect no consul, since the tabooridden priest could not command an army. Refusing to accept his illegal deposition, Cinna rallied a legion to the Popular cause and marched on Rome. Other troops under Q. Sertorius and Marius, who had returned from Africa, converged on the city. The Optimate resistance was ineffective, and Rome fell to the Populares after a siege. With the fierce hatred of a vindictive old man, Marius unleashed a reign of terror against old enemies and new rivals. While Octavius and a few others were formally tried and executed, Marius's henchmen hunted down and murdered many Optimates on the orders of the aged general. After five days, Cinna and Sertorius intervened and massacred Marius's agents, but not until they had effectively thinned the ranks of the Optimates. Fulfilling the omen of the seven eagles, Marius was chosen consul for 86 together with Cinna, but the old warlord died a few days after taking office. Had he perished at Sulla's hands in 88 or earlier by natural causes, Marius would have passed into history as a patriotic hero equal to Camillus or the Scipios. Instead, he died a bloodstained butcher.

In the next few years, Rome was dominated by the Populares, and Cinna held the consulship from 86 to 84. The Sullan legislation was abrogated, and its author was declared an outlaw. Meanwhile, Sulla had

[37] Velleius Paterculus 2.19.4.
[38] The sources often confuse Sulla's acts in 88 and his later legislation as dictator. The sequence followed here seems most probable.

arrived in Greece, laid siege to Athens, and plundered the sacred treasures of Delphi. When his troops stormed Athens in 86, the last stand of Greek democracy was crushed in a bloodbath. While Sulla defeated large Pontic armies in Boeotia, one of Cinna's generals, Flaccus, who had been sent to oust Sulla but dared not after his victories, carried the war to Asia. There, Flaccus was murdered by his own lieutenant, a fanatical Marian, C. Flavius Fimbria, who inflicted a major defeat on the king. Had Sulla's fleet under Lucullus cooperated, the war might have ended with the capture of Mithridates, who had already lost the support of the Asian population by his despotic cruelties. However, Sulla was anxious to return to Italy, and the weary king and the outlawed general came to terms in 85, for both needed peace desperately. Agreeing to evacuate conquered territory and pay an indemnity of 2,000 talents, Mithridates was recognized as the friend and ally of Rome. Sulla then marched against Fimbria, won over his troops, and drove to suicide the man who had beaten Mithridates. No wonder Sulla believed in his luck. To punish Asia, he imposed a crushing indemnity of 20,000 talents and billeted his troops in the luckless cities. Unable to pay the sum and again at the mercy of the publicans, the Asian cities went hopelessly in debt to raise the funds. Meanwhile, Cinna was preparing to lead an army to fight Sulla in the East, but his troops mutinied and slew the consul in 84. Either Cinna or his successor, Cn. Papirius Carbo, finally enrolled the Italians and freedmen in all the tribes of the Assembly, hoping to win Italian support in the forthcoming confrontation with Sulla.

In 83, Sulla landed in Italy with 40,000 veterans and began his final bid for power. The alternative was defeat and death, but he had no doubt that his miraculous luck would hold. Marian forces were defeated or won over, and many ambitious young men rallied to the Sullan cause —Crassus, whose father had been slain by Marius; Metellus Pius, the son of Marius's old rival; and Pompey, who raised an army of clients to fight for Sulla. In 82, the Marian consuls were Carbo and Marius's son, but the Sullan forces were triumphant; the younger Marius was driven to suicide, and Pompey hunted down and slew Carbo. To forestall an Italian rally on behalf of the Populares, Sulla announced that he would respect the distribution of Italians in all the tribes of the Assembly, and the dynast kept his word. Since the Italian Revolt, the Samnites had hated Sulla, and Telesinus raced to seize Rome and "destroy the Roman wolves in their lair." [39] By the Colline Gate, Sulla met the Samnites and with Crassus's aid defeated them in a savage battle. Occupying the capital, Sulla addressed the Senate with a speech punctuated by the cries of

---

[39] Velleius Paterculus 2.27.2.

Samnite prisoners who were being massacred nearby. On his orders, cities that had resisted were leveled, and Sulla's fury was unrelenting toward Samnium, where he came close to exterminating the brave highlanders. Toward Roman opponents, Sulla was just as merciless. After the first wave of murders, he systematized the execution of his victims by posting proscription lists offering cash for their heads. The property of the proscribed was confiscated, and their descendants were forbidden to ever hold political office. Not only Populares and suspected foes but even Optimates with large fortunes perished, for Sulla needed money and land to reward his followers. Though some acts of selfless heroism are reported, many Romans profited from the proscriptions by denouncing friends and relatives. At least 90 senators and 2600 *equites* perished as Sulla's vengeance reached into every province. Ten thousand confiscated slaves were freed and became Sulla's clients and loyal agents. In time, Sulla settled over 100,000 veterans on seized lands throughout Italy and relied on them to preserve his policies. Yet even his loyal lieutenants felt Sulla's arbitrary wrath, and he had one general cut down for asking to hold the consulship. When his aides questioned his ferocity, Sulla coolly compared his victims to lice that had to be destroyed before any serious work could be done.

Late in 82, Sulla took up the task of reorganizing Roman politics. A prominent Marian turncoat proposed that Sulla be made dictator for an indefinite period with authority to "write laws and settle the state." The cowed Centuriate Assembly quickly confirmed the extraordinary dictatorship that gave Sulla both *imperium* and powers undreamed of by Roman dictators of the past. Most of his legislation probably took place in 81. While not doctrinaire, Sulla hoped to create a system that would curb the popular assemblies, reinvigorate the senatorial oligarchy, and prevent military coups. The key to the Sullan system was the supremacy of the Senate, and he restored its monopolies on the juries that heard complaints of extortion in the provinces. The dictator widened the judicial authority of the Senate by having its juries try other major crimes —murder, treason, assault, electoral bribery, and graft.[40] To fill the depleted ranks of the Senate, he appointed new senators, including 300 *equites,* and raised the membership to about 600. The new Senate was made up largely of Sullan appointees, and he hoped that the incorporation of so many *equites* would lessen the tension between the two classes. To preserve his handpicked Senate, Sulla neglected to appoint censors. For some time, ex-quaestors had been enrolled in the Senate. The dictator confirmed the practice which added twenty ex-quaestors

[40] The size of the juries probably varied. In 52 B.C., Milo was convicted by a jury of 51. Normally, praetors presided over these courts.

each year, but he insisted that quaestors be at least 30 years old, praetors 39, and consuls 42. Thus, he hoped, no one would hold an office with *imperium* until he had spent almost a decade in the Senate and been conditioned to its views, and Roman armies would be commanded only by mature, safe men. The number of praetorships was fixed at eight, which together with the two consuls provided ten ex-magistrates each year to hold provincial governorships. By Sulla's decree, governors were limited to one year in office and forbidden to leave their province or wage war on their own initiative. The Po Valley was made the province of Cisalpine Gaul. Not only did the dictator elevate the Senate, but he also degraded the Tribal Assembly by emasculating the tribunate. Henceforth, tribunes could not propose legislation without the Senate's approval, and their veto powers were somehow limited. Above all, a tribune could not subsequently hold a higher office, and no one of ambition or ability would want to destroy his career by becoming a tribune. If Saturninus's program of grain at low prices was still in effect, Sulla revoked it at this time. Having curbed popular government and restored the domination of the Senate, Sulla abdicated his dictatorship in 79 and walked the streets of Rome as a private citizen, quipping that there was no one left for him to fear. Perhaps poor health prompted his retirement from public life. At his country estate, the former dictator hunted, fished, and finished his highly egotistical memoirs a few days before his death in 78. His followers and veterans provided Sulla with a magnificent funeral, but posterity remembered him as a bloody despot.

To celebrate his phenomenal luck, Sulla had constructed an imposing sanctuary at Praeneste dedicated to the goddess Fortuna. His political order was less durable, for the arbitrary arrangements troubled many Optimates who preferred to manipulate the old system, rather than change it drastically. Though conservatives had opposed individual tribunes, the tribunate was still a venerable institution. While Optimates welcomed the buttressing of the Senate, the oligarchs would have to rise to the occasion, now that Sulla had made Rome safe for oligarchy again. Above all, whatever settlement he made in Roman political life, "Sulla could not abolish his own example."[41] The client armies remained an essential and dangerous part of the new Rome, and Sulla had demonstrated what an unscrupulous general could do with soldiery. In the future, Roman generals would not balk at overthrowing the Republic, for Sulla had shown the way. In the bloodbaths of Sulla and Marius and in those to come, no man could doubt that, as Shakespeare said, "Rome is but a wilderness of tigers."

[41] Syme, *The Roman Revolution*, p. 17.

CHAPTER SIX

The old order passes

The reasons why institutions fail and societies change are complex, and simplistic explanations should evoke automatic suspicion. Sometimes external causes—droughts, plagues, or foreign invasions— can unsettle a nation, or its leadership may prove inadequate because of personal factors. In every case, a society faces problems, and its solutions or lack of response set a course for the future. As an empire, Rome was a failure, for the institutions of a city-state were inadequate for ruling vast territories and myriad nations. The empire needed a professional bureaucracy and some concern for the governed. Unpaid, elected magistrates mismanaged the lives of millions, who had even worse to fear from brutal soldiers and greedy publicans. As an imperial people, the Romans of the Republic had little grasp of the responsibilities that come with power, and the ruling class viewed the empire as an inexhaustible source of tribute. When desperate provincials had risen in Spain or the East, the Romans crushed them with savage repressions and ignored legitimate complaints. Even the Romans' own kinsmen in Italy had been forced to place a dagger at Rome's throat before the Republic granted them citizenship. The empire was based on conquest, and to maintain it, Rome had to remain a militaristic state, now dangerously dependent upon hired soldiery. In the background lurked the menace of slave revolts, for Italy was filled with sullen captives. The ease with which Romans practiced manumission relieved some of the pressure, but the congregation of large groups of slaves on *latifundia* remained a constant source of danger. To some degree, the problem of urban poverty had been relieved by the Gracchan land program and colonies, yet the slums of Rome were still filled with proletarians whose votes were coveted by politicians. The client army had solved the shortage of military manpower, but the Republic was at the mercy of generals, who could use their troops in fierce power struggles. The Republic meant much to the ruling class, but less to most Roman citizens, who cherished peace and order above all. When the Republic fell, few

172

mourned, but there had always been the possibility of rejuvenation if all classes had been willing to sacrifice selfish ends to preserve popular government. Perhaps it is too much to expect altruism from any people when decision making has been entrusted to mercenaries and their commanders.

THE GRAVEDIGGERS OF THE REPUBLIC

The collapse of the Roman Republic amid corruption, intrigue, and civil war is a familiar story, for the last decades of Republican Rome are well-documented, perhaps too well-documented. The major sources are the bitter monographs of Sallust, the partisan memoirs of Caesar, the catty correspondence and hyperbolic speeches of Cicero, and histories written during the Imperial Era when the Republic was an antiquarian oddity. The theme that emerges from these writings is bleak—a hopelessly corrupt society dragged toward autocracy by power-mad generals. Tacitus, for example, observes: "Gaius Marius, whose origin was of the humblest, and Lucius Sulla, who outdid his fellow nobles in ruthlessness, destroyed the republican constitution by force of arms. In its place, they put despotism. After them came Gnaeus Pompey, who, though more secretive, was no better, and from then on the one and only aim was autocracy."[1] While much of the indictment is true, it is warped by hindsight and gives the impression of inevitability to events that need not have happened.

Despite riots in the Assemblies, the Republic was not overthrown by the urban masses, and its fall has no awful implications for popular government, for Rome was an oligarchy, and it was the oligarchs who failed. The Republic was pulled down by the ceaseless struggles of a few proud men, who did not shrink from subversion and civil war to advance their ambitions or protect their dignity. Yet the dynasts did not want civil war, and even Caesar turned to autocracy only as a last expediency. Since a handful of men held the center of the political stage, personality conflicts were decisive factors. Because the Roman political system was not representative, the bulk of the citizenry in Italy took no interest in the political life of the distant city-state to which they all legally belonged. Within Rome, the urban poor were manipulated as pawns by politicians, who were equally willing to use armies for their ends. The Late Republic was corrupt and violent, the Senate inept and the Assemblies rowdy, but even if a miraculous reformation had cleansed the Senate and the electorate, the client armies still menaced

[1] Tacitus *Historiae* 2.38, trans. Kenneth Wellesley (London: Penguin Books, 1964), pp. 103–4.

the Republic whenever their commanders had the nerve to employ them.

The Sullan system was predicated on the ability of the Optimate nobility to sustain the dominance of the Senate. After the dictator's resignation, the leading figures at Rome were Sulla's henchmen, who, however, proceeded to undermine his laws. The *equites* were not content with the elevation of a few of their class into the Senate, for they had lost control of the courts. Though badly hurt by the proscriptions, the Populares were still active, and Sulla's downgrading of the tribunate and censorate had given them a rallying point, one which even conservatives had to admit was just. In 78, the consul, M. Aemilius Lepidus, courted the Populares by resuming the sale of cheap grain and recalling exiles, though he himself was a Sullan creature who had profited from the proscriptions. Among the returning Populares was Marius's young nephew, C. Julius Caesar, who had defied Sulla by refusing to divorce his wife, Cinna's daughter Cornelia. In Etruria, evicted farmers battled Sulla's veterans who had been assigned their land. Sent to restore order, Lepidus gambled on a coup and tried to rally the farmers in a major revolt. One of the generals sent by the Senate to deal with Lepidus was Gnaeus Pompeius, who was not a senator and legally too young to hold a command, but the Senate had need of his talents. The ambitious son of a ruthless Optimate father, Pompey had earned a reputation for brutality serving Sulla. In 77, Lepidus was defeated and soon died, but many of his troops joined Marian rebels in Spain. Surrendering on a safe-conduct, Lepidus's lieutenant, M. Junius Brutus, was executed by Pompey, who earned the lifelong hatred of Brutus's young son and namesake. Impressed by Pompey's ability, the Senate next gave him a command in Spain, again violating a Sullan law, for Pompey still was not a senator. Sulla had sarcastically given him the epithet Magnus, but Pompey took the name seriously.

In Spain, Q. Sertorius had gathered a force of Marian exiles and challenged the Sullan Senate in the name of the old Republic. A man of imagination, Sertorius had once despaired of the Sullan triumph and asked pirate friends to transport him to the utopian Isles of the Blessed in the Atlantic, but the corsairs did not wish to make the voyage, and the Marian chief was forced to become a resistance leader. To fill his legions, he rallied the oppressed Spaniards and added a nationalist dimension to his rebel movement. To substantiate his claim to represent the legal government of Rome, Sertorius set up a Senate in exile. Since he had only one eye, the barbarians believed that Sertorius was Hannibal returned.[2] Playing on their superstition, the wily leader claimed that

---

[2] On Hannibal, Sertorius, Civilis, and a possible connection with the Wotan cult, see T. W. Africa, "The One-Eyed Man Against Rome," *Historia* 19 (1970): 528–38.

a pet doe brought him revelations from the goddess Diana. The Spaniards were devoted to the charismatic Sertorius, who skillfully used guerilla tactics against the Senate's general Metellus Pius and twice defeated the vain Pompey. In 75, Mithridates sent money and ships to aid the Spanish revolt, and Pompey was only saved from defeat by the military skill of Metellus. Finally reinforced from Italy, Pompey used superior numbers to wear down the rebels. When Metellus put a price on his head, Sertorius was assassinated by a Roman renegade in 72. However, parts of Spain remained unpacified for half a century, and Sertorius was added to the pantheon of Popular martyrs. His ego inflated by the Spanish war, Pompey returned to Italy.

Meanwhile, another Sullan henchman, M. Licinius Crassus, had saved Rome from Spartacus. After winning his spurs at the Colline Gate, Crassus had accumulated a fortune during the proscriptions. Later he added to his wealth by investing in mines and real estate and soon became the richest man in Rome. Since the city had no fire department, Crassus maintained a brigade of slaves who put out conflagrations after he had bought the buildings from their distraught owners. In time, half of the Senate would be in debt to the multimillionaire, who quipped that no one was really rich who could not support a private army. Despite his riches, Crassus lived frugally, but like his peers he wanted glory in war and power in politics. In 73, a band of gladiators had broken out of their barracks in Campania and fled to the hills under the leadership of a forceful Thracian, Spartacus, who proclaimed a war of liberation for all slaves. As thousands of slaves flocked to join him, Spartacus formed a large army of fierce Celts and Cimbrians whom he trained to stand up to the Roman legions. After defeating Roman armies, he marched his slave horde to Cisalpine Gaul in 72, for the slaves wished to break up into national units and seek out their homelands, but the leaders persuaded them that smaller groups would be hunted down by the pursuing Romans. The lure of plundering Italy was also a strong motive, and the slave army returned to the South. In 71, the Senate gave Crassus six legions to deal with Spartacus. After a difficult campaign, the millionaire finally defeated the slaves, and Crassus celebrated his victory by crucifying 6,000 captives along the Appian Way. Rome was never again troubled by a major slave revolt.

Crassus loathed Pompey who, on his way back from Spain, had crushed a band of rebel slaves and then claimed credit for saving Italy from the servile threat. However, the rivals were also practical men, whose legions were encamped near Rome and could intimidate the government. Joining forces, they forced the Senate to grant Pompey a triumph illegally and allow him to run for the consulship, although he was still underage. The plutocrat Crassus had connections with the *equites,* and both men needed Popular support. Despite their blood-stained Sullan past, Crassus and Pompey became Populares and were elected consuls for 70. Never having sat in the Senate, Pompey had to employ a handbook on procedure prepared by Varro. To pay off their political debts, the two consuls, who had been Sulla's loyal lieutenants, completed the dismantlement of the Sullan system. Since 75, former tribunes had been eligible to hold higher offices, and now Crassus and Pompey restored the tribunate to its previous powers. They also revived the censorate to expel "undesirable elements" (their enemies) from the Senate, and citizenship was restored to former rebels who had fought for Lepidus and Sertorius. The newly converted Populares, Crassus and Pompey, were not the only Sullans to repudiate the dictator—his own handpicked Senate had twice violated his laws to give armies to Pompey, and political bossism flourished behind the facade of senatorial rule.

Though he never held a high office, the wily P. Cornelius Cethegus had manipulated both the Senate and the Assemblies and disbursed favors to men of greater renown. According to Cicero, Cethegus was so knowledgeable of public affairs that he wielded power in the Senate as if he had been a consular noble.[3] Once a lackey of Marius, he had switched to Sulla, made a fortune during the proscriptions, and played a major role behind the scenes during the 70s. Another dubious Sullan henchman was C. Verres, whose venality contributed to the low reputation of the Optimate era. As governor of Sicily, he had mercilessly exploited the islanders and abused Roman citizens. Unfortunately for Verres, his victims included some of Pompey's clients, and in 70 the infamous governor was tried and convicted for his crimes. Though Verres retired to Massilia to enjoy his ill-gotten wealth in exile, the trial made a great reputation for the relentless prosecutor, Marcus Tullius Cicero, an eloquent quaestor from Arpinum. Distantly related to Marius, Cicero came from an equestrian family and had chosen a career in law and oratory. Ambitious, able, and vain, he had served under Pompey's father and was now a partisan of the son. So scandalous had been Verres's mismanagement of Sicily, as portrayed by Cicero, that the Senate lost its monopoly on the courts. By a law passed in 70, juries were to be drawn in equal numbers from senators, *equites,* and rich commoners. Little was left of the Sullan settlement, and the aristocracy had only itself to blame for losing the privileges that Sulla had bestowed upon them.

In the East, Mithridates had again threatened Rome, and new wars promised glory for ambitious nobles. In 75, Nicomedes IV of Bithynia

---

[3] Cicero *Brutus* 48.178.

had died without heirs and bequeathed his nation to Rome, but Mithridates occupied the country to keep it out of Roman hands. One of the consuls in 74 was a fastidious epicure and patron of the arts, L. Licinius Lucullus, whose luxurious life style is still remembered in the term "Lucullan." Despite his elegant ways, Lucullus was a capable soldier and had served Sulla well, and he may have been the sole officer who joined the revolutionary march on Rome in 88. To get the Eastern command for himself and a command against pirates for his friend, M. Antonius, Lucullus contrived an affair with Cethegus's mistress, who persuaded the politico to provide the desired assignments. A poor choice, the easy-going Antonius was soon defeated by the pirates of Crete, who were allies of Mithridates. Dying not long after, Antonius is best remembered as the father of a more famous Antony. However, Lucullus was an apt pupil of Sulla and a harsh disciplinarian. Sweeping Mithridates from Bithynia, he pursued the king into Pontus and defeated him by 72. While the king fled to Armenia, Lucullus settled the affairs of Asia where the provincials had become hopelessly indebted by the impositions of Sulla. The proconsul reduced the debts from 120,000 to 40,000 talents and set a maximum interest rate of twelve percent. Though the grateful provincials established festivals in his honor, Lucullus had angered the *equites* at Rome, who plotted his downfall. When Tigranes of Armenia refused to surrender Mithridates to Roman envoys, Lucullus invaded Armenia in 69 and won a spectacular victory against overwhelming odds. Once overlord of much of Anatolia, Syria, and northern Mesopotamia, the Armenian monarch was a formidable foe, and his defeat added to Lucullus's military glory, which made Pompey jealous. In 68, Lucullus pushed farther east but his men tired of his iron discipline and mutinied. The following year, Mithridates, who had escaped from Armenia, was again active in Pontus and inflicted defeats on the Romans, but Lucullus received no support from his fellow governors, and discontent among his troops was fanned by his opportunistic brother-in-law, P. Clodius Pulcher. At Rome, the jealous Pompey and the *equites* engineered Lucullus's replacement by an unimportant proconsul who soon made way for Pompey himself. Stripped of his commands, Lucullus had a stormy meeting with Pompey in Galatia and returned to Rome an embittered man. Disgusted with politics, the fallen general abandoned himself to a life of pleasure and would emerge from his gardens only to revenge himself on Pompey. Divorcing Clodius's sister on grounds of immorality, he married Cato the Younger's sister who was no better. Eventually, Lucullus died insane. His permanent contribution to posterity was the cherry trees that he had introduced from Pontus to Europe.

During Lucullus's absence from Rome, Pompey and the Populares had put the restored tribunate to good use. In 67, the tribune C. Cornelius made praetors render decisions consistent with the edict that they proclaimed at the beginning of their year in office, and possibly even with the edicts of their predecessors. Thus the praetorian edicts evolved into a body of laws. Cornelius's colleague, A. Gabinius, passed legislation against bribery of the Senate: foreign envoys were forbidden to borrow money at Rome, and the Senate was required to receive embassies promptly instead of delaying them until a bribe was offered. More important was the problem of the pirates of Cilicia and Crete, whose fleets terrorized the seas and imperiled the grain shipments to Rome. The buccaneers kidnapped prominent Roman travelers and held them for ransom—Caesar was one of their victims. To crush the pirates, Gabinius proposed an extraordinary military command for Pompey with 6,000 talents, 120,000 troops, 500 ships, 24 legates of praetorian rank, and authority over all coastal lands for fifty miles inland. Though there was great opposition to so much power being held by one man (especially Pompey), Gabinius's bill passed the Assembly, and Pompey promptly carried off his assignment with great success. He may have lacked the flair of Sertorius and the nerve of Lucullus, but Pompey was a talented organizer and deployed his forces in coordinated attacks on the corsairs. Within three months, his aides cleared the seas of pirates and took their fortresses in the East. Crete was made a Roman province, and in Cilicia Pompey settled captured pirates as farmers instead of crucifying or selling them. While many men had contributed to the great victory, the crushing of the pirates was Pompey's supreme achievement, and both his popularity and self-esteem reached new heights. The reliance on one individual to solve a pressing problem cast an ominous note for the future, and many prominent men fretted over Pompey's paramount role in the state.

In 66, the tribune C. Manilius procured more fields for Pompey to conquer by granting him Lucullus's former command against Mithridates, a war that had almost been won. Both Cicero and Caesar supported Manilius's bill, and Cicero's speech in defense of Pompey included a frank confession of brutal Roman methods in the East:

> Words cannot express, gentlemen, how bitterly we are hated among foreign nations owing to the wanton and outrageous conduct of the men whom of late years we have sent to govern them. For, in those countries, what temple do you suppose has been held sacred by our officers, what state inviolable, what home sufficiently guarded by its closed doors? Why, they look about for rich and flourishing cities that they may find an occasion of a war against them to satisfy their lust for plunder.[4]

[4] Cicero *pro lege Manilia* 65, trans. H. Grose Hodge (Cambridge, Mass.: Harvard University Press, 1927), p. 77.

Ironically, Lucullus was one of the few Romans to treat provincials decently, and the lauded Pompey would return from the East a multimillionaire. With superior forces, Pompey drove Mithridates from Pontus and moved on to humble Tigranes in Armenia. Fleeing to the Crimea, the Pontic king became involved in squabbles with his children. In 63, besieged by his son Pharnaces, Mithridates despaired and committed suicide. Despite his great abilities, the king had failed in his long contest with Rome. Had he been more sincere with his allies in the 80s, Mithridates might have succeeded in his role of champion of the Hellenistic East.

Moving southward, Pompey ended the defunct Seleucid monarchy and imposed Roman order on Syria, which became a province in 62. In Palestine, he intervened in a civil war between rival Hasmonean princes and seized Jerusalem in 63. Though he was careful to spare the treasures in the Temple, Pompey abolished the Hasmonean crown and left Judea under the control of the Hasmonean High Priest, Hyrcanus. From the Crimean kingdom—through Galatia and Cappadocia in Anatolia, Commagene and lesser principalities along the Euphrates—to the Nabataean state at Petra, a string of client kingdoms was set up or confirmed by Pompey to serve as buffers against the Parthians. Armenia, too, became a buffer state between the two superpowers. At Alexandria, the feeble Ptolemy XII Auletes was more noted as a flute player than a statesman, but like other client monarchs, the Egyptian king bought Roman favor with substantial bribes. To the provinces of the East, Pompey brought law and order, and he established many cities, but the conqueror also imposed the publican's yoke and almost doubled Rome's tax revenues. From the loot of the Eastern campaigns, Pompey gave 16,000 talents to his troops, and his own wealth must have been enormous—"he could have bought Crassus out without feeling the pinch." [5] Moreover, the proconsul had added kings and cities to his clientage. In 62, he returned to Rome and celebrated a spectacular triumph in 61. Giddy with adulation, Pompey "the Great" prepared to enjoy the unquestioned supremacy he had won, but his enemies had been waiting for him to disarm. When he disbanded his legions, Pompey's laurels quickly faded, and his foes broke the prestige of the proud dynast.

While Pompey had been absent in the East, politics at Rome had continued its hectic pace. In 65 Crassus was a censor, and his protégé, Caesar, an aedile. An ambitious patrician, C. Julius Caesar was a gifted orator and shrewd politician, but he lacked wealth and relied on Crassus for backing. As Marius's nephew and Cinna's son-in-law, Caesar was a prominent *Popularis* and treated the masses to extravagant games

[5] E. Badian, *Roman Imperialism in the Late Republic* (Pretoria: University of South Africa Press, 1967), p. 73.

Pompey. Copenhagen, Ny Carlsberg Glyptothek. *The Ny Carlsberg Glyptothek.*

during his aedileship. Though Caesar kept ties with Pompey, Crassus considered him a valuable ally and a good investment. At Caesar's urging, Crassus tried to extend citizenship to the inhabitants of Cisalpine Gaul who lived north of the Po River, but Crassus's foes were not willing to let him add so many voters to his clientage, and despite its merits the proposal foundered. To match Pompey's Eastern success, Crassus proposed the annexation of Egypt with himself or Caesar as governor and promised the *equites* tax contracts and the masses Egyptian grain. However, Pompey's man, Cicero, defeated the bill. Less reputable than Caesar was another crony of Crassus, L. Sergius Catilina, a patrician opportunist who had bloodied his hands in Sulla's service but might be useful against Pompey. Supposedly, Catiline was involved in an abortive plot to murder his rivals for the consulship for 65, but the affair is obscure and Crassus would not have spent good money on so harebrained a scheme. In 64, however, Crassus supported Catiline and a mediocrity, C. Antonius, as candidates for the consulship in 63, but the third candidate was the eloquent Cicero, who persuaded the electorate that Catiline was too unsavory to hold office. Many voters admired the *eques* from Arpinum for aspiring to the consulship, and Cicero and Antonius won the consular elections, but defeat at the polls did not remove Catiline as a force in politics.

In 63 Rome narrowly escaped a revolution that had social implications. With the support of Crassus and Caesar, the tribune, P. Servilius

Rullus, proposed a massive program to resettle the urban poor on public lands in Italy and the provinces and pay the expenses with funds from recent conquests. While Crassus hoped to use the public lands as a political bargaining point when Pompey's veterans returned and expected farms from the state, Rullus's program appealed to the hard-pressed urban masses. However, to frustrate Crassus and aid Pompey, Cicero misrepresented the social benefits of Rullus's bill and brought about its defeat. The consul also blocked Caesar's attempt to restore the rights of the descendants of Sulla's victims. Running for the consulship for 62, Catiline sensed the desperation of the masses and promised to abolish all debts if he were elected; he also threatened violence if he were not. Though aimed primarily at the poor, an abolition of debts also appealed to improvident aristocrats and to Sulla's veterans who had not prospered as farmers. As a friend of the masses, Catiline's sincerity may be doubted, but his debt proposal alienated Crassus and the *equites,* and the violent streak in Catiline made voters in all classes nervous.

Defeated in the election, Catiline proceeded with a widespread conspiracy to create disorder in Italy, burn the city of Rome, and seize power in the chaos. The nobles in the plot included a praetor who was an ex-consul, but since Sulla, revolutionary aristocrats were no novelty. The conspirators assembled troops in Etruria and negotiated with a Gallic tribe for horsemen. Luckily, a mistress of one of the conspirators betrayed the plot, and Crassus, who had contacts in many quarters, passed additional information to Cicero. In the Senate, the consul denounced Catiline to his face and assumed emergency powers that had been granted at the first news of danger. Followed by many of the urban poor who believed in him, Catiline was able to flee to his forces in Etruria, but at Rome five of the leading conspirators were implicated by treasonable letters, and Cicero ordered their arrest. During a lively debate in the Senate, Caesar pleaded that the traitors be imprisoned for life, but the implacable Cato the Younger insisted on the death penalty. Though he equivocated during the debate, Cicero promptly had the five prisoners executed without a formal trial.[6] Early in 62, loyal troops under the nominal command of the consul C. Antonius defeated Catiline's rebel forces, who died fighting bravely beside their leader; their standard was a faded Eagle once born by Marius's men. Vilified in Cicero's speeches and in a lurid monograph by Sallust, Catiline became a stock villain in history, a Roman Richard III—at best, he aped the worst in Sulla. Yet many of the poor had believed in Catiline, and some

---

[6] One of those executed was the ex-consul P. Cornelius Lentulus Sura, the stepfather of Antony, who never forgave Cicero for his death.

had died for him. Years later, his grave was still strewn with flowers. To quiet the masses, Cato as tribune passed a law in 62 that provided grain at about one-third of the market price. The grain program benefited about 200,000 recipients and cost the state 1250 talents annually. However dubious his character, Catiline had stirred up discontent among the urban poor and forced an arch-conservative to inaugurate Rome's first dole.

For his role in suppressing the Catilinarian conspiracy, the Senate granted Cicero the title, "Father of his Country," and the vain orator took it seriously. For the rest of his life, he boasted of his hour of glory and wrote various accounts of it which disagree on details. As a "new man," Cicero was insecure, and although an ally of Pompey, he needed the approval of the hereditary nobility and became a spokesman for the Optimates. Cicero viewed himself as a man of the middle who could lead a coalition of responsible nobles and *equites* against demagogic Populares. Yet he had few clients and no power base—his sole strength was his oratory, and that was up for hire. Equivocating and calculating, Cicero was a master of compromise and never let principles interfere

Cicero. Rome, Vatican Museum. *Alinari—Scala.*

with political profit. Early in 62, he survived harassment by tribunes sympathetic to Catiline, and his vanity was ruffled by an abortive attempt to have Pompey recalled from the East to crush the Catilinarians.

Compared to Cicero, whom he despised, M. Porcius Cato the Younger seemed a tower of rectitude. Unflinching, unreasoning, and self-righteous, he was a parody of his great-grandfather and cloaked his fierce biases as statements of principle. Cato loathed Caesar as a wastrel and the lover of his sister, Servilia, and he hated Pompey who had slain his kinsman Brutus in 78. Spiteful toward his foes, Cato was willing to wreck the commonwealth, if need be, to harm them. Although he claimed to be a Stoic, Cato was overly fond of wine, and he handed over his wife to his friend, the famed orator Q. Hortensius, who had taken a fancy to her. Willing to sacrifice principles for Optimate aims, Cato was not adverse to bribery in elections, and he deliberately created a dole for political purposes. Meanwhile, Caesar, who had been elected Pontifex Maximus in 63, was now a praetor. After the death of his wife Cornelia in 68, he had married Sulla's granddaughter, Pompeia, but she had caught the eye of the notorious P. Clodius Pulcher. In pursuit of Pompeia, Clodius infiltrated a religious gathering which was taboo for men, but he was discovered. On the grounds that his wife must be "above suspicion," Caesar divorced Pompeia and later married the highborn Calpurnia. Since Caesar's own amours were many, the episode was taken as a joke by Roman high society, but Cato insisted that Clodius be tried for sacrilege. At the trial in 61, Caesar refused to testify, but Cicero broke the alibi of Clodius, who would have been convicted if Crassus had not bribed the jury to acquit him. Clodius was now anxious to take revenge on Cato and Cicero.

When Pompey returned from the East and disbanded his legions, his varied foes put aside their differences to destroy him. Dazzled with his own achievements, Pompey expected a grateful Rome to ratify the Eastern settlement and furnish land for his 40,000 veterans. In 60, the Senate called upon its Eastern expert, Lucullus, who quibbled over each detail of Pompey's arrangement in the East. Although Lucullus soon returned to his gardens, Crassus and Cato continued the attack and prevented the Assembly from granting land to the veterans. Humiliated and helpless because his men were disarmed, Pompey looked about for new allies. Meanwhile, his enemies fell out among themselves. With the backing of Crassus and Cicero, the *equites* asked for rebates on overbid tax contracts in Asia, but the self-righteous Cato blocked the bill. To further harass the *equites,* Cato made the bribery of juries a criminal offense. Cicero's comments on Cato's intransigence are apt and self-revealing:

The opinions he delivers would be more in place in Plato's Republic than among the dregs of humanity collected by Romulus. That a man who accepts a bribe for the verdict he returns at a trial should be put on trial himself, is as fair a principle as one could wish. Cato voted for it and won the Senate's assent. Result, a war of the *equites* with the Senate, but not with me. I was against it. That the tax collectors should repudiate their bargain was a most shameless proceeding. But we ought to have put up with the loss in order to keep their good will. Cato resisted and carried the day. Result, though we've had a consul in prison and frequent riots, not a breath of encouragement from one of those who in my own consulship and that of my successors used to rally round us to defend the country. "Must we, then, bribe them for their support?" you will ask. What help is there, if we cannot get it otherwise? [7]

Having humbled Pompey and infuriated Crassus, Cato offered Caesar a gratuitous insult.

Senatorial permission was required for a triumph, and commanders were expected to wait with their troops outside the walls of Rome until the Senate approved the celebration. Returning from a command in Spain, Caesar wished to enter the city to campaign for the consulship before marching in triumph with his troops, but Cato opposed the request. The ambitious Caesar forfeited the triumph and won the election with Crassus's generous backing, but his colleague for 59 was Cato's son-in-law, M. Calpurnius Bibulus, whose election had also been aided by bribery. To further harass Caesar, Cato provided that the new consuls should be assigned to policing the backwoods of Italy after their year in office. As a Roman noble, Caesar lusted for military fame, and he had been deprived of both a triumph and the prospect of future glory. The vindictive Cato had overplayed his hand, however, for Caesar was friendly with both Crassus and Pompey. Though normally at odds, Crassus and Pompey had been dealt with shabbily, and they responded to Caesar's overtures to form a loose political partnership, the First Triumvirate. Individually, the three dynasts were at the mercy of Cato and the Optimates, but no rival coalition could withstand the combined weight of Crassus's money, Caesar's shrewdness, and Pompey's veterans, who might even fight if Pompey had the nerve to lead them. To seal the bargain, Pompey married Caesar's only child, Julia; although begun as a typical Roman political match, the marriage soon became a union of love.

Although it lacked legal status, the First Triumvirate was a constellation of power, irresistible in a Rome where politicians were corrupted

---

[7] Cicero *ad Atticum* 2.1, trans. E. O. Winstedt (Cambridge, Mass.: Harvard University Press, 1912), I, 109.

by bribery and intimidated by riots and threats of violence. As consul in 59, Caesar tried to cooperate with the Senate, but his efforts on behalf of Pompey and Crassus were rebuffed by Cato's faction. Turning to the Assembly, Caesar asked for land for Pompey's veterans, but his colleague, Bibulus, obstructed the bill with the usual devices—tribunician vetoes and reports of bad omens—whereupon Pompey's men rioted and Bibulus was driven from the Forum, covered with refuse. Impressed by the show of force, the Assembly passed the land bill, which Caesar soon augmented with another law, seizing land in Campania for veterans and fathers of three children. Pompey's Eastern settlement was promptly ratified, and Crassus's business allies received rebates of one-third of the Asian tax contracts. Other laws were enacted to curtail bribery and unauthorized actions by provincial governors, and a daily bulletin was issued, listing legislation, edicts, and Senate debates. Since Bibulus stayed home and issued vain reports of unfavorable omens, wags dubbed the year 59 the "consulship of Julius and Caesar." In purely monetary terms as well, the triumvirate was a profitable partnership, for Caesar and Pompey extorted 6,000 talents to guarantee Ptolemy XII as king of Egypt. However, to equal Crassus, Caesar needed more money, and to approach Pompey's prestige, military victories and a client army of veterans were essential. Since a colonial war in Gaul would provide all these things, Caesar received a five-year command over Cisalpine and Transalpine Gaul. In 58 he left Rome to seek glory and wealth on the Gallic frontier.

Before his departure, Caesar as Pontifex Maximus had permitted the patrician opportunist, P. Clodius Pulcher, to assume plebeian status in order to hold the tribuneship. Although an ally of Caesar, Clodius had ambitions of his own and sought power through demagoguery and violence. As tribune, he forbade the use of omens to block legislation and expanded Cato's dole into a program of free grain for the resident citizenry of Rome.[8] While both laws had merit, the new dole was an obvious bid for popular support, and its rationale was not humanitarian concern for the poor, but the right of the Roman people to enjoy the profits of empire. Clodius had a score to settle with Cicero and drove the orator into exile for having executed the Catilinarian conspirators without a trial. When Cicero sought Pompey's protection, the triumvir slipped out the back door of his home, and Cicero left Italy, a sad and wiser man. Another of Clodius's foes was removed when Cato was sent to organize Cyprus as a province. Though the Senate had earlier forbidden the existence of private clubs (as opposed to conventional social

[8] The monthly ration of free grain was five *modii* (1¼ bushels) and was probably only given to adult male citizens who resided in Rome. About 260,000 took advantage of Clodius's dole.

and religious groups), Clodius legalized political *collegia* that were in effect gangs of toughs who browbeat voters and assaulted his enemies. Since Rome lacked a police force, its residents were particularly vulnerable to gangsterism of this sort. The Optimates had their own hoodlum chief in T. Annius Milo, whose thugs battled Clodius's gangs in the Forum and the back alleys of Rome. The caliber of Late Republican Roman politics can be gauged by the offices held by the two gangsters: Milo was tribune in 57 and praetor in 55, and Clodius was tribune in 58 and aedile in 56. When Pompey tried to have Cicero restored from exile, Clodius threatened to murder the triumvir in the Senate. In 57, however, Pompey secured the recall of Cicero and assumed a five-year authority over the grain supply for Rome, but the command did not include *imperium*. The following year, driven from Alexandria by a popular uprising, Ptolemy XII sought Pompey's assistance in regaining his throne, but Crassus blocked a new military command for Pompey, and the king was not restored until later. In 56, stresses within the triumvirate brought Caesar briefly back to northern Italy, and the coalition was repaired at a conference in Luca. Hoping for patronage, 120 senators followed Pompey and Crassus to Luca where the triumvirs agreed to extend Caesar's Gallic command for five more years and to give Crassus and Pompey the consulships for 55. Pompey would then receive the governorship of Spain and Cyrene with six legions, and Crassus Syria with authority to attack Parthia. Cicero, who had been trying to alienate Pompey from Caesar, quickly shifted and sought to ingratiate himself with Caesar, who was not fooled and made the vain orator defend henchmen of the triumvirs in court.

After violence in the elections, Crassus and Pompey served as consuls in 55, and the latter dedicated a handsome theater, the very building in which Caesar would be slain a decade later. In 54, Pompey assumed his promised proconsular commands but governed the provinces through legates without leaving Rome. Crassus, however, had hurried to Syria to launch an unprovoked assault on Parthia. Always jealous of Pompey, the old dynast was piqued by Caesar's success in Gaul, and he hoped for new laurels in the East. Even though a hostile tribune had put a solemn curse on his expedition, Crassus was resolved on war, but he underestimated his enemy. Under the Arsacid kings, Parthia was a loose feudal kingdom, stretching from Iran to the Euphrates and controlling the overland trade routes from China. Originally Iranian nomads, the Parthians left most administrative matters in the hands of Hellenistic bureaucrats. Though nominally Zarathustrian, the state cult was frankly polytheistic, and the Arsacids were so tolerant of the diverse religions within their realm that the Jews of Palestine hoped vainly that the Parthians would supplant the Romans in the East. Unlike the Romans, the Parthians disdained infantry and had developed a highly effective cavalry force, made up of mailed knights (cataphracts) and mounted archers. Riding heavy chargers but lacking stirrups, the cataphracts could be unseated in a pitched battle, but the mounted archers on their swift ponies supplied a firepower unequaled in antiquity. In 53, the overconfident Crassus marched his legions into Mesopotamia where they encountered a major Parthian army near Carrhae. The Parthian general, Surenas, was a master of logistics and supplied his archers in the field with arrows brought in by camel trains. Herded together by the cataphracts, the Romans were exposed to a rain of arrows from all directions and suffered terrible losses. At a parlay with the Parthians, Crassus was killed in a scuffle, and his head was sent as a trophy to the Arsacid king, who permitted it to be used as a stage prop in a performance of Euripides' *Bacchae*. Luckily for Rome, the monarch was jealous of Surenas's ability and had the general executed. In 51, Syria was defended against Parthian raiders by Crassus's quaestor, C. Cassius Longinus, who had led the survivors back from Carrhae. Although the Arsacids did not pursue their advantage after Carrhae, the Eagles of Crassus's legions were proudly displayed as proof of Parthian prowess and Rome's greatest defeat in the East. Apart from the great blow to Roman prestige, the death of Crassus widened the cleavage between Pompey and Caesar, who could tolerate each other as triumvirs but not as rivals for primacy in the political life of Rome.

THE CAESAREANS

The political squabbles of the Republican leaders degenerated into a civil war from which Caesar emerged as victor and dictator, but he was soon struck down by his irreconcilable foes. Then a prolonged power struggle between the Caesarean chiefs ended with the triumph of Octavian who, as Augustus, established the Imperial system. Both in antiquity and in modern times, historians have sought to dignify the sordid story as a conflict of principles. While sentimental Republicans claim that liberty was overthrown by tyrants, admirers of Caesar and Augustus insist that an incompetent oligarchy was replaced by a responsible monarchy.[9] Despite the claims of propagandists, the issues were never so

[9] The great German historian Theodor Mommsen saw Caesar as a messianic hero who overthrew a cabal of corrupt reactionaries. To him, Cato was a "stupid Don Quixote," Pompey an inflated sergeant major, and Caesar "the perfect man." An ardent liberal, Mommsen loathed Junkers and projected nineteenth-century German politics into the Roman past. Because of his magisterial contributions to the study of Roman law and inscriptions, Mommsen had enormous

elevated, for the civil wars were personality conflicts between men whose prestige and political survival were at stake. All of the contestants were products of the same system and subscribed to the same ideology. Since Sulla, dictatorship and client armies had become acceptable political tools, and Caesar was no ideologue blazing the way for monarchy. At Rome, autocracy won by default. When the oligarchs fell out and one man beat down all opponents, autocratic rule was the unintended result, and a nation wearied by civil strife did not care. Whatever had been the role of the people in the past, the Late Republic was a closed circle of oligarchic privilege, and only the client armies were willing to fight for the quarreling dynasts. The fact that the empire was better off under Imperial rule does not mean that Caesar crossed the Rubicon with that lofty aim in mind. The fall of the Republic was also not the result of class struggles, for the middle and lower classes stayed aloof from the wars of the dynasts. Although the civil wars produced momentous changes, the ultimate consequences were not intended or anticipated, and the war between Caesar and Pompey need not have occurred if the two dynasts had been less vain and Cato less vindictive.

Witty, urbane, and shrewd, Gaius Julius Caesar was the ablest of the Roman leaders of his generation. He was an effective orator, an accomplished writer, and a ladies' man of some renown; all three traits made him admired at Rome. Tall, lean, slightly bald, and foppish in his dress, Caesar was at home in high society as well as the military camp. Prodigal with money to buy votes or reward his soldiers, he was moderate in his personal habits and indifferent to good food and wine. He was also epileptoid, a factor that may have contributed to his sober regimen. Intellectually, Caesar was an Epicurean but, like Sulla, he had an almost mystical faith in his own luck. Politically, he was a Marian *Popularis,* and there is nothing in his early career to suggest a propensity for monarchy. Unlike Marius, Sulla, and Cato, Caesar was not vindictive, and he freely pardoned defeated Roman foes. His enemies, of course, were not grateful for owing their lives to Caesar and his celebrated clemency was not applied to barbarians; his campaigns in Gaul were brutal colonial wars. Yet Caesar's attitude toward provincials was enlightened, for he was generous in bestowing Roman citizenship. To the poor at Rome, he seemed a friend, and the masses were genuinely fond of him. The devotion of his troops brought Caesar victory in Gaul and in the civil war. His self-confidence reassured his supporters and irritated his foes. Like all Roman nobles, Caesar was proud and defensive when his dignity was challenged.

authority, and his vision of Caesar as a savior was often accepted uncritically. More recently, antifascist historians have damned the Roman dictator for the sins of the ersatz Caesars of the twentieth century.

Caesar. Rome, Palazzo dei Conservatori. *Alinari—Scala.*

In Gaul, Caesar won great prestige, expelling German invaders and conquering the Celts who had originally asked him to intervene. Savage against the Germans, Caesar slaughtered women and children as well as warriors, and Cato denounced him for war crimes. After an ineffectual sally into Britain in 54, Caesar subdued rebels in Gaul and Belgium, but in 52 news of political troubles at Rome prompted a major uprising under the Gallic chieftain, Vercingetorix. At the siege of Alesia, Caesar was caught between a Celtic force in the town and a relief army outside the Roman lines. After hard fighting, Vercingetorix was defeated and surrendered; later he was strangled after Caesar's triumph at Rome. In 51 Caesar crushed the last holdouts of Gallic resistance and cut off the hands of prisoners of war to warn the Celts of the price of freedom. So devastated was Gaul by the Roman conquest that perhaps a third of the adult males were dead and another third were enslaved, and Caesar could only impose a light tribute on the exhausted Celts. However, the victor had become a multimillionaire through war booty, and his underlings had similarly enriched themselves. Caesar was free to take on his political foes at Rome where Cato's faction was energetically plotting his downfall.

At the conference of Luca in 56, the triumvirate had been patched up, but two deaths had seriously weakened Caesar's position. In 54 his daughter, Julia, had died in childbirth, and her baby, too, was dead within a few days. Had Julia lived, Pompey might not have joined the anti-Caesarean faction, for his love for her was great. When Caesar offered to divorce Calpurnia and marry a daughter of Pompey, however, the proposal was spurned. In 53 Crassus perished in Parthia, and the tripartite balance of power was ended. Wooed by Optimate flattery, Pompey gradually drifted into Cato's camp and married the daughter of Q. Metellus Scipio, a conservative politician of dubious reputation. Meanwhile, political violence and electoral bribery had accelerated, and the elections for 52 dissolved into rowdyism and chaos, for Milo was running for consul and Clodius for praetor. Early in 52, Clodius was murdered by Milo's thugs, but his forceful widow, Fulvia, rallied the Clodian supporters, who burned their hero's body in the Senate building, which also went up in flames. Shocked at last, the Senate proclaimed martial law and authorized Pompey to bring troops into Rome and impose order. To legalize his new role, Pompey was made sole consul with the blessings of Cato, who put aside his concern for constitutional niceties and his personal loathing of Pompey to bind the dynast closer to the Optimates. As a sop to Caesar, the absent proconsul was to be allowed to run for the consulship in absentia, but that contingency never took place. On trial for the murder of Clodius, Milo received a lukewarm defense from Cicero and was exiled to Massilia. Pompey's soldiers stationed near the jury had encouraged a prompt verdict.

To restore constitutional forms, Pompey took a consular colleague, his father-in-law, Scipio. He also extended his own military command in Spain for five years without similarly accommodating Caesar, whose Gallic command would soon expire—the exact date of its expiration is disputed. In 51, the Optimate clique tried to relieve Caesar of his troops since the Gallic war was over, but Caesar's tribunes protected his interests in Rome. As usual, Pompey vacillated and played a double game: "He thinks one thing and says another," complained Cicero, "and yet he is not quite clever enough to disguise his desires." [10] In 50, Caesar gave up two legions, supposedly to be sent to Syria, but Pompey kept them in Italy. While the consul, C. Claudius Marcellus, wished to strip Caesar of his command by a specific date, a Caesarean tribune, C. Scribonius Curio, proposed that both Caesar and Pompey surrender their legions, and the Senate approved the mutual disarmament by a vote of 370 to 22. Cato's faction vetoed the proposal and rejected the Senate's overwhelming declaration for peace. Despite Caesar's urgent entreaties to Pompey for a compromise, Pompey accepted command of all troops in Italy from Marcellus.

In January 49, Scipio urged that Caesar be declared a public enemy if he did not surrender his legions, and the Optimates passed a declaration

[10] Cicero *ad Familiares* 8.1.3.

of public emergency, despite the vetoes of Caesarean tribunes who then fled to the proconsul in Cisalpine Gaul. Ostensibly, both Caesar and Pompey had legality on their side, for the former was defending the tribunate and the latter was opposing a rebellious proconsul. The real issue, of course, was not legality but survival for Caesar, whose foes were using the vain Pompey to destroy him. Suetonius cites the views of Caesar and his contemporaries on the situation:

> Marcus Cato often declared and took oath too, that he would impeach Caesar the moment he had disbanded his army. It was openly said, too, that if he was out of office on his return, he would be obliged, like Milo, to make his defense in a court hedged about by armed men. The latter opinion is the more credible one in view of the assertion of Asinius Pollio, that when Caesar at the battle of Pharsalus saw his enemies slain or in flight, he said word for word: "They would have it so. Even I, Gaius Caesar, after so many great deeds, should have been found guilty, if I had not turned to my army for help." [11]

Rancorous and foolhardy, Cato's clique had pushed Pompey and Caesar into war in order to crush the latter. Faced with political extinction if he submitted, Caesar gambled on revolution and crossed the Rubicon River, the boundary between Italy and Cisalpine Gaul.

Since the civil war was a struggle of dynasts and noble factions, the people of Italy held aloof and ignored Cato's war cry that the Republic was in peril. Virtually unopposed, Caesar seized the peninsula and Rome itself as Pompeian troops defected to his banners. However, he was unable to prevent Pompey and his followers from transporting a large force to Greece, where Pompey rallied his Eastern clients and hoped to repeat Sulla's strategy. After vacillating, Cicero joined Pompey, but other conservatives, including C. Claudius Marcellus, quickly capitulated to Caesar as did eager opportunists of every persuasion. At Rome, Caesar appropriated the state treasury, which his foes had forgotten to take with them, and placed his henchmen in office. The residents of Cisalpine Gaul north of the Po finally received full citizenship. While Caesar subdued the Pompeian legions in Spain and added them to his army, Curio tried to seize Africa for the Caesarean cause but was defeated and slain by Juba, the client monarch of Numidia. Briefly assuming the dictatorship, Caesar reassured the business community that he was no Catiline, for he ordered the payment of private debts. However, he pleased the masses by subtracting previous interest payments from the balances due. He also recalled exiles and restored the rights of

[11] Suetonius *Divus Iulius* 30.3–4, trans. J. C. Rolfe (Cambridge, Mass.: Harvard University Press, 1913), I, 43.

the descendants of Sulla's victims. Receiving the consulship for 48, Caesar invaded the Balkans but failed to take the port of Dyrrhachium by siege. Fearful that the Pompeians would strike at Rome while he was in Greece, Caesar retreated to Thessaly, hoping that Pompey would follow. Luckily, Pompey took the bait and pursued Caesar to Pharsalus where a decisive battle was fought. Though his forces greatly outnumbered Caesar's, Pompey's troops were no match for Caesar's veterans, and Pompey himself was handicapped by his peers who nagged at his leadership and bickered over the political fruits of the expected victory. When the tide of battle turned against him, Pompey collapsed into despondency. Caesar's triumph was complete, the Pompeian survivors joined his legions, and many proud senators took advantage of his clemency. Once the most powerful man in Rome, now the broken shield of the Optimates, Pompey fled to Egypt but was beheaded when he stepped ashore. The Egyptian government wished to ingratiate itself with Caesar, who deplored the murder but was no doubt relieved that his rival was dead.

Arriving in Egypt, Caesar intervened in a power struggle between young Ptolemy XIII and his sister, Cleopatra VII, who soon became the Roman's mistress. Intelligent and crafty, skilled in languages and statecraft, Cleopatra was no beauty, but she had style and modeled herself on the great Macedonian queens of the past. At twenty-one, she captivated the aging Caesar, who defeated and slew Ptolemy XIII and made her queen-consort to her other brother, Ptolemy XIV.[12] Perhaps Caesar also gave her a former Ptolemaic possession, Cyprus. In 47 the Roman dynast took a brief holiday, touring the sights of the ancient land with Cleopatra. He then hurried northward to Pontus where Pharnaces, the client king of the Crimea, had attacked and defeated Caesar's legate. Caesar's Pontic campaign was brief and successful, and the East was securely in his grasp. Meanwhile, his dictatorship had been renewed but Antony had ineptly governed Italy as Caesar's Master of Horse. An able soldier, fond of wine and women, M. Antonius had married Clodius's ambitious widow, Fulvia, but government was not his forte. He could not even control a mutiny among troops who were being readied for the invasion of Africa where Cato, Scipio, and Juba still challenged Caesar. Returning to Italy, Caesar restored order and replaced Antony with M. Aemilius Lepidus, whose father had led an abortive rebellion in 78. As consul in 46, Caesar invaded Africa and crushed his foes; Scipio died in battle, and Juba and Cato committed suicide. Responding to Cicero's pamphlet praising Cato as the last champion of the Repub-

---

[12] Later, Cleopatra had her brother-husband murdered and ruled Egypt alone. She followed Caesar to Rome and returned to Egypt after his death.

Cleopatra. *American Numismatic Society, New York.*

lic, Caesar took time to write a tract attacking Cato, who nevertheless became a legendary hero to sentimental historians.[13] Yet, more than any other Roman, the irascible Cato had contrived the crises that destroyed the Republic. Caesar's dictatorship was extended for ten years, and he celebrated a magnificent triumph, emphasizing his victories in Gaul, Egypt, Pontus, and Africa but discreetly ignoring the defeat of Pompey. In 45, Caesar stamped out the last pockets of Pompeian resistance in Spain, and his dominance of the empire was complete. The tasks of peace, however, proved as grueling as those of war.

His enemies slain or submissive, Caesar was free to settle Rome's affairs as he saw fit, but he had grown impatient with Republican forms. Sulla, he said, had been a fool to give up power.[14] The legal basis of his own authority was the dictatorship, which gave Caesar control of the army through *imperium* and also the right to override other magistrates. Hoping to corrupt the opposition with kindness and patronage, Caesar pardoned his enemies and scheduled them for high offices, but not all were grateful and many resented their dependence on a former peer. He expanded the Senate to nine hundred members and filled its ranks with former *equites* and even provincials, but the dictator spoke first on every topic, and the senators were expected to rubber-stamp his proposals. Caesar also recommended candidates and legislation to the voters in the Assemblies who followed the leads of his henchmen. The person of the dictator was made sacrosanct, and all senators took personal loyalty oaths to him. With obsequious professions of gratitude, the Senate showered Caesar with honors and renamed the seventh month July.

[13] So potent was the legend of the righteous Cato that Dante made him the guardian of Purgatory.
[14] Suetonius *Divus Iulius* 77.

Ironically, Caesar's most lasting legislation was calendric, for he abolished the chaotic calendar of the past and established the Julian year of 365¼ days.

A similar breadth of vision was applied to the problems of Rome and the empire. Governors were encouraged to be generous with grants of citizenship, and Caesar's close friend and financial agent was a rich Spaniard from Cadiz, L. Cornelius Balbus, who had been enfranchised by Pompey. Doctors and scholars who migrated to Rome were made citizens, and freedmen were allowed to hold offices in provincial cities. Asia and Sicily were freed from the extortions of publicans. At Carthage, Corinth, and other provincial towns, Caesar resettled about 100,000 of the surplus population of Rome. He also established colonies of veterans in the provinces. In the capital, the dictator reduced the number of recipients of the dole from 320,000 to 150,000, but he provided employment for the urban poor with public works. In rural areas, landowners were obliged to fill a third of their labor force with free workers. To encourage Italian agriculture, nobles were ordered to invest half of their wealth in land. A new gold coin, the *aureus,* worth 25 denarii, was issued, and the pay of the army was doubled. At Rome, the troublesome political clubs were abolished, but guilds and religious associations were still permitted, and the Jews of Rome considered Caesar their patron. To spread culture, Varro was commissioned to assemble a public library in the capital, but the project was not realized until Pollio opened the first public library in 39. Like Sulla, Caesar passed sumptuary legislation, but as usual, attempts to curb luxury were ineffective. In general, Caesar was an enlightened ruler whose laws benefited the people of Rome and their subjects, but his autocratic presence paralyzed the institutions of the Republic and reduced both nobles and masses to dependence on his imperious will. When critics accused him of wanting a crown and a kingly title, the master of Rome snapped that he was above kings—he was Caesar.[15] Early in 44, his dictatorship was extended for life, and Rome was locked into a military despotism, however benevolent.

Caesar's ultimate plans for Rome will never be known, for the dictator was preparing an invasion of Parthia to avenge Crassus when he was assassinated. Perhaps the aging dynast, who was now fifty-five, wearied of the thankless task of taming the oligarchs and yearned for the simpler demands of war where he could anticipate his customary success. If so, he was avoiding the responsibilities of power. Always practical, Caesar deposited his will with the Vestal Virgins and insisted that his nearest male relative, his young grandnephew C. Octavius (Oc-

---

[15] Suetonius *Divus Iulius* 79.2.

tavian), accompany him on the expedition, but neither man ever reached Parthia. In 44 the dictator was consul for the fifth time, and his colleague was Antony. The ranking praetors were M. Junius Brutus and his brother-in-law C. Cassius Longinus; both had fought for Pompey but accepted Caesar's bounty. Under their leadership, about sixty senators conspired to murder their benefactor on the grounds that his extraordinary powers had undermined the Republic—i.e. eclipsed the oligarchs. Caesar's arrogance and sarcasm infuriated the proud Cassius, and even favored Caesareans, such as Decimus Brutus, were jealous enough to join the conspiracy, but the plotters wisely excluded the equivocal Cicero from their plans. The motives of Marcus Brutus were mixed. An aloof noble with intellectual pretensions, he cherished an abstract loyalty to the Republic which allowed him to mask personal drives as ideological concerns. Brutus admired and aped his uncle, Cato, and completed the identification by marrying Cato's daughter, Porcia, after the deaths of Cato and her husband Bibulus in the civil war. As the son of Caesar's former mistress, Servilia, Brutus had received special favors from Caesar, but he deeply resented the older man. Since Pompey had slain his father, Brutus also hated Pompey and had snubbed him in public until the civil war. Yet when the crisis broke in 49, Brutus backed his father's murderer against his mother's lover, a neat solution to an Oedipal problem. Whatever their personal motives, the assassins claimed to be rescuing Republican liberty from a tyrant.

Ignoring rumors of plots against his life, Caesar disbanded his personal bodyguard and was cut down by a handful of senators at a meeting of the Senate on March 15, 44. Of the twenty-three wounds he received, only one in the chest was fatal. Had he survived the attack, Caesar would surely have outdone Sulla in vengeance. An able soldier and intelligent administrator, Caesar had not been a messiah and had not sought monarchy. As a proud patrician, he had been willing to fight to protect his dignity and career. Faced with total victory over his foes, Caesar settled for autocracy and enjoyed his new-found power and glory. With more tact, he might have survived, but he had grown impatient with the game of politics as played at Rome. Had Pompey won, he too would probably have demanded a paramount role and been assassinated by the irreconcilable oligarchs.[16] On the Ides of March, a great talent was wasted, but Caesar had caused his own death by sparing his enemies. The lesson was not lost on Octavian.

Caesar's murder did not permanently damage the Caesarean cause, for the self-styled "Republicans" failed to carry out a thorough purge of the dictator's prominent followers. Though Cassius advised killing An-

[16] Plutarch *Pompey* 75.4.

Obverse: Brutus. Reverse: Liberty Cap and Daggers (the Ides of March).
American Numismatic Society, New York.

tony, Brutus opposed further bloodshed, and the assassins soon effected
a compromise with the Caesarean leaders. Though Caesar's acts and appointments were ratified, his murderers received amnesty. Presumably,
the public business would continue undisturbed by the Ides of March,
but Antony had other plans. At an emotional funeral for Caesar, Antony roused the masses by reading the dictator's will that left his gardens and cash bequests to the Roman people. As the public turned
against the assassins, Brutus and Cassius prudently departed for duties
in the East. In control at Rome, Antony granted land to Caesar's veterans and assumed command of four legions, but his role as chief of the
Caesareans was dimmed, for in the will Caesar had adopted young Octavian and left the bulk of his fortune to the eighteen-year-old boy.
Though Antony despised him and Cicero saw him as a pawn to be used
against the Caesareans, Octavian was an ambitious and crafty youth,
who now possessed a fortune and a magic name. Short, slight, and
sickly, he had curly blond hair, bad teeth, and a piercing gaze. As Caesar's "son," Octavian was popular with the army and the masses, and he
began hiring a private force of mercenaries. Meanwhile, Antony made
himself governor of Cisalpine and Transalpine Gaul for five years and
marched north to oust Decimus Brutus from Cisalpine Gaul. In his absence, Cicero made a bid for power and rallied the Senate with a vicious attack on Antony, whom he accused of aiming at a dictatorship.
Though both were Caesareans, the consuls, A. Hirtius and C. Pansa,
marched against Antony. To further split the Caesareans, the Senate
raised Octavian to senatorial rank, legalized his private army, and sent

him with the consuls. In 43, Hirtius and Pansa drove Antony across the Alps, but both consuls died in the campaign and Octavian took over their troops. Assuming that Antony would soon be disposed of, the Senate proclaimed him a public enemy and gave Brutus and Cassius *imperium* over the eastern provinces, where they soon extorted vast sums. A naval command was provided for Pompey's son, Sextus Pompeius, who had been leading a minor Pompeian resistance in the West. No longer considering him important, the Senate denied Octavian a triumph, but he proved himself Caesar's heir by marching on the capital and forcing his election as consul. After distributing cash to his soldiers, the "boy" (as Cicero called him) revoked the amnesty on the assassins and joined forces with Antony, who had returned from Gaul with the Caesarean generals, Lepidus and C. Asinius Pollio. Cowed by the Caesareans, the Senate authorized the avenging of Caesar's murder and granted Antony, Octavian, and Lepidus emergency powers as triumvirs for five years.

Unlike the First Triumvirate, the Second Triumvirate was a legal entity, and the partners divided the Western provinces among themselves. To fill their coffers and crush their opponents, the triumvirs revived the

Octavian. Rome, Museo Capitolino. *Alinari—Scala.*

Sullan techniques of butchery and confiscation and proscribed 300 senators and 2000 *equites*. Combining the cruelty of youth with ambition,
Octavian outdid Antony and Lepidus in the proscriptions. Since the
triumvirs needed money, their victims were largely *equites,* but Antony
personally spared the wealthy *eques,* T. Pomponius Atticus, who had
managed the business affairs of Cicero and Cato. Both shrewd and humane, Atticus had friends in all camps. When Antony was outlawed,
Atticus had protected Fulvia, and now, secure of Antony's favor, he
took care of Servilia. Atticus's friend Cicero fared less well, for the
triumvir hated the orator who had slain his stepfather and tried to destroy Antony. Cicero was hunted down and killed; his head and hands
were displayed in the Forum. To sanctify their cause, the triumvirs deified Caesar, and to guarantee their power, they filled the Senate with
henchmen who were often of low birth. Opportunists who profited from
the proscriptions formed a powerful faction with a vested interest in the
success of the triumvirs. In 42 Antony and Octavian invaded Greece
where Brutus and Cassius had collected a large army. At Philippi, Antony defeated first Cassius and then Brutus, but the inexperienced Octavian made a poor showing in the battle. Both Cassius and Brutus
committed suicide, and the latter became a martyr in the eyes of pro-
Republican writers. As befitted Cato's daughter, Porcia too killed herself
months before the news of her husband's defeat. "The noblest Roman of
them all," Brutus had been a contradictory character. In 50, he had tried to
extort 48 percent interest from provincials on Cyprus and pushed two
decrees through the Senate to legalize the usury.[17] Yet Brutus slew Caesar for being "above the laws." With such defenders, the loss of the Republic was no tragedy.

The triumvirate was now strained by success. Inflated by the victory
in Greece, Antony and Octavian reduced Lepidus's holdings to Africa
on the pretext that he was Brutus's brother-in-law and had been plotting
with Sextus Pompeius, whose fleet controlled Sicily. In 41, while Antony toured the East, Octavian confiscated lands in Italy to reward his
veterans, but his high-handed measures provoked riots, and Antony's
brother and Fulvia tried to turn the discontent to Antony's advantage.
Driven from Rome, the Antonian leaders held out in Perusia until the
town succumbed to siege early in 40. Though he savagely sacked Perusia, Octavian spared Antony's brother and wife; the latter fled to
Greece and soon died. Though Antony had not authorized the fiasco in
Italy, Octavian feared a possible alliance between Antony and Pompeius and so married Scribonia, an older woman who was related to
Pompeius. The brief and unhappy match produced Octavian's only

---

[17] Cicero *ad Atticum* 5.21–6.3.

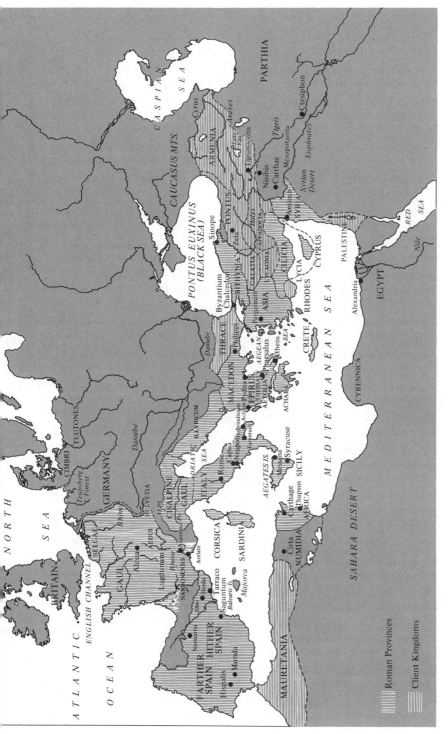

Map 3. The Empire in 40 B.C.

child, Julia. Although cautious and without military talent, Octavian
had become a serious rival to Antony, largely because he realized his
own limitations and relied on the skills of two loyal *equites:* the Etruscan *bon vivant,* C. Maecenas, and a childhood friend, M. Vipsanius
Agrippa. A military man of great ability, Agrippa had acquired wealth
by marrying Atticus's daughter with Antony's blessings.

When Syria was menaced by a Parthian raid, Antony returned to
Italy to recruit troops, but Octavian closed Brundisium to him and civil
war threatened. However, a pact (the Peace of Brundisium) was negotiated by Maecenas for Octavian and Asinius Pollio for Antony, dividing
the empire between the dynasts. Ignoring Lepidus in Africa, Octavian
received the West and Illyria and Antony the East with recruiting rights
in Italy. To seal the bargain, Antony married Octavian's sister, Octavia,
whom the sources agree was both beautiful and virtuous; in time, the
marriage produced two daughters, both named Antonia. In 39, Sextus
Pompeius's attacks on the grain fleets caused a food shortage and bread
riots at Rome where Octavian was almost killed. Antony rescued him
from the mob—and lived to regret it. The triumvirs soon came to terms
with Pompeius and recognized his authority in the isles of the West, but
Octavian divorced Scribonia, for he had fallen in love with Livia, the
nineteen-year-old wife of Tiberius Claudius Nero, a supporter of Antony. Although she had a son by Nero and was pregnant with a second,
her husband accommodated the triumvir and divorced Livia, who
promptly married Octavian. While he had no love for her sons (Tiberius and Drusus) nor she for his daughter (Julia), the marriage of Octavian and Livia was a happy union that would last over fifty years.

As all readers of Shakespeare know, Antony too was amorous at this
time, though the chief attraction of Cleopatra was the wealth of Egypt.
For her part, the queen needed a powerful ally among the Roman decision makers to maintain her client kingdom in a world run by Rome. In
41 Antony had called her to account for backing Cassius, for the pragmatic Cleopatra had supplied funds to her former lover's murderer
when the assassins were preparing war against the Caesareans. At a
spectacular meeting in Tarsus, Cleopatra charmed the triumvir and became his mistress. Once Caesar's bedmate, she settled for Antony and
in time bore him three children: twins, a boy and a girl, and another
son. Her family also included an older boy, Caesarion, whom she
claimed was sired by Caesar. In 37, without divorcing Octavia, Antony
married Cleopatra and gave her Cyprus and slices of Cilicia and Syria;
though the areas were still client states under Rome, the Ptolemaic empire was being rebuilt. However, Antony was also generous with other
client rulers in the East, and he set up Herod as king of Judea, though
Cleopatra, who coveted Palestine, loathed the man. In 36, the triumvir

invaded Parthia through Armenia, and though he briefly won control of Armenia in 34, the war was a fiasco and Cleopatra refused to supply him with more funds.

Meanwhile, the fortunes of Octavian were rising in the West. In 38, he had contemplated suicide after failing to wrest Sicily from Sextus Pompeius, but Agrippa took over the war and Maecenas persuaded Antony to furnish ships. In 37, when Agrippa was consul, the triumvirate was legally renewed to expire in 33. By 36, Agrippa had decisively defeated Pompeius in a great naval battle, and the vanquished leader was soon slain in the East on Antony's order. When Lepidus tried to seize Sicily, his troops defected to Octavian who then deprived him of any public role other than that of Pontifex Maximus which he had held since 44. Lepidus lingered for decades in political oblivion as the chief priest of Rome. Having assumed the military title of *Imperator* [18] for victories that Agrippa had won, Octavian later campaigned against Illyrian tribes to gain a military reputation. More importantly, he was given the sacrosanctity of a tribune and gained popularity with a large-scale building program in the capital. The food and water supplies of Rome were improved, and the triumvir was conspicuous in his devotion to the older Roman cults as he assumed a new role as the champion of the West against his rivals in the East. In 34, Antony alienated public opinion at Rome by asking for confirmation of his grants of Eastern territories to his children by Cleopatra, though the areas were to remain client states of Rome. In 33, he offered to resign as triumvir if Octavian would do the same, but Octavian was consul and ignored the proposal. With customary Roman abusiveness, the rivals exchanged mutual charges of debauchery and tyranny. Because Octavian eventually won, his propaganda became enshrined in the historical tradition of a drunken Antony trapped in the coils of the "serpent of the Nile."

By 32 the triumvirate had expired, and the consuls were Antony's men; many in the Senate supported Antony, though most had misgivings about his Egyptian queen. However, Octavian was resolved to destroy Antony and willing to overthrow the constitution to achieve his aim. When the consuls tried to censure Octavian for his attacks on Antony, a tribune vetoed the proceedings and Octavian brought armed supporters to the next meeting of the Senate and dismissed the government. While the consuls and three hundred senators fled to Antony, Octavian seized Antony's will from the Vestal Virgins and publicized an edited version that emphasized the favors to Cleopatra's family and recognized Caesarion as Caesar's son. Appealing to anti-Eastern preju-

---

[18] Under the Empire, all rulers were automatically styled *Imperator,* and the word eventually evolved into the English title "emperor."

dices, Octavian proclaimed a holy war against Cleopatra in defense of Roman civilization. In Italy and the Western provinces, the cities swore allegiance to Octavian, not to the Republic which he promised to restore once the crusade had ended. In the new civil war, few men emulated the integrity of Asinius Pollio, who refused to fight for Cleopatra or against his friend Antony, remarking that he would hold aloof from the quarrel and be the prize of the victor.[19] In 31, Octavian as consul led his forces to Greece where Antony and Cleopatra had accumulated a large army and navy. However, the Antonian chiefs bickered incessantly, and like Pompey, Antony collapsed at the final crisis. At Actium, Agrippa won a major naval victory, and Cleopatra fled to Egypt followed by Antony, whose leaderless legions capitulated to the victor. In 30, after a brief resistance, Antony killed himself when Octavian occupied Egypt. Rather than grace a Roman triumph, the queen too slew herself, probably with an asp. Seizing the treasures of the Ptolemies, Octavian made Egypt his private possession and not a property of the Republic. Though he executed Caesarion and Antony's son by Fulvia, the victor spared Antony's children by Cleopatra who marched in his triumph and were later raised by Octavia. Like his adoptive father fifteen years earlier, Octavian was supreme master of the Roman world and intended to exploit his power to the utmost, but he would not repeat Caesar's errors.

Caesar had been contemptuous of the oligarchs; Octavian posed as a champion of the Senate and won their loyalty with patronage and deference. Yet, he never surrendered the power he had seized through chicanery and butchery. To legalize his acts, Octavian retained the consulship from 31 to 23. Returning to Rome, he disbanded many legions and gave the veterans lands in Italy and the provinces. Perhaps 100,000 veterans were settled as farmers and clients of Octavian, who could afford to contribute his own funds to such projects, for he was now the richest man in the empire with holdings in every province. In 28, he purged the Senate and later restricted it to 600 respectable members with high property holdings. Since Octavian was the *Princeps Senatus,* his paramount role in the state was acknowledged by the unofficial title of Princeps (or leading man). In 27 with a grand theatrical gesture, Octavian "restored the Republic" and "abdicated" his extraordinary powers while the senators shouted in protest and begged him to continue to serve the state, so great was their devotion to the constitution. Sighing that he had no other choice, the artful Princeps accepted a ten-year grant of *imperium* with control of the crack combat legions in Syria, Gaul, and parts of Spain. Amid other honors, the Senate bestowed on

[19] Velleius Paterculus 2.86.3.

him the name of Augustus, which had connotations of divinity; he already was the son of a god. The effusive senators also renamed the eighth month August. In his memoirs, Augustus claims:

> I refused to accept any power offered me which was contrary to the traditions of our ancestors. . . . When I had extinguished the flames of civil war, after receiving by universal consent the absolute control of affairs, I transferred the Republic from my own control to the will of the Senate and the Roman people. . . . After that time, I took precedence over all in rank, but of power I possessed no more than those who were my colleagues in any magistracy.[20]

The Princeps thus cloaked his supremacy with legalistic humbug and avoided the fate of Caesar. The Senate willingly aided the deception, for they knew that the revered Augustus was still the bloodstained Octavian, and few senators were willing to risk the fates of Brutus and Cassius.

In 23, the consul A. Terentius Varro Murena, who was Maecenas's brother-in-law, was involved in a conspiracy against the Princeps. Prosecuted by Augustus's stepson Tiberius, the plotters were condemned and executed, and Murena's disgrace forced Maecenas into retirement. The affair had shaken Augustus, whose regime was still not yet a way of life. To provide another empty honor for the nobles and also more candidates for proconsular positions, Augustus gave up the consulship as an annual office for himself and held it again only in 5 and 2 B.C. Moreover, the Republican habit of appointing a suffect consul to fill an unexpected vacancy in the office soon became an Augustan policy, whereby a number of favored men might hold the magistracy in one year, two as eponymous consuls and the rest as suffect consuls. In return for his generosity, the Princeps received tribunician powers for life and proconsular *imperium* throughout the entire empire.[21] Even senatorial provinces were subject to his military authority, and every act of the state could be negated by his tribunician veto. During a grain shortage in 22, the Roman masses begged Augustus to accept the dictatorship, but, though assuming responsibility for supplying grain to the city, the Princeps declined the dangerous title of dictator, for he was sated with power and remembered the end of the last dictator.

The pillars of the Principate were tribunician powers, proconsular *imperium,* and the towering prestige of the Princeps, who suggested pol-

---

[20] *Res Gestae Divi Augusti* 1.6; 6.34.

[21] In 19 Augustus probably received "consular" *imperium* to control troops and conduct courts in Italy, and the powers of a censor in order to revise the roster of the Senate.

icy to a dutiful Senate and recommended candidates and legislation to the obedient Assemblies. By 12 B.C. Lepidus was dead and Augustus was Pontifex Maximus. He eagerly rebuilt abandoned shrines and revived ancient cults. A handsome expression of Augustan sentiment was the Altar of Peace with its superb bas-reliefs displaying both the imperial family and majestic symbols of peace and plenty. A religious conservative, Augustus hoped to be a second Numa, and the masses tried to respond. If the Augustan reformation was somewhat forced, the devotion of the people to the Princeps was real, for the armies were under control, and his regime meant an end to civil strife. Both popular devotion and artful statecraft favored the growth of a ruler cult. Throughout the provinces, cities erected altars to the gods, Rome and Augustus, and with awesome oaths, the peoples of the empire swore to uphold and defend both the Princeps and his family. The civic calendars of municipalities throughout the empire soon bore new festivals commemorating episodes in the life of Augustus and his relatives. Less effective than his religious propaganda were Augustus's laws on morality, which encouraged large families and punished adultery. Worried that Eastern freedmen were "polluting" the Roman body politic, the Princeps imposed restrictions on the large-scale freeing of slaves and civic disabilities upon many freedmen. Though born at Rome, Augustus had been raised in a small Italian town, and his views on religion, race, and marriage were those of a sincere bigot. Even on his deathbed, he warned against freeing slaves and extending citizenship to provincials, but the future of the empire required more liberal policies, and his successors increasingly followed Caesarean guidelines on these matters. In foreign affairs, the pragmatic Augustus preserved peace with the Parthians who returned Crassus's standards to his stepson Tiberius. With peace in the East, the flow of luxury goods from China and India was unimpeded. In the Balkans the frontier was extended to the Danube, a defensible border, and in Germany Augustus tried to push the boundary of the empire to the Elbe River. In A.D. 9, the German chieftain Arminius massacred three legions under P. Quinctilius Varus in the Teutoburger Wald,[22] and Augustus had to be satisfied with the Rhine as a frontier. Similar probes into Nubia and Southern Arabia were also abortive. To contemporaries, it seemed that the Roman empire had reached its "natural" borders, and the Mediterranean world looked forward to the *Pax Romana:* internal peace under the eternal rule of Rome.

Students of politics may ponder the paradox that Augustus succeeded

---

[22] A leader of great ability, Arminius had served with the Roman armies and attained the rank of an *eques*. Though the Romans refused an offer to have him poisoned, the German chieftain was later murdered by his own henchmen.

A panel from the *Ara Pacis* showing members of the imperial family. Rome. *Alinari—Scala.*

A panel from the *Ara Pacis* showing the Earth Mother surrounded by symbols of fertility and plenty. Rome. *Alinari—Scala.*

where Caesar had failed precisely because he was a lesser man. With the arrogance of genius, Caesar had scoffed at political forms and humiliated his former peers—even worse, he made them owe their lives to him. But Augustus could think and act on a lower level, and he used both cruelty and flattery with great success. Since he believed in some of them himself, the Princeps did not despise the lies that men live by. There is much truth in Gibbon's acid-etched portrait of the Princeps:

> The tender respect of Augustus for a free constitution which he had destroyed can only be explained by an attentive consideration of the character of that subtle tyrant. A cool head, an unfeeling heart, and a cowardly disposition, prompted him at the age of nineteen to assume the mask of hypocrisy, which he never afterwards laid aside. With the same hand, and probably with the same temper, he signed the proscription of Cicero and the pardon of Cinna. His virtues, and even his vices, were artificial; and according to the various dictates of his interest, he was at first the enemy, and at last the father, of the Roman world. When he framed the artful system of the Imperial authority, his moderation was inspired by his fears. He wished to deceive the people by an image of civil liberty, and the armies by an image of civil government. The death of Caesar was ever before his eyes. . . . Augustus was sensible that mankind is governed by names; nor was he deceived in his expectation that the Senate and people would submit to slavery, provided they were respectfully assured that they still enjoyed their ancient freedom.[23]

Of course, the Senate and the people were not fooled, and the Princeps was treated with the servility that autocrats must learn to endure. Nevertheless, the Principate was genuinely popular with all classes, and the system endured for centuries. Without imposing the indignity of kingship on the Romans, Augustus had taken the burden of decision making from the Senate and Assemblies. Freed of responsibility, the nobles could hold high offices and govern provinces without worrying about policy making, and the voters in the Assemblies had only to heed the advice of the Princeps. The real Republic had not only been bloody and chaotic; it had been demanding as well. Under the new order, the loss of liberty seemed a small price to pay for freedom from responsibility.

Much of the Augustan system had precedents in the recent past. Rome had known military coups, dictators, and purges before, and Pompey had been sole consul and had held extraordinary military commands. The holding of multiple offices by one man was Augustus's clever contribution to the edifice of autocracy. However, his regime was revolutionary, not merely in its violent origins but in the composition of

[23] Gibbon, *Decline of the Roman Empire,* I, 70–71.

the new elite who often rose from the ranks of the *equites*. The post-Caesarean era was a time of opportunity for men of merit. As consuls, Agrippa and Pollio were "new men," and in 40 the Spaniard L. Cornelius Balbus had been the first provincial to hold a consulship. The prime example of a "new man" was the Princeps himself, for his grandfather had been a small-town banker without political or social pretensions. His father, C. Octavius, was more ambitious and had reached the praetorship in 61, two years after Augustus was born. Though his mother, Atia, was the daughter of Caesar's sister, Augustus was not a noble until he was adopted in Caesar's will. His stepsons, who were blueblooded Claudians, outranked Augustus in Roman society. Yet the upstart Princeps had taken the wife of a patrician and triumphed over Sextus Pompeius, Lepidus, and Antony—all nobles. In the new order, merit would be more important than lineage, and new names would fill the Senate. Not only did the Principate replace Republican oligarchy, but the Princeps and his successors gradually changed the composition of the aristocracy.[24] The new elite were either henchmen of the emperors or loyal civil servants. Moreover, under the Empire, governors were paid salaries, and most were more honest and efficient than the grasping nobles of the past had been.

Whatever its merits and achievements, the old order had ended, and the course of Roman history was set on the star of autocracy. Everyone was aware that a new era was being born in the bloody strife of the civil wars, and Cato and Brutus fell on their swords in despair as well as pride. The attitudes of common men were expressed by Vergil in his *Ninth Eclogue,* which dealt with men whose farms had been expropriated to provide land for Octavian's veterans:

> Daphnis, why study the ascent of constellations that have had their day?
> See how Olympian Caesar's star has climbed into the sky—
> the star to gladden all our corn with grain
> and paint the grapes with purple on the sun-bathed hills.
> Graft your pears, Daphnis, now; your children's children will enjoy the fruit.[25]

The poet, too, had lost land in the expropriations, but he now enjoyed the patronage of Augustus. Millions more, less vocal and favored than Vergil, reaped the fruits of the Principate.

---

[24] So few patricians were left by the Late Republic that Augustus and his successors were obliged to create new patrician families.

[25] Vergil, *Ecloga* 9.46–50, trans. E. V. Rieu (Baltimore, Maryland: Penguin, 1954), p. 109.

THE GOLDEN AGE OF LATIN LITERATURE

In politics, the first century B.C. was a sordid era, but socially it was a time of great sophistication, and intellectually the Romans came of age. Swollen with a mixed population of diverse origins, the city of Rome had become a cosmopolitan center, and the ramshackle tenements of the poor stood next to stately mansions and imposing public buildings. Wild animal shows and increasingly numerous gladiatorial combats raised public entertainment to new heights of spectacle, if not of good taste. Except in the countryside, the old religion of Rome had become outmoded, and many citizens turned to novel cults that promised immortality and to charlatans who practiced astrology at the curbside. Among the intelligentsia, astrology and Neopythagorean mysticism were preached by Cicero's scholarly friend, P. Nigidius Figulus, whose pedantry frightened off casual readers. Under the eclectic umbrella of Neopythagoreanism, intellectual dabblers sought insights in numerology and revelations in magic and obscure oracles. The astrological succession of the Age of Aries by that of Pisces aroused in many Romans a sense of expectation that a new era was dawning, and the Etruscan doctrine of *saecula* seemed to confirm a turning in the wheel of time. However threadbare in reality, these speculations reflected a vitality and curiosity in Roman thought which would not have pleased Cato the Elder.

In upper-class circles, the role of women—always legally low but socially high—reached new heights as divorce became commonplace and the family ceased to be the center of every woman's life. Still dominated by males, Roman society included more women of stature. Wags sneered that Fulvia had housebroken Antony before Cleopatra got him, and in 44 Servilia promised Cassius that "she would see to it" that his appointment as grain commissioner would be withdrawn.[26] Despite her pose as a simple Roman matron, Livia was Augustus's confidant and an active schemer in politics. Sallust's sketch of Sempronia, who had some vague connection with Catiline, summarized the emancipated woman of the times:

> Fortune had favored her abundantly, not only with birth and beauty, but with a good husband and children. Well educated in Greek and Latin literature, she had greater skill in lyre-playing and dancing than there is any need for a respectable woman to acquire, besides many other accomplishments such as minister to dissipation. There was nothing that she set a smaller value on than seemliness and chastity, and she was as careless of her reputation as she was of her money. Her passions were so ardent that she more often made advances to men than they did to her. . . . She could

[26] Cicero *ad Atticum* 15.11.

write poetry, crack a joke, and converse at will with decorum, tender feeling, or wantonness; she was in fact a woman of ready wit and considerable charm.[27]

This formidable lady, whose husband was consul in 77, was far removed from the waxen heroines of early Republican legend.

The last decades of the Republic were a glorious era for oratory, and the Forum and Senate echoed with the impassioned pleas of Cicero and his contemporaries. Indispensable as a weapon in politics, oratory was raised to a high art by the nobles and would-be nobles of Rome, and the ability to speak well and at length was essential for success. Salted with invective and swollen with hyperbole, speeches were not always meant to be taken seriously, and many were published in a polished form quite different from that in which they were delivered. Despite personal abuse and inaccurate statements of facts, oratory was one of the great achievements of the Republic, for freedom of expression was unrestrained and men spoke what they felt. Free speech and free thought did not survive the Republic. The prince of orators was the glib Cicero, who wrote treatises on the art of persuasion.[28] His total literary output was prodigious, for his interests were wide and his method eclectic. Even in letters to friends, he could not resist digressing on learned matters and such varied topics as the Sicilian historian Philistus or the Roman use of obscene words.[29] Making no pretensions as to originality, Cicero in his many treatises popularized Greek philosophic and scientific works for Roman readers and enriched the Latin language with a new vocabulary. Generally, he was a skeptic in philosophy with a vague respect for the divine and a penchant for ethical platitudes. The Roman Republic, as Cicero conceived it, was based on warmed-over Stoic concepts of natural law, and he supported this notion with bits of dubious history in his treatises the *Republic* and the *Laws*. Banal at best, his political thought was laced with Optimate clichés about the horrors of land reform and demagogic tribunes, and he believed, like Locke, that the purpose of society was to protect private property. With regard to divination and astrology, however, Cicero took a negative position, convinced by reading Carneades and Panaetius that the two pseudosciences were humbuggery. To remind posterity of his heroic stand in 63, Ci-

---

[27] Sallust *Bellum Catilinae* 25.1–6, trans. S. A. Handford (Baltimore, Maryland: Penguin, 1963), p. 193.

[28] It may have been his brother, Q. Cicero, who wrote an informative election manual, the *Commentariolum Petitionis,* which recommends that candidates appeal to emotion and promise more than they intend to deliver. The tract also mentions the prevailing chicanery and bribery at Rome and can still be read with profit by those who aspire to political careers.

[29] Cicero *ad Familiares* 9.22; *ad Quintum fratrem* 2.13.4.

cero wrote two long pompous poems on his consulship, but later critics scoffed at such lines as: *"O fortunatam natam me consule Romam."* [30] An inveterate letter writer, his correspondence with Atticus and other friends is an invaluable source for the times, though the image of Cicero that emerges from these letters is that of a petty man and political trimmer. Whatever his limitations as a thinker and a man, Cicero was a master of Latin prose, and his influence on European thought has been considerable.

To the ancients, historiography was a blend of rhetoric and truth as seen by the author, and Roman historians continued to create the national past, albeit with varying biases. A partisan of Sulla, L. Cornelius Sisenna wrote a much-admired account of the Sullan era, but only fragments survive. Also lost is the universal history in Greek of the period from 145 to 78 by Pompey's friend, the Syrian polymath Posidonius of Apamea, who was a prominent Stoic and a dabbler in science. Interested in primitive peoples, his ethnological descriptions of European barbarians are preserved by Diodorus and Strabo. Conservative in politics, Posidonius damned the Gracchi and Marius and criticized Hellenistic rebels against Rome, for he viewed the Roman dominion as an act of Providence to bring order to mankind. Ideally, Roman rule of the world could restore the primitive Golden Age when philosopher kings governed justly, but Posidonius also emphasized that luxury and arrogance undermined even model regimes. His Stoic cant and advocacy of astrology impressed many Romans, although Cicero had the good sense to reject the latter. Interest in the origins of the Republic prompted the propagandistic histories of Sisenna's friend C. Licinius Macer and other annalists whose works have been discussed in an earlier chapter. The first Latin biographer was a friend of Cicero and Catullus, Cornelius Nepos, who wrote brief, inept lives of Roman and foreign heroes; Plutarch admired and used him. The antiquarian M. Terentius Varro issued a collection of 700 Greek and Roman lives, complete with portraits. He also composed a *Life of the Roman People,* presumably a social history. To defend their posthumous image, many prominent Romans wrote autobiographies. Caesar's trim and partisan accounts of the Gallic and civil wars have survived, but the memoirs of Sulla and Augustus exist only in fragments. Sulla had a cavalier attitude toward statistics, and Caesar too was careless with figures.

A major loss is the history of C. Sallustius Crispus, which covered the post-Sullan era from the Popular viewpoint. Though a former supporter of Caesar, Sallust was not in favor with the triumvirs, and he took a dim view of politics in general. Addicted to sardonic epigrams,

[30] Juvenal 10.124.

the historian moralized heavily in his two extant monographs on Jugurtha and Catiline. To shame the Roman aristocracy, he portrayed Jugurtha and Marius sympathetically and sketched Catiline as the epitome of patrician viciousness. In what was probably a veiled jibe at Octavian, Sallust treated both Caesar and Cato with respect. Under Augustus, Pompeius Trogus wrote a survey of world history relying on Timagenes and other Greek sources: the work survives in an epitome by Justin, who probably lived in the third century A.D. A more ambitious universal history from prehistory to Augustus was written by a Sicilian Greek, Diodorus Siculus, who was a careless compiler but preserved large fragments of more respectable Hellenic historians. Abler but pedantic was the Greek scholar, Dionysius of Halicarnassus, who wrote a long history of early Rome down to Pyrrhus, which is a useful supplement to Livy; he was also a literary critic of some stature. Once tutor to Cleopatra's children and then secretary to Herod, Nicolaus of Damascus was a prolific Greek author who wrote on Augustus and also composed a universal history which was utilized by Josephus and others. The historical work of another Greek savant, Strabo of Pontus, has perished, but his geographic survey of the Mediterranean world, rich in ethnic and historical data, has survived. Though often criticized for his errors in mathematics and astronomy, Strabo was a perceptive student of anthropology and noted that institutions, not geography, were the determining factors in human development. More compatible with Roman pride was the ethnology advocated by the engineer Vitruvius Pollio, whose handbook on architecture and mechanics is a valuable source on ancient technology. Adapting Aristotle to Roman needs, Vitruvius insisted that the benign climate of Italy produced a master race, designed by nature to rule the brutish tribes of the cold North and the effete nations of the lazy South.

The two greatest Republican historians were Livy and Pollio. Like Augustus, T. Livius came from a conservative Italian town and disliked the sophistication of Late Republican Rome. A native of Patavium in Cisalpine Gaul and inexperienced in public life, Livy relished rustic virtues and the old-time religion and saw them as the causes of Rome's rise to supremacy. In a massive and dramatic history of Rome from the kings to Augustus, he idolized the remote past, criticized the "moral decline" of the post-Hannibalic era, and bemoaned the civil wars. So great was his artistry that Livy's work replaced the earlier annalists on whom he relied often uncritically, but his history was so long (three times the length of Gibbon) that it was soon reduced to digest form. Though he teased the historian as a "Pompeian," Augustus found Livy's historical epic useful propaganda for his own program of social and religious reformation. On one occasion the emperor suggested a

version of a historical episode that contradicted all the sources—Livy
dutifully inserted Augustus's revision of history.[31] In his preface, Livy
confessed that contemporary history was a dangerous field, and that he
felt safer as well as more sympathetic in the golden haze of the early
Republic, however dubious it might be as history.

A quite different personality was C. Asinius Pollio, who had fought
under Caesar, served as consul in 40, and refused to follow Octavian
against Antony. A realist in politics and independent by nature, Pollio
wrote a major history of Rome from 60 to 42, a topic fraught with danger in the new order. He also began the practice of public readings
which Roman historians used to publicize their works. In his history, which
no longer exists but was used by Appian and Plutarch, Pollio treated
Caesar and his rivals impartially and gave a rounded picture of his own
benefactor, Antony. Earlier, when lampooned by Octavian, Pollio made
a classic pun on the man of the proscriptions: "I am saying nothing in
reply, for it is asking for trouble to write (*scribere*) against a man who
can write you off (*proscribere*).[32] Later, he protected the outspoken
Greek historian Timagenes, who had defied the Princeps. A caustic
critic, Pollio disputed Caesar's statistics, sneered at Cicero, and charged
Sallust with affectation and Livy with provincialism, but he was also the
patron of Vergil and Horace. The tone of his history can be gauged
from Horace's ode:

> Pollio! your page records the fate
> Of Rome, her crimes, her wars, her feuds,
> Their causes and vicissitudes,
> Since brave Metellus ruled its state,
> The sport of Fortune, the array
> Of leaders banded to betray,
> And Roman armor crimsoned o'er
> With yet unexpiated gore.
> A high but perilous task! you tread
> O'er fires with treacherous ashes spread.
> . . . As I read, I seem to hear
> The clarion bray; the trumpet's breath
> With quivering thunder smites mine ear;
> Methinks I see the war-horse quail
> Before yon wall of flashing mail,
> And warriors, wan with sudden fear,
> Trembling at coming death;
> And chiefs careering o'er the plain
> With no ignoble battle-stain,

---

[31] Livy 4.20.5–11.   [32] Macrobius *Saturnalia* 2.4.21.

> And all that's best on earth subdued
> Save Cato's iron fortitude.[33]

Unlike Livy, Pollio was what William James called "tough-minded," a major virtue in a historian.

For Latin poetry, the first century B.C. was a Golden Age, graced by Lucretius, Vergil, and Horace, and the lesser lights of Catullus, Tibullus, Propertius, and Ovid. A gifted poet, C. Valerius Catullus was a young gentleman from Verona who became involved in amorous adventures at Rome and died in the late 50s. His most famous mistress was Clodius's promiscuous sister, Clodia, the object of lovely lyrics and later of obscene abuse, for Catullus was a master of latrine verse as well as erotic poetry of great sensitivity. Love was the principal theme of the somewhat artificial elegiac poets, Propertius and Tibullus; the former enjoyed the patronage of Maecenas and Augustus, while the latter was a dependent of the Augustan general, M. Valerius Messalla Corvinus. Of particular interest are six charming poems included in the *Fourth Book* of Tibullus; actually written by Messalla's ward, Sulpicia, the poems deal with her passion for a young man. While some Roman poets anticipated Eliot and Pound in pedantry and allusiveness, Sulpicia's verses were the unaffected expression of a young lady in love. Once part of Messalla's circle and a close friend of Propertius and Tibullus, P. Ovidius Naso became a court poet under Augustus, but he somehow offended the Princeps and was banished to a wilderness outpost, Tomis on the Black Sea, where he died a decade later. Lively and polished, Ovid was a born storyteller, and his popularized myths, the *Metamorphoses,* have always been favorites. More poignant are the plaintive poems from Tomis in which he begged to be released from bitter winters and barbaric neighbors. His *Fasti* is a poetic calendar and a rich source of Roman religious lore, but more readers are drawn to his witty *Art of Love* with its sound advice:

> Words have a magical power to mitigate many shortcomings:
> If she is blacker than tar, *tanned* is the term to employ.
> Cross-eyed? She looks like Venus! Albino? Fair as Minerva!
> Thin as a rail? What grace lies in her willowy charm!
> If she's a runt, call her *cute;* if fat, *a full-bodied woman:*
> Dialectic can make grace out of any defect.[34]

---

[33] Horace *Odes* 2.1, trans. S. E. DeVere, in C. J. Kraemer, Jr., ed., *The Complete Works of Horace* (New York: Modern Library, 1936), pp. 182–83.

[34] Ovid *Ars amatoria* 2.657–662, trans. R. Humphries (Bloomington: Indiana University Press, 1957), p. 150.

Obviously, Ovid spoke from experience, for both sexes relish flattery.

Although the minor poets sang the praises of love—sometimes in a strained tone—Rome's first great poet, T. Lucretius Carus, took a dim view of the effects of passion. Serious to the point of fault, Lucretius was a philosophic missionary who tried to convert Rome to Epicureanism by popularizing the atomic theory and ethical quietism of Epicurus in a majestic didactic poem, *On the Nature of Things*. Little is known of his life, but he died at the age of forty-four probably in 55 and by his own hand, Jerome assures us, "driven mad by a love potion." Saints, however, rarely have a good word for Epicureans. Although the poem was not finished, Cicero and his brother saw the manuscript and praised the author despite Cicero's hostility to Epicurus. With great artistry, Lucretius explained the atomic structure and workings of the universe and described the evolution of man and society with frequent comments on the baleful effects of gold and ambition. Above all, he attacked religion, both the state cult and its new rivals, as an opiate that dulled foolish men's fear of death:

> Like children trembling in the blinded dark
> And fearing every noise, we sit and dread
> The face of light, and all our fears are vain
> Like things the child has fancied in the dark.
> This fear, this darkness of the mind, we break
> Not by the sun, the glittering shafts of day,
> But by perception of the natural truth.[35]

Presumably, the gospel of Epicurus would banish all the bogies of fear and their noxious spawn—superstition and priestcraft. Though Cicero apparently published the poem, Lucretius's lofty sermons had little effect on Rome. All classes dabbled in mystery cults, and Augustus would soon rejuvenate the state religion and add Caesarean deities to the pantheon. To politically minded Romans, Epicurus's plea to follow a quiet, simple life was unrealistic. Caesar and Cassius endorsed the cosmology of Epicurus, but both were political activists. Though Lucretius and his saintly master counseled moderation in all things, the wealthy classes of Rome delighted in spectacular banquets and *la dolce vita;* they preferred to be epicures, not Epicureans.

Less austere was the genial poet Q. Horatius Flaccus, who was born in Apulia. Short and fat, Horace was the son of a freedman who had prospered and provided him with a good education. While studying in Athens, he had succumbed to youthful idealism and joined Brutus at Philippi, but at the first sounds of battle the future poet ran away. A

---

[35] Lucretius 3.87–93, trans. Jack Lindsay, in L. R. Lind, ed., *Latin Poetry*, p. 22.

few years later, perhaps occasioned by the siege of Perusia, the theme of flight reappears in his moving *16th Epode,* which denounces civil strife and advises the Romans to migrate to the blissful Isles of the Blessed in the Atlantic where peace and plenty abound—the same sentiment gripped Sertorius in the grim Sullan era. However, Horace's fortunes improved, for he became a friend of Vergil and was introduced to Maecenas, who subsidized talented authors to support the programs of Augustus in their writings. Although he admitted to be "a pig from Epicurus's sty," Horace composed liturgical hymns for the pious Princeps, and with tongue in cheek, the man who had fled at Philippi assured his countrymen: *"Dulce et decorum est pro patria mori."* [36] With greater sincerity, Horace sang the joys of wine and love and the advantages of an apolitical life of moderate pleasure. From the spectacle of the passing seasons, Horace drew a sensible moral and expressed it in memorable verse:

> The snow, dissolved, no more is seen;
> The fields and woods, behold, are green;
> The changing year renews the plain;
> The rivers know their banks again; . . .
> The changing year's successive plan
> Proclaims mortality to man.
> Rough Winter's blasts to Spring give way;
> Spring yields to Summer's sovereign ray;
> And Winter chills the world again.
> Her losses soon the moon supplies,
> But wretched man, when once he lies
> Where Priam and his sons are laid,
> Is nought but ashes and a shade.
> Who knows if Jove, who counts our score,
> Will rouse us in the morning more?
> What with your friend you nobly share,
> At least you rescue from your heir.[37]

Unlike the prim Lucretius, Horace advised men to seize the moment and savor the joys of life before eternal darkness closed in.

The greatest Roman poet, P. Vergilius Maro, came like Livy from Cisalpine Gaul. A native of Mantua, Vergil lost his family farm during Octavian's confiscations, but his artistic skills won him the successive patronage of Pollio, Maecenas, and the Princeps himself, who showed great favor to the poet. Tall, swarthy, and sickly, Vergil was a

---

[36] Horace *Odes* 3.2.
[37] Horace *Odes* 4.7, trans. Samuel Johnson, in C. J. Kraemer, Jr., ed., *Complete Works of Horace,* p. 285.

shy, retiring man, and although a confirmed homosexual, he was called "the Virgin" by the townspeople of Naples, where he lived much of his later life. A sincere love of the Italian countryside pervades his *Georgics,* but the earlier pastoral poems, the *Eclogues,* often follow Theocritean patterns. Written in 40, the *Fourth Eclogue* is an extraordinary poem, heralding the dawn of a new Golden Age of universal peace and freedom from want, presided over by a male child who was about to be born. The intense emotion of the work reflects the false hopes of the Peace of Brundisium, and the wonder child was the expected baby of Antony and Octavia, who turned out to be a girl. Insistent that Rome should have a national epic, Augustus commissioned Vergil to compose a major poem worthy of the topic. Trying to outdo Homer, the Roman poet produced the *Aeneid,* a monument to his artistry and Augustan propaganda. In the first six books (which parallel the *Odyssey*) the Trojan prince Aeneas wandered from Asia to Africa and at last to Italy, where he settled and sired the Roman race. His mother was Venus, who was also the divine ancestress of the Julian house. Aeneas had fled from burning Troy with his father on his back and the household gods in his arms. Though he dallied with Dido at Carthage, the hero put aside the African queen (unlike Antony) and fulfilled his destined task in Italy. In the sixth book, Aeneas visited the underworld, like Odysseus, and saw the future pattern of Roman history to Actium. Vergil propounded a Neopythagorean afterlife of immortality and rebirth where evil men were punished and men of the future waited to be born. In the last six books (which correspond to the *Iliad*), Aeneas fought for survival and supremacy with the Italian princes and battered down their champions, as Caesar and his adopted son overcame their noble opponents. Unsatisfied with the *Aeneid,* Vergil wished to destroy the manuscript, but Augustus ignored his dying request and preserved the poem for posterity. It would have been a crime against the state as well as art to burn a poem in which Jupiter promised the Romans dominion without end, an empire unbounded in time or space.[38]

As Livy enshrined the legends of the Republic, Vergil gave poetic expression to the mythical origins of Rome, rivaling the epics of Homer. Though riddled with praise of the Princeps, his family, and his views, the *Aeneid* was a magnificent achievement, and its author was a poet of world significance. Like Homer, Dante, Milton, and Goethe, Vergil crystallized the beliefs of his society in dramatic symbols that were artistically valid. Dutiful, pious, and brave, Aeneas was the model that the new order held up to the Roman people and sanctified with the aura of antiquity. Only pedants cared about the real past, and Livy had

[38] Vergil *Aeneid* 1.278.

shown how flexible was history. In unforgettable lines, Vergil portrayed the Romans as they saw themselves:

> Others I doubt not will hammer the flexible bronze to soft
> features;
> Skilfully draw from the marble a latent and livelier resemblance;
> Plead with a craftier tongue, each his cause; in tracing the
> skyway,
> Measure with rods, thus truly foretelling the course of the
> planets.
> Thou, though, O Roman, consider as thy task the ruling of
> nations,
> This be thine art: to found and to foster a law that is peaceful,
> Sparing the vanquished and vanquishing any who dare to oppose
> thee.[39]

It was a lofty task to be overseers of the world, and the passing fads of art seemed ephemeral decorations amid the granite monuments of an eternal empire. To a degree, all artists were now in the service of the man who ruled the master race. Their pockets crammed with Augustus's gold, Vergil and Horace basked in the sunshine of patronage, but they were no longer free to be other than the Princeps's men. The new era was one of subservience for artists wherever art and politics touched. Lucretius was lucky, for he had died before art had become a concern of the state, and his doctrinaire blasphemies would not have pleased the new Numa.

[39] Vergil *Aeneid* 6.847–853, trans. J. S. Untermeyer, in Hermann Broch, *The Death of Virgil* (New York: Pantheon Books, 1945), pp. 313–14.

CHAPTER SEVEN

The immense majesty

> Credit has been restored in the Forum, strife has been banished from the Forum, canvassing for office from the Campus Martius, discord from the Senate house; justice, equity, and industry, long buried in oblivion, have been restored to the state. The magistrates have regained their authority, the Senate its majesty, the courts their dignity. . . . All citizens have either been impressed with the wish to do right, or have been forced to do so by necessity. . . . When was the price of grain more reasonable, or when were the blessings of peace greater? [1]

So wrote a middle-class Roman in A.D. 30, expressing the admiration for the Principate felt by all who benefited from the new order. For two centuries, the Mediterranean world prospered, more or less, under what Pliny the Elder called "the immense majesty of the Roman Peace." [2] It mattered little that it was the peace of despotism, for the Romans and their subjects were tired of war, and peace and order were acceptable at any price. The era was a time of Caesars when the merits and flaws of autocracy were revealed in stark contrast. It was also a time of cultural unification and the spread of Roman citizenship to diverse nations until one world, homogeneous at least on the surface, stretched from the borders of Scotland to the Syrian desert. However, the Roman Empire was a world without freedom, in which coercion by the state was commonplace and servility became a way of life.

For many aspects of life in the Imperial era, there is abundant evidence—inscriptional, documentary, and literary—but the emperors present a particular problem, inherent in the study of autocracy. Social, institutional, and cultural history can be inferred from a variety of sources, but the central problem in political history is decision making, and in authoritarian states, decisions are made behind closed doors. As

---

[1] Velleius Paterculus 2.126.2–3, trans. F. W. Shipley (Cambridge, Mass.: Harvard University Press, 1955), p. 317.
[2] Pliny the Elder *Naturalis Historia* 27.3.

for the personalities and motives of decision makers, their images are inflated by propaganda and honest adulation as well as distorted by libels and casual gossip. Early in the third century, the historian Cassius Dio described a major difficulty that has plagued students of the Roman Empire. After describing the establishment of the Principate in 27 B.C., Dio comments:

> In this way, the government was changed at that time for the better and in the interest of greater security; for it was no doubt quite impossible for the people to be saved under a republic. Nevertheless, the events occurring after this time cannot be recorded in the same manner as those of previous times. Formerly, as we know, all matters were reported to the Senate and to the people, even if they happened at a distance. Hence all learned of them and many recorded them, and consequently the truth regarding them, no matter to what extent fear or favor, friendship or enmity, colored the reports of certain writers, was always to a certain extent to be found in the works of the other writers who wrote of the same events and in the public records. But after this time, most things that happened began to be kept secret and concealed, and even though some things are perchance made public, they are distrusted just because they cannot be verified; for it is suspected that everything is said and done with reference to the wishes of the men in power at the time and of their associates. As a result, much that never occurs is noised abroad, and much that happens beyond a doubt is unknown, and in the case of nearly every event a version gains currency that is different from the way it really happened. Furthermore, the very magnitude of the empire and the multitude of things that occur render accuracy in regard to them most difficult.[3]

Students of other authoritarian regimes know that this problem is not confined to Roman history. Dio's words are relevant for modern democracies when public knowledge of executive decisions is restricted by security concerns or obscured by propaganda.

For the inner history of the Principate, we must rely largely on the hostile histories of Tacitus, the often scandalous biographies of Suetonius, the highly unreliable *Historia Augusta,* and the work of Dio himself. With these conflicting authors, it is difficult to know where truth actually lies. In an authoritarian state, individuals who have access to the head of government—whether advisers or close friends—affect decision making and are more important than legislative forms that mask the realities of power. To a great degree, Imperial history is court history, and the wives and favorites of the emperors loom large. With few

---

[3] Cassius Dio 53.19.1–4, trans. E. Cary (Cambridge, Mass.: Harvard University Press, 1955), VI, 243–45.

exceptions, less information is available on the able governors and face-less civil servants who went quietly about their business and kept the empire intact and functioning whether the remote ruler at Rome was a benefactor or a tyrant. As for the masses at the bottom of the Roman pyramid, evidence of the agony and frustration of their lives is provided by the petitions and complaints they presented.

THE HERITAGE OF AUGUSTUS

In A.D. 14, when Augustus died at the age of seventy-six, "the young men had been born since the battle of Actium, most of the older generation during the civil wars. How many were left who had ever seen the Republic?" [4] Tacitus's rhetorical question emphasizes the importance of longevity in history. Though always in poor health, Augustus had the iron constitution of a chronic hypochondriac and survived the harsh and inane treatment that passed for advanced medicine in ancient Rome. Outliving his friends and foes, he controlled Rome for half a century. With his revolutionary past forgotten, Augustus became a national institution and the Principate a way of life. Exhausted by political chaos and civil war, the Roman people became accustomed to the autocrat, who assured them that the Republic was still in effect with a few modifications. However, these "minor changes" made him an emperor.

In modern times, much ink has been spilled over the precise legal relationship between the Principate and the Senate and Assemblies. The early emperors made considerable efforts to buttress their regime with legalistic props, and Mommsen wistfully imagined a diarchy in which the emperor and Senate shared power. Yet even the most conservative senators had no doubts that the reigning Caesar was not "first among peers" but their master, however distasteful the fact might be. As Tacitus and others testify, the activities of the Senate were conducted under the eye of the emperor, who, even if he were not a tyrant, was still the source of patronage. Legally, it was important than an emperor's acts be ratified (before or after the event) by the conventional forms of the Republic, but in effect, the ratification was automatic. Though legal antiquarians delight in the complexities of the *Tabula Hebana*,[5] the fact remains that the forms of the Republic atrophied even in the early

---

[4] Tacitus *Annales* 1.3.

[5] The *Tabula Hebana* describes elaborate voting procedures whereby a select assembly of senators and *equites* nominated candidates for consulships and praetorships under Augustus and Tiberius. The document does not concern actual elections or the emperor's role in recommending candidates.

Principate. The legal authority of the Princeps was a constellation of consular, proconsular, tribunician, and censorial powers, and as Pontifex Maximus, the emperor was also head of the state religion. When Vespasian occupied the throne in A.D. 70 a *lex de imperio* was passed to confirm his powers "as was permitted to the deified Augustus, Tiberius, and Claudius":

> He may make a treaty with whomsoever he wishes. . . . He may convene the Senate, make or withdraw a motion, and make a resolution of the Senate by motion and division. . . . When the Senate is convened by his wish and authority or order or command or in his presence, all the proceedings shall be deemed to be legal and maintained just as if the Senate had been convened and summoned according to law. . . . Whomsoever he has commended to the Senate and Roman people as candidates for any magistracy, office, command, or administration of any matter and to whomsoever he has given or promised his support, at the several elections the candidatures of such persons shall be given special consideration. . . . Whatever he shall deem to be conducive to the interests of the Republic and the majesty of things divine and human, public and private, he shall have the right and power to do and act accordingly, as had the deified Augustus, Tiberius, . . and . . . Claudius.[6]

Since the final clause was a carte blanche for absolutism, the Republican pose of the emperors—deferring to consuls and allowing the humbug of elections and legislation by the Senate and Assemblies—was an exercise in public relations, a necessary concern even to autocrats. Emperors who played the game well were remembered fondly while arbitrary rulers were hated, but the degree of control was no less under "good" emperors than under tyrants. In Ovid's words, *"res est publica Caesar"*—the state is Caesar.[7]

Under the shadow of the Princeps, the Assemblies legislated and elected officials, but their acts endorsed his suggestions. In the interest of efficiency, Tiberius transferred consular elections to the Senate. Though the last known comitial law was passed in A.D. 98, the Assemblies existed in some ghostly form into the early third century, but their function had become so ethereal that there is no record of their final evaporation. As the Assemblies meant nothing, the voice of the people was expressed in demonstrations and chants at large public gatherings. Particularly at the Circus Maximus, immense throngs shouted opinions and petitions to the imperial box, and astute emperors usually paid heed to the mood of the crowd. The Senate was more easily cowed, for its members were known to the emperor. While always prestigious, the

---

[6] Dessau, *ILS* 244, trans. A. H. M. Jones, II, 42.   [7] Ovid *Tristia* 4.4.15.

Senate was essentially a rubber stamp for imperial policies, and its most productive function was to provide governors for some provinces and staff various governmental boards. The Senate also served as a court for important cases, such as treason, and invariably the senators condemned those few among their ranks who had forgotten their servile role and criticized the emperor.[8] Though a few outspoken senators were martyred by tyrants, the notion that the senatorial order was a consistent or effective opposition group is a myth and can be easily dispelled by reading Tacitus and Pliny the Younger. Since its members had to meet high property qualifications, the Senate became in effect a hereditary body filled by the sons of the aristocracy. In time, men of more merit *(equites* from the bureaucracy and career officers) would eventually reach senatorial rank, but the infusion of fresh blood did not provide the Senate with a backbone, for the new men were loyal agents of the regime. Even in the early Principate, when the old nobility still sat in the Senate, the integrity of the august fathers was illusory, and their demeanor exasperated responsible emperors. With characteristic frankness, Claudius scolded the Senate:

> If you approve of this, conscript fathers, signify so at once forthrightly, and in accordance with your real convictions. If you do not approve, find other remedies, but do so within the walls of this chamber, or if you wish to take more time perhaps, take it, providing that you remember that you will have to state your opinions whenever you are convened. It is unseemly and inconsistent with the dignity of this house, conscript fathers, that only one consul designate should deliver an opinion, copied word for word from the speech of the consuls, and the rest should say the word "agreed," and then when they have left the chamber: "We did speak." [9]

Similar servility by the Senate prompted Tiberius's famous quip: "Men fit to be slaves." [10]

To advise him in matters of high policy, Augustus established a council of twenty senators, including the consuls and members of the imperial family, and its decisions had the force of law. Since the emperor represented the "general will" of the Roman people, the imperial council also received the "appeals to Caesar" that replaced the old appeals to the Centuriate Assembly. Under the successors of Augustus, the composition of the imperial council was less formal, and the powerful body was the circle of friends of the emperor. Many of these close

---

[8] Roman law encouraged informers and prosecutions for treason (*maiestas*), for the informer prosecuted the case and received a quarter of the convicted man's property; the state took the rest.

[9] *BGU* 611, trans. A. H. M. Jones, II, 280.   [10] Tacitus *Annales* 3.65.

advisers held high office, and the Praetorian and urban prefects were conspicuous in the *consilium principis*. Among Augustus's major innovations for the city of Rome was the establishment of a police force, first three and later four cohorts of riot troops under the urban prefect who was always a senator. To combat the constant threat of fire in the metropolis, seven cohorts of firemen, *vigiles,* also served as a night watch and were organized under a prefect who was an *eques.* Two other prefects, also *equites,* commanded nine (later ten) cohorts of Praetorian Guards, who protected the emperor's person and patrolled the imperial palace on the Palatine Hill. An elite corps, the Praetorian Guards were pampered and well paid, and at a few crucial junctures in Roman history, their prefects aspired to be kingmakers, for the Guards were the main military force at Rome. As an institution, the Praetorian Guards were modeled on the Republican custom of a praetor in the field designating a body of troops as his bodyguards. The imperial council, too, reflected the tendency of the great nobles of the Republic to rely on a small group of friends and aides. Despite their awesome position as masters of the Roman world, the emperors conducted their affairs in a makeshift manner, and much of the clerical work in the palace was done by their slaves or freedmen, who acquired considerable power in spite of their lowly status. As the executive hub of the empire, the emperor was besieged with petitions that dealt with trivial matters as well as those of greater import. Augustus, for example, spent time answering an appeal from the town of Cnidus regarding responsibility for the death of a rowdy who had been brained by a chamber pot while trying to break into a house.[11] There is ample evidence that emperors handled matters that should have been delegated, and that the rulers actually dictated much of the correspondence that in other societies would be issued in their name. Though eventually secretariats for correspondence and finance evolved, the Principate lacked the advantages of a cabinet system, and its absolutism was tempered by the general inefficiency common to ancient governments, for communications were slow and records primitive by modern standards.

The finances of the Principate were a tangled affair, and their precise structure is still not clear. Theoretically, the Senate administered the funds of the commonwealth, but the Senate did nothing without Caesar's approval. In provinces governed by imperial legates, the emperor's agents (procurators) collected taxes, and eventually the procurators extended their activities to provinces under senatorial governors. As the supreme warlord of Rome, the emperor needed to reward his veterans, and Augustus established a separate treasury, the *Fiscus,* to provide bo-

[11] *ARS,* p. 124.

nuses for them. Sales taxes, inheritance taxes, and a tax on manumission fed the *Fiscus*. For many expenses, the rulers simply spent the enormous revenues of the imperial estates, a vast empirewide conglomerate of wealth and land, swollen by confiscations and the voluntary donations of rich men who protected their heirs by including the emperor in their wills. The stupendous wealth of the imperial estates permitted the emperors to shower money on the army and even on the residents of Rome from time to time. Made up of twenty-five legions and various auxiliary units, the imperial army was a sizeable force. About 130,000 citizens served for twenty years with the legions and received land or cash when they retired; about the same number of provincials served as auxiliaries, often as cavalry, and earned citizenship upon retirement. As individual farmers or grouped in settlements, veterans helped to spread the leaven of Roman civilization throughout the empire. The bulk of the armies were stationed in frontier provinces governed directly by the Princeps; older, less effective troops policed the quiet senatorial provinces. Though loyal to the house of Augustus, the troops were a potential danger, should a Princeps alienate the military or a group of generals decide to risk a coup d'état.

Within the empire were a number of client kingdoms, such as Mauretania, Thrace, Cappadocia, Commagene, and Judea, which were absorbed as provinces during the first century A.D. As the private estate of the emperor, Egypt was an anomaly governed by an *eques,* and senators were forbidden to visit it without Caesar's express permission. Though there are few statistics and no certainty, the population of the empire was about fifty million in the time of Augustus. In 28 B.C. the census of citizens recorded 4,063,000; by A.D. 14, the number was 4,937,000; under Claudius, the census was 5,984,072.[12] Throughout the empire, both citizens and subjects swore oaths of fealty to the emperor and his family, and in the Eastern provinces he was worshiped as a god; in Italy and the West, it was more common that the *genius* of the emperor received religious honors. Though Jews were exempted from the imperial cult, prayers for the emperor were offered in the Temple at Jerusalem. In part, the imperial cult was a contrived propaganda device to instill a sense of cohesiveness among the peoples of the empire, but it was also an honest expression of gratitude and dependence on the figure who embodied peace and order. Lest intemperate critics undermine the consensus of opinion in the new order, Augustus harassed subversive writers and had their books burned by order of the Senate.

In any autocracy, succession to power is a serious problem, com-

---

[12] It is more than likely that women and children were included in the imperial census, which would explain the discrepancy between the last known Republican figure of 900,000 in 69 B.C. and the number of over four million in 28 B.C.

monly solved by establishing a dynasty. As a good Italian burgher, Augustus was devoted to his family, and despite the humbug of a restored Republic, he insisted that the Principate remain in the possession of his own blood line. In spite of his love for Livia, the Princeps had no intention of passing the throne to either of her sons, Tiberius and Drusus, who were adults and commanded armies on the German frontier. Augustus, who had no son of his own, intended his daughter Julia to breed his heirs. In 25 B.C. he married her to his nephew, M. Marcellus, the son of Octavia and the one-time foe of Caesar, C. Claudius Marcellus, —the boy was both a blood relative and a useful link with the old patrician nobility. The grooming of Marcellus as the imperial heir pleased neither M. Agrippa, the Princeps's right hand, nor Livia, who lobbied for her own children. In 23 Augustus was gravely ill and, thinking that he would die, gave his signet ring to Agrippa as the strong man of the regime. When he recovered, the Princeps bestowed proconsular *imperium* on Agrippa and sent him to the East, probably to remove friction between Agrippa and Marcellus. Late in the same year, Marcellus died without issue, and Augustus decided to reconcile both Agrippa's ambition and his own plans for Julia. In 21, Agrippa divorced his wife, Marcella,[13] and married Julia despite the differences in their ages. As the broodmare of the Principate, Julia bore Agrippa three sons, Gaius, Lucius, and Agrippa Postumus, and two daughters, Julia the Younger and Agrippina the Elder. The delighted Augustus gave tribunician powers to Agrippa and adopted Gaius and Lucius as his heirs. Meanwhile, Livia had arranged profitable marriages for her sons: Tiberius had married Vipsania, Agrippa's daughter by his first wife, and Drusus had married Antonia, the daughter of Octavia and Antony. Before his death in 9 B.C., Drusus had produced Germanicus, Claudius, and Livilla, who married Tiberius's son, Drusus the Younger.

When Agrippa died in 12 B.C., Livia acted promptly and forced Tiberius to divorce Vipsania and marry the widowed Julia, a tragic alliance of a reserved man and a vivacious woman who was indifferent to him and hated his mother. Promptly, the fertile Julia bore Tiberius a boy, but the baby soon died and with it Livia's hopes to wrest the succession from Agrippa's sons. Though he received tribunician powers, Tiberius soon lost favor with Augustus. To flaunt her contempt for Livia, Julia took lovers until Tiberius could no longer bear the humiliation and retired to Rhodes in 6 B.C. Even Augustus could not ignore Julia's conduct, and the severe old Princeps banished her to an island; a similar punishment was also inflicted on two of her children, Julia the

[13] By 28 B.C., Augustus's niece, Marcella, had replaced Attica as Agrippa's wife. The marriages of Agrippa are a barometer of his importance to the new order.

Younger and Agrippa Postumus, whose lives did not conform to Augustan standards of morality. By A.D. 2, Tiberius had returned to Rome but not to the good graces of Augustus, who doted on his adopted heirs, Gaius and Lucius. Though the aged emperor expected to be succeeded by his grandsons, chance factors blighted his hopes. Death by natural causes took Lucius in 2 and Gaius in 4, and Augustus in his grief turned to Tiberius and adopted him as heir with tribunician and proconsular powers. Livia's triumph was complete, and the old nobility must have smiled—the upstart brood of Augustus and Agrippa were thwarted, and a Claudian would get the throne. However, Augustus was still determined that his descendants would inherit the Principate. Although he relied on Tiberius to preserve the regime, the emperor forced Tiberius to bypass his own son, Drusus the Younger, and adopt as heir his own nephew, Germanicus, who was the grandson of Octavia and married to Julia's daughter, Agrippina the Elder. With this arrangement, the Princeps intended that Tiberius would be succeeded by Germanicus, whose children had the blood of Augustus in their veins. Even from the grave, the iron will of the first emperor would control the lives of the imperial family. In 14, Augustus died quietly at the age of seventy-six.[14] An arch dissembler, he had solved the riddle of power and set the pattern for centuries of peace and public order, but the legacy of Augustus was a despotism dependent upon the military. While the citizens of Rome and the subject peoples were sincere in their devotion to the new order, the principal bastion of the Principate was not public affection but the sanction of force implicit in control of the armies. Whether benefactor or tyrant, the emperor was a warlord, and a ruler who was not master of the legions would be their puppet.

Augustus's successor, Tiberius, was an experienced administrator who ruled the empire efficiently and frugally. Tall and nearsighted, he affected a stern manner that reflected his cynical and suspicious nature. When he reached the throne, Tiberius was fifty-five years old and scarred by resentment. Unloved as a stepson, cuckolded by Julia, and snubbed by courtiers when he lost favor with Augustus, the bitter Tiberius took little pleasure in power that had come too late after too many frustrations. To discourage a possible rallying point for dissenters, the emperor executed Agrippa Postumus, and he also eased into retirement the elderly Livia, who had hoped to control policy in the new regime. Though consular elections were transferred to the Senate, Tiberius despised the senators and always addressed them with heavy sar-

---

[14] Also in A.D. 14, Julia died of neglect in captivity. Her mother, Scribonia, had shared her exile, but her unforgiving father had left instructions that Julia was not to be buried in the family tomb. In A.D. 28, Julia the Younger died similarly in exile.

casm. He deified Augustus but repeatedly refused divine honors for himself. A religious conservative, Tiberius tried to suppress Druidism in Gaul and the Isis cult at Rome, and once he expelled Jews from the capital. Too stingy to spend much on public entertainment, he was disliked by the masses at Rome. While Tiberius's son, Drusus, subdued a major military mutiny in the Balkans, the imperial heir, Germanicus, waged ineffectual campaigns on the German border. Touring the East, the vain Germanicus quarreled with the governor of Syria, Cn. Calpurnius Piso, who was Tiberius's watchdog. When the popular prince died of fever in 19, Piso was suspected of having poisoned him and committed suicide after a sensational trial at Rome. Germanicus's widow, Agrippina, was convinced that Tiberius had arranged her husband's death. At any rate, he refused her request to remarry, for her children were descendants of Augustus and presented a threat. With Germanicus gone, the emperor made Drusus his heir but the young man died in 23, and Tiberius became increasingly dependent on the Praetorian prefect, L. Aelius Sejanus, who was his only close friend. In effect a prime minister, the ambitious Sejanus encouraged the emperor to withdraw from the capital, which he hated, and seclude himself on Capri, where Tiberius spent his time debating with scholars and astrologers and pouring over dispatches from Rome. When Livia died in 29, Tiberius did not emerge from his retreat to attend her funeral. The dowager empress's death left Sejanus free to attack Agrippina and her family on charges of conspiracy, and within four years, she and her two oldest sons had died in prison. Though Tiberius had given him a free hand in these and other treason trials, Sejanus had his own private goal in destroying Agrippina, for the prefect was secretly aspiring to the throne. To gain control of Tiberius's grandson, Gemellus, Sejanus asked to marry Drusus's widow, Livilla, but the emperor refused the request and intended to designate Gemellus and Agrippina's surviving son, Gaius, as his heirs.

In 31, Sejanus had proconsular *imperium* and was expecting tribunician powers, but he was apparently toying with the idea of a coup d'état. At any rate, old Antonia feared for the safety of her grandson, Gaius, and sent him to Capri together with a loyal freedman, Pallas, who persuaded Tiberius that Sejanus was a threat. Taken by surprise while presiding over the Senate, Sejanus was denounced by Tiberius's agents, who had secured the support of the Praetorian Guards. The senators, who had abased themselves before Sejanus, now joyfully condemned him to death. His innocent children also perished in the purge, and his wife committed suicide after sending Tiberius a note informing him that Sejanus had earlier seduced Livilla and that the pair had poisoned Drusus. Contrary to Lord Acton's epigram, Sejanus had not been corrupted by power, for he had played Tiberius false all along. Betrayed by his only friend, the emperor drank heavily and became morose in his last years while Sejanus's supporters fell victim to treason trials. Though he often intervened in the interest of justice, the frequency of treason trials was a blot on Tiberius's reign both before and after the fall of Sejanus. However, the prefect had been responsible for many of the prosecutions,[15] and to a degree, the trials reflected a severity that was also extended to inept governors, such as Pontius Pilate. Despite his frugality, the emperor bestowed funds on Asian cities damaged by earthquakes, and he rebuilt parts of Rome that had been destroyed by fire. In 33, the emperor inadvertently caused a financial panic by ordering creditors to invest two-thirds of their capital in Italian land. When the creditors called in debts, Tiberius had to advance interest-free loans to debtors. Because he squandered little on pomp or games, the treasury acquired an enormous surplus under Tiberius, who was equally conservative in foreign affairs and avoided wars of expansion. Having made Gaius and Gemellus his heirs, Tiberius died in 37 lonely and bitter on Capri. Along Augustan guidelines, the elderly emperor had ruled Rome with great care, but his personal life had been a series of cruel rebuffs.

Ignoring Tiberius's will, the Senate recognized Gaius alone as emperor, probably because the twenty-five year old prince had the backing of the Praetorian Guards. Tall, lean, and hollow-eyed, Gaius was almost bald despite his youth. Astute in the cruel ways of politics, he soon executed Gemellus as a possible rival. The son of Germanicus and Agrippina, Gaius had spent his childhood in his father's camp where he wore a tiny uniform, and the soldiers had nicknamed him Caligula (Little Boots). His youth had been less happy, for he witnessed Sejanus's destruction of his mother and brothers. As emperor, Gaius presents an enigma, for a hostile tradition details the extravagant and cruel deeds of the "mad Caligula," who thought himself a god and committed incest with at least one of his sisters. Indeed, Gaius was arbitrary, wasteful with public funds, and savage to suspected traitors and former allies of Sejanus. His insistence upon being worshiped as Jupiter would have caused a revolt in Judea had his whim been enforced in that touchy province. Perhaps the emperor was a megalomaniac, or maybe he merely wished to imitate Hellenistic monarchs. Though cruel and suspicious, Gaius was threatened by real conspiracies and had to banish his sister, Agrippina the Younger, for her complicity in a plot. There is, however,

---

[15] In 25, Sejanus engineered the trial of the historian A. Cremutius Cordus for praising Brutus and Cassius. Condemned by the Senate which ordered his books burned, Cordus committed suicide. Tacitus's account (*Annales* 4.34–35) of the case has relevancy for our times as well.

another tradition about Caligula, who restored books burned by Augustus and Tiberius and returned consular elections to the people, and it was widely believed that his grandfather, Drusus, and father, Germanicus, had Republican sympathies. Early in his brief reign, the emperor was severely ill and may have suffered a nervous breakdown. At any rate, contemporaries claimed that Gaius was epileptic, tormented by insomnia, and subject to disturbing visions. By 41, his cruelty and squandering of public monies prompted a major conspiracy to replace the tyrant with his uncle, Claudius, who was Germanicus's brother and could rely on the dynastic loyalties of the legions. The leaders of the plot were Praetorian officers and a powerful freedman, Callistus, who had earlier persuaded Gaius to spare Claudius as an inoffensive nonentity. While one officer assassinated Caligula, other Praetorians murdered the empress and her infant daughter to remove any possible rivals to Claudius. Still loyal to the dead emperor, Caligula's German bodyguards scoured Rome and slew some of the assassins, but Claudius hid in the palace until a detachment of Guardsmen found him and hurried him to the safety of the Praetorian camp. Meanwhile, some senators spoke wildly of restoring the Republic, but the urban cohorts withdrew support after originally backing the proposal, and the masses openly favored the continuance of the Imperial system. On Claudius's behalf, the Jewish prince, Herod Agrippa, an old friend of Caligula, negotiated with the senators and won their approval when Claudius guaranteed consular elections to the Senate. The new emperor rewarded his envoy by restoring the Herodian kingdom and placing Herod Agrippa on the throne. The Praetorian Guards received a sizeable bonus, setting a precedent that subsequent emperors ignored at their peril.

At fifty, the emperor Claudius was a tall, handsome, white-haired man, affable and fond of food and drink, but since infancy he had suffered from a severe neurological disorder. While walking, Claudius stumbled, and when agitated he slobbered; at all times his head shook and he frequently stammered. His childhood had been unhappy and his later years dangerous. With typical Roman contempt for weakness, Augustus and Livia had despised Claudius and considered him a disgrace to the imperial house; Tiberius had shared their distaste, and Caligula had made him the butt of cruel jokes. For consolation, Claudius turned to books and wine and became a scholar, studying history under Livy. An enthusiastic antiquarian, he wrote authoritative works on Carthage and Etruria as well as a history of Rome to 44 B.C., thus avoiding the delicate topic of Augustus's bloody rise to supremacy. Like Augustus and Tiberius, Claudius composed an autobiography to defend himself before posterity. As emperor, he displayed great interest in administrative details and worked long hours on affairs of state. To win the re-

spect of the legions, Claudius presided over the conquest of Britain in
43. The island became a province, but the barbarous Britons were restive for many years. Under Claudius, the client kingdoms of Mauretania
and Thrace were also made into provinces. At Ostia, he added a new
harbor to enlarge the facilities that served as the port of Rome. In religious matters, Claudius was conservative. In 49, he expelled Jews from
Rome for arguing about "Chrestus," and in Gaul he tried to suppress the
Druids but with little success. As a historian, the emperor was aware
that Rome had grown great by absorbing the talents of former foes, and
he was generous in granting citizenship to provincials. At Lyons, an inscription preserves an address by Claudius replete with pedantic allusions to historical precedents, defending his admission of Gallic aristocrats into the Senate; Tacitus's paraphrase of the speech is more
readable.[16] Perhaps Claudius's liberalism was heightened by the fact
that he had been born at Lyons. So conscientious was the Princeps that
he spend unnecessary hours listening to trivial legal disputes.

The regime of Claudius accelerated the concentration of power in the
hands of the emperor. In the interest of efficiency, he put imperial appointees in control of the public treasury and increased the authority of
procurators in senatorial provinces. Moreover, Claudius rationalized the
flow of public business to the palace by delegating trusted freedmen to
specialized duties. As the emperor's administrative assistant (*ab epistu-
lis*), Narcissus screened all correspondence and decided its importance;
Callistus handled petitions, and the secretary (*a rationibus*), Pallas,
dealt with financial matters. Though they peddled patronage and took
graft like freeborn bureaucrats, the freedmen were capable and efficient,
and their offices were a long overdue development in the creation of a
functional autocracy. Respectful toward the Senate, Claudius was impatient with the servility of many senators, but he learned to fear the ambitions of some nobles, and a number of conspiracies were crushed during his reign. Though a diligent ruler, Claudius was vulnerable as a
man, for he was fond of women and unlucky in his choice of wives. The
empress Messalina was a sensuous beauty who bore him two children,
Britannicus and Octavia, but she was also faithless and conspired with
one of her lovers to overthrow Claudius. At Narcissus's insistence, the
forbearing emperor reluctantly ordered her executed in 48. Pallas soon
persuaded Claudius to marry his own niece, Agrippina the Younger, a
haughty young woman who lusted for power as Messalina had relished
sensuality. Fiercely ambitious, she had once conspired against her
brother, Caligula, and she now dominated the easygoing Claudius. By a

---

[16] See Dessau *ILS* 212, trans. A. H. M. Jones, II, 112–14 and Tacitus *Annales* 11.23–25.

prior marriage to a brutal and mediocre descendant of Antony, Cn. Domitius Ahenobarbus, Agrippina had a son, Nero, and she was determined that he would replace Claudius. Bypassing Britannicus, the infatuated emperor adopted Nero as his heir and married him to Octavia. An intelligent and personable youth, Nero was groomed for the succession by his mother and her allies, Pallas, Seneca, and Burrus. Despite his servile origin, Pallas had acquired great wealth and power and was accorded special honors by the Senate; gossip labeled him Agrippina's lover. An able Gallic soldier, Sextus Afranius Burrus was a Praetorian prefect, and Nero's tutor, L. Annaeus Seneca, was a scheming intellectual from Spain who had once been exiled for adultery with Agrippina's sister. In 54, the cabal seized power when Claudius died after eating a dish of mushrooms, poisoned perhaps by Agrippina.

The new emperor, Nero, was a blond, blue-eyed, attractive youth of seventeen with an interest in art and a taste for Greek culture. Promising to model himself on Augustus, he deified Claudius and announced that clemency would be the motto of his reign. While Nero devoted himself to art and pleasure, his elders struggled savagely for power. The first to fall was Narcissus, who was driven to suicide. Outmaneuvered by Seneca and Burrus, Agrippina lost control of her son, and Pallas was forced into retirement. When the frustrated Agrippina turned to Britannicus, Nero became alarmed and had his stepbrother poisoned in 55. Hoping to reach Nero through his wife, Agrippina tried to win the confidence of Octavia, but the wily Seneca distracted the emperor with a beautiful freedwoman, Acte, who could never aspire to be more than a mistress. With Agrippina immobilized, Seneca was the power behind the throne, and in Nero's name he ruled the empire with efficiency while also filling his own pockets. Though Seneca's greed may have caused a rebellion in Britain, the Neronian regime generally appointed excellent men to govern the provinces. On the lower Danube, one far-sighted governor settled 100,000 barbarians on Roman soil, giving them a civilized way of life and Rome new recruits for the army. By 58, Nero had hoped to repeal indirect taxes, but despite some tax reform, the emperor's tastes were too expensive to allow much relief. A patron of the arts, Nero attracted many intellectuals to his court, including Seneca's nephew, the poet Lucan, and the aesthete Gaius Petronius, who became the "arbiter of taste." As a Hellenist, Nero sponsored Greek athletics and drama at Rome, and as a poet of sorts, he recited his own verses on stage, to the amusement of the crowd and the disgust of old-fashioned Romans. Meanwhile, Agrippina fretted in retirement, composing a bitter pamphlet that defamed Tiberius, who had killed her mother; Caligula, whom she had tried to depose; Claudius, whom she had cuckolded and probably poisoned; and Nero, who had betrayed

Nero. *American Numismatic Society, New York.*

her.[17] Fearing that his formidable mother might conspire against him, Nero had Agrippina murdered in 59, but matricide is a heavy burden even for an emperor.

After the death of Agrippina, Nero visibly degenerated and became corpulent, debauched, and cruel. By 62, Burrus had died of natural causes, and his successor, C. Ofonius Tigellinus, encouraged Nero's excesses. Without Praetorian support, Seneca withdrew from court into an uneasy retirement. Infatuated with the beautiful Poppaea Sabina, Nero first divorced and then murdered Octavia. Though he married Poppaea, she later died after Nero kicked her while she was pregnant. In 64, much of Rome was damaged by a terrible fire, and many people lost their lives or possessions in the flaming tenements. Though the emperor was energetic in supplying relief for the victims, suspicions arose that Nero had started the fire to make room for a huge new palace, the Golden House. To quiet the rumors, Nero blamed the fire on an unpopular sect, the Christians, and tortured some as antisocial arsonists, but the Roman masses were not fooled and openly sympathized with the unlucky scapegoats. More constructive were Nero's efforts in rebuilding the city with wider streets, more stone buildings, and convenient cisterns. To pay for the reconstruction of Rome and a war in Armenia, the emperor devaluated currency and confiscated the property of suspected traitors. In 65, Tigellinus uncovered an inept conspiracy to replace Nero with a mediocre noble, C. Calpurnius Piso, and many prominent men, including Seneca and Lucan, were slain or made to commit suicide. In later purges, even the elegant Petronius was forced to take his own life, but he left a vituperative will denouncing Nero's crimes. More respectable than Petronius was the Stoic senator P. Thrasea Paetus, who idolized Cato the Younger and was forced to commit suicide for opposing the regime. The Senate shared in the guilt of Nero's reign of terror, for the august fathers condemned their peers and many senators readily became informers in hopes of self-preservation or gain.

---

[17] Agrippina's sensational document provided much unsubstantiated scandal for Tacitus, Suetonius, and other writers.

Meanwhile, Rome's most prominent general, Cn. Domitius Corbulo, had successfully wrested control of Armenia from the Parthians and made it a satellite state of the Roman empire. Amid splendid pomp at Rome, Nero crowned the Parthian prince, Tiridates, king of Armenia in 66. The emperor then made a triumphant tour of Greece where he was deluged with flattery and responded by exempting the province from tribute, a privilege later canceled by Vespasian. Though Nero was popular in the Eastern provinces, a major revolt broke out in Judea, and the able Vespasian was dispatched to suppress the Jewish rebels. Morbidly suspicious, the emperor suddenly struck at the general staff, and during his tour of Hellas, he forced Corbulo to commit suicide. Although Corbulo had been a scheming careerist, the commanders of the Rhine legions soon suffered the same fate. Nero's rash actions ignored the Principate's dependence on the armies, and the legions responded by sweeping away the Princeps. In 68, generals in Gaul, Spain, and Africa rose against the tyrannical emperor. Although the Gallic revolt was suppressed, Tigellinus deserted Nero, and the other Praetorian prefect, Nymphidius Sabinus, threw the support of the Guards behind Galba, the rebel general in Spain. Condemned by the Senate as a public enemy, Nero tried to escape from Rome and killed himself to avoid capture. His final words were, "What an artist dies in me!" However, many Romans believed that Nero had escaped, and in the years that followed, various pretenders posed as the fugitive emperor. Although the Senate had loathed him, Nero had been popular with the Roman masses and Eastern provincials. In folk belief, he became a "once and future king" who was lurking somewhere beyond the frontier and would one day return in glory. A sinister variant of the Nero legend was provided by Christians who hated him as the "first persecutor" and feared his return. In the Apocalypse of John, Nero appears as the "beast from the earth" whose "human number" is "666." Almost as hostile was the image of the degenerate tyrant, preserved by Tacitus and other senatorial writers. Although not mad like Caligula, Nero had been extravagant and headstrong, blinded by his "artistic" ego, and his break with the army was an act of supreme folly that doomed the Julio-Claudian dynasty.

According to Tacitus, the overthrow of Nero "excited all the legions and their generals, for the secret of the empire had been divulged—that emperors could be made elsewhere than at Rome." [18] Accordingly, various army groups struggled to win the throne for their commanders, and Rome submitted to four emperors in the unhappy year of 69. The Senate had accepted as emperor the elderly general, S. Sulpicius Galba, who had been a protégé of Livia. A severe, stingy old man, he arrived

---

[18] Tacitus *Historiae* 1.4.

from Spain and infuriated the Praetorian Guards by refusing to pay for their support. The frugal emperor also failed to reward them for slaying their prefect, C. Nymphidius Sabinus, who had ousted Tigellinus but was aspiring to the throne himself. In Africa, other troops removed a general who had risen against Nero but did not support Galba. On the Rhine, the legions rose on behalf of another general, Vitellius, who had been a friend of Claudius. Earlier, the governor of Lusitania, Otho, had supported Galba and expected to be his heir, but the aged emperor adopted the aristocratic L. Calpurnius Piso. A worldly young man who had obligingly handed over his wife, Poppaea, to Nero, M. Salvius Otho bribed the Praetorians to murder Galba and Piso in January 69. As emperor, Otho tried to reinstate the memory of Nero, but he also drove Tigellinus to suicide. Forced into civil war by the advance of Vitellius's army, Otho was defeated in April at Bedriacum and slew himself to prevent further hostilities. In view of his previous life, Otho's noble end came as a surprise. The new emperor, Aulus Vitellius, was a fat, middle-aged glutton and ill at ease on the throne. Although he executed the murderers of Galba, he had little control over his own troops. Meanwhile, the legions in Syria and Judea declared for Vespasian, who occupied Egypt and left his son, Titus, to complete the siege of Jerusalem. The Danubian legions also supported Vespasian and invaded Italy, defeating a Vitellian army near Cremona in October and sacking the town for good measure. At Rome, Vespasian's brother, the urban prefect Flavius Sabinus, persuaded Vitellius to abdicate, but the Praetorian Guards and the masses prevented the move. Sabinus and the urban cohorts seized the Capitoline Hill and perished there when Vitellian forces stormed it. During the melee, the venerable temple of Jupiter went up in flames. Late in December, the Danubian legions reached Rome and defeated the Vitellians in fierce street fighting while the urban populace watched idly. The victorious troops captured the wretched Vitellius and tortured him to death. Early in January 70, Vespasian's aides arrived in the capital and restored order. Except for a brief moment of enthusiasm for Vitellius, the people of Rome had held aloof from the generals' struggle for power, and the millions in the provinces were indifferent to a conflict that did not concern them. The issue was never autocracy but only the name of the autocrat, and that was not worth a civil war. During the agony of 69, nationalists in Gaul and Batavia had risen against a seemingly divided Rome, and a barbaric messiah, Civilis, had seized Roman garrisons on the Rhine.[19] The

---

[19] Like Arminius, Civilis was a Roman citizen and had served as an officer in the Roman army. He was also a Batavian prince, appealed to native superstitions, and made his revolt a holy war against Rome. A one-eyed charismatic figure, he may have exploited legends of Hannibal and Sertorius.

burning of the Capitol was a welcome omen to Gallic Druids and German shamans, and in far-off Jerusalem fanatic Jews took heart at the news. However, in both East and West, the might of the legions crushed the rebels who looked in vain for divine assistance. Despite the trauma of 69, the unity of the empire was unshaken, and the Roman army was securely in possession of the throne.

THE "GOLDEN AGE" OF ROME

Although the Julio-Claudian family had fallen from power, the Augustan principle of dynastic succession remained ingrained in the Principate. The triumph of Vespasian placed a new dynasty—the Flavian house—on the throne, and even the "adopted emperors" of the second century usually tried to keep power in the hands of their own kinsmen. Under the Empire as under the Republic, Romans thought in family terms and trusted familiar names in authority. To all classes, the Principate was a legitimate form of government, and both the armies and the masses had become accustomed to dynastic succession. Both Otho and Vitellius had claimed continuity with Nero, and Vespasian was adamant that the throne should be passed on to his own sons. In the fierce struggles of 69, the Roman army had proven its enormous importance in the state, and no future emperor would reign in safety without the approval of the legions.

Secure in the support of the army and thoroughly businesslike, the Flavian dynasty provided a quarter century of responsible government and laid the foundations for the "Golden Age" of the second century. The new emperor, T. Flavius Vespasianus, was a stocky, middle-aged man with a quick wit and a realistic grasp of the empire's needs. His father had been a tax collector, and the Flavians did not forget their equestrian origins. With the backing of Narcissus, Vespasian had enjoyed political and military success under Claudius, but he had offended Nero by falling asleep during one of the artist-emperor's recitals. Luckily, Nero needed a capable general to deal with the Judean revolt, and Vespasian received the command in Palestine that he parlayed into a crown during the power scramble of 69. A shrewd usurper, Vespasian exploited rumors that a world ruler would emerge from the East. The stratagem was suggested by the Jewish priest Josephus, who had thrown himself on the Roman's mercy and hailed him as a messiah. Long a widower, Vespasian had two grown sons, Titus and Domitian. An experienced general, Titus gained a reputation for ruthlessness when he sacked Jerusalem in 70. Domitian was an intelligent youth but eclipsed by Titus's glory and jealous of his brother. To curb the Guards' potential for meddling, Vespasian reduced the number of Praetorian cohorts, which had been increased by Vitellius, and appointed the stern Titus as their prefect. Though the affable emperor ignored most critics, Cynic anarchists were banished from Rome, and Titus dealt harshly with real traitors. Since the treasury had been almost emptied by Nero's extravagance and the disorders of 69, Vespasian raised taxes and restored the solvency of the state. Frugal in his living habits, the bourgeois emperor spent little on luxury and accumulated a large surplus in the treasury. Yet, through careful financial management, he was able to restore the ruined Capitol and build public works. On the land once covered by Nero's Golden House, Vespasian began construction of the Colosseum. In administrative posts, he tended to rely on *equites,* and many were promoted to senatorial rank. Aware that the Roman elite should represent the empire as well as Italy, the emperor added many able provincials to the Senate. Despite his obvious competence, Vespasian was abused in the Senate by an irascible Stoic, Helvidius Priscus, who was the son-in-law of Thrasea Paetus and had been exiled under Nero. Determined to emulate Paetus even in martyrdom, Priscus badgered the forbearing emperor until Vespasian finally lost his temper and ordered his execution. The Priscus affair was an unfortunate blot on the reputation of one of the most responsible emperors.

In 79 Vespasian died of fever; at the last moment, he struggled to his feet to die erect as a Caesar should. His successor, Titus, was an esteemed war hero and an extremely handsome man. Some Romans had criticized his love affair with the Herodian princess, Berenice, and others feared his reputation for harshness. However, Titus had already sent his Jewish mistress home, and his brief reign was singularly mild. The Colosseum was opened with spectacular games, and the emperor assisted victims of a fire at Rome and also those who fled from Pompeii and Herculaneum when Vesuvius erupted. Since Titus had no son, Domitian was designated as his heir, but relations between the two brothers were strained. In 81 Titus died of fever, and Domitian ascended the throne.

At thirty, Domitian was tall, ruddy-complexioned, and handsome; later he became bald and wrote a poem on the care of hair. He was married to Domitia, the daughter of the famed general Corbulo, but they had no children, and the emperor soon took Titus's daughter, Julia, as his mistress. Like his father, Domitian was a conscientious administrator and made many excellent appointments. During his reign, capable provincials, such as Trajan and Tacitus, held high positions. Legalistic by temperament, Domitian insisted on efficiency and justice in his courts, and he severely punished Vestal Virgins who had fallen from grace. He forbade the castration of children, harassed homosexuals, and

Interior of the house of the Vettii, a wealthy family of Pompeii. *Alinari— Scala.*

drove prostitutes from the streets of Rome. Though he wrote off debts to the state that were five years overdue, the emperor skillfully managed finances and sponsored public constructions. He also raised military pay and was popular with the armies. To encourage cereal crops, Domitian ordered that the acreage devoted to viticulture be reduced, but the policy was not fully implemented. In Britain, Roman power was extended by an able Gallic general, Cn. Julius Agricola, who was later recalled because the emperor was jealous of his success—or so Agricola's son-in-law, Tacitus, claims. On the Danube frontier, Domitian warred with varying success against the Marcomanni and Quadi, powerful coalitions of tribes in the region of Bohemia. In Dacia (now Rumania), the barbarian king, Decebalus, had created a formidable state, and his army defeated more than one Roman force. When the war against Dacia ended in a stalemate peace, Domitian tried to neutralize Decebalus with subsidies and lent him the service of Roman engineers. Though an able and efficient ruler, Domitian had an imperious personality and was susceptible to flattery, letting courtiers address him as "Lord and God." Impatient with critics, he twice banished philosophers from Italy. However, the regime did not become tyrannical until an abortive military revolt on the Rhine in 88 alarmed Domitian about subversion. The emperor became increasingly accessible to informers, and at night he brooded over the gloomy memoirs of Tiberius. Becoming paranoid with fear, Domitian imagined plots everywhere. By 93, a reign of terror descended on the capital, subversive books were burned, and real and imagined traitors were hurried to execution. As usual, the Senate joined in a fervid purge of its more courageous members. In 96, Domitian executed his innocuous cousin, Flavius Clemens, and exiled Clemens's wife, although she was the emperor's niece and her children had been made his heirs.[20] The purge of a Praetorian prefect and other palace officials panicked their successors into forming a real conspiracy, which was joined by a threatened senator, Nerva, and even the empress Domitia. An agent of the conspirators stabbed the emperor to death. Though he often complained that no one believes in assassination plots until one succeeds, the fear-crazed Domitian had caused his own death by terrifying his household into preventive action. In no sense was the murder of Domitian a protest against autocracy, only a blow against an autocrat gone mad.

Caught off guard by the assassination of Domitian, the high command could not offer a replacement before the Senate had seized the initiative and elevated as emperor the elderly M. Cocceius Nerva, who had been privy to the plot against his predecessor. Old, inoffensive, and childless, Nerva had the virtues of a modern pope—he could not found a dynasty and would soon die, leaving a vacancy to be filled by one of his former peers. While the emperor tried to buy Praetorian support with a generous bonus, the Senate hoped to recover its honor by damning the memory of Domitian and harassing his henchmen. Neither Nerva nor the Senate was successful. Recriminations reached ludicrous lengths, and Nerva had to restrain the new wave of informers. Busts of Brutus, Cassius, and Cato appeared in the home of an *eques* who had been Domitian's administrative assistant and managed to retain the post under Nerva and Trajan. Though Nerva had forgotten the "secret of the empire," the generals had not, and the legions were restive over the death of the popular Domitian. In 97, the Praetorian Guards threatened Nerva with violence if he did not punish the assassins of Domitian, and the helpless old man gave in to their demands. In desperation, the frightened emperor turned to the generals for aid and was advised to adopt the commander of the Rhine legions, Trajan, whose friends had engineered Nerva's humiliation. By bullying Nerva, the army regained

[20] Since Clemens and his wife were charged with "atheism and Jewish customs," Christians later appropriated them as martyrs and saints, but it is more likely that the pair was interested in Judaism, which was in ill repute in the Flavian era.

control of a throne that had been won at a considerable price in soldiers' blood in 69 and lost by accident in 96. Within a year of the adoption of Trajan, Nerva was dead and Trajan's cousin, Hadrian, raced to Cologne to notify the general that he was now emperor.

In 98, the Principate passed to a career soldier from Spain, M. Ulpius Traianus, who was in his forties and was the first non-Italian emperor. Fond of life in the camps, Trajan was a blunt, honest man who enjoyed drinking with his officers and was happiest in command of troops. His adoption by Nerva was probably contrived by his close friend, L. Licinius Sura, who was subtler than Trajan. Widely read and interested in the arts, Sura was the ablest of Trajan's cronies, who were usually generals and preferably Spaniards—Sura was both. To quiet rumors of his complicity in the coup of 97, the emperor disciplined the Praetorian Guards and executed their prefect, who might be an embar-

Trajan. London, British Museum.
British Museum.

rassment to the new regime. On Sura's advice, Trajan was careful to conciliate the Senate and assumed the pose of an Augustan Princeps in contrast to the "despot Domitian." Accordingly, the senators admired the new emperor, and Pliny the Younger delivered a fawning panegyric that hailed Trajan as Jupiter's viceroy on earth. However, the realities of the regime can be seen in the correspondence between Trajan and Pliny, who as governor of Bithynia was dependent on imperial approval for trivial decisions. Other letters of Pliny reveal the irresponsibility of the "liberated" Senate; when Trajan allowed the use of secret ballots, some senators scribbled witticisms and obscenities on them.[21] While solicitous to honor the Senate as an institution, Trajan relied on his imperial council and was an autocrat, albeit a popular one. With wealth from his conquests, the emperor was lavish with public works and built great baths at Rome and a handsome Forum dominated by a high column celebrating his war in Dacia. To a degree, taxes were lessened, and a welfare system was instituted to assist the poor in raising children. So generous an emperor earned a reputation as a benefactor with all classes, and posterity has remembered him fondly.[22]

Although an able administrator, Trajan's first love was the army, and he was anxious to extend the empire beyond Augustan limits. With the aid of the Moorish general Lusius Quietus, he reduced Dacia to client status in 102. Later, Decebalus rebelled, was defeated, and committed suicide in 106. Since Dacia was rich in gold mines, Trajan annexed it as a province, and Roman colonists moved north of the Danube. In the East, the kingdom of the Nabataean Arabs was made a Roman province; its picturesque capital of Petra was a valuable link with the Red Sea trade routes. In 110, the death of Sura deprived Trajan of a close and valued friend. It also left Hadrian with few allies in the military circle about the emperor. Since Trajan and his wife, Plotina, had no children, Hadrian, who was his cousin and had been his ward, had hopes of being adopted as the imperial heir. However, the young Spaniard was not popular with Quietus and the expansionist clique who were increasingly influential with the emperor. Still, Hadrian was married to Trajan's grandniece Sabina and had the support of the empress Plotina. A squabble with Parthia over control of Armenia gave Trajan an opportunity to wage a great war in the East. After sweeping through Armenia, he invaded Mesopotamia and took the Parthian capital, Ctesiphon, in 115. Pressing southward, the emperor reached the Persian Gulf, where thoughts of Alexander and India quickened his imagina-

---

[21] Pliny the Younger *Epistulae* 3.20, 4.25.

[22] Since a pleasant legend provided Trajan with a posthumous conversion to Christianity, Dante was able to enroll the Roman emperor among the saints in Paradise.

Scene from Trajan's Column of soldiers helping wounded comrades. Rome.
Alinari—Scala.

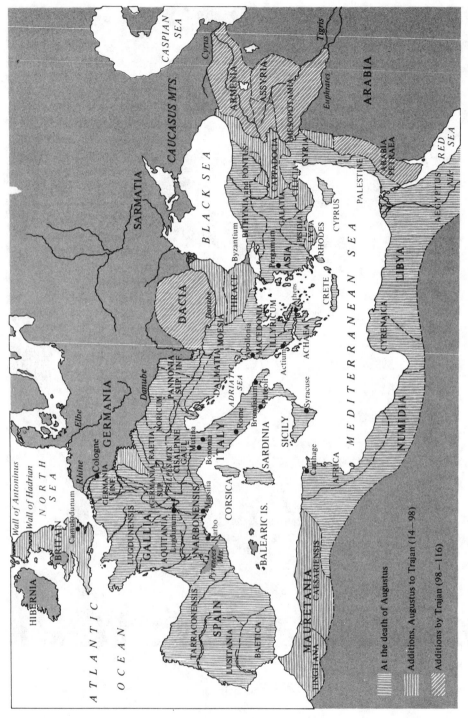

Map 4. The Empire to the Death of Trajan, A.D. 117.

tion. However, in his rear, Parthian agents and messianic pretenders had stirred up major revolts of Jews throughout the Near East. By 116, Quietus had put down the revolt in Judea, but the Parthians retook much of the conquered areas. Ill with dropsy and aware that his conquests in the East were evaporating, Trajan retired to Antioch in 117. There he suffered a stroke but tried to return to Rome, dying en route in Cilicia. Though Trajan had not designated an heir, Plotina and the Praetorian prefect favored Hadrian and concealed the emperor's death until Hadrian could be notified that the dying Trajan had adopted him in a document that was signed by Plotina. The deathbed adoption aroused suspicions which were not quieted by the prompt execution of Trajan's valet who might have told a different story. Since 114, Hadrian had been governor of Syria, and his elevation to the throne was hailed by his legions. Faced with a *fait accompli,* the Senate grudgingly accepted him as emperor.

The new emperor, P. Aelius Hadrianus, was a tall, athletic Spaniard, forty-one years old, and regal in manner. To hide a blemish on his chin, he wore a beard, and facial hair quickly became fashionable after two

Hadrian. London, British Museum.
British Museum.

and a half centuries of well-shaved Romans. A highly opinionated intellectual with a passion for Greek culture, Hadrian loved to argue with scholars but preferred to win the debates, and he relished old-fashioned writers such as Ennius and Cato. With the indefatigable curiosity of a "Renaissance man," the emperor was an amateur architect, artist, sculptor, poet, and astrologer. His marriage to Sabina was childless and unhappy, and Hadrian consoled himself with a handsome boy, Antinous, who was his constant companion. Though derided by his foes as a Hellenist and a dilettante, the emperor was a hard-headed realist and governed the empire conscientiously. Shortly after assuming the throne, he dismissed Quietus from the Judean command and abandoned Trajan's policy of aggression in the East. When it became obvious that Hadrian intended to keep the empire within its current limits, Quietus and three other generals of consular rank plotted to remove him, but the emperor learned of the conspiracy and struck first. In 118, the four prominent generals were summarily executed, and the Senate was not relieved or convinced when Hadrian demoted the Praetorian prefect for having exceeded his orders in slaying Quietus and the others. Although he promised that in the future senators would be judged by their peers, relations between Hadrian and the Senate were strained throughout his long reign. Perhaps to mollify public opinion, the emperor canceled a large number of overdue debts to the state, and he promised to review similar debts every fifteen years. Hadrian also subsidized impoverished senators and continued Trajan's welfare program for poor children. In the imperial staff, the emperor often replaced freedmen with *equites*. He also intensified the policy of promoting distinguished *equites* to senatorial rank, thus eroding the distinction between the two orders. In dealing with legal matters, Hadrian admitted jurists to the imperial council, and he authorized the African jurist L. Salvius Julianus to revise and codify the praetorian edicts in a fixed form alterable only by an emperor. Hadrian's legislation on the treatment of children and slaves was humanitarian, but it is difficult to know how effective such laws were. More lasting were his public works at Rome—the great vault of the Pantheon and his circular mausoleum (now the Castel Sant' Angelo). At Tivoli, Hadrian built an elaborate estate and added replicas of locales that had pleased him during his travels, for the emperor was a compulsive tourist.

While he disavowed military expansion, Hadrian did not neglect the army and kept the legions at peak efficiency by constant training and frequent unannounced inspections. Restless by nature, he spent most of the years from 120 to 131 traveling about the empire, checking account books and dropping in at frontier posts to join the troops in exercises. On the northern border of Britain, the emperor built a permanent wall to hold back the fierce Picts of Scotland. In Germany, less elaborate fortifications bridged the exposed gap between the Rhine and the Danube. At Athens in 128, Hadrian completed the great Temple of Zeus that had been begun six centuries earlier. Two years later, he was touring Egypt when his beloved Antinous drowned in the Nile. Grief-stricken, Hadrian deified the dead youth and built a sacred city in his honor. Also in 130, the emperor visited Palestine and ordered that Jerusalem be rebuilt as a major center complete with a temple to Jupiter. It is possible that, as a Hellenist unsympathetic to oriental customs, the emperor further angered the Jews by forbidding circumcision. By 132 a new messiah, Bar Cochba, rallied the country folk of Palestine in a fierce war of resistance that was waged with great ferocity by both Jews and Romans. After enormous casualties, the revolt was crushed in 135 and Hadrian imposed severe restrictions on the practice of Judaism in Palestine. Aging and ill with dropsy, the childless emperor turned his attention to the choice of an heir. In 136 he adopted a handsome but undistinguished friend, L. Ceionius Commodus, who assumed the name of L. Aelius Caesar. Hadrian's elderly brother-in-law, L. Julius Servianus, had hoped for the honor for himself or his grandson, and the pair were driven to suicide when the emperor suspected them of plotting against the new heir. At best a pleasant mediocrity, Aelius Caesar was tubercular and died in 138. Frustrated by the unexpected death of his first choice, Hadrian now adopted a middle-aged senator, T. Aurelius Antoninus, who had acquired a good reputation serving the state. However, the emperor forced Antoninus to adopt as his heir Lucius Verus, the son of the late Aelius Caesar, and the boy was then betrothed to Antoninus's daughter, Faustina. Like Augustus with Tiberius, Hadrian had made a grudging adoption and tried to arrange the next generation of heirs. Antoninus was allowed to also adopt his own nephew, Marcus Aurelius, who was already betrothed to Verus's sister. In his final illness, Hadrian suffered so greatly that he begged his attendants to kill him, but none dared obey the emperor, whose agonies ended in summer 138. The Senate, which had hated and feared him, did not wish to deify Hadrian, a customary honor for good emperors, but Antoninus insisted on the formality and earned the epithet Pius.

Wealthy, kindly, and unassuming, Antoninus Pius was a conscientious emperor, but he lacked Hadrian's driving energy and did not tour the provinces. Although the British frontier was pushed farther north and secured with a wall, the military power of Rome waned during Antoninus's long reign. Disorders in the provinces were subdued, but the legions grew lax under an emperor who had no military experience. While active in philanthropy, Antoninus was a frugal man and accumulated a large surplus in the treasury. However, he gave too little attention to imperial defense. Unlike the flamboyant Hadrian, Antoninus preferred the quiet of country life and was an avid fisherman. His own family had come from Gaul, and he had married into an ambitious senatorial family from Spain, the Annii Veri, who had engineered the betrothal of young Marcus Aurelius to the daughter of Aelius Caesar. However, soon after Hadrian's death, Marcus's aunt persuaded her husband, Antoninus, to reverse Hadrian's plan to make Lucius Verus the principal heir. Lucius was pushed aside, and Marcus married Antoninus's daughter, Faustina. An easygoing youth, Lucius was content to take second place to Marcus who was carefully trained to assume his ultimate role in government. A solemn and bookish young man, Marcus took his duties seriously and fortified his resolve with the cold principles of Stoicism. When the elderly Antoninus died in 161, Marcus was forty years old and Lucius thirty-one.

An incongruous pair, Marcus Aurelius and Lucius Verus ascended the throne as joint emperors, the first sharing of imperial authority in Roman history. To further link the two rulers, Lucius married Marcus's

Marcus Aurelius sacrificing on the Capitol. Rome, Museo dei Conservatori. *Scala Fine Arts Publishers, New York.*

daughter, Lucilla, but he aided little in affairs of state. Weak and frivolous, Lucius was despised by Marcus, who detested court life and found the imperial office a heavy burden. Although she bore him thirteen children, Faustina was a vivacious woman and gossips claimed that she was not always faithful to her somber husband, whose philosophizing was often boring.[23] Though Stoicism was his principal crutch in life, Marcus was also addicted to the opiates in his daily dose of theriac, a presumed preventive against poison, which was prepared by the court physician, Galen.[24] The theriac was useful, too, in easing the physical pains of the emperor whose health was generally poor. Despite his ailments, he was diligent in the time-consuming tasks of administration. Marcus, though an intellectual, spent much of his reign in war. Encouraged by the weak frontier defenses resulting from Antoninus's frugality and laxity, fierce enemies assaulted Rome in both the East and the North. In 162, Lucius was sent to Syria to repel a Parthian invasion, but the playboy emperor spent his time in Antioch while the able C. Avidius Cassius carried Roman arms into Mesopotamia and sacked Ctesiphon. Lucius returned to Rome in 165 and celebrated a great triumph, but his troops brought back a plague which ravaged much of Italy and spread to the Rhine and Danube regions as well. The loss of life was great, and religious hysteria seized the populace, who turned on Christians as scapegoats. Striking while Rome was weakened by pestilence, the Marcomanni and Quadi swarmed across the Danube and invaded northern Italy in 167. To meet the emergency, the two emperors enlisted slaves and gladiators, marched north, and defeated the barbarians in 168.

In 169, Lucius died of apoplexy, but Marcus did not select another colleague, for he had decided to reserve the throne for his own son, Commodus. Preoccupied with the barbarians, the emperor waged campaigns in southern Germany. In 175, a false rumor of his death prompted the legions in Syria to raise Avidius Cassius as emperor; the usurper had been encouraged by a letter from Faustina who believed that Marcus was dead and hoped that Cassius would protect her son. However, the revolt was quickly crushed and Cassius was slain by loyal troops. In Germany, Marcus failed in his efforts to extend the borders of the empire into central Europe, but he had the foresight to enlist Germans in the Roman army and settle some tribes on abandoned lands south of the Danube, thus pumping fresh blood into the lifestream of

---

[23] If the rumors are true, Marcus was not the only preoccupied king in history to be cuckolded by a fecund queen.

[24] The sources are discussed by T. W. Africa, "The Opium Addiction of Marcus Aurelius," *Journal of the History of Ideas* 22 (1961): 97–102. See also Edward C. Witke, "Marcus Aurelius and Mandragora," *Classical Philology* 60 (1965): 23–24.

the empire. The wars had been costly, and the treasury was low. Meanwhile, Commodus had been advanced to various honors and was made co-emperor in 177. Three years later, he was campaigning with his father when Marcus died in Vienna. According to legend, the dying emperor advised his aides to "go to the rising sun." Tiberius had said the same words with reference to Caligula, but Marcus thought better of his son and hoped that with good advisers he would rule well. While his dynastic aim was in keeping with earlier precedents, Marcus Aurelius had sadly misjudged the capacities of his son.

In 180, Commodus was nineteen years old and totally unqualified to be emperor. Tall, blond, and athletic, he rejected the intellectualism of his father and wanted to be a gladiator. A skilled archer, Commodus could have gone down in history as a sportsman prince if Marcus had made Avidius Cassius co-emperor and allowed his son to rule under the guidance of an older, abler man. However, misplaced paternal affection left Commodus to rule alone. Making a quick peace in Germany, he hurried to Rome to enjoy his new role and entrusted decision making to a series of corrupt Praetorian prefects. Commodus spent much of his time wasting public funds and killing animals in the arena. In 182, the rambunctious emperor was surprised by an assassination attempt engineered by his sister, Lucilla, who had once been Lucius's empress and had ambitions for her current lover. Though the plot failed, Commodus suspected the Senate of complicity and began sporadically to purge its ranks. In time, the rowdy ruler lost touch with reality and became a megalomaniac, insisting that Rome be renamed Commodiana. Imagining himself Hercules, he dressed in a lion's skin and carried a club. Late in 192, Commodus contrived an insane scheme to rule enthroned as a gladiator and with a government of gladiators. Rather than perish with their mad master when the inevitable fall came, the Praetorian prefect and Commodus's mistress Marcia decided to replace him with a respected senator, Pertinax. Despite his debauched life, the emperor was difficult to kill, but at last he was strangled to death. By his escapades, the imperial lunatic had disgraced his office, and his extravagant spending depleted what little was left in the treasury after the wars of Marcus Aurelius. As with the death of Domitian, the murder of Commodus was a palace plot against a despot who had become too dangerous for his underlings. A similar scenario also followed: The Senate installed one of its members as emperor; the Praetorian Guards got out of hand; and the Roman army soon reclaimed the throne. Within five months of the assassination of Commodus, a general was installed as emperor at Rome.

Except for the bizarre reign of Commodus, the emperors of the second century had been a commendable lot, and posterity has termed their era the Golden Age of Rome. The classic expression of this view was made by the great British historian Edward Gibbon in his *History of the Decline and Fall of the Roman Empire*. In 1776 Gibbon insisted:

> If a man were called to fix the period in the history of the world during which the condition of the human race was most happy and prosperous, he would without hesitation name that which elapsed from the death of Domitian to the accession of Commodus.[25] The vast extent of the Roman empire was governed by absolute power under the guidance of virtue and wisdom. The armies were restrained by the firm but gentle hand of four successive emperors, whose characters and authority commanded involuntary respect. The forms of the civil administration were carefully preserved by Nerva, Trajan, Hadrian, and the Antonines, who delighted in the image of liberty and were pleased with considering themselves as the accountable ministers of the laws. . . . The labors of these monarchs were over-paid by the immense reward that inseparably waited on their success, by the honest pride of virtue, and by the exquisite delight of beholding the general happiness of which they were the authors.[26]

From such Utopian heights, of course, it was straight downhill into the pit of despotism and religiosity that was the Late Empire. Gibbon's hyperboles came right from the heart. As a man of the Enlightenment, he admired philosopher kings who tossed Christian fanatics to lions. As a good Tory, he imagined that the Romans had found a golden mean between the anarchy of democracy and the genetic problems that arise in a hereditary monarchy. Like Machiavelli, Gibbon believed that an adoptive system predicated on merit had produced a Golden Age. Throughout Roman history, adoptions were common, but merit rarely entered into consideration, least of all when a throne was at stake. Nerva had been bullied into adopting Trajan, who probably did not adopt Hadrian at all. Hadrian's first choice of an heir was "opposed by all" and rightly so, and Antoninus was only adopted to keep the throne warm for Lucius Verus. With Marcus Aurelius, Plato's dream was realized with a philosopher as king, but Marcus ignored the merits of Avidius Cassius and handed the empire to his own worthless flesh and blood. To be sure, the five "good emperors" were for the most part excellent rulers, but no one planned it that way. Intrigue, whim, and accident produced a succession of five able rulers.

Gibbon's notion of the second century as an age of justice and pros-

[25] This famous sentence parodies a line in William Robertson's *History of Charles V*, and the tone of the paragraph recalls a passage in Fielding's *Tom Jones*. Both authors were favorites of Gibbon and familiar to readers in 1776.
[26] Gibbon, *Decline of the Roman Empire*, I, 78.

perity was a reflection of eighteenth-century views. For men of property, the Roman empire was a fine place in which to live, and even the Christian polemicist Tertullian had kind words for the achievements of the City of Man:

> The world is every day better known, better cultivated, and more civilized than before. Everywhere roads are traced, every district is known, every country opened to commerce. Smiling fields have invaded the forests; flocks and herds have routed the wild beasts; the very sands are sown; the rocks are broken up; the marshes drained. There are now as many cities as there were formerly cottages. Reefs and shoals have lost their terrors. Wherever there is a trace of life, there are houses, human habitations, and well-ordered governments.[27]

Such, at its best, was the world that Rome had made.

Perhaps one hundred million people lived within the borders of the empire. Trade flourished, goods passed peaceably over excellent roads, and centers of production spread from Mediterranean lands to the outer provinces. Once produced at Arretium in Italy, red-glazed pottery was now made in factories in Gaul. More expensive was fine glassware from the Levant where the techniques of glass blowing were discovered early in the first century A.D.[28] Beyond the frontiers of the empire, Roman merchants traveled as far as India, and an embassy from Ceylon had visited Claudius. In the first century A.D., sailors from the West had learned the seasonal secret of the Indian Ocean monsoon winds, and a diligent traveler could reach the Malabar Coast only four months after leaving Puteoli. The luxury trade with the East brought fabulous profits to middlemen, and Pliny the Elder complained that Rome exported fifty million sesterces annually for baubles and gems from India.[29] While draining the empire of gold, the luxury trade benefited only a few merchants and their wealthy customers. More beneficial and lasting in effect was the passion of the emperors and the aristocracy for public benefactions, bestowing baths, arches, aqueducts, amphitheaters, and colonnades on cities throughout the empire. Every provincial town aspired to be a miniature Rome, and the local gentry donated enormous sums for public constructions and upkeep. Through philanthropy, some of the wealth of the upper class was turned to public use, and the mania for building provided employment for the urban poor. Obviously there

---

[27] Tertullian *de anima* 30, trans. F. W. Walbank, *The Awful Revolution* (Liverpool: Liverpool University Press, 1969), p. 19.

[28] According to an unlikely tale, flexible glass was also developed, but Tiberius forbade the invention for fear that it would undermine the value of precious metals.

[29] Pliny the Elder *Naturalis Historia* 6.101.

was a limit to imperial generosity, for Dacia was Rome's last great booty, and future contributions from an emperor came either from his own purse or from public funds. At the municipal level, overextended philanthropists sometimes put themselves in debt to beautify their communities. Whatever their motives—personal vanity, public spirit, or local pride—the imposing ruins of their works still stand and often bear the name of the benefactor.

Roman philanthropy was not limited to public buildings. Though Rome had no state educational system, the emperors endowed professorial chairs, and local magnates often paid the salaries of teachers in small towns. The emperors relieved doctors of obligatory state service if they practiced medicine in their own communities or at Rome, "everyone's home town." Since it was difficult for poor parents to raise children, and unwanted babies were frequently exposed, wealthy men set up funds to support the needy children of a community. An example of such philanthropy is provided by an inscription, recording the grant of a rich benefactor to the African town of Sicca:

> To my dearly beloved fellow-townsmen of Sicca, I wish to give 1,300,000 sesterces. I trust you, my very dear fellow-townsmen, to ensure that from the interest of five percent on that capital 300 boys shall receive subsistence grants and 200 girls, the boys to receive ten sesterces a month from the age of three to fifteen, the girls eight sesterces a month from the age of three to thirteen. The selection is to be made from citizens or from inhabitants of the city, provided these latter are staying within its boundaries. It will be best, if you agree, that the selection should be made by the annual magistrates, a replacement being found immediately in the case of a child who reaches the upper age limit or who dies, so that the number of beneficiaries may never fall short.[30]

Because of high infant mortality, no provision was made for children under three years of age; it was best to wait until a baby had survived for three years. Pliny the Younger was even more generous to the townspeople of Comum, and Pliny's master, Trajan, institutionalized the support of poor children through the alimentary program, whereby wealthy landowners were asked to borrow a sum from the state and pay five percent interest on the loan. The total amount of interest had already been calculated as sufficient for the upkeep of a specific number of children, and Trajan made a distinction in payments for legitimate (boys: 16 sesterces per month, girls: 12) and illegitimate (boys:12, girls: 10) recipients. Since the landowner had to pledge more than ten times

[30] Dessau, *ILS* 6818, trans. J. P. V. D. Balsdon, *Life and Leisure in Ancient Rome* (London: The Bodley Head, 1969), pp. 89–90.

the value in land as security for the loan, the alimentary program did not affect poor farmers, and the rich who received the loans probably reinvested the money at current interest rates (12 percent) instead of making improvements on their estates. The emperor's concern for the children of the poor was not wholly altruistic, for Pliny the Younger notes that boys who were raised with state aid would one day receive pay as soldiers from the same source.[31] Begun by Nerva and enlarged by Trajan, the alimentary program was widespread in second-century Italy and later spread to the provinces.

Although the presence of Rome was visible everywhere and increasing numbers of provincials received citizenship, the Roman empire was not a nation state but a legal patchwork of lands belonging to the Roman people together with the territories of cities and tribes bound to Rome by a variety of treaty relationships. In most matters, the cities governed themselves through elected officials, but the supremacy of the Caesars superseded any meaningful rights that might be claimed by an old ally or "friend of Rome," and everyone within the empire knew it. Even in the time of Augustus, the cities competed in sycophancy, filling their calendars with holidays to commemorate important dates in the lives of the emperor and his family, and creating priesthoods to celebrate such events as the assumption of the toga of adulthood by an adolescent heir of the ruler. Two centuries of groveling conditioned the "allies and friends of Rome" to remember their place in the Roman scheme. Under Antoninus Pius, the Greek rhetorician Aelius Aristides delivered a famous oration in praise of Rome, under whose eternal leadership the world enjoyed a perpetual holiday while the cities glistened in prosperity and contentment. Aristides, however, also lifted the veil and exposed the fabric of life in the empire:

> Since the constitution is a universal one and, as it were, of one state, naturally your governors rule not as over the property of others but as over their own. Besides, all the masses have as a share in it the permission to [take refuge with you] from the power of the local magnates, [but there is] the indignation and punishment from you which will come upon them immediately if they themselves dare to make any unlawful change. Thus, the present regime naturally suits and serves both rich and poor. No other way of life is left. . . . It is not safe for those to rule who have not power. . . . Accordingly, all are held fast and would not ask to secede any more than those at sea from the helmsman. As bats in caves cling fast to each other and to the rocks, so all from you depend with much concern not to fall from this cluster of cities.[32]

[31] Pliny the Younger *Panegyricus* 26.3.
[32] Aelius Aristides *ad Romam* 65–66, 68, trans. J. H. Oliver, "The Ruling Power," *Transactions of the American Philosophical Society* N.S. 43 (1953): 902.

For those who lived under the Roman Peace, there were no options left, and they huddled like bats in a cave.

If Rome provided peace, the price was taxation, and Roman officials were diligent in collecting revenue. As the home of the master race, Italy was exempt from direct taxation, but everyone in the empire paid indirect taxes (sales, customs, manumission) and "crown gold," periodic donations to the emperor. In the provinces, all residents and even Roman citizens paid direct taxes (a land tax and a poll tax) unless they belonged to a privileged community, perhaps a former military colony with "Italian rights," or were specifically exempted as individuals. Generally, provincials had no such immunity, and their only consolation was that the emperor's procurators were less rapacious than the publicans of the Republic. After an overzealous governor had squeezed excessive taxes from Egypt, Tiberius warned him, "Shear my sheep, but do not flay them." [33] Responsible governors would intervene in times of famine with food relief or price controls. During Domitian's reign, there was a serious famine in Asia Minor and Anatolia, and a governor imposed a maximum price of one denarius for a quarter bushel of grain when profiteers were demanding far more. Since the normal price was half a denarius, even the governor's maximum represented a hardship for the poor, but prices could be worse, for the Third Horseman of the Apocalypse cried: "A quart of wheat for a denarius, and three quarts of barley for a denarius." [34] The intervention of Roman authorities in local affairs had negative as well as positive aspects. When the bakers' guild of Ephesus went on strike for higher bread prices, the governor forbade the bakers to assemble and their leaders to strike and threatened severe punishments for disobedience. Concern for public order was obsessive with the Romans, who viewed most associations as potentially subversive. As governor of Bithynia, Pliny asked Trajan to authorize a municipal fire brigade for the town of Nicomedia and promised that it would be properly supervised. Although Rome had a fire department, the emperor refused to permit one for the provincial city: "We must remember that it is societies like these which have been responsible for the political disturbances in your province, particularly in its towns. If people assemble for a common purpose, whatever name we give them and for whatever reason, they soon turn into a political club." [35] Trajan grudgingly confirmed a mutual benefit society in another town because of a standing treaty, but he insisted: "In all other cities which are subject to our own law, these institutions must be forbidden." [36] Since the Hellenistic cities had a long history of rowdi-

---

[33] Cassius Dio 57.10.5.   [34] Apocalypse of John 6.6.
[35] Pliny the Younger *Epistulae* 10.34.   [36] Pliny the Younger *Epistulae* 10.93.

ness and factional strife, the emperor forbade any organization that might conceivably disturb the Roman peace.

Despite the intrusiveness of the Roman state, the cities enjoyed prosperity and growth under the rule of the emperors, and the Golden Age of Rome was certainly golden for the *bourgeoisie*. However, the majority of the inhabitants of the empire were rural, not urban, and the peasants received little benefit, other than the vaunted Roman peace, from the people who dwelt in the cities. Like Rome itself—the symbol of civic life—the towns were centers of administration and consumption. Handsome buildings were inscribed with the names of public benefactors, but not with the names of the peasants from whose labor the wealth of the elite was drawn. In Rostovtzeff's apt phrase, the cities were "hives of drones." [37] Like all ancient societies, the Roman empire was an economic iceberg. While a highly visible urban minority basked in affluence, the overhelming mass of the people was submerged in poverty, a nation in the depths. Even in the cities, most people were poor, for industry was minimal and wages were low. The philanthropy that characterized the age was aimed in part at reducing the revolutionary potential of the poor. At the bottom of society were a sizeable number of slaves, but the total slave population was shrinking because of the frequency of manumission and the dwindling number of captives from war. Pliny the Younger grumbled over freedmen who advanced too high on the social ladder, and satirists sneered at slaves who were the spoiled pets of rich women. The lot of most slaves, however, was miserable.[38] In the *Golden Ass*, Lucius Apuleius depicts a pitiful scene in a mill operated by slaves:

> Ye gods, what a pack of runts the poor creatures were! . . . Their skins were seamed all over with the marks of old floggings, as you could easily see through the holes in their ragged shirts that shaded rather than covered their scarred backs; but some wore only loin-cloths. They had letters branded on their foreheads, and half-shaved heads and irons on their legs. Their complexions were frightfully yellow, their eyelids caked with the smoke of the baking ovens, their eyes so bleary and inflamed that they could hardly see out of them, and they were powdered like athletes in the arena, but with dirty flour, not dust.[39]

[37] Mikhail Rostovtzeff, *The Social and Economic History of the Roman Empire*, 2d ed. (Oxford: Clarendon Press, 1957), I, 380.

[38] An important exception were administrative slaves in the imperial service, a high percentage of whom had free-born wives. A managerial cadre, they were skilled and well-paid and could anticipate high posts as freedmen.

[39] Apuleius *Metamorphoses* 9.12, trans. Robert Graves (New York: Farrar, Straus, and Giroux, 1969), p. 202.

As evidence for the treatment of slaves, this passage and comparable descriptions of servile misery outweigh the pleas of philosophers who urged masters to treat slaves humanely. Even Seneca's moving *Epistle 47*, a classic argument for humanity toward slaves, makes its point by describing the indignities endured by domestic slaves, who were among the best treated of the servile population. Unfortunately, few Romans were philosophers, and fewer still were humanitarians.

In view of the national myth of the virtues of rustic life in Rome's remote past, the plight of the peasantry was one of the bitterest ironies in Roman history. Since slaves were expensive and sometimes troublesome, the great landowners of the Imperial era gradually abandoned the plantation system and rented their land in small parcels to tenant farmers (*coloni*) who were free men but not freeholders. In the past, moralists had bemoaned the dwindling of sturdy yeomen; now, free farmers were returning in greater numbers, but as sharecroppers in economic bondage and without the political rights of their Republican ancestors. Pliny the Elder noted the trend with displeasure: "Large estates have been the ruin of Italy, and are now proving the ruin of the provinces too—half of Africa was owned by six landlords, when the emperor Nero put them to death." [40] With backbreaking drudgery, the *colonus* produced the wealth of the elegant gentry who grace the pages of literature and history. Even if a farmer happened to own his own land, he was at the mercy of local officials who lived in nearby towns. In discussing the effects of malnutrition on the rural populace, Galen indicts the greed of the magnates in the cities:

> The city-dwellers, as it was their custom to collect and store enough grain for the whole of the next year immediately after the harvest, carried off all the wheat, barley, beans, and lentils, and left to the peasants various kinds of pulse—after taking quite a large proportion of these to the city. After consuming what was left in the course of the winter, the country people had to resort to unhealthy foods in the spring; they ate twigs and shoots of trees and bushes and bulbs and roots of inedible plants. [41]

Despised as bumpkins, the peasants received no sympathy from townsmen and little justice from representatives of the imperial government. The farmers' produce was grabbed by landlords and tax collectors, and the peasants were bullied by soldiers and officials who might seize their animals or force them to serve as guides or laborers. Alluding to such

[40] Pliny the Elder *Naturalis Historia* 18.35. ·

[41] Galen *de Probis Pravisque Alimentorum Succis* 1 (Kühn, VI, 749–50), trans. F. Millar, *The Roman Empire and its Neighbours* (London: Weidenfeld and Nicolson, 1967), p. 208.

impositions, Jesus had counseled: "If someone in authority forces you to go a mile with him, go two miles" cheerfully.[42] Epictetus, a former slave, offered a practical piece of advice: "If a soldier on service with the emperor lays hands on your donkey, give it up and do not resist or grumble, for if you do, you will only get a beating and lose the poor beast anyway." [43] On estates of the emperor, tenant farmers were exposed to excessive demands to perform forced labor for wealthy men who had leased the lands from imperial procurators. In Africa, exasperated *coloni* appealed to Commodus:

> Please help us, and since we are poor peasants who scrape a living by the toil of our hands and are not a match for a lessee who makes himself agreeable by profuse gifts in the eyes of your procurators with whom, as one succeeds the other, he is acquainted in virtue of his lease; take pity on us and by your sacred rescript deign to order that we should not furnish more than is due under the Hadrianic law and according to the letters of your procurators, that is three times two days work, so that by the kindness of your majesty, we, your rustic home-born slaves and foster sons of your estates, born in your service, may no longer be troubled by the lessees of the fiscal lands.[44]

The petitioners were not really "rustic slaves," but their families had worked the imperial estates so long that they went with the property. Luckily for these *coloni,* Commodus heard their plea favorably, and they wisely preserved the correspondence in an inscription. However, most cries for justice went unheard in the Roman world.

If the poor carried the heaviest loads, the upper and middle classes in the provinces were not without burdens, for they were coerced into performing services for the state. In the Hellenistic East, obligatory state services (liturgies) were a time-honored device for getting bureaucratic work done free, and the gentry usually accepted the duties with good grace as honors of a sort. The collection of taxes or supervising land surveys and water supplies were commonly imposed on local magnates who performed the services gratis. Lacking an elaborate bureaucracy, the Roman empire had found similar techniques expedient, and the obligations gave civic leaders the illusions of self-government. Even when the official responsible for tax collection was expected to pay deficiencies himself, the wealthy class could take pride in playing the role of public benefactors. Since membership in the city councils (*curiae*) was generally monopolized by a few families, the class of municipal officials (*decuriones, curiales*) tended to become hereditary, and so did the bur-

---

[42] Matthew 5.41.   [43] Epictetus *Dissertationes* 4.1.79.
[44] S. Riccobono *FIRA* ² 1.103, trans. A. H. M. Jones, II, 297–98.

dens of office. As long as the communities and their leaders enjoyed prosperity, the system was bearable, but should times change for the worse, the obligatory services could become onerous, even disastrous in the matter of taxes.

Even in the Golden Age, the middle class found liturgies burdensome, and it is noteworthy that individuals who were legally immune found themselves obliged to perform services for the state. Under Antoninus Pius, a desperate physician in Egypt complained to the prefect:

> Contrary to the prohibition, I have been impressed as a superintendent of sequestrated property. . . . , and through laboring on this task for the last four years, I have become quite impoverished, my lord; wherefore I entreat you, my preserver, to have pity on me and order me now to be released from my task, in order that I may be able to recover from the effects of my labors, having at the same time appended precedents by which complete exemption from compulsory services is granted to persons practicing the profession of medicine, especially to those who have been approved like myself.[45]

In another case, a doctor complained, "I have treated these very persons who have nominated me for a public service." The prefect replied, "Perhaps you treated them unskilfully." [46] Soldiers who had looked forward to an unencumbered retirement might find themselves subject to an illegal liturgy, as did an irate veteran in Egypt under Marcus Aurelius:

> It has been decreed, my lord, that after their discharge veterans should have a five-year period of repose. In spite of this regulation, I was molested two years after my discharge and arbitrarily nominated for a public duty, and from then till now, I have been on duty without a break. Such a prolonged burden being universally forbidden in the case of natives, much more ought the rule to be observed in the case of myself who have served such a long time in the army. Wherefore I have been compelled to have recourse to you with a righteous request, and I ask you to secure for me an equivalent period of repose in accordance with the decree on this subject, in order that I may be able to attend to my own property, being an elderly and lonely man, and may be grateful to your fortune for ever.[47]

In the case of the soldier as well as the doctor, legal immunity had not saved them from being dragooned into a liturgy. Had they been wealthier, a judicious bribe could have spared them such treatment.

---

[45] A. S. Hunt and C. C. Edgar, *Select Papyri* (Cambridge, Mass.: Harvard University Press, 1934), II, 271 (No. 283).
[46] Ibid., II, 169 (No. 245).   [47] Ibid., II, 275 (No. 285).

The power of the Roman state was most evident in the cities and garrisons that dotted the empire, but Caesar's hold was less secure in remote areas—mountains, forests, and wilderness—where banditry was rife. A frequent task of the Roman army was chasing brigands, and some bands were of considerable size. Widespread brigandage is a common symptom of an agrarian society weakened by poverty and frustration. In the *Golden Ass,* Apuleius lists the important factors in recruiting bandits: "Some of the local lads might have to be impressed and kept loyal by a sense of fear, some would be attracted by a prospect of loot and come forward as volunteers, others would be only too pleased to exchange a life of drudgery for membership in a company that exerted an almost sovereign power."[48] Fear, profit, escape from toil, and a sense of power—any or all might turn a peasant or an army deserter into a bandit, and runaway slaves often became brigands. Under Commodus, an army deserter named Maternus raised a large force of bandits and terrorized parts of Spain and Gaul. A man of imagination, he sometimes stormed jails and freed prisoners to augment his band. Intent on assassinating the emperor, Maternus came to Rome in disguise but was betrayed and executed. While bandits preyed on all classes, some outlaws posed as champions of the poor and became popular heroes. The Roman Robin Hood was Bulla Felix, who led a band of 600 men in Italy late in the second century. Many of his followers were slaves who had run away from imperial estates, and Bulla turned loose a captured centurion with a defiant protest against injustice: "Fetch this message to your masters: Feed your slaves, so that they do not have to become bandits." [49] Captured at last, Bulla was asked by the famed prefect Papinian why he was a robber, and the outlaw replied, "Why are you a prefect?" [50] Although comforting to the masses, the heroics of Bulla accomplished nothing in lessening the oppressiveness of the Roman state. The same soldiers who pursued bandits browbeat the peasantry, and the prevalence of brigands was used to justify the importance of the military in local areas, for soldiers were the policemen of the Roman empire. Dressed in civilian clothes, soldiers also served as secret police and lured unwary commoners into making seditious comments about the emperor. Epictetus warned his fellow Romans to beware of *agents provocateurs* who were soldiers in disguise.[51] So useful to the emperors was the secret police that it became a separate corps (*frumentarii*). However, the secret police not only spied on suspected persons but also extorted bribes from the innocent and guilty alike.

Within the Roman world dwelt a great number of ethnic groups, tribes, and former nations, all with cultures other than that of the domi-

---

[48] Apuleius *Metamorphoses* 7.4, trans. Graves, p. 153.   [49] Cassius Dio 77.10.5.
[50] Cassius Dio 77.10.7.   [51] Epictetus *Dissertationes* 4.13.5.

nant Romans. Though Roman citizenship was widespread and the provincial elites might aspire to senatorial status, the conquered peoples preserved cultural continuity particularly among the rural population. For administration, business, and literature, Latin was the official language in the West as were Greek and Latin in the East. While the culture of the elite was exclusively Greco-Roman, local cultures were easily discernible below the surface. In the provinces, native languages were still in use, and local gods were readily Romanized as aspects of Jupiter or another appropriate Latin deity. In times of stress, separatist movements often assumed a nationalistic aspect. In Gaul, various rebels set up ephemeral "Gallic empires," and many provinces witnessed revolts led by would-be liberators. Tacitus describes a tribal messiah who stirred up central Gaul in 69:

> A certain Mariccus, a Boian of the lowest origin, pretending to divine inspiration, ventured to thrust himself into fortune's game and to challenge the arms of Rome. Calling himself the champion of Gaul and a god, for he had assumed this title, he had now collected 8000 men and was taking possession of the neighboring villages of the Aedui, when that most formidable state attacked him with a picked force of its native youth, to which Vitellius attached some cohorts, and dispersed the crowd of fanatics. Mariccus was captured in the engagement and was soon after exposed to wild beasts, but not having been torn by them, was believed by the senseless multitude to be invulnerable, till he was put to death in the presence of Vitellius.[52]

In suppressing Mariccus, Rome played off the tribes against each other, for not all Gauls were willing to shake off the Roman yoke. A more typical nationalist was the army deserter, Tacfarinas, whose "bandit" forces terrorized Numidia in the time of Tiberius. When he promised to drive the Romans from Africa, "the penniless and the desperate" flocked to his standards. Though a master of guerrilla tactics, Tacfarinas was finally crushed by the legions.

Despite strong ties of native culture, the comforts of civilization were an important incentive for Romanization among the former barbarians of the West. Adopting Roman ways meant a better standard of living as well as the psychological lift of identifying with the conquerors. With a moralistic aside on the vices of civilization, Tacitus commented on Romanizers in Britain, a land that had seen fierce native revolts:

> They who lately disdained the tongue of Rome now coveted its eloquence. Hence, too, a liking sprang up for our style of dress, and the toga became

[52] Tacitus *Historiae* 2.61, trans. A. J. Church (New York: Modern Library, 1942), p. 512.

fashionable. Step by step they were led to things that dispose to vice, the lounge, the bath, the elegant banquet. All this in their ignorance, they called civilization, when it was but a part of their servitude.[53]

Tacitus to the contrary, the British had once painted themselves blue and were surely better off with hot baths, central heating, and a Mediterranean cuisine. In the East, the material benefits of Roman rule were criticized in an episode recounted in the Babylonian Talmud:

> Rabbi Judah and Rabbi Jose and Rabbi Simeon were sitting, and Rabbi Judah, son of proselytes, was sitting with them. Rabbi Judah began and said: "How excellent are the deeds of this nation! They have instituted market-places, they have instituted bridges, they have instituted baths." Rabbi Jose was silent. Rabbi Simeon ben Yohai answered and said: "All that they have instituted they have instituted only for their own needs. They have instituted market-places to place harlots in them; baths, for their own pleasure; bridges, to collect toll." Judah, son of proselytes, went and reported their words, and they were heard by the government. They said; "Judah who exalted shall be exalted; Jose, who remained silent, shall be banished . . . ; Simeon who reproached shall be put to death." [54]

The treatment of the rabbis according to their attitude toward Rome is significant, and the division of views was probably representative of public opinion in the empire. A third admired Rome and were content, a third fretted in anger, and a third "remained silent." [55]

Opposition to Roman rule not only produced fierce revolts but also an underground literature of great virulence. Although rebels were always crushed by the legions, some of their litanies of hate have survived to dispel the illusion of a contented empire spun by apologists for Rome. Under Domitian, the author of the Apocalypse of John expressed Christian and Eastern resentments of "Babylon the Great," the harlot of the seven hills, whose "merchants were the great men of the earth, and all nations were deceived by her sorcery." With vicious glee, the writer anticipated the imminent overthrow of Rome by the wrath of heaven: "Alas, alas, for the great city that was clothed in fine linen, in purple and scarlet, bedecked with gold, with jewels, and with pearls! In one hour, all this wealth has been laid waste." [56] Similar fantasies were evoked by the so-called *Sibylline Oracles,* a hodgepodge of prophecies,

---

[53] Tacitus *Agricola* 21, trans. Church, p. 690.

[54] *Babylonian Talmud, Sabbath* 33b, trans. Moses Hadas, "Roman Allusions in Rabbinic Literature," *Philological Quarterly* 8 (1929): 373.

[55] Alexander Hamilton noted the same proportions in American attitudes toward Britain during the Revolutionary War.

[56] Apocalypse of John 18.16.

largely Jewish and Christian but also integrating pagan and topical themes. Written in Greek and covering events over four centuries, the oracles are difficult to date, but the author of a late second-century passage cries for vengeance against the empire:

> Inexorable wrath shall fall on Rome; a time of blood and wretched life shall come. Woe, woe to thee, O land of Italy, great, barbarous nation! . . . No more under slavish yoke to thee will either Greek or Syrian put his neck, barbarian or any other nation; thou shalt be plundered and shalt be destroyed for what thou didst, and wailing aloud in fear, thou shalt give until thou shalt all repay.[57]

The very fervor of such passages reflected a frustrated rage that was impotent against the armed might of Rome and could only indulge in fantasies of the sudden collapse of the oppressor and the exaltation of his victims. Less frenzied but bitterly anti-Roman are a collection of papyri, the *Acts of the Pagan Martyrs,* that celebrate the heroics of upper-class Alexandrians who defied various emperors and called them tyrants and brigands to their faces. Often the offense of the Romans was favoring the Jews of Alexandria in their constant quarrels with pagans, but the basic grievance of the martyrs was the impotence of the once independent Alexandrians under an unheeding and arrogant alien rule.

Since most of them were illiterate, the views of Western barbarians, who opposed the expansion of the empire, have not been preserved, but Tacitus put an eloquent speech into the mouth of the Caledonian chieftain, Calgacus, who rallied the tribesmen to battle Agricola:

> There are no tribes beyond us, nothing indeed but waves and rocks, and the yet more terrible Romans, from whose oppression escape is vainly sought by obedience and submission. Robbers of the world, having by their universal plunder exhausted the land, they rifle the deep [with their fleet]. If the enemy be rich, they are rapacious; if he be poor, they lust for dominion; neither the East nor the West has been able to satisfy them. Alone among men, they covet with equal eagerness poverty and riches. To robbery, slaughter, plunder, they give the lying name of empire; they make a solitude and call it peace.[58]

Since Tacitus was no renegade, his indictment of insatiable imperialism may have been intended for Trajan to heed.[59] While the speech does not

---

[57] *Oracula Sibyllina* 8.93–95, 124–129, trans. Naphtali Lewis & Meyer Reinhold, *Roman Civilization* (New York: Columbia University Press, 1955), II, 417.

[58] Tacitus *Agricola* 30, trans. Church, p. 695.

[59] There are comparable passages in Tacitus's model, Sallust, and in Pompeius Trogus, who may be repeating Timagenes. The Roman capacity for self-criticism is too often overlooked.

preserve Calgacus's words, it surely expresses the sentiments of the patriot chiefs who tried to resist conquest by Rome.

On close examination, the Golden Age of Rome was the surface glitter on an era of polished brass. Even Gibbon admitted that "the military force was a blind and irresistible instrument of oppression," [60] and
its baleful effect was felt in the palace as well as on the masses. Imperial Rome had much law but little justice, and the prosperity of the
few shone more brightly against the dark background of poverty in
which most men languished. If military despotism was the answer to
Republican anarchy and incompetence, the cure was as fatal as the disease, for the patient never recovered. There is considerable truth in
Kurt von Fritz's glum verdict: "The history of the Roman empire under
Augustus' successors is the history of a long-drawn-out agony, and this
includes the age of the Antonines, which Gibbon believed to have been
the happiest period in the history of mankind." [61] Yet, in the grim history of empires, the faults of Rome are not unique, and the scope and
duration of its achievements are impressive. Most of the emperors were
hard-working and productive, and the system functioned well even
under a few "bad emperors," despite an occasional spasm of lunacy.
Public order and peace are taken lightly only by those who have never
suffered under anarchy and war. While the extinction of liberty at
Rome was tragic, few societies past or present can really be considered
"free." How common is social and economic justice today? What imperial power ever cosmopolitanized itself as did Rome, shared its citizenship so broadly, or admitted provincials to the elite and to the throne
itself? The Roman empire became an integrated society, and it was the
only lasting international order that Europe has known.

BODIES AND SOULS

The nerve center of the empire was Rome, a sprawling urban mass
with about one million inhabitants. To the great city came couriers and
envoys, aspiring politicians and social climbers, merchants and artists,
intellectuals and mountebanks. Swollen beyond the "Servian" walls, the
city was congested, noisy, and filled with jerry-built wooden tenements.
The apartment houses were firetraps, but rents were high, for space was
at a premium. Building codes were not always enforced, and the collapse of tenements was almost as common as the frequent fires that ravaged the city. Except for a few major thoroughfares, the streets of

---

[60] Gibbon, *Decline of the Roman Empire*, I, 78.
[61] Kurt von Fritz, *The Theory of the Mixed Constitution in Antiquity* (New
York: Columbia University Press, 1954), p. 254.

Rome were narrow and winding, jammed by day and dangerous by night, for they were not lighted and criminals lurked in the shadows. Thanks to the energies of Agrippa and subsequent commissions, great aqueducts kept the city well supplied with water, but only the rich had it piped into their homes. The poor lacked toilets in their tiny apartments and had to tote chamber pots to nearby cesspools—less civic-minded Romans simply emptied the pots over the railings of the balconies that girded the tenements. All classes, however, enjoyed public baths with steam rooms, exercise courts, and swimming pools. The first public bath was built by Agrippa, and the emperors Nero, Trajan, Caracalla, and Diocletian constructed enormous vaulted baths for the people of Rome. One appreciative worldling celebrated the pleasures of Rome in his epitaph:

> Women and wine and baths bring life's decline.
> Yet, what is life but women, baths, and wine.[62]

He forgot to mention bread. The emperors provided about 200,000 citizens of the capital with wooden chits redeemable for one and a quarter bushels of grain a month. Though the dole helped a poor man feed his family, the state did not provide clothing or rent, and the Roman masses worked hard to subsist in the city. Only the rich were indolent, and Rome was a bustling center of business and small industry. Many of the lower classes were employed in transportation and construction. If much of the city was shoddy, the rest was imposing with stately temples and public buildings, large statuary and triumphal arches, for the Romans equated grandeur with size. The Colosseum held 50,000 spectators, and the Circus Maximus seated a quarter of a million avid racing fans. Despite the discomforts of life in the city, Imperial Rome was exciting and a showplace for tourists.

Urban life invites satire, and the sins and squalor of Rome were pilloried in the witty, biting verses of D. Junius Iuvenalis, who lived in its slums early in the second century. Juvenal's Rome was a bedlam of crime and vice, upper-class decadence and lower-class loutishness, a grotesque cartoon of urban blight and human folly. Society women, Jews, and Greeks fare badly in his poems as do gluttons, hypocrites, and the masses, whose sole concern, Juvenal insists, was "bread and games." [63] Like all satirists, Juvenal was an indignant moralist, and his scathing epigrams should not be taken too seriously. Among the social vermin swatted by Juvenal and similar writers were the ubiquitous legacy hunters, who fawned on elderly and childless people of means. The

---

frequency of the theme in literature has led some social historians to infer a low birth rate, at least among rich Romans, but there are no statistics, and demography requires hard data. On the other hand, there is abundant literary and epigraphic evidence of a desire for children, and the existence of childless couples does not prove the efficacy of the crude methods of contraception, but rather the staggeringly high rate of infant mortality. Of greater importance than any imaginary drop in the birth rate was the sociological shift in the ruling class demonstrated by the new names of elite families in the Imperial era. Pliny the Elder noted that the homes of the aristocracy were no longer decorated with busts of famous ancestors but with works of art [64]—having no pedigrees, the new aristocracy displayed its wealth. Since the Imperial system emphasized public service and promoted *equites* to the Senate, the old nobility was replaced by an aristocracy of merit. The new nobles, Tacitus tells us, betrayed their bourgeois origin by the simplicity of their life style—conspicuous consumption and gastronomic orgies went out with the Julio-Claudians.[65] The frequency of gout in the late first century was due less to overeating than to lead water pipes, for lead poisoning produces painful swellings in the joints. Despite the picture given by ancient moralists and modern films, the Romans were not particularly decadent, and most Americans would find the Roman way of life rather plain.

At Rome, much public entertainment was free and some was spectacular. The public enjoyed pageants and musical shows, acrobats and magicians, trained animals and exotic beasts. A favorite crowd pleaser was a tightrope-walking elephant. Extremely popular were the chariot races in the Circus Maximus where the wild devotion of fans sometimes erupted in riots. The most famous fan clubs were the Blues and the Greens, whose rivalry was intense. Roman entertainment also included public executions and gladiatorial combats, for the Romans were not squeamish about pain and death. Though Cicero and Pliny the Younger defended the games as educational,[66] the real appeals were sadism and spectacle. Both Augustus and Trajan sponsored gladiatorial games with 5000 pairs of combatants. Since a good gladiator represented a major investment in money and training, not all fights were to the death, and the crowds would not tolerate harm done to favorite champions. Nevertheless, the arena games were bloody and often fatal, and Seneca considered them revolting and sadistic.[67] He mentions men who committed

[64] Pliny the Elder *Naturalis Historia* 35.4–5.   [65] Tacitus *Annales* 3.55.
[66] Cicero *Tusculanae Disputationes* 2.(17) 41, and Pliny the Younger *Panegyricus* 33.
[67] Seneca *Epistulae ad Lucilium* 7.3–5.

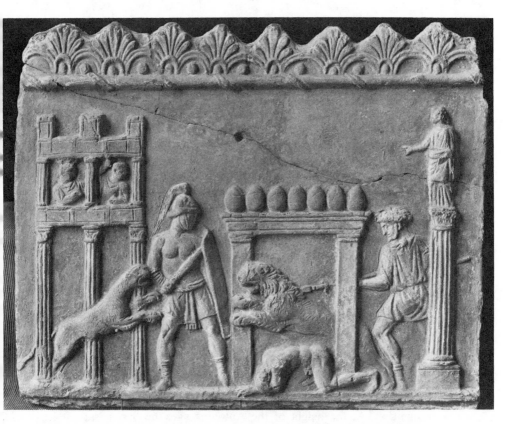

Scene of gladiators in the Circus. Rome, Museo Nazionale delle Terme.
Alinari—Scala.

suicide rather than die to amuse an audience.[68] Christians were also
critical of the games and of public entertainment in general, and none
more so than Tertullian:

> So it comes about that a man who will scarcely lift his tunic in public for
> the necessities of nature, will take it off in the Circus [69] in such a way as
> to make a full display of himself before all; a man who guards the ears of
> his maiden daughter from every smutty word, will himself take her to the
> theater to hear words of that sort and to see gestures to match; the man
> who when he sees a quarrel on the streets coming to blows will try to
> quiet it or express his strong disapproval, will in the stadium applaud
> fights far more dangerous; he who shudders at the body of a man who
> died by nature's law the common death of all, will, in the amphitheater,
> gaze down with most tolerant eyes on the bodies of men mangled, torn in
> pieces, defiled with their own blood; yes, and he who comes to the specta-
> cle to signify his approval of murder being punished, will have a reluctant

[68] Seneca *Epistulae ad Lucilium* 70.20, 23, 26.
[69] Under a broiling sun, the audience in the Circus was uncomfortable in the
heat, and some of them removed their outer clothing for comfort.

gladiator hounded on with lash and rod to do murder; the man who calls
for the lion as the punishment for some notorious murderer, will call for
the rod of discharge for a savage gladiator and give him the cap of liberty
as a reward.[70]

In his antitheses of virtue and vice, Tertullian implies that the average
Roman was a model of morality when not at the games, the theater, or
the races. As for the "debased mob" at Rome, the masses rioted in A.D.
61 to prevent the execution of innocent slaves, and a year later they
protested on behalf of Nero's wronged wife, Octavia. Both episodes are
reported by Tacitus, who was not a friend of the commons.[71] It should
also be noted that theater audiences listened to recitations of classics
and loudly applauded dramatic readings of Ennius's verse.[72] Apparently, not all Roman tastes were brutal or frivolous.

The Romans did not lose their sense of humor under the Empire.
Most likely, the Neronian courtier C. Petronius is the author of an extravagant comic novel, the *Satyricon,* that survives only in fragments.
With great verve, Petronius parodied contemporary poets, Greek peder-
astic romances, and Roman life in general. The best-known character in
the book is the wealthy freedman, Trimalchio, who embodied the vulgar
nouveaux riches. Juvenal's witty satires were less fanciful and have a
bitter undertone, and modern urbanites may read them with a smile of
recognition. At the height of the Antonine age, the Syrian satirist Lucian of Samosata used comic Greek dialogues to scathe humbuggery and
human weakness wherever he found it. Like H. L. Mencken, Lucian
took a dim view of religious zeal and intellectual pretension and delighted in debunking fanatics and poseurs. Another provincial wit was
the African rhetorician L. Apuleius, who made his fortune by marrying
a rich widow but had to defend himself in court on a charge of having
beguiled the lady through magic. His successful defense speech has survived and is a fascinating account of current superstitions. Apuleius's
masterpiece is the Latin novel, the *Golden Ass,* based on an earlier
Greek tale by Lucius of Patras which was also used by Lucian in a less
successful sketch. The basic plot deals with a rich young man who ran
afoul of a witch in Thessaly, a notorious center of the black arts, and
was transformed into a donkey, in which form he had various adventures until at last the spell was broken when the ass ate roses. With
great skill and bawdy humor, Apuleius expanded the story with details
of life in the empire, elaborated on witches and mendicant eunuch
priests (whom he despised), added a charming novella on the romance

[70] Tertullian *de Spectaculis* 21, trans. T. R. Glover (Cambridge, Mass.: Harvard
University Press, 1931), p. 283.
[71] Tacitus *Annales* 14.42–45, 59–61; Cf.15.44.   [72] Aulus Gellius 18.5.3.

of Cupid and Psyche, and transformed the tale into an allegory of man's redemption from bestiality through faith in the goddess Isis. One of the great picaresque novels of all time, the *Golden Ass* is a valuable source on social conditions in the provinces.

The cosmopolitanism of the Imperial era is reflected in the galaxy of Latin writers who were born in Spain and graced the first century. An able rhetorician of Cordova, L. Annaeus Seneca, wrote on the art of oratory with ample examples and composed a history of his own times— born during the First Triumvirate, he died in Caligula's reign. An old-fashioned man, Seneca the Elder suggested that the history of Rome followed the life cycle of a human and had reached old age. His famous sons were the philosopher-politician Seneca and Gallio, who as governor of Greece refused to hear Jewish complaints against Paul; a third son was the father of Lucan. L. Annaeus Seneca the Younger is a paradoxical figure. A Stoic philosopher, he wrote voluminously on moral questions and so loftily that later Christians fancied that he must have been converted by Paul. Though a humane man, Seneca composed a nasty satire on the apotheosis of Claudius and a number of grisly dramas that inspired the Elizabethan Tragedy of Blood. He was interested in natural history and believed in the progress of science: "The people of the coming generation will know much that we do not know; much is reserved for ages which will have forgotten our names: the world is a tiny thing, except that it contains questions enough for all the world." [73] A born businessman, Seneca managed a vineyard in Italy so well that he sold it for four times its original price ten years later. Despite his advocacy of philosophy, the Stoic was a worldly courtier who lived in a grand style and was briefly banished for adultery. A schemer, Seneca plotted with Agrippina and then betrayed her, and as Nero's chief administrator, he filled his pockets with bribes and public funds. Though the man besmirched the philosopher, Seneca died well when Nero drove him to suicide. His nephew, Lucan, wrote a lurid epic on the civil war between Pompey and Caesar, crammed with sensational scenes and horrific descriptions of witchcraft. Amid the bombast, Lucan could deliver superb epigrams: "Pompey could allow no man to be his equal, and Caesar no man to be his superior. . . . The winning cause pleased the gods, but the losing cause pleased Cato." [74] Regrettably, the poet lacked Cato's fortitude, and when suspected of complicity in the Piso conspiracy, he denounced his innocent mother, hoping vainly to win Nero's favor.

Spain produced the agricultural expert L. Junius Columella, who wrote on estate management and denounced absentee landlords. The re-

[73] Seneca *Quaestiones Naturales* 7.30.   [74] Lucan *Bellum Civile* 1.125–28.

nowned rhetorician M. Fabius Quintilianus was also a Spaniard; he earned handsome fees as a teacher and was the tutor of Domitian's heirs. In his classic work on the training of an orator, Quintilian provides extensive details on ancient education as well as the actual practice of oratory in the law courts of his day. His fellow Spaniard, the poet M. Valerius Martialis, flattered Domitian but satirized many aspects of Roman society, including orators:

> It's not a case of poisoned cup, assault, or slitting throats;
> I've had to have my neighbor up for stealing my three goats.
> You dwell on Punic faith and fury, Pontic wars and Cannaes,
> But this they're asking on the jury, "Prove he stole the nannies."
> And now with gestures various, you've told in ringing notes
> Of Sulla, Mucius, Marius, please mention my three goats.[75]

Martial's complaint nicely illustrates the empty flamboyance of contemporary rhetoric as well as the prime occupation of orators under the Empire, that of advocate. Not long afterwards, Tacitus wrote a dialogue on oratory emphasizing that great oratory had died with the Republic, for real eloquence requires topics of significance and freedom of speech.

Despite the generosity of various emperors, the Greeks did not fare well under the Empire, for Hellas was economically stagnant and unemployment was high. The Greeks viewed the prosperity of their neighbors in Asia with considerable jealousy. Yet Hellenic culture enjoyed a resurgence, primarily because the Roman ruling class valued the heritage of the Greek past and was willing to pay handsome fees to clever Greek intellectuals. Rhetoric was a highly prized specialty under the "Second Sophistic," a cultural label for the Greek "sophists" who traveled about the empire, displaying their oratorical talents and teaching those who could afford to pay. Many were superb showmen, and not all were Hellenes by birth though Greek was the language with which they dazzled audiences. After years as a wandering philosopher, Dio of Prusa became a successful sophist and won the patronage of Trajan. The Gallic sophist Favorinus was part of Hadrian's stable of intellectuals until he lost the emperor's favor and was banished. Exceptional in many ways, Favorinus was a eunuch by birth and an opponent of astrology, the accepted "science" of the day. The most famous sophist was the Athenian multimillionaire, Herodes Atticus, who was consul in 143. A philanthropist on a grand scale, he donated public buildings at Athens and elsewhere in the empire. Despite his generosity, the Athenians complained that Atticus had not given them all the money due them in his father's will; ungraciously, he pointed out the debts his country-

[75] Martial 6.19, trans. "T. W. M.", *Greece and Rome* 9 (1940): 116.

men still owed to his family. The lordly Atticus also squabbled with other sophists and with prominent Romans. More importantly, he favored the classic Attic style of the time of Critias. The most interesting of the sophists was Aelius Aristides, whose oration *To Rome* epitomized provincial faith in Rome as the supreme benefactor. An extremely neurotic hypochondriac, Aristides was plagued by a variety of psychosomatic ills and almost incapacitated by asthma until he began to dream of revelations from Asclepius. The god of medicine prescribed a harsh regimen, odd diets, and icy baths that allowed the neurotic orator to "earn" his health and go on to a successful career. At times, Aristides' contact with Asclepius bordered on a mystical experience, and his account of his illnesses and cures are of great interest to students of religion, medicine, and mental aberration.

Under the Empire, historians were active, though Tacitus growls that objective history died at Actium and all subsequent writers (except himself) were either sycophants or libelers.[76] A retired officer, Velleius Paterculus, who had served under Tiberius, wrote a brief history of Rome enlivened with sketches of minor as well as major figures and digressions on colonies, provinces, and literature. His praise of Sejanus as the model "new man"[77] is a lone voice of approval in a chorus of defamation. Various senators, including Pliny the Elder, tried their hands at history, but their writings have perished. Perhaps the greatest loss is the work of an opportunistic courtier, Cluvius Rufus, which may be the source of Josephus's detailed account of the overthrow of Caligula and succession of Claudius. Most of Augustus's official account of his reign (*Res Gestae Divi Augusti*) has survived, but not his memoirs or those of Tiberius, Claudius, Vespasian, or Hadrian. The sensational material in extant writers is based on works of vilification by senatorial authors and Agrippina's vindictive pamphlet exposing the sins of the imperial house. Under Vespasian's patronage, the Jewish priest Flavius Josephus chronicled in Greek an account of the revolt in Judea, showing the Romans in a favorable light and the Jews as misled by fanatics. The most famous Greek writer on historical topics was a gentle Boeotian scholar, Plutarch, who had powerful friends in Trajan's Rome. Neither a historian nor a biographer, he utilized the lives of renowned Greeks and Romans as didactic sermons to illustrate the need for virtue and piety. Widely read and fond of digressions, Plutarch filled his *Parallel Lives* with interesting data and citations from authors now lost, but his methodology was selective and his portrayal of famous men was inconsistent. Nevertheless, his concern with personality traits made the sub-

---

[76] Tacitus *Historiae* 1.1. See also John Wilkes, "Julio-Claudian Historians," *Classical World* 65 (1972): 177–203.
[77] Velleius Paterculus 2.127–28.

jects come alive, and Shakespeare easily transferred Plutarch's Roman heroes to the stage. Like Plutarch, the Greek Pausanias had an antiquarian love of the past and composed a tourist guide to Hellas, accurately describing monuments and famous places and less accurately recounting historical anecdotes. Another Greek, Arrian, who was governor of Cappadocia under Hadrian, wrote on India and on Hellenistic and Parthian history. While his life of Alexander the Great is a reliable and sensible work, one may question Arrian's reason for trusting Ptolemy's memoirs—that a king would have been ashamed to lie! In the Antonine era, an Alexandrian Greek, Appian, wrote a summary of Rome's wars and used Pollio as a major source for a valuable account of the civil wars. In Latin, the African Florus produced a similar but less detailed epitome based largely on Livy. Florus endorsed the elder Seneca's opinion that Rome had reached senility, but he quickly added that Trajan was rejuvenating the empire. The Antonine scholar Aulus Gellius preserved much antiquarian lore and bits of literature in a patchwork compendium called the *Attic Nights*. Though more interested in grammar than in history, Gellius produced a valuable collection of tidbits for browsers. A similar mine of material is Plutarch's *Roman Questions,* in which the Greek scholar tried unsuccessfully to explain odd or archaic religious practices of the Romans.

The two major figures in Latin historiography under the Principate are Tacitus and Suetonius. Probably a native of Narbonensian Gaul, Cornelius Tacitus married the daughter of the famed general, Agricola, and advanced his career under the Flavian emperors. In Domitian's Senate, he participated in purges and was psychologically scarred by the experience. After experimenting with a dialogue on oratory, a laudatory sketch of Agricola, and a moralistic essay on the Germans, Tacitus tried to exorcise his guilt with two major historical works, the *Histories* (from Galba to Nerva's accession) and the *Annals* (from Tiberius to Nero)—much of the *Annals* has survived, but only the events of A.D. 69 in the *Histories*. Like his model Sallust, Tacitus was bitter, biased, and addicted to sardonic epigrams. Loathing the memory of Domitian, he painted the Principate in dark colors and etched the emperors in acid as tyrants or fools. To preserve the illusion of objectivity, Tacitus recounted good as well as evil deeds, but he used innuendo and journalistic tricks to ensure that the worst possible interpretation would be made. The historian became gloomier as he grew older, and some passages seem veiled attacks on Trajan and Hadrian. The Republic, too, earned his scorn, and he sneered at senatorial martyrs whose heroics had won them fame without damaging the tyranny. Tacitus's savage sketches of the Julio-Claudians still dominate the popular notion of Roman emperors, but his treatment of senators under pressure is more useful for students of history. A speech in which a former friend of Nero defends himself was an apology for Tacitus as well:

> I acquiesce in the present, and while I pray for good emperors, I can endure whomsoever we may have. It was not through my speech any more than it was through the judgment of the Senate that Thrasea fell. The savage temper of Nero amused itself under these forms, and I found the friendship of such a prince as harassing as others found their exile. Finally, Helvidius may rival the Catos and the Bruti of old in constancy and courage; I am but one of the Senate which bows to the same yoke.[78]

Tacitus, too, had mastered the art of survival, but he had bloodied his hands in the process and tried to wash them with ink.

A lesser writer but happier man was C. Suetonius Tranquillus, who served as Hadrian's secretary until banished from court for some slight to the empress Sabina. Like Plutarch, he was fascinated by personalities and relished data that threw light on the lives of famous men. Most of his biographies have been lost, but his lives of Caesar and the emperors to Domitian have survived and have always been popular, for Suetonius never neglected a good scandal or a bizarre character trait. While in the palace, he had access to the imperial archives and often quotes original documents, such as letters of Augustus belittling young Claudius. Though Suetonius was a sensible man and capable of critical judgments, his taste for sensationalism set an unfortunate precedent for subsequent Roman biographers. The epistles of Tacitus's friend C. Plinius Caecilius Secundus (Pliny the Younger), concern the life and times of an Italian gentleman who sat in Domitian's Senate and served Trajan as a governor in Bithynia. Of special interest are letters dealing with the work habits of his uncle Pliny the Elder, the eruption of Vesuvius, the degradation of being a senator under Domitian, and the investigation of Christians in Bithynia.[79] The tenth book of the epistles contains official correspondence between Pliny and Trajan and throws invaluable light on the imperial system. The letters of the Numidian rhetorician M. Cornelius Fronto, once tutor and later friend of Marcus Aurelius, deal largely with the imperial family and add a human dimension to famous figures who often appear as mere types in the pages of formal historians. In the letters between the emperor and the scholar, a recurring topic is illness, and Marcus Aurelius and Fronto tried to outdo each other in the gravity of their pains, real and imagined. Being introspective and self-centered, intellectuals are often hypochondriacs—Seneca was one, and while not pathological like Aristides, Marcus Aurelius and Fronto took a peculiar pride in poor health.

[78] Tacitus *Historiae* 4.8, trans. Church, p. 598.
[79] Pliny the Younger *Epistulae* 3.5, 6.16, 6.20, 8.14, 10.96.

For sick bodies and minds, philosophy is often a palliative if not a cure. Under the Principate, philosophizing was a popular escape for sensitive men. Although admired, the Stoic martyrs who died at the hands of tyrants were not typical of the age. Stoicism had become less stiff-necked and blended with Cynicism, which lost its radical tone of anarchic defiance, despite the antics of a few street corner Cynics. The intellectual trends of the time were eclectic, and ethics were viewed as more important than the rationalistic absolutes of Plato and Aristotle. Though the main aim of philosophy was to provide peace of mind, some thinkers expressed concern for the poor and criticized social injustices that had not moved many intellectuals in the past. In the first century, the Stoic C. Musonius Rufus protested against gladiatorial games, mistreatment of slaves, the exposure of unwanted children, and the double standard in sexual morality. Marriage, he argued, should be based on love and mutual respect, and it is as unworthy for a husband to sleep with a slave as it would be for his wife to seek similar pleasures. The philosopher even disapproved of any sexual intercourse not intended to beget children. In 69, Rufus tried to dissuade the Flavian troops from storming Rome and was almost mobbed for his efforts. His disciple, Dio of Prusa, was banished from Rome by Domitian and became a wandering Cynic, but he ended his days as a wealthy orator in his native Bithynia. In his orations, Dio often displays a concern for the plight of the masses, whose poverty he had shared, but he had no solution other than moving the urban poor back to farms and relying on the generosity of Trajan. Another disciple of Rufus was a former Phrygian slave, Epictetus, whose gentle teachings have been preserved by the historian Arrian. An advocate of resignation, he preached the brotherhood of man and the futility of holding grudges—criminals should be forgiven, not punished. According to Epictetus, man should live unencumbered by family or property, for freedom is impossible when one gives hostages to society. Pain and fear must also be overcome, and the only true misfortune is that we allow life to shatter the serenity that philosophy provides.

Peace of mind is not easily attained by those who occupy a throne, as Marcus Aurelius ruefully learned. At heart a Thoreau, he felt imprisoned by the imperial office and sought comfort in the stern tenets of Stoicism. In his spare moments, the philosopher king jotted down his melancholy reflections in Greek together with favorite quotations from sages of the past. Like Job and Ecclesiastes, the notebooks of Marcus Aurelius make gloomy reading—life is like "scummy bath water," and man is (as Epictetus said) "a soul dragging about a corpse"; human achievements are futile, and the future will only repeat the sordid follies of the past. Yet Providence and Marcus expect every man to do his duty as a Stoic and a Roman, to serve without flinching, and to endure the horror that is life until death provides release in a diffusion of atoms. "Always think how ephemeral and worthless human things are," he writes, "and what was yesterday a little mucus tomorrow will be a memory or ashes. . . . Be like a rock against which the waves dash unceasingly, but it is not moved." [80] While Marcus Aurelius poured out his anguish to himself, a gentle old Epicurean, Diogenes of Oenoanda in Lycia, tried to bring comfort to ordinary men by inscribing a summary of Epicurus's doctrines on a public wall, prefacing the inscription with these words:

> Having arrived by our years at the sunset of life, and expecting at any time now to depart out of the world with a glad song and a heart filled with happiness, we have decided, lest we be snatched away too soon, to offer some help to the rightly disposed. . . . It is only right to help those who are to come after us, since they too belong to us, though not yet born. And finally, love for mankind bids us render aid to strangers passing by. [81]

No doubt, some passers-by found consolation in the inscription, for the gospel of Epicurus was one of comfort. [82] At the close of the second century, a Greek doctor, Sextus Empiricus, composed three books that demolished the existing philosophic systems with careful logic and offered a civilized skepticism in their place. However, Sextus Empiricus achieved only a hollow victory, for neither skepticism nor its rivals could shelter men from the traumas of the third century. In the coming era, philosophers would embrace subjectivity and mysticism.

Rarely innovators, the Romans exploited the technology of the past on a grand scale and with considerable success. At Rome and every major city, great aqueducts brought tons of water for washing and bathing. With justifiable pride, the water commissioner for Rome, Frontinus, [83] boasted of the aqueducts in the capital: "With such an array of indispensable structures, carrying so many waters, compare, if you will, the idle Pyramids or the useless, though famous, works of the Greeks!" [84] Equally impressive were the great Roman roads that stretched

---

[80] Marcus Aurelius 4.48–49.

[81] F. C. Grant, *Hellenistic Religions* (Indianapolis: Bobbs-Merrill, 1953), p. 161.

[82] Found in the ruins of Herculaneum, another Epicurean text offers the "Fourfold remedy": "Nothing to fear in God; Nothing to feel in Death; Good can be attained; Evil can be endured."

[83] After a successful military career, S. Julius Frontinus served Nerva and Trajan managing the water supply for Rome and wrote an informative tract on the subject.

[84] Frontinus *de Aquis urbis Romae* 1.16.

The Pont-du-Gard. This aqueduct near Nimes in southern France was built during the last quarter of the first century B.C. *Courtesy French Government Tourist Office.*

Interior of a factory. Rome, Mostra Augustea. *Alinari—Scala.*

through the provinces and were unequaled until modern times. In colder climes, Roman engineers devised hypocaustic central heating for the homes of the rich. Although water mills had been invented by the first century B.C., they do not seem to have been employed much, and a flour mill using water power does not appear until the fourth century A.D., but as usual our evidence is incomplete. In first-century Gaul, Pliny the Elder observed reaping machines: "On the vast estates in the provinces of Gaul, very large frames fitted with teeth at the edge and carried on two wheels are driven through the grain by a team of oxen pushing from behind; the ears thus torn off fall into the frame." [85] Since the reaper does not seem to have been used elsewhere, its employment was probably related to local labor shortages. When an engineer offered Vespasian a labor-saving machine for use in construction work, the paternalistic emperor rewarded the inventor but refused to employ the machine, quipping that if he did, who would feed the poor? [86] Because the urban masses needed the work that the machine could do better, the Roman state opted for human employment rather than technological advance. Moderns who equate machinery with progress are often disturbed that the Romans did nothing with the gadgetry that had been devised at Alexandria to amuse the Ptolemies and produce temple miracles. The Hellenistic inventors had contrived automata moved by pneumatic and hydraulic pressures, and Hero of Alexandria was experimenting with a steam turbine in the first century A.D. [87] Though they had replaced the Ptolemies as patrons of the Museum, the Roman emperors had little interest in moving toys, and the resources of the Roman state were committed to war, pomp, and the everyday needs of the empire. The wealthy classes spent their money on land, luxury, and philanthropy, putting the need for prestige ahead of the profit motive. [88] Even if some enterprising Roman capitalists had invested in scientific research and sparked an industrial revolution, the buying power of the poverty-stricken masses was too low to purchase the new products, and the wages of free labor were not likely to rise when skilled slaves were available to compete for jobs. [89]

Except for Archimedes and a few others, the educated class in antiq-

---

[85] Pliny the Elder *Naturalis Historia* 18.296.   [86] Suetonius *Vespasian* 18.

[87] The calendric "computer" found off Antikythera illustrates the refinement of Greek gadgetry in the first century B.C. Among Hero's inventions was a vending machine that dispensed holy water when a coin was dropped in a slot.

[88] On the important topic of the failure of antiquity to produce an industrial revolution, see the comments of H. W. Pleket, "Technology and Society in the Greco-Roman World," *Acta Historiae Neerlandica* 2 (1967): 1–25, and M. I. Finley, "Technological Innovation and Economic Progress in the Ancient World," *Economic History Review* 18 (1965): 29–45.

[89] Rostovtzeff, *Roman Empire,* I, 350–51.

The tomb of the Haterii showing construction machinery. Rome, Museo Profano. *Alinari—Scala.*

uity did not consider mechanics a respectable science, because too many common people had knowledge of it. The favored sciences were medicine and astronomy, both of which required an education and had mysterious sidelines in faith healing and astrology. Though Greek medicine was highly regarded, the Romans had little patience with the theoretical squabbles of rival medical schools. In the reign of Tiberius, Aulus Cornelius Celsus continued the encyclopedic tradition of summarizing specialized knowledge for practical use by laymen. His survey of medicine has survived and was decidedly an improvement over older witch doctor methods.[90] The greatest of the encyclopedists was Vespasian's friend Pliny the Elder, whose *Natural History* is a storehouse of information on the ancient world and its beliefs. A voracious reader, he indiscriminately filled thirty-seven books with an amazing clutter of facts and fables on astronomy, geography, animals, plants, minerals, history, medicine, magic, and odd lore. Credulous here and critical there, Pliny's curiosity was inexhaustible and he perished like a true scientist, overcome by volcanic gas when he ventured too close to the erupting Vesuvius. Assessing contemporary science, Pliny noted that few discoveries were being made and that even the knowledge of the past was often neglected, though travel was safe and easy and the emperors were generous patrons. Yet science had flourished amid the wars and insecurity of the Hellenistic Age because, Pliny claimed, the "ancients" had hoped to win immortality by advancing knowledge. In his own day, he complained, science was dying because profit was the only motive.[91] Although his analysis was simplistic, Pliny had sensed the slowing down of science and a stilling of the spirit of quest.

The second century witnessed the great synthesis of astronomy by Ptolemy and of medicine by Galen. Like the Roman world, the two major sciences were reduced to order, and it is fitting that Galen compared his unification of medical knowledge to the Roman road system in Italy.[92] A skilled doctor and voluminous writer, Galen of Pergamum won fame at Rome and became the court physician of Marcus Aurelius and Commodus. His writings constitute not only a corpus of medical knowledge but also a unified view of man in the cosmos. Because of his experiments in dissection, Galen succumbed to the spell of teleology and saw the hand of God in the delicate mechanism of the body, even in the heel. Rejecting materialism, he accepted astrology and sympathetic magic and revived the Hippocratic doctrine of four humors in the

---

[90] To cure epilepsy, Celsus advised purgatives, bleeding, shaving the head, and cauterizing the scalp, but he deplored the expedient of drinking the "hot blood" of a freshly-slain gladiator.

[91] Pliny the Elder *Naturalis Historia* 2.117–18.

[92] Galen *de Methodo Medendi* 9.8 (Kühn X, 633).

body, corresponding to the four basic elements (earth, air, fire, and water). As the harmony of the four elements constitutes order in the macrocosm of nature, so a balance of the humors is health in the microcosm of the human body, and an imbalance results in disease. His religious faith as well as his vast knowledge made Galen a popular authority in late antiquity and a medical canon in the Middle Ages. Nothing is known of the life of Claudius Ptolemaeus other than that he made astronomical observations at Alexandria late in the reign of Hadrian. Though he wrote on optics, music, and geography, his masterwork was the grand synthesis of astronomy which the Arabs called *Almagest*. Borrowing the concept of eccentric orbits and epicycles from the Hellenistic astronomers Apollonius and Hipparchus, Ptolemy utilized his own careful observations and sketched a geostatic universe harmoniously ordered by mathematical laws. The moon and five planets moved in epicycles on eccentric orbits that were centered at hypothetical points in space moving about a stationary earth at the center of the cosmos. Also geared to a point near the earth, the sun's orbit was eccentric rather than epicyclic. Brilliantly conceived and supported by fresh observations, the Ptolemaic system soon became an astronomical canon and held sway for fourteen centuries.[93] Like Galen, Ptolemy was a deeply religious man:

> Mortal though I be, yea ephemeral, if but a moment
> I gaze up at the night's starry domain of heaven,
> Then no longer on earth I stand; I touch the Creator,
> And my lively spirit drinketh immortality.[94]

It is not surprising that Ptolemy was also an astrologer, and his *Tetrabiblos* was a popular handbook on astral determinism. As Vitruvius had used climate to justify Roman dominance, Ptolemy employed the stars and explained national characteristics and Roman superiority on astrological grounds. While Aries and Mars made the Jews atheists and rebels, Ptolemy claimed, Mars, Leo, Sagittarius and the Sun made the Italians "independent, warlike, clean, magnanimous, masterful, benevolent, and cooperative." [95] Though Ptolemy's accommodation of "science" to Roman pride was gratuitous, other astrologers practiced their art at the imperial court and earned handsome fees and appointments. Couched in mathematical terms and buttressed with astronomical data, astrology en-

---

[93] Even Copernicus retained the epicycles and eccentric orbits of the Ptolemaic system, which was finally overthrown by Kepler.

[94] *Anthologia Palatina* 9.577, trans. R. Bridges, *The Oxford Book of Greek Verse in Translation* (Oxford: Clarendon Press, 1938), p. 643.

[95] Ptolemy *Tetrabiblos* 2.66; 3.161–62.

joyed the aura of a science and provided a sense of certainty about the workings of Providence. However, its occult aspects eclipsed its scientific side in the troubled third century.

So pervasive was the religiosity of the third and subsequent centuries that there is a tendency among some scholars to label the first and second centuries as an Age of Enlightenment at least among the educated elite. Yet there is abundant evidence of devotion among all classes to both conventional gods and newer deities. If the state cult tended to petrify into formalistic ritual, private prayers to the gods were sincere and frequent, and there was a steady growth in popularity of deities from the East—Isis, Serapis, and Mithras. On walls at Pompeii, devotees of Isis scrawled the names of political candidates favored by Isis's followers in the impending municipal elections. While a few philosophers smiled at conventional religion, most of their colleagues accepted the gods as manifestations of a single divine principle but nonetheless real entities who could influence men's lives. The lurid descriptions of witches and necromancy in Lucan and Apuleius reflect a widespread interest in and fear of the black arts. Magic amulets and charms were widely used, and even enlightened men observed popular superstitions if only out of habit. In the reigns of Nero and Domitian, Rome was visited by a Neopythagorean prophet from Cappadocia, Apollonius of Tyana, who was reputed to be a wonder-worker and credited with raising the dead. Despite the aura of wizardry that he encouraged, Apollonius was a religious reformer, a vegetarian opponent of animal sacrifices, and a devotee of sun worship. After his death, he became a cult hero. Less flamboyant was the second-century Neopythagorean, Numenius of Apamea, whose influential writings accelerated the drift of philosophy into theosophy. In the time of Marcus Aurelius, a theurgist called Julianus composed the *Chaldaean Oracles,* which soon became a sacred text for spiritualists and mystagogues. Conventional religion appealed to Plutarch, who was a priest of Delphi, but he too was interested in Egyptian beliefs. Too much has been made of Plutarch's complaint about a decline in religious faith, symbolized in a charming tale about the announcement in the time of Tiberius that "great Pan was dead." [96] More cogent was his worry over the shrunken prestige of Delphi, which he sensibly attributed to the depopulation of Greece.[97] Nothing short of a revival of archaic Hellas would have satisfied the pious Plutarch, but there was no lack of religion in his world. Rather, other gods were replacing the Olympians and strange prophets were abroad.

One of the oddest of the new prophets was the neurotic Peregrinus

[96] Plutarch *Moralia* 419B–E. Perhaps the story had its origins in the ritual lament for Tammuz.

[97] Plutarch *Moralia* 414A.

who earned the nickname Proteus because of his shifting spiritual pos-
tures. Born into a wealthy family in the province of Asia, he was
plagued by Oedipal guilt over the death of his father and became a restless wanderer. In Palestine, Peregrinus was attracted to Christianity,
rose rapidly in the sect, and was even imprisoned until a perceptive
governor saw through his posing and denied him martyrdom. Released
from prison, he stayed with the Christians until they rejected him for
eating food from a temple feast. Next, Peregrinus became a mendicant
Cynic, tried asceticism as a fakir in Egypt, was expelled from Rome for
reviling Antoninus Pius, baited Herodes Atticus and stirred up riots in
Greece, and finally immolated himself at Olympia in 165. Impressed by
his fiery death, the populace quickly deified the man who had narrowly
escaped being a Christian saint. Less reputable was the Paphlagonian
prophet Alexander of Abonuteichos, who rigged up a human mask for
a tame snake and delivered oracles in the name of the reptilian deity.
Dubbed Glycon, the serpent was supposed to be Asclepius the divine
healer. With showmanship and cunning, Alexander built the oracle into
a booming business and culled gullible Romans of high position. As the
cult of Glycon spread abroad, the prophet contrived impressive rites
that included injunctions to expel "atheists, Christians, and Epicureans." Through well-wishers at court, Alexander imposed on Marcus
Aurelius and promised the emperor victory over the barbarians if he
would toss two lions into the Danube. However, the lions swam the
river and were clubbed to death by the barbarians who then routed the
Romans. Despite such occasional slips, Alexander's success was un-
abated and the Glycon cult survived his death. Although an outrageous
charlatan, Alexander had satisfied the spiritual needs of some Romans
with his pageantry and messages from heaven. Both Alexander and Peregrinus are the subjects of indignant essays by Lucian, whose running
battle with religion indicates its vitality in his world.

One of the more popular deities in the Golden Age was the kindly
god of healing Asclepius, who was worshiped in both human and serpent form. Whatever progress had been made in knowledge of physiol-
ogy and disease, the practice of medicine was still limited by ignorance
of the causes of infection and the inability to perform interior surgery
because internal bleeding could not be stopped. Because of the limitations of ancient medicine, physicians never lost the need for religious
aid, and difficult cases were turned over to Asclepius, in whose sanctu-
aries patients slept and waited for the god to appear to them in dreams
and effect cures. Though the ancients were quite aware of the physical
and psychological causes of dreams, they did not dispense with the
primitive notion that some dreams were messages from the divine; thus,
one did not dream about a god; rather, the god actually visited men in

Asclepius. Rome, Museo Capitolino. *Alinari—Scala.*

dreams. Many psychosomatic cures were effected through dreams, and shrines of Asclepius were filled with grateful testimonials and votive offerings as Lourdes is today. Though founded on an illusion and often debased for profit, faith healing can be a reality, and many Romans owed their lives to their faith in Asclepius. Had the sophist Aristides not "been visited by the god," he would have died of asthma. Marcus Aurelius thanked the gods for their "help in dreams on how to avoid spitting blood." [98] Naturally, Galen had frequent dream visitations from Asclepius, who advised him on literary and medical matters and even directed the doctor to perform an operation on himself. With great common sense, the god forbade Galen to visit the plague-ridden battle front in the Marcomannic war.

Heaven could cure spiritual ills too. Apuleius's *Golden Ass* is an allegory of his own redemption through initiation into the mysteries of Isis, the holy mother and divine principle behind all things. A dabbler in magic and a slave to sensuality, he had become "an ass" and wandered through a world filled with pain and folly until a vision of Isis showed the way to salvation and true manhood. Despite the humor of the novel, its climax is a religious tract of great intensity, an invitation to join Apuleius at the feet of Isis:

[98] Marcus Aurelius 1.17.

Holiest of the Holy, perpetual comfort of mankind, you whose bountiful grace nourishes the whole world; whose heart turns toward all those in sorrow and tribulation as a mother's to her children; you who take no rest by night, no rest by day, but are always at hand to succour the distressed by land and sea, dispersing the gales that beat upon them. Your hand alone can disentangle the hopelessly knotted skeins of fate, terminate every spell of bad weather, and restrain the stars from harmful conjunction. The gods above adore you, the gods below do homage to you, you set the orb of heaven spinning around the poles, you give light to the sun, you govern the universe, you trample down the powers of Hell. At your voice the stars move, the seasons recur, the spirits of earth rejoice, the elements obey. . . . My voice is unequal to uttering all that I think of your majesty—no, not even if I had a thousand tongues in a thousand mouths and could speak for ever. Nevertheless, poor as I am, I will do as much as I can in my devotion to you; I will keep your divine countenance always before my eyes and the secret knowledge of your divinity locked deep in my heart.[99]

Nothing could better illustrate the appeal of mystery cults than this moving hymn.

Since the Golden Age was not as pleasant as Gibbon imagined, many Romans turned to the gods for comfort or certainty, and the trend toward personal religion and direct contact with the divine accelerated. Yet few men were visionaries, fewer still were saints, and the mystery cults accommodated only a minority. Most Romans were satisfied with traditional religion and conventional morality; old idols and festivals were familiar, and temple feasts were fun. When the pressures of life became overwhelming in the third century, this comfortable religion would lose its hold on many, but, for the time being, smoke rose from the altars, and prayers were intoned to familiar figures of stone and wood. Some ancient philosophers sneered at cult images, and most moderns have a conditioned bias against idolatry. Happily, an eloquent defense of idols and religious tolerance was made by the sophist Maximus of Tyre, who lived in the Antonine era:

God Himself, the father and fashioner of all that is, older than the Sun or the Sky, greater than time and eternity and all of the flow of being, is unnameable by any lawgiver, unutterable by any voice, not to be seen by any eye. But we, being unable to apprehend His essence, use the help of sounds and names and pictures, of beaten gold and ivory and silver, of plants and rivers, mountain-peaks and torrents, yearning for the knowledge of Him, and in our weakness naming all that is beautiful in this world after His nature. . . . Why should I further examine and pass judgment about images? Let men know what is divine, let them know: that is

[99] Apuleius *Metamorphoses* 11.25, trans. Graves, pp. 282–83.

all. If a Greek is stirred to the remembrance of God by the art of Pheidias, an Egyptian by paying worship to animals, another man by a river, another by fire—I have no anger for their divergences; only let them know, let them love, let them remember.[100]

Infinitely preferable to the narrow exclusiveness of monotheism, this statement of sanity and understanding would be drowned out by strident voices in the coming age.

[100] Maximus of Tyre *Oratio VIII* 10, trans. G. Murray, *Five Stages of Greek Religion* (Boston: The Beacon Press, no date), pp. 77–78.

CHAPTER EIGHT

A kingdom
of iron and rust

*A*ccording to Cassius Dio, the Roman Empire after the death of Marcus Aurelius degenerated from "a kingdom of gold into one of iron and rust." [1] Dio's image of "iron and rust" can be extended to cover the third and early fourth centuries: an era of foreign wars, frequent usurpations, the unbridled dominance of the military, and the rude extinguishing of Republican survivals. However, metaphors can be misleading, and the preceding age of the Antonines was hardly very golden. The makeshift policies of third-century rulers that ultimately coalesced into the grinding oppression of the fourth century were largely based on precedents in the first and second centuries. Under the rubric of military necessity, Roman society became increasingly regimented, and the luxury of Augustan hypocrisy was discarded in the process. According to some scholars, Rome became an "oriental despotism." In the new era, the emperors did adopt a few details of costume and protocol from the Persians, but there is nothing particularly "oriental" about the Late Empire. The roots of tyranny went deep into the Greco-Roman past, and Roman despotism was an indigenous growth. Though discernible in art, literature, and religion, Eastern elements in Roman life should not be overemphasized. Like the notion of "oriental despotism," the theme of "Eastern mysticism" subverting "Western rationalism" is an inaccurate value judgment. In the third and fourth centuries, there was a heightening of religiosity that culminated in the triumph of Christianity, but the causes of this mood lay in the mounting difficulties of life within the empire. The emergence of a totalitarian state and the rush to religion were twin responses to the same crisis of the spirit.

The major domestic difficulties of the Roman empire were military mutinies, rampant inflation, increased demands upon all classes by the state, and (according to some emperors) subversion by religious dissi-

[1] Cassius Dio 72.36.4.

dents. Some of these problems were directly related to foreign pressures, for Rome was seriously menaced by hostile peoples in Europe and Asia who at times invaded the empire in force. In the East, the feeble Arsacid dynasty was replaced by the energetic Sassanids, who revived Persia as a major power and challenged Roman control of the Levant. While Rome's foe in Iran was a civilized nation, primitive tribes lurked beyond the Danube and Rhine barriers and on the northern coasts of the Black Sea. The warlike tribes of Germany were eager to raid the prosperous towns and farms of the West, and nomadic horsemen, such as the Sarmatians, threatened the Balkans. The most formidable of the Germanic peoples were the Goths, who dwelt in Scandinavia at the beginning of the Christian era and had drifted southeastward to the Ukraine and the Crimea by the third century. Tall, fierce, and blond, the Goths had long mustaches and uncut hair and worshiped Thor the Thunderer and Tiwaz-Wotan, the god of battles. Hygiene was not a Gothic virtue, and most Romans found the odor of Goths and other barbarians offensive. What they lacked in cleanliness, the barbarians made up in valor and strength, and consequently they were valued as mercenaries and feared as foes. Along the borders of the Roman empire, the tribesmen absorbed bits of Roman civilization and a taste for luxury. Some barbarians earned pay serving with the Roman armies, but most preferred to raid the empire and carry off goods and women. Enriched with booty and subsidies from nervous Roman governors, the tribal chieftains were often wealthy. Their gold and silver attracted Greek and Roman merchants who journeyed northward and risked the danger of dealing with barbarians to peddle luxury goods and fine weapons. Despite the acculturative effects of contact with the Romans, the barbarians relished predatory warfare and delighted in rape, pillage, and the sheer joy of battle.

With good reason, the peoples of the Roman empire dreaded the barbarians and viewed them much as Ovid had depicted his savage neighbors at Tomis:

> Greater hordes of Sarmatae and Getae go and come upon their horses along the roads. Among them there is not one who does not bear quiver and bow, and darts yellow with viper's gall. Harsh voices, grim countenances, veritable pictures of Mars, neither hair nor beard trimmed by any hand, right hands not slow to stab and wound with the knife which every barbarian wears fastened to his side. . . . They have more of cruel savagery than wolves. They fear not laws; right gives way to force, and justice lies conquered beneath the aggressive sword. With skins and loose breeches, they keep off the evils of the cold; their shaggy faces are protected with long locks.[2]

[2] Ovid *Tristia* 5.7.13–20, 46–50, trans. A. L. Wheeler (Cambridge, Mass.: Harvard University Press, 1924), pp. 237–39.

Rowdy and unpredictable in times of peace, the barbarians were fearsome when they took the warpath and crashed through the defenses of the empire. The terrible raids of the Goths and other northern bands added a nightmarish dimension to the troubled third century.

Though the turbulent third and early fourth centuries were filled with significant developments, the extant sources are few and poor. For the emperors, sketches by the fourth-century epitomizers Aurelius Victor and Eutropius survive as well as the notorious *Historia Augusta,* an unreliable gallery of imperial biographies from Hadrian to Carinus. More reliable is the account of his own times by the Severan historian, Cassius Dio, which exists only in fragments. The period from 180 to 238 is covered by the Syrian historian Herodian, who was a contemporary, and some help on the later third century is provided by the sixth-century writer Zosimus, who relied on Dexippus and Eunapius. Eusebius preserves valuable material on the history of Christianity and his hero, Constantine. Luckily, papyri and inscriptions provide some documentary evidence, and Diocletian's decree on wages and prices is an invaluable source on economic matters. It is a pity, however, that so important an era produced no great historian. "The period is like a dark tunnel," complains a modern authority, "illumined from either end and by rare and exiguous light wells in the interval. One cannot do much more than follow out the known tendencies of the Severan age, at the same time looking forward to the state of affairs which appears under Diocletian, and thus hope to grope one's way through the intervening darkness." [3] Despite the dimness of our sources, it was an era of momentous changes and striking personalities.

THE ARMY AND THE THRONE

Soon after the assassination of Commodus had extinguished the Antonine dynasty, the Roman army reclaimed the throne, but first two ephemeral emperors—one pathetic, the other contemptible—flashed briefly across the screen of history. On the first day of 193, the Senate had elevated one of its members, P. Helvius Pertinax, to replace Commodus. Though his father was a freedman, Pertinax had enjoyed a distinguished career under Marcus Aurelius and Commodus. Frugal and conscientious, the new emperor alienated the Praetorian Guards, who murdered him after a reign of only 87 days. Ignoring the legions, the Praetorian prefect auctioned the throne to an overambitious senator, M. Didius Julianus, who foolishly thought that he could buy power. To le-

[3] A. H. M. Jones, *The Later Roman Empire 284–602* (Norman: University of Oklahoma Press, 1964), I, 23.

gitimize his regime, Julianus executed the assassins of Commodus. While the cowed Senate accepted the new ruler, the masses at Rome loudly protested the murder of Pertinax and the usurpation by Julianus, and rioters briefly seized the Circus Maximus. Meanwhile, the legions had reacted predictably to the tragic farce in Rome. Three generals—C. Pescennius Niger in Syria, D. Clodius Albinus in Britain, and L. Septimius Severus on the Danube—grasped for the imperial authority. Closest to the capital, Severus marched on Rome where the Praetorians promptly abandoned Julianus and the Senate accepted Severus as emperor. Having reigned only a few weeks, Julianus was slain in the palace. His stern successor disciplined the Praetorians by executing the killers of Pertinax and disbanding the rest of the Guards. Severus recruited a new Praetorian Guard from veterans of his legions and sought support for his regime by deifying the late Pertinax. For the next half-century, the Severan dynasty ruled Rome.

Short in stature, L. Septimius Severus was a dominating personality and a harsh military realist. Born in Africa, he spoke Latin with a provincial accent and had married a Syrian beauty, Julia Domna, because she had an imperial horoscope. Her father was the hereditary priest of the sun-god of Emesa, Elagabal. To secure his regime, the emperor had to solve the problem of his rivals, Albinus and Niger. Adopting Albinus as his heir, Severus marched against Niger in the East and defeated him in 194. Niger was slain in flight, and cities that had supported him were punished. In 196 Severus tried to legitimize his dynasty by claiming a connection with the Antonine family and deifying Commodus. He also announced that his oldest son, Caracalla, would be the imperial heir. Betrayed and angry, Albinus led a revolt in the West but was defeated and slain by Severus near Lyons in 197. The luckless city of Lyons was sacked for harboring rebels, and the Senate was purged of all who were suspected of having supported Albinus. The confiscated properties of his enemies were added to Severus's private estates. Since Parthia had backed Niger, the emperor invaded Parthian territory, sacked Ctesiphon, and annexed portions of northern Mesopotamia. His victories perpetuated Roman preoccupation with the East, and in undermining the shaky Arsacids, Severus unwittingly fostered the rise of the abler Sassanids.

The tone of the Severan regime reflected the driving, authoritarian temper of the emperor, who was at work before dawn and demanded efficiency and honesty from his subordinates. A frank militarist, he increased the army's pay and often promoted centurions to equestrian rank. Despite some currency devaluation, the frugal Severus accumulated a treasury surplus and was still able to sponsor public works and alimentary subsidies in the provinces. Concerned with performance more than titles, he disdained the Senate and relied increasingly on *equites* in the imperial administration. The Severan ideal was a military camp run with precision on fixed rules, and the regime employed distinguished Syrian jurists, Papinian and Ulpian, to buttress the monarchy with legal interpretations. Since law and justice are not synonymous, it was fitting that the pillars of Severan absolutism were lawyers and soldiers. Throughout the second century, legal distinctions between classes had been increasing until only *honestiores*—senators, *equites,* municipal gentry, and the military—retained the old privileges of immunity from torture and the right of appeal to the emperor on capital convictions. The mass of the population were *humiliores* with few rights and no privileges. The hardships of the common people were aggravated when Severus provided free rations for the army and imposed a tax in kind on farmers, who were already subject to impositions from the military. To assist him in affairs of state, the emperor relied on an old friend and kinsman from Africa, the Praetorian prefect C. Fulvius Plautianus. A pale, nervous, fat man, the prefect soon attained a position of power greater than that once held by Sejanus. Arrogant and greedy, Plautianus quarreled with Julia Domna and married his daughter to Caracalla, who loathed the girl. In 205 the crown prince persuaded Severus that the high-handed Plautianus was a threat to the throne. Like Sejanus, the prefect was executed by an emperor who had once relied upon him as his closest friend. The lawyer Papinian succeeded Plautianus as Praetorian prefect. While he had no illusions about Caracalla and his brother Geta, Severus insisted on dynastic succession and hoped that their mother, Julia Domna, would restrain his rowdy sons when they finally held imperial power. After an indecisive campaign against the wild tribes of Scotland, Septimius Severus died at York in 211. According to Cassius Dio, the dying emperor had advised his sons to maintain family harmony, enrich the soldiers, and scorn everyone else.[4]

For a time, Caracalla and Geta ruled as joint emperors, but the brothers detested and feared each other. In 212, on Caracalla's orders, Geta was struck down in the palace and died in their mother's arms. For opposing the crime, Papinian too was killed, and Geta's supporters were purged from the army. A headstrong and violent man, Caracalla also executed his own wife. As Severus's son, he had ambitions to be a conqueror and eventually fancied himself Alexander reborn. However, he was short, his health was poor, and he was tormented by nightmares. Eccentric in dress and manner, the emperor derived his nickname from the long Gallic cloak (*caracalla*) that he wore. At Rome, he built the

[4] Cassius Dio 76.15.2.

Caracalla. Rome, Villa Albani. *Alinari—Scala.*

enormous Baths of Caracalla. Despite the murder of Geta, Julia Domna loved Caracalla and provided a stable influence on him, working behind the scenes to effect policy. A woman of intellectual interests, the dowager empress was a generous patroness to writers and men of learning. The most famous act of Caracalla was an edict in 212 granting citizenship to all residents of the empire except *dediticii* (a vague term for conquered or stateless persons)—how many people were thus excluded is not known. The purpose of the edict was additional revenue, for only Roman citizens paid inheritance taxes and the emperor had just increased such taxes and those on manumission. Though he raised the army's pay, Caracalla debased currency. After successful campaigns on the Rhine and Danube, he planned a war against Parthia and armed a phalanx in Macedonian fashion. Visiting Egypt, Caracalla turned his troops loose on the irreverent Alexandrians when they mocked his pose as the new Alexander. While on the Parthian border in 217, the emperor was assassinated by agents of the Praetorian prefect, Macrinus, who was fearful of the suspicious Caracalla. Soon after her son's death, Julia Domna died, perhaps by suicide. For some time, she had been ill with cancer of the breast.

The brief reign of Macrinus was only an interlude in the Severan era. A soft-spoken Moroccan lawyer, M. Opellius Macrinus was the first non-senator to seize the throne, but he was not a military man and had little support from the army. His rapid downfall was engineered by

Julia Domna's ambitious sister, Julia Maesa,[5] who convinced the legions in Syria that her grandson, Varius Avitus, was Caracalla's bastard. Loyalty to the Severan house was still strong, and in 218 Macrinus was defeated and slain by troops who supported the pseudo-Severan Avitus. Fearful of the army and bribed by Maesa, the Senate accepted the fifteen-year-old Avitus as emperor, but even the worldly residents of Rome were not prepared for their new ruler, who was a priest of the sun-god of Emesa, Elagabal, and called himself Elagabalus. A mincing, rouged, bejeweled transvestite, Elagabalus squandered public funds on extravagant luxuries and effeminate favorites. His mother, Soaemias, encouraged his escapades and hoped to rule the state through her bizarre son, but Julia Maesa was the *de facto* empress of Rome with the title, "Mother of the Armies and the Senate." In a burst of henotheism, Elagabalus proclaimed Elagabal the official deity of the empire and built a magnificent temple at Rome to house the black stone cone that was the earthly form of the solar god. Worried over public outrage at the emperor's antics, Julia Maesa forced Elagabalus to adopt his young cousin, Severus Alexander, whose mother, Julia Mamaea, had raised him free from vice. Since Alexander was an obvious replacement, Soaemias tried to have him and her sister killed. However, old Maesa turned to the Praetorian Guards who murdered Elagabalus and his mother and elevated Alexander to the throne in 222.

Since the new emperor was only thirteen years old, his grandmother and his mother ruled in his name and placed the ambitious jurist Ulpian in the Praetorian prefecture. Within a year, Ulpian was slain by the guardsmen, and his patroness, Julia Maesa, soon died of natural causes. The dominant figure in Alexander's regime was Julia Mamaea, who modestly styled herself "Mother of the Emperor, Armies, Senate, Fatherland, and Whole Human Race." Her son was a cipher whose virtues were magnified by unreliable writers to emphasize the vices of his unsavory predecessor. Apparently, a gesture was made to reconcile the Senate, for a number of senators served on the imperial council. There was the usual building program and perhaps some tax relief, and state control may have been extended to guilds that supplied the city of Rome with food and clothing. Though Elagabal was returned to Emesa, the trend toward oriental cults continued, and the private chapel of Severus Alexander contained statues of Orpheus, Abraham, Jesus, and Apollonius of Tyana, a likely pantheon for a Syrian prince whose mother was interested in Christianity. Mamaea and her son probably

[5] Julia Maesa's husband had been a consul, and her daughters, Soaemias and Julia Mamaea, had married well. The husband of Soaemias and father of Elagabalus was a senator, and though the father of Severus Alexander was an *eques,* Julia Mamaea's first husband was a consul.

viewed the four saints as great magicians. Though he rescued Mesopotamia from the Sassanids in 232, the military prestige of the emperor was not high, and the legions resented the role played by his mother in affairs of state. On the Rhine frontier, Alexander and Mamaea tried to buy off the troublesome Alemanni, but the Roman army wished to fight the barbarians. In 235, the surly legionaries raised an able general, Maximinus, as emperor, and Severus Alexander and his mother were murdered near Mainz. While the armies had respected Septimius Severus and Caracalla, the dominance of the dowager empresses had discredited the later Severans in the soldiers' eyes. Yet, with the exception of the founder of the dynasty, the Severan women had been stronger than the men of the family. A permanent result of the Severan era was an increase in the number of senators from Africa and the East.

The half-century that followed the overthrow of the Severan dynasty was a hectic time of domestic insecurity and major incursions by the barbarians of the North. Compounding Rome's problems, Persia enjoyed a spectacular revival under the Sassanid dynasty. In Roman minds, Parthia represented the ancient glories of Darius and Xerxes, and Trajan and Caracalla had been obsessed with defeating the King of Kings. Under the Sassanids, the Persian empire became a reality again and a serious danger to the Roman presence in the Near East. Originally a priestly family, the Sassanids were Iranian princes who had exploited Arsacid weakness to win independence and topple the Parthian rulers. In 224 the Sassanid leader, Ardashir, defeated the last of the Arsacids, occupied Ctesiphon, and became the new King of Kings. With the aid of his son Shapur, Ardashir conquered a widespread empire at the expense of the Romans, the Armenians, and the Kushans of the Indus Valley. Succeeding his father in 242, Shapur I ruled for thirty years and expanded the Sassanid realm, absorbing Roman Mesopotamia, Armenia, and the Kushan kingdom. In 260 he defeated and captured the Roman emperor, Valerian. With captive Roman engineers, the king constructed roads and bridges and a large dam at Shushtar. To commemorate his victories over Rome, Shapur covered a rock cliff near Bishapur with inscriptions and reliefs depicting Valerian cringing at his feet. A man of culture, he ordered translations into Pahlavi of Greek and Indian texts on astronomy, philosophy, and medicine. Though a devout Zoroastrian, Shapur tolerated other religions, but there is no reliable evidence that he was interested in the prophet Mani or his creed. Despite the king's pragmatic attitude toward religious dissent, Zarathustrianism was the state church of the Persian realm, and the Magian clergy were zealous and intolerant. During the Arsacid era, the Zoroastrian cult had succumbed to syncretism, but the Sassanids sponsored a "Back to Zarathustra" movement and hymns and texts were collected into a sacred canon, the *Avesta*. Piety and nationalism blended in the interests of the state, which relied on the Magi for support and allowed priests to preside at civil trials. Unlike the feudal Parthians, the Sassanids created a centralized state with key positions in the hands of royal princes and a network of authority reaching to village headmen who were dependents of the king. While the Persian economy rested on a tenant peasantry, the empire contained many large cities where trade was brisk and profitable. The Persians served as middlemen for Chinese silks and Indian spices, which were much desired in Roman markets. Though the peasants derived no benefit from urban prosperity, the revenues of the Sassanid state were considerable, but much of the national wealth was wasted on royal splendor and war. Like the Parthians, the Sassanid army emphasized cavalry and firepower, and the Romans dreaded the charging cataphracts and mounted archers of Iran. The Persian armed forces also included levies from the tribes of Central Asia. Luckily for Rome, the emphasis on mobility made the Persians impatient with prolonged campaigns, and their invasions of the Roman empire were only grand-scale raids, no matter how destructive or humiliating to Roman prestige. After Shapur's death in 272, the Persian empire faltered under inept or unlucky kings, who lost control of Armenia, Upper Mesopotamia, and the Kushan realm by the end of the third century.

While Persia enjoyed a renaissance of power, the Roman empire was almost wrecked by internal crises. Despite serious external threats, the Roman army ignored the security of the empire, and for five decades, it set up and unseated emperors at will and plundered the populace in sporadic civil wars. In the fifty years between Severus Alexander and Diocletian, nineteen emperors occupied the precarious throne, and an even greater number of would-be usurpers claimed the imperial title. While Goths and Persians battered at the defenses of the empire, the Roman army indulged in an orgy of mutiny, and few emperors could rely on more than the legions under their immediate command. At times, entire blocks of provinces were separated from the control of the central authority. Though many were men of ability, most emperors were cut down before they could restore discipline to the army and peace to the empire. During the chaos, currency was frequently debased, inflation raged unchecked, and marauding soldiers pillaged towns unmercifully. Since the armies were made up largely of peasant recruits, the famed Russian historian, Mikhail Rostovtzeff, interpreted the disorders of the third century as a class war of the rural masses against the pampered *bourgeoisie* of the cities.[6] Furthermore, some emperors came

---

[6] Unsurpassed in his ability to utilize archeological evidence, Rostovtzeff was probably the most influential ancient historian of our times. His major works,

from humble origins, and the urban classes suffered grievously and loudly during the constant crises. However, Rostovtzeff had been seared by the Bolshevik Revolution, and his notion of a "Red Army" in the third century is anachronistic. In fact, the Roman armies plundered peasants cruelly, and no self-made emperor viewed himself as an avenging angel against the urban rich. What is most noteworthy is that the Roman empire remained intact after this time of troubles. Rome survived as a result of the heroic efforts of various emperors, the disunity and relatively small numbers of barbarian raiders, Shapur's failure to annex the Levant, and the great resources of the empire in men and supplies. During the permanent crisis, however, the future of Rome looked bleak.

During the military anarchy, most emperors tried to establish dynasties and elevated their sons as Caesars, which had long been an official title for the heir of a reigning Augustus. So prevalent was disloyalty, however, that few dynasties survived the brief reigns of their founders. In 235, the discredited Severan family had been overthrown by supporters of Maximinus Thrax, a man of immense size and physical strength. Born a Balkan peasant, he had joined the army, risen through the ranks, and become a respected general. Resenting him but fearful of the legions, the Senate accepted Maximinus as emperor. He raised military pay and campaigned successfully against barbarians on the Rhine and Danube. Exasperated by high taxes, a group of plantation owners in Africa rose in rebellion in 238 and set up an elderly noble, M. Antonius Gordianus, as emperor. Endorsed by the Senate, Gordian and his son were soon slain by Maximinus's supporters in Africa. On news of his death, the Senate elected two of its members, M. Clodius Pupienus and D. Caelius Balbinus, as co-emperors, but popular pressure forced the pair to adopt Gordian's grandson as the imperial heir. The stern Maximinus was hated by the masses at Rome, who battled his Praetorians until a large part of the city was burned in the riots. Invading Italy, Maximinus was killed by his own troops who wearied of the discomforts of a civil war. The triumph of his enemies was short-lived, for Pupienus and Balbinus were soon butchered by the untamed Praetorians and Gordian III became emperor at the age of thirteen. The boy was dominated by his capable father-in-law, the Praetorian prefect Timesitheus, who defended the Danube frontier and took Gordian on a campaign to rescue Syria from Shapur's raiders. Though the Persian threat was contained, the prefect died of disease in the East, and the young emperor was slain by mutinous troops in 244.

According to rumor, the murder of Gordian III was engineered by

Social and Economic History of the Roman Empire and *Social and Economic History of the Hellenistic World,* are modern classics.

Philip the Arab who had succeeded Timesitheus as Praetorian prefect. In any case, the legions raised Philip as emperor. A practical man, he made peace with Persia and gave up Roman claims on Armenia. At Rome, the Arab emperor tried to win public approval by curbing the secret police, who were overzealous in locating tax dodgers. In 247 the millennium of the city of Rome was celebrated with impressive rites and great pageantry by an Augustus who had been born in what is now Jordan. Like Severus Alexander, Philip was indulgent toward Christians, and his son may have joined the sect. Later legends credited Philip as the first Christian emperor.[7] When rebels rose in Syria and barbarians attacked the Balkans, the worried Philip wished to resign, but the urban prefect Decius dissuaded him. Sent to command troops on the Danube, Decius was elevated by them as emperor, supposedly against his will. In 249 Philip died in battle against the rebels. Another version of these events has Decius plotting at Rome and sending assassins to kill Philip in the Balkans. The confusion over Philip's death illustrates the contradictory propaganda obscuring his reign. Pagan writers defamed the pro-Christian Arab to exalt Decius, who was a pagan bigot, and Constantinian apologists attacked Philip's memory because Constantine's foe, Licinius, was his descendant.

A wealthy landowner from the Balkans, Decius was popular with the Senate, for he was conservative in politics and religion. Convinced that the ills of Rome were caused by divine displeasure, the emperor launched the first empire-wide persecution of Christians in 250. His attention to religious subversion was soon distracted by barbarian invasions of Dacia and Thrace. Twice defeated by the Goths, Decius died in battle against them in 251. The remnant of his army raised to the throne a general, Trebonianus Gallus, who bribed the Goths to withdraw across the Danube, but the barbarians continued to menace the frontier. At Rome and elsewhere, plague broke out, and various provinces were ravaged by disease during the next fifteen years. When Gallus and his ephemeral successor, Aemilianus, perished in military mutinies in 253, the armies rallied at last behind a popular general, Valerian, who shared the throne with his adult son Gallienus. Like his friend Decius, Valerian was a senator and a bigoted pagan, but apparently the gods were not grateful for his attempts to eradicate Christianity, for an extraordinary series of calamities marred his reign. While Alexandria was devastated by plague, the provinces of the East were attacked by both Persians and barbarians. In the West, Gallienus defended Gaul and later drove the Alemanni from Italy, but his father

---

[7] Jerome and Orosius claim that Philip was a Christian; if so, he celebrated the millennium of Rome with pagan rites. However, Decius's hostility to Christians was due in part to the bond between them and Philip.

was less successful in the East. In great war fleets, the Goths crossed the Black Sea and pillaged the cities of Asia Minor. Meanwhile, Persian horsemen harassed Syria, and in 258 Shapur himself invaded the province and sacked Antioch. Valerian tried to stem the Persian advance but was repeatedly defeated, and in 260 he fell into Shapur's hands. Flush with victory, the King of Kings led his army into Anatolia, but the Persians mistreated the local population who might otherwise have viewed them as liberators. Despite his spectacular success, Shapur's invasion was only a great raid for booty, and as he withdrew, his troops were harried by Odaenathus and other Roman commanders. A client of Rome, Odaenathus was the ruler of Palmyra, an important caravan stop on the border of Syria, and he provided cataphracts and archers for the war against Shapur. In Gallienus's name, Odaenathus recovered northern Mesopotamia but was unable to rescue Valerian, who died in captivity in Persia. According to legend, the Roman emperor's skin was stuffed with straw and hung in a Magian temple, but the tale seems only wishful thinking on the part of Christians.

During Gallienus's reign as sole ruler, the Roman empire almost came apart. Yet, like Hadrian, the emperor was intelligent, energetic, and interested in arts and letters. Lacking his father's bigotry, Gallienus in 261 halted the persecution of Christians, returned confiscated property to the bishops, and gave the church recognition as a legal religion. Beset by many crises, the emperor needed support wherever he could find it. He had less success with political dissidents. In 260 the legions in Gaul, Spain, and Britain had set up an able general, Postumus, as emperor, and Gallienus was unable to regain control of the West. However, the usurper served the interests of the empire by driving marauding barbarians from his provinces. In the East, other generals rose in revolt, but a loyal marshal, Aureolus, restored order in the Balkans, and Odaenathus put down rebels in Syria. Still active against the Persians, the Palmyran prince was showered with honors by Gallienus. To meet the threat of the barbarians in Europe, the emperor adopted a strategy of defense in depth rather than depending on fortified frontiers. He established strongholds behind the borders and increased the cavalry to add greater mobility to the armies of Rome. The emphasis on cavalry raised their commanders to new prestige and excited the ambition of some. Since the military situation required professionalism, Gallienus ignored senators in the assignment of commands and relied on *equites* who had long service with the army. In 267, Gothic fleets swarmed through the Aegean, and the barbarians sacked Ionia and burned the great temple of Artemis at Ephesus. On his way to fight the invaders, Odaenathus was murdered by rival Roman generals, and the throne of Palmyra passed to his widow, Zenobia. In 268 a horde of Goths and

Heruli attacked Greece by land and sea; the ancient towns of Athens, Sparta, Corinth, and Argos were pillaged and put to the torch. As the barbarians moved northward through the Balkans, Gallienus marched from Italy and inflicted a major defeat on them at Naïssus. Unable to enjoy his victory, the emperor had to return to Milan where Aureolus had risen in revolt. During the siege of the city, Gallienus was assassinated by two ambitious generals, Claudius and Aurelian. Though one of the ablest Roman rulers, Gallienus fared badly at the hands of conservative historians, who resented his treatment of the Senate and his toleration of Christianity. His image fell further when Constantine claimed descent from one of the murderers of Gallienus.

With the accession of Claudius II, who was from Illyria, the throne became the prize of a series of emperors from the Balkans. Claiming that the dying Gallienus had named him as successor, Claudius was recognized as emperor by the Senate. Though Aureolus submitted and was slain, the new emperor was ignored by the rebel regime in Gaul, and Zenobia occupied Egypt and parts of Asia Minor. While she recognized Claudius as emperor, the Palmyran queen had become a troublesome vassal. Before dealing with Zenobia, Claudius drove the remaining Goths from the Balkans, but his life was cut short by plague in 270. With the Senate's support, his brother Quintillus claimed the throne, but the army elevated the cavalry commander, Aurelian, and Quintillus committed suicide. A ruthless soldier whose motto was "Hand on Hilt," Aurelian was determined to restore order in the Roman world. With luck and ability, he succeeded. To protect the sprawling capital from marauders, the emperor encircled Rome with a new wall, twelve miles long, portions of which still stand. With dispatch, Aurelian crushed rebellious generals and drove barbarians from Italy and the Danube provinces. However, he was a realist and abandoned the exposed portion of Dacia north of the Danube to the Goths. Meanwhile, Zenobia had refused to recognize Aurelian's authority and was reigning as Queen of the East. A woman of beauty and intelligence, she claimed descent from Cleopatra, and her court at Palmyra included the Greek philosopher Longinus, whom Eunapius called "a living library and walking Museum." [8] In 272 Aurelian moved against Zenobia, and near Antioch and again at Emesa, his cavalry defeated her cataphracts. In the campaign against Zenobia, the emperor claimed to have seen visions of Apollonius of Tyana and the Syrian sun-god, Elagabal; he attributed to the latter his victory over Palmyra. Faced with a Roman siege, Zenobia asked the Persians for aid, but Shapur was dead and his successor failed to act. Fleeing from Palmyra, Zenobia was captured by the Romans;

[8] Eunapius *Vitae Sophistarum* 456.

she tried to appease Aurelian by blaming her past conduct on the advice of Longinus and other courtiers. The emperor accepted the queen's lame excuse and executed her advisers when the city surrendered. After Aurelian withdrew with Zenobia, Palmyra rose on her behalf in 273 and was destroyed by the Romans. A wealthy Alexandrian, Firmus, had also tried to salvage Egypt for the queen, but he was easily defeated by Aurelian. With the East secure, the emperor marched against the Gallic rebels who were now led by the elderly and timid Tetricus. In 274 Tetricus deserted his own army and submitted to Aurelian, thus restoring the West to the central authority. At Rome, the emperor celebrated the restoration of imperial unity with a splendid triumph and paraded Zenobia and Tetricus before the crowds. No longer dangerous to Aurelian, Tetricus was given an administrative post and Zenobia received a pension and a villa at Tivoli.

Although most of his reign was occupied with warfare, Aurelian tried to deal with some of the pressing problems of his time. The deflated currency was replaced by a new coinage with little gold or silver content. Like Hadrian and Marcus Aurelius, the emperor burned overdue public debts, and he replaced the grain dole at Rome with a daily allowance of baked bread and a monthly allotment of pork, olive oil, and salt. Perhaps the augmented dole was intended to feed refugees who had crowded into the city during the barbarian invasions. Aurelian may also have nationalized the guilds of food suppliers for the capital. In gratitude to Elagabal, the emperor promoted the solar deity of Emesa to be the universal god of the empire, and the new cult of Sol Invictus, the unconquerable sun, became extremely popular with the army. Impatient with inefficiency and corruption, Aurelian dealt severely with incompetent or dishonest officials. A secretary who feared his vengeance forged a purge list in the emperor's name and sent copies to generals whose names were on the false roster. With military promptness, the fearful officers murdered Aurelian in 275. The "Restorer of the World" deserved a better fate.

Despite the reunification of the empire, the imperial succession was still a hectic affair. According to tradition, Aurelian was succeeded by an elderly senator, Tacitus; it is very likely that he was an ex-general. By 276 Tacitus was dead, and the throne was seized by an able general, Probus, who like Aurelian came from the Danube provinces. A thorough man, Probus secured the frontiers of the empire by driving Franks and Alemanni from Gaul and other barbarians from the Balkans. His generals protected Egypt from desert tribesmen, and a number of military mutinies were suppressed. Like Marcus Aurelius, Probus admitted a large number of barbarians into the empire and enrolled many in his armies, a convenient form of recruitment. Not all barbarians were reliable, and a band of Franks stationed in Pontus grew homesick, seized ships, and terrorized coastal towns in the Mediterranean. After sacking Syracuse, the Franks escaped into the Atlantic and made their way to their home in the North. Despite such lively episodes, the empire under Probus enjoyed a kind of security. In time of peace, the emperor put his troops to constructive work, building roads and planting vineyards. In 282 a group of discontented soldiers murdered him. The armies chose a new emperor, the Praetorian prefect Carus, who was probably an Illyrian. After rescuing the Balkans from barbarians, Carus launched a successful campaign against Persia, but he died near Ctesiphon in 283, supposedly struck by lightning. More likely, the emperor was killed by the Praetorian prefect Aper, who was the father-in-law of Carus's son and successor, Numerian. Abandoning the war with Persia, Numerian died of disease in 284, but the high command accused Aper of killing him and executed the prefect at Nicomedia. The fall of Aper was contrived by an ambitious officer, Diocletian, who was then elevated as emperor. In the West, Numerian's brother Carinus had been reigning as co-emperor, and he quickly marched against Diocletian with a large force. In 285 the troops of Diocletian were almost defeated in a hard-fought battle in the Balkans, but with victory in sight, Carinus was assassinated by a man whose wife he had seduced, and the leaderless Western legions accepted Diocletian as emperor. If the story of Carinus's indiscretion is true, the fate of the Roman empire was decided, not on the battlefield, but in the boudoir. At any rate, Diocletian, whose military skills were limited, had won control of the empire, and the history of Rome had reached a new watershed.

THE TOTALITARIAN STATE [9]

No empire could have continued to suffer the shocks and stresses that Rome had endured for half a century, and the recent power struggles seemed to herald a new round of usurpations that would undo the constructive work of Aurelian and Probus. Fortunately for the Romans, the new emperor was a forty-year-old pragmatist who halted the chaos of the third century and buttressed the empire with a series of reforms that gave it a new lease on life. For good and ill, Diocletian consolidated the totalitarian trends of the past and put all elements of society in a state of perpetual mobilization. He also added some touches of his own personality. A Dalmatian of humble origin, probably the son of a freed-

[9] The use of the term "totalitarian" does not imply that the Roman state ever achieved total control over its subjects. No recent despotism has attained that goal, and the Roman empire was appallingly inefficient by modern standards.

man, Diocletian was a man of intense practicality who had risen through his own merits and worshiped order and efficiency. In Gibbon's words:

> His abilities were useful rather than splendid: a vigorous mind, improved by the experience and study of mankind, dexterity and application in business; a judicious mixture of liberality and economy, of mildness and rigor; profound dissimulation under the disguise of military frankness; steadiness to pursue his ends; flexibility to vary his means; and above all, the great art of submitting his own passions, as well as those of others, to the interest of his ambition, and of coloring his ambition with the most specious pretences of justice and public utility. Like Augustus, Diocletian may be considered as the founder of a new empire. Like the adopted son of Caesar, he was distinguished as a statesman rather than a warrior; nor did either of those princes employ force, whenever their purpose could be effected by policy.[10]

No flamboyant conqueror, Diocletian was a realist who delighted in administration and outfoxed the warlords. In modern times, he would have been a successful corporation executive or First Secretary of the Communist Party in the Soviet Union. The emperor's realism, however, was diluted by his years with the military: he believed in government by decree and assumed that orders would always be carried out.

Since he relished the title of *Dominus* (Lord), the system of Diocletian and his successors is sometimes labeled the Dominate. There is no harm in the term as long as it is realized that the Principate had been abandoned long before Diocletian, and that the Principate itself was a hypocritical mask for autocracy. In many ways, Diocletian was a very conservative ruler, anxious to maintain Roman laws and customs, and his innovations usually had precedents. Under the Republic, the authority of magistrates had been collegiate and Marcus Aurelius, Valerian, and other emperors had shared their thrones. Diocletian too was willing to distribute the burden of authority onto shoulders other than his own. The emperor established a Tetrarchy with two senior Augusti and two junior Caesars, but there was no doubt that he was chairman of the board. After twenty years of rule, Diocletian and his colleague resigned and elevated the Caesars as Augusti. At the time of his abdication, Diocletian was in poor health, but it is probable that he had earlier promised the Caesars that the Augusti would step down after a specific number of years.[11] The grim lessons of the third century had revealed the insatiable ambition of generals, and a guaranteed time for promotion to

[10] Gibbon, *Decline of the Roman Empire*, I, 351.
[11] It is noteworthy that Galerius later intended to abdicate after twenty years in power, but his death intervened.

the rank of Augustus would relieve a Caesar of the temptation to mutiny. Such a system would provide an orderly succession and free the
empire from the recurring nightmare of revolution in the camps. Since
his predecessors had often been murdered, Diocletian protected himself
from assassination by hiding behind a host of secretaries and courtiers.
The size of the court rapidly expanded, and functionaries bore titles of
increasing pompousness. To inflate his image, the emperor became the
earthly representative of Jupiter—his person was sacred, and imperial
portraits featured a golden nimbus about the sovereign's head. Gorgeous
costumes added to the ersatz charisma of the ruler. Since Aurelian, it
had been common for Roman emperors to wear a diadem, and Diocletian affected jeweled footwear and wore robes of cloth of gold. Whether
such finery was designed to awe the masses or merely gratify a poor boy
who had made good, sartorial splendor was now the hallmark of a
Roman emperor. Protected by a wall of protocol and pageantry, the emperor became a remote figure, if not quasi-divine, at least superhuman.

Like all reformers, Diocletian could not anticipate the total results of
his acts. Though he glittered in public, the emperor spent most of his
time busy at his desk; some of his successors, however, would become
distracted by the pomp of the court and the unreal life of the palace.
Although lords of the Roman world, the emperors were isolated by the
court, and those who would reach them had to bribe their way through
a gauntlet of attendants. Strong men like Diocletian dominated their
courtiers, but a weak emperor could become a puppet of his own servants, and even able rulers were dependent on secretaries and aides who
screened what the imperial eyes would see. In the heart of the palace,
the emperor and his family were attended by eunuchs, a common practice in wealthy households. Since Roman law forbade castration, these
eunuchs were slaves imported from Armenia or Persia; though foreigners, constant proximity gave them more access to the ruler than was
enjoyed by senators and generals. As Overseer of the Sacred Bedcham-
ber, the chief eunuch was a powerful figure and the final and most
costly obstacle in the arduous task of reaching the emperor. In a totalitarian system, eunuchs seemed to be ideal attendants. Dependent solely
on the emperor for their position, they had neither a past nor a future;
as slaves of foreign origin, they had no local ties to be exploited. Without wives or children, eunuchs had no stake in family politics which
flourished under the Empire as under the Republic. Yet, in fact, the
eunuchs were constantly involved in cabals and their greed was notorious. Denied normal pleasures, they lusted for money and power. Their
machinations and itching palms became serious problems in the Late
Roman Empire.

In no sense was Diocletian a doctrinaire ideologue. Much of his reign was spent combating foreign and domestic enemies, and his policies were responses to military or social crises. While the results may have been totalitarian, the intent was Roman and conservative, and the methods were extemporized to meet the needs of the moment. When Diocletian began his reign, Gaul was being ravaged by Franks and Alemanni, and the Gallic peasantry were in despair. Infuriated at a state that taxed them heavily but could not protect them from invaders, bands of peasants (Bacaudae) rose in revolt in Central Gaul and added to the disorders of the time. To deal with the crisis in the West, Diocletian relied on the military skills of his friend Maximian, a rough and ready general of peasant origin, who promptly smashed the Bacaudae and drove the barbarians back across the Rhine. In 286 Diocletian raised Maximian to share the throne as the Augustus of the West. In the slogans of the regime, the new emperor played the earthly Hercules to Diocletian's Jupiter. The following year, an ambitious general, Carausius, set up a rebel state in Britain and seized the port of Boulogne as well. Unable to cope with Carausius or his successor Allectus, the two emperors concentrated on more immediate threats. The Eastern Augustus campaigned successfully on the Danube and in Syria and imposed a vassal king on Armenia. By 293 he had crushed a revolt in Egypt. The same year, the Tetrarchy was established. Conceding that the task of defending the empire was too great for the Augusti, Diocletian expanded the number of emperors to four, appointing as his Caesar a capable general of humble origin, Galerius. Maximian chose as his Caesar another skilled soldier, Constantius, whose nickname was Chlorus (pale). All four emperors were from the northern Balkans, and Constantius was already Maximian's son-in-law, having put aside his concubine, the barmaid Helena, to marry Theodora, the stepdaughter of the Western Augustus. Not to be outdone, Galerius divorced his wife to marry Diocletian's daughter, Valeria. Constantius's son by Helena, Constantine, was sent to live at Diocletian's court.

Bound by marriages and personal loyalties, the four emperors issued laws jointly but maintained separate courts and minted their own coins. Guarding the Eastern frontier, the senior Augustus resided at Nicomedia where he had first seized power. His Caesar, Galerius, kept a close watch on the lower Danube from a fortress in the Balkans. At Milan, Maximian guarded the upper Danube and upper Rhine, while his Caesar, Constantius, protected Gaul from a headquarters at Treves. After wresting Boulogne from Allectus, Constantius invaded Britain in 296 and subdued the rebels. Later, he inflicted a major defeat on the Alemanni. Meanwhile, Galerius and Maximian were active defending the empire from other barbarians. In 297 Diocletian crushed a serious revolt in Egypt that may have been connected with a reaction to his mon-

Tetrarchs (Diocletian, Maximian, Galerius, Constantius Chlorus). Venice, St. Marks Basilica (northwest corner). *Alinari—Scala.*

etary reforms, for he abolished the mint at Alexandria when he recovered the province. Taking advantage of the Roman's troubles, the Sassanid king, Narses, overran Armenia and Syria and defeated Galerius near Carrhae. In 298 Galerius was reinforced by troops from the Balkans and recovered his prestige with a smashing attack on the Persians. When the Romans took Ctesiphon, Narses begged for peace and surrendered Armenia and portions of Upper Mesopotamia. The victory over Persia gave Galerius an importance among the Tetrarchs second only to Diocletian. In 301 the senior Augustus could counsel his subjects: "We must be grateful for a world that is tranquil and reclining in the embrace of the most profound calm, and for the blessing of a peace that was won with great effort." [12]

The "profound calm" of which Diocletian boasted was similar to the quiet of a prison, for in a piecemeal fashion, he had erected a massive pyramid of absolutism and oppression. As a military man, national defense was his paramount concern, and the emperor expected every Roman to do his duty without questioning. Already hard-pressed, the

[12] Frank *ESAR*, V, 311.

peoples of the empire had to shoulder additional burdens to support a never-ending military effort, an expanding bureaucracy, and four imperial courts. In his zeal for decrees, Diocletian revealed the delight of a true organization man in paperwork and the apparatus of administration. A self-made man, the emperor had little respect for the hereditary aristocracy and excluded senators from most governmental posts. Like many of his predecessors, he relied on *equites,* not only because of their experience, but also because they were more grateful for advancement. Only Asia, Africa, and Italy were administered by senators, and Italy lost its ancient immunity from the land tax. Since provincial governors had stirred up mutinies in the third century, Diocletian fragmented the provinces into about one hundred new provinces, governed by *equites* and grouped into twelve large administrative districts (dioceses). The diocesan governors (vicars) were also *equites* and reported to the Praetorian prefects of their respective emperor. In frontier provinces where armies were concentrated, Diocletian separated civilian and military authority, disarming the governors and placing the troops under a general who was responsible to the diocesan marshal. The increasing division between civil and military officials soon converted the Praetorian prefects into finance ministers. At every level of officialdom, the bureaucracy was expanded, and opportunists sought jobs in the lower echelons of government, especially as financial officers. Despite the emperor's efforts, the system swarmed with parasites. Though Diocletian disbanded the corrupt secret police, the totalitarian state required a new network of spies who proved to be just as vicious. Since every Roman was theoretically subject to conscription, local officials had to provide levies of recruits or sufficient money to hire soldiers in their place. Barbarians too served as mercenaries in the armies of Rome, and bands of alien soldiery served as auxiliary troops. Though the size of a legion may have been reduced, the number of legions was increased, and probably half a million men were under arms, an enormous burden for the state. Disdaining the mobile concepts of Gallienus and his successors, Diocletian emphasized fixed frontier defenses and concentrated troops in force on the borders. To guarantee support and supplies for the armies, the emperor nationalized most arms factories and much of the transport facilities in the empire.

To meet his mounting expenses, Diocletian stabilized the currency with a new silver coin and reformed the tax structure. To facilitate army requisitions, many taxes were paid directly in manufactured goods or agricultural products. The state assessed landowners on the estimated productivity of each unit (*iugum*) of farm land, pasture, or orchard that one laborer could work; the tax on the *iugum* was payable in kind. A head tax (*caput*) on laborers and tenants was payable in cash, and both land and head tax assessments were to be revised every fifteen years. In 297 the prefect of Egypt explained the tax system:

> Our most providential emperors, Diocletian and Maximian Augusti and Constantius and [Galerius] most noble Caesars, having seen that the levies of the public taxes take place in such a way that some people get off lightly and some are overburdened, have determined to root out this most evil and pernicious practice in the interest of their provincials and to lay down a salutary rule whereby the levies shall be made. I have therefore publicly given notice how much has been assessed for each [unit] according to the quality of the land and how much on each head of the peasants, and from what age and to what age, according to their published divine edict and the schedule annexed thereto, and I have issued copies of them in my edict. So the provincials, seeing that they have received great benefits, must take care that they make their payment with all speed according to the divine regulations and do not wait to be compelled. All must fulfill their obligations with the greatest zeal, and if anyone be found doing otherwise after such great benefits, he will be punished.[13]

How peasants felt about their "great benefits" can be inferred from the frequency with which oppressed tenants abandoned their farms and ran away. The thankless task of supplying deficit taxes for a community fell upon municipal officials (*decuriones, curiales*) who could be bankrupted by a bad harvest. In addition to various liturgies, the local gentry had to subdue rural discontent and recapture runaway tenants. While the rising tax burden oppressed the lower and middle classes, the great landowners who made up the senatorial class avoided paying their share of taxes by bribing state officials and the secret agents who spied on everyone.

One of the most malignant problems of the third century was a rampant inflation, aggravated by war and swollen governmental expenditures. Diocletian's policy of collecting taxes in kind was a concession to the bitter realities of a devaluated currency. Ironically, his monetary reforms had encouraged speculation in coins among officials who knew in advance that the money would change. Ever-rising prices harmed even that most favored group, the military, and Diocletian complained that, "sometimes in a single purchase, a soldier is deprived of his bonus and salary." [14] Heedful of the suffering of his people, the emperor decided to halt inflation by decree. In 301 he issued an edict that specified maximum prices, wages, and freight charges and ordered the death penalty for violators. The edict is an invaluable glimpse at what were considered fair prices at the turn of the fourth century, and details on the quality of products and specifics of services provide a unique spotlight

---

[13] Aurelius Isidorus No. 1, trans. A. H. M. Jones, *History of Rome*, II, 267–68.
[14] Frank *ESAR*, V, 314.

into what is usually the Stygian darkness of economic history in antiquity. For eight denarii, a Roman could buy either two pints of Celtic beer, four of Egyptian beer, a pint of Phoenician honey, a pound of beef, a half pound of best quality salted pork, eight oysters, a half pound of sardines, twenty cabbages, ten large beets, eight eggs, twenty apples, two fine sewing needles, or a three-pronged hay fork. For two denarii more, he could buy a pound of hair rope. Sixty denarii was the price of either a peck of barley, two pints of Falernian wine, three pounds of ham, a pair of chickens, a pound of garlic, five pounds of ordinary olive oil, a pair of purple slippers, or thirty pounds of kindling wood. For one hundred denarii, the consumer could purchase either a peck of wheat, a peck of dried kidney beans, a pair of soldier's boots, a plow with a yoke, a pound of goose down, a pound of washed Asturian wool, or a pound of frankincense. For two hundred denarii, he could have a peck of rice or one fattened hen pheasant or goose. A peacock cost three hundred denarii, a military saddle five hundred, and a hooded African cloak fifteen hundred. The finest quality soldier's mantle sold for four thousand denarii, a pound of white silk twelve thousand, a pound of refined gold fifty thousand, and a pound of purple dyed raw silk one hundred and fifty thousand. Daily wages with maintenance for a farm laborer, mule driver, water carrier, or sewer cleaner were twenty-five denarii, a carpenter or baker received fifty denarii a day with maintenance, and a top quality linen weaver forty with maintenance. A barber or a checkroom attendant at the baths could charge two denarii a customer, while a notary received ten denarii for a hundred lines. For each pupil per month, an elementary school teacher could demand fifty denarii, a teacher of architecture one hundred, and a teacher of rhetoric two hundred and fifty. For pleading a case, a lawyer received one thousand denarii. The items and services cited are only a sample of the many entries that have survived of this valuable document.[15] From other sources, it is estimated that a legionary's annual pay with donatives was 7500 denarii. Though well-intentioned, Diocletian neglected to establish a minimum wage for any profession or allow for legitimate market fluctuations. No precursor of socialism, the conscientious emperor simply tried to stop inflation and protect his subjects from overcharging profiteers. However, the edict was indifferently enforced, and greedy merchants braved the death penalty to hoard goods and sell them on the black market. By the time of Constantine, the edict on maximum prices and wages was no longer in effect.

[15] A convenient edition as of 1940 is that of T. Frank, *ESAR,* V, 305–421. A sample of recently discovered material is provided by Kenan T. Erim and Joyce Reynolds, "The Copy of Diocletian's Edict on Maximum Prices from Aphrodisias in Caria," *Journal of Roman Studies* 60 (1970): 120–41.

Subversion is a matter of great concern to despots, and during the war against Narses, Diocletian had briefly persecuted the Manicheans under the mistaken impression that they were Persian sympathizers. Though a devout pagan, he had no quarrel with Christianity, which had been a legal cult since 261. Many of his courtiers were Christians, even some of the eunuchs, and a Christian church stood opposite the imperial palace in Nicomedia. So order-conscious an emperor as Diocletian had no interest in disturbing a large law-abiding minority. In 299, however, Christian courtiers made the sign of the cross "to ward off demons" while a pagan sacrifice was being conducted in Diocletian's presence. When the priests complained of sacrilege, the pious emperor ordered that everyone in the palace should offer worship to the gods or be beaten. Though Diocletian's anger soon cooled, Galerius insisted on extending the demands to the army in order to purge Christian officers. Probably Galerius's zeal was real, for his mother was a pagan bigot who urged him to eradicate the enemies of the gods. Diocletian was reluctant to unleash a full-scale persecution until Galerius unnerved the aging Augustus by producing an anti-Christian oracle from Apollo at Miletus. Even then, Diocletian wished to avoid bloodshed—such is the testimony of the Christian professor Lactantius, who was at the court and had no love for Diocletian.[16] In 303 the senior Augustus issued an edict banning Christian rites and confiscated churches and books; he also cancelled the legal immunity of Christian *honestiores* from torture. When two mysterious fires broke out in the palace, Galerius persuaded Diocletian that the blazes were the work of Christian arsonists. With more edicts, the Caesar of the East launched a thorough persecution, imprisoning and executing recalcitrant Christians. In Syria and Palestine, the persecutors were especially brutal, but in the West, Maximian and Constantius were indifferent to the "Christian menace."

While Galerius concentrated on affairs in the East, Diocletian visited Rome for the first time in his life to celebrate his twentieth year in power. The ancient city and its rowdy crowds were not to his liking, but he ordered enormous baths built to commemorate his visit. A year later, the Augustus, who was now sixty, suffered a serious illness that left him in poor health. In 305, urged on by Galerius, Diocletian resigned his imperial powers and made Maximian also retire into private life. The Western Augustus's grudging compliance suggests that promises of abdication had been made earlier to the Caesars, Galerius and Constantius, who now became Augusti. Though both Maximian and Constantius had grown sons, Maxentius and Constantine respectively, the two princes were passed over in the selection of new Caesars. Galerius's

---

[16] Lactantius *de Mortibus Persecutorum* 11.

nephew, Maximinus Daia, was appointed Caesar of the East, and Severus, who was a drinking companion of Galerius, became the Western Caesar. Ignoring the power plays of his protégé, Diocletian retired to a fortified villa at Salonae in Dalmatia where he spent his final days working in his garden. To moderns, the abdication of Charles V springs to mind, but Diocletian was following the precedent of Sulla. Unlike the dictator, Diocletian's old age was filled with grief, for he lived to see the Tetrarchy destroyed by the struggles of new dynasts and his own wife and daughter slain in the strife. Caesar had been right, he surely mused —only fools abdicate and leave themselves naked to their enemies. To complete the irony, the ex-emperor also lived to see the Christians basking in the patronage of Constantine, the prime wrecker of the Tetrarchy. A broken man, Diocletian must have welcomed death when it came, probably in 313.

Despite a fondness for strong drink, Galerius was a capable ruler, but he lacked Diocletian's ability to control the ambitions of colleagues. Under Galerius, the Tetrarchy collapsed in a new round of power struggles; the ultimate victor was Constantius's son, Constantine. Born in the Balkans and poorly educated, Constantine had learned the military arts in frontier wars under Galerius's direction, but he was in effect a hostage at Nicomedia to insure his father's cooperation. In 306 Constantius insisted that Constantine join him in a campaign against Scottish tribes, and Galerius reluctantly allowed the ambitious prince to escape his grasp. Within a few months, the Augustus of the West was dead, and the legions in Britain elevated Constantine as his replacement, but Galerius accepted him only as a Caesar and promoted Severus to be the senior emperor in the West. The luckless Severus soon faced a major revolt at Rome where the populace and the Praetorian Guards resented the ancient capital's eclipse in the new order. Maximian's son, Maxentius, exploited the mood of Rome to seize power in the city, and his father gladly hurried out of retirement to aid him. To gain Constantine as an ally, Maximian presented him with the title of Augustus and his daughter, Fausta, for a wife. Though he already had a son, Crispus, by a concubine, Minervina, Constantine welcomed the marriage with Fausta, but he made no move to assist Maximian and Maxentius, who were more than a match for Severus and had extended their control to Spain and Africa. Unable to retake Rome, Severus surrendered to Maximian and was later murdered. In 307, Galerius too was unable to subdue the rebels, but Maximian quarreled with his son and fled to Constantine in Gaul. In 308 Galerius persuaded Diocletian to restore order by presiding over a conference that established a new Western Augustus, Licinius, who was a friend of Galerius. Constantine and Maximinus Daia were recognized as Caesars, Maxentius was proclaimed a public enemy, and Maximian was ordered back into retirement. Unwilling to abandon his claim as an Augustus, Constantine bided his time and warred successfully against barbarians on the Rhine. In 310 his troublesome father-in-law, Maximian, tried to stir up a revolt in Gaul, but the movement collapsed and he committed suicide. While his children by Fausta had imperial blood, Constantine wanted a stronger dynastic base for his ambitions, and he now announced that his father was descended from Claudius II. A divine sanction was added when Constantine claimed that Sol Invictus and the goddess Victoria had appeared to him and promised world dominion and thirty years of power. More earthly support was provided by Licinius who encouraged Constantine to challenge Maxentius. Spain had already defected from Maxentius, and a revolt in Africa further undermined his prestige; the loss of African grain caused food shortages in Rome. While Licinius engaged in a sporadic struggle with Maximinus Daia, Constantine prepared to dispose of Maxentius.

Distracted by the breakdown of the Tetrarchy, Galerius had lost interest in Christians, but his nephew Maximinus Daia was a devout pagan who wished to revive the religious fervor of the masses. Despite Daia's zeal, however, persecution had failed to crush the Christian movement. In 311 Galerius was seriously ill and regretted both the failure of the persecution and its divisive effect on society. On his deathbed, the Eastern Augustus rescinded the persecution and restored universal freedom of religion. Confiscated property was returned to the bishops, and the dying emperor asked Christians to pray for his health. Although Daia continued to harass Christians after Galerius's death, the senior Augustus had revoked the empire-wide persecution that had never had much effect in the West. The struggle between Constantine and Maxentius was purely political, and Maxentius's sole involvement with Christianity was the expulsion of two rival popes from Rome to prevent disorders in the city. In 312 Constantine invaded Italy and marched a small army of veterans to Rome where Maxentius abandoned the walls that had withstood Severus and Galerius. Prestige required a pitched battle outside the city, but Constantine's cavalry won the day and Maxentius and many of his troops died when a pontoon bridge collapsed into the Tiber. Before the battle of the Mulvian Bridge, Constantine had dreamed that he would triumph if his soldiers' shields bore an emblem ⚡ which to Christians was the Greek monogram for Christ and to pagans a solar sign of Sol Invictus. The emblem was used, and Constantine believed that it had brought him victory. Years later, the emperor assured Eusebius that he and "his whole army" had seen a cross over the sun with the words, "Conquer with this," and that he had been honored with a vision of Christ in a dream that night.[17] Whatever the truth, the blend of Christian and pagan solar themes was characteristic of Constantine, who was grateful to the Christian god of battles but had no wish to antagonize pagans.

Occupying Rome, Constantine disbanded the Praetorian Guards, who had backed his opponent, and when he later abolished the *vigiles,* the ancient city was left without a paramilitary police force. In 313 the emperor repaid his debt to the Christian god by granting Christian clergy the exemption from obligatory state service that was enjoyed by pagan priests. At Milan, he and Licinius endorsed the policy of religious toleration proclaimed by Galerius two years earlier. Now married to Constantine's sister Constantia, Licinius clashed with Maximinus Daia and defeated him in battle; the fallen dynast died in flight. To remove any potential rallying points for rebels, Licinius proceeded to exterminate the families of former emperors. His most famous victims were Galerius's widow and her mother, who was Diocletian's wife. Though allied by marriage, the victorious emperors, Constantine and Licinius, were jealous of each other, and quarrels over territorial jurisdiction flared into open warfare. By 316 the two rulers concluded an uneasy truce and divided the empire with Constantine holding the West and Licinius the East. The Caesars of the new order were Constantine's sons, Crispus and Constantine II, and Licinius's infant son. Later, Licinius grew impatient with Christian doctrinal disputes and dismissed the sectarians from his court and army. As the patron of Christianity, Constantine made war against his brother-in-law, who was defeated in 324 in a campaign in which Crispus distinguished himself. Because Constantia pleaded for his life, Licinius was spared, but Constantine soon repented his leniency and had the former emperor strangled. The Roman empire was now in the grip of one man, who believed in dynastic succession and not collegiate rule. Constantine was the sole Augustus and his sons were Caesars; the throne was once again a family affair.

Like Diocletian, Constantine was a firm advocate of an all-powerful state. Unlike Diocletian, however, he favored senators over *equites* and placed members of the aristocracy in high positions. Perhaps this policy was an attempt to placate conservative pagan senators who resented his radical religious views. Under his regime, Roman society became stratified along class and occupational lines approaching a caste system.

[17] Lactantius, who reports the plausible dream of the emblem, knows nothing of this miracle. Even Eusebius admits that the story of the cross in the sky would be unbelievable had he not heard it from the pious old emperor himself. Yet, he made no mention of it in his *Ecclesiastical History* but only in the florid biography of Constantine that was written after the ruler's death.

While there was still some social mobility, many occupations essential to national defense were made hereditary, and evasion of them was a crime. Though favored officials were promoted to senatorial rank, the municipal gentry were tightly locked into their unenviable positions:

> No judge shall attempt to grant exemption from compulsory municipal services to any decurion, nor shall he free anyone from the municipal council by his own judgment. For if any man should be impoverished by a misfortune of such kind that he needs to be assisted, his name must be referred to Our Wisdom, so that an exemption from compulsory municipal services may be granted to him for a limited space of time.[18]

The luckless decurions were also forbidden to escape their duties by joining the clergy. At the bottom of society, the wretched tenant farmers (*coloni*) were reduced to serfdom:

> Any person in whose possession a *colonus* that belongs to another is found, not only shall restore the aforesaid *colonus* to his birth status but also shall assume the capitation tax for this man for the time that he was with him. *Coloni* also who meditate flight must be bound with chains and reduced to a servile condition, so that by virtue of their condemnation to slavery, they shall be compelled to fulfill the duties that befit freemen.[19]

Despite such severe laws, desperate *coloni* continued to run away.

While an expanding web of regulations enmeshed the lower and middle classes, the senatorial class easily avoided its obligations by bribing officials, and the corruption of both judges and administrators was a standing scandal. While Diocletian had relied on spies, Constantine revived the secret police, but they were notoriously corrupt and of little help to him. In repeated edicts, the emperor thundered vainly against the inequities of Roman justice. Even his solicitation of evidence of misconduct only provided new sources of blackmail for informers. The army was easier to control, and Constantine completed the separation of civil and military powers in government. Unlike Diocletian, he distrusted fixed defenses and built an elite mobile force with a major emphasis on cavalry and mercenary specialists. Though silver coins continued to depreciate, Constantine issued a stable gold coinage, but most taxes were collected in kind, and taxation was increased to feed the insatiable appetite of the state. A minor but sizeable item of expense was the emperor's personal fondness for elaborate ceremonials and costly

[18] *Theodosian Code* 12.1.1, trans. Clyde Pharr (Princeton: Princeton University Press, 1952), p. 342.
[19] *Theodosian Code* 5.17.1, trans. Pharr, p. 115.

costumes.[20] His most expensive whim was the conversion of the old city of Byzantium on the Bosporus into a "New Rome," a capital named Constantinople after its patron. Strategic for both trade and war, the city was not far from Diocletian's Nicomedia, and its selection reflected a shift in the empire's center of gravity to the East. To rival old Rome, the new capital was filled with public building and boasted its own Senate, made up largely of social upstarts. Immigrants to the city were lured with cash bequests and a grain dole, and its residents could enjoy public games and horse races in the magnificent Hippodrome. Though dedicated in 330 with both pagan and Christian rites, Constantinople was to be a Christian city symbolic of a new era in Roman history.

The nature of Constantine's private religious beliefs has been the cause of much controversy. A shrewd and practical politician, he had no desire to anger the pagan majority, and he was equivocal in the symbols on his coins and in the support of pagan rites. However, his patronage of Christianity was public policy after 312. Like Aurelian, Constantine had experienced a vision of Sol Invictus, who was also the favored god of his father, Constantius. For a time, he may have confused Christ with the solar deity, but it was Christ whom he credited with the victory at the Mulvian Bridge. It was a time of belief in magic and visions, and Constantine was grateful to the god who had given him victory over his enemies. The emblem ☧ was now on his banners, and crucifixion was abolished as a form of punishment. An uneducated man, Constantine was not interested in the fine points of theology; he was satisfied with Christ as a Lord of Hosts. Probably the organizational strength of the church, as demonstrated by its survival under persecution, also appealed to the emperor, who was a usurper in need of support and appreciated the tenacity of the sect. Another factor was the large Christian population in the domains of his rivals; there were few Christians in the West. At his court, Constantine was surrounded by bishops, and their number and influence increased in Constantinople. As he grew older, his devotion to religion intensified, and he built many churches. In the fourth century, it was common to postpone baptism until late in life, and Constantine delayed the rite until he was on his deathbed, a wise precaution for a politician.

As an emperor and patron of Christianity, Constantine felt free to intervene in church affairs. In 317 the emperor had tried to oblige the Western bishops by persecuting the Donatists in Africa. A puritanical sect, the Donatists insisted that major sins (such as surrendering the Scriptures during persecution) invalidated the efficacy of priests, and

---

[20] Like Hadrian, Constantine affected hair styles. Since the emperor was clean-shaven, beards soon became unfashionable.

Constantine. Rome, Palazzo dei Conservatori. *Alinari—Scala.*

the emperor was aware that the same rigorous logic might be applied against a Christian ruler. After harassing the African heretics for three years, Constantine gave up the persecution and restored freedom of religion. Like Galerius, he had learned the folly of trying to subdue fanatics by force. Pagans were too numerous to be threatened, and the state had need of their services, but Constantine's favoring of Christians undoubtedly stimulated conversions. Because he hoped that Christians would provide a unifying force in his realm, the emperor was furious when Catholics and Arians began quarreling over the relationship between Christ and God the Father, "an unprofitable discussion" in his eyes. To restore order to the Christian community, Constantine convened an ecumenical council at Nicaea in 325 and presided over the opening session. The council's endorsement of the Catholic position reflected the emperor's support of the Western clergy, and he confined clerical privileges to those who accepted the Nicene decision. No doctrinaire theologian, Constantine wanted religious unity at all costs and later refused to back the Catholic champion Athanasius, whom he considered a divisive figure. Though his piety increased with age, the emperor saw himself as head of the church as well as the state, truly God's viceroy on earth. He even claimed to be a bishop for the laity. Such notions were consistent with Roman tradition but potentially dangerous for the church. Constantine set the pattern of Caesaropapism that would characterize the Byzantine world.

The first Christian Roman emperor presided over an empire that was generally secure. His forces repelled a Gothic invasion at the Danube, and large numbers of Sarmatian nomads were admitted as settlers in the Balkans. After her son had become a patron of the church, Constantine's mother, Helena, became a Christian and busied herself with pious acts, including the building of a number of churches. In Palestine, the elderly lady was delighted to find a cross that she was sure was the gibbet on which Jesus had died. Her son was in need of such relics, for he was gravely troubled by domestic tragedies in the imperial family. In 326 the empress Fausta had tried to protect the succession of her own children by destroying Constantine's son by Minervina, Crispus, who was a favorite of Helena. When Fausta denounced Crispus for trying to rape her, the outraged Constantine had him executed, but Helena later convinced the emperor that Fausta had lied, whereupon he had his wife steamed to death in her bath. Grief-stricken over the duplicity of Fausta and the death of his innocent son, Constantine became increasingly suspicious and solicited rumors from informers. At the same time, he craved loyalty and bought the friendship of courtiers with excessive gifts. Despite the execution of Fausta, her sons were still groomed for imperial roles. Constantius II, Constantine II, and Constans served their father as Caesars as did two nephews. In 337 there was danger of war with Persia, and Constantine was planning a campaign in the East when he fell fatally ill. Knowing that he was dying, the emperor decided to risk baptism and received the rite at the hands of an Arian bishop. Like his predecessors, the dead Constantine was made a god by the Senate at Rome, and the Byzantine Church later declared him a saint "equal to the apostles." As a Christian, he hardly qualified for the former honor, nor as a man for the latter.

Lauded by Christian apologists, Constantine was detested by pagans, and his reputation has not been high among modern skeptics. Gibbon sneered:

> He pursued the great object of his ambition through the dark and bloody paths of war and policy; and, after the victory, he abandoned himself without moderation to the abuse of his fortune. . . . As he gradually advanced in the knowledge of truth, he proportionably declined in the practice of virtue.[21]

To Jacob Burckhardt, Constantine was an insincere opportunist, "an egoist robed in purple," who played the role of a Bonaparte for Roman Christianity. Henry Adams saw the emperor "using the Cross as a train of artillery which, to his mind, it was," and compared the patron of

[21] Gibbon, *Decline of the Roman Empire*, II, 310.

Christianity to a modern stockbroker who "merged all uncertain forces into a single trust, which he enormously overcapitalized and forced on the market." [22] Certainly Constantine was a worldly man, bloodspattered like most emperors and impatient with the fine points of theology. Yet he was sincerely in awe of Christian magic and willing to turn his back on a thousand years of pagan tradition. Religiously, Constantine was a revolutionary who put the Roman state under the protection of a new god and into the hands of sectarians. The effect on Rome and subsequent world history was enormous.

THE DARK NIGHT OF THE SOUL

W.H. Auden has aptly dubbed our own time "the age of anxiety," a label that can equally apply to the Late Roman Empire. In the troubled third century, a resident of the Roman empire would have been obtuse not to be anxious, for his world was tumbling down amid wars, rebellions, and inflation. Accordingly, the literature of the time was escapist or religious, and occultism flourished. The shift to otherworldliness was reflected in art as classical realism was gradually abandoned for cruder stylizations. Two famous portraits, the realistic bust of Caracalla and the heavy-featured face of Constantine with his eyes turned heavenward, illustrate the trend in art. In more mundane fields, the evidence of widespread anxiety is overwhelming. Many petitions survive in which despairing provincials begged the emperors for redress of grievances that were never resolved. Rostovtzeff noted the significance of queries put to an oracle in Egypt:

> "Shall I be sold up?" is an inquiry which clearly refers to confiscation of property. The same question is put in a different form, "Is my property to be sold by auction?" Other typical questions are: "Am I to become a beggar?", "Shall I take to flight?", "Shall I become an envoy?", "Am I to become a member of the municipal council?", "Shall my flight come to an end?", "Shall I receive my salary?", and so on. One sees what were the great perils that threatened a man's career. They arose from the interference of the state with the life of the individual. [23]

Appointment as a councillor or an envoy meant financial ruin. Other papyri complain of the ruinous impositions upon the citizenry made by billeted troops. In provinces torn by civil war or exposed to barbarian

---

[22] Henry Adams, *The Education of Henry Adams* (New York: Modern Library, 1931), pp. 478, 479.

[23] Rostovtzeff, *Roman Empire*, I, 479–80.

invasions, numerous coin hoards have been found, mute testimony that wealth could only be saved by burying it in the ground. Of course, the worried men who buried these particular hoards never lived to dig them up again. Life within the empire became intolerable, emperors changed with bewildering frequency, and marauding bands of barbarians penetrated previously safe regions. In the mounting insecurity, the mood of the Roman populace became neurotic, and many men began a mental exodus from an unpleasant reality into worlds of fantasy.

Except for philosophy, most of the literature of the third century was second-rate. In the Severan era, an Asian senator, Cassius Dio, wrote a competent history of Rome in Greek, celebrating the achievements of the remote Republic and endorsing the authoritarian state as a historical necessity. Characteristically, Dio began his writing career with a pamphlet on the dreams and portents that foretold the glory of Septimius Severus. Like Livy, Dio was obsessed with omens, but he was an eyewitness to important events under Commodus and the Severi. Much inferior to Dio and prone to inflated rhetoric was a Syrian civil servant, Herodian, who composed a history in Greek of the emperors from Commodus to Maximinus Thrax. A better historian, the aristocratic Dexippus of Athens, wrote on Hellenistic and Roman history to 270, but his works survive only in fragments. A man of action as well as letters, Dexippus helped to defend Attica against the Goths; Polybius would have approved of him. Whatever the merits of Greek historians, Latin historiography was feebly represented by a Severan senator, Marius Maximus, who imitated Suetonius and recounted court scandals from Nerva to Elagabalus; his work was an important source for the infamous *Historia Augusta*. The taste of the time also ran to digests, usually compiled by Greeks. Valuable fragments of lost writers were preserved by Diogenes Laertius, who wrote an inept biographical history of philosophy. Athenaeus of Naucratis assembled a collection of quotations on dining and luxury as well as occasionally more important topics. Animals and historical anecdotes interested Aelian who, though an Italian, wrote in Greek. Fiction was extremely popular, the more escapist the better, and the most famous Greek novels were written in this period. With great charm, Longus described the rustic romance of Daphnis and Chloe, a minor masterpiece of pastoralism indebted to Hellenistic models. Unlike Longus, Heliodorus in his *Aethiopica* emphasized melodrama and improbable adventures in far-off lands. In the works of Heliodorus and his second-century predecessors, Chariton and Achilles Tatius, incredibly beautiful and chaste heroines were frequently at the mercy of lecherous villains who threatened them with torture if they resisted amorous advances. The themes of attempted rape and sadism added a tone of morbid eroticism to these novels that not

only titillated general readers but also excited some Christians to emulate the martyrs of romance. A readable blend of fiction and fact was
provided by Philostratus's biography of Apollonius of Tyana, which
was filled with miracles, trips to strange lands, and edifying encounters
of the sage with the tyrants, Nero and Domitian. Widely read, the book
was written at the urging of Julia Domna, who realized the propaganda
value of Apollonius as an apostle of solar henotheism. Later, in the bitter struggle against Christianity, pagans invoked Philostratus's tract to
show that polytheism had saints as appealing as Jesus.

An interesting passage in a work of literary criticism, traditionally
attributed to Longinus, reflects the burden that imperial tyranny imposed on intellectuals:

> In our own day, we learn righteous slavery as children, we are all but
> swaddled in its customs and practices while our minds are still tender; we
> have never tasted of the most beautiful and most creative spring of lan-
> guage. By this, I mean freedom, and so we turn out to have no genius ex-
> cept for flattery. . . . As in the case of the dwarfs whom we call Pygmies,
> not only do the cages in which they are kept stunt their growth, but their
> bonds, if I am rightly informed, actually make their bodies shrink; so
> slavery of every kind, even the best, could be shown to be the cage and
> common prisonhouse of the soul.[24]

Modern critics have preferred to assign this tract to an unknown writer
of the first century A.D. It is not impossible, however, that an archaizing
savant like Longinus wrote it. If he is the author, Longinus may have
hoped for greater freedom at Zenobia's court than he could expect
under Aurelian's heavy hand. At any rate, the image of the artificial
dwarfs fits the intelligentsia of any authoritarian regime.

Except in mathematics,[25] the scientific thought of late antiquity was
undistinguished, though it is unfair to label the era as one of decline.
Rather, scientists coasted on their oars after the successful syntheses of
Galen and Ptolemy. The interests of intellectuals turned from nature to
supernatural matters. Since there had never been any serious conflict
between science and religion, scientists acquiesced in the drift toward
occultism, unaware that one day religious zealots would attack science
as sinful. Long before Christian fanatics launched a frontal assault, ancient science had fatally embraced the occult. Magic was widely practiced by intellectuals who sought to master an unpleasant present by re-

---

[24] Longinus *On the Sublime* 44, trans. G. M. Grube (Indianapolis: Bobbs-Merrill,
1957), p. 57.
[25] Alexandria boasted such able mathematicians as Diophantus in the third century
and Pappus in the fourth; the former used techniques similar to algebra.

viving the techniques of a primitive past. Through theurgy, gods and demons were invoked to foretell the future or work parlor tricks. Inextricably intertwined with astronomy, astrology shifted its emphasis from material effluences from the stars to the notion of personalities in the heavens. Once almost abstractions, the planetary gods became malevolent demons who were accessible to prayers and might be controlled by magic rites. The pervasive pessimism of the age combined with a dualism ultimately derived from Platonism to downgrade matter into something evil, and those men who wished to master or understand matter became magicians in spite of themselves. The occultizing of science trapped chemistry in the bog of alchemy and left it in the hands of fantasts and charlatans. Though indifferent to science in general, the Roman state took a dim view of alchemists who could change the appearance of metal and might be allied with counterfeiters. Probably for this reason, Diocletian confiscated and burned alchemical texts in Egypt. The Roman book burning came too late to prevent the spread of the *Revelations of Hermes Trismegistus,* a bizarre collection of theosophical works that were heavily laced with astrology and alchemy and purported to be the "secret wisdom" of ancient Egypt. Immensely popular with intellectual dabblers who wished to "penetrate behind the veil of mystery," the Hermetic texts sanctified silliness with exotic names and debased science in the interest of a pompous superstition.

In most societies, formalistic religion serves a useful function, providing a sense of social solidarity and continuity with the past. In troubled times, however, men need the gods on a personal level, interceding to avert disaster or at least supplying bliss in another life. Though the evidence is fragmentary, it appears that mystery cults partially eclipsed the old gods of the Greco-Roman world, although the ancient deities still received state support, and neglect of a god by polytheists does not imply disbelief. The mystery religions promised immediate contact with the divine and immortality for the initiated, and their appeal was great among uprooted individuals, such as soldiers, merchants, and the floating population of large cities. Impotent and insecure in ordinary life, the initiate through his cult had direct access to forces that controlled the universe; he was privy to mysteries denied to outsiders, and he had the enormous satisfaction of belonging to the elect. Since admission to a mystery cult guaranteed immortality, initiates were usually charged a fee, a small price for such a boon. The widespread cult of Isis combined the aura of the exotic with the appeal of a maternal figure. Her closest rival was the Great Mother, Cybele, whose consort Attis was annually castrated and killed but rose again, a symbol of vernal rebirth. By late antiquity, the cult of the Great Mother had incorporated a spectacular rite, the *taurobolium,* in which a worshiper was drenched with the

Isis, holding an Egyptian ritual
rattle and a jar of water from the
Nile. Rome, Museo Capitolino.
Alinari—Scala.

blood of a freshly slain bull. A less expensive version of the ritual featured the sacrifice of a ram. The redemptive power of blood was also an
aspect of the most successful mystery cult, Christianity, the members of
which were figuratively "washed in the blood of the Lamb."

While the cults of Isis and Cybele celebrated mother goddesses, one
of the most famous mystery cults featured a masculine deity, Mithras,
and limited its membership to males. Once an Aryan solar god in Iran,
Mithras had survived Zoroastrian downgrading and resurfaced in grand
style in the Arsacid era. Though the god preserved Persian dress, his
cult reached the West and was popular among Cilician pirates in the
first century B.C. Slowly spreading through the cities and garrisons of
the Roman empire, Mithraism was a flourishing religion in late antiquity
and especially popular among soldiers and merchants. The initiates of
Mithras were promised eternal bliss in the afterlife. Here on earth, they
were organized in a hierarchical religious order, observed a strict moral
code, and conducted ceremonies that included a baptism, a sacred supper, and the revelation of mysteries. From garbled literary allusions and
iconography, the outline of the Mithraic myth can be discerned. Born
from a rock, the god was a rainmaker who pursued and slew a heavenly
bull that probably represented an animal form of Mithras himself. At a
divine banquet, the sun paid Mithras homage and absorbed part of his
divinity by eating a portion of the bull. The Mithraic ceremonies imitated episodes in the myth. So much did some elements in Mithraism

resemble Christian rites that outraged Christians were sure that demons had concocted the cult to parody "the true faith." However, the similarities were only the common property of many religions. Some moderns have felt that Mithraism was a serious rival to Christianity, but a cult confined to males could hardly hope to become the dominant religion of any society.

Mithraism was not the only spiritual product of Persia to reach the Roman empire, for a world religion, Manicheism, emerged from the Sassanid realm in the third century. During the Zoroastrian revival, the pessimism of the time infected the dualism of Zarathustra by emphasizing the dominance of evil in the world. True believers could be sure that the good god, Ahura Mazda, would eventually triumph in the universe, but for the time being the earth lay in bondage to the evil spirit, Ahriman, and the followers of Ahura Mazda had a difficult struggle before them. This tilting of dualism in favor of darkness and evil reflected a contempt for matter that characterized the gnostic mood of the Middle East in the early centuries of the Christian era. About 242, a Syriac-speaking native of Mesopotamia, Mani, announced that he was the last of the great prophets and had been sent to restore the true teachings of Zarathustra, the Buddha, and Jesus which had been corrupted by their followers. The creed of Mani transcended all national boundaries and superseded all religions. Despite the legend that Shapur favored Mani, it is unlikely that the great conqueror had any interest in the unworldly prophet. To the Magi, Mani was a heretic and they martyred him about 276, but devoted missionaries carried his message to the Roman empire and later to China. According to Mani, the world lay in darkness and was ruled by demonic forces, but the human soul was a particle of light yearning to be reunited to the original heaven of light from which it had fallen eons ago. At times, the high god of light sent divine messengers to try to liberate the particles. The messenger Jesus had almost rescued Adam by persuading him to taste the Tree of Knowledge, but the forces of evil devised Eve and recaptured mankind. To Manicheans, sex was always the ally of darkness. Later, Jesus returned to earth and was again foiled by the demons, but they only crucified his phantom on Calvary. At last, Mani was sent to show the true path of redemption through a spiritual elite of celibate saints, who avoided sex and meat and liberated light particles by eating vegetables in which souls were trapped. To support the saints, a lesser order of "hearers" were allowed to live more mundane lives, after which they would be reborn as the elect. The ascetic regimen of the saints appealed to neurotic personalities, and the missionary zeal of Manicheans gave the religion considerable momentum. Conservative Romans disdained it as a Persian superstition, and Diocletian briefly harassed Manicheans as probable subversives. However, the creed of Mani attracted guilt-ridden individuals such as Augustine, and its appeal as a universal church was strong among some urban dwellers. Yet, Mani had arrived too late on the historical scene, and Christianity had preempted much of his potential following. The severity of Manichean life was too demanding for most Romans or Persians, and the dominance of bishops in the Christian Roman empire made the Manichean saints unwelcome in the West. Ironically, Manichean tenets reappeared in the Byzantine world among the Paulicians and Bogomils.

Common to the mystery cults and to Manicheism was an overwhelming syncretism, a blending of ideas, deities, and rituals from various religious sources. Some themes were almost omnipresent, such as mystic numbers: the seven seals of the *Apocalypse of John,* the seven stages of the Mithraic fraternity, the seven metals of the alchemists, the seven planetary demons who were the "archons of the age." In the major pagan cults, it was common for the cult deity to absorb competing gods,

A syncretic relief from Modena, depicting the Orphic god of light and creation, Phanes, standing in the cosmic egg, surrounded by the Zodiac and the four winds. Sometimes, the evil spirit of Zoroastrianism, Ahriman, is shown similarly with the serpent about his body, and this icon may have some Mithraic significance, for more than one sect used it. Modena, Galeria Estense. *Galeria Estense.* Photo: *Thames and Hudson.*

and Isis became a divine force lying behind all other divinities, at least to her followers. Similar claims were made for the ersatz Ptolemaic god, Sarapis, whose great temple, the Serapeum, was one of the main tourist attractions at Alexandria. Politically, the trend toward syncretism encouraged henotheism, the elevation of one god to dominate the pantheon. After the fiasco of Elagabalus, the sun god of Emesa, Elagabal, found favor with Aurelian and ruled the Roman heaven as Sol Invictus. Soldiers who joined the Mithraic cult simply blended the two gods into Mithras Sol Invictus. Constantine had visions of both Sol Invictus and Christ and probably confused the two. From the notion that all gods were aspects of one deity, the step was more easily made to Christian monotheism, though it was difficult for many Romans to accept the intolerant exclusiveness of the new creed. For pagan intellectuals, the concept of one god behind the myriad cults was a philosophical commonplace. Yet it was the intelligentsia who most stubbornly resisted the rigidity of monotheism and clung to old gods and rites.

The triumph of religiosity over reason was illustrated in the evolution of Neoplatonism, the last important philosophic development in ancient thought. By blending rationalism and mysticism, the Neoplatonists bridged the gulf between the limited world of science and reason and the boundless, timeless realm of the occult. Across that bridge, wise men moved slowly and hesitantly, but fools and fantasts scurried pellmell. While it emphasized the mystic elements in Plato's thought, Neoplatonism was actually a blend of many philosophic trends. In the second century, the Neopythagorean mystic Numenius had insisted that mortals could communicate with the divine through meditation:

> One must withdraw far from the things of sense and enter into solitary communion with the Good, where is no human being nor any other creature nor body great or small, but only a kind of divine desolation which in truth cannot be spoken of or described, where . . . the Good itself [is] at rest with peace and friendliness, the Sovereign Principle riding serene above the tides of Being.[26]

The influence of Numenius's writings on Neoplatonists was so great that critics accused Plotinus of plagiarizing his works. However, Plotinus was an intellect of the first rank and, though eclectic, was no plagiarist. Early in the third century, he studied at Alexandria under the saintly Ammonius Saccas, a former Christian turned pagan, whose other pupils included Origen and Longinus. Hoping to visit India, Plotinus joined

---

[26] Eusebius *Praeparatio Evangelica* 11.2, trans. E. R. Dodds, *Pagan and Christian in an Age of Anxiety* (Cambridge: Cambridge University Press, 1965), pp. 93–94.

the Persian expedition of Gordian III but was forced to return home when the emperor died. Moving to Rome, he became a renowned teacher of philosophy and won the favor of Gallienus, who promised to rebuild a ruined Pythagorean town in Campania as a city of sages, Platonopolis, but nothing came of the plan. By 270 the great philosopher was dead, but a disciple, Porphyry, edited his hastily-written essays. Unlike many of his contemporaries, Plotinus disdained astrology and magic and opposed the gnostic notion that the material world was evil. A pantheist of sorts, he was prone to mystic experiences. In Porphyry's words:

> Good and kindly, singularly gentle and engaging . . . pure of soul, ever striving toward the divine which he loved with all his being, he labored strenuously to free himself and rise above the bitter waves of this blood-drenched life; and that is why to Plotinus . . . that God appeared . . . four times during the period that I passed with him.[27]

Like Numenius and Pascal, Plotinus had found what he sought in the "divine desolation."

Although mystic ecstasies are indescribable, Plotinus attempted to communicate what sometimes happened after prolonged contemplation of the ultimate divine reality:

> Many times it has happened: lifted out of the body into myself; becoming external to all other things and self-encentered; beholding a marvellous beauty; then, more than ever, assured of community with the loftiest order; enacting the noblest life, acquiring identity with the divine; stationing within It by having attained that activity; poised above whatsoever within the Intellectual is less than the Supreme; yet, there comes the moment of descent from intellection to reasoning, and after that sojourn in the divine, I ask myself how it happens that I can now be descending.
> . . . The vision baffles telling. . . . There were not two; beholder was one with the beheld; it was not a vision compassed but a unity apprehended. The man formed by this mingling with the Supreme must—if he only remember—carry its image impressed upon him; he is become the Unity, nothing within him or without inducing any diversity; no movement now, no passion, no outlooking desire, once this ascent is achieved; reasoning is in abeyance and all Intellection and even, to dare the word, the very self; caught away, filled with God, he has in perfect stillness attained isolation; all the being calmed, he turns neither to this side nor to that, not even inwards to himself; utterly resting, he has become very rest. He belongs no longer to the order of the beautiful; he has risen beyond beauty; he has overpassed even the choir of the virtues; he is like

[27] Porphyry *vita Plotini* 23, trans. Stephen MacKenna, *Plotinus' Enneads,* 3d ed. (London: Faber & Faber, 1962), p. 17.

one who, having penetrated the inner sanctuary, leaves the temple images behind him. . . . It was a going forth from the self, a simplifying, a renunciation, a reach toward contact and at the same time a repose, a meditation towards adjustment.[28]

Such extraordinary experiences would confirm any philosophy. On the other hand, the ecstatic bliss of the mystic resembles the contentment of infancy with its untroubled rest and lack of definition of self. Though obstinately reticent about his childhood, Plotinus told Porphyry that he still suckled the breasts of his nurse at the age of eight.

In Porphyry, Plotinus had a worthy disciple who in old age also achieved a mystic experience. A brilliant but neurotic scholar from Tyre, Porphyry had studied under Longinus at Athens before becoming the devoted aide of Plotinus. Despite the serene presence of Plotinus, he was prone to suicidal longings, but he busied himself in work. A prolific writer on many topics, Porphyry was an able polemicist, defending both vegetarianism and the ancient gods. To confound Christians, he carefully studied the Old and New Testaments, pounced on contradictions, and realized that the *Book of Daniel* was a product of the era of Antiochus IV. With similar acumen, Porphyry detected some pagan texts as late forgeries. However, he accepted magic and oracles on principle and was enthusiastic over theurgy. In his eyes, the gods were benevolent daimons provided by God for simple folk who could not join Plotinus in the stratosphere of philosophy. Porphyry's disciple, Iamblichus, completed the intellectual shoring-up of paganism. A Syrian theosophist of middling intelligence, Iamblichus responded to the Christian triumph under Constantine with a counterblast of gullible fanaticism, defending any pagan absurdity and accepting the claims of all theurgists. Enlisting the sages of the past in the pagan cause, he portrayed Pythagoras and other philosophers as wizards and cast an aura of shamanism over much ancient thought. Within three generations, Neoplatonism had degenerated into a creed where philosophy was invoked to defend quackery and superstition, and learned men seriously attended seances and displays of parlor magic.

When faced with danger or an unpleasant situation, it is natural for animals to flee, and men have often reacted to troubled times with flights into unreality. "Things fall apart; the center cannot hold," wrote Yeats, "Surely some revelation is at hand." In the third century, simple men groveled before idols or sought admission into mystery cults. Intellectuals, too, tried to elude an unbearable reality by escaping into fantasy. The tidal flow into religiosity is aptly described by E.R. Dodds:

[28] Plotinus *Enneads* 4.8.1; 6.9.10–11, trans. MacKenna, pp. 357, 624.

As Festugière has rightly said, "misery and mysticism are related facts."
From a world so impoverished intellectually, so insecure materially, so
filled with fear and hatred as the world of the third century, any path that
promised escape must have attracted serious minds. . . . The entire culture, pagan as well as Christian, was moving into a phase in which religion was to be coextensive with life, and the quest for God was to cast its
shadow over all other human activities.[29]

Under the Christian Roman empire, this intellectual revolution was
brought to completion.

[29] Dodds, *Pagan and Christian,* pp. 100–1.

CHAPTER NINE

The Christian Revolution

And what rough beast, its hour come round at last,
Slouches towards Bethlehem to be born?

W. B. Yeats

*T*he conversion of Constantine was a revolutionary event. By gaining control of the emperor, Christians dominated the center of power in the Roman state and maintained it under his successors, all but one of whom were Christians. The Late Roman Empire was a Christian society, despite the importance of individual pagans and the fact that the majority of the population was pagan in the early fourth century. When the century ended, pagans were an embattled minority, and the Christian church was inextricably linked with the Roman state. Like all revolutions, the triumph of Christianity meant a change of personnel in positions of power and prestige. Being ideological in nature, the revolution altered society by requiring specific beliefs in matters of religion, a notion new to Roman life. In everyday morality, nothing changed, for the Roman people were no better or worse as Christians than they had been as pagans. However, the ideological emphasis on the overriding importance of the next world slowly changed men's habits of thought. Heresy became a matter of concern for the state, and society accepted with approval activities such as asceticism and monasticism that were antithetical to traditional Roman mores. Gradually, the City of Man lost ground to the City of God. Naturally, Christian statesmen did not cease the pursuit and enjoyment of power, nor did laymen display any lack of enthusiasm for pleasure and profit, but society agreed unanimously that the interests of the soul were paramount when a conflict with secular matters arose. Pagan or Christian, the Roman state always tried to win the favor of Heaven, but the ancient gods were primarily concerned with rites and were indifferent to the private regions of the mind. The Christian god, however, was a jealous deity, and his servants pried into men's consciences. Christian rulers paid heed to

325

plotting bishops and raving fakirs, whom the Caesars of old would have scorned.

In many respects, the history of Christianity in antiquity follows a paradigm that is common to many religions. Its founder was a charismatic prophet, critical of an established religion and opposed by its priests. Dead, the prophet was deified by his followers and his message was expanded by other personalities. To survive, the struggling sect acquired an administrative elite who led it through factional strife and periods of persecution. Eventually, the church became a highly organized and socially acceptable body, run by priests and hostile to prophets and critics. Specifically, Christianity began as a radical Jewish heresy, became a mystery cult suspect to the authorities, slowly acquired respectability, and developed into a hierarchical corporation that made a fitting partner to the Roman state. As Socrates would have been silenced in Plato's Republic, so Jesus would not have fared well under the church triumphant. Successful revolutionaries have no tolerance for dissenters. Yet the image of the anticlerical preacher, Jesus the disturber of the status quo, could not be erased from Christianity, no matter how splendid and unreal theologians made the deified Christ. The dichotomy between organizational Christianity and Christian radicalism gave the evolution of the church a schizoid quality. Not only did worldly success result in a deep sense of guilt, but unruly saints became an embarrassment to the episcopate, for they were too reminiscent of Jesus the man.

Of the world's major religions, Christianity is one of the best documented in terms of historical development. Although the Gospels are very shaky sources, the Pauline epistles and much of the New Testament give valuable insights into the mentality of the second generation of Christians. By Hellenistic standards, the *Acts of the Apostles* is not a bad work despite its artificial speeches and glossing over controversies. A propaganda tract aimed at Roman readers, *Acts* is based in part on the memoirs of a companion of Paul, but the author of *Acts* gives three contradictory versions of Paul's traumatic vision on the road to Damascus, and he may have been ignorant of the Pauline letters or deliberately suppressed evidence. In the second and third centuries, an increasing body of Christian literature throws light on the church and its problems, and pagan observers provide a different point of view. The bedrock of church history is the *Ecclesiastical History* of Constantine's friend Eusebius, who had a bishop's bias but quoted documents and authors whose works no longer survive. His successors in antiquity were lesser historians, but moderns have created a massive scholarly literature that is extremely valuable on textual and historical problems but often sectarian in interpretation. To view church history in the light of later religious disputes in medieval and modern times is an approach that Livy and his predecessors would have approved, but anachronistic notions only obscure the role of Christianity in antiquity.

A SHOOT FROM JESSE, A STAR OUT OF JACOB

Christianity originated as a protest movement within Judaism, which itself had evolved from protests against the ancient Canaanite cults of the Hebrew kingdoms. In impassioned poetry, the prophets had denounced idols, orgies, and human sacrifice and remodeled the national deity, Yahweh, into a universal god. Eventually, he became the only god. A strong theme of social criticism against despotic government and the unfeeling rich ran through much of the prophetic literature, and some militant groups advocated pastoralism and puritanism as the only fit environment for a pious people. Sanctified with the aura of the legendary lawgiver Moses, the religion of the prophets was accepted by some later rulers of Judah. After the fall of the Judean kingdom and the sojourn of some Hebrews in Babylonia, a theocratic state was established at Jerusalem under the protection of the Persian empire. The priests who controlled the temple state intensified the rigidity of "Mosaic" law with dietary prohibitions, ritual demands, and exclusive attitudes toward gentiles. The bond with the national god was viewed as a covenant between Yahweh and his chosen people, who were obligated to obey the conglomeration of laws that made up the way of life which is Judaism. The emphasis on ceremonialism and legalism overwhelmed the message of the prophets whose major thrust had been ethical, and some later books of the Old Testament express an anticlerical tone that hearkened back to Amos. Another secular note was added by nationalists who yearned for a revival of the Davidic monarchy. As Judaism tried to maintain a precarious balance between clericalism and the prophetic tradition, the religion was subject to considerable cultural influence from its neighbors. From the Zoroastrian Persians, the Jews absorbed a populous demonology replete with a prince of evil, Satan, and the notion of an afterlife in which men would be rewarded or punished for their deeds on earth. When Greek rule supplanted Persian domination of the Near East, Hellenistic skepticism and cosmopolitanism influenced many Jews in both Palestine and the far-spread communities of the Diaspora. Alexandria had a large Jewish population, and the translation of the Hebrew scriptures into Greek in Ptolemaic Egypt reflected the degree to which Diaspora Jews had lost touch with traditional Judaism.

Eroded by the cosmopolitan trends of the Hellenistic age, Judaism was suddenly reinvigorated when Antiochus IV foolishly intruded into the religious and personal squabbles of the Hellenist and conservative factions at Jerusalem. Assuming that all Jews were as "liberal" as the Hellenists, the king tried to transform Yahweh into a form of Zeus and established pagan rites in the Temple in 167. When conservative Jews opposed the new policy, they were harshly dealt with by Seleucid authorities. In the countryside, resistance erupted under the leadership of the Hasmonean family, whose chief, Judas Maccabeus, was practical enough to fight on the sabbath. By 164, the Seleucid government revoked its policy, and the Maccabean forces celebrated the cleansing of the Temple with the first Hanukkah. The brief persecution had awakened a new militancy in conservative Jews who soon ousted the Hellenists from control of Jerusalem. When the Seleucid kingdom was torn by dynastic strife, the brothers of Judas Maccabeus established themselves as heads of the Palestinian state "until a true prophet should arise." Though they skillfully won independence for their tiny nation and protection through a Roman alliance, the Hasmonean priest-kings were primarily Hellenistic despots, concerned with power and territorial expansion. John Hyrcanus subdued the Samaritans, and his brutal son, Alexander Jannaeus, conquered Galilee and various Greek cities on the coast and across the Jordan.

A bitter civil war between the sons of Jannaeus prompted Roman intervention. In 63 B.C. Pompey abolished the Judean monarchy but retained Hyrcanus II as high priest and ethnarch of Judea. The power behind Hyrcanus was a shrewd Arab, Antipater, who brought aid to Caesar at Alexandria and later provided funds for Cassius. Antipater's son Herod was a protégé of Antony, who set him up as king of Judea after Hyrcanus had been overthrown by a Parthian invasion. Despite Cleopatra's hostility, Herod kept Antony's favor until Actium, after which the king switched his allegiance to Augustus. Able and ruthless, Herod taxed his subjects heavily and rebuilt the Temple on a grand scale. He also subsidized the Olympic Games and was popular with the Greeks under his rule. The high priests were royal appointees, and rabbis who criticized Herod's lapses from Judaic law were slain. When the king executed members of his own family who had plotted against him, Augustus quipped that he would rather be Herod's pig than his son. On Herod's death in 4 B.C., Augustus divided Palestine among three of the king's sons. Judea went to Archelaus, who proved so inept that the emperor deposed him in A.D. 6 and made the region a Roman province. The new status of Judea occasioned a famous census. Although other parts of Palestine were ruled by Herodian princes, the Roman presence was evident everywhere, and the governor kept a wary eye on the Jews from his coastal headquarters at Caesarea.

The Maccabean revolt had unleashed intense religious feelings that did not abate under long years of Hasmonean misrule and Herodian tyranny. Far more than their coreligionists of the Diaspora, the Jews of Palestine were dominated by rigid conservatives who clung to the Law and castigated backsliders. Discredited by the episode of Antiochus IV, the Hellenist faction receded in Palestine, which became a stronghold of narrow religiosity. Originating in the "Pure" (*Hasidim*) followers of Judas Maccabeus, the Pharisees insisted on a strict interpretation of the Law and fretted over its obscurities and fine points. This concern prompted careful attention to the scriptures and the commentaries of distinguished teachers or rabbis, whose prestige often rivaled that of the priesthood. Due to Pharisaic obsession with the written law, village schools flourished and a limited knowledge of the scriptures was available to any intelligent layman. No doubt many Pharisees were nitpicking legalists for whom the letter of the Law killed its spirit, but others managed to transcend a literal and stifling creed. Under Herod, the famed rabbi Hillel observed that the whole Law was contained in the injunction to love one's neighbor—"all else is commentary." Another great Pharisee, Saul's teacher Gamaliel, opposed the persecution of Christians. While the Pharisees were the most popular sect, their rivals, the Sadducees, wielded great influence among the upper classes and dominated the priesthood. Unlike the Pharisees, the Sadducees sneered at angels and immortality, and some suggested that the awesome Yahweh permitted mankind a measure of free will. Damned by their critics as worldly and lax, the Sadducees represented an older and less rigorous type of Judaism, but there is no reason to question their sincerity. When Pompey took Jerusalem in 63 B.C., Sadducee priests refused to interrupt the Temple services and were cut down at the altar. No Maccabean fanatic could ask for a greater proof of devotion.

Whatever their faults, the Hasmonean and Herodian kings provided security for the upper classes, who also accepted the alien rule of Rome as a bulwark of law and order. Less able to satisfy the greed of kings and publicans, the poverty-stricken masses resented the established order, whether native or Roman, and turned to wishful hopes for liberation and vengeance on their oppressors. In an earlier time, the prophet Joel had promised that, before the Day of the Lord when Yahweh would rescue his people,

> your sons and your daughters shall prophesy,
> your old men shall dream dreams,
> and your young men shall see visions.[1]

Apocalyptic fancies permeated Hasmonean and Roman Palestine as discontented elements dreamed of a miraculous savior, who would descend

[1] Joel 2.28.

with armies of angels to smite the rulers of the earth and establish an invincible empire of Israel. A Maccabean document, the *Book of Daniel,* had depicted a favored agent of Yahweh, the Son of Man, who would rout the heathen, and the *Apocalypse of Enoch* further described his imminent arrival and the terrors of the awful Day of the Lord. To many Jews, the national savior would be a Davidic prince, the Messiah or "Anointed One," a king in his own right but aided by the hosts of heaven. Centuries earlier, Isaiah had hoped for a king of Judah, "a shoot from Jesse," under whom the poor and the meek would receive justice, and peace would prevail.[2] Probably the bliss of the coming reign was only flattery for King Hezekiah, but Isaiah's hyperboles were incorporated into the wishful fantasies of the Messianic age. Other colorful tales congealed about the imminent savior—"He who is coming." The prophet Elijah would first return to announce the arrival of the Messiah, whose formal appearance would be accompanied with great cataclysms of nature and horrendous slaughters of his enemies. Only a saving remnant, those Jews who *really* kept the covenant, would be spared to enjoy the new Israel and lord it over other nations. The greater the national despair and the more hopeless the reality of resistance to Rome, the more brightly burned the apocalyptic dream. Psychologically, the Messiah was a paranoid delusion shared by a society, a wish figure of power and revenge conjured up to compensate for frustration and humiliation. Socially, the Messianic expectation provided hope for resistance movements and consolation for the downtrodden, who believed that soon the sun would darken and the Messiah would arrive to confound their enemies. Ironically, the notion of the imminent Day of the Lord and the appearance of the Messiah gave rise to a new religion that would prove a bane to Jews.

So repellent was the existing order that some ultrapharisaic Jews rejected not only the world but their own coreligionists and withdrew into desert communities where they lived ascetic lives and prepared for the Day of the Lord. These groups, the Essenes, viewed themselves as the "saving remnant" of Israel and cherished the writings of a mysterious prophet, the Teacher of Righteousness, who had been persecuted by the "wicked priest" (probably a Hasmonean king). The Essene order was hierarchical, and the elect practiced monastic communism. Some rigorists even embraced celibacy, unusual among Judaic puritans since Hebraic tradition considered fertility a blessing from God. Yet the author of the *Wisdom of Solomon* had taken an unorthodox view on sex:

> Blessed is the barren woman who is undefiled,
> who has not entered into a sinful union;

[2] Isaiah 11.1–9.

> she will have fruit when God examines souls.
> Blessed also is the eunuch whose hands have done no lawless
> deed,
> and who has not devised wicked things against the Lord;
> for special favor will be shown him for his faithfulness,
> and a place of great delight in the temple of the Lord. . . .
> For the end of an unrighteous generation is grievous.
> Better than this is childlessness with virtue.[3]

While the lesser orders of Essenes did not abandon marriage or property, all were conscious of belonging to a unique and favored community.

The Teacher of Righteousness had set the tone for the Essene movement:

> My eyes have gazed on that which is eternal,
> on wisdom concealed from men,
> on knowledge and wise design (hidden) from the sons of men;
> on a fountain of righteousness
> and on a storehouse of power,
> on a spring of glory (hidden) from the assembly of flesh.
> God has given them to His chosen ones
> as an everlasting possession,
> and he caused them to inherit
> the lot of the Holy Ones.
> He has joined their assembly to the Sons of Heaven
> to be a Council of the Community,
> a foundation of the Building of Holiness,
> an eternal Plantation throughout all ages to come.[4]

While only the Essene Council was equal to the Sons of God, all Essenes could do the Lord's will. Though outside observers considered Essenes to be pacifists, the Dead Sea Scrolls reveal the community at Qumran as highly militant and eager to wage war against the Children of Darkness, in particular the legions of Kittim (Rome). Although some of this literature is prophetic rhetoric, there is also concern for practical military affairs such as combat order and sanitation, and magic slogans are prescribed to be written on banners and weapons. The Qumran Essenes were preparing to do battle on the Day of the Lord, and in this fervor they perished in the great revolt of A.D. 66–70. Except for the advocacy of violence, many Essene themes appear in early Christianity, and it would be odd if the Essene sect had no influence on Jesus.

[3] Wisdom of Solomon 3.13–14, 19; 4.1.
[4] *Qumran Community Rule,* XI, trans. G. Vermes, *The Dead Sea Scrolls in English* (Baltimore: Penguin Books, 1962), pp. 92–93.

To the Romans, the Jews were a strange people with bizarre customs and narrow-minded doctrines. Philosophers smiled at the arrogance of monotheism, and pious pagans resented the notion that their cherished deities were "false gods." In 139 B.C. the Senate had expelled Jewish missionaries from Rome, and the emperor Tiberius reacted to a scandal involving Jewish swindlers by ousting a number of Jews from the capital. Perhaps the anti-Semitic Sejanus was behind the action. In A.D. 49 Claudius expelled some Jews who were quarreling over "Chrestus." However, the Roman empire was not intolerant in religious matters if only because it had no desire to stir up hostilities in the provinces. The state tried to suppress Druidism in Gaul because it encouraged rebels, but the official charge was human sacrifice, which also prompted the suppression of a cult in North Africa. Diocletian's edict against the Manicheans was prompted by the erroneous fear that they were Persian spies. As for Jews, the attitude of Rome was indulgent toward a venerable and widespread religion. Both Caesar and Augustus favored the Jews, and the latter exempted them from the imperial cult. In return, prayers for the emperor were offered daily in the Temple at Jerusalem. Throughout the empire, Jews suffered no disabilities, and in Alexandria, they wielded considerable power. The most renowned of Alexandrian Jewish intellectuals was the philosopher Philo, who sought to reconcile the Torah and Plato and subjected the scriptures to allegorical interpretations. At times, quarrels between Jews and Greeks in Alexandria erupted into violence, but Claudius enforced the rights of Jews after a bloody anti-Semitic riot. Amid the various fads for exotic cults at Rome, Judaism won few converts, but it did attract sympathizers, including Nero's empress, Poppaea.

In Palestine, Roman governors ruled with a heavy hand, but most carefully avoided offending the religious sensibilities of the local populace. While the priesthood and the upper classes supported Rome, the masses seethed with discontent, and Messianic pretenders had little difficulty gathering a following. The Roman authorities dealt harshly with such "brigands," and Pontius Pilate, who ruled Judea from 26 to 36, was particularly brutal. The tragedy of Jesus was only a minor episode during Pilate's troubled governorship. After repeated complaints to Rome, Pilate was recalled by Tiberius and exiled to Gaul by Caligula. When Caligula wished to install a statue of himself in the Temple, the Roman authorities procrastinated until the tactless emperor was dead, and there was no need to execute an order that would have provoked a major revolt. In 41, Claudius restored the Judean monarchy and bestowed it on his friend, Herod Agrippa, a grandson of Herod the Great. A colorful opportunist whose checkered career is described by Josephus, Herod Agrippa was a highly unorthodox Jew and tried to display his newfound piety by harassing Christians. When the king died in 44, Judea and Galilee reverted to Roman control, and his son, Agrippa II, received only a tiny fraction of the kingdom. Had he lived longer, Agrippa I might have stabilized the Herodian kingdom, and Palestine would have been spared the horrors of the great revolt and the destruction of the Temple.

The new Roman regime in Judea was particularly inept, and the region was soon on the verge of rebellion. Jewish collaborators were often murdered by fanatic Zealots who were dedicated to revolt, and unemployment in Jerusalem swelled the ranks of the discontented. In 66 a major revolt broke out, and the Zealots seized Jerusalem, but many Jews held aloof and others, such as Agrippa II, aided the Romans. Sent by Nero, Vespasian crushed the rebel forces in the countryside and left his son, Titus, to complete the siege of Jerusalem. Within the beleaguered city, three factions struggled for power while the populace starved, but some fanatics hoped for rescue by an army of angels. In 70, the Romans stormed the city and massacred many of the survivors. The Temple and much of the city burned, and the treasures of the Temple were taken as booty to Rome. At Masada and elsewhere, the Romans eradicated the last holdouts of resistance. As punishment, the tithe that Jews formerly sent to the Temple was now paid to the Roman treasury. With the loss of the Temple, the priesthood and the Sadducees passed from history and were replaced by rabbis and a Pharisaic adherence to the Law. As local synagogues rose in importance, it became necessary to agree on a canon of scripture. At Jabneh (Jamnia), the academy of Johanan ben Zakkai emphasized the authority of the rabbinate and established the present canon of the Hebrew Bible during the reign of Domitian. In Rome, Vespasian's friend, the Jewish priest Josephus, wrote a pro-Roman account of the great revolt and an apologetic history of his people in Greek. Though he obscured his own dubious career as rebel and turncoat, Josephus was a major Hellenistic historian and a valuable source on both Jewish and Roman history. Despite Josephus's efforts, Roman attitudes toward Jews were cool, and the writings of Tacitus and Juvenal display a peevish anti-Semitism.

Though the revolt in Palestine had been dramatically crushed, former rebels and Messianic pretenders stirred up new resistance among Jews in the second century. While Trajan was engaged in his Parthian campaign, Jewish fanatics rose in Cyrene, Egypt, and Cyprus as well as in Palestine. Probably Parthian intrigue was involved in the risings, which were savage in nature and ruthlessly put down. In 132 Palestine again erupted after Hadrian announced a ban on circumcision and his intent to build a pagan temple in Jerusalem. The famed rabbi Akiba hailed the rebel leader Shim'on Ben Cosiba as Bar Cochba (Son of the Star), alluding to the "star out of Jacob" of *Numbers* 24.17. According to Cassius Dio, the Palestinian revolt was suppressed with great loss of life, and both Akiba and his Messiah died at Roman hands. Though Antoninus Pius relaxed the severe policies of Hadrian, there are obscure references to later disorders in Palestine. Apparently, some Jews backed the abortive revolts of Avidius Cassius and Niger, but Rome had no quarrel with Judaism per se. In the third century, Palestine was quiet, and rabbinical studies flourished in Galilee. In the Severan era, the *Mishnah,* a major collection of legal opinions, was compiled by Judah the Prince, and later scholars assembled the *Mishnah* and other compilations of commentaries and popular lore into the *Talmud.*[5] Revolts having failed, the Jews of the Roman empire took refuge in books, and the *Talmud* became as authoritative as the scriptures. Ironically, the bookishness of Talmudic religion ran counter to the agrarian basis of Judaism. Ancient cult practices and laws were reinterpreted often in highly fanciful ways, and major rabbis acquired the aura once held by the Temple priests. Despite its narrowness, Talmudic Judaism was a useful defense mechanism and more effective than the violence that sporadically broke out among the Jews of Palestine. When Rome adopted Christianity, the Jews needed internal bulwarks, for many clergymen were anti-Semitic and insisted that the emperors impose disabilities on Jews. By the fifth century, Jews were unwelcome sojourners in the Roman empire and the barbarian successor states. Eventually, the Muslim conquest rescued the Jews of the Near East from Christian oppression.

THE BEGINNINGS OF CHRISTIANITY

It is too often forgotten that Jesus was a Jew in a Roman world and that Christianity developed within the context of that world. A lowborn prophet, Jesus challenged the Judaic religious establishment, announced the imminent Day of the Lord, and was executed as a traitor to Rome. Whatever he had claimed to be, his followers and new converts transformed him into a universal savior whose cult gradually won a place in Roman society. As a prophet, Jesus was in the radical Jewish tradition and probably had much in common with the Essenes. His brief career is inconceivable without the Messianic hysteria of the time. Moreover, Jesus preached a social message, and his impact was all the greater be-

---

[5] In the fifth century, the active Jewish community in Mesopotamia produced the *Babylonian Talmud,* which is fuller and more authoritative than the *Palestinian Talmud.* Later Jews viewed the *Babylonian Talmud* as divinely inspired.

cause the Judaic establishment was bogged down in ritualism and legalism. A charismatic figure could easily appeal to frustrated Jews who yearned for the thunderous tones of Amos and Isaiah. For the historian, the major problem is to determine what exactly Jesus said and did; the subsequent development of Christianity is much better documented.

The earliest accounts of the life of Jesus are four Greek tracts, the Gospels, which are attributed to Mark, Matthew, Luke, and John even though the first three books are anonymous. After Jesus' death, his followers had recounted his words and deeds in oral accounts that were later incorporated into the written Gospels. Since Mark, Matthew, and Luke generally agree on events, scholars term them "synoptic." Supposedly based on the reminiscences of Peter, Mark begins with Jesus' adult life and ends with a brief account of his resurrection. A simple, forceful work, the Gospel of Mark prophesied the fall of Jerusalem in vague apocalyptic terms and may predate A.D. 70. Matthew and Luke utilized Mark and another collection of stories and sayings. Strongly Judaic, Matthew tried to connect Jesus' life with Old Testament prophecies and parallels. Often overdone, this technique casts suspicion on some matters that may be true, since many men have tried to model their lives on a paradigm in the past. To the simple story of Mark, Matthew added a miraculous birth for Jesus, a Davidic ancestry through Joseph, Herod's slaughter of infants, and a flight into Egypt; the latter item was a parallel with Israel's history, and the others were standard Near Eastern king myths. In the Flavian era, a gifted writer composed the Gospel of Luke and the *Acts of the Apostles;* both works were aimed at Roman readers. Adding some memorable parables and more details of Jesus' life, Luke provided a different Davidic genealogy for Jesus and dropped the tales of Herod's massacre and the flight into Egypt. By the end of the first century, the Gospel of John had appeared, presumably based on the reminiscences of the apostle John, who ignored the birth legends and elaborated on the passion and resurrection of Jesus. Highly personal, well written, and at times spiteful toward Peter, the Gospel of John is philosophic and filled with comments that are sometimes confused with quotations. Its strong gnostic flavor made it highly suspect to the early church. From Mark to John, the figure of Jesus expanded into that of a divinity.

Though accepted as canonical in the second century, the Gospels are filled with implausibilities and contradictions, such as the crucial details of the first Easter. Mark and John ignore the birth and childhood of Jesus, and Matthew dated his birth in the reign of Herod the Great (4 B.C. or before), although Luke connected it with the census held by P. Sulpicius Quirinius (A.D. 6). According to Luke, Jesus was "about thirty years old" in the fifteenth year of the reign of Tiberius (A.D. 29).[6] This information prompted a sixth-century monk, Dionysius Exiguus, to determine the beginning of the Christian Era; he was reassured by certain astrological events that had occurred in what is now the year A.D. 1. It goes without saying that the exact year of Jesus' birth is unknown. Chronological dilemmas are the least of the many problems that afflict New Testament scholars.[7] Not only did the authors of the Gospels have strong biases, but later editors added passages to support various controversies in the early church. According to Matthew, Jesus' mission was to the lost sheep of Israel alone, but John insists that it included "other sheep of mine, not belonging to this fold," the gentiles.[8] So fallible are the Gospels and so difficult is it for moderns to accept wonder tales, that the Bultmann school of Form Criticism has rejected both the miracles and the dubious history as borrowed legends and reduced Jesus to a string of "authentic sayings," acceptable to Bultmann's theology. Rather than arch-skepticism, Form Criticism is a modern form of gnosticism that transforms Jesus into the pure Word who is never really incarnate. Secular scholars need not go so far, for the Gospels can be studied with the same techniques that are used for Philostratus's life of Apollonius and the more creative passages in Livy. The historicity of Jesus is confirmed by unsympathetic Roman historians and a passing comment by Josephus, though the latter passage has been "improved" by Christian editors. More important is the primary evidence in the letters of Paul, who knew the apostles and was aware of the crucifixion. Whatever else remains obscure, Jesus was a real man who influenced other men and died an ignominious death. To the question, "to what purpose," the historian can offer only probable answers.

During the prefecture of Pontius Pilate, Palestine was disturbed by numerous religious agitators. None was more picturesque than the ragged ascetic, John the Baptist, who haunted the desert and announced the imminent Day of the Lord. Like the Greek Cynics, he disdained government and property and delighted in attacking men in authority. A teetotaler, John may also have disapproved of sex. His eloquent harangues impressed the masses, and many of his followers washed their sins away in the waters of the Jordan. Eventually, John clashed with the client king of Galilee, Herod Antipas, and his wife Herodias, at whose

---

[6] Luke 3.1, 23.

[7] Connoisseurs of esoterica can savor the apocryphal gospels of the second century which feature not only charming wonder tales but also the repentance and martyrdom of Pilate and an attempt by Tiberius to convert the Senate to Christianity. Yet some of the scrappy material found in Egypt may preserve actual sayings of Jesus that were ignored by the canonical Gospels.

[8] Matthew 10.5; 15.24. John 10.16.

request the puritanical prophet was executed. Among the crowds baptized by John was a carpenter from Galilee, Jesus, who may have been a relative and who was also obsessed with the Day of the Lord and the need for a new way of life for Israel. A common man with little education, Jesus may have been influenced by the Essenes. There are stories of his contact with messengers (*angeloi*) in the desert, and his praise for "those who are eunuchs for the sake of the Kingdom of Heaven" may reflect the views on celibacy of the Essene elite. When he assumed a prophetic role, Jesus was rejected by his neighbors, and his own brother, James, did not accept his claims until after Jesus' death. A teetotaling vegetarian ascetic, James prayed so often that "his knees grew hard like a camel's," [9] and his fanaticism may have prompted Jesus' disdain for excessive piety and religious formalism. Jesus' emphasis on ethics and faith as superior to ritualism and rabbinical scruples was rooted in the anticlericalism of the peasantry and their distrust of priestly pomp and learning. Ritualistic Judaism could be expensive, and the complexities of the Law weighed heavily on the poor. When Jesus insisted that the sabbath was made for man and not man for the sabbath, the religious Establishment was both shocked and irritated at the presumption of a country bumpkin. However, the new prophet was no simple rustic, and Herod Antipas feared that he was John risen from the dead.

A charismatic figure, Jesus was a faith healer whose cures awed the masses and lent credence to his claims. Like his contemporaries, he believed in demons and viewed his ability to soothe lunatics as a victory over demonic forces. The prophet was also an eloquent speaker who addressed simple folk through parables. At ease with workingmen and social outcasts, Jesus easily won the loyalty of a handful of laborers who followed him about and relished the role of disciples. Their leader was a fisherman, Simon, whom Jesus nicknamed "Rock" (*Cephas* in Aramaic, *Petros* in Greek) despite his tendency to equivocate under pressure. With fierce sarcasm, Jesus denounced the rich as oppressors of their brothers and damned priests and Pharisees as nitpicking hypocrites. Like Amos, he cried that justice and kindness had priority over rituals and customs. Like Hosea, Jesus emphasized the overwhelming mercy of Yahweh, but he also portrayed the Day of the Lord in grim colors. A novel note was introduced when Jesus counseled pacifism and forbade resistance to violence. Perhaps he was influenced by Deutero-Isaiah in his notion that the passive sufferings of the righteous would somehow atone for their or Israel's sins. Though the famous injunction to "love one's neighbor as one's self" was a quotation from

[9] Eusebius *Historia Ecclesiastica* 2.23.

Leviticus,[10] Jesus apparently felt that a community based on love was the long awaited Kingdom of God and was present among his audiences if they would only act upon it. In such a society, all would be the Sons of God mentioned by the Psalmist and the *Wisdom of Solomon,* and Jesus, who already felt such love, was in this sense Yahweh's son.

Did Jesus claim to be the Son of Man of apocalyptic prophecy, the Messiah who would conquer on the Day of the Lord and distribute honors to his loyal followers? Embarrassed that this assertion would make Jesus either mad or in error, some modern scholars have denied that Jesus ever claimed to be the Messiah, even though Peter hailed him as such. Yet Pilate, who had no interest in Jewish religious notions, was persuaded that the Galilean prophet posed as some kind of king and deserved execution as a traitor to Rome. Moreover, Jesus' enemies mocked him as a would-be Messiah. He seems to have sought a martyr's death in going to Jerusalem to confront the priests. The author of *Fourth Maccabees* (also echoed in the *Talmud*) insisted that martyrs atoned for the sins of the nation. Probably Jesus believed that he was chosen to be a national scapegoat whose death would usher in the Day of the Lord, a nonviolent Son of Man. Filled with such dreams, he went to Jerusalem and was cheered by the Passover crowds. Horrified by the moneylenders and merchants in the Temple, Jesus instigated a riot that overturned their stalls. Yet he shrank back from the Zealots who urged a revolt against Rome, and his equivocating words about rendering to Caesar the things that were Caesar's lost him the support of the crowds. Long resentful of his sweeping criticism, the priests could have ordered Jesus stoned as a blasphemer, but they preferred to denounce him to Pilate as a traitor. The Roman obliged them, and the prophet died in agony and despair on a cross, deserted by his followers. While Jesus was under arrest, Peter three times denied even knowing him; the prophet deserved better of his apostles.

While the story and personality of Jesus are appealing, the ancient world was well-supplied with sages as kind as Epictetus and martyrs as noble as Socrates. Apollonius of Tyana, too, was a wonder-worker, and every temple of Asclepius had its authenticated miracles. However, three days after his death, Jesus' tomb was found empty, and the risen prophet was glimpsed by a neurotic woman, Mary Magdalene, from whom he had "cast out seven devils." Skeptical at first, Peter and the other disciples soon began to see the resurrected Jesus; their conviction was proportionate to their guilt over having deserted him. Though the appearances ceased after a few weeks, the apostles were sure that Jesus would quickly return in Messianic splendor, for he had promised to do

[10] Mark 12.31. Leviticus 19.18.

so during their lifetime. Filled with enthusiasm, the apostles began to preach the message of Jesus the Messiah (*Christos* in Greek). Although the gods Osiris and Dionysus had also risen from the dead, the Christ was a man who had triumphed over death as would all who accepted him. The mystery cults promised immortality in the next world, but the Christ would soon judge the living and the dead. In the near future, the sky would be split and Jesus would descend with his angelic hosts. In the fervor of their faith, the apostles set up a communist society in which the faithful shared their goods and received "each according to his needs." As the community expanded, it quickly abandoned communism, but charity and brotherhood continued to be major Christian virtues.

The central problem for the emerging church was its relationship to Judaism. Was Christianity a universal religion or only a Jewish heresy? As the brother of the prophet, James assumed leadership of the community at Jerusalem, and upon his death, he was succeeded by a cousin of Jesus. Conservative in everything except the identity of the Messiah, James insisted on the observance of Mosaic law and Jewish customs, despite the opposition of the Hellenist faction of Diaspora Jews who saw Christianity as a new religion. Even Peter conceded that circumcision and food taboos discouraged gentile converts, but outspoken Hellenist criticism of conventional Judaism led to sporadic harassment of the new sect. Among the militant foes of the Christian movement was a fanatic Pharisee from Tarsus, Saul, who was probably born a Roman citizen but may have acquired that status; in any case, he is better known as Paul, the name of his family's patron or possibly his sponsor. A traumatic vision on the road to Damascus turned Paul from a persecutor into an equally zealous defender of Christianity. As a Diaspora Jew oriented toward a broader world, he embraced the Hellenist position and urged that gentile Christians need not adopt Judaic practices. Although originally suspect because of his past, Paul became a successful missionary in Asia and Hellas, and through his efforts and those of less famous men, gentiles soon outnumbered Jews in the Christian communities. By the time of the reign of Claudius, there were Christians at Rome and elsewhere in Italy. While sympathetic to the Hellenists, Peter equivocated when James objected to the suspension of Judaic practices, but Paul confronted the "two pillars" of the church and badgered them into accepting his position. Since the Hellenist churches were richer than the community at Jerusalem, Paul could reinforce his arguments with promises of financial aid. Eclipsed by the Hellenist victory, the Jerusalem Christians migrated beyond the Jordan during the great revolt against Rome and faded from history. Perhaps the later Ebionite sect, which rejected Pauline views and emphasized a Jewish Christianity, evolved from these refugees. Although Peter's fate is obscure, a strong tradition insisted that he migrated to the capital and died there under Nero. Hence, future bishops of Rome claimed to be successors of Peter and heirs to his position among the apostles.

Despite the diversity of its contents, the New Testament is essentially a Pauline document, dominated by the epistles of the great apostle and reflecting the historical views set forth by the author of Luke and *Acts*. Only briefly do we glimpse rival Christian leaders, some of whom are only names to us, or sense the wilder winds of faith that fanned those who babbled "in tongues" and picked up serpents. The eschatological delirium of the *Apocalypse of John* has excited heretics throughout the ages, and any man of property would be unnerved by the revolutionary fervor of the Epistle of "James":

> You have piled up wealth in an age that is near its close. The wages you never paid to the men who mowed your fields are loud against you, and the outcry of the reapers has reached the ears of the Lord of Hosts. You have lived on earth in wanton luxury, fattening yourselves like cattle— and the day for slaughter has come.[11]

Such sentiments did not endear Christian extremists to the Roman state. Most Christians, however, followed the example of Paul, the loyal Roman, who endorsed slavery and insisted on total submission to the civil authorities except in matters of worship.

The towering figure in the early church was Paul, who elevated the cult of Jesus the Messiah into a universal religion. By sheer force of personality and the eloquence of his writings, he set his stamp indelibly on the Christian movement. A wiry little man with thin hair and a hooked nose, Paul was impatient with opposition and petulant when crossed; he often quarreled bitterly with the other apostles and reserved diplomacy for Roman officials and potential converts. Heir to the Hellenistic culture of Tarsus and schooled in rabbinic lore under Gamaliel, Paul considered Peter a bumpkin and James old-fashioned. Unlike the other apostles, Paul was unmarried, and his antipathy to sex elevated celibacy into a Christian ideal which some of Jesus' utterances seemed to sanction. He also complained of a "thorn in the flesh" and was subject to seizures characterized by flashes of light and ecstatic visions; one such episode triggered his conversion. Apparently, the apostle was epileptoid like Muhammad and Dostoevsky, and his thoughts were permeated with notions of guilt and the helplessness of man in the hands of God. Denounced for profaning the Temple at Jerusalem, Paul stood on his rights as a Roman citizen and appealed his case to the emperor, but

[11] James 5.3–5.

Nero was not interested. At Rome, the apostle squabbled with the Christian community and considered his own missionary work a failure. Perhaps he died a martyr's death in the capital, or maybe he fulfilled his ambition to carry the "good news" to Spain. The author of *Acts* discreetly ignored the last days of the Apostle to the Gentiles.

The achievement of Paul was not limited to missionary activity, for he was the dominant intellectual force in the Christian movement, and his epistles became canonical. Paramount among Paul's views was the concept of original sin, Adam's fall from grace, which was occasioned by a woman. To aid sinful mankind, God had bestowed the Jewish Law as a temporary expedient, but the Law was a burden and Paul resented the guilts it provoked in his troubled mind. Man was marred by Adam's sin, the Jews were in bondage to the Law, and the material world was governed by demonic powers, the archons in the planets. Although mankind was unworthy, God in his infinite mercy sent his son, Jesus, to break the yoke of the Law and free all men from sin by a supreme act of atonement. The ignominious death of the Christ was really a sacrifice for all mankind:

> Jews call for miracles, Greeks look for wisdom; but we proclaim Christ —yes, Christ nailed to the cross; and though this is a stumbling-block to Jews and folly to Greeks, yet to those who have heard his call, Jews and Greeks alike, he is the power of God and the wisdom of God.[12]

By his martyrdom, Jesus had restored the heritage squandered by Adam, and he would soon return in splendor to judge the living and the dead. It was urgent that the message be spread to all who would heed before the awful events of the Day of the Lord. Yet God had not intended that all men would be saved—from the beginning of time, the divine potter had designed some vessels for beauty and others for destruction. His grace could not be earned and only partially justified by faith in his son. God required that men practice good deeds, but virtue alone did not warrant salvation; otherwise pagans would be saved. Himself unworthy of grace, Paul nonetheless had been rescued by the divine whim, and so would the elect be spared when they embraced Jesus as the Christ.

The grim vision of Paul has attracted other disturbed men from Augustine to Luther and many moderns, but the apostle offered his readers more than predestination. He begged Christians to emulate that overriding love that Jesus had preached and demonstrated by dying for mankind:

[12] I Corinthians 1.22–24.

I may speak in tongues of men or of angels, but if I am without love, I am a sounding gong or a clanging cymbal. I may have the gift of prophecy and know every hidden truth; I may have faith strong enough to move mountains; but if I have no love, I am nothing. I may dole out all I possess, or even give my body to be burnt, but if I have no love, I am none the better. . . . Love will never come to an end. Are there prophets? their work will be over. Are there tongues of ecstasy? they will cease. Is there knowledge? it will vanish away. . . . There are three things that last forever: faith, hope, and love; but the greatest of them all is love.[13]

Although gongs and cymbals refer to pagan rites, the thrust of this eloquent passage was against Christian pride in prophecy, ecstasy, and martyrdom. Although he tore Jesus from Judaism and made him into a world savior, Paul had captured the essential message of love preached by a man whom he had never seen.

Slowly, Christianity had spread from Palestine through Syria, Egypt, and Asia and eastward beyond the Euphrates. The Christian communities were small and scattered, but their enthusiasm was high because they were sure that they were the elect. In the eastern provinces, peasants as well as city dwellers were attracted to the new cult, but in Hellas, Italy, and the West, Christianity was most successful in urban areas. While alienated Romans of all classes joined the church, the bulk of Christians were poor and uneducated, and pagan critics sneered at them as sectarian rabble. Unlike other mystery cults, the rites of Christianity were simple, and no initiation fees were charged. Baptism by water washed away the sin of Adam, and some zealots contrived a surrogate baptism for dead relatives. At weekly meetings to which only the faithful were admitted, Christians ate bread and drank wine, believing that these substances had been miraculously transformed into the body and blood of their god. To Paul, the magic of the sacramental meal was so powerful that sinners would die after partaking of it. At Christian services, portions of the Gospels and other revered writings were read aloud. Since the readers needed to refer quickly to selected passages, the codex or modern form of book was more convenient than the traditional papyrus rolls of antiquity. The emerging churches soon produced their own organizational apparatus with an overseer or bishop, who was elected by the congregation to supervise affairs and administer funds. Aping Roman custom, the bishops of major cities assumed authority over the clergy in surrounding towns and rural areas. The episcopal leaders were frequently in correspondence with one another, and their consensus on rites and scriptures produced an orthodoxy that triumphed

[13] I Corinthians 13.1–3, 8, 13.

over religious dissenters. While internally suppressing prophets and overexuberant congregations, the bishops had to maintain good relations with the civil authorities. Paternalistic and sometimes imperious, the bishops adjusted the church to the needs of the world, rallied their flocks in times of trouble, and preserved a continuity of belief and practice. Thanks to their efforts, the faithful survived the shock that the second coming of Christ was not imminent.

Without the episcopal system, the Christian movement would have succumbed to centrifugal force and shattered into ephemeral sects, for its ranks were filled with enthusiasts and wild saints. Spurious gospels and apocryphal scriptures proliferated until the bishops determined the canon of the New Testament. In second-century Rome, the New Testament still included the *Wisdom of Solomon* and the *Apocalypse of Peter* but did not yet incorporate *Hebrews, James, Peter I* and *II,* and *John II* or *III.* The need for a canon was crystallized by the threat of Marcionism. In Asia, the scholarly Marcion rejected the Old Testament and limited the New Testament to the Pauline epistles and an edited Gospel of Luke. Influenced by gnostic thought, Marcion considered Yahweh an inferior deity who had created an imperfect world. To set things right, the high god of light sent Jesus into the material world, but the Marcionite Jesus was not human and his death was only symbolic. At the other extreme of heresy, the Montanists of Phrygia took scripture too literally. The Gospel of John had promised that a messenger, the Paraclete, would precede the second coming, and Montanus claimed that he was the Paraclete. Aided by prophetesses, he announced the imminent end of all things and set up a New Jerusalem in the village of Pepuza, from which his missionaries spread the awesome tidings. Exemplary puritans, the Montanists fasted and forbade sexual relations, and their extremism found a sympathetic defender in the African polemicist Tertullian. The bishops of Asia, however, could not tolerate the independent authority of Montanist prophecy and condemned the sect as heretical. Surviving for centuries, the Montanists of Phrygia were finally outlawed by the Byzantine state, locked themselves in their churches, and set fire to the buildings.

While the bishops may be accused of locking Christianity in the fetters of orthodoxy, the alternative was worse, for Marcion had shown the dangers implicit in gnosticism. Gnostic thought permeated portions of the Gospel of John, and gnostic notions occurred elsewhere in the New Testament. Like the Christian enthusiast, the gnostic knew through a personal revelation what lesser men did not. What exactly gnostics knew varied, for there was no uniformity in gnostic systems, though some common patterns emerge from such diverse material as the *Gospel of Truth,* the *Gospel of Thomas,* the *Secret Book of John,* and the *Odes of*

Solomon. Essentially, gnosticism was a hybrid of Hermetic lore, de-based Platonism, Jewish mysticism, and exotic Christianity. To most gnostics, the material world was a realm of evil and darkness, created by an inferior demiurge and ruled by planetary demons. The true home of human souls was in a heaven of light, from which God sent his per-sonified thought, the Logos, to save mankind, but the Logos was cap-tured by the demons. Later, God dispatched another savior, such as Jesus or Simon Magus, to rescue the Logos and enlighten mankind. A Samaritan Messiah who had an encounter with Peter, Simon was a colorful figure with a flare for magic. He soon became a gnostic deity. Through revelation or the savior, men received knowledge (*gnosis*) of their true nature and an awareness of God and the heaven of light. Some gnostics provided elaborate mythologies to explain the fall of man and the Logos, and they spotted allegories in Judaic and pagan lore. Consistent with their hatred of matter, gnostics usually disdained sex and admired asceticism. Though Christian gnostics were condemned as heretical in the second century, gnostic doctrines underlay Manicheism and reappeared in medieval heresies.

Despite its bizarre aspects, gnosticism appealed to those Christians who deeply distrusted the world and the flesh. Orthodox Christianity in-sisted that all of God's creations were good, yet asceticism and celibacy were venerated as means to escape the snares of Satan. Even the great-est Christian philosopher before Augustine, Origen of Alexandria, suc-cumbed to gnostic views although he opposed heretical gnostic systems. An immensely learned man, he probably studied under Ammonius Sac-cas, the teacher of Plotinus. According to Eusebius, Origen in his youth was disturbed by the lures of the flesh and solved the problem by cas-trating himself. More plausible are the stories of his friendly contacts with Julia Mamaea and Philip the Arab. A prolific writer and popular teacher, Origen labored to buttress Christianity with scholarship and produced an edition of the Bible with the Hebrew and Greek texts in parallel columns. The crudities and contradictions in the Bible were ex-plained as allegories. Origen's theology was highly unorthodox. Origi-nally, all souls were with God, but everyone except the Logos failed to adore him and fell into lower status. Some became angels or demons and others humans, but all were caught within cycles of rebirth until rescued by the Logos. Ultimately, all souls would return to God after they had accepted the *gnosis* revealed by the Logos who appeared on earth as Jesus. Even Satan would repent, and Hell would be emptied. The grand design was like a ladder on which souls were climbing, sometimes slipping back, but all would eventually reach the top through the aid of the Logos. While inferior to God, the Logos was divine, as was the Holy Spirit,[14] and the three combined to form the Trinity but its members did not have equal rank. While Origen's system maintained free will for all souls, its novelties shocked orthodox clergymen, who later condemned his views as heretical. Origen, who died as a result of abuse suffered in the persecution under Decius, had tried to construct a Christian philosophy albeit on semi-gnostic terms.

While gnostics and heretics made up the picturesque fringe of Christianity, the vast majority of Christians were not attracted to esoteric doctrines and lived quiet lives no different from those of their pagan neighbors except in matters of worship. In the second century, the author of the *Address to Diognetus* assured the pagan world that Christians were not dangerous cranks:

> Now Christians are not different from the rest of men in where they live, in their speech, or in their clothing. For they do not dwell in their own private cities, they use no special language, nor does their external life present anything remarkable. . . . They live as luck will have it either in Greek or non-Greek cities; they follow local usage in their dress, food, and way of life; and yet they manifest a marvelous and admittedly strange way of life in their society. They live in their own native cities, but as though they were strangers. They participate in everything as citizens, and yet carry out their obligations like aliens. Every foreign city is their native land, and every native city a foreign country. They marry and have babies like the rest of men, but they do not expose their infants. They share a common table but not a common bed. Though in the flesh, they do not live according to the flesh; though living on earth, their citizenship is in heaven. They obey the established laws, yet in their private lives they go beyond the laws. They love all men, yet all men persecute them.[15]

While odd in their beliefs and unjustly harassed on occasion, the author insists, Christians were good citizens and perhaps better than most.

Though Tertullian snorted that "Christians are made, not born," [16] many were hereditary Christians and lacked the arrogance of converts, and few, whatever their origin, were saints. Confident of their place in the next world, they had no desire to dwell in this world as in a vale of tears. As fragile humans, Christians sinned and expected to be forgiven, and the church accommodated itself as a religion for ordinary men and not merely the apocalyptic elect. Callistus, bishop of Rome from 217 to

[14] The notion of a Holy Spirit, equal to the Father and the Son, was derived from the account of the "holy spirit" that inspired the apostles on Pentecost. (Acts 2.4)

[15] *Address to Diognetus* 5, trans. H. A. Musurillo, *The Fathers of the Primitive Church* (New York: Mentor, 1966), pp. 147–48.

[16] Tertullian *Apologeticus* 18.4.

222, compared the church to Noah's ark filled with all manner of animals, some clean and others unclean. His enemy Hippolytus claimed that Callistus was an embezzler and former convict who had wheedled his way into the ranks of the clergy. At any rate, the bishop was a practical man who forgave apostates and allowed ladies of rank to live openly with men of lower status, even slaves. Though married in the eyes of the church, such women were legally concubines, and the policy horrified rigorists such as Hippolytus and Tertullian. Nevertheless, the worldly-wise compromises of Callistus made further inroads into the ranks of the aristocracy possible, for women were more easily converted than men and it was absurd to expect them to embrace celibacy. Similarly, few individuals could withstand the rigors of martyrdom, and it was quixotic to deny readmission to repentant Christians who had apostatized under pressure. If the blood of martyrs was the seed of the faith as Tertullian insisted, episcopal practicality and cagey compromises allowed the church to grow and gain recruits from all classes until its numerical strength was sufficient to withstand the severe persecutions of the third century.

THE TRIALS AND TRIUMPH OF CHRISTIANITY

As long as the Roman state did not recognize Christianity as a legal religion, the position of even pragmatic Christians was precarious, and that of fanatics was dangerous. Whatever their other merits as citizens, Christians denied one of the basic tenets of Roman society, the existence of the gods who protected the empire and whose rites could not be neglected without dire consequences. While pacifism ceased to be a Christian habit after the first century, Christian soldiers would not offer pagan religious sacrifices. Pagan parents were saddened when children mocked the faith of their fathers, and the dogmatism of Christianity seemed arrogant to intellectuals. Christian rejection of traditional *pietas* was an affront to Rome itself. Centuries later, Pope Gregory the Great looked back on the early church:

> Those saints at whose tomb we are now standing lived in a world that was flourishing, yet they trampled upon its material prosperity with their spiritual contempt. In that world, life was long, well-being was continuous, there was material wealth, there was a high birth-rate, and there was the tranquility of a lasting peace; and yet, when that world was still so flourishing in itself, it had already withered in the hearts of those saints.[17]

[17] Gregory the Great *Homiliae Quadraginta in Evangelica* 28, trans. Arnold J. Toynbee, *A Study of History* (London: Oxford University Press, 1939), IV, 60–61.

Patriotic Romans were deeply offended that venerable beliefs which had satisfied Scipio and Augustus and sustained the empire were contemptible in the eyes of sectarians who worshiped a convicted felon and who offered no proof for their own beliefs other than fervent assertions of faith.

Polytheistic and indifferent to creeds, the Roman state had no interest in private religious beliefs. According to Tiberius, the gods could look after themselves even in matters of sacrilege.[18] However, Rome expected that all citizens and subjects would participate in the official cult as proof of their loyalty. Only Jews were exempted from the rites of the state cult, and originally Christians were confused with Jews. By the reign of Nero, the distinction was apparent, and the new sect was viewed as a "degenerate Eastern cult," but the state took no action to suppress it. The handful of martyrs who died at Rome under Nero were scapegoats for the great fire of 64 and were executed as "antisocial arsonists." During the first and second centuries, individual Christians might be hauled into court on some charge and there confronted with the judge's order to demonstrate their loyalty by offering to the gods; upon refusal, they would be condemned, for Roman officials did not tolerate defiance. Roman bureaucrats, however, had more important things to do than hunt down sectarians, despite persistent rumors that their secret rites included cannibalism and incest. According to legend, Domitian interviewed two men of the family of Jesus and dismissed them as harmless. Although active in law courts at Rome, Pliny the Younger had never seen a Christian before he went to Bithynia and was faced with popular denunciations of the sect. After a thorough investigation, he was satisfied that the Christians had committed no civil crimes, but he was equally convinced that their obstinacy in court should not go unpunished. Trajan confirmed Pliny's action:

> They should not be sought out, but if they are accused and convicted, they must be punished. Yet, whoever denies that he is a Christian and proves it by worshiping our gods, shall obtain pardon on his repentance, however suspicious his past conduct may be. However, papers that are presented unsigned ought not to be admitted in any charge, for they set a very bad precedent and are unworthy of our age.[19]

Christians, too, were entitled to the full measure of Roman justice.

The legal position of Christianity in the Roman empire is the source of much controversy. Christian propagandists exaggerated the number of martyrs, and apologists for Constantine have obscured the role of pagan emperors. Yet evidence of imperial policy is sparse, and tales of

---

[18] Tacitus *Annales* 1.75.   [19] Pliny the Younger *Epistulae* 10.97.

martyrs are often unreliable. A *religio licita* was one permitted by the state, and the legality of any religion, except the venerated state cult, was subject to the whim of the emperor. By modern standards, Roman criminal law was vague, and magistrates had great latitude in interpreting and enforcing its provisions. Unless a reigning emperor stated his policy on the sect, the treatment of Christians was a local affair and varied greatly. Even during persecutions, some magistrates were lax while others were severe. Accounts of martyrs are not a safe barometer of imperial policy unless it is known that a particular emperor (e.g. Decius) opposed Christianity. Modern Americans may recall that an unpopular group need not be illegal for its members to be prosecuted on other charges. Similarly, even a public policy of toleration does not save individuals from harassment by determined bigots.

During public calamities, such as plagues or invasions, when it seemed that the gods were angry, the populace might denounce Christians as the culprits and force local officials to take action against them. Even educated men such as Fronto believed that Christians were sexually promiscuous and ate babies baked in pies at their clandestine ceremonies. His friend Marcus Aurelius loathed "atheists and traitors who do vile things behind closed doors," and dismissed the heroics of martyrs as theatrical and fanatic.[20] During his reign, a severe persecution took place against the Christians of Lyons, but later Commodus's mistress, Marcia, favored the sect and harassment abated. The grim Septimius Severus dealt harshly with the sect in Africa, and a moving account is preserved of the martyrdom of a young matron, Perpetua, whose dreams in jail are of great psychological interest. The other Severan rulers were sympathetic to Christianity, and Origen was received at court. Philip the Arab's favorable attitude toward the church prompted a conservative reaction under Decius, who was the first emperor to attempt an empire-wide persecution. With typical Roman confidence in documents, Decius insisted on loyalty oaths from suspected Christians:

> To the commissioners of sacrifices from Aurelia Demos, without patronymic, daughter of Helena and wife of Aurelius Irenaeus, of the quarter of the Hellenium. I have always been accustomed to sacrifice to the gods, and now also in your presence, in accordance with the command, I have made sacrifice and libation and tasted the offering, and I request you to certify my statement. Farewell. (Signed.) I, Aurelia Demos, have presented this declaration. I, Aurelius Irenaeus, wrote it for her as she is illiterate. (Attested.) I, Aurelius Sabinus, *prytanis,* saw you sacrificing. (Dated.) [21]

[20] Marcus Aurelius 3.16; 11.3.   [21] Hunt, *Select Papyri,* II, 353–55 (no. 319).

Wily Christians simply purchased such certificates. According to Origen, the number of martyrs before the reign of Decius was very small,[22] and Clement of Alexandria noted that some were pathological types who denounced themselves to startled Roman judges.

Originally, Valerian allowed Christians at his court, but he later harried the church when troubles overtook his reign. In 261 his son, Gallienus, reversed the official policy and granted Christianity recognition as a legal religion.[23] So confident did the church become that the Syrian clergy asked Aurelian to unseat a heretical bishop, Paul of Samosata. The last major persecution, that by Galerius, was the most severe, but the church was strong enough to survive, and the persecution was halted by its author when failure was apparent. Though Maximinus Daia was a bigot, the harassment of Christians by Licinius was brief and politically motivated, for Constantine had become a champion of the church. In summary, the hostility of the Roman state toward Christianity, though savage at times, had been sporadic. Most pagan emperors were indifferent to Christianity; some had openly favored the sect; and only a handful tried to eradicate it. By pagan standards, the Roman state was unduly lax, for the Christians were subversives who fully intended to destroy the traditional religion of Rome.

From the beginning, Christianity had been engaged in a struggle to win the minds of men, but the grounds for battle shifted once the apostolic age had passed and the second coming was no longer imminent. Enthusiasts were still unhinged by the prospect of the end of all things, but the church adapted itself for life in this world, and it desperately wanted respectability. In the second century, Justin Martyr and other apologists pleaded that Christians were exemplary citizens and that the truths of the Gospel had been anticipated by Socrates. Most pagans were not impressed, and the Alexandrian Platonist, Celsus, made a frontal assault on Christian claims. A cursory student of the Bible, Celsus noted contradictions in the scriptures and asked how the Biblical god of wrath could be reconciled with the Christian god of love. To Celsus, Christianity was a dangerous counter culture, preached by uneducated rascals who feared disputes with men of learning but corrupted children with wild tales and taught them to defy their parents and teachers. Christians reminded Celsus of "worms wriggling about on a manure heap and saying to one another: 'God has revealed to us all that has to be; he cares not for the rest of the world.' " [24] Origen troubled to write

---

[22] Origen *Contra Celsum* 3.8.

[23] Eusebius, *Ecclesiastical History* 7.13, quotes a letter of Gallienus assuring the Egyptian bishops that they can rely on his recent decree "that none may molest you."

[24] Origen *Contra Celsum* 4.23.

an elaborate reply to Celsus's charges. Christians had a vitriolic champion in Tertullian, whose polemics against pagans and rival Christians knew little restraint. In one of his quieter moods, the African convert assured the world that Christians prayed for the emperors: "We pray for them long life, a secure rule, a safe home, brave armies, a faithful Senate, an honest people, a quiet world, and everything for which a man and a Caesar can pray." [25] He added that Christians had a special self-interest in the preservation of the empire, for the world would end when Rome fell and not even the faithful looked forward to the horrors of the last day.[26]

Another third-century apologist, Minucius Felix, composed an elegant dialogue to convince the upper classes of the merits of Christianity. He also neatly summarized the pagan notion of Christianity:

> A gang of discredited and proscribed desperadoes band themselves against the gods. Fellows who gather together illiterates from the dregs of the populace and credulous women with the instability natural to their sex, and so organize a rabble of profane conspirators, leagued together by meetings at night and ritual fasts and unnatural repasts. . . . A secret tribe that shuns the light, silent in the open but talkative in hid corners; they despise temples as if they were tombs; they spit upon the gods; they jeer at our sacred rites. . . . What a pitch of folly! What wild impertinence! present tortures they despise, yet dread those of an uncertain future; death after death they fear, but death in the present they fear not: for them, illusive hope charms away terror with assurances of a life to come.[27]

In short, Christianity was the revolt of the unwashed and unreasoning, but Minucius Felix countered by pointing out the follies of paganism and glossing over Christian doctrines that would be difficult for a Roman gentleman to accept. Probably the most learned critic of Christianity was the Neoplatonist Porphyry, who studied the Bible with care, but he also believed in demons, magic, and theurgy and could not attack the Christians as irrationalists. When philosophers despaired of reason, they were defenseless against Christianity and could only seek support in class appeals to snobbishness.

Early Christian literature was filled with bitter comments on "the passing age" and the irrelevancy or evil of the existing order. The faithful frequently boasted that their true citizenship was in heaven, but much of this attitude was doctrinaire rhetoric, for most Christians were fully integrated into Roman society and did not wish its collapse. Yet

---

[25] Tertullian *Apologeticus* 30.4.   [26] Tertullian *Apologeticus* 32.1.
[27] Minucius Felix *Octavius* 8.3–5, trans. Gerald H. Rendall (Cambridge, Mass.: Harvard University Press, 1940), pp. 335–37.

one of the attractions of the new religion was the hope it offered of a new order based on Christ-like love. The lure of the supernatural, to which both pagans and Christians responded, was a symptom that all was not well in the Roman world. The intelligentsia were uneasy over invasions and military mutinies, and they were troubled by guilt over glaring injustices and social contradictions. This sense of flaw was echoed by the bishop of Carthage, Cyprian, who was martyred under Valerian. The world had become senile, he alleged, and he cited an apparent decline in productivity and population, but the root of the matter was social:

> You complain of the aggression of foreign enemies; yet, if the foreign enemy were to cease from troubling, would Roman really be able to live at peace with Roman? If the external danger of invasion by armed barbarians were to be stamped out, should we not be exposed to a fiercer and heavier civil bombardment on the home front, in the shape of calumnies and injuries inflicted by the powerful upon their weaker fellow citizens? You complain of crop-failures and famine; yet, the greatest famines are made not by drought but by rapacity, and the most flagrant distress springs from profiteering and price-raising in the grain trade. You complain that the clouds do not disgorge their rain in the sky, and you ignore the barns that fail to disgorge their grain on terra firma. You complain of the fall in production and ignore the failure to distribute what is actually produced to those who are in need of it. You denounce plague and pestilence, while really the effect of these scourges is to bring to light or bring to a head, the crimes of human beings: the callousness that shows no pity for the sick, and the covetousness and rapine that are in full cry after the property of the dead.[28]

A Christian society, presumably, would abolish social ills, or so believed many converts including Cyprian. While no longer a "religion for rabble," Christianity retained the rhetoric of love and justice preached by Jesus.

When Christianity became the favored religion within the empire, its members were only a minority of the population, despite their strength in numbers. The reasons for the Christian victory are varied. Politically, they had won the patronage of an emperor, Constantine, who swept aside the remnants of Diocletian's Tetrarchy and ruled supreme. Despite the horrors inflicted on individuals during the persecutions, the pagan state had been characteristically inefficient in suppressing a cult that threatened the established religion. Ironically, the fortitude of martyrs had a great appeal to idealistic spectators who became interested in a faith worth dying for, and relics of noted martyrs were cherished by

[28] Cyprian *ad Demetrianum* 10, trans. Toynbee, *Study of History*, IV, 121–22.

Jesus as the Good Shepherd. Vatican, Lateran Museum. *Alinari—Scala.*

Christians everywhere. Despite defections by individuals, the discipline of the church and its episcopal cadre was impressive, and the popular election of bishops provided a sense of decision making for common people that was absent in secular politics. Under stress, the church allowed weak Christians to apostatize and welcomed them back when the crisis had past, and similar compromises in everyday morality made the religion palatable for ordinary men. Thus, Christianity had become a hereditary religion for many Romans, a way of life in which they felt comfortable. Unlike the rival mystery cults, the church charged no fees and recruited many converts who might have turned to Isis or Mithras if they could have afforded it. The poor also welcomed the charities performed by the clergy and pious laymen, and even its enemies admitted that Christians fed the unfortunate. The paternalism of the church attracted men crushed by poverty or discarded by society. For those alienated by urban loneliness or rootlessness, Christianity offered the comfort of belonging to a group and the pride of being one of God's elect. For the young, conversion was a means to reject the parents and their ways. Intellectually, the simplistic doctrines of Christianity cut through the clutter of polytheism and the obfuscations of philosophy—thus, the Gospel satisfied both the uneducated commoner and the world-weary intellectual. Since irrationality already permeated the world of learning, Christianity could not be faulted as "a degenerate superstition carried to extravagant lengths," as Pliny the Younger had once called it.[29] To many Romans, it was now the hope of the world.

The Christian millennium dawned with Constantine, but the empire was not transformed into a kingdom of saints. While conversions increased, many new Christians were opportunists, climbing on the winning bandwagon. As the wealth of the church grew, the clergy were able to extend their charitable activities, but substantial treasure was invested in building churches to rival the pagan temples in splendor. Once a radical sect, Christianity became a staunch bulwark of the established order, now that the state was in "godly hands." Secure at the top of society, the Christian leadership made no move to lessen the sufferings of those on the bottom, the miserable peasantry and dehumanized slaves, apart from pious injunctions to landlords and owners to practice Christ-like mercy. The full significance of the Christian revolution was felt in other fields. Until the Christian victory, the totalitarian state was incomplete, for the emperors of the past had controlled only the bodies of their subjects, not their minds. The Christian goal was the total conquest of souls, and it now enlisted the aid of the state. The weight of imperial authority was brought to bear against heretics and pagans. Ultimately, the church intended to destroy paganism root and branch, but neither Constantine nor his immediate successors were willing to embark on so drastic a course. The pressure on pagans was gradually increased until Theodosius I launched a major assault on the ancestral religion in 391. The victory of Christianity was the triumph of a revolutionary ideology, contemptuous of the past and intolerant of dissent.

To effect the revolution in Roman society, the church had first to put its own house in order. With bishops advising the emperor at court, the secular arm could be used against heretics, and Constantine was persuaded to persecute the Donatists in Africa, but the effort was a failure. To Constantine, Christianity meant religious cohesion, and his concern was with unity, not theology. As a Westerner, his religious views reflected those of Western bishops, especially Ossius of Cordova who served the emperor as an ecclesiastical expert. Theological speculation was more to Greek tastes, and the practical Westerners were satisfied with the mystery of the Trinity. However, the theological problems of the relationship between the Father and the Son had long been a bone of contention among heretics and Christian philosophers. In 318 the issue came to a head in Alexandria when an ascetic priest, Arius, insisted that the Son and Holy Spirit were derivative from and inferior to the Father. As the controversy spread, the Arian position was con-

[29] Pliny the Younger *Epistulae* 10.96.8.

demned and supported by rival synods. To Constantine, the theological issue was a squabble over "these small and very insignificant questions," but he was furious at the division in Christian ranks. In 325, the emperor convened an ecumenical council at Nicaea in Bithynia, attended by over 220 bishops but only three or four from the West; the bishop of Rome sent two priests to represent him. Advised by Ossius, Constantine presided at the council and influenced its decision in favor of the Trinity. The council formulated a creed using the Greek word *homoousios* to express the consubstantial nature of the Father, Son, and Holy Spirit. Since the term was not derived from scripture, theology was added to revelation as a source of Christian doctrine. Most of the bishops accepted the Nicene creed, and even the extreme Arians submitted within two years, for the emperor withheld clerical privileges from those who resisted.

To a theological purist, the emperor's post-Nicene attitude toward the Arians seems paradoxical. Despite his endorsement of the Trinity, he had no desire to inquire too deeply into the consciences of the clergy, and he insisted that recanting Arians not be penalized. Constantine was especially angry over the anti-Arian stance of the new bishop of Alexandria, Athanasius, who was adamant against heretics. Though short in stature, Athanasius was a towering personality who spent most of his life in ecclesiastical disputes and was often exiled for his views. In 333, Constantine ordered that Arius's writings be burned,[30] but he later granted the heresiarch an audience and seemed satisfied of his orthodoxy. Athanasius, who had just been deposed by rival clerics, also appeared before Constantine and almost won over the ruler to his cause, but the bishop's enemies notified Constantine that Athanasius had threatened to call out the longshoremen of Alexandria on strike and prevent the grain fleet from sailing to the capital. The emperor promptly exiled Athanasius to Gaul where he remained until after Constantine's death. Unable to profit from his rival's fall, Arius died in 335, and two years later Constantine was dead. Ironically, the dying emperor had received baptism from an Arian bishop. As a secular ruler concerned with the welfare of all his subjects, Constantine did well to avoid the extreme anti-Arian position of Athanasius, but his meddling in religious matters set an unfortunate precedent for future emperors. The blame must be shared by ecclesiastical politicians who appealed to the power of the throne. The principle that the emperor was head of the church, Caesaropapism, was extremely dangerous, for not all rulers would be orthodox and the involvement of the secular arm transformed

---

[30] Constantine had also ordered the burning of Porphyry's anti-Christian polemics, but the books still circulated in 448 when Theodosius II held another literary bonfire.

Christian sarcophagus of the third century, utilizing classical forms as symbols of initiation into Christianity. Probably, Jonah represents faith, the praying figure—prayer, the philosopher—study of Holy Writ, and the shepherd—salvation through Christ; the final scene is the last stage in initiation—baptism. Rome, S. Maria Antiqua. *Alinari—Scala.*

religious disputes into political affairs. The church soon realized that the price of success over dissent was subordination to imperial authority.

The relationship of Christianity to secular culture was ambivalent. While educated men had no desire to abandon the Greek and Latin classics, much classical literature was imbued with pagan thought and myths, and the reason of scientists and philosophers often clashed with revelation. The dangers of "too great learning" were made explicit by a group of heretics in third-century Rome, who "studied Euclid, admired Aristotle and Theophrastus, and almost worshiped Galen"; they also altered the scriptures and applied dialectical reasoning to matters of faith.[31] Such scandalous doings prompted Tertullian's famous outburst: "What has Athens to do with Jerusalem, the Academy with the Church? . . . We have no need for curious disputation after Jesus Christ, nor for inquiry after the Gospel!"[32] Similar views were expressed by another African convert, Arnobius, who wrote a sarcastic attack on pagan beliefs. Even more dyspeptic was the Sicilian astrologer Firmicus Maternus, who was converted to Christianity under Constantine. In his polemic against paganism, he urged the state to extirpate "false gods" and their worshipers and cited as a laudatory precedent the

[31] Eusebius *Historia Ecclesiastica* 5.28.13–14.
[32] Tertullian *de Praescriptione Haereticorum* 7.

persecution of the Bacchic cult under the Republic. The doleful deaths of those emperors who had opposed Christianity were recounted with relish by another convert, the African Lactantius, who had been a pupil of Arnobius, taught Latin rhetoric at Diocletian's court, and later tutored Constantine's son Crispus. In his apologetic work, Lactantius asserted the merits of revelation and faith over mere human reason and was willing to reject the spherical shape of the earth. Yet he quoted the Sibylline Oracles and Hermes Trismegistus as valid authorities in matters of prophecy. To Lactantius, the Roman world was old and ill, and within two centuries it would fall under the heel of an oriental tyrant as a preliminary to the end of all things. The pessimism of Lactantius reflected middle-class despair, for he was a bitter critic of the secular policies of Diocletian and saw no hope in the Constantinian state.

The most famous Constantinian apologist was an erudite bishop, Eusebius of Caesarea, who wrote prolifically in defense of the faith and in celebration of the Christian triumph. His apologetic works are crammed with references to authors now lost, and he welded Christianity to classical culture by claiming that Plato and other sages were either inspired by Biblical truth or had somehow intuited it. The *pax Romana* had been divinely designed to make the world safe for Christianity, which was the culmination of all that was good in the past. The hero who completed the divine plan, Constantine, was glorified in a panegyrical biography that contains much useful material. Eusebius's masterpiece was a history of the church, written with an episcopal bias and glossing over unpleasantries such as the Arian controversy, in which his own position was open to question. Nevertheless, Eusebius quoted extensively from many valuable documents and early Christian authors. Thanks to his pedantry, the development of Christianity can be reconstructed with some assurance. As enunciated in his oration on Constantine's thirtieth year in power, the political views of Eusebius provided an ideological bulwark for the Christian Roman monarchy and its Byzantine successor. As God rules the universe, the emperor governs mankind, and he is literally the chosen agent of God:

> Our emperor, His friend, acting as interpreter to the Word of God, aims at recalling the whole human race to the knowledge of God; proclaiming clearly in the ears of all, and declaring with powerful voice the laws of truth and godliness to all who dwell on the earth. . . . Invested as he is with a semblance of heavenly sovereignty, he directs his gaze above and frames his earthly government according to the pattern of that divine original, feeling strength in its conformity to the monarchy of God.[33]

[33] Eusebius *Tricennalian Oration* 2.4; 3.5, trans. J. Stevenson, *A New Eusebius* (London: Society for Promoting Christian Knowledge, 1957), pp. 391–92.

The Roman emperor was as divine as he could be while still remaining a Christian. In part, the roots of Eusebian monarchism lay in the inflated rhetoric of Pliny the Younger and the propaganda of Diocletian, but the transfigured ruler-figure was more than just Heaven's viceroy— he was divinely inspired and privy to revelations denied to ordinary mortals. Not only had Christianity completed the edifice of totalitarianism, but Eusebius revived the Hellenistic concept of a god-king. Not all Christians were willing to accept this notion, which was rejected in the West, but it became the ideology of Byzantium.

While Constantine may have been the first Christian emperor (although that distinction may rightfully belong to Philip the Arab), the Roman empire was not the first society to embrace Christianity. Since apostolic times, missionaries had been active in the Syriac regions, and the king of Osroëne in northwestern Mesopotamia was converted late in the second century. By the end of the third century, the ruler of Armenia had accepted Christianity. The fourth century witnessed the Christian triumph in the Roman empire, the conversion of Ethiopia, and the spread of missionaries among the Goths. In spreading its control over diverse peoples, the church adopted practical compromises with local customs and even with cherished aspects of paganism. Devoted to the old gods of the soil, rural peoples retained them in the guise of Christian saints to whom the farmers could pray for rain and good crops. Wonder-working trees continued to be objects of devotion, although their magic powers of bestowing fertility on women were no longer credited to a heathen god but to the intercession of a saint. The bones of famous martyrs were cherished as potent fetishes. The widespread solar cult was incorporated by Constantine, whose views of Christ were alloyed with his old devotion to Sol Invictus. In 321 the emperor reserved Sunday as a holiday for Christians, and in 336 the birthday of Sol Invictus, December 25, was arbitrarily chosen as Christmas. A mosaic still survives under Saint Peter's in Rome which shows Christ as a solar deity in Apollo's chariot. Although adamant on doctrinal matters, the church realized the pragmatic benefits of syncretism and accepted traditional folkways and artistic motifs. The clergy were more concerned with heresy than with festivals. Through sensible accommodation, Christianity was eased into the lives of the masses.

CHAPTER TEN

The end of
the Roman world

> The rise of a city, which swelled into an empire, may deserve, as a singular prodigy, the reflections of a philosophic mind. . . . The story of its ruin is simple and obvious; and, instead of inquiring why the Roman empire was destroyed, we should rather be surprised that it had subsisted so long.[1]

So mused Edward Gibbon, the most eminent historian of Rome's fall. With hindsight, moderns view the Late Roman Empire with greater clarity than those who lived in it, unaware that a great tragedy was unfolding. "Except the Lord keep a city, the watchman waketh but in vain," the Psalmist had warned,[2] but Christians were now sure that the Lord was watching over the eternal city. Buttressed with the Gospel and the decrees of Diocletian, the Constantinian state was a powerful structure. Within the empire, dissent was crushed, and on the borders, the barbarians were kept at bay for half a century. Even major defeats such as the battle of Adrianople did not forebode permanent damage to an empire that had survived the catastrophes of the third century. While men know that they are mortal, societies rarely admit as much, and the ideology of the empire insisted that Rome was eternal. Yet, the perpetuity of the Roman empire proved to be illusory within two lifetimes. A man born in the year of Constantine's death might live to see the eternal city occupied by barbarians. Another man, born during the sack of Rome, would witness the dissolution of imperial authority in the West, the barbarization of the Western provinces, and the contraction of the remains of the empire within a Byzantine shell. A world that had lasted for half a millennium ceased to exist.

The sources for Late Imperial history are varied and interesting.

---

[1] Gibbon, *Decline of the Roman Empire*, IV, 161.   [2] Psalms 127.2.

Much of the literature is ecclesiastical and reflects the spiritual mood of the time as well as clerical disputes and comments on current problems. Such are the writings of Synesius, Jerome, and Augustine. Pagan views are well represented in the works of the emperor Julian, the rhetorician Libanius, and the senator Symmachus. A particularly important source is the *Theodosian Code,* a compilation of imperial decrees from 313 to 438, which presents a grim picture of regimentation. Like all legal codes, it must be used with caution, for even the subjects of despots do not always obey the laws, however dire the consequences may be. Nevertheless, the code presents the Roman world the way the state wished it to be, and those who disobeyed it did so at their peril. The fourth century produced the last great Latin historian, Ammianus Marcellinus, a minor biographer, Aurelius Victor, and a literary curiosity, the *Historia Augusta.* Early in the fifth century, Orosius explained Roman history from a Christian point of view, while Eunapius and Olympiodorus were major pagan historians. Later, Priscus was an accurate observer whose account of the Huns is especially valuable. Also important is the history of the Goths written by Cassiodorus and summarized by Jordanes in the sixth century. Among historians, the last pagan voice was that of Zosimus, who wrote a partisan account of the "decline and fall" of the empire.

Besides the usual difficulties in ascertaining facts under a despotism, the historians of the Late Empire had an additional obstacle in the rivalries between the Western and Eastern emperors after 395. The Greek historian, Eunapius, deplored the informants upon whom he had to rely:

> It was not possible to include in the history any accurate information about Western affairs in the time of the eunuch Eutropius, for the great distance of the journey by sea caused news to be stale and spoiled by time. . . . Any persons who had traveled there on business or on military service and were in a position to obtain information on political events brought back reports which were prejudiced and partial and conformed to their own whim and pleasure. So, if one brought face to face, like witnesses in a law court, three or four of them who gave contradictory accounts, there was a great verbal struggle: . . . "How did *you* learn that? Where did Stilicho see *you?* Would *you* have recognized the eunuch?" So that it was a considerable task to compose their quarrels. Of the traders (who had been to the West), not a single one said anything that was not false or such as he thought would bring him profit.[3]

For modern historians, the problem is further complicated by the fragmentary survival of much of the ancient sources. For many episodes,

[3] Eunapius, fragment 74, trans. E. A. Thompson, "Olympiodorus of Thebes," *Classical Quarterly* 38 (1944): 46.

the history of Rome's final years must be pieced together from "rags and patches" and partisan pleas.

THE CHRISTIAN ROMAN EMPIRE

The Christian Roman empire was a world that Constantine made when he added dynastic succession to the system of Diocletian and wedded the church to the state. His third contribution, the reinvigoration of the senatorial class, unintentionally undermined the autocratic structure of Roman society. Nevertheless, Constantine and his successors tried to perfect the arts of despotism and reduce the empire to the rule of bishops and bureaucrats. In the words of Ortega y Gasset, under such regimes "the people are converted into fuel to feed the mere machine which is the state. The skeleton eats up the flesh around it. The scaffolding becomes the owner and tenant of the house." [4] Though the emperors were conscientious, the effectiveness of government was weakened by the corruption of eunuchs at court, the favored role of the senatorial class, and the fear engendered by the secret police everywhere. The oppressiveness of the Roman state intensified without a compensating increase in efficiency. The needs of the armies and a swollen bureaucracy sapped the limited resources of the empire, and the state had no solution to the problem beyond tightening the screws of tyranny. Unfair taxation and injustice in law courts were recurring complaints in the fourth and fifth centuries. There is much truth in Rostovtzeff's harsh judgment:

> There was almost nothing positive except the fact of the existence of the empire with all its natural resources. The men who inhabited it had utterly lost their balance. Hatred and envy reigned everywhere: the peasants hated the landowners and the officials, the city proletariate hated the city *bourgeoisie*, the army was hated by everybody.[5]

One reason for the general dissatisfaction was that two major elements in society, the church and the senators, did not pull their weight. Whatever good was done by individual clergymen, the church was a parasite on the empire. Not only were men of ability diverted from secular life into religious roles, but pious men and rulers endowed the church with large amounts of property that were lost as sources of revenue for the

[4] J. Ortega y Gasset, *The Revolt of the Masses* (New York: Norton, 1957), p. 122.
[5] Rostovtzeff, *Roman Empire*, I, 505.

state. Church property was only subject to land taxes, and the state often returned the funds in direct subsidies. Equally parasitical was the senatorial nobility, the pampered elite of the Late Empire.

While the *Theodosian Code* depicts a monolithic autocracy, the realities of life in the Christian Roman empire reveal a powerful noble class, basking in the favor of the emperors and avoiding legitimate tax demands. Though the policy was not in the interest of the state, Constantine and his successors revived the senatorial class after its eclipse in the third century. High positions in the government were given to senators, and able civil servants were promoted to senatorial rank. In the East, the Senate at Constantinople was largely made up of new appointees, but in the West, the Senate at Rome was crowded with old established families who held great amounts of land. Prominent among the great families of the West were the Anicii, the Probi, and the Ceionii. The wealth of Western senators was enormous, and both Ammianus Marcellinus and Olympiodorus testify to the splendor of their huge palaces at Rome and the conspicuous consumption that characterized their lives. The famous Symmachus, "a senator of moderate means," spent a ton of gold on games to celebrate the praetorship of his young son; another senator spent twice as much on his son. Though some of the Anicii embraced Christianity, many of the great families were stubbornly pagan, and the Christian emperors bought their support with patronage, elevating their members to consulships and prefectures and overlooking their venality in office. At a time when the state was desperate for revenue, the great landowners of the West avoided their just share of taxation by bribing officials or passing the burden on to their tenants. Since the senators policed themselves lightly, the situation was not unlike the abuses that had undermined the old Republic. Despotism sufficed to crush freedom of thought and outbreaks by the anguished poor, but it did not prevent corruption from draining the resources of society into private hands.

For good or ill, Constantine insisted on dynastic succession and had trained his sons as Caesars. At his death in 337, the throne passed jointly to Constantius II, who governed the East, and his brothers, Constans and Constantine II, who ruled the West. The Eastern Augustus was an Arian, and the Western rulers were Catholics. Christian principles did not prevent Constantius from ordering the slaughter of the male descendants of Constantius Chlorus, except for himself, his brothers, and two cousins, Gallus and Julian, whose father died in the dynastic purge. In the West, Constantine II quarreled with Constans and died in a civil war in 340. A decade later, Constans perished in a military mutiny which was suppressed with great loss of life by Constantius, who, like his father, claimed a vision of the Cross before the decisive battle. The empire could ill afford the depletion of military manpower in these struggles. The ablest of Constantine's sons, Constantius was fastidious in manner and suspicious by nature. Pious to a fault, he promoted the Arian cause and deposed Athanasius, who had returned to Alexandria. The emperor angered conservatives by removing the Altar of Victory from the Senate chamber at Rome and passed some ineffectual laws against public pagan rites. In need of a Caesar, Constantius appointed his cousin Gallus to the post. The new Caesar was headstrong and oppressive, and his harsh administration of Antioch prompted loud complaints from the unhappy city. In 354 Gallus was executed on a charge of treason. The emperor then turned to his cousin Julian, appointed him Caesar, and gave him his sister's hand in marriage. In Gaul, Julian successfully battled bands of Franks and Alemanni, but his new prestige disturbed Constantius, whose eunuchs intrigued against the Caesar. In 360 the emperor ordered a major troop movement from Gaul to deal with the threat of Persia, but the Gallic legions mutinied and elevated Julian as emperor. On his way to fight the rebels, Constantius suddenly died of fever, and Julian assumed the throne in 361 without a civil war.

The new emperor was a short, bearded young scholar, ascetic in habit and addicted to mysticism. Though raised a Christian, Julian had been converted to paganism by conservative professors and the theurgist, Maximus of Ephesus, who awed him with seances and miracles. Probably the murder of his closest kin by the pious Constantius also contributed to Julian's distaste for Christianity. Once on the throne, he proclaimed the restoration of the old religion as the official cult, but his paganism was saturated with Neoplatonism and theurgy. A puritan at heart, the emperor tried to remodel the pagan priesthoods on Christian standards, but the pagan laity mocked his prim notions on religion. More effective was an imperial ban on Christian teachers of Greek and Latin literature, which Julian hoped would drive a wedge between Christianity and the educated classes. Unintentionally, his policies relaxed tension within the church, and Christians in the East did not hesitate to riot when pagan mobs threatened their sacred buildings. In the mounting chaos, the emperor deposed Athanasius, whom he had restored to Alexandria. In secular affairs, Julian was more productive; he reduced some taxes and eliminated unnecessary officials at court. Ambitious for military glory, the emperor invaded Persian Mesopotamia and died there of wounds in 363, his hopes of conquest shattered like his dreams of a pagan renaissance. Though he failed to stem the tide of Christianity, the imperial apostate had put new heart into the pagan cause.[6]

[6] Julian's adviser Maximus later won the favor of Valens, but the theurgist became involved in a court conspiracy and was executed in 370. A picturesque charlatan, he had gone far in an age of gullibility.

After the death of Julian, the throne passed from the family of Constantine into the hands of a new military dynasty. In 363 the army on the Eastern front elevated as emperor a young officer, Jovian, who made peace with Persia by surrendering all territories won by Rome since the time of Diocletian. Though a Catholic, he decreed religious toleration for both pagans and Arians. In 364 Jovian was overcome by poisonous fumes in a newly-plastered, unventilated bedroom. A cabal of generals picked as his successor a capable commander from the Balkans, Valentinian I, who appointed his brother, Valens, Augustus of the East, and his own son, Gratian, Caesar of the West. The senior Augustus was a Catholic but tolerant in religious matters. Valens, however, was an ardent Arian and harassed Catholics in the East, but he did not disturb Athanasius, who died in 373, a formidable champion of orthodoxy to the end. A harsh man, Valentinian disliked Greeks and intellectuals, and he forbade Romans to marry barbarians. Worried over peasant disorders, the emperor prohibited civilians from owning weapons, but he also strove for honesty in government and appointed new officials as public defenders. While battling barbarians on the Danube, Valentinian died of a stroke in 375. As Western Augustus, he was succeeded by Gratian, who was a Catholic but shared his throne with his Arian half-brother, Valentinian II. To link the Valentinian dynasty with the house of Constantine, Gratian had married a daughter of Constantius II. A dilettante, he was fond of literature and hunting and left decision making to his advisers. A Spanish general, Theodosius, who had served the empire well, fell victim to court intrigue and was executed. In disgrace, the fallen general's son, also named Theodosius, retired to Spain, but a sudden turn of events in the East would soon put him on the throne.

North of the Danube, the tribes were on the move. Though still warlike barbarians, some Goths had embraced Christianity after a fellow Goth, Ulfilas, had preached the Gospel among them. An inspired missionary, he created a Gothic alphabet based on Greek and Latin letters and translated much of the Bible into Gothic. By the end of the fourth century, the majority of Goths had abandoned paganism, but most were Arians as Ulfilas had been. In the middle of the century, the Huns emerged from the steppes and overwhelmed the Alans and Ostrogoths who lived in the Ukraine. A coalition of nomadic tribes from Central Asia, the Huns were superb horsemen and expert archers. Fierce in war, they terrified the Romans, who described them as short, ugly, brutal, and bestial, but later Rome employed Hun mercenaries. In 376 the Huns drove the Visigoths out of Dacia across the Danube into the Roman empire. When the refugees asked to settle on Roman soil in return for service with the imperial army, Valens agreed, but his agents failed to feed the homeless Visigoths, and Roman slavers tried to buy their women and children. Furious at such treatment, the Gothic

Theodosius I flanked by Valentinian II and Arcadius. Madrid, Real Academia de la Historia. *Hirmer Fotoarchiv München.*

warriors rose in arms and ravaged the Balkans. Though Gratian was coming to his aid, Valens grew impatient and attacked the Visigoths near Adrianople in 378. The Eastern Augustus and two-thirds of his army died in the battle. Not only had Roman manpower been squandered, but the psychological effect of the Gothic victory was great on both barbarians and Romans. In 379 Gratian called the surprised Theodosius from Spain and appointed him as Valens's successor. With more diplomacy than fighting, the new Augustus pacified the Goths, gave them land in the Balkans, and enlisted large numbers of them in his depleted army. For centuries, the empire had utilized Germanic mercenaries, but Theodosius made a crucial departure from precedent when he allowed the barbarians the status of federates, subject to Rome but ruled by their own chiefs and laws. Theodosius and strong leaders could control the barbarians, but weak emperors found themselves at the mercy of unruly federates. The presence of shaggy German generals at court and in the high command irritated Greeks and Latins and added an element of ethnic conflict to further weaken the troubled empire.

Fond of reading history, Theodosius fancied that he bore a physical resemblance to his fellow Spaniard, Trajan. The emperor had two sons, Arcadius and Honorius, but since his wife was dead, he married Gratian's sister who bore him a daughter, Galla Placidia. Despite a quick temper, Theodosius was a conscientious ruler, but he spent money lavishly and was a Catholic bigot. Though baptized late in life, his zeal for orthodoxy was unbounded. Indifferent to Jews, Theodosius loathed Arians and issued a momentous decree in 380:

It is Our Will that all the people who are ruled by the administration of Our Clemency shall practice that religion which the divine Peter the Apostle transmitted to the Romans, as the religion which he introduced makes clear even unto this day. It is evident that this is the religion that is followed by the Pontiff Damasus, . . . according to the apostolic discipline and the evangelic doctrine . . . of the Holy Trinity. We command that those persons who follow this rule shall embrace the name of Catholic Christians. The rest, however, whom We adjudge demented and insane, shall sustain the infamy of heretical dogmas, their meeting places shall not receive the name of churches, and they shall be smitten first by divine vengeance and secondly by the retribution of Our own initiative, which We shall assume in accordance with the divine judgment.[7]

The Arian bishop of Constantinople was deposed, and heretics suffered civil disabilities. In 381, Theodosius prompted an ecumenical council at Constantinople, which emphasized the equality of the Trinity and insisted that the bishop of Byzantium had precedence over all clergymen except the bishop of Rome, "because Constantinople is New Rome." Pope Damasus was not enthusiastic over the statement of Byzantine prestige. Although he was a zealous Catholic, Theodosius criticized worldly clerics and had little patience with the abuse of sanctuary in churches.

In the West, Gratian had fallen under the influence of the bishop of Milan, Ambrose, who persuaded him to abandon the title of Pontifex Maximus, which his predecessors had retained. The formidable Ambrose also insisted on the removal of the Altar of Victory which Julian had restored to the Senate chamber, and the bishop prevented Valentinian II from returning it, despite an eloquent plea by the distinguished senator Symmachus. In 383 Gratian perished in a military mutiny led by a Spanish general, Magnus Maximus, whom Theodosius briefly recognized as an emperor in order to buy time. Maximus earned the dubious distinction of being the first Roman ruler to execute a heretic when he slew Priscillian, the leader of an unorthodox sect of puritans in Spain and Gaul. By 388 Maximus was overthrown and executed by Theodosius, who left young Valentinian II in nominal control of the West. When the townspeople of Thessalonika murdered some imperial officers in 390, Theodosius ordered a massacre in which 7,000 civilians died. Later, at Milan, Ambrose denied the emperor the sacraments unless he confessed his guilt for the recent atrocity. As a dutiful Catholic, Theodosius obeyed and accepted a light penance. Ambrose had scored a major point in forcing a Roman emperor to accept the moral authority of the church in a secular matter. Such incidents foreshadowed the medieval world.

The fine hand of Ambrose may also be discerned in Theodosius's

[7] *Theodosian Code* 16.1.2, trans. Pharr, p. 440.

crusade against paganism, the final break with traditional Rome. Though he had retained pagans in the government and entrusted his oldest son to a pagan tutor, the emperor was persuaded to forbid the public display of paganism. In 391 he banned pagan rites, closed the Delphic oracle, and forbade the Olympic Games. Since many temples were richly endowed, the Christian state made a handsome profit seizing treasures and lands in the antipagan program. At Alexandria, a Christian mob stormed the Serapeum and destroyed other venerable temples. In the disorders, many books perished when the temple libraries were looted. In 392 the antipagan campaign provoked a major revolt in the West where conservative senators backed a coup d'état by the Frankish marshal, Arbogast, who murdered Valentinian II and replaced him with a puppet emperor, the rhetorician Eugenius. Though a nominal Christian, Eugenius favored the old religion, and Arbogast and the leading senator, Virius Nicomachus Flavianus, were devout pagans. The rebels were encouraged by a convenient oracle which announced that the magician Peter would enslave the world in the name of Christ for only 365 years, and that the hour of deliverance was at hand.[8] Probably the scholarly Nicomachus discovered or concocted the oracle. Unfortunately, the gods did not heed the prayers of their followers when Theodosius marched on Italy in 394 with a large army and such able generals as the Goth Alaric and the Vandal Stilicho. In a major battle, the rebels were defeated and their leaders, Arbogast and Nicomachus, committed suicide. The luckless Eugenius was executed by Theodosius, whose triumph sealed the doom of paganism as a viable religion in the Roman world. Ironically, the emperor believed that the empire would now be secure in the hands of his heirs, Arcadius and Honorius, whom he had earlier elevated as Augusti despite their youth. In 395 Theodosius died at the age of fifty; two years later, Ambrose too was dead. The emperor's hopes proved to be vain, for the Roman empire began to crumble in the generation after his death. The future belonged to the church that Ambrose had defended so energetically.

The literature of the fourth century was rarely first-rate. Christian clerics produced tendentious tracts on pious topics, and theologians obfuscated the Trinity and other mysteries with tortuous Greek reasoning. Since Origen, the theologians of Alexandria tended to interpret scripture allegorically, but their bitter rivals in Antioch insisted on a literal interpretation of Holy Writ. To propagandize the merits of monastic life, Athanasius wrote an extremely popular biography of the Egyptian monk Antony. The little book won many converts, and Augustine claimed that two members of the secret police turned to God after read-

---

[8] Augustine *de Civitate Dei* 18.53.

ing it.[9] The hagiographic literature that followed in the wake of Athanasius's *vita Antonii* was related to the cult of saints fostered by the leadership of the church. Popes like Damasus and bishops like Ambrose diligently collected the relics of martyrs and publicized miracles associated with these potent fetishes. On the pagan side, the emperor Julian wrote polemics against Christianity and lyric descriptions of his mystic visions of the supreme deity, Helios, who was manifest in the sun and attended by the conventional gods of paganism. Solar henotheism was a common theme in late pagan thought. Julian's Neoplatonist friend, Sallustius, composed a tract that intellectualized the gods and disavowed the crudities of myth. The Greek rhetoricians Libanius and Themistius also defended the pagan cause but largely on conservative grounds. Their writings are valuable sources for the social history of the time, and Libanius tells us much about life in Antioch. Despite their paganism, both Libanius and Themistius enjoyed the patronage of Christian emperors, and the latter was the tutor of Arcadius. Gratian too was educated by a pagan literary figure, the Gallic poet Ausonius, who wrote charming Latin verses and a memorable description of the Moselle River. His Christian counterpart, the Spaniard Prudentius, defended both the church and the Christian state and celebrated martyrs in grisly verses. Totally artificial was an effort by the Greek poet Quintus Smyrnaeus to continue the *Iliad*. The Latin poet Avienus translated obsolete Hellenistic works on astronomy and geography and tried to turn Livy into verse. These retreats to a distant past were typical of many Roman intellectuals, who sought escape in art and pedantry.

The Latin historians of the fourth century were a mixed lot. The African official S. Aurelius Victor briefly described the emperors from Augustus to Constantius II, condemned military usurpers, and praised provincials (especially Africans). Other pagans produced sketches of emperors and Republican worthies and wrote on the origin of Rome; the civil servant Eutropius composed a short digest of Roman history to enlighten the uneducated Valens. The militant pagan senator Flavianus Nicomachus edited Livy, translated Philostratus's life of Apollonius, and wrote annals of his own time that are not extant. His conservative views were shared by the author of the *Historia Augusta,* a motley collection of biographies of emperors and pretenders from Hadrian to Carinus. Although portions are demonstrably fictional, this bizarre work sometimes reflects good sources. A propaganda tract for the pagan reaction, the *Historia Augusta* celebrates the Senate and the family of Constantius Chlorus and generally denigrates emperors who favored Christianity. The author also criticizes rulers who made their own sons

[9] Augustine *Confessiones* 8.6.

imperial heirs. The last great Latin historian, Ammianus Marcellinus, was a pagan but less impressed by the Roman Senate. A native of Antioch who had served under Julian, he idolized the pagan emperor and had no use for Gallus, Constantius II, or barbarians. Toward Christianity, Ammianus was discreetly impartial. An imitator of Tacitus, he wrote a history of the empire from Nerva to the death of Valens and devoted more than half the book to contemporary events. His later years were spent at Rome, where he observed with disgust the venality and arrogance of the senatorial class. A member of the oppressed middle class, Ammianus despised the spoiled grandees of Italy and criticized the injustices of imperial tyrants. The historian had harsh words for an urban prefect who, during a food shortage in 383, expelled foreigners from Rome but exempted 3,000 dancing girls and other theatrical types. Perhaps Ammianus was one of the temporary exiles from the capital.

In 366 the city of Rome was disturbed by a riotous papal election. Ammianus's account of the episode offers valuable insights on triumphant Christianity:

> Damasus and Ursinus, burning with a superhuman desire of seizing the bishopric, engaged in bitter strife because of their opposing interests; and the supporters of both parties went even so far as conflicts ending in bloodshed and death. . . . In the struggle, Damasus was victorious through the efforts of the party which favored him. It is a well-known fact that in the Basilica of Sicininus where the assembly of the Christian sect is held, in a single day a hundred and thirty-seven corpses of the slain were found, and that it was only with difficulty that the long-continued frenzy of the people was afterwards quieted. Bearing in mind the ostentation in city life, I do not deny that those who are desirous of such a thing ought to struggle with the exercise of all their strength to gain what they seek; for when they attain it, they will be [secure], . . . enriched from the offerings of matrons, ride seated in carriages, wearing clothing chosen with care, and serve banquets so lavish that their entertainments outdo the tables of kings. These men might be truly happy, if they would disregard the greatness of the city behind which they hide their faults, and live after the manner of some provincial bishops, whose moderation in food and drink, plain apparel also, and gaze fixed upon the earth, commend them to the Eternal Deity and to his true servants as pure and reverent men.[10]

Thus did the Christian clergy and its leaders appear to a thoughtful pagan.

[10] Ammianus Marcellinus 27.3.12–15, trans. John C. Rolfe (Cambridge, Mass.: Harvard University Press, 1952), Vol. III, pp. 19–21.

In 384, the urban prefect of Rome, Q. Aurelius Symmachus, clashed with Ambrose over the proposed restoration of the Altar of Victory in the Senate chamber. In a famed oration, the pagan Symmachus reminded Valentinian II of the venerable rites that had sustained the Romans against Hannibal and the Gauls and that were now to be discarded. The old and the new religion, Symmachus argued, could exist side by side:

> One may recall the list of princes of both religions and of both views; the earlier of them observed the ceremonies of the forefathers; the later ones did not set them aside. If one does not imitate the reverence of the former, at least let him imitate the tolerance of the latter! . . . Grant us, I pray you, the right to pass on to our descendants what we ourselves received as children. The love of tradition is a mighty force. . . . It is on behalf of the ancestral, the native gods that we plead for tolerance. It is all one and the same, whatever god any particular man adores. We all look up to the same stars; heaven is common to all; the same world surrounds every one of us. Whatever rests above these—each in his own wisdom seeks to know the truth. It is not by one single path that we arrive at so great a mystery.[11]

The altar had become a symbol, not merely of the ancestral religion, but of its right to exist. Doctrinaire Christians would concede no toleration, and Ambrose bullied Valentinian into rejecting the plea. Such acts of bigotry drove desperate conservatives to support the revolt of Eugenius. Unlike his kinsman Nicomachus, Symmachus held aloof from the confrontation with Theodosius, but he had earlier been an eloquent spokesman for tolerance. Yet his speech had been in vain, and the twilight of paganism was fast approaching.

Another voice crying in the wilderness was the anonymous author of the tract *De Rebus Bellicis,* which proposed new armaments to upgrade the Roman defense posture but also dealt with social and economic ills that weakened the empire. Since Valentinian I was interested in gadgetry, the pamphlet was probably addressed to him with its proposals for new frontier fortifications, improved artillery, scythed chariots, and a warship with paddle wheels to be powered by oxen on treadmills. Valentinian was faced with peasant revolts, and the author of the tract argued that the disorders were caused by official corruption and the oppression of the poor by the rich. In frank terms, the writer depicted the agony and rage of the masses:

> From some kind of blind folly, there ensued an even more extravagant passion for gold [among the rich]. . . . This store of gold meant that the

---

[11] Symmachus *Relatio III* 3–10, trans. F. C. Grant, *Ancient Roman Religion* (New York: Bobbs-Merrill, 1957), pp. 247–50.

houses of the powerful were crammed full and their splendor enhanced to
the destruction of the poor, the poorer class of course being held down by
force. But the poor were driven by their afflictions into various criminal
enterprises, and losing sight of all respect for law, all feeling of loyalty,
they entrusted their revenge to crime. For they often inflicted the most
severe injuries on the empire, laying waste the fields, breaking the peace
with outbursts of brigandage, stirring up animosities, and passing from
one crime to another, supported usurpers. . . . It was not bravado that
inspired them.[12]

With equity in taxation and honesty in government, the author continued, these disorders would not have occurred and Roman troops could
have fought the real enemy across the frontiers. Ironically, the author
thought that a codification of laws would promote honesty in government. Though he might have been receptive, the emperor never saw the
pamphlet, for no courtier would pass on a tract that offered excuses for
rebels and condemned the great landowners of the Senate. The Roman
state and its ruling class relied on force to suppress outbreaks in rural
areas without relieving the causes that drove desperate men to revolt. If
the anonymous author had been heeded, the constructive social criticism
of De Rebus Bellicis might have helped the empire to weather the coming storms of the fifth century.

THE END OF A WORLD

Whether of men or of nations, death is never attractive, but it is a
topic of absorbing interest since we are all mortal. The melancholy fate
of the Roman empire has a symbolic dimension that excites the imagination of moralists and monocausal cranks. Whatever its flaws, Rome
was the only lasting political unity that Western Man has known, and
the image of the Pax Romana takes on a nostalgic glow in times of anarchic nationalism. The Roman empire is still an impressive symbol of
secular power, awesome in its extent and duration. When such an edifice topples, men ask: "How have the mighty fallen?" There is no single
answer, though there have been silly attempts at one. Historical causa-
tion is always complex, for men do things for various concurrent reasons, and they do not necessarily intend the results of their acts. The
verdict of history can be correct about an event but wrong about its
causes, for the occurrence of something does not mean that it had to
occur. Many things happen purely by chance, and sometimes important

---

[12] De Rebus Bellicis 2.1–3, trans. E. A. Thompson, A Roman Reformer and Inventor (Oxford: Clarendon Press, 1952), p. 110.

things do. Whether the hand of God or the dialectic, destiny may be safely discounted, but the whimsical goddess, whom the Greeks called Tyche and we label chance, must be taken into account. While much of history is susceptible to rational analysis, the rest is the result of random factors.

There is little doubt that the Roman empire was weaker than anyone suspected when the barbarians began to push across its borders. "The decline of Rome was the natural and inevitable effect of immoderate greatness," Gibbon moralized, "The stupendous fabric yielded to the pressure of its own weight." [13] Though a nice epigram, this notion is no more than the Nemesis of Herodotus or Lucretius's image of lightning striking the tallest tree. Perhaps there is more to Gibbon's claim that Christianity had a deleterious effect on the empire, though the Romans did not become either saints or pacifists with the triumph of the Gospel. To the end, Christian Roman armies fought as bravely as the legions of old. However, the church did drain off potential revenue through pious endowments, and men of talent often abandoned the service of the state to find peace in clerical life. The empire could ill afford either loss. The constant demands of the army and the bureaucratic state exhausted the basically agrarian economy of Rome, and the chronic shortage of funds was not helped by recurrent cycles of inflation or the deliberate evasion of taxes by great landowners. Bribery of officials and the notorious lack of justice in courts of law weakened the efficiency of the state and undermined the confidence of the masses in the Roman government. While there is insufficient data for precise statements on demographic matters, there is considerable evidence of a manpower shortage in the Late Empire. Abandoned farms, shrunken cities, great losses of life in war or pestilence, all suggest a contracting population. There is no need to invoke fantasies of sterility or "misbreeding," though the Christian craze for celibacy prevented some conceptions. A smaller population placed greater demands on the survivors, and it is significant that soldiers and workers in the state armories were branded to discourage them from running away. An additional problem was the disarming of the peasantry to prevent rural rebellions. While this policy protected Rome from its own subjects, the masses were unable to function as militia and defend the countryside when the frontier defenses were breached and invaders swept aside the imperial armies. Since the populations of the barbarian tribes were not enormous, the ease with which they penetrated the empire suggests serious weaknesses within the Roman world.

Ratiocination on the fall of Rome must deal with the fact that the Eastern provinces survived while the West succumbed to the barbarians.

---

[13] Gibbon, *Decline of the Roman Empire,* IV, 161.

Part of the explanation lies in geography—the invaders came across the Rhine and the Danube. While the Balkans received the brunt of many invasions, the barbarians passed on to loot Italy and the West. Constantinople was impregnable, Asia Minor was generally safe, and Egypt and Syria were distant. Though exposed to Persian raids, the provinces of the East were never permanently lost until the Muslim conquest. The Hellenistic East was more urbanized, more populous, and richer than the West; the resources of the East were simply greater. In the East, the ruling class tended to be careerists who owed their fortunes and loyalty to the state, but the entrenched aristocracy of the West were great landowners who could survive the collapse of imperial authority. Despite centuries of Romanization, the veneer of urban civilization in the West proved very thin when the unity of the Roman world was shattered. Later, when the Roman East fell to the Arabs, urban civilization did not wither away in the lost provinces. In a sense, the Hellenistic world outlasted its Roman conquerors..

Yet exposure to hostile neighbors does not doom a strong society, and even inefficient despotisms have lasted for centuries. The personalities of decision makers are crucial factors in history. Authoritarian states are particularly dependent upon the abilities of their leaders, and most Roman emperors of the fifth century were a sorry lot, unable to cope with continuing crises. In Gibbon's words,

> The happiness of an hundred millions depended on the personal merit of one or two men, perhaps children, whose minds were corrupted by education, luxury, and despotic power. The deepest wounds were inflicted during the minorities of the sons and grandsons of Theodosius; and after those incapable princes seemed to attain the age of manhood, they abandoned the church to the bishops, the state to the eunuchs, and the provinces to the barbarians.[14]

Even powerful states cannot endure incompetent rulers for long. Thus, a conjunction of factors brought down the Roman world: serious domestic problems, inadequate rulers, and persistent pressures from aggressive neighbors. Since the barbarian invasions did not engulf the Romans in a tidal wave of humanity, capable emperors might have pulled the empire through, as in the third century. On the other hand, Rome could have endured idiots in high places as long as the barbarians were not at the gate. How long the empire could have withstood the social pressure caused by misgovernment and oppression must remain an open question. If the fifth century had been a time of peace, the prime task of the emperors would have been to relieve the plight of the peasantry. Per-

14 Ibid., IV, 165.

haps, as Cavafy intuited, "the barbarians were a kind of solution." Despotic Rome never had to face up to peasant demands for justice, as the Republic had once faced up to Italian insistence on citizenry. Instead, a series of contingent crises wrecked the empire before the Roman state was forced to choose between reform and extinction.

The history of the last century of the Roman empire is filled with folly, pettiness, and lost opportunities. On his death in 395, Theodosius had left a unified empire in the hands of his two sons, the Eastern Augustus Arcadius and the Western Augustus Honorius. Since both were young and incompetent, their father had provided them with strong protectors. In the East, a Gallic official, Rufinus, was the power behind Arcadius, and the Western strongman was the Vandal general, Stilicho, who had married Theodosius's favorite niece. Division of the empire was a long-standing and practical device for sharing the immense responsibilities of imperial authority, but after 395 the division became a force for disunity as the rival courts engaged in bitter jurisdictive quarrels and fierce personality conflicts in the names of puppet emperors. Honorius was a calamity. Moronic in appearance and act, he spent his time raising chickens. Though twice married to daughters of Stilicho, he was probably impotent; his feeble affection was reserved for his strong-willed half-sister, Galla Placidia. Stupid and ill-tempered, Arcadius was not much better, but he managed to produce an heir. His Frankish wife, Eudoxia, was a stronger personality who later deposed the famed John Chrysostom as bishop of Constantinople. Originally, Rufinus had wanted Arcadius to marry his daughter, but Stilicho could not tolerate a strong rival in the East and arranged to have Rufinus murdered. The weak Arcadius then fell under the influence of a corrupt eunuch, Eutropius, who encouraged the marriage with Eudoxia. Stilicho soon learned that Eutropius was more dangerous than Rufinus.

While Arcadius sat on the throne, the Eastern court was a nest of intrigue. Greek politicians and German generals struggled for power, and Eutropius and Eudoxia became bitter enemies. Taking advantage of the situation, the ambitious king of the Visigoths, Alaric, rose in revolt and began to ravage the Balkans. Since Arcadius could not control the Gothic federates, Stilicho landed troops in Greece and probably hoped to add the Balkans to his domains. To dislodge the uninvited Westerners, Eutropius instigated a rebellion in Africa that endangered the food supply for Rome and forced Stilicho to return to Italy. In order to put down the African revolt, the Vandal general withdrew troops from Gaul and seriously weakened the Rhine defenses. Eutropius then appointed Alaric marshal of Illyricum and probably suggested that he move his tribesmen into Italy, though the Goth needed no encouragement. In 399 the sinister eunuch was overthrown by Eudoxia and other enemies, but

Stilicho with his wife and son. Monza, Cathedral Treasury. *Alinari—Scala.*

the Visigoths marched on Italy and their ranks were swollen by other barbarians who were fleeing from the Huns. While the armies of Stilicho and Alaric fought sporadically, the court of Honorius withdrew permanently from Rome to the relative safety of Ravenna. After a raid on northern Italy, the Vandals, Alans, and Suebi crossed the Rhine in 406 and fell upon Gaul. In 407 a Roman general in Britain rose in revolt and stripped the island of most of its troops when he invaded Gaul, where he was eventually defeated. When the cities of Britain asked for protection from Saxon raiders, Honorius told them to "look to their own defenses," and the province gradually slipped from Roman control. In Italy, a similar policy of feebleness prevailed when the Visigoths threatened Rome. The Senate paid Alaric a large bribe that merely whetted his appetite. The collapse of the Western empire had begun.

As long as Stilicho was alive, the barbarian threat to Italy was contained, but the high-handed Vandal had made many enemies at Honorius's court and his feeble son-in-law feared him. In 408 Arcadius died and was succeeded by his young son, Theodosius II, over whom Stilicho wished to impose a regency. The Western warlord also planned to employ Alaric's forces against the invaders and pretenders who were disturbing Gaul. However, Stilicho's enemies convinced Honorius that a Germanic plot was afoot to take over both halves of the empire, and the foolish emperor ordered Stilicho's arrest and execution. Delighted that his foe was gone, Alaric promptly extorted another ransom from the Roman Senate. In 409 the Gothic king supported an attempt by the urban prefect, Attalus, to claim the Western throne, but the usurper's regime did not survive food shortages in the city of Rome. After failing to break through the walls of Ravenna, Alaric decided to abandon Italy and occupy Africa, sacking Rome on the way. Since the Celtic assault in 387 B.C., the ancient city had not fallen to a foreign enemy, but after a brief siege in 410, Rome was betrayed to the Goths who pillaged it for three days. As good Arians, the barbarians spared the churches, but the civilian population suffered greatly, and Honorius's sister, Galla Placidia, was among the captives. At Rhegium, the Visigoths awaited a fleet to transport them to Africa, but a storm destroyed the ships and Alaric suddenly died. Together with a great treasure, the Gothic king was buried in the Busento River. His successor, Athaulf, led the Visigoths to southern Gaul. Meanwhile, the Vandals, Alans, and Suebi had moved into Spain. In 414 Athaulf married Placidia and was persuaded by her to try to restore the power of Rome with Gothic arms. According to Orosius, the barbarian king had earlier intended to destroy the Roman empire, but he realized the incapacity of his fierce followers to build a Gothic empire in its place, and his wife converted him to the Roman cause.[15] In 415 their mutual hopes foundered when Athaulf was assassinated by Gothic dissidents. His widow was sent to Ravenna where she soon dominated her witless brother. The adventures of Galla Placidia among the Goths illustrate the impotence of the Western empire, as does an imperial decree in 416 that absolved Romans of crimes committed when they had been forced to join the invaders. The edict also dealt with the difficulty of recovering plundered possessions.[16]

Powerless to stop the invaders, the court of Ravenna decided to play the barbarians against each other, for the tribes were bitter rivals. Enlisted as federates, the chiefs were given Roman titles and ordered to combat other barbarians. One Roman general, Constantius, utilized the Visigoths against the barbarians in Spain, crushed a pretender in Gaul, and won the hand of Placidia as his reward. In 421 Constantius III was elevated as Augustus by his brother-in-law, Honorius, but he died the same year. By 423 Honorius too was dead; his successor was Valentinian III, the infant son of Constantius and Placidia. For the first twelve years of his reign, Valentinian was under the regency of his mother, who arranged his marriage with Eudoxia, the daughter of Theodosius II. Meanwhile, the Vandals had crossed from Spain to Africa in 429, and within a decade, their king, Gaiseric, had established a powerful state at Carthage. During his long reign, Vandal fleets terrorized shipping in the Western Mediterranean. Like most of his contemporaries, Gaiseric despised Valentinian, whose principal interests were sports and hunting. In 440 the Vandal menace prompted the emperor to revoke the ban on civilians bearing arms, but the order only reflected his inability to protect them. Luckily, Valentinian could exploit the military abilities of a capable Roman marshal, Aetius, who crushed peasant rebels and Burgundian barbarians in Gaul. Earlier in his career,

---

[15] Orosius 7.43.5–7.   [16] *Theodosian Code* 15.14.14.

Aetius had served under Alaric and later with the Huns, and he soon put his knowledge of both Goths and Huns to good use. In central Europe, the Hun king, Attila, had created a large empire of subject tribes, and he preyed upon the Eastern Roman empire, ravaging the Balkans and extorting huge subsidies. Turning his attention to the West, "the Scourge of God" invaded Gaul in 451 but was defeated by a coalition of Romans and Visigoths under the command of Aetius. Undaunted, Attila led his hordes against Italy in 452, but disease had weakened his forces, and according to legend, Pope Leo I warned the king that he would meet the same fate as Alaric if he sacked Rome. For whatever reason, Attila withdrew from Italy and died a year later. With his death the Hun empire disintegrated.

The Western Roman empire did not outlive Attila by more than two decades. In 454 Aetius succumbed to court intrigue and was slain by the ungrateful Valentinian, who was himself murdered by two retainers of Aetius in 455. The absurd tragedy had been devised by a scheming aristocrat, Petronius Maximus, who seized the throne and forced Valentinian's widow to marry him. Within a few months, the usurper was killed by a mob at Rome while a Vandal force approached the city, supposedly at the invitation of the irate Eudoxia. Invited or not, the Vandals thoroughly plundered Rome and carried off Eudoxia and her children. To replace the unlamented Maximus as emperor, the Visigoths backed a Gallic noble, Avitus, who was deposed and hustled off to a bishopric by Ricimer in 456. A barbarian kingmaker, Ricimer dominated Italy until his death in 472, ruling through a series of imperial puppets and holding the Vandals and Ostrogoths at bay. Ricimer's nephew set up another figurehead ruler who was deposed in 474 by an emperor selected by the Eastern court. A year later, the new ruler was ousted by a former associate of Attila, Orestes, who made his own young son emperor. The boy's name, Romulus Augustulus, was a fitting omen. In 476, Orestes' troops mutinied under a German warlord, Odoacer, who deposed the child Romulus and ended the farcical series of shadow emperors in the West. Accepting the nominal authority of the Eastern emperor, Odoacer ruled Italy as a barbarian prince. A year earlier, the Visigoths in Gaul had severed all formal ties with Constantinople. Such acts had more symbolic value than content, for the barbarian kings had generally gone their own ways, whether or not the emperor was their nominal overlord. Constantinople was far away, its military might did not frighten them, and there had been no lack of pretenders and puppets in the West to issue empty titles to barbarian rulers. The Western Roman empire had long since ceased to be a reality.

Looking back on the calamities of the fifth century, the Byzantine

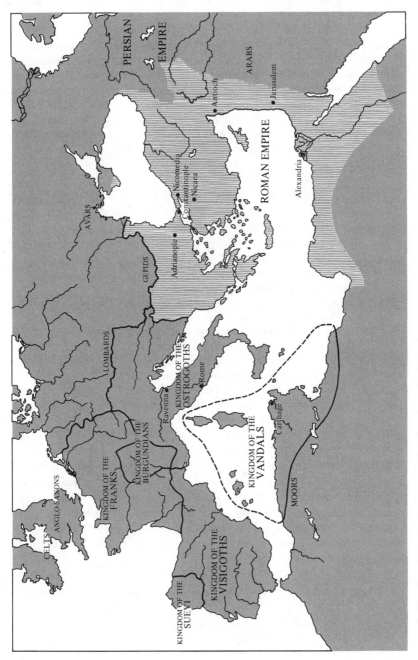

Map 5. The Empire and the Germanic Kingdoms in 527.

historian Zosimus claimed that Valens in 378 had seen a dreadful omen of the ills to come:

> The body of a man was seen lying on the road, like one who had been lashed from top to toe, altogether immobile save that his eyes were open and looked upon those who approached him. . . . He was reckoned neither as alive (because his entire body was motionless) nor yet was wholly dead (because his sight remained unimpaired). . . . The portent bespoke the condition of the state, which would continue to suffer beatings and lashings, like a person breathing out his last, until it was completely destroyed by the wickedness of its magistrates and rulers.[17]

The image of helpless agony was fitting, and it is noteworthy that Zosimus blamed the Roman leadership for the pitiful plight of the empire. If the state could not save itself, how helpless must common people have felt amid the horrors of the invasions!

In a moving poem, a Gallic monk, Orientus, expressed the fear that gripped all classes during the barbarian invasions:

> Murder in ambush or in open brawls!
> Starvation strangles those whom fury spared.
> The sorrowing wife with spouse and children falls.
> In bond with his own slaves, the lord is snared.
> Here food for dogs they lie; or homes on fire
> give to the ravished dead a funeral pyre.
> In village, villa, cross-roads, district, field,
> down every roadway and at every turning,
> death, grief, destruction, arson are revealed.
> In one great conflagration, Gaul is burning.[18]

It was a time of gutted villages and burning farms, raped women and murdered men, families separated and lives broken beyond repair. In rural areas, one of the few places of safety was the fortified villa of a noble. Many free peasants voluntarily became *coloni* to receive protection with the magnates, whose retainers fought off foreign marauders and whose influence kept the dreaded Roman officials away. As this trend increased, quasi-feudal growths festered in the corpse of the Roman world.

Fearsome as the barbarians were, they appeared as deliverers to some Roman peasants who were tired of being bullied by tax collectors

---

[17] Zosimus 4.21, trans. James J. Buchanan and Harold T. Davis (San Antonio: Trinity University Press, 1967), p. 154.

[18] Jack Lindsay, *Song of a Falling World* (London: A. Dakers, 1948), pp. 200–1.

and soldiers. As more provinces slipped from Roman control, the tax burdens of the remaining regions of the empire increased, and contemporary evidence was unanimous in charging that the rich passed the new assessments on to the poor. At best, the masses had a difficult time under Roman rule, but theoretically the laws applied fairly to all citizens. In practice, the great landowners bribed officials to adjust the assessments in their favor, and the same venality reduced the law courts to travesties of justice. Only the rich could afford the costs of litigation, and in any case the judges could be bought off. So oppressive was life within the empire that many peasants preferred the rude ways of the barbarians and ran away to join the invaders. In 376 miners in the Balkans had fled to the Goths and aided their raiding parties as guides.[19] In the early fifth century, peasants in Spain joined the Visigoths, "preferring poverty among the barbarians to paying taxes with anxiety among the Romans." [20] In Gaul, the clergyman Salvian observed the same conditions:

> The poor are being robbed, widows groan, orphans are trodden down, so that many, even persons of good birth, who have enjoyed a liberal education, seek refuge with the enemy. . . . They seek among the barbarians the Roman mercy. . . . Although these men differ in customs and language from those with whom they have taken refuge, and are unaccustomed . . . to the nauseous odor of the bodies and clothing of the barbarians, yet they prefer the strange way of life they find there to the injustice rife among the Romans. So you find men passing over everywhere, now to the Goths, now to the Bacaudae,[21] or whatever other barbarians have established their power anywhere, and they do not repent of their expatriation, for they would rather live as free men, though in seeming captivity, than as captives in seeming liberty. Hence, the name of Roman citizen, once not only much valued but dearly bought, is now voluntarily repudiated and shunned and is thought not merely valueless but even almost abhorrent.[22]

How many Romans actually deserted the empire is unknown, but their numbers were sufficient to attract attention, and the flight was symptomatic of grave social ills in Roman society.

In 449 the historian Priscus accompanied a Byzantine embassy to the camp of Attila, where he encountered a renegade Greek who denounced the inequities of life within the Roman empire:

---

[19] Ammianus Marcellinus 31.6.6.   [20] Orosius 7.41.7.

[21] Salvian included the peasant rebels, the Bacaudae, because they were independent of Roman authority and refugees flocked to them as to the barbarians.

[22] Salvian *de Gubernatione Dei* 5.5, trans. Eva M. Sanford (New York: Columbia University Press, 1930), pp. 141–42.

Among the Romans . . . on account of their tyrants, all men are not allowed to use arms. For those who do use them, the cowardice of their
generals, who cannot support the conduct of war, is more perilous. In
peace, moreover, experiences are more grievous than the evils of the
wars, on account of the very heavy taxes and the wrongs suffered at the
hands of wicked men, since the laws are not imposed on all. If the trans-
gressor of the law be of the monied class, it is not likely that he pays the
penalty of his wrongdoing; if he should be poor and ignorant of how to
handle the business, he endures the penalty according to the law—if he
does not depart life before his trial. For the course of these cases is long
protracted, and a great deal of money is expended on them. . . . No one
will even grant a court to a wronged man unless he lays aside some
money for the judge and his attendants.[23]

Though Priscus responded in defense of the empire, he could not convince the former Roman who preferred to live among the Huns.

Not all discontented Romans ran away; some rose against their oppressors, and peasant revolts were common in the Late Empire. In
Gaul, the rural rebels were called Bacaudae, perhaps a term of Celtic
origin. Late in the third century, Maximian had crushed a major Bacaudic rising, but peasant rebels were still active in the time of Valentinian I. In Africa, rural discontent merged with Christian radicalism,
and bands of extreme Donatists, known as Circumcellions, terrorized
the countryside, plundering villas and rich farms and manhandling their
owners, who were likely to be Catholics. According to Augustine, the
rural terrorists sometimes blinded their victims with lye and vinegar.
While religious fanaticism contributed to their ferocity, the Circumcellions delighted in forcing masters to change places with their slaves.
Similar acts of symbolic levelling are recorded of the Bacaudae who
controlled parts of northwestern Gaul in the fifth century. In the
words of a contemporary writer, "men live there under the natural law.
There's no trickery there. Capital sentences are pronounced there under an
oak tree, and . . . even rustics perorate, and private individuals pro-
nounce judgment. You can do anything you like there."[24] Apparently,
the rebels set up "people's courts," and Salvian suggests that they maintained a separate "barbarian" state. Though some of the rebels may
have been Celtic nationalists, the basic element in the Bacaudic movement was rural desperation. Other "Bacaudae" were active in Spain.
With Visigothic aid, Aetius subdued the main strongholds of the Gallic
Bacaudae. The frequency and intensity of these jacqueries reveal the ex-

[23] Priscus, fragment 8, trans. C. D. Gordon, *The Age of Attila* (Ann Arbor: University of Michigan Press, 1960), pp. 86–87.
[24] *Querolus* 16, trans. E. A. Thompson, "Peasant Revolts in Late Roman
Gaul and Spain," *Past and Present* 2 (1952): 18.

tent of peasant misery. When the barbarians invaded in force, the Roman empire was already distracted by serious internal disorders. "Its fall was announced by a clearer omen than the flight of vultures," Gibbon remarks, "The Roman government appeared every day less formidable to its enemies, more odious and oppressive to its subjects." [25]

While the West crumbled before the barbarians, the Hellenistic East survived, its resources in men and money largely removed from the paths of invasions. The Eastern Augusti were also generally better men than their Western counterparts, and even those who lacked executive drive often had capable advisers. Theodosius II, who ascended the throne in 408, was a pious, gentle prince, heavily under the influence of his sister, Pulcheria, who served as regent during his childhood and later drove his wife from the court. Pulcheria also quarreled with the bishop of Constantinople, Nestorius, who insisted that Mary was the mother of Jesus the man but not the god. Though he was deposed as a heretic, the views of Nestorius were popular in the Syriac regions, and Nestorianism was adopted by the Christians who lived in the Persian empire. Theodosius was interested in education and founded a Christian university in the capital to rival the pagan schools at Athens. In foreign affairs, he had little success, for his generals failed to dislodge the Vandals in Africa or protect the Balkans from the Huns. Attila was bought off with huge annual subsidies. However, the emperor did improve the fortifications of Constantinople, and his walls (with later additions) protected the city for a thousand years. In 438 he published the first codification of Roman laws since the Twelve Tables, the *Theodosian Code*. Like the Western emperors, Theodosius was dependent on Germanic soldiers, and the Alan general Aspar wielded great influence at the court.

When Theodosius II died in 450, Aspar and Pulcheria picked as his successor a Thracian officer, Marcian, who married the aging princess in order to preserve continuity with the Spanish dynasty. With the empress's enthusiastic support, an ecumenical council met at Chalcedon in 451 to repudiate Nestorianism and confirm the Nicene pronouncements on Christ. However, the decisions at Chalcedon did not halt the rise of Monophysitism, a loose term for a variety of Christological beliefs that emphasized one nature of Christ over the other, usually the divine over the human. Bitter conflicts between orthodox believers and Monophysites soon disturbed the Eastern Roman empire. A man of peace, Marcian avoided foreign wars, but he also refused to pay tribute to Attila, whose death saved Byzantium from Hun vengeance. While he favored the senatorial class in tax relief, the emperor was a careful administra-

---

[25] Gibbon, *Decline of the Roman Empire,* III, 480.

tor and left a full treasury at his death in 457. Again Aspar selected a
Thracian officer as emperor, but Leo I resented the dominance of the
marshal, whose power rested on German soldiery. In 468 Leo entrusted
his brother-in-law with a major expedition against the Vandals, but the
attack was a disastrous failure that squandered much of the surplus
funds left by Marcian. Since Aspar had approved the ill-fated campaign, his prestige slipped, and the emperor began intrigues with a
corps of Isaurian troops from Asia Minor. Their leader, Zeno, married
Leo's daughter. In 471 the Isaurians supported the emperor when he
had Aspar murdered. The act of treachery ended the role of Germanic
kingmakers at Constantinople. Unlike its Western counterpart, the Byzantine court had shaken off the barbarian yoke. Though an unsavory
crew, the Isaurians were Easterners. When Leo died in 474, control of
the Eastern empire passed to Zeno and the Isaurians.

Despite the troubles of the time, the fifth century was an age of considerable literary activity. In Greek, the Egyptian poet Nonnus wrote a
rambling epic on the god Dionysus. Another Greek poet, Musaeus,
showed more competence in a long work on the fabled lovers, Hero and
Leander. More topical were the Latin verses of Claudian of Alexandria,
who like Ammianus Marcellinus achieved mastery in a borrowed
tongue. Though a pagan, Claudian served Honorius as a court poet and
heaped praise on Stilicho and abuse on the eunuch Eutropius. Another
pagan poet, Rutilius Namatianus, wrote a memorable account of his trip
home from Rome to Gaul during the invasions of the early fifth century.
The poet had no love for barbarians, monks, or Jews, and though he
spoke of the eternity of Rome, he was witnessing its death throes. The
Gallic poet Paulinus of Nola ably defended Christianity in letters and
verses. Though schooled by Ausonius in the classics, he had rejected
the old religion and found serenity as a Christian clergyman. Two Gallic monks, Sulpicius Severus and Salvian, produced major works. Severus wrote a competent history of the church and an influential life of
Martin of Tours. Social injustice was the dominant theme of Salvian's
bitter tract, *On the Government of God,* which denounced Roman oppression and inherited wealth and exaggerated the virtues of barbarians.
An important Gallo-Roman writer was Sidonius Apollinaris, whose father-in-law was the ephemeral emperor Avitus. After a checkered career at the imperial court, Sidonius returned to Gaul and became a
bishop. His letters are valuable documents on life under the barbarians
and reflect the narrow views of the collaborating gentry. In Africa, the
scholarly Martianus Capella wrote a tortuous allegory on the seven liberal arts which later caught the imagination of medieval educators.
More interesting are the writings of Synesius of Cyrene, a country gentleman turned bishop, who despised both theurgists and ascetic monks.

He warned the emperor Arcadius against relying on German troops, and he protected his own flock against oppressive officials. Though a bishop, Synesius had been a Neoplatonist and a friend of Hypatia, and he did not accept the Christian dogma of the resurrection of the body. Another unconventional bishop was the eloquent John Chrysostom, who studied under Libanius and had a stormy career at Constantinople. Christlike in his love for the masses, he castigated the rich and gave his own possessions to the poor. A foe of the empress Eudoxia, John was twice banished and died in exile. In interpreting scripture, he favored the literal approach of the school of Antioch. In the middle of the fifth century, a Byzantine official, Priscus, wrote a highly readable history of his time. His eyewitness report on a visit to Attila's court is vivid and perceptive. While the Hun generals wore finery and feasted off silver, Priscus noted, Attila dressed simply without any regal ornaments and ate a modest supper out of a wooden dish. Possessed of immense power, the great Hun did not need the theatrical trappings of a Byzantine emperor.

In the fifth century, pagans felt distaste for the present and a passion for the past. At Rome, conservative senators wrote commentaries on Vergil and lovingly edited Livy. Typical of this partisan scholarship was the *Saturnalia* of Macrobius, who centered his book on Vergilian themes and packed it with antique lore. Significantly, the setting of the work is a symposium attended by Symmachus, Flavianus Nicomachus, and other heroes of the pagan reaction. The Greek historians Eunapius of Sardis and Olympiodorus of Thebes were also pagans. Though both their histories survive only in fragments, Eunapius's gallery of Neoplatonists and theurgists, *Lives of the Sophists,* is extant. His comments on "black-robed vermin" (monks) and the "spiritual darkness that has engulfed the world" reflect the bitter despair of the pagan intelligentsia. Symbolic of their plight was the tragic fate of Hypatia. A mathematician and Neoplatonist, she was one of the few women to attain intellectual prominence in antiquity. In 415 Hypatia was lynched by a Christian mob instigated by the bishop of Alexandria. Her circle of friends had included both Synesius and Palladas. A poor schoolmaster in Alexandria, Palladas was a soured man who wrote scathing epigrams on the absurdity of life. Appalled by the Christian triumph, he expressed the defeatist mood of many pagans:

> We men of Hellas live now turned to dust,
> Feeding on naught but dead men's buried hopes;
> For all the world today's tossed upside down.[26]

---

[26] *Anthologia Palatina* 10.90, trans. F. L. Lucas, *Greek Poetry for Everyman* (Boston: Beacon Press, no date), p. 371.

While other pagan scholars retreated into antiquarian studies, Palladas and Eunapius proclaimed the grim truth, that the surviving pockets of paganism would soon be swamped in a rising sea of Christian bigotry.

While the church in the East produced theologians and episcopal politicians, the Western church contained bishops as aggressive as Damasus and Ambrose and saints as lively as Jerome. Born in Dalmatia about 347, Jerome was educated at Rome and never lost his love for the classics. Equally drawn to asceticism, he felt guilt over his lust for literature and had a famous anxiety dream in which he was whipped for being a better Ciceronian than a Christian. As a hermit in Syria, he kept in contact with Christian intellectuals in the East. Returning to Rome, he served as Damasus's secretary and was prompted by the pope to translate the New Testament into Latin. After the death of Damasus, Jerome resided in Palestine and produced a Latin translation of the Old Testament. Since the second century, Latin translations of Holy Writ had existed, but Jerome's elegant version, the Vulgate Bible, was more authoritative and won general acceptance in the West by the seventh century. Jerome wrote prolifically on many religious subjects, and his letters reveal much about Roman high society, for he was a popular figure in fashionable salons. Obsessed with sex, Jerome persuaded a number of aristocratic women to embrace lives of virginity. In his writings, he was prone to overstatement and often acrimonious. With fierce sarcasm, he scathed hypocritical monks and shallow Christians, and his rage was unbounded toward heretics. In gentler moments, Jerome could describe the pagan Pontifex Maximus cradling a Christian granddaughter in his arms. Despite his petulance and hyperboles, the Christian champion offered useful insights into the complex problems of his time, and he never ceased to be a patriotic Roman. "A dreadful rumor has reached us from the West," he wrote in 410, "The city which had taken the whole world was itself taken." [27] The preface to his commentary on Ezekiel summed up his anguish at the fall of Rome: "The bright light of all the world was quenched. . . . The whole universe had perished in one city." A Ciceronian to the end, Jerome died in 420.

Though he and Jerome did not get along, Augustine of Hippo is a major figure in the history of Christian thought. To the student of late antiquity, the African saint presents a familiar paradigm. A professional intellectual, Augustine abandoned reason for faith; despite strong sexual drives, he became a celibate cleric; though a Roman, he turned his back on the world. Born at Carthage in 354, Augustine received a good education and became a professor of Latin rhetoric, but he never mastered Greek. His father was a pagan but his mother, Monica, was a

---

[27] Jerome *Epistulae* 127.12.

devout Christian who greatly influenced her son. Brooding over the meaning of human existence, Augustine turned to Manichean dualism, skepticism, Neoplatonism, and finally Christianity. His spiritual odyssey is described movingly in his *Confessions.* However, the professor also found time to keep a mistress who bore him an illegitimate son. Anxious to advance his career, Augustine, with his mother, mistress, and son, moved to Rome in 383. He soon attracted the attention of Symmachus who arranged for him to receive an academic appointment in Milan. There Augustine came under the influence of Ambrose, and Monica never ceased pushing her son toward conversion to Christianity. A practical Roman mother, she also persuaded him to send his mistress back to Africa in order that he might marry a wealthy young heiress. However, the marriage plans fell through, and Augustine took another mistress. On the verge of conversion, he still prayed: "Lord, make me chaste, but not yet." [28] In 386 the troubled professor was idly perusing the New Testament when he heard a child say to its playmate, "Pick it up and read." By chance, he turned to a passage condemning sensuality and accepted the omen as a divine call. Embracing Christianity, Augustine was confirmed in his new faith by a mystic experience. Soon afterwards, Monica died and her son returned to Africa where he became a clergyman and eventually bishop of Hippo.

Amid his episcopal duties, Augustine wrote prolifically in support of orthodoxy as he conceived it. He championed the monastic movement, bitterly assailed heretics, and insisted that the state persecute religious dissent. Since he saw his own conversion as proof of divine grace, Augustine adopted a strict Pauline position on predestination and opposed the British cleric Pelagius, who believed in free will and the inherent goodness of man. In defense of the doctrine of original sin, Augustine insisted that unbaptized infants would be damned even though they had committed no sin. As a philosopher, he was consistent in affirming that Christian faith took precedence over mere reason; thus, science was secondary in any conflict with Holy Writ. The sack of Rome in 410 prompted pagans to sneer that the city had been punished for abandoning the gods. To refute the charge, Augustine's Spanish protégé, Orosius, wrote a digest of Roman history that emphasized the calamities that had afflicted the empire in its pagan past. However, Orosius held a Eusebian view of the providential role of Rome. The events of 410 were so spectacular and symbolic that Augustine decided to answer the pagans with a major work, *The City of God,* in which the ephemeral City of Man was contrasted with the eternal City of God. The dichotomy of two cities had been used by earlier writers; both Seneca and

---

[28] Augustine *Confessiones* 8.7.

Marcus Aurelius had contrasted the towns of mankind with the City of Zeus, which is the universe. More recently, an African Donatist, Tyconius, had written on "Babylon" and "Jerusalem," but Augustine outdid his predecessors. To him, the City of Man was based on self-love while the City of God negated the self. The fall of the Roman empire was lamentable but not surprising, for secular society was based on robbery, violence, and fraud and was doomed to decay. The Romans were only the most successful brigands in history, and their empire must perish as had the wicked kingdoms in the Bible. Even a Christian Rome was not eternal, for pious emperors could not erase the taint of the City of Man. However, Christians belonged to the City of God, which was not the church but the totality of saints on earth and in heaven. Since the City of God could never fall, it was of little importance that the City of Man was crumbling. Ironically, the Vandals were at the gates of Hippo when Augustine died in 430.

The intellectual malaise of the Christian Roman world produced a craze for celibacy and asceticism. While most Christians lived normal sexual lives, extremists made a cult of celibacy and imposed it on the clergy, who were not uniformly enthusiastic about such rigors. Since celibacy had a Pauline (though not apostolic) sanction, the majority of clergymen accepted it as a test of moral strength, and most leaders of the church were either unmarried or had put aside their wives. Though not all priests were celibate, their bishops were, and all Christians were lyric in their praise of perpetual virginity at least as an ideal. Probably the repression of sexuality contributed to the sharp tempers of the church fathers and the fierceness of their polemics. To keep the flesh subdued, celibate Christians tamed their bodies with long fasts, sleepless nights, and self-inflicted pain. They also avoided bathing, for Augustine and others feared that a pious virgin or a monk might succumb to temptation in the bathtub. Such godly concern resulted in poor hygiene among clerics, but no doubt it increased the odor of sanctity. Not to be outdone by mere celibates, ascetics mortified the flesh with severe tortures and rigorous privation. In their zeal, the ascetics wallowed in filth and pain, willing devotees of what Baudelaire called le culte de la plaie et l'amour des guenilles. Sensualists in spite of themselves, they masked masochism as piety. While Augustine and most saints were content with sexual privation and cautionary discomforts, the ascetics strove for the ultimate in self-torture and performed extraordinary acts of mortification.

For bizarre behavior, no one excelled the Christian fakirs of Syria:

> Symeon Stylites went through a whole gamut of mounting types of asceticism. By birth, he belonged to a family of prosperous farmers. Before he

was twenty, he began to wear a cord round his body which chafed his skin till the blood ran; he had himself "buried" for two years; he beat off sleep by continually standing. In February 412, he abandoned the monastery where he had lived to that date and . . . [moved to a village.] He lived there in a cell, but had himself walled up for the forty days of Lent, a procedure which he repeated on two occasions. Later, he climbed a neighboring mountain and lived within an encircling wall under the open sky, at first fettered to the place by an iron chain. Soon afterwards, he climbed on a rock about three feet high, whose top gave him not more than two square yards for movement. He spent five years on this pedestal, then adopted higher and yet higher rocks, until he took to pillars. . . . In the end, he reached the goal of his desires on the top of a pillar about 70 feet high, where he stood for thirty years, till his death [in 459.] . . . The platform on the top was at most only four square yards, and there he lived in continuous prayer accompanied by a rhythmical falling on his knees and bowing his forehead to the platform.[29]

A generation later, a great church was built around the pillar to honor the athlete of God. Throughout the Near East, other fakirs dazzled both emperors and commoners with their antics. Since the masses viewed them with awe, imperial officials sought the support of the saints in rallying public opinion. High on his perch, Symeon was not totally removed from society, and he persuaded Theodosius II not to restore a confiscated synagogue to Jews. Later in the century, Daniel Stylites backed the Isaurians against Aspar and helped Zeno weather a major crisis. As individuals, the Christian fakirs represent the outer limits of piety and pathology, but it is significant that they could also play a political role. Apparently, it was easier for saints to overcome the flesh and the Devil than it was to discard the world completely.

Flight from the world was the motivating factor in the monastic movement which originated in Egypt and Syria in the fourth century and spread to the West in the fifth. Earlier saints had sought solitude, and no place was more isolated than the desert. There, solitary hermits hoped to shake off the world through prayer and privation. In the words of one monk: "Unless a man can say in his heart, 'I alone and God are in the world,' he shall not find peace." [30] As the repute of the holy hermits grew, it was difficult for them to maintain their cherished isolation, for disciples flocked to the desert to dwell near and imitate the saints. Slowly, monastic groups coalesced, and wise abbots kept the monks busy with manual work as well as penance and prayer. Many monks were merely refugees from life who despaired of the troubled

---

[29] Hans Lietzmann, *A History of the Early Church* (London: Lutterworth Press, 1953), IV, 170–71.

[30] Pelagius *Verba seniorum* 11.5.

Roman world and sought sanctuary with God. Others were highly neurotic and became crazed with religion. When these troubled men went mad and saw demons, their hallucinations were often sexual. Their fellow monks were greatly edified, and the temptations of Saint Antony became legendary. A whole body of pious literature arose to spread the inspiring stories of Antony and other monastic heroes. These pious biographies were replete with miracles and crowded with demons; "a mass invasion of devils into historiography preceded and accompanied the mass invasion of barbarians into the Roman empire." [31] When not grappling with demons, the monks sometimes descended upon the cities of the East, an unwashed and rowdy horde of fanatics, to riot on behalf of clerics and causes they championed. Filthy in appearance and fierce in manner, the monks were formidable foes who did not hesitate to challenge the state that they despised. While sleek bishops feared the emperor's wrath and the loss of privilege, monks usually came from the lower classes and spoke out frankly against officials and policies that angered the masses. More ambitious monks insinuated themselves at court and joined political cabals, but most confined their interests to religion. The monastic life also attracted men of the caliber of Augustine and Jerome, who took a dim view of misbehaving monks. As troubles overwhelmed the West, monastic groups developed there as havens in what were thought to be "the last days." Other Westerners became monks because they were weary of secular life, and some were as able as Martin of Tours, who gave up a military career. A kindly man who promoted charity for the poor and opposed the persecution of heretics, Martin was a model Christian. Unfortunately, many monks were undisciplined vagabonds, and some were religious lunatics who saw fearsome visions and terrified the masses with hysterical sermons. A few monks were outright charlatans who peddled false relics and charms to gullible peasants. The popes and bishops disapproved of monkish antics, but, as often as not, the masses encountered the church principally through monks or semiliterate priests who were not much better.

AFTER THE DELUGE

While no one denies the events of the fifth century, it is sometimes said that the Roman empire never fell, since elements of Roman life survived in the West and Constantinople was still a going concern. Carried to its logical extreme (as Gibbon did), this view holds that the

---

[31] Arnaldo Momigliano, *The Conflict between Paganism and Christianity in the Fourth Century* (Oxford: Clarendon Press, 1963), p. 93.

Roman empire fell when the Turks took Byzantium in 1453, unless one accepts the Russian position that Moscow is the Third Rome. By the same whimsical terms, the Holy Roman Empire was still viable when its ghost was laid to rest in 1806. It is too often forgotten that an empire is a thing of the mind as well as pieces of territory and tax accounts. "Though certainly related to events and external realities," a recent scholar has noted, "empire is a phenomenon of intellectual history." The end of the Roman world can be demonstrated in "that awareness of empire lost, which is in the nature of a meditation upon the past and a sense of the observer's present. . . . So considered, the end of empire—elusive and ambiguous as it is at the level of events—becomes a concrete datum of intellectual history." [32] By the end of the fifth century, men knew that the Roman empire had fallen although Byzantium claimed to carry on the imperial heritage. Whatever pose the authorities at Constantinople might assume, the entity which survived in the East was not the Roman empire of the past. That vast realm had been created by Italians, and its rulers were Latin in culture and generally Western in origin. For the most part, the Hellenistic East had received short shrift from the Roman state. During the fourth century, tensions had grown between the old and the new Rome, and in the fifth century the dichotomy was clear. The Roman empire was pagan and secular, and its ways were rooted in the distant past. The Byzantine empire was Christian and obsessed with religion, the product of a recent revolution in men's thought. While the Roman empire was international, the culture of Byzantium was Greek, and its Hellenic tone became more strident when the Western provinces were lost. Reality does not lie in names and titles. In both East and West, there were consuls in the fifth century, but they were imperial appointees, and eunuchs and poets held the office. Though the consulship survived, it would be whimsical to claim that the Republic had survived. Rather, venerable names masked new realities. So, too, despite Byzantine rhetoric, the Eastern empire did not preserve the Roman empire but transformed its remains into something different, a totally Eastern, completely Christian society.

In the devastated West, a new, rude society took form as barbarian chiefs carved kingdoms out of the wreck of the Roman empire. Prolonged periods of violence had upset communications, and the lack of imperial unity ruined commerce. Urban life visibly degenerated, the educated class dwindled, and knowledge of Greek became rare. The eclipse of education, however, meant little to a peasantry that had never

---

[32] Walter Goffart, "Zosimus, The First Historian of Rome's Fall," *American Historical Review* 76 (1971): 438, 429.

known its pleasures. Without the Roman empire to sustain its towns, the West reverted to rustic ways and ignorance of the outside world. While making use of whatever Roman talent they could find, the barbarian kings generally failed to integrate their tribesmen with the conquered populations who were left to live under what passed for Roman law. Religious differences separated Arian barbarians from Catholic Romans, and the old ban on intermarriage was usually preserved. Once the invaders had settled down, the Roman aristocracy easily accommodated themselves to the new order. Generally, their estates were intact,[33] and the barbarians provided military security in return for taxes. Though the barbarians had a monopoly on military offices, the Roman nobility was predominant among the higher clergy where they could put their literary and administrative skills to good use. While barbarian kings and their warriors brawled over territorial quarrels, the old Roman ruling class maintained its dominance in the agrarian economy and supplied the bishops who made up the civilian elite of the new nations. Though Rome had fallen, the nobles had not.

In the fifth century, four major barbarian kingdoms had risen in the West—the Vandals, Visigoths, Ostrogoths, and Franks. In Britain, Saxon war bands preyed on the defenseless islanders, and the remnants of Roman civilization were quickly eroded. In the warmer climate of Africa, the Vandals established a powerful state at Carthage under Gaiseric, who had led them from Spain in 429 and ruled with a strong hand until his death in 477. His ability matched his longevity, and Gaiseric strove to create an effective autocracy at the expense of Vandal nobles and Roman landowners. The king ruthlessly subdued the former and seized the lands of the latter for his followers. Aware of the importance of sea power, he maintained a powerful war fleet, and once again the Western Mediterranean was a "Carthaginian" lake. In 455 a Vandal force sacked the city of Rome. The Vandal kingdom withstood Byzantine assaults and local discontent. Recently converted from paganism, Gaiseric was a militant Arian and persecuted Catholics as did his successors. A dynastic squabble at Carthage prompted the intervention of Justinian, whose armies invaded Africa and overthrew the Vandal state in 534. The Byzantine government suppressed Arianism, restored estates to the Roman nobles, and enslaved the Vandals, whose military prowess had obviously declined. Once, however, the name of Vandal was synonymous with destructive ferocity.

The Visigoths had a checkered history. Before entering the Roman empire, they were probably the most economically advanced of the bar-

---

[33] In theory, the nobles surrendered a third of their lands to the invaders, and later the Visigoths and Burgundians claimed two-thirds, but these legal provisions were not uniformly carried out.

barians, for agriculture was widespread in Gothic Dacia and literacy was not unknown. After the battle of Adrianople, the Visigoths had great military prestige, and they functioned mainly as federates, theoretically in the service of Rome but often rampaging freely through the empire. Despite Alaric's sack of Rome, the Visigoths were useful against rival barbarians in Gaul and Spain. Athaulf's dream of a Gothic reinvigoration of the Roman empire was never realized, and the Goths' Catholic subjects fretted under an Arian regime. In southwestern Gaul and eastern Spain, the Visigoths established a flourishing kingdom, and in 475 their ruler, Euric, cut off even nominal ties with the empire. His successor, Alaric II, issued a brief summary of Roman law for the benefit of his non-Gothic subjects. In 507, Alaric was slain in battle by Clovis, and the victorious Franks reduced the Gothic holdings in Gaul to a small strip of territory in the South. From a capital at Toledo, the Visigoths ruled much of Spain with a light hand. Though Arians, the kings were tolerant of Catholics and Jews. In 552 the Byzantines seized two strongholds on the southern coast. In 589 the Visigothic state adopted Catholicism as the official religion and began severe repressions of Arians and Jews. Despite some cultural activity as witnessed by the encyclopedic writings of Isidore of Seville, the seventh century was a grim era in Spain, and the troubled kingdom was easily overwhelmed by the Muslims in 711.

Under the Huns, the Ostrogoths were an obscure tribe, and they roamed in the Upper Balkans after Attila's death. Among the rival Ostrogothic chiefs, Theodoric emerged as a strong king but only after a long struggle for dominance. Familiar with the Byzantine court, he meddled in its tortuous politics and backed the emperor Zeno during a major crisis. Later he broke with Zeno and threatened Constantinople. To rid himself of the dangerous Ostrogoths, the emperor authorized Theodoric to unseat Odoacer, who had ruled Italy as a barbarian king since 476. Leading his people into Italy, Theodoric defeated his rival in 490, occupied Ravenna in 493, and there murdered Odoacer and massacred his followers. As king of Gothic Italy, Theodoric was nominally a vassal of Constantinople. He took pains to placate the Roman aristocracy, leaving all administrative posts in their hands, and preserved the ban on intermarriage between Romans and barbarians. On the other hand, the Ostrogoths alone made up the armed forces, and legal disputes between Romans and Goths were settled in Gothic military courts. Generally, Italy was prosperous under Theodoric, but there was friction between Romans and Ostrogoths. Though an Arian, the king was impartial toward Catholics and was asked to arbitrate a disputed papal election in 498. While unable to write himself (he used a stencil to sign documents), Theodoric patronized scholars and maintained as splendid a court at Ravenna as the times would allow. Nevertheless, in 524, the monarch executed Boethius and other prominent senators for plotting with the Byzantines. His relations with the papacy also deteriorated at this time. In 526 Theodoric died, but his image survived in Germanic legends as Dietrich von Bern. Theodoric's capable daughter, Amalasuntha, ruled as regent for her young son, but her pro-Byzantine policies angered the Gothic aristocracy who overthrew and slew her in 535. The fall of Amalasuntha gave Justinian a pretext to invade Italy, and for the next two decades, Byzantine and Gothic armies battled until the peninsula was devastated, and Rome itself was largely in ruins. The final victory of the Byzantines in 554 doomed the Ostrogoths as a nation, and the abuses of Justinian's officials made all residents of Italy yearn for the "golden age" of Theodoric. Shortly after Justinian's death in 565, the fierce Lombards moved into northern Italy.

The Franks were rowdy German pagans who had long disturbed the Rhine frontier. In the third and fourth centuries, their incursions into Gaul had been brief but destructive. In 406, the Frankish tribes and the Alemanni had invaded Gaul in force, and they continued to harass the hard-pressed provincials. Aetius managed to contain the Franks, who became token allies of the empire. One Frankish tribe, the Salians, occupied the region around Tournai. About 481 the ruthless, ambitious Clovis became king of the Salian Franks. Gradually, he extended his control over northeastern Gaul through conquest and treachery. Some rival princes were defeated, others were assassinated, and Clovis did not spare his own kinsmen. By 486, he had overrun the domains of a Roman warlord, Syagrius, in northwestern Gaul. His next major victory was over the Alemanni, and in the decisive battle, Clovis invoked the aid of the god of his Catholic wife. Impressed by the victory, the Frankish king renounced paganism and became a militant Catholic. Religious zeal provided Clovis with a convenient pretext for his aggressive designs on the Visigoths: "It grieves my soul that these Arians should hold a part of Gaul; with God's help, let us go and conquer them and take their territories." [34] By 507 the Frankish monarch had conquered the Visigoths and seized most of their holdings in Gaul. Though the war against the Goths was publicized as a crusade for orthodoxy, many Catholics had fought for the Arian Goths against the predatory Franks. At Paris, Clovis established a capital for the swollen Frankish realm. Like Constantine, he viewed the church as a valuable ally and considered himself supreme over the bishops in his kingdom. In 511 Clovis died at Paris. His successors, the Merovingian dynasty, were weak and brutal rulers, whose misdeeds are recorded in the lively pages of Gre-

---

[34] Gregory of Tours *Historia Francorum* 2.37.

gory of Tours's *History of the Franks*. Though a greater future lay in store for the Franks under the Carolingians, Clovis had created a kingdom and a nation, and his alliance of the Frankish monarchy with the Catholic church had far-reaching effects in centuries to come.

While the barbarians converted Roman provinces into kingdoms, the major beneficiary of the fall of the Roman state in the West was the papacy, which alone had universal pretensions and did not hesitate to challenge the emperors of Constantinople as mere secular rulers. In a time of chaos and transition in the West, the bishops of Rome provided continuity with the past and authority in the present, for the popes claimed to be vicars of Christ, and their prestige was enormous in an age which was saturated with religion. The primacy of Peter was less palatable to the great bishops of the East, who accorded their colleague at Rome much honor but jealously guarded their own prerogatives. Couched in ambiguous phrases, the pronouncements of ecumenical councils, such as Chalcedon, could be interpreted as subtle affronts to the papacy. Sometimes on doctrine, more often on jurisdictive matters, the popes clashed with the Eastern bishops and their imperial master. In the West, the emperors were enthusiastic supporters of the papacy if not of individual popes. In 445, Valentinian III issued a famous decree:

> Since the primacy of the Apostolic See has been confirmed by the merit of Saint Peter . . . by the dignity of the city of Rome, and also by the authority of a sacred synod, no illicit presumption may strive to attempt anything contrary to the authority of that See; for the peace of the churches will finally be preserved everywhere only if the Church universal acknowledges its ruler.[35]

When the Western empire ceased to exist, the papacy continued to develop on an imperial model, and strong popes sought to control the new nations through the higher clergy.

While a new barbaric world emerged in the West, the Hellenistic East evolved rapidly into the Byzantine world. In 474 the Isaurian general Zeno had succeeded his father-in-law, Leo, as master of Byzantium. His reign was troubled by major revolts, and at one time a rival seized control of the capital, but Zeno overcame all the rebels. Since one pretender was backed by pagans who vainly hoped to restore the past, the emperor responded by persecuting some prominent pagans, but embers of the old faith still flickered, not only among conservative intellectuals but also in rural areas.[36] The philosophical academies at Ath-

---

[35] *Novels of Valentinian III* 17, trans. Pharr, p. 530.

[36] As late as the early tenth century, the old gods were worshiped in remote parts of the Peloponnesus, and the emperor Leo VI had to send troops to suppress the cults.

ens were still pagan and included luminaries such as the Neoplatonist Proclus, whose writings later influenced Muslim and medieval thinkers. The Ostrogoths gave Zeno more trouble than did the pagans, but the wily emperor managed to divert Theodoric into Italy. Squabbles between Catholics and Monophysites disturbed the empire, and Zeno was concerned over discontent in Syria and Egypt, which were Monophysite strongholds. As a gesture to the Monophysites, the emperor issued an official statement of religious belief that circuitously abrogated the decisions of Chalcedon. Though Zeno was trying to restore unity among his people, his rapprochement with heretics infuriated the orthodox and led to schism with the papacy. When Zeno died in 491, his widow appointed and married his successor, Anastasius, an administrator skilled in financial matters. The new emperor freed himself of Zeno's Isaurians and drove them from the capital. He fought inconclusive wars against the Persians and was faced with incursions of Slavs and Bulgars into the Balkans. Unable to control the new barbarian threat, Anastasius strengthened the fortifications of Constantinople. Like Zeno, he tried to accommodate the Monophysites, but his policy caused riots in the capital and a serious revolt in the army. The emperor survived these crises, which were partially related to his tax reforms. A diligent tax collector, he favored the commercial class and townsmen over the landowners and peasants of the countryside. When he died in 518, Anastasius left a full treasury and a well-organized government, both of which would be exploited by Justinian. Anastasius was succeeded by an elderly general, Justin, who had once been a peasant in Illyricum and had never learned to write. The new emperor revoked the religious policy of his predecessors and restored good relations with the papacy. Ironically, Justin sent support to the Monophysite king of Ethiopia for the invasion of Yemen. Ostensibly, the move was to protect Christian Arabs from persecution by a Jewish king, but the Ethiopians had imperial ambitions and Justin was anxious to counter Persian influence in Arabia. Nearer to home, the Byzantine government was unable to halt the Slavic invasion of the Balkans. Justin's most important role in history was to advance the career of his nephew, Justinian, who became emperor on Justin's death in 527.

Like the fall of Rome, the reign of Justinian represents a watershed in history. In many ways, some symbolic, he closed the door on antiquity and brought Byzantium into the Middle Ages. In 529 the emperor suppressed the academies at Athens and drove the pagan philosophers into exile. He also harassed Jews and dealt harshly with heretics. Justinian was the last Eastern emperor whose native language was Latin. In the capital, the emperor built a great domed cathedral, Hagia Sophia, a stunning tribute to triumphant Christianity. Hoping to revive past

glory, Justinian conquered Italy, Africa, and a bit of Spain, but the new
empire was Byzantine, not Roman, and most of the Western holdings
were lost in the next century. Moreover, the costs of the wars in the
West and the emperor's extensive building programs consumed the treasury surplus built up by Anastasius and strained the resources of the
empire. While posing as the restorer of the Roman world, Justinian was
powerless to protect the Balkans from Slavs and Bulgars, who ravaged
towns and farms and made attacks on Constantinople. On the Eastern
front, the Byzantines faced a determined foe in Persia, and Sassanid
troops sacked Antioch in 540. After prolonged fighting, a stalemate was
reached in 561 on condition that Byzantium pay an annual tribute to
Persia. The victories in the West were small compensation for weakness
in the East. The defeat of the Vandals was achieved by Justinian's
ablest marshal, Belisarius, who also campaigned for many years in

Justinian flanked by clergymen and courtiers. Ravenna, S. Vitale. *Scala
Fine Arts Publishers, New York.*

Italy, but the emperor grew suspicious of the general and Belisarius fell dramatically from favor. The final victory over the Ostrogoths was won by a eunuch, Narses, whose holding of a military command would have shocked Cato or Augustus.

The emperor and his consort were unconventional; Justinian's father was a peasant, and the empress, Theodora, had been a prostitute. A tiny, strong-willed woman, she had kept her husband from fleeing the capital during the Nika revolt in 532; Narses and Belisarius subdued the rioters. Active in court intrigue, Theodora supported the Monophysites although her husband was devoutly orthodox. The emperor freely made theological pronouncements that sometimes embarrassed his adherents. Toward the Monophysites, his policy was alternately conciliatory and repressive, and his meddling in theology caused another break with the papacy. Nevertheless, Justinian's pose as the liberator of western Catholics from Arian oppressors forced him into stands that alienated the Monophysites of Egypt and Syria. Always in need of money, the emperor taxed his subjects heavily and looked about for new sources of revenue. To break the Persian hold on the silk trade from China, Justinian encouraged the Ethiopians to develop a route through the Indian Ocean, but the plan failed. Luckily, silkworms were somehow smuggled from China, and the Byzantines were able to create a state monopoly of silk production. A tireless worker, Justinian devoted much time to administration and commissioned a massive collection of laws that appeared in revised form in 534. This great work, the *Corpus Juris Civilis,* consists of the Code, imperial decrees from Hadrian to 534; the Digest, extracts of legal treatises; the Institutes, an introduction to Roman law; and the Novels, decrees issued after 534 and written in Greek. To Byzantine and medieval legalists, the *Corpus Juris Civilis* was a fount of law; to modern scholars, it is an extremely rich source of evidence on antiquity. To the people who had to live under its stern decrees, the great code was an instrument of grinding tyranny. After 541, the consulship, the last relic of a forgotten Republic, became an office held only by the emperors. In 542 and 543 the empire was devastated by outbreaks of bubonic plague as severe as the Black Death of medieval Europe. Stricken himself, the emperor survived the plague, but in 548 his beloved Theodora died of cancer. In 565 Justinian died, and the throne passed to his witless nephew, who inherited an empire swollen in size, drained of its wealth, and torn with discontent.

Under inept emperors, the Byzantine empire was a dinosaur— immense size and power directed by a tiny brain. But even under capable rulers, much of its efforts were counterproductive. The Byzantines inherited a tradition of Roman-Persian conflict, and both empires wasted men and treasure in futile wars that ceased only long enough to allow the combatants to recover for the next bout. Emperors and generals in Byzantium and Persia gained prestige in these costly wars, and bitter memories of mutual atrocities fanned the embers of hatred. Religious antagonism between Christians and Zoroastrians added to the permanent struggle. The only rational motive for the wars was to win control of the border regions that supplied tough peasants as recruits for the imperial armies. Since the West was no longer a recruiting ground, the Byzantines had need of the hardy farmers of Anatolia and Armenia. Yet the wars consumed the product for which they were fought and also wasted the revenues of the state. Nevertheless, the Byzantines and Persians continued to exhaust themselves in perpetual conflict. In both empires, the tax burden on provincials was heavy, and both states added to the misery of their subjects by imposing ideological conformity. The Sassanids periodically harassed Christians and other dissenters, and the Byzantines tried repeatedly to crush Monophysitism in Egypt and Syria. In the provinces of both realms, religious resentment blended with economic discontent and local pride. Late in the fifth century, the Persian empire was imperiled by a revolt of the Mazdakites, an esoteric religious sect that advocated communal use of women and property. Widespread among the peasantry, the Mazdakite communists were suppressed with great severity. Although their protests were limited to riots and other minor disorders, the Egyptians and Syrians resented the religious and economic policies of Byzantium. Though no one knew it, time was running out for the two great empires. Five years after the death of Justinian, Muhammad was born, and an irresistible force would soon rise out of Arabia, overrun the Sassanid realm, and sweep into Syria and Egypt where the provincials welcomed the Muslims as liberators.

Whatever its faults and despite the miasma of theology which hung over it, the Byzantine world was urban, education was respected there, and the classics of antiquity were cherished. The reign of Justinian was described in various works by a first-rate historian, Procopius, who was a confidant of Belisarius. After the emperor's death, however, Procopius released a malicious secret history that depicted Justinian as the Antichrist. Both the quality of his major history and the abusiveness of the secret history were in the classical tradition. In the West, however, civilization lost ground with each generation. A darkening night of ignorance closed in on the new nations, and education was largely confined to the clergy, whose horizons were narrow at best. To its credit, the church played a custodial role in preserving the remnants of Latin culture, but clerical scholars had a marked preference for digests and inept handbooks. The main effort in preserving and copying books took place in the relative peace of monasteries. Though mendicant monks were still unruly, settled monastic communities were more often disciplined and productive. A major figure in monastic reform was the abbot of Monte Cassino, Benedict, who lived during the Gothic era in Italy. In his famous regulations which were models for monasteries in the centuries ahead, Benedict employed a very Roman sense of order and practicality, keeping his monks equally busy with prayer, study, and manual labor. A monastery devoted essentially to intellectual pursuits was set up by the Roman senator Cassiodorus, who had served Ostrogothic kings and supported the Byzantine occupation of Italy. His letters are valuable sources on contemporary events, and his *History of the Goths* (in a digest by Jordanes) has survived; its interest lies not only in its contents but in the author's attempt to reconcile Goths and Romans and to convince both groups that Byzantine rule was in their interest. Cassiodorus also wrote a popular work on the seven liberal arts and had his monks translate Greek texts into Latin. Naturally, most of the translations were of ecclesiastical interest.

Two writers of the early sixth century, one Eastern and one Western, represent the last glow of the twilight of antiquity. Taking Polybius as his model, the Greek historian Zosimus described the decline and fall of the Roman empire to 410. As a pagan, he attributed the collapse of the empire to the abandonment of the ancient religion and portrayed Constantine and Theodosius as villains. For sources, Zosimus relied heavily on Eunapius and Olympiodorus, but he did not trouble to reconcile their divergent estimates of Stilicho. Conservative in politics as well as religion, Zosimus spied a fatal flaw in the establishment of autocracy by Augustus, and he spoke knowingly of the tyranny and corruption inherent in the imperial system. In the Christian city named after Constantine, the pagan Zosimus looked back wistfully to a Republican Rome that revered the ancestral cults. In Italy, the Roman senator Boethius held high office under Theodoric, but in 522 he and other senators conspired with agents of Justin. Their motives were probably religious, since Boethius was a sincere Catholic and Justin was an orthodox ruler, but Roman resentment of barbarian kings also played a role. Convicted of treason, Boethius was imprisoned for two years during which he wrote a memorable *Consolation of Philosophy*. In 524, Theodoric ordered him tortured and killed. Whether traitor or martyr, Boethius was primarily an intellectual in love with the best of Greek and Roman thought. Although he wrote theological treatises, he also feared that the secular wisdom of the past was in serious danger of being lost in an age of dwindling culture and religious enthusiasm. Boethius translated important Greek works on logic and compiled handbooks on mathematics, music, and astronomy, thus passing on Aristotle, Euclid, and Ptolemy to Latin readers. While there is no doubt that he died a Christian, Boethius in prison turned to philosophy for comfort, and his *Consolation* made no mention of Christianity. Rather, he consoled himself with concepts of God and virtue that had sustained Socrates and Epictetus.

There is irony in the efforts of Boethius to keep the fires of intellect burning as an Ice Age of ignorance and superstition overwhelmed the West. To Christian zealots, science and philosophy were potentially dangerous. Although an admirable war-god and miracle worker, the god of the Bible was an ignoramus in scientific matters, for Holy Writ preserved the obsolete beliefs of ancient Mesopotamia. The earth was flat, with waters below and waters above, hence the deluge of Noah, but Greek astronomers insisted that the earth was round and that only celestial bodies were in the sky. The conflict between science and scripture troubled Augustine and other Christian thinkers, who nevertheless had to concede that revelation was superior to reason. In any case, astronomy was tainted by astrology, and the devil enjoyed snaring proud men with baubles of knowledge. Isidore of Seville warns:

> Let the monk beware of reading the books of gentiles and heretics. It is better for him to be ignorant of their pernicious doctrines than through making acquaintance with them to be enmeshed in error.[37]

Luckily, Isidore did not follow his own precepts, for he was a diligent, if uncritical encyclopedist. He was also a rarity, a learned man in a dark age. Even in brighter times, Christian cranks had denounced profane learning, and the author of the third-century *Didascalia Apostolorum* had warned:

> Avoid all books of the heathen. For what hast thou to do with strange sayings or laws or lying prophecies which also turn away from the faith them that are young? . . . If thou wouldst read historical narratives, thou hast the Book of Kings; but if philosophers and wise men, thou hast the Prophets. . . . If thou wish for songs, thou hast the Psalms of David; but if thou wouldst read of the beginning of the world, thou hast the Genesis of the great Moses. . . . All strange writings therefore which are contrary to these wholly eschew.[38]

Such narrow views might be tolerated as eccentricity in a time when education was flourishing, but the post-Roman world could ill afford willful ignorance and disdain of knowledge. The scientific heritage of the past, filled with error and folklore, was feeble enough without being to-

---

[37] M. L. Laistner, *Thought and Letters in Western Europe A.D. 500 to 900* (London: Methuen, 1957), p. 121.

[38] *Didascalia Apostolorum* 12, trans. M. L. Laistner, *Christianity and Pagan Culture in the Later Roman Empire* (Ithaca: Cornell University Press, 1951), p. 50.

tally discarded as the work of demons. Occultism and demonology were delusions shared by both Christians and pagans, but at least a pagan did not commit heresy if he doubted the myths of the poets or the humbug of priests and augurs. The Christian revolution had succeeded too well.

At the end of the sixth century, when the peninsula was still prostrate from the Gothic-Byzantine wars, the ferocious Lombards preyed upon the suffering peoples of Italy and menaced Rome, where the pope was forced to bribe them to withdraw. The occupant of the papacy was a Roman aristocrat, Gregory the Great, who was both the spiritual and temporal ruler of central and southern Italy. To contemporaries, he was the "consul of God," [39] but his realm was impoverished and Rome was only a shadow of its former self. Its condition a reflection of the times, the city was filled with ruins, and its population had drastically shrunk. Surveying the pitiable state of the city and its inhabitants, Gregory was reminded of Ezekiel's prophecy of a seething pot and its seeming fulfillment in the fate of Rome:

> What Rome herself, once deemed the Mistress of the World, has now become, we see—wasted away with afflictions grievous and many, with the loss of citizens, the assaults of enemies, the frequent fall of ruined buildings. . . . Of this city, it is well said, "The meat is boiled away and the bones in the midst thereof." . . . For where is the Senate? Where is the People? The bones are all dissolved, the flesh is consumed, all the pomp of the dignities of this world is gone. The whole mass is boiled away, . . . for the Senate is no more, and the People has perished. . . . Rome is, as it were, already empty and burning. But what need is there to speak of men when, as the work of ruin spreads, we see the very buildings perishing.[40]

The words of the Pontifex are a fitting conclusion for a history of Rome.

[39] Bede *Historia ecclesiastica* 2.1.

[40] Gregory the Great *Homiliarum in Ezechielem Prophetam* 2.6.22–23, trans. F. H. Dudden, *Gregory the Great* (New York: Longmans, Green, & Co., 1905), II, 19–20.

Epilogue

Throughout the regions which made up the Roman empire, now stand thousands of ruins—shattered walls and aqueducts, pillars and broken statuary, ironic triumphal arches—spores of a once vital entity, relics of lost grandeur. To the simple Saxons, the gutted villas in Britain, though overgrown with weeds, had seemed the "work of giants." Pilgrims to eighth-century Rome were awed by the Colosseum and circulated a proverb about the great amphitheater:

> As long as the Colosseum stands, Rome shall stand;
> when the Colosseum falls, Rome will fall;
> when Rome falls, the world will fall.[1]

For Montaigne, the antique ruins outshown the glitter of Renaissance Rome: "Her very ruin is glorious and grandiose; she still retains in the tomb the symbol and image of empire." Like other visitors to Rome, Gibbon was excited by propinquity with the past:

> At the distance of twenty-five years, I can neither forget nor express the strong emotions which agitated my mind as I first approached and entered the eternal city. After a sleepless night, I trod with a lofty step the ruins of the Forum; each memorable spot where Romulus stood or Tully spoke or Caesar fell, was at once present to my eye.[2]

Poets, such as Keats, were drawn to Rome, "where its wrecks like shattered mountains rise," and Henry Adams was not the only historian to sit where Gibbon had sat on the Capitoline Hill and ponder the mutability of power. Wherever they exist, Roman ruins prompt thoughtful men to consider not only the grandeur of the past and the achievements and errors of the Romans, but also the impermanence of human accomplishment, the worm in the heart of things.

[1] Gibbon, *Decline of the Roman Empire,* VII, 317.
[2] Edward Gibbon, *Autobiographies* (London: J. Murray, 1897), p. 267.

Recommended reading list

GENERAL

Badian, E. *Studies in Greek and Roman History*. Ithaca: Cornell University Press, 1968.

Baldson, J. P. V. D. *Life and Leisure in Ancient Rome*. New York: McGraw-Hill, 1969.

Bickerman, E. J. *Chronology of the Ancient World*. Ithaca: Cornell University Press, 1968.

The Cambridge Ancient History. Vols. 7–12. Cambridge: Cambridge University Press, 1928–39.

Cary, M. *Geographical Background of Greek and Roman History*. Oxford: Clarendon Press, 1949.

————. *History of Rome*. 2d ed. New York: St. Martin's Press, 1954.

Crook, J. *Law and Life of Rome*. Ithaca: Cornell University Press, 1967.

Daube, D. *Roman Law: Linguistic, Social, and Philosophical Aspects*. Chicago: Aldine Press, 1969.

Dunbabin, T. J., *The Western Greeks*. Oxford: Clarendon Press, 1948.

Earl, D. C. *The Moral and Political Tradition of Rome*. Ithaca: Cornell University Press, 1967.

Finley, M. I., ed. *Slavery in Classical Antiquity*. Cambridge: Heffer, 1968.

Frank, T., ed. *An Economic Survey of Ancient Rome*. 5 vols. Baltimore: Johns Hopkins Press, 1933–40.

Jolowicz, H. F. *Historical Introduction to the Study of Roman Law*. Cambridge: Cambridge University Press, 1954.

Jones, A. H. M. *The Cities of the Eastern Roman Provinces*. 2d ed. Oxford: Clarendon Press, 1971.

403

————. *The Greek City from Alexander to Justinian*. Oxford: Clarendon Press, 1966.

————. *A History of Rome Through the Fifth Century*. 2 vols. New York: Harper & Row, 1968–70.

————. *Studies in Roman Government and Law*. New York: Praeger, 1960.

Larsen, J. A. O. *Representative Government in Greek and Roman History*. Berkeley and Los Angeles: University of California Press, 1955.

Lewis, N. and Reinhold, M. *Roman Civilization*. 2 vols. New York: Columbia University Press, 1967.

Magie, D. *Roman Rule in Asia Minor*. 2 vols. Princeton: Princeton University Press, 1950.

Mommsen, T. *Römisches Staatsrecht*. 3 vols. Leipzig: Hirsel, 1887–88.

Nicholas, J. K. B. M. *Introduction to Roman Law*. Oxford: Clarendon Press, 1964.

Sherwin-White, A. N. *The Roman Citizenship*. Oxford: Clarendon Press, 1939.

Stahl, W. *Roman Science*. Madison: University of Wisconsin, 1962.

Westermann, W. L. *The Slave Systems of Greek and Roman Antiquity*. Philadelphia: American Philosophical Society, 1955.

Wirszubski, C. *Libertas as a Political Idea at Rome during the Late Republic and Early Principate*. Cambridge: Cambridge University Press, 1950.

ROMAN REPUBLIC

Adcock, F. E. *Roman Political Ideas and Practice*. Ann Arbor: University of Michigan Press, 1959.

Alföldi, A. *Early Rome and the Latins*. Ann Arbor: University of Michigan Press, 1965.

Astin, A. E. *Scipio Aemilianus*. Oxford: Clarendon Press, 1967.

Badian, E. *Foreign Clientelae*. Oxford: Clarendon Press, 1958.

————. *Roman Imperialism in the Late Republic*. 2d ed. Oxford: Basil Blackwell, 1968.

Beloch, K. J. *Römische Geschichte bis zum Beginn der punischen Kriege*. Berlin: de Gruyter, 1962.

Bloch, R. *The Etruscans*. New York: Praeger, 1958.

————. *The Origins of Rome*. New York: Praeger, 1960.

Boren, H. C. *The Gracchi*. New York: Twayne Publishers, 1968.

Botsford, G. W. *The Roman Assemblies,* New York: Macmillan, 1909.

Broughton, T. R. S. *The Magistrates of the Roman Republic*. 2 vols.

and supplement. New York: American Philological Association, 1951–52.

Brunt, P. A. *Italian Manpower 225 B. C.–A. D. 14.* London: Oxford University Press, 1971.

———. *Social Conflicts in the Roman Republic.* London: Chatto and Windus, 1970.

Earl, D. C. *Tiberius Gracchus, A Study in Politics.* Brussels: Latomus, 1963.

von Fritz, K. *The Theory of the Mixed Constitution in Antiquity.* New York: Columbia University Press, 1958.

Gelzer, M. *Caesar; Politician and Statesman.* Translated by P. Needham. Cambridge: Harvard University Press, 1968.

———. *Cicero und Caesar.* Wiesbaden: Franz Steiner Verlag, 1968.

———. *Kleine Schriften.* 3 vols. Wiesbaden: F. Steiner, 1962–64.

———. *Pompeius.* 2d ed. Munich: F. Bruckmann, 1959.

———. *The Roman Nobility.* Translated by R. Seager. Oxford: Blackwell, 1969.

Gjerstad, E. *Early Rome.* 4 vols. Lund: Gleerup, 1953–66.

———. *Legends and Facts of Early Roman History.* Lund: Gleerup, 1962.

Grimal, P., ed. *Hellenism and the Rise of Rome.* Translated by A. M. S. Smith. New York: Delacorte Press, 1968.

Gruen, E. S. *Roman Politics and the Criminal Courts, 149–78 B.C.* Cambridge: Harvard University Press, 1968.

Heitland, W. E. *The Roman Republic.* 3 vols. 2d ed. Cambridge: Cambridge University Press, 1923.

Hill, H. *The Roman Middle-Class in the Republican Period.* Oxford: Basil Blackwell, 1952.

Holleaux, M. *Rome, la Grèce et les monarchies hellénistiques au IIIe siècle avant J.-C. (273–205).* Paris: E. de Boccard, 1969.

Holmes, T. R. *The Roman Republic and the Founder of the Empire.* 3 vols. Oxford: Clarendon Press, 1923.

Lintott, A. W. *Violence in Republican Rome.* Oxford: Clarendon Press, 1968.

Marsh, F. B. *History of the Roman World from 146 to 30 B. C.* 3d ed. London: Methuen, 1964.

McDonald, A. H. *Republican Rome.* London: Thames and Hudson, 1966.

Michels, A. K. *The Calendar of the Roman Republic.* Princeton: Princeton University Press, 1967.

Mommsen, T. *The History of Rome.* 5 vols. London: Bentley, 1894.

Münzer, F. *Römische Adelsparteien und Adelsfamilien.* Stuttgart: Metzler, 1920.

Pallottino, M. *The Etruscans*. London: Penguin, 1955.

Powell, T. G. E. *The Celts*. New York: Praeger, 1958.

Rostovtzeff, M. *Social and Economic History of the Hellenistic World*. 3 vols. Oxford: Clarendon Press, 1953.

Salmon, E. T. *Roman Colonization under the Republic*. Ithaca: Cornell University Press, 1969.

————. *Samnium and the Samnites*. Cambridge: Cambridge University Press, 1966.

Scullard, H. H. *The Etruscan Cities and Rome*. London: Thames and Hudson, 1967.

————. *From the Gracchi to Nero*. 2d ed. London: Methuen, 1963.

————. *History of the Roman World from 753 to 146 B. C.* 3d ed. London: Methuen, 1969.

————. *Roman Politics 200–150 B. C.* Oxford: Clarendon Press, 1951.

————. *Scipio Africanus; Soldier and Politician*. Ithaca: Cornell University Press, 1970.

Seager, R., ed. *The Crisis of the Roman Republic: Studies in Political and Social History*. Cambridge: Heffer, 1969.

Staveley, E. S. *Greek and Roman Voting and Elections*. Ithaca: Cornell University Press, 1972.

Stockton, D. *Cicero: A Political Biography*. London: Oxford University Press, 1971.

Syme, R. *The Roman Revolution*. London: Oxford University Press, 1960.

Taylor, L. R. *Party Politics in the Age of Caesar*. Berkeley: University of California Press, 1949.

————. *Roman Voting Assemblies from the Hannibalic War to the Dictatorship of Caesar*. Ann Arbor: University of Michigan Press, 1966.

————. *Voting Districts of the Roman Republic, the Thirty-five Urban and Rural Tribes*. Rome: American Academy in Rome, 1960.

Thiel, J. H. *Studies on the History of Roman Sea-Power in Republican Times*. Amsterdam: North-Holland Publishing Co., 1946.

Toynbee, A. J. *Hannibal's Legacy: The Hannibalic War's Effects on Roman Life*. 2 vols. Oxford: Clarendon Press, 1965.

Treggiari, S. *Roman Freedmen during the Late Republic*. Oxford: Clarendon Press, 1969.

Walbank, F. W. *Philip V of Macedon*. Cambridge: Cambridge University Press, 1940.

Warmington, B. H. *Carthage*. London: Pelican, 1964.

ROMAN EMPIRE

Abbott, F. F. and Johnson, A. C., *Municipal Administration in the Roman Empire*. Princeton: Princeton University Press, 1926.

Africa, T. W. *Rome of the Caesars*. New York:·Wiley, 1965.

Alföldi, A. *A Conflict of Ideas in the Late Roman Empire*. Oxford: Clarendon Press, 1952.

Arnheim, M. T. W. *The Senatorial Aristocracy in the Later Roman Empire*. Cambridge: Cambridge University Press, 1972.

Balsdon, J. P. V. D. *The Emperor Gaius*. New York: Oxford University Press, 1934.

Barrow, R. H. *Slavery in the Roman Empire*. New York: Barnes and Noble, 1968.

Birley, A. *Marcus Aurelius*. Boston: Little, Brown, 1966.

———. *Septimius Severus*. London: Eyre & Spottiswoode, 1971.

Boak, A. E. R. *Manpower Shortage and the Fall of the Roman Empire in the West*. Ann Arbor: University of Michigan Press, 1955.

Bowersock, G. W. *Augustus and the Greek World*. Oxford: Clarendon Press, 1965.

———. *Greek Sophists in the Roman Empire*. Oxford: Clarendon Press, 1969.

Burckhardt, J. *The Age of Constantine the Great*. Translated by Moses Hadas. New York: Pantheon Books, 1949.

Bury, J. B. *History of the Later Roman Empire from the Death of Theodosius I to the Death of Justinian*. New York: Dover Publications, 1958.

Carcopino, J. *Daily Life in Ancient Rome* Translated by E. O. Lorimer. New Haven: Yale University Press, 1940.

Charlesworth, M. P. *Trade-Routes and Commerce of the Roman Empire*. 2d ed. New York: Macmillan, 1926.

Cochrane, C. *Christianity and Classical Culture*. Oxford: Clarendon Press, 1944.

Crook, J. M. *Consilium Principis*. Cambridge: Cambridge University Press, 1955.

Dill, S. R. *Roman Society from Nero to Marcus Aurelius*. 2d ed. New York: Meridian, 1956.

———. *Roman Society in the Last Century of the Western Empire*. 2d ed. New York: Macmillan, 1906.

Dodd, C. H. *New Testament Studies*. Manchester: Manchester University Press, 1933.

Dodds, E. R. *Pagan and Christian in an Age of Anxiety*. Cambridge: Cambridge University Press, 1965.

Duff, A. M. *Freedmen in the Early Roman Empire*. 2d ed. Cambridge: Heffer, 1958.

Ferguson, J. *The Religions of the Roman Empire*. Ithaca: Cornell University Press, 1970.

Frend, W. *Martyrdom and Persecution in the Early Church*. New York: Doubleday, 1967.

Garnsey, P. *Social Status and Legal Privilege in the Roman Empire.* London: Oxford University Press, 1970.

Gibbon, E. *The History of the Decline and Fall of the Roman Empire.* Edited by J..B. Bury. 7 vols. London: Methuen, 1896–1900, with revisions, 1909–14.

Gordon, C. D. *The Age of Attila.* Ann Arbor: University of Michigan Press, 1960.

Hammond, M. *The Antonine Monarchy.* Rome: American Academy in Rome, 1959.

————. *The Augustan Principate in Theory and Practice.* Cambridge: Harvard University Press, 1968.

Jonas, H. *The Gnostic Religion.* Boston: Becaon Press, 1958.

Jones, A. H. M. *Constantine and the Conversion of Europe.* New York: Macmillan, 1949.

————. *The Later Roman Empire, 248–602 A. D.* 3 vols. Oxford: Basil Blackwell, 1964.

Laistner, M. L. W. *Christianity and Pagan Culture in the Later Roman Empire.* Ithaca: Cornell University Press, 1951.

Lietzmann, H. *A History of the Early Church.* 2 vols. London: Lutterworth Press, 1953.

Lot, F. *The End of the Ancient World and the Beginnings of the Middle Ages.* New York: Harper Torchbooks, 1961.

MacMullen, R. *Constantine.* New York: Dial Press, 1970.

————. *Enemies of the Roman Order.* Cambridge: Harvard University Press, 1966.

————. *Soldier and Civilian in the Later Roman Empire.* Cambridge: Harvard University Press, 1963.

Marsh, F. B. *The Reign of Tiberius.* Cambridge: Heffer, 1959.

Millar, F. G. B. *The Roman Empire and Its Neighbors.* New York: Delacorte Press, 1968.

Momigliano, A. *Claudius, the Emperor and His Achievement.* New York: Barnes and Noble, 1961.

————., ed. *The Conflict between Paganism and Christianity in the Fourth Century.* Oxford: Clarendon Press, 1963.

Neill, S. *The Interpretation of the New Testament.* Oxford: Clarendon Press, 1964.

Nock, A. D. *Conversion.* Oxford: Clarendon Press, 1933.

Ogilvie, R. M. *The Romans and Their Gods in the Age of Augustus.* London: Chatto and Windus, 1969.

Oost, S. I. *Galla Placidia Augusta: A Biographical Essay.* Chicago and London: University of Chicago Press, 1968.

Parker, H. M. D. *History of the Roman World, 138–337 A. D.* rev. ed. London: Methuen, 1958.

Piganiol, A. *L'empire chrétien. (323–395)* Paris: Presses Universitaires de France, 1947.

Reynolds, P. K. B. *The Vigiles of Imperial Rome.* London: Oxford University Press, 192(.

Rogers, R. S. *Studies in the Reign of Tiberius.* Baltimore: Johns Hopkins Press, 1943.

Rostovtzeff, M. *Social and Economic History of the Roman Empire.* 2 vols. 2d ed. Oxford: Clarendon Press, 1957.

Rowell, H. T. *Rome in the Augustan Age.* Norman: University of Oklahoma Press, 1962.

Salmon, E. T. *History of the Roman World from 30 B. C. to 138 A. D.* 6th ed. London: Methuen, 1968.

Seeck, O. *Geschichte des Untergangs der antiken Welt.* 2 vols. Stuttgart: J. B. Metzler, 1921.

Sherwin-White, A. N. *Racial Prejudice in Imperial Rome.* Cambridge: Cambridge University Press, 1967.

———. *Roman Society and Roman Law in the New Testament.* Oxford: Clarendon Press, 1963.

Starr, C. G. *The Roman Imperial Navy.* Ithaca: Cornell University Press, 1941.

Syme, R. *Colonial Elites.* New York: Oxford University Press, 1958.

Taylor, L. R. *The Divinity of the Roman Emperor.* Middleton, Conn.: American Philological Association, 1931.

Walbank, F. W. *The Awful Revolution: The Decline of the Roman Empire in the West.* Liverpool: Liverpool University Press, 1969.

Weaver, P. R. C. *Familia Caesaris. A Social Study of the Emperor's Freedmen and Slaves.* Cambridge: Cambridge University Press, 1972.

Webster, G. *The Roman Imperial Army of the First and Second Centuries A. D.* London: A. and C. Black, 1969.

Yavetz, Z. *Plebs and Princeps.* Oxford: Clarendon Press, 1969.

HISTORIOGRAPHY

Adcock, F. E. *Caesar as a Man of Letters.* Cambridge: Cambridge University Press, 1956.

Dorey, T. A., ed. *Latin Biography.* New York: Basic Books, 1967.

———., ed. *Latin Historians.* New York: Basic Books, 1966.

Earl, D. C. *The Political Thought of Sallust.* Cambridge: Cambridge University Press, 1961.

Evans, J. A. S. *Procopius.* New York: Twayne Publishers, 1972.

Laistner, M. *The Greater Roman Historians.* Berkeley and Los Angeles: University of California Press, 1947.

Millar, F. G. B. *A Study of Cassius Dio.* Oxford: Clarendon Press, 1964.

Momigliano, A. *Studies in Historiography.* New York: Harper Torchbooks, 1967.

Ogilvie, R. M. *A Commentary on Livy, Books I–V.* Oxford: Clarendon Press, 1965.

Syme, R. *Ammianus and the Historia Augusta.* Oxford: Clarendon Press, 1968.

————. *Emperors and Biography: Studies in the Historia Augusta.* Oxford: Clarendon Press, 1971.

————. *Sallust.* Berkeley and Los Angeles: University of California Press, 1964.

————. *Tacitus.* 2 vols. Oxford: Clarendon Press, 1958.

Thompson, G. *Ammianus Marcellinus.* Cambridge: Cambridge University Press, 1947.

Walbank, F. W. *A Historical Commentary on Polybius.* 2 vols. Oxford: Clarendon Press, 1957.

————. *Polybius.* Berkeley and Los Angeles: University of California Press, 1972.

Walsh, P. G. *Livy, His Historical Aims and Methods.* Cambridge: Cambridge University Press, 1961.

Genealogical charts

Chart 1: THE AEMILII, THE CORNELII SCIPIONES, AND THE GRACCHI

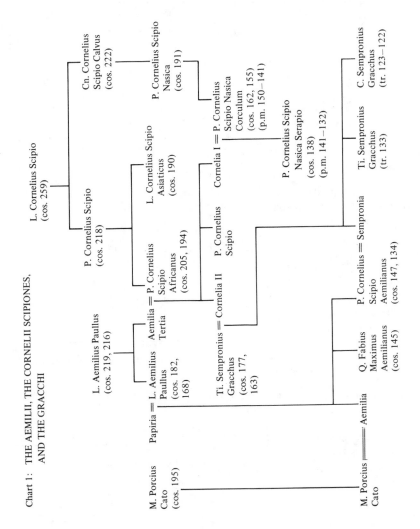

cos. = consul
p.m. = pontifex maximus
tr. = tribune

413

Chart 2: THE GRACCHAN ALLIANCE

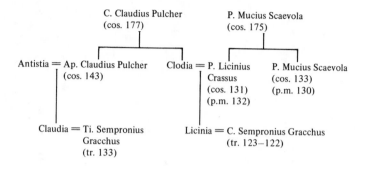

Chart 3: THE MARITAL CONNECTIONS OF SULLA,
MARIUS, CAESAR, AND POMPEY

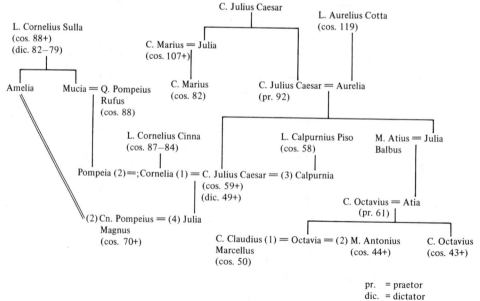

pr.   = praetor
dic. = dictator
+   = more than one year

414

Chart 4: THE MARITAL CONNECTIONS OF CATO AND BRUTUS

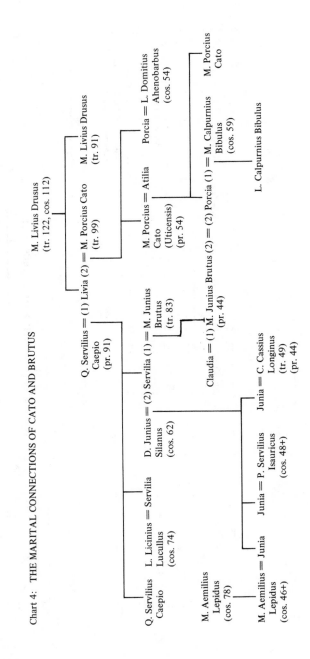

Chart 5: THE JULIO-CLAUDIAN DYNASTY

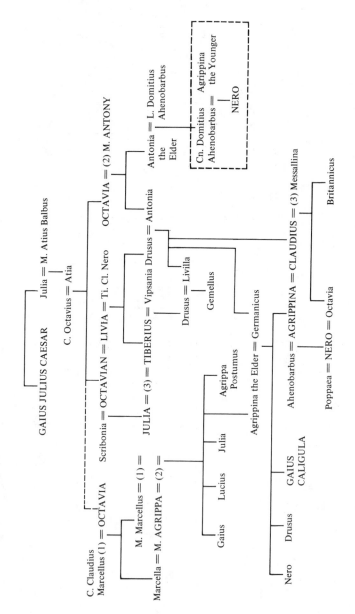

Chart 6: THE HASMONEAN AND HERODIAN DYNASTIES

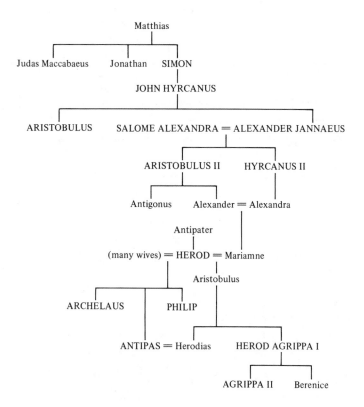

Chart 7: THE FLAVIAN DYNASTY

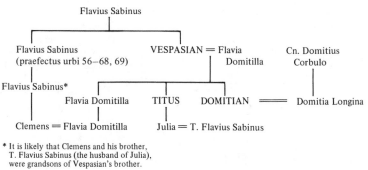

* It is likely that Clemens and his brother,
T. Flavius Sabinus (the husband of Julia),
were grandsons of Vespasian's brother.

Chart 8: THE ANTONINE DYNASTY

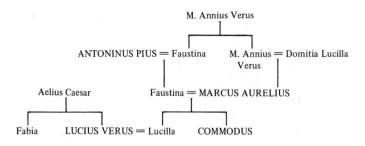

Chart 9: THE SEVERAN DYNASTY

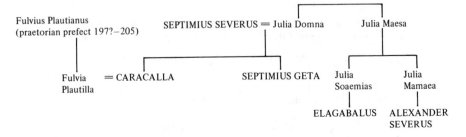

Chart 10: THE CONSTANTINIAN DYNASTY

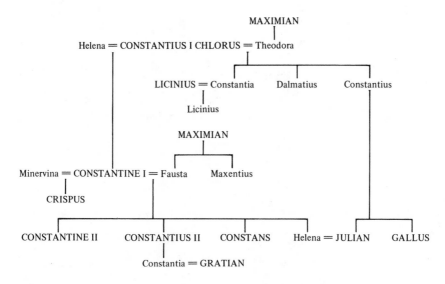

Chart 11: THE VALENTINIAN-THEODOSIAN DYNASTY

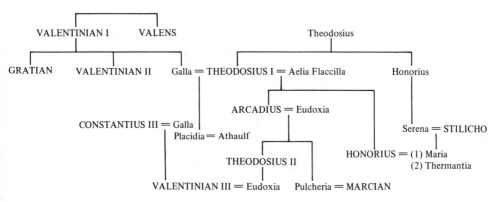

Index

Abbreviations used in this index: cos. = consul; Imp. = emperor; tr. = tribune.

Achaeans, 112–13, 130–31, 133, 135
Acilius, Manius, 159
Acragas (Agrigentum), 29–32, 118, 126
Actium, 202
Acts of the Apostles, 326
Acts of the Pagan Martyrs, 261
Adams, Henry, 313–14, 401
aedile, 52, 57, 63
Aelian, 315
Aelius Caesar, L., 245
Aemilianus (Imp.), 294
Aeneas, 38, 45, 216
Aetius, 375–76, 380
Aetolians, 61, 112, 126, 130–33
Agathocles, 33, 36, 100, 104, 113, 116, 127, 147
Agricola, 237, 261, 270
Agrippa, M. Vipsanius, 200–201, 207, 225
Agrippa Postumus, 225–26
Agrippina the Elder, 225, 227
Agrippina the Younger, 230–32, 267, 269
Alaric, 366, 373–75, 391
Alaric II, 391
Albinus, D. Clodius, 287
Alexander of Abonuteichos, 280
Alexander of Epirus, 32, 58
Alexander the Great, 109, 116, 270, 288
Alexandria, 109
alimentary program, 251–52
Allectus, 301
Amalasuntha, 392

Ambrose, 78, 365–67, 369, 385
Ammianus Marcellinus, 359, 361, 368
Ammonius Saccas, 321, 344
Amos, 337
Anastasius (Imp.), 394
Andriscus, 135
Antigonus III, 113
Antinous, 244–45
Antiochus III, 110, 112, 123, 129, 131–32, 135, 140, 151
Antiochus IV, 110, 134, 327–28
Antipater, 328
Antonia, 225, 227
Antoninus Pius (Imp.), 245–46, 249, 280
Antonius, C., 180–81
Antonius, M. (father of Antony), 177
Antonius, M. (Antony, triumvir), 76, 177, 181, 192, 196–98, 200–202, 207–8, 212, 328
Antony (monk), 366, 388
Aper, 298
Apollo, 12, 33, 306
Apollonius of Tyana, 279, 290, 296, 316
Appian, 212, 270
Apuleius, L., 254, 258, 266–67, 279
Aquilius, Manius, 166
Arbogast, 366
Arcadius (Imp.), 364, 366–67, 373–74
Archelaus, 328
Archidamus, 32
Archimedes, 101, 126
Ardashir, 291

Arians, 312, 353–54, 362–63, 365, 390–
    92
Aricia, 49
Aristarchus of Samos, 109, 113
Aristides, Aelius, 252, 269, 281
Aristodemus, 29, 30, 49
Aristonicus, 157–58
Aristotle, 9, 30, 103, 105, 146, 355, 398
Arius, 353–54
Armenia, 177, 201, 233, 291
Arminius, 204, 234
army, development of, 47, 50, 56,
    115–16, 127, 150–51, 162–63, 224,
    233, 238, 258, 303
Arnobius, 355–56
Arrian, 270, 272
Asclepius, 83, 269, 280–81
Aspar, 381–82
astrology, 45, 114, 208–9, 278, 317
Athanasius, 312, 354, 362–63, 366
Athaulf, 375, 391
Athenaeus, 315
Athens, 31, 104, 169, 296
Attalus I, 111
Attalus III, 156–57
Attica (wife of Agrippa), 200, 225
Atticus, T. Pomponius, 198, 200
Attila, 376, 381, 383
Auden, W. H., 314
Augustine, 78, 83, 105, 359, 380, 384–
    86, 388, 399
Augustus (Octavian), 40, 76, 88, 187,
    194–98, 200–204, 206–7, 210–12,
    216, 220–26, 229, 264, 269, 328,
    332
Aurelian (Imp.), 296–97, 349
Aurelius Victor, 359, 367
Ausonius, 367, 382
Avidius Cassius, C., 247–48
Avienus, 367
Avitus (Imp.), 376

Bacaudae, 301, 379–80
Bacchic cult, 12, 144–45, 356
Bachofen, Johann, 21
Balbinus (Imp.), 293
Balbus, L. Cornelius, 194
banditry, 258
Bar Cochba, 245, 333–34

Baudelaire, Charles, 386
Belisarius, 395–96
Benedict, 398
Berenice, 236
Bestia, L. Calpurnius, 161
Bibulus, M. Calpurnius, 184–85, 195
Bithynia, 132, 134, 163, 166, 176, 240
Blossius, C., 157–58
Boethius, 392, 398–99
Britain, 107, 230–31, 237, 244–45, 259,
    301, 390
Britannicus, 230–31
Brutus, Decimus, 195–96
Brutus, L., 38
Brutus, M. Junius (legate 77 B. C.),
    174, 183, 195
Brutus, M. Junius (tyrannicide), 146,
    195–96, 198, 207, 214, 228, 238
Buddhism, 319
Bulla Felix, 258
Bultmann, Rudolf, 336
Burckhardt, Jacob, 313
Burrus, 231–32

Caepio, Q. Servilius, 162, 164
Caesar, C. Julius, 40, 146, 160–61,
    173–74, 178–81, 183–85, 187–94,
    206, 210, 214, 267, 328
Caesar, L. Julius (cos. 90 B. C.), 165–
    66
Caesarion (Ptolemy XV), 200–202
calendar, 80, 137, 194, 204, 252
Calgacus, 261
Caligula. See Gaius Caligula
Callistus (freedman), 229, 230
Callistus (pope), 345–46
Calpurnia, 183, 190
Camillus, 38, 55–56, 162
Cannae, 125
Capua, 10, 17, 30, 58–59, 125–26, 128,
    148
Caracalla (Imp.), 287–89
Carausius, 301
Carbo, C. Papirius (cos. 120 B. C.),
    157–58, 161
Carbo, Cn. Papirius (cos. 82 B. C.), 169
Carinus (Imp.), 298
Carneades, 145, 209
Carrhae, 187

Carthage, 17, 28–31, 33, 57, 88, 101–5, 117–29, 136–37, 141–42, 159, 168, 194, 375, 390
Carus (Imp.), 298
Cassiodorus, 359, 398
Cassius Dio, 219, 284, 288, 315
Cassius Longinus, C., 146, 187, 195–96, 198, 208, 214, 228, 238, 328
Castor and Pollux, 12, 49, 83
Catiline, 180–82, 211
Cato the Elder, 43, 45, 61, 65, 70, 72, 76, 79, 84, 93, 97, 127, 132, 134, 136–37, 139, 142–45, 147–49, 151, 244
Cato the Younger, 146, 161, 177, 181–85, 188, 190–93, 195, 207, 232, 238, 267
Catullus, C. Valerius, 210, 213
Celsus, A. Cornelius, 277
Celsus of Alexandria, 349
Celts, 9, 17, 105–6, 111, 122, 128
censor, 54, 59, 62, 87
Centuriate Assembly, 47, 50–51, 54, 58, 60, 62, 121, 170
Cethegus, P. Cornelius, 176–77
Chalcedon, Council of, 381, 393
Christians, 144, 232, 238, 247, 264, 271, 280, 294–95, 306, 308–9, 311, 318–19, 325–26, 333–57, 362, 366–68, 371, 381, 383–88, 390
Christmas, 85, 357
Chrysostom, John, 373, 383
Cicero, M. Tullius, 1, 9, 41, 44–45, 52–53, 63, 71, 90, 93, 96–97, 103, 140, 153, 161, 167, 173, 176, 178, 180–83, 185–86, 190–92, 196–98, 208–10, 212, 214
Cicero, Q. Tullius, 209
Cilicia, 163
Cimbri, 162
Cincinnatus, 50
Cineas, 117
Cinna, L. Cornelius, 168–69, 174, 179
Circumcellions, 380
Circus Maximus, 78, 221, 263–65
Civilis, 234
Claudian, 382
Claudius (Imp.), 18, 22, 48, 222, 224–25, 229–30, 235, 250, 269, 332
Claudius II (Imp.), 296, 308

Claudius, Appius (decemvir), 52
Claudius Caecus, Appius, 59, 65, 117
Claudius Caudex, Appius, 118
Claudius Pulcher, A., 155–56, 158
Claudius Pulcher, P., 119
Claudius Quadrigarius, Q., 44
Clemens, Flavius, 238
Clement of Alexandria, 349
Cleomenes III, 113, 135
Cleonymus, 32
Cleopatra VII, 192, 200–202, 208, 296, 328
client, 71–72
Clodius Pulcher, P., 177, 183, 185–86, 190
Clovis, 391–92
Cluvius Rufus, 269
Coelius Antipater, L., 44
coinage, 70, 194, 297, 310
coloni, 255–56, 310
Colosseum, 236, 263, 401
Columella, 267
Commodus (Imp.), 247–48, 256, 277, 286–87, 348
Constans (Imp.), 313, 361
Constantine (Imp.), 302, 306–14, 351, 353–54, 356–57, 360–61
Constantine II (Imp.), 309, 313, 361
Constantinople, 311
Constantius Chlorus (Imp.), 302, 306–7
Constantius II (Imp.), 313, 361–62
Constantius III (Imp.), 375
constitution, Roman, 61–66, 121, 147, 168, 170–71, 193, 203, 206, 220–21, 223, 299, 309
consul, 51, 54, 57, 62–63, 147, 171, 203, 229, 389, 396
Corbulo, Cn. Domitius, 233, 236
Corinth, 130, 135, 141, 194, 296
Coriolanus, 50
Cornelia (mother of the Gracchi), 76, 96, 155, 157–59
Cornelia (wife of Caesar), 174, 183
Cornelius, C., 178
Corpus Juris Civilis, 396
Crassus, M. Licinius, 146, 169, 175–76, 179–81, 183–87, 190
Crassus, P. Licinius, 155, 157–58
Cremutius Cordus, A., 228
Crispus, 307, 309, 313, 356

Croton, 26–27, 29, 33, 35
Cumae, 10, 17–18, 26, 29–31, 33
Curial Assembly, 51, 62
Curio, C. Scribonius, 190–91
Cybele, 317–18
Cynics, 114, 272, 280
Cyprian, 351
Cyrene, 163

Dacia, 237, 240, 251
Damasus, 365–66, 368, 384
Daniel Stylites, 387
Dante, 34, 193, 240
Decebalus, 237, 240
Decius (Imp.), 294, 348
Decius Mus, P. (cos. 340 B.C.), 89–90
Decius Mus, P. (cos. 295 B.C.), 60, 90
Decius Mus, P. (cos. 279 B.C.), 90
Delphi, 106, 279
Dexippus, 286, 315
Diana at Aricia, 12, 46
Dictator, 51, 125, 193
Didius Julianus (Imp.), 286–87
Dido, 38, 102, 216
Diocletian (Imp.), 298–307, 319, 356
Diodorus Siculus, 45, 210–11
Diogenes Laertius, 315
Diogenes of Oenoanda, 273
Diognetus, Address to, 345
Dion, 32
Dionysius I, 32, 36, 104, 147
Dionysius II, 32
Dionysius Exiguus, 336
Dionysius of Halicarnassus, 15, 30, 40–
    41, 44, 71, 211
Dio of Prusa, 268, 272
Dodds, E. R., 323–24
dole, 182, 185, 194, 263, 297
Domitia, 236, 238
Domitian (Imp.), 235–38, 268, 270,
    347
Domitius Ahenobarbus, Cn., 231
Donatists, 311–12, 353
Druids, 106–7, 227, 230, 235
Drusus (son of Livia), 200, 225, 229
Drusus (son of Tiberius), 225–27
Drusus, M. Livius (tr. 122 B.C.), 159
Drusus, M. Livius (tr. 91 B.C.), 165
Ducetius, 31

Ebionites, 339–40
Egypt, Ptolemaic, 109–10, 112, 115,
    134, 179–80, 192, 202
Elagabal, 287, 290, 296–97, 321
Elagabalus (Imp.), 290
Empedocles, 33, 35
Engels, Friedrich, 21
Ennius, Q., 67, 146, 244
Epictetus, 256, 272
Epicureans, 114, 188, 214, 272
Epicurus, 114, 145–46, 214–15
Epirus, 133–34
equites, 63, 148–49, 159–60, 162, 165–
    66, 170, 176–77, 207, 222, 295,
    303, 309
Eratosthenes, 105, 109
Essenes, 330–31, 337
Ethiopia, 74, 357, 394, 396
Etruscans, 7, 9, 14–25, 28, 45, 47–49,
    55–57, 59–60, 82, 165
Eudoxia (wife of Arcadius), 373, 383
Eudoxia (wife of Valentinian III), 375–
    76
Eugenius, 366, 369
Euhemerus, 146
Eumenes II, 112, 131–34, 157
Eunapius, 286, 296, 359, 383, 398
eunuchs, 300
Eunus, 155, 158
Euric, 391
Eusebius, 286, 308–9, 326, 344, 356–57
Eutropius (eunuch), 373, 382
Eutropius (historian), 286, 359, 367

Fabius Maximus, Q., 86, 121, 124–25,
    127
Fabius Pictor, Q., 43–44, 50, 71, 115,
    118, 124, 146
Fannius, C., 159
Fausta, 307–8, 313
Faustina, 245–47
Favorinus, 268
fetiales, 87–88
Fimbria, C. Flavius, 169
Firmicus Maternus, 355–56
Flaccus, L. Valerius, 169
Flaccus, M. Fulvius, 158–59
Flamininus, T. Quinctius, 130–31, 140,
    143, 147, 151
Flaminius, C., 121–22, 124, 128

Flavius, Cn., 59
Florus, 270
Franks, 298, 301, 391–93
Frazer, James, 12
freedmen, 59, 64, 74, 152, 214, 230, 266
Fregellae, 141, 158
Frontinus, 273
Fronto, 271, 348
Fulvia, 190, 192, 198, 208
Fustel de Coulanges, Numa, 81

Gabinius, A. (tr. 139 B. C.), 154
Gabinius, A. (tr. 67 B. C.), 178
Gaiseric, 375, 390
Gaius (grandson of Augustus), 225–26
Gaius Caligula (Imp.), 227–30, 332
Galba (Imp.), 233–34
Galba, Sulpicius, 139
Galen, 247, 255, 277–78, 281, 355
Galerius (Imp.), 299, 302, 306–8, 349
Galla Placidia, 364, 373, 375
Gallienus (Imp.), 294–96, 322, 349
Gallio, 267
Gallus (brother of Julian), 361–62
Gallus (Imp.), 294
Gamaliel, 329, 340
Gaul, 153, 188–89, 374
Gauls, 38, 42, 55–57, 59–60, 100, 158, 259
Gellius, Aulus, 270
Gellius, Cn., 43
Gelon, 30, 103
Gemellus, 227–28
Germanicus, 225–27, 229
German tribes, 107–8, 188, 204
Geta (Imp.), 288
Gibbon, Edward, 107, 206, 211, 249, 262, 299, 313, 358, 371–72, 381, 401
Glabrio, M'. Acilius. *See* Acilius, Manius
gladiators, 10, 21, 78, 248, 264–66
Gnostics, 319, 343–44
Goethe, Johann Wolfgang von, 39
Gordian I (Imp.), 293
Gordian III (Imp.), 293
Gospels, 335–36
Goths, 285, 295–96, 363–64, 373–76, 390–92, 398

Gracchus, Gaius, 149, 153, 156–61, 165
Gracchus, Tiberius the Elder, 137, 151–53, 156
Gracchus, Tiberius the Younger, 122, 139, 155–58, 164–65
Gratian (Imp.), 363–65, 367
Greeks, 17, 25–36, 100–102, 111–13, 116–18, 126, 129–31, 133–35, 167, 169, 233, 268
Gregory of Tours, 393
Gregory the Great, 346, 400

Hadrian (Imp.), 239–40, 243–45, 249, 268–71
Hamilcar, 30
Hamilcar Barca, 119, 122–23
Hamilton, Alexander, 260
Hannibal, 58, 116, 123–24, 126–29, 132, 147, 174, 234
Hanno (explorer), 103
Hanno "the Great," 119–20, 124
Hardy, Thomas, 3
Hasdrubal (brother of Hannibal), 127
Hasdrubal (Punic governor of Spain), 123
Hasmoneans, 111, 134, 328
Heine, Heinrich, 78
Helena, 302, 313
Heliodorus, 315
Helvidius Priscus, 236, 270
Hermes Trismegistus, 317, 356
Hero of Alexandria, 275
Herod, 200, 211, 328, 335
Herod Agrippa I, 229, 332–33
Herod Agrippa II, 333
Herod Antipas, 336–37
Herodes Atticus, 268–69, 280
Herodian, 286, 315
Herodias, 336
Herodotus, 15, 17, 33
Hiero I, 30–31, 35
Hiero II, 101, 117–18, 120, 125
Hillel, 329
Himilco, 103
Hirtius, A., 196–97
Historia Augusta, 219, 286, 315, 359, 367–68
historiography, 15, 26, 30, 36, 39–41, 43–45, 61, 72, 91, 124, 187–88,

historiography (*cont.*)
    210–13, 219, 228–29, 231–32,
    269–71, 286, 292–93, 309, 315,
    326, 359–60, 367–68, 383, 385,
    388, 397, 398
Homer, 25, 145
homosexuality, 147–48, 236, 290
Honorius (Imp.), 364, 366, 373–75,
    382
Horace, 87, 212, 214–15, 217
Horatius Cocles, 38, 49
Hortensius, Q., 60
Hosea, 337
Huns, 363, 376, 380–81, 383
Hypatia, 383
Hyrcanus, John, 328
Hyrcanus II, 179, 328

Iamblichus, 323
Iberians, 107, 137
Iguvine Tablets, 12–13
Isaiah, 330
Isidore of Seville, 391, 399
Isis, 114, 279, 281–82, 317–18

James (apostle), 337, 339
James, William, 213
Jannaeus, Alexander, 328
Jerome, 294, 359, 384
Jesus, 256, 290, 319, 326, 334–38, 344
Jews, 110, 134, 179, 186, 194, 224,
    227–28, 230, 233, 238, 243, 245,
    260, 269, 327–34, 347, 387, 391,
    394
Joel, 329
Johanan ben Zakkai, 333
John the Baptist, 336–37
Jordanes, 359, 398
Josephus, 211, 235, 269, 333
Jovian (Imp.), 363
Juba, 191–92
Jugurtha, 161–62, 211
Julia (daughter of Augustus), 200,
    225–26
Julia (daughter of Caesar), 184, 189
Julia (daughter of Titus), 236
Julia Domna, 287–89, 316
Julia Maesa, 290
Julia Mamaea, 290–91, 344
Julian (Imp.), 359, 361–62, 365–66

Julianus Salvius, L., 244
Julia the Younger, 225–26
Jupiter, 83, 98, 146, 300
Justin (historian), 211
Justin (Imp.), 394
Justinian (Imp.), 390, 392, 394–97
Justin Martyr, 349
Juvenal, 263, 266, 333

Keats, John, 401
Kushans, 291

Lactantius, 306, 309, 356
Laelius, C., 155–56
Latins, 46, 49–50, 56–58, 117, 159–60,
    164–66
law, Roman, 53, 78–79, 244, 288, 359,
    381, 396
Lawrence, D. H., 14–15
Lemuria, 84
Lentulus Sura, P. Cornelius, 181
Leo I (Imp.), 382
Leo I (pope), 376
Leonidas, 36
Lepidus, M. Aemilius (cos. 78 B.C.),
    174, 176
Lepidus, M. Aemilius (triumvir), 197–
    98, 200–201, 204, 207
Libanius, 359, 367
Licinian law, 56, 149, 156
Licinius (Imp.), 294, 307–9, 349
Ligurians, 7, 9
Ligustinus, Spurius, 151–52
Lipari Islands, 27, 119
liturgies, 256–57
Livia, 200, 208, 225–27, 229, 233
Livilla, 225, 227
Livius Andronicus, 146
Livy, 9, 10, 16, 19, 22, 32, 40–45, 50,
    123–24, 130, 133, 148, 151–53,
    211–13, 270, 367, 383
Lombards, 392, 400
Longinus, 296, 316, 321, 323
Longus, 315
Lucan, 231–32, 267, 279
Lucian, 266, 280
Lucilius, C., 147
Lucilla, 247–48

Lucius (grandson of Augustus), 225–26
Lucretius, 214, 217
Lucullus, L. Licinius, 167, 169, 177–79, 183
Lupercalia, 85
Lusitanians, 139
Lusius Quietus, 240, 243–44

Macaulay, Thomas, 39–40
Macedon, 112–13, 115, 130, 132–33, 135
Macer, C. Licinius, 44, 54, 210
Machiavelli, Niccolò, 249
Macrinus (Imp.), 289–90
Macrobius, 88, 383
Madison, James, 61
Maecenas, C., 18, 200–201, 203, 215
Magnus Maximus (Imp.), 365
Mago (agricultural writer), 105
Mago (Barcid), 127
Mago (Punic general), 103
maiestas, 164, 222, 228
Mani, 291, 319
Manicheans, 306, 319–20, 385
Manilius, C., 178
Marcella, 225
Marcellus, C. Claudius, 190–91, 225
Marcellus, M. Claudius (cos. 214 B. C.), 126
Marcellus, M. Claudius (nephew of Augustus), 225
Marcia, 248, 348
Marcian (Imp.), 381–82
Marcion, 343
Marcomanni, 237, 247
Marcus Aurelius (Imp.), 245–49, 271–73, 277, 280-81, 348, 386
Marius, C., 9, 71, 93, 160–65, 167–69, 173, 179, 188, 211
Marius Maximus, 315
Marius the Younger, 169
Mars, 12, 38, 83–85
Marsi, 165
Martial, 268
Martin of Tours, 382, 388
Mary Magdalene, 338
Masada, 333
Masinissa, 127–28, 136, 161
Massilia, 27, 106, 123, 153, 158

Maternus, 258
Maxentius, 306–8
Maximian (Imp.), 301–2, 306–8
Maximinus Daia (Imp.), 307–9, 349
Maximinus Thrax (Imp.), 291, 293
Maximus of Ephesus, 362
Maximus of Tyre, 282–83
Mazdakites, 397
Messallina, 230
Messana, 101, 117–18
Messiah, 330, 334, 338–39
Metellus, L. Caecilius, 98
Metellus Numidicus, Q. Caecilius, 161, 164
Metellus Pius, Q. Caecilius, 169, 175
Metellus Scipio, Q., 190, 192
Milo, T. Annius, 170, 186, 190
Minervina, 307, 313
Minucius Felix, 350
Mithras and Mithraism, 318–20
Mithridates VI, 166–67, 169, 175–76, 179
Mommsen, Theodor, 121, 187
monasticism, 387–88, 397–98
Monica, 384–85
Monophysites, 381, 394, 396–97
Montaigne, Michel de, 401
Montanus, 343
Musaeus, 382
Musonius Rufus, C., 272

Nabis, 130–31, 135
Naevius, Cn., 146
Narbonensian Gaul, 158
Narcissus, 230, 235
Narses (eunuch), 396
Narses (Sassanid king), 302, 306
Neoplatonism, 321–23, 394
Neopythagoreans, 208, 279, 321–23
Nepos, Cornelius, 210
Nero (Imp.), 231–35
Nerva (Imp.), 238, 249
Nestorius, 381
New Testament, 148, 260, 323, 326, 335–36, 340, 343, 363, 384
Nicaea, Council of, 312, 354
Nicolaus of Damascus, 211
Nicomachus Flavianus, Virius, 366–67, 383
Nicomedes III, 163

Nicomedia, 298, 302
Niger, C. Pescennius, 287
Nigidius Figulus, P., 208
Nonnus, 382
Numa, 38, 40, 46–47, 76, 87
Numantia, 139, 141, 155, 157, 159, 161
Numenius, 279, 321
Numerian (Imp.), 298
Numidia, 103, 120, 123, 127, 136, 161–62, 259
Nymphidius Sabinus, C., 233–34

Octavia (sister of Augustus), 200, 226
Octavia (wife of Nero), 230–32, 266
Octavian (Octavius, C.). See Augustus (Octavian)
Octavius, Cn., 168
Octavius, M., 156
Odaenathus, 295
Odoacer, 376, 391
Ogulnian law, 59
Old Testament, 323, 327, 333, 384, 399
Olympiodorus, 359, 361, 383, 398
Opimius, L., 158–61
Optimates, 160–61
Orestes, 376
Orientus, 378
Origen, 321, 344–45, 349
Orosius, 294, 375, 385
Ortega y Gasset, José, 360
Osroëne, 357
Ossius, 353–54
Ostrogoths, 376, 391–92, 394, 396, 398
Otho (Imp.), 234–35
Ovid, 213–14, 221, 285

Palladas, 383–84
Pallas, 227, 230–31
Palmyra, 295–97
Panaetius, 146, 209
Pansa, C., 196–97
papacy, 368, 393
Papinian, 258, 288
Parentalia, 84
Parmenides, 28, 33, 35
Parthia, 186–87, 194, 204, 240, 247, 292
patricians, 51–54, 57, 92, 207
patron, 71–72

Paul (Saul of Tarsus), 267, 326, 339–42
Paulinus, 382
Paullus, L. Aemilius (cos. 216 B.C.), 125
Paullus, L. Aemilius (cos. 168 B.C.), 68, 133, 136, 143
Paul of Samosata, 349
Pausanias, 270
peasant revolts, 301, 369–70, 379–80, 397
Pelagius, 385
Peregrinus Proteus, 279–80
Pergamum, 111–12, 129, 134, 156–58, 166
Perpetua, 348
Perseus, 132–33, 135
Pertinax (Imp.), 248, 286–87
Peter (apostle), 337–40, 366
Petronius, C., 231–32, 266
Petronius Maximus (Imp.), 376
Phalaris, 29
Pharisees, 329
Pharnaces, 192
Pharsalus, 191–92
Philip V, 74, 112, 122, 125–26, 129–32, 140, 151
Philippi, 198
Philip the Arab (Imp.), 294, 344, 348
Philistus, 36, 209
Philo, 332
Philolaus, 35
Philostratus, 316, 367
Pilate, Pontius, 228, 332, 336, 338
Pindar, 31, 35
Piso, C. Calpurnius, 232
Piso, Cn. Calpurnius, 227
Piso, L. Calpurnius, 234
Piso Frugi, L. Calpurnius, 43–44, 145, 155
Plato, 32, 34–35, 146, 249
Plautianus, 288
Plautus, 73, 146
plebeians, 51–54, 57, 63, 92
Pliny the Elder, 90, 108, 149, 250, 255, 264, 269, 271, 275, 277
Pliny the Younger, 222, 240, 251–54, 264, 271, 347, 353
Plotina, 240, 243
Plotinus, 321–23

Plutarch, 23, 40, 44, 79, 210, 212, 269–70, 279
Pollio, C. Asinius, 191, 194, 197, 202, 207, 211–13, 215, 270
Polybius, 29, 45, 56, 61, 66, 68, 78, 85, 91, 94, 100, 113, 115, 117–20, 122–24, 133–34, 137, 139, 145, 147, 155, 159
Pompeia, 183
Pompeii, 236, 279
Pompeius, Sextus, 197, 200–201, 207
Pompey, 96, 146, 161, 169, 173–76, 178–80, 183–86, 188–89, 191–92, 195, 210, 267, 329
Pontifex Maximus, 86
Pontius Telesinus, 165, 169
Pontus, 166
Poppaea Sabina, 232, 234, 332
Populares, 160–61
population, 115, 224, 250, 262, 264, 371
Porcia, 195, 198
Porphyry, 322–23, 350
Porsenna, Lars, 18, 29, 49
Posidonius, 7, 146, 150, 210
Postumus (Imp.), 295
praetor, 57, 62–63, 121, 171
Princeps Senatus, 65, 202
Priscillian, 365
Priscus, 359, 379–80, 383
Probus (Imp.), 297–98
Proclus, 394
Procopius, 397
proletarians, 59, 63–64, 152, 154, 156–57, 172
Propertius, 24–25, 37, 213
prosopography, 72
Prudentius, 367
Ptolemy (astronomer), 278, 398
Ptolemy IV, 101, 110
Ptolemy VI, 134
Ptolemy VIII, 134
Ptolemy XII, 179, 185–86
Ptolemy XIII, 192
Ptolemy XIV, 192
Pulcheria, 381
Pupienus (Imp.), 293
Pyrrhus, 58, 90, 101, 112, 116–17, 146
Pythagoras, 29, 33, 35, 79, 323
Pythagoreans, 27, 29, 35

Quadi, 237
quaestor, 51, 63, 171
Quintilian, 268
Quintillus, 296
Quirinius, P. Sulpicius, 335
Qumran, 331

race, attitudes on, 74–75, 204
Ravenna, 374, 391–92
Regulus, M. Atilius, 119
religion
    Carthaginian, 104–5
    Celtic. *See* Druids
    Christian. *See* Christians
    Etruscan, 22–24
    Germanic, 107, 285
    Greek, 12, 33–35
    Judaic. *See* Jews
    Persian. *See* Zoroastrianism
    Roman, 12–13, 46, 57, 59, 81–91, 125, 144, 146, 163, 204, 208, 224, 279-83, 297, 300, 317, 321, 366, 383, 393–94
Remus, 38
Rhodes, 111, 129, 134, 167
Romulus, 37–38, 40
Romulus Augustulus (Imp.), 376
Rostovtzeff, Mikhail, 140, 254, 292–93, 314, 360
Rufinus, 373
Rullus, P. Servilius, 180
Rutilius Rufus, P., 162, 165

Sabina, 240, 271
Sabines, 9, 38, 46
Sabinus, Flavius, 234
Saguntum, 123
Sallust, 9, 142, 173, 181, 208, 210–12, 261, 270
Sallustius, 367
Salvian, 379–80, 382
Samnites, 9–11, 57–60, 117, 125, 165–66, 169–70
Sarmatians, 285, 313
Sassanids, 285, 287, 291–92, 302, 362–63, 396–97
Saturnalia, 85
Saturninus, L. Appuleius, 164
Scaevola, P. Mucius, 41–42, 155

science, 113–14, 277–78, 316–17, 399
Scipio, P. Cornelius, 127
Scipio Aemilianus, 61, 68, 77, 136–37, 139–40, 146–48, 154–55, 157–58
Scipio Africanus, 96, 127–29, 132–33, 136, 143, 146–47, 155–56
Scipio Asiaticus, Lucius, 132, 155
Scipio Nasica Corculum, P., 136, 145
Scipio Nasica Serapio, P., 154, 156–58
Scribonia, 198, 226
Sejanus, L. Aelius, 227–28, 269, 332
Seleucids, 110–11, 115, 131–32, 134, 179, 328
Sempronia (Roman bluestocking), 208
Sempronia (sister of the Gracchi), 155, 158
Senate, 51, 58, 60, 62, 64–65, 94, 128, 170, 222, 240, 309, 361
Seneca the Elder, 267, 270
Seneca the Younger, 24, 74, 82–83, 85, 231–32, 255, 264, 267, 271, 385
Serapeum, 321, 366
Sertorius, Q., 71, 168, 174–76, 178, 215, 234
Servilia, 183, 195, 208
Servius Tullius, 38, 40, 47–48
Severus, F. Valerius (Imp.), 307
Severus, L. Septimius (Imp.), 287–88, 315
Severus, Sulpicius (historian), 382
Severus Alexander (Imp.), 290–91
Sexto-Licinian land law, 56
Sextus Empiricus, 273
Shakespeare, William, 171, 270
Shapur, 291–92, 319
Sibyl, 33, 87
Sibylline Oracles, 260–61
Sicily, 26, 29–32, 35, 100–101, 104, 117–21, 155, 163, 176
Sidonius Apollinaris, 382
Silius Italicus, 55
Simon Magus, 344
Sisenna, L. Cornelius, 210
slavery, 21, 53, 58, 60, 70, 72–74, 107, 112, 130, 134, 143–45, 149–50, 154–55, 157–58, 163, 172, 175, 204, 254–55, 272
Smyrnaeus, Q., 367
Soaemias, 290
Sol Invictus, 297, 308, 311, 321, 357

Spain, 122–23, 126–28, 137, 150, 154, 239, 267, 375
Sparta, 21, 27, 61, 113, 130–31, 296
Spartacus, 175
Stilicho, 359, 366, 373–74, 382, 398
Stoics, 114, 146, 210, 232, 236, 246–47, 267, 272–73
Strabo, 210–11
Suetonius, 191, 219, 271
Sulla Felix, L. Cornelius, 161–62, 165, 167–71, 173, 177, 188, 210
Sulpicia, 213
Sulpicius Rufus, P., 167
Sura, L. Licinius, 239–40
Surenas, 187
Syagrius, 392
Sybaris, 26–27, 29, 103
Syme, Ronald, 91, 93
Symeon Stylites, 386–87
Symmachus, 359, 361, 369, 383, 385
Synesius, 383
Syphax, 127
Syracuse, 26, 30–32, 100–101, 118, 120, 126, 128, 298

Tacfarinas, 259
Tacitus (historian), 108, 173, 219–20, 222, 230, 233, 236–37, 259–61, 264, 266, 269–71, 333
Tacitus (Imp.), 297
Talmud, 260, 334
Tarentum, 26–27, 32–33, 36, 58, 116–17, 159
Tarquins, 17, 28, 38, 47–48, 87
taxation, 55, 70, 121, 148, 224, 253, 288, 303–4, 361
technology, 101, 126, 211, 275
Terence, 75, 146
Terramara culture, 5
Tertullian, 250, 265–66, 346, 350, 354
Tetricus, 297
Teutones, 162
Themistius, 367
Theocritus, 101
Theodora (wife of Constantius Chlorus), 302
Theodora (wife of Justinian), 396
Theodoric, 391–92, 398
Theodosian Code, 359, 381
Theodosius I (Imp.), 353, 363–66, 373

Theodosius II (Imp.), 354, 374, 381, 387
Thor, 107, 285
Thrasea Paetus, P., 232, 236
Tiberius (Imp.), 200, 203–4, 222, 225–26, 228–29, 250, 253, 332, 336
Tibullus, 213
Tigellinus, C. Ofonius, 232–33
Tigranes I, 177, 179
Timaeus, 26, 36, 45, 85, 102
Timagenes, 211, 261
Timesitheus, 293
Timoleon, 32, 104
Tiridates, 233
Titus (Imp.), 234–36
Tiwaz, 107, 285
Trajan (Imp.), 236, 238–40, 243, 249, 251, 253, 261, 264, 268, 270, 333, 347, 364
Tribal Assembly, 53, 60, 63–64, 166, 171
tribune, 52–53, 63, 171
Trogus, Pompeius, 45, 211, 261
Tubero, Q. Aelius, 44
Twelve Tables, 52–53, 72, 78

Ulfilas, 363
Ulpian, 288, 290

Valens, 362–63, 367
Valentinian I (Imp.), 363, 369, 380
Valentinian II (Imp.), 363, 365–66, 369
Valentinian III (Imp.), 375–76, 393
Valeria, 302, 309
Valerian (Imp.), 291, 294–95, 349
Valerius Antias, 44

Vandals, 374–76, 390, 395
Varro, C. Terentius, 125, 128
Varro, M. Terentius, 9, 22, 41, 44–45, 47, 69, 74, 83, 87, 149, 194, 210
Varro Murena, A. Terentius, 203
Varus, P. Quinctilius, 204
Veii, 16, 25, 55, 69, 88
Velleius Paterculus, 168, 218, 269
Vercingetorix, 189
Vergil, 9, 33–34, 45, 102, 146, 207, 215–17, 383
Verres, C, 176
Verus, Lucius (Imp.), 245–47, 249
Vespasian (Imp.), 233–36, 269
Vesta, 83
Vestal Virgins, 83
Vesuvius, 271
Villanovan culture, 5, 7
Viriathus, 139
Visigoths, 363–64, 373–76, 390–92
Vitellius (Imp.), 234–35
Vitruvius Pollio, 211
Volscians, 9, 50, 57

women, position of, 21, 27, 36, 75–77, 96–97, 152, 204, 208–9, 213, 272, 291, 383

Yeats, W. B., 323, 325

Zaleucus, 27
Zeno (Imp), 382, 387, 391, 393–94
Zenobia, 295–97
Zoroastrianism, 186, 291, 318–19, 327, 397
Zosimus, 286, 378